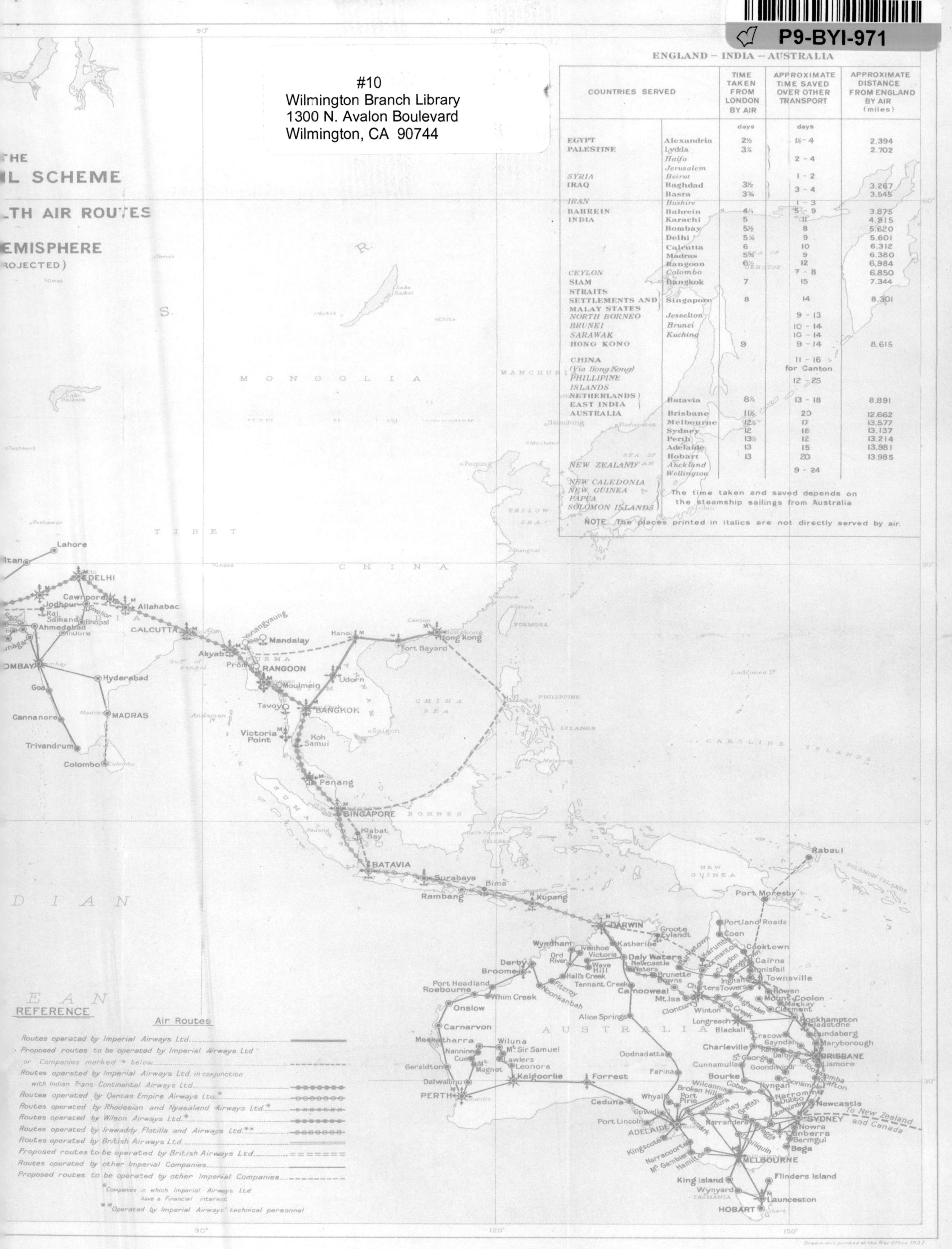

ENGLAND – INDIA – AUSTRALIA

COUNTRIES SERVED		TIME TAKEN FROM LONDON BY AIR	APPROXIMATE TIME SAVED OVER OTHER TRANSPORT	APPROXIMATE DISTANCE FROM ENGLAND BY AIR (miles)
		days	days	
EGYPT	Alexandria	2½	1½ - 4	2,394
PALESTINE	Lydda	3⅛	2 - 4	2,702
	Haifa			
	Jerusalem			
SYRIA	*Beirut*		1 - 2	
IRAQ	Baghdad	3½	3 - 4	3,267
	Basra	3¾		3,545
IRAN	*Bushire*		1 - 3	
BAHREIN	Bahrein	4¼	5 - 9	3,875
INDIA	Karachi	5	11	4,915
	Bombay	5½	8	5,620
	Delhi	5¼	9	5,601
	Calcutta	6	10	6,312
	Madras	5¾	9	6,380
	Rangoon	6½	12	6,984
CEYLON	*Colombo*		7 - 8	6,850
SIAM	Bangkok	7	15	7,344
STRAITS SETTLEMENTS AND MALAY STATES	Singapore	8	14	8,301
NORTH BORNEO	*Jesselton*		9 - 13	
BRUNEI	*Brunei*		10 - 14	
SARAWAK	*Kuching*		10 - 14	
HONG KONG		9	9 - 14	8,615
CHINA *(Via Hong Kong)*			11 - 16 for Canton	
PHILLIPINE ISLANDS			12 - 25	
NETHERLANDS EAST INDIA	Batavia	8¼	13 - 18	8,891
AUSTRALIA	Brisbane	11½	20	12,662
	Melbourne	12½	17	13,577
	Sydney	12	18	13,137
	Perth	13½	12	13,214
	Adelaide	13	15	13,981
	Hobart	13	20	13,985
NEW ZEALAND	*Auckland*		9 - 24	
	Wellington			
NEW CALEDONIA, *NEW GUINEA*, *PAPUA*, *SOLOMON ISLANDS*	The time taken and saved depends on the steamship sailings from Australia			

NOTE. The places printed in italics are not directly served by air.

REFERENCE

Air Routes

- Routes operated by Imperial Airways Ltd.
- Proposed routes to be operated by Imperial Airways Ltd or Companies marked * below
- Routes operated by Imperial Airways Ltd. in conjunction with Indian Trans-Continental Airways Ltd.
- Routes operated by Qantas Empire Airways Ltd.*
- Routes operated by Rhodesian and Nyasaland Airways Ltd.*
- Routes operated by Wilson Airways Ltd.*
- Routes operated by Irawaddy Flotilla and Airways Ltd.**
- Routes operated by British Airways Ltd.
- Proposed routes to be operated by British Airways Ltd.
- Routes operated by other Imperial Companies
- Proposed routes to be operated by other Imperial Companies

*Companies in which Imperial Airways Ltd have a Financial interest

**Operated by Imperial Airways' technical personnel

SMITHSONIAN

ATLAS OF WORLD AVIATION

CHARTING THE HISTORY OF FLIGHT FROM THE FIRST BALLOONS TO TODAY'S MOST ADVANCED AIRCRAFT

DANA BELL

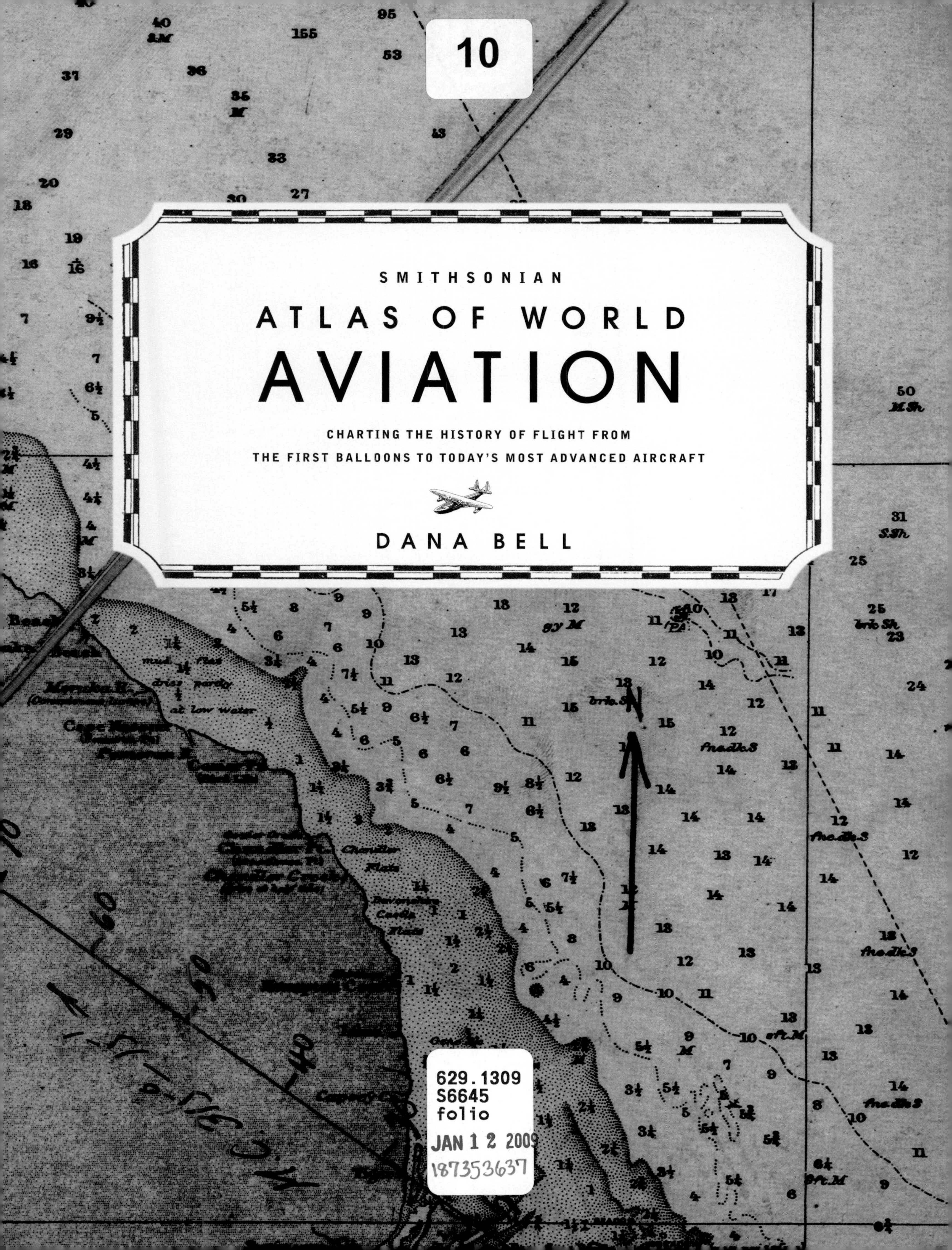
SMITHSONIAN
ATLAS OF WORLD
AVIATION
CHARTING THE HISTORY OF FLIGHT FROM
THE FIRST BALLOONS TO TODAY'S MOST ADVANCED AIRCRAFT
DANA BELL

HarperCollins books may be purchased for educational, business, or sales promotional use.
For information please write:
Special Markets Department
HarperCollins Publishers,
10 East 53rd Street
New York, NY 10022.

BUNKER HILL PUBLISHING
www.bunkerhillpublishing.com
This book has been designed and produced by
Bunker Hill Publishing,Inc.
285 River Road
Piermont, New Hampshire 03779

FIRST EDITION

Designed by Sterling Hill Productions

Library of Congress Cataloging-in-Publication Data

Smithsonian atlas of world aviation / Dana Bell. -- 1st ed.
p. cm.
Includes index.
ISBN 978-0-06-125144-3
1. Aeronautics--History--Pictorial works. 2. Historical geography--Maps.
3. World history. I. Bell, Dana. II. Title.

TL515.S525 2008
629.1309--dc22

2007047574

ISBN: 978-0-06-125144-3

Printed in China
10 9 8 7 6 5 4 3 2 1

DEDICATION

For Dad, who taught me to love maps and aviation.

Contents

PIONEER AVIATION

The Beginnings of Human Flight

1 Man Takes to the Air
2 Buoyant Flight
8 Winged Flight
12 Four Flights at Kitty Hawk

The Ascent of the Airplane

14 The Wrights in Europe
16 The New Pioneers
20 Europe's Great Races
22 The First Aeronautical Charts
24 The Race Across America

WORLD WAR I

26 Fledglings and the Great War
28 Over the Trenches
32 The Italian Campaign
38 The Yanks are Coming
42 Bombers over England
44 Formations & Maneuvers
46 Closing Positions
48 Armistice

BETWEEN THE WARS

50 The Golden Years
52 Into the Stratosphere

Across America

54 Delivering the Mail
56 Marking the Airways
58 Non-Stop Coast to Coast
60 The Emerging Airlines
64 The Transcontinental Airline
66 Route Maps and Sectionals
70 The Domestic Airways

Linking Europe

72 The Early Airlines
74 The Zeppelin Liners
76 European Air Transport in the 1930s
80 Far East Connections
82 Britain to Australia
84 Into Africa

Across the Oceans

86 The First Atlantic Crossings
90 Atlantic Crossings after Lindbergh
96 Kingsford-Smith and the *Southern Cross*
98 Exploring with the Lindberghs
100 Pan American and the Great Flying Boats

Around the World

102 The 1924 Round the World Flight
106 Circumnavigation Record Flights

Pan America

108 The Pan American Goodwill Flight
110 Pan American to South America
112 Aviation in Latin America

The Frozen Wastes

114 Exploring the Arctic
116 Exploring the Antarctic

WORLD WAR II

War in Europe

118 Lightning War
120 The Battle of Britain
122 Reaping the Whirlwind
124 Airborne Radar
126 Hunting the U-Boat
128 US Stations in Britain
130 Cross-Channel Attack
132 Allied Continental Landing Fields

War Over the Pacific

134 Pearl Harbor
136 Naval Aviation over the Pacific
140 Bombing Japan
144 Eyes over the Pacific
146 America's Air Forces

Grid Maps

148 Wright Field's Crash Map
150 The US Image Grid

The World's Largest Airline

152 The Air Transport Command
158 The ATA and the WASPs

POST WAR

Post War Military

160 Cold War Military Aviation
162 The Berlin Airlift
164 Air War over Korea
166 The Small Wars
168 Vietnam
170 The Gulf Wars
174 Modern Military Aircraft

Post War Research – The X-Planes

178 Pushing the Envelope

Post War Airlines

184 The Postwar Airlines
194 The Growth of a Modern Airport

Controlling the Airspace

196 Modern Flight Charts
198 Helicopter Route Charts
200 VFR Terminal Area Charts
202 Sectional Aeronautical Charts
204 Jeppesen Enroute Low Altitude Charts
206 World Aeronautical Charts
208 Operational Navigation Charts
210 IFR Enroute High Altitude Charts
212 Jet Navigation Charts
214 Jet Navigation High Altitudes

APPENDICES

216 National Aircraft Markings
222 National Civil Aviation Codes
226 Bibliography
228 Index
230 Photo Credits

384
N18196
FLY - EASTERN AIR LINES

INTRODUCTION & ACKNOWLEDGMENTS

Some time back, Trish Graboske, Publications Officer at the National Air and Space Museum mentioned that publisher Ib Bellew was looking for someone to help with a book project he was developing. The book was to be an historical atlas of aviation, and I was immediately hooked. Ib was already known within the Museum for a number of interesting and successful projects, but this one promised to be, at least in my view, the most fascinating yet. The links between flight and cartography offered endless possibilities.

We've been able to create maps to show the locations and routes of historical events; we've located maps and charts used in the events themselves, and located maps created with the aid of airborne photography and radar. Even the maps used for aerial navigation tell a story, the symbols (or lack thereof) reflecting the instrumentation and navigational aids available over the years. The project has been as exciting as I had expected, and it was a rare week that didn't introduce me to some new historical detail, whether navigational, cartographic, or aeronautical.

A subject of this size requires many hands, and I have many people to thank for their support.

Ib Bellew and Carole Kitchel Bellew of Bunker Hill Publishing created and fostered this project, and included me in the effort. Bunker Hill's editor Rob Chirico reviewed and tuned the manuscript, improving the clarity of the final text.

Donna Sanzone of HarperCollins offered her insight and helpful suggestions.

Patricia J. Wynne also offered help on many levels and prepared the special maps and illustrations created for this volume.

Peter Holm, Abrah Griggs, and Sylvie Vidrine at Sterling Hill Productions were responsible for design and layout, and offered additional creative input.

The staff at the NASM Archives - my former co-workers - made many great discoveries, many of which found their way into these pages. I owe a great deal to Marilyn Graskowiak (Chief), Dan Hagedorn, Katharine Igoe, Allan Janus, Mark Kahn, Kristine L. Kaske-Martin, Melissa A. N. Keiser, Brian Nicklas, David Schwartz, Paul Silbermann, Barbara Weitbreck, Patricia Williams, and Larry Wilson.

In the NASM Aeronautics Department, Tom Crouch, Ron Davies, Peter Jakab, and Bob van der Linden help answer my many questions and steer me to useful resources.

The FAA provided critical support when I needed it most. This work has benefitted from the input of Christo G. Cambetes, Terry M. Layton, Brad W. Rush, and Paul Turk.

I've also received important input and guidance from a number of other individuals including:

Barry L. Spink at the USAF Historical Research Agency; Carol Nickisher, who helped with materials relating to her grandfather, W. B. Voortmeyer; Italian researcher Gregory Alegi; Suzanne Yeonopolus at Jeppesen; David H. Klaus at Meteor Productions; and Jerry Crandall at Eagle Editions.

As always, I appreciate the help all these folks have provided. In the end, however, should any mistakes turn up in the following pages, they are mine alone.

Man Takes to the Air

Today we take the existence of aircraft for granted. A little more than a century ago, a balloon ride was a thrill for anyone fortunate enough to have the opportunity to go aloft. Equipped with new gasoline, diesel, or electric engines, dirigible airships were offering the new possibilities in commercial and military aviation. By 1903, a handful of aspiring aviators had flown gliders, some launching their hand-built craft from hilltops, with a few carried aloft to drop from balloons. Newspapers had already carried fanciful tales of spectacular flights by gifted tinkerers who had mated engines to their gliders; the report that two Dayton bicycle makers had flown over North Carolina could be easily dismissed as just another journalistic invention.

But the four flights of Orville and Wilbur Wright began a new era in the story of flight, a pioneering era where the public eventually recognized that powered flight was possible, even if it might somehow prove useless. In the years before World War I, aircraft could perform few tasks reliably. The aeroplane, in its many developing guises, had instead become the chosen mount of contemporary sportsmen, many flying designs of their own invention. (The wisdom of their experimentation was frequently refuted by the hundreds of aircraft that never left the ground, or quickly returned to earth with disastrous results.) The word "contraption," while not created simply to describe these pioneering aircraft, proved a frequently deserved synonym.

Grooms steady startled horses as Orville Wright and passenger soar above in a Wright Model A. The flight was one of a series of European demonstrations conducted in 1908.

The Wrights' first flights in December 1903 did not immediately, in any substantive way, change the world forever. The brothers' secretive natures initially kept most of the details of their invention hidden from competitors and the public. Several years would pass before the nature of their accomplishment was widely recognized, and even more years would be needed to develop the airplane into a military tool or an accepted mode of transportation.

By today's standards, the world of 1903 was exceptionally slow. Fast steamships were cutting some travel times: the record Atlantic crossing was 5 days, 11 hours, and 5 minutes; the record between Southampton to Capetown was just over two weeks; and an average steamship needed eight or nine days to connect Seattle with Anchorage, Alaska. The cost of building and operating steamships meant that a large number of cargo ships still traveled under sail. The record wind-powered freight between Australia and the UK stood at 67 days (since the Suez Canal was not designed for sailing ships). Much heavy freight from New York to San Francisco still traveled by sail; in the days before the Panama Canal opened, the record for that trip, through the Straits of Magellan, stood at just over 89 days.

By land, steam trains were the fastest, most consistent form of transportation. A train across the US needed some 100 hours, while the the Orient Express carried passengers and mail between Paris and Constantinople in just over 67 hours. Gasoline-engined motor cars were used for some short trips (if the roads were adequate), but horse-drawn vehicles, camel caravans, and shoe leather, still carried most of the world's people and goods on overland routes.

During the pioneering years, aviation did nothing to change any of these travel times. As an aid to aerial navigation, trains often guided aviators racing between cities, and those trains rarely ran at full speed. Even when an aircraft set a new speed record, it carried no passengers or substantial freight for any distance.

Although pioneer aviators saw their capabilities developing at an astounding rate, the first ten years of powered flight were really little more than the long, shallow flat at the beginning of a new learning curve. These first aviators learned new lessons of science, engineering and mechanics, of navigation and piloting. Some of them became household names, entertained by royalty, and surrounded by fans and the press. And even when the least among them flew by, everyone looked up. A great many died in their aircraft; others were seriously injured. Some started with an idea and soon found themselves prosperous. Others invested all they owned and soon found themselves penniless. But the pioneers of aviation did what pioneers have always done: they blazed new trails.•

Roland Garros soars above the crowd at the beginning of the 1911 Paris-to-Madrid race.

Buoyant Flight

While most early flight legends and attempts involved imitations of bird wings, invocations of magic, or acts of faith, the eighteenth century's first successful flights drew on a new understanding of air as matter - a fluid with mass and volume. Archimedes developed principles of bodies floating in liquids some two hundred years BC, but took two millennia before philosophers would apply those principles to gases. The recognition that an object weighing less than the air it displaced was buoyant and would float seems to have attracted Italian Jesuit Francesco de Lana around 1670. De Lana designed an early "lighter-than-air" craft, buoyed by four twenty-foot-diameter copper spheres. By pumping the air out of the spheres, de Lana expected he could reduce the vehicle's total weight to the point it would float through the skies. The pious theoretician never built his craft, believing that such a vehicle would fly against the will of God. His crisis of conscience was for naught, however - the good brother never recognized that the external air pressure would have crushed his copper spheres long before they reached neutral buoyancy.

Some forty years later, another Jesuit with a different interpretation of God's will found a bit more success in his experiments. On 8 August 1709, Father Laurenço de Gusmão demonstrated an unmanned hot air balloon to João V, King of Portugal. The balloon reportedly rose a short distance before crashing to earth and setting some of the king's furnishings afire. The Brazilian-born de Gusmão showed no inclination to continue his aeronautical experiments.

In 1766, British scientist Henry Cavendish discovered that "inflammable air" (a gas we now refer to as hydrogen) was much lighter that air. Others in the scientific community surmised that a light bladder filled with hydrogen would rise, though no experiments would be recorded for sixteen years. It was Tiberius Cavallo, an Italian scientist living in Britain, who, in 1782, first tried floating hydrogen-filled paper bags. The bags failed to rise, but Cavallo correctly theorized that the hydrogen gas had leaked through the bag without providing the expected buoyancy.

Gusmão and Cavallo were each working with gases that would equal the ambient air pressure while weighing less than the air. It is unclear how well Gusmão understood what he created - by heating the air inside his balloon, he increased its pressure. As the heated air expanded to match the external air pressure, it became less dense, and the balloon became buoyant. As the air inside the balloon cooled, buoyancy was lost, and the device descended. Cavallo used hydrogen, a light-weight gas that did not require heat or increased pressure to provide buoyancy. But the tiny hydrogen molecules were prone to migrating through most light-weight balloon fabrics, and the entire balloon would descend as more hydrogen escaped.

In November 1782, the same year that Cavallo's paper bags failed to fly, Frenchman Joseph Montgolfier inflated a silken bag with

On 21 November 1783, Jean-François Pilâtre de Rozier and the Marquis d'Arlandes became the first humans to rise above the earth in an untethered aircraft. The beautifully decorated montgolfièr transported them five miles in just under a half hour.

One of the world's earliest photographs of a balloon, this Ambrotype shows the inflation of John Steiner's balloon at Erie, Pennsylvania, on 18 June 1857. By the 1850s many balloonists relied on coal gas (an explosive mixture of methane, hydrogen, carbon monoxide and ethylene) for buoyancy. While not as light as hydrogen, coal gas was far less expensive and much easier to procure.

heated air from his fireplace. Amazed as the bag floated around his room, Montgolfier wrongly surmised that captured smoke was providing the lift. (He failed to recognize that burned gases, vapors, and particles made smoke heavier than air - only the expanded, heated, smokey air provided any buoyancy. Working with his brother Etienne through the next spring, Montgolfier was ready for a public demonstration in June 1783. On the 4th, the brothers inflated a paper-lined linen bag over a fire built in the marketplace at Annonay. Eight men held the 30-foot-diameter "aerostat" with increasing difficulty until told to release their lines. The hot air balloon then soared to an altitude of over 6,000 feet, cooled, and came to earth more than a mile away.

Almost at the same time, J. A. C. Charles (another French inventor) was developing his first hydrogen balloon. Using a rubberized silk bag (to slow the migration of the hydrogen molecules), Charles first launched his invention in August 1783. When one spectator commented on the uselessness of the new invention, his companion - American Benjamin Franklin - asked, "What use is a newborn baby?" Alas, the Age of Enlightenment was not an age of universal enlightenment - superstitious provincials destroyed the balloon when it eventually descended near their village.

Charles and the Montgolfiers would have a busy autumn. On 19 September, three animals were sent aloft in a "montgolfièr" (as all hot-air balloons were then known); the following month, people were carried aloft in captive montgolfières. On 21 November, Jean-François Pilâtre de Rozier and the Marquis d'Arlandes made the first free ascent, a 25-minute flight that carried them more than five miles from their launch point. On 1 December, Charles and a passenger launched in a "charlière." The flight lasted more than two hours, and the balloon traveled more than 25 miles. Manned flight was a reality; only time would tell what the newborn would become.

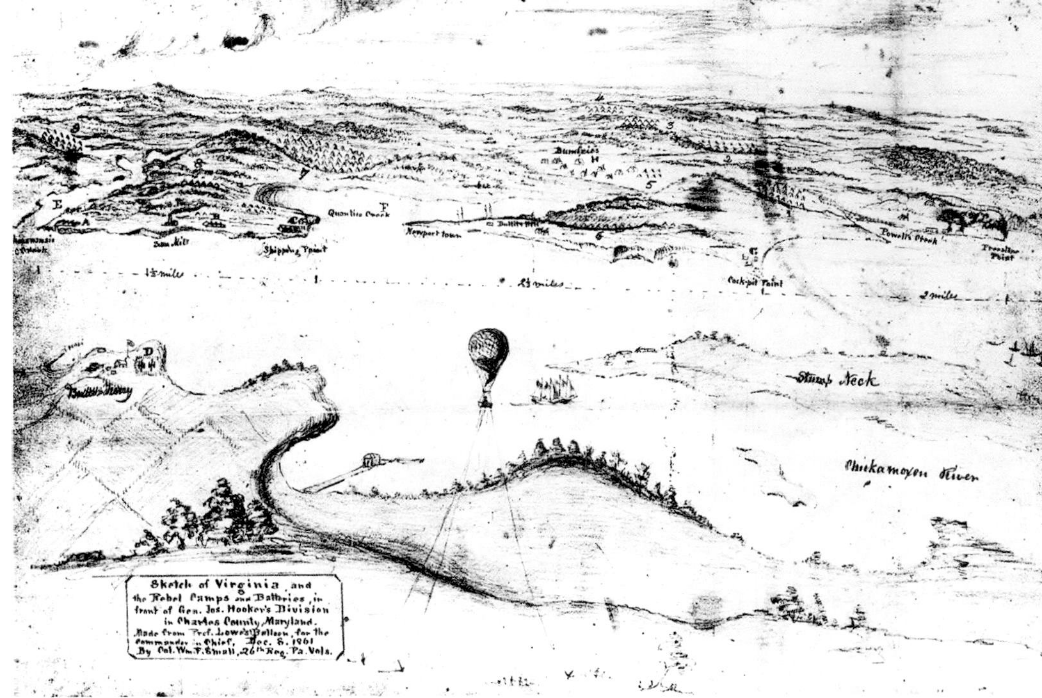

The inflation of Professor Thaddeus Lowe's balloon *Intrepid* in 1861 saw a return of military aviation. The French armies had briefly used tethered balloons for reconnaissance during the Revolution (though Napoleon closed the air arm in 1802), and the Austrians had dropped a number of light bombs from balloons at the 1849 siege of Venice.

Although early balloons gained some control over the third dimension, they lost all influence over the other two: at the mercy of the winds, the montgolfières and charlières could rise and descend, but could only drift across the terrain. In September 1784, Italian aeronaut Vincent Lunardi thought he had achieved some control using oars in a balloon flown over London. But the oars used by Lunardi and several subsequent balloonists could do little to influence an airship's course. Even if a rower could move the balloon basket, the motion was quickly damped by the pendulum action as the basket swung below the envelope. By the late 1700s, several designers were creating elongated balloons to lessen wind resistance to forward motion, but without an effective power source and drive system, the guided airship remained a mirage on the horizon.

The nineteenth century saw some limited successes in the invention of a dirigible (or steerable) airship. In Britain, Sir George Cayley proposed propeller-driven balloons in 1816, an idea tested in 1850 on Hugh Bell's human-powered locomotive balloon. France's Henri Giffard used a 3hp steam engine to drive a three-bladed prop, guiding his elongated balloon at 5mph for 17 miles in 1852. Giffard's countryman Henri Dupuy de Lôme introduced a muscle-powered dirigible in 1872, the same year that Germany's Paul Haenlein drove his airship with a coal-gas-powered internal combustion engine. None of these designs could be considered successful, however. In each case, the power source provided too little thrust for the weight added. In 1884 France's Charles Renard and A. C. Krebs experimented with an electric motor for powering their airship *La France* in the world's first controllable, powered flights. *La France* was able to exceed 15mph and complete a circuit without landing, but the battery-powered electric motors limited range.

The gasoline-powered internal combustion engine, invented in Germany by Karl Benz in 1885, offered the first glimpse of a light-weight, reliable power source. Three years later, countryman Hermann Wölfert built the first of his gasoline-engined airships. Wölfert's designs were underpowered and difficult to maneuver. Although subsequent designs showed some improvement, Wölfert was killed in the crash of his third dirigible in 1897.

Improvements in the internal combustion engine would assure a reliable power plant for airships (and soon for aeroplanes), but many advances would wait until the twentieth century. On early dirigibles power and steering changes originated in a suspended control car. Cables translated any alteration in direction or speed to an overhead framework, while other cables translated the movement to the pressurized balloon envelope. It is easy to understand the difficulty aeronauts encountered when attempting any sort of precise movement in these "non-rigid" airships. One solution was the introduction of a keel attached to the balloon envelope. The first airship with this design was *Le Jaune* (named for its yellow covering), a French airship designed by brothers Paul and Pierre Lebaudy. First flown in November 1902, this "semi-rigid" airship was a remarkable success, flying 23 miles in May 1903, then covering 61 miles in under three hours in June. Semi-rigid airships would remain popular with French and Italian designers into the early 1930s.

But the giant airships, capable of carrying great payloads over long distances, would be fully rigid designs, with skeletons supporting the main structure, power units, and control cars. Inside the structure, individual gas cells would provide buoyancy - with the loss of pressure in one cell no longer signaling a catastrophic failure of the entire airship. Despite many earlier nineteenth century designs and prototypes, the construction of the first successful rigid airship would fall to Germany's Count Ferdinand Adolf August Heinrich von Zeppelin. Zeppelin's first airship, the LZ 1, took to the air in July 1900 with a disappointing lack of control. LZ 2, flying in January 1906, proved equally uncontrollable; the airship was destroyed by winds the night after its only flight. But LZ 3, which flew with larger stabilizers and control surfaces in October 1906, was a marked success. At a time when few airplanes showed any control, range, or speed, the LZ 3 maneuvered steadily for two hours at a speed near 30 mph. Other designers would create their own rigid airships, but for three decades the public would call any giant dirigible a "Zeppelin." •

Early Zeppelin airships were built in this floating hangar/factory on Lake Constance. Here, the LZ 1 nears completion in 1900.

Alberto Santos-Dumont began his first dirigible experiments in 1898. Three years later, he electrified Paris with this flight to the Eiffel Tower in his latest non-rigid airship. The flight earned the Brazilian-born aeronaut a 100,000 franc prize.

RIGHT: The *California Arrow* was a 52-foot, non-rigid, hydrogen airship built by Captain Thomas Scott Baldwin in 1904. Baldwin powered the dirigible with an engine built by Glenn Curtiss, who was then known as a motorcycle racer and designer.

ABOVE: A week after the French aviation show at Reims, the Germans opened their own international exposition in Frankfurt.

TOP LEFT: The rapid advances in the aeronautical sciences convinced Walter Wellman and Melvin Vaniman that dirigibles were ready to cross the Atlantic in 1910. Together with two mechanics, a navigator, a radio operator, and one obstreperous cat, the two aeronauts left Atlantic City, New Jersey, in their airship *America* on 15 October 1910. Plagued by failing engines, the *America* was rescued by the steamer SS *Trent* after three days.

CENTER LEFT: The advent of the airship did not spell the end of the free balloon. This French card shows the excitement of balloon races at Reims on 26 August 1909.

The first Schütte-Lanz dirigible, the S.L.1, in flight over Mannheim, Germany, in late 1911. Schütte-Lanz designers favored a wooden skeletal structure, rather than the aluminum structure used by Zeppelin.

Melvin Vaniman's second attempt to cross Atlantic came two years after the *America's* loss. On 2 July 1912, Vaniman and his crew of four died when this improved hydrogen airship exploded off the coast of Atlantic City, New Jersey.

Distorted by a panoramic camera and by it own weight, John A. Morrell's giant airship prepares for takeoff at Berkeley, California, on 23 May 1908. The 450-foot-long non-rigid airship is carrying sixteen people, all of whom would soon be injured when the single-cell envelope ripped, venting the entire supply of hydrogen, to crash to the ground from an altitude of 300 feet. No one died, but Morrell's plans for an American passenger airship line could not be resuscitated.

The US Army's first airship, known simply as *Signal Corps No.1*, compared poorly with the designs being evaluated in France, Germany, and even Britain. The airship is seen during evaluation flights in August 1908, flown by Thomas Baldwin (standing aft) and Glenn Curtiss.

Winged Flight

The ancients have left us many legends and tales of flying men, but little theory to explain why such attempts would have worked. With today's understanding of aerodynamics, few grant any credence to these stories. By the Middle Ages men were strapping wings to their arms and jumping from towers, roofs, and city walls. They now had basic theories about imitating birds; they soon had the injuries to refute those theories. During the Renaissance, artist and scientist Leonardo da Vinci investigated flight, producing numerous designs for helicopters and ornithopters. But even the great Leonardo's vision was clouded by fundamental misconceptions about the nature of air, lift, and power, and none of his inspirations had any hope of lifting a man off the ground.

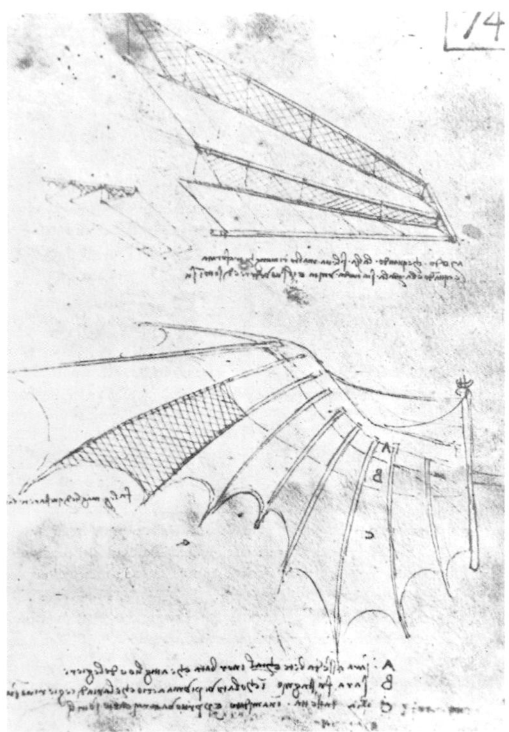
Working in the late fifteenth century, Leonardo da Vinci created this study of a wing. Note the reversed handwriting - using his left hand, Leonardo wrote backward in a code that somehow confused many of the master's contemporaries.

The eighteenth century brought the Age of Enlightenment. Where "philosophy" had once ruled the study of all things physical, the new fields "science" and "engineering" suggested not just different names, but entirely new approaches to how things worked and how new things could work. The success of the early balloonists inspired many, including the young Briton George Cayley (1773-1857), who focused his attention on the problem of heavier-than-air flight. In 1804 Cayley built a whirling arm to help with his study of fluid forces on adjustable planes and airfoils. He was soon building model and full-sized gliders, discovering the advantages of dihedral (a wing's upward inclination) and stabilizing tail surfaces. In 1809 he presented his first scientific paper on aerial navigation. One of his 1849 gliders lifted a 10-year-old boy on a down-hill run; Cayley's 1853 glider reportedly carried his coachman - who apparently soon decided it wiser to find a new employer.

For all his innovation and discovery, Cayley concentrated primarily on lift and drag; a lightweight powerplant and a system of control would occupy other minds for the rest of the century. In1842, another Briton, William Samuel Henson, moved toward construction of the first powered airplane when he patented his aerial steam carriage. Five years later he tested a large model built with the assistance of John Stringfellow. Despite a twenty-foot wingspan and twin pusher props, the craft achieved little more than a long glide. Henson moved to other pursuits, but Stringfellow made a second attempt in 1848. The new, smaller model was a bit more successful, but not enough to convince Stringfellow to continue his experiments. (New discoveries brought Stringfellow back to aviation in 1868, but his new triplane design was a failure.)

In France, Felix du Temple built a number of successful clockwork- and steam-powered models in the late 1850s. One of du Temple's models was the first airplane to rise off the ground under its own power. In 1874, du Temple would build a full-sized aircraft powered by a hot-air engine. Launched down an inclined ramp, the craft is usually credited as the first to lift a man off the ground, if only for a quick leap or hop.

Another Frenchman studying powered flight in the 1870s was Alphonse Pénaud, who built and flew rubber-band powered helicopters, ornithopters, and airplanes. His "Planophore," which flew 40 yards in 11 seconds, led to the design of an 1876 amphibious aircraft with retractable landing gear, a control column for rudders and elevators, a glazed canopy, and two

Photographed late in his life, Sir George Cayley was the first to successfully bring a modern scientific approach to aviation.

The modern model depicts one of Sir George Cayley's nineteenth-century helicopter designs. Four elaborate screws were to provide lift, while a fifth propeller moved the craft forward. Not all of Cayley's designs were successful....

tractor props. The design, like so many of the era, was never built. Pénaud died a suicide at age 30 in 1880.

Other French innovators continued the quest. In 1890 Clément Ader tested his steam-driven *Eole* claiming the craft had flown about 164 feet. Ader, however, was unable to repeat his alleged success when demonstrating his *Eole III* to the French government in 1897.

Renowned British inventor Sir Hiram Maxim turned his attention to aviation in the 1890s. He designed and built a giant aircraft with a 110-foot wingspan and a gross weight of over 3-1/2 tons. Charging down the launch rail in 1894, the machine strained free the ground, coming to a hard landing with minor damage. Maxim announced that he had solved the problems of propulsion and lift, but declined the opportunity for further experimentation in the field.

In Germany, Otto Lilienthal took a less direct, more studied approach to powered flight. Between 1891 and 1896 he designed, built, and flew a series of gliders. Raising a conical hill, so that he could always take off into the wing, Lilienthal made over 2,000 glides. His first powered design, which was to use a carbonic acid gas motor to drive flapping wing tips, never flew; Lilienthal died in the crash of one of his gliders on 9 August 1896.

Scotsman Percy Pilcher was one of many influenced by the great Lilienthal; the German personally guided Pilcher through the basic principles when the Scot came to visit in 1895. Returning home, Pilcher built a series of highly successful gliders, including the *Hawk*, which set a world gliding record of 250 yards in 1897. In 1898 Pilcher started the design of a new engine and a propeller-driven aircraft, but in September 1899 the canny Scot died, as his mentor had three years earlier, in a glider crash.

American Octave Chanute was another great influence in aerial navigation. Assembling known accomplishments in aviation, Chanute published a series of magazine articles which were subsequently assembled in the popular book *Progress in Flying Machines* in 1894. Chanute was a well known lecturer, explaining the latest discoveries to audiences in North America and Europe. Chanutes own gliders, which first flew in 1896, also added to the body of knowledge, though they were never as successful as those built by his friends Orville and Wilbur Wright.

Samuel Pierpont Langley, the head of the Smithsonian Institution, is best remembered for his failed attempts at powered manned flight in the months and weeks before the Wright brothers' successes. As is oft remembered, Langley's *Aerodrome A* crashed from its houseboat launch platform on 7 October 1903, and again on 8 December. But for twelve years prior to his great failures (which he attributed to problems with the catapult launch system), Langley designed and flew the most successful model aircraft of the day. In the end, Langley failed to deliver a powered, man-carrying aircraft, and he failed publicly using public funds. Regardless of the launch system, Langley's *Aerodrome A* could not have flown safely - there were too many structural and design flaws that would only become obvious with improved understandings of aeronautical science. But history has somehow treated Langley more harshly than his contemporaries, nearly all of whose designs for manned, powered airplanes also failed. When Langley died on 27 February 1906, only two other humans had built and flown an airplane, and both of theirs names were Wright.

Orville and Wilbur Wright had been interested in flying since youth. The death of Lilienthal, whom they admired greatly, seems to have given the brothers the final push into their own experiments. Like Lilienthal, the Wrights decided to explore models and gliders first, learning to fly safely, then planning to add power. They would succeed where all others had failed. •

Otto Lilienthal amazes the small crowd gathered for the demonstration of an early monoplane glider. This drawing is dated 1893.

Hiram Maxim's giant steam-driven biplane made a short hop in 1894; the success was enough for Maxim, who moved on to other projects.

Joining the Wright Brothers at Kill Devil Hills in 1902, Octave Chanute experimented with a new triplane glider. The pilot was Augustus Herring.

Clement Ader's 1897 *Eole III* was displayed in Paris in 1908, eleven years after its evaluation by the French government. Although Ader reported success, the government revealed in 1910 that the craft's wheels had never left the ground.

The *Hawk* was Percy Pilcher's most successful glider, carrying him to a gliding distance record soon after it was built in 1897. The glider suffered a structural failure in 1899, carrying Pilcher to his death.

Octave Chanute began his first glider experiments in 1896, using A. M. Herring as pilot. Although built after the Lilienthal gliders, this early Chanute biplane's wings have dihedral.

Perched atop it's houseboat catapult, Langley's *Aerodrome A* was photographed on 7 October 1903, shortly before its first crash into the Potomac River.

Four Flights at Kitty Hawk

Planning to move from kites into man-carrying gliders and powered aircraft, Orville and Wilbur Wright recognized the need for an appropriate test site. In late 1899 they wrote the US Weather Bureau for help finding locations known for relatively constant, moderate winds (of about 15 mph), generally fair weather, and open, level ground. This correspondence, along with advice from Octave Chanute and others, would lead them to Kitty Hawk, North Carolina.

In 1900, Kitty Hawk was little more than a post office on a series of desolate, treeless, wind-swept barrier islands known as the Outer Banks. Today the Outer Banks are a popular vacation destination, but a turn-of-the-century survey would have identified more shipwrecks than homes. That privacy and seclusion was exactly what was needed by two brothers hoping to develop and test an operable flying machine, but the seclusion came with a price - all supplies and materials would have to be boated across from the mainland. (The regular mail boat ran from Manteo on Mondays, Wednesdays, and Fridays; the causeways and bridges that now cross the sound would be built decades later.)

The brothers first visit was in September 1900. They tested their new tethered, man-carrying glider with mixed success. Living in a tent, but supported and encouraged by the few locals living in Kitty Hawk, the Wrights recognized that they were still a long way from their goal. They returned home to Dayton, leaving in late October but resolving to return the next year.

In July 1901 they built a shed at Kill Devil Hills, just south of Kitty Hawk. The shed offered better shelter than their old tent and gave room to erect and store their new machine. (In the early years, the Wrights called each of their aircraft "the machine.") But this 1901 glider also failed to perform as expected, and the Wrights were dejected and grim as they closed up camp and headed home in late August.

Experiments conducted in Dayton led to an improved glider design. Back on the Outer Banks in September 1902, the brothers began a series of highly successful free glides in October. They were joined briefly by Octave Chanute and Augustus Herring, who tested an ineffective glider of Chanute's design. But the Wrights' new glider flew superbly, and did so under near-perfect control. The brothers made between 700 and 1,000 flights that October, tweaking their aircraft and teaching themselves to fly. An enthusiastic Orville wrote home, "...we now hold all the records! The largest machine we handled in any kind of weather, made the longest distance glide [American], the longest time in the air, the smallest angle of descent, and the highest wind!!!" As they locked their glider in the shed in late October, the Wrights were aware the goal was in sight. The brothers would develop their 1902 design into a powered aircraft, and return the next year.

In September 1903, the Wright brothers returned to Kill Devil Hills, rebuilt their shed (which had suffered some damage in the previous winter's storms), and added a second, larger shed. The new shed would serve as hangar for a new machine - one with a single gasoline engine driving twin, pusher propellers. After reacquainting themselves with

This October 1932 image shows the newly completed Wright Memorial Shaft, a 60-foot high pylon which, in November, would be dedicated to the Wrights and their achievements. A path connected the memorial to a 10-ton granite boulder, installed in 1928 to mark the launch point of the first four flights. The flights launched directly away from the future site of the tower atop Kill Devil Hill.

December 1903, and "the machine" sits atop its launch rail at Kill Devil Hills. The Wrights built the smaller of their two sheds in 1901; they constructed the second shed in September 1903 to store the larger powered aircraft.

the flight characteristics of the 1902 glider (which survived the year in fine condition), the Wrights decided they were ready.

They assembled a sixty-foot wooden launch rail (which they dubbed "the Grand Junction Railroad"), mounted a wheeled dolly on the rail, and balanced the machine atop the dolly. A coin flip selected Wilbur for the first flight attempt. After a portable battery started the engine, the machine raced forty feet down the rail, rose into the air and flew a hundred feet before stalling to earth. The elevator and one of the landing skids were damaged, but Wilbur was uninjured. It was December 14, 1903.

Neither brother considered this first attempt a successful flight, but both sensed that first flight was close. Repairs and weather delayed the next attempt for three days. On the morning of December 17th, the Wrights raised a signal flag to notify the local lifesaving station that, despite high winds, they were ready to try again. Four members of the station crew (W. C. Brinkley, John Daniels, W. S. Dough, and A. D. Etheridge) and Nags Head teenager Johnny Moore walked up to help and observe. This time Orville took the controls. Again, the machine rose into the air after traveling two-thirds of the launch rail; Daniels snapped the shutter of the Wrights' camera, recording the iconic image as Wilbur stood to the right. After a twelve-second flight, the machine slid to a safe landing in the sand, 120 feet from its launch point. Although many would later question the reports, the first heavier-than-air, man-carrying, powered airplane had flown successfully.

Alternating at the controls, Orville and Wilbur completed three more flights that day, each in a relatively straight line. After the fourth flight, which lasted almost a minute and covered 852 feet, a sudden wind gust flipped the machine causing extensive damage; the aircraft never flew again. The Wrights would later name their early aircraft *Flyers*, and this machine would be known as the *1903 Flyer* or the *Kitty Hawk Flyer*. Today the Wright *1903 Flyer* occupies a place of honor in National Air and Space Museum in Washington, DC.

Ever-present Atlantic winds made launching the 1902 Glider a breeze. With Orville at the controls, Wilbur and a neighbor steady the aircraft as they trot across the summit of Kill Devil Hill.

The Wrights would develop their subsequent *Flyers* closer to home, but in May 1908 spent two weeks at Kill Devil Hills relearning the controls of their 1905 Flyer. Orville returned again in October 1911, testing an automatic stabilization system on a new glider. Orville's final visit to the Kitty Hawk campsite came in November 1932, at the dedication of the completed Wright Brothers National Memorial.

Today that 60-foot-high granite memorial is part of a National Park, with a museum, reconstructions of the sheds, and markers showing the distances flown in 1903. •

The Wrights in Europe

After 1903, Orville and Wilbur Wright began a quiet program of improvement on their invention. In Europe, the occasional reports of their successes were greeted with skepticism, and the brothers themselves were widely regarded as *bluffeurs.* The Wrights worked in relative secrecy, partially due to their self-effacing natures, but primarily to prevent what both feared would become the inevitable theft of their design.

In Europe, particularly France, aircraft were often developed on a more public stage. In October 1904, Ernest Archdeacon and the Aéro-Club de France offered a 3,000-franc prize for the first airplane to cover a distance of 25 meters, an additional 1,500 francs for the first flight of 100 meters, and 50,000 francs for the first flight around a one-kilometer circle. It would be two years before the first prize was claimed. On October 23rd, 1906, Brazilian-born aeronaut Alberto Santos-Dumont covered a distance of approximately 50 meters. On November 12th, Santos-Dumont again amazed observers with two flights, one of 86.6 meters in just over 7 seconds, and the second of 220 meters in less than 22 seconds. Already adored for his spectacular dirigible flights, *le petit Santos* was quickly recognized as the father of heavier-than-air flight.

With such amazing successes to their credit, it is little wonder that Europe's aviators were suspicious of the Wrights' 1905 claim to have flown a 24-mile circuit in just over 38 minutes. Using published sketches and accounts of the Wright gliders, Ernest Archdeacon and Robert Esnault-Pelterie had already built rudimentary imitations of the Americans' machines. When these aircraft failed to perform, the experience reinforced disbelief in the Americans' accomplishments.

The brothers toured Europe in 1907, hoping to sell their invention to European governments, but refusing to uncrate and demonstrate the Model A they had brought along. In May 1908, Wilbur returned to France. His plans to demonstrate the Flyer's capabilities were initially thwarted when the machine, which had languished at the Le Harve customs office since the previous year, was found to have been damaged. Orville shipped new parts from America, while Wilbur repaired and adjusted what he could. The delays fueled local incredulity, and the aircraft would not be ready for flight until August 8th. On that day, at Hunaudières racecourse, a single warm-up flight of one-and-three-quarters minutes changed the face of European aviation for ever. Two graceful, effortless circles and a smooth landing stunned the expectant crowd, which included some of France's greatest aviators. Louis Blériot proclaimed, "A new era in mechanical flight has commenced... it is marvelous... Wright is a genius. He is the master of us all!" A shocked Léon Delagrange remarked, "We are beaten! We just don't exist!" The Aéro-Club de France, long-time critics of the Wrights, repudiated its earlier rejections of the Wright claims, as "...the greatest error of the century!" In the UK, the British Aeronautical Society wrote, "That Wright is in possession of a power which controls the fate of nations is beyond dispute."

In a nation that adored its aviators, the *bluffeur* was suddenly a public hero. Wright's quiet demeanor and working class tastes (sleeping in the shed with his aircraft, carrying his lunch pail) only added to the man's mystique. He was lovingly dubbed "Old Oilcan," a pun on the French pronunciation of his name (*Vieille Burette*) that somehow managed to reflect his strong, and understated character.

ABOVE: Wilbur Wright and passenger draw the attention of French farmers during an early demonstration flight.

LEFT: Viewed from the grandstands, the Wright Model A is prepared for a demonstration flight at the Le Mans race course.

Between August 8th and 13th 1908, Wilbur made nine flights at Hunaudières. He then moved to a larger field at Camp d'Auvours, seven miles east of Le Mans, demonstrating the Flyer in 104 flights between August 21st and the year's end. Orville joined his brother in 1909, and in April the two performed 42 demonstrations near Rome before returning home. In August 1909, Orville returned to Europe for several demonstration flights at Tempelhof, Germany.

The brothers left Europe with companies contracted to build and sell Wright aircraft and train aviators to fly them. But more importantly, they left European designers with an awareness that future designs must maneuver along three axes. The revolution in European design would not be far behind.

ABOVE: During one of his first French demonstration flights, Wilbur Wright carried French Captain Paul N. Luca-Girardville as passenger.

RIGHT: Photographed at the controls of his Model A, Wilbur Wright prepares for another demonstration flight at Hunaudières, July 1908.

BOTTOM: The Wright Model A skims the field at Centocelle, near Rome. The photo was taken from a captive balloon.

The New Pioneers

Although the Wrights flew at the end of 1903, almost three years elapsed before the next country (France) would produce a successful heavier-than-air craft. The French would soon dominate the market, and through 1911 the historic first flights over most nations would be made in French Voisins, Farmans, and Blériots. •

HARRY HOUDINI
born: ERIK WEISZ; later EHRICH WEISS
(24 March 1874 – 31 October 1926)
Hungarian-born American Harry Houdini was already famous as an escape artist, magician, and movie star when he arrived in Australia in 1910. Late the previous year, Houdini had purchased (and learned to fly) a French Voisin biplane in Germany. Erecting the aircraft at Diggers Rest, just outside Melbourne, the "handcuff king" made the first successful flight in Australian skies on 16 March 1910.

	FLIGHT #	
1903	1	December 17 - USA - Wright brothers - Wright Biplane - Kitty Hawk, NC
1906	2	October 23 - France - Alberto Santos-Dumont - Santos-Dumont Biplane - Paris
	3	?? - Denmark - J. C. Ellehammer - Ellehammer Biplane - Lindholm
		Many sources cite Ellehammer's attempt of 23 September as the first successful "flight" of a European aircraft. However, this claim is generally discounted because the aircraft was tethered to the ground during the entire hop. Ellehammer would succeed later in 1906, but the date of that flight is not recorded.
1908	4	May 15 - Italy - L. Delagrange - Voisin Biplane - Rome
	5	May 26 - Belgium - H. Farman - Voisin Biplane - Ghent
	6	June 8 - England - A. V. Roe - Avro Biplane - Brooklands
	7	June 18 - Holland - E. Lefebvre - Wright Biplane - The Hague
	8	November 24 - Germany - A. Zipfel - Voisin Biplane - Berlin
	9	December- Scotland - Lt. Lancelot D. L. Gibbs - Dunne Biplane - Blair Atholl
		Gibbs made a number of bounds and hops in the Dunne D.4 at Blair Atholl in late October; he eventually flew 40 yards in December.
1909	10	February 23 - Canada - J. A. D. McCurdy - Silver Dart Biplane - Baddeck, N.S.
	11	April 23 - Austria - G. Legagneux - Voisin Biplane - Vienna
	12	July 25 - Russia - Van der Schrouff - Voisin Biplane - Odessa
	13	July 29 - Sweden - G. Legagneux - Voisin Biplane - Stockholm
	14	October 17 - Hungary - L. Bleriot - Bleriot Monoplane - Budapest
	15	October 30 - Rumania - L. Bleriot - Bleriot Monoplane - Bucharest
	16	November 15 - Algeria - R. Metrot - Voisin Biplane - Blida
	17	December 2 - Turkey - P. de Caters - Voisin Biplane - Constantinople
	18	December 15 - Egypt - P. de Caters - Voisin Biplane - Abbassia
	19	December 28 - South Africa - Albert Kimmerling - Voisin Biplane - East London
	20	December 31 - Ireland - Ferguson - Ferguson Monoplane - Hillsborough
1910	21	January 8 - Mexico - Alberto Braniff - Voisin Biplane - Mexico City
	22	February 2 - Argentina - H. Bregi - Voisin Biplane - Burzaco
	23	February - Brazil - G. Ruggerone - H. Farman Biplane - ?
	24	February - Cuba - H. Bregi - Voisin Biplane - Havana
	25	February 10 - Spain - J. Mamet - Bleriot Monoplane - Barcelona
	26	March 13 - Switzerland - Engelhard - Wright Biplane - St.-Moritz
	27	March 16 - Australia - Harry Houdini - Voisin Biplane - Diggers Rest
	28	April 21 - Portugal - Julien Mamet - Bleriot XI Monoplane - Lisbon
		Some sources credit A. Zipfel with Portugal's first successful flight in December 1909. Zipfel took off and flew without problem, however, he crashed his Voisin Biplane on landing.
	29	August 21 - Chile - Cesar Copetta - Voisin Biplane - Santiago
	30	October 14 - Norway - C. Cederstrom - Bleriot Monoplane - Etterstadt
	31	December 15 - Indochina - C. Van der Born - H. Farman Biplane - Saigon
	32	December 17 - India - H. Pequet - Humber Monoplane - Allahabad
	33	December 19 - Japan - Y. Tokugawa - H. Farman Biplane - Tokyo
1911	34	February - Peru - Juan Biélovucic - Voisin Monoplane - Lima
	35	February 9 - New Zealand - V. Walsh - Howard-W right Biplane - Papakura
	36	February 21 - Philippines - Bud Mars - Baldwin Red Devil Biplane - Manila
	37	February 21 - China - R. Vallon - Sommer Biplane - Shanghai
	38	December - Madagascar - Jean Raoult - Bleriot Monoplane - Tananarive

J. C. "BUD" MARS, born: JAMES D. McBRIDE (8 March 1876 – 25 July 1944)
At the age of fourteen, James McBride ran away from home, changing his name to Bud Mars and finding work as a circus acrobat performer. In 1892, the teenage Mars met balloonist Thomas S. Baldwin and began an eighteen-year career as a touring balloonist, parachute jumper, and dirigible pilot. After learning to fly airplanes in early 1910, Mars joined Glenn Curtiss' exhibition team, touring the US and Canada. The year ended with Mars joining Thomas Scott Baldwin for a Pacific demonstration tour of Baldwin's Red Devil biplanes. In February 1911, Mars made the first flight in the Philippines. After Baldwin and the rest of the team returned to the US, Mars continued his with own tour of the Far East through June. In 1912, Mars retired from demonstration flying.

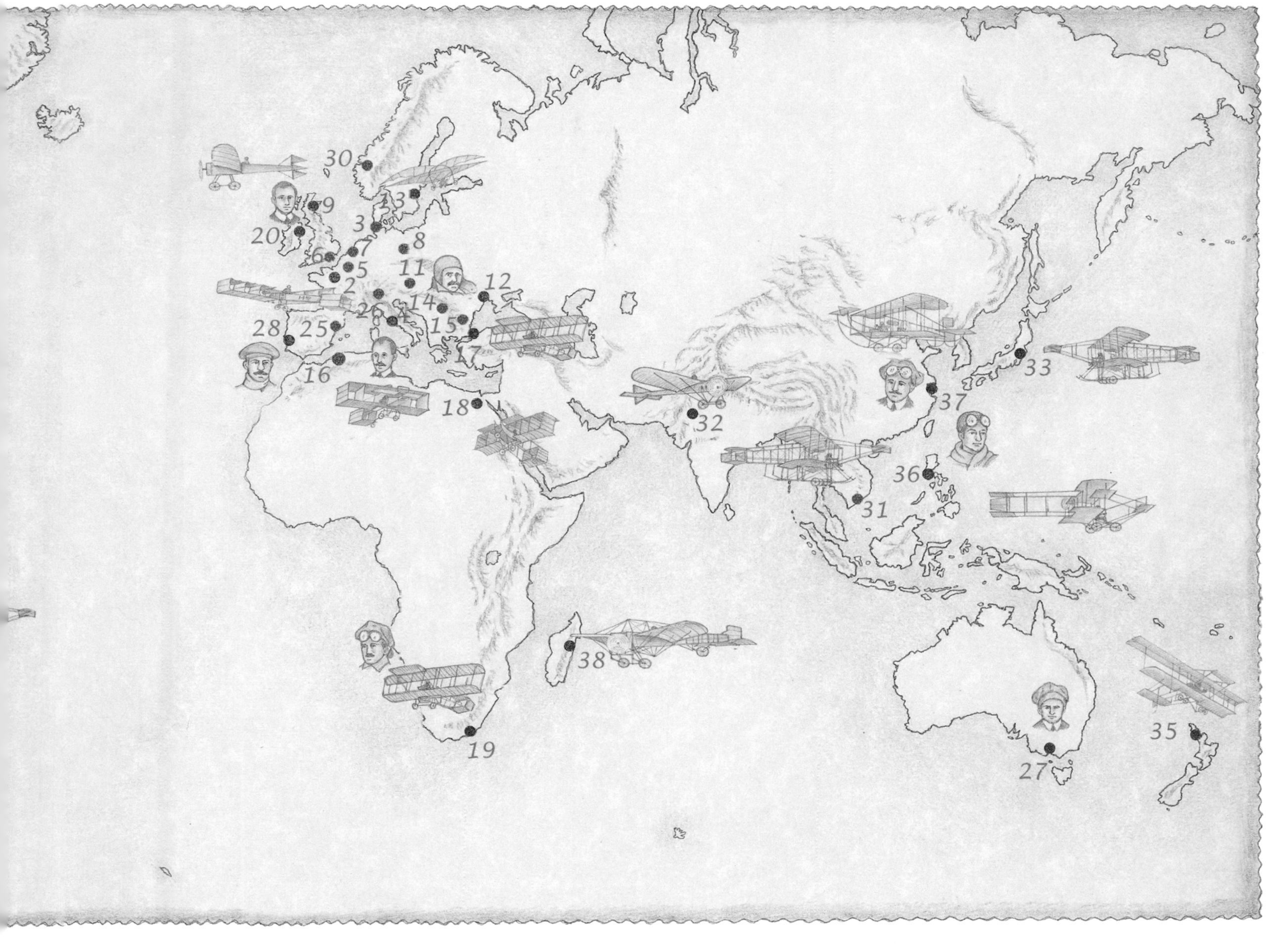

ALBERTO SANTOS-DUMONT
(20 July 1873 – 23 July 1932)
His work with dirigible airships had already made Alberto Santos-Dumont the toast of Paris when he turned his attention to heavier-than-air craft in 1904. Subsequent experiments with were rewarded on 23 October 1906 with the first flight of his Model 14*bis*. Most of Europe would recognize Santos-Dumont as the inventor of the airplane, a claim later discounted by recognition of the Wright brothers' achievements. Santos-Dumont would die in 1932 in his native Brazil, where he is still recognized as the Father of Aviation.

Charles K. Hamilton hangs on as one of Israel Ludlow's 1905 gliders is towed aloft in New York. A year later, Ludlow himself would be severely injured in a crash of one of the aircraft; he would remain partially paralized until his death in 1960.

The Blériot IX was easily the most influential monoplane of its day - it was produced in the hundreds and imitated by designers in every flying nation. This example was actually flown by its designer, Louis Blériot, at an early aerial demonstration.

In August 1909, The Great Week of Aviation at Reims drew Europe's aviation elite and hopefuls for a series of races and contests. Here, France's Eugène Lefebvre in a Wright Biplane, leads Henri Fournier in his Voisin. Two days later, Fournier would escape injury in a crash; less fortunate, Lefebvre would die at the controls of his Wright in early September.

Helping hands push Jean Olieslangers' Blériot out of a tidal pool as Rawlinson's Farman buzzes in over the surf. The competitors were entered in one of a series of races held at Nice in April 1910.

London's *Daily Mail* hired Henri Salmet to tour Britain as a good-will ambassador for aviation and good journalism. His flights included this demonstration at the seaside resort at Margate in August 1913.

Europe's Great Races

Many factors affected aviation's remarkable growth in the decade following the Wrights' first flight; for many, the promise of prize money was certainly a major influence. Among the best known prizes were three offered by the London *Daily Mail* in June 1909. One prize posted £1,000 for the first British-built airplane and British pilot to fly a mile, taking off and landing at the same point. Another £1,000 was offered for the first pilot and airplane of any nation to cross the English Channel. And the third offer, renewing a prize first announced in 1906, promised £10,000 for the first flight between London and Manchester.

With the French and Americans already logging some substantial distance flights, the first British one-mile flight was a nudge to a lagging domestic aviation industry; that flight would be completed by J. T. C. Moore-Brabazon on 30 October 1909. While British aviation would continue to grown, the French continued to expand their lead. Less than five years later, Frenchman Roland Garros would have flown across the Mediterranean, with his countryman Jules Védrines carrying a passenger 2,500 miles from France to Egypt. Through July 1914, lucrative prizes would encourage new aviation developments, with several nations preparing to attempt the first crossing of the Atlantic. The pioneering races would end in August as World War I drew the talents of designers and pilots into combat.

Six long-distance races, three of them sponsored by the *Daily Mail*, illustrate the dramatic increases in the ranges of pioneering aircraft. •

25 July 1909 - Blériot crosses the English Channel. The *Daily Mail* prize for crossing the English Channel would draw five competitors. All elected to fly from the French coast, but only two would actually attempt the flight. The first was Hubert Latham, who took off in his Antoinette monoplane on 19 July; six miles into the flight, his engine quit. Both aircraft and aviator were safely recovered from the Channel's gentle waves by a French destroyer.

A few days later, a replacement Antoinette arrived - but so did the fifth competitor. Louis Blériot and the eleventh monoplane of his own design would take off two days later during the pre-dawn calm. Latham, with his more powerful engine, rushed to launch and overtake his competitor mid-Channel, but increasing winds forced another delay.

Flying without a compass, Blériot found himself lost above a surface haze that obscured both coasts. The cliffs of Dover eventually drew his attention to the west, where his aircraft was damaged in a rough landing. The 22-mile flight had taken 36 minutes; when Blériot landed Britons joyfully accepted a new hero even as they recognized that their island was now vulnerable to attack from the air. (The first bombing raid was little more than five years away.) Blériot's eleventh aircraft became the sire of a line - hundreds of Type XIs would be built at the Blériot factory, with many more built by international licensees and imitators.

Louis Blériot stands atop his model XI prior to his flight across the English Channel.

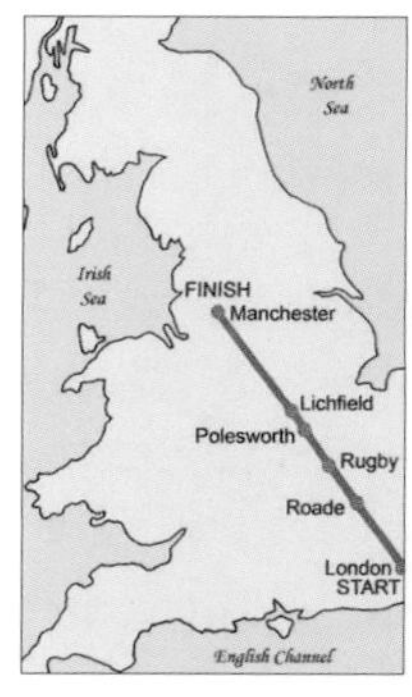

27-28 April 1910 - London-Manchester Race. Offering one of aviation's first great prizes, the *Daily Mail* promised £10,000 to the first aviator to fly the 185 miles between London and Manchester in less than 24 hours. As with the cross-Channel flight, a single successful flight constituted a victory - there was no requirement for multiple entrants.

So it was that Englishman Claude Grahame-White left London in his French Farman biplane on 23 April 1910. Louis Paulhan, the only announced competitor, had not yet left France. Paulhan seemed unconcerned by Grahame-White's start – the poor reliability of early aircraft and engines suggested that the Frenchman was still likely to get his opportunity. Indeed, Grahame-White flew within 62 miles from Manchester when violent headwinds forced him to land. As he awaited better conditions, a sudden, heavy gust flipped his machine and caused enough damage to end all flying for several days.

Four days later, his Farman repaired, Grahame-White was back in London - but so was Louis Paulhan. Despite severe winds, Paulhan took off that afternoon. The English pilot rushed to catch up, taking to the air an hour later. Darkness forced both aviators to land, with Paulhan still 60 miles in the lead. After a brief rest, Grahame-White took off at 2:00 the next morning, reasoning that a night flight - however risky and unconventional - was his only chance of closing the gap. Warned of the Englishman's approach, Paulhan launched at 4:16. Unaware that engine problems had forced Grahame-White to land only six miles to the south, Paulhan raced to Manchester with one eye over his shoulder. In an hour and a quarter, victory was his.

Paulhan would fly the route again in 1950, celebrating the fortieth anniversary of his first inter-city flight. On that occasion he was strapped into the back seat of an RAF Gloster Meteor jet. The flight took 48 minutes.

Another British race won by a Frenchman; Louis Paulhan and his Henri Farman biplane are surrounded by an enthusiastic crowd at the completion of the London-Manchester race.

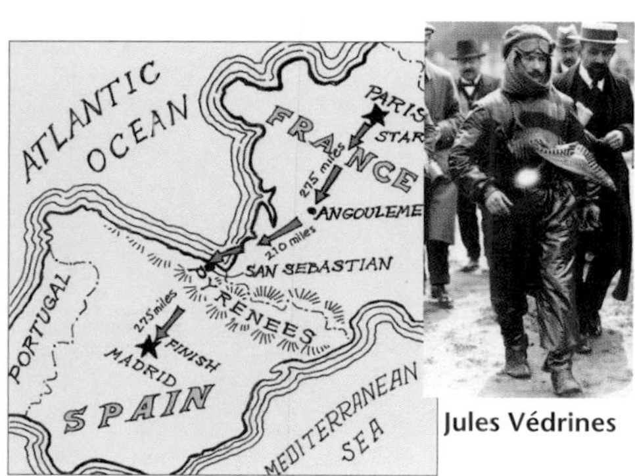

Jules Védrines

22-24 May 1911 – Paris-Madrid Race. The London-Manchester race inspired other intercity prizes and ushered in an era of long-distance attempts. In April 1911, France's Pierre Prier set a new non-stop, point-to-point record, flying the 250 miles from London to Paris at an amazing average speed of 64mph. A month later, on 21 May, a field of 28 aviators gathered for the Paris-Madrid race. While a $30,000 purse waited at the end of the 874-mile course, death marked the beginning. Crowd control was always an issue at these early races, and when one aviator returned for an emergency landing, he found the field covered with spectators. His forced landing would injure the French prime minister and kill the minister of war. Another aviator, Jules Védrines, wrecked his Blériot while avoiding the crowd; he was able to borrow a Morane Borel before the race restarted the next day. By late on the 23rd, mechanical difficulties and weather had eliminated all but three competitors; additional mechanical problems soon grounded all but the hotheaded Jules Védrines, who flew his borrowed Morane Borel to Madrid on the 24th. The celebrations kept Védrines in Spain so long that he almost missed the start of the next great race from Paris to Rome.

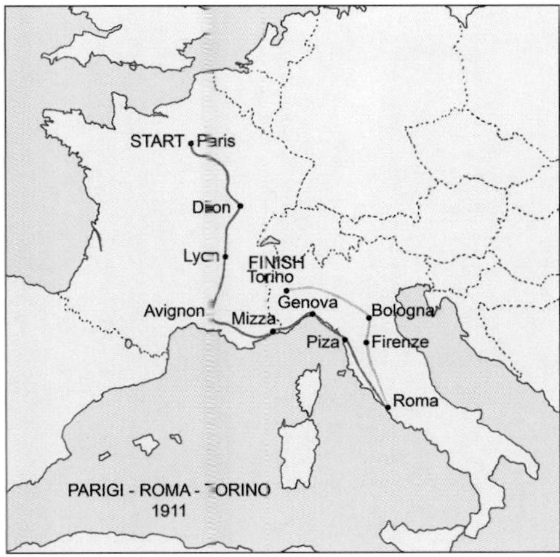

Exhausted by the time he arrived in Rome, Lieutenant Jean Conneau stands with the support of an enthusiastic crowd. Conneau raced as Andre Beaumont; the French military insisted that each of its pilots adopt a *nom de course* when participating in civilian events.

28 May – 5 June 1911 - Paris to Rome (Torino). Celebrations of the 50th anniversary of Italian independence included an international race from Paris to Rome. Although twenty aviators registered for the competition, only twelve were able to takeoff when the race began on the morning of 28 May 1911. By the first evening, only two racers (Roland Garros and Roger Conneau) had reached Avignon with several other racers delayed along the route.

On the third day, Conneau was delayed, forced to replace a sabotaged engine; the race had become subject of heavy betting, and several sportsmen evidently found Conneau's success an expensive proposition. Garros arrived at Genova before his competition left Nice; he would later receive a special gold medal as the first contestant to reach Italy. Garros ended the day with an over-water flight (under the watchful eyes of an Italian naval escort) to Pisa.

The fourth day saw a reversal, with Garros crash landing just outside Pisa. While he ordered a replacement aircraft from France, Conneau flew by, reaching Rome that evening. Garros arrived in Rome the next day, 1 June, followed by Andrea Frey on the 3rd, and Renato Vidart on the 5th.

Although organizers had planned to extend the race from Rome to Torino, only Andrea Frey would attempt this northward journey. Lost in the fog, he wrecked his aircraft in a crash near Viterbo on 12 June. Trapped in the wreckage for thirteen hours, Frey suffered only a broken jaw; his survival was attributed to Frey's early use of a flight helmet. The Torino attempt was enough to earn Frey a consolation prize and a gold medal.

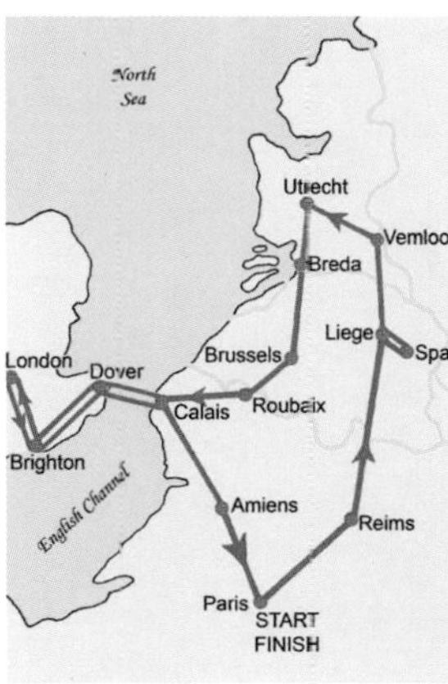

18 June – 7 July 1911 - European Circuit. With a top prize of £20,000, the 1911 European Circuit race drew a field of 53 aviators. The three-week race covered four countries and included two Channel crossings. The three best known airmen - Védrines, Conneau, and Garros - were entered, but many of the challengers lacked the experience for a cross-country race of almost 1,100 miles.

At the official start outside of Paris, spectators again crowded the field; nearly 200 were injured as mounted police drove them back to safety. At 6:00am the first racer took to the air, followed by 42 others at two-minute intervals. Eleven airmen would not start, and two of those who did died a few minutes after taking off. Additionally, a French military aviator assigned to escort the racers died in the crash of his Blériot. Five more would crash on the first leg, one with serious injuries.

Eight completed the first leg that day; a one-day delay of the race allowed ten more to catch up. Over the next three weeks, each airman suffered his share of setbacks, and even the leaders were flying replacement engines, wings, or landing gear. On 7 July, Rene Vidart became the first to complete the race; Conneau, however, would be the overall winner, with a total flying time of 58 hours 38 minutes. Garros was second, four hours behind, followed by Vidart, eleven hours behind Garros, and finally Védrines, flying a replacement aircraft after wrecking his starting machine in Brussels. All would be soon be preparing for the Circuit of Britain race.

22 - 26 July 1911 - Circuit of Britain. Lord Northcliff and the *Daily Mail* again offered a huge prize to encourage advances in British aviation. Fifteen of the thirty aircraft entered were British, but even a top prize of £10,000 could not remake an industry overnight.

Crashes in pre-race flight tests eliminated three aircraft, two of them British. Another Briton was banned from the race for "buzzing" (a term that had not yet been invented) the Henley Rowing Regata. Seven more withdrawals whittled the field to nineteen starters (eleven British), including favorites Védrines and Conneau.

In all, four would finish the race, though none would die in the attempt. On the 26th, Védrines, who had the fastest aircraft, took second to Conneau, the superior navigator. A week later, Britain's James Valentine would land in his French Deperdussin, and a day after that, American-born Briton Samuel Cody brought in his home-built aircraft, nicknamed the *Flying Parish Church.* The British press, which had sponsored a worthy race, was quick to note that every aircraft designed by a British company had failed to finish.

1911 was a good year for Jean Conneau (aka Andre Beaumont), who won the Paris-Rome Race and the circuits of Europe and Britain. Besides the support of a fine racing team, Conneau's navigational training helped guide him to the right field when other aviators lost their ways.

Ground handlers await Rene Vidart's release signal at the beginning of the European Circuit. Three weeks later, Vidart would be the first to cross the finish line, coming in third overall when flight times were totaled.

The First Aeronautical Charts

One of the first aviation maps ever printed, this beautiful 1909 German topo (topographical map) covered most of the Rhineland, and a portion of Alsace-Lorraine. The key (below, right) shows a range of pastel shades marking every fifty meters of ground height and style of markings for political boundaries, major thoroughfares, and population centers.

Perhaps the real story of this map is what it doesn't show. No markings depict landing fields or airports - few existed, and most contemporary aviators tried to stay close to the field they had just left. Nor were there any beacons or aerial markers. Latitudes and longitudes are marked in the borders, but not laid out across the map itself. And most indicative of the limited range and instrument capability of the early aviator, there is no indication of magnetic north! A compass rose or magnetic declination arrow, standard on all other navigational maps, was of little use when few aircraft or aviators carried a compass.

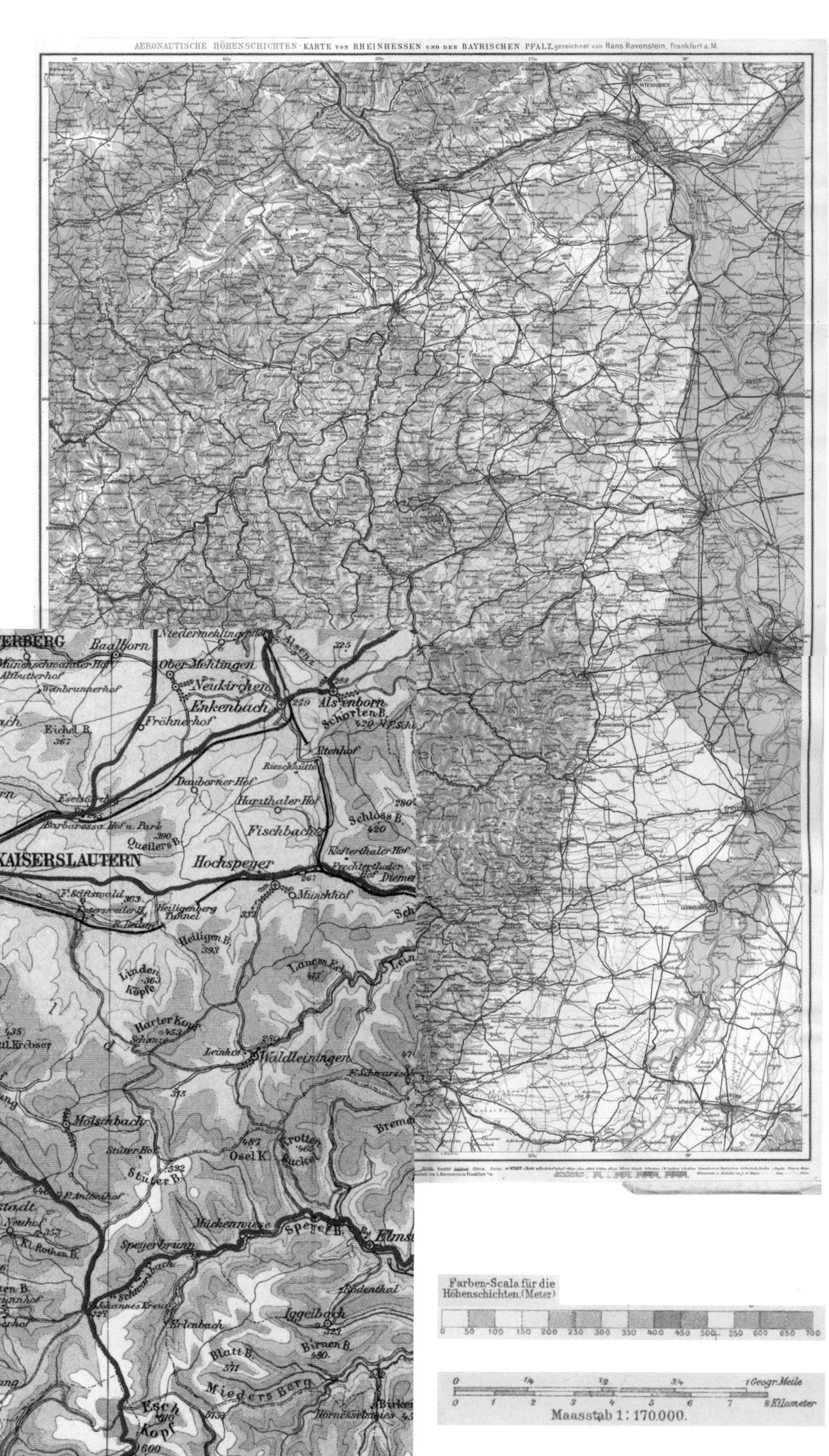

Hans Grade built the first German airplane in 1907, making his first flight in October 1908. By 1910, Grade had established his first pilot school and aircraft factory, soon exporting his designs across Europe and Asia. This monoplane is a Grade 1911 design.

The Albatros firm, which would become a famous for its World War I fighter designs, began by producing copies of Farman biplanes in 1910.

The years before World War I saw many inspired designers turning to aviation, then soon forgotten. Little is known about Paul Fiedler, for example, who apparently designed this large monoplane in 1911.

The Taube (Dove) was one of Germany's most successful prewar designs. Produced for sport flying by a number of European factories, the aircraft was also used for observation duties at the beginning of World War I.

The Race Across America

One of those inspired by Louis Paulhan's victory in the London-to-Manchester race was American publisher William Randolph Hearst. With aircraft now connecting two great cities, Hearst reasoned that aviation should be capable of flying between the US East and West Coasts. In September 1910, Hearst posted a $50,000 prize for the first aviator to depart by 10 October 1911, and complete the flight within thirty days. While many, including the Wright bothers, protested that aviation had not progressed to the point that such a flight would be possible, the Aeronautical Society presented Hearst with a medal for his "contribution and inspiration toward the advancement of aeronautics."

For a year, Hearst's challenge went unanswered. Finally, in September 1911, four contenders threw their hats into the ring. Newly minted aviator Calbraith Perry "Cal" Rodgers became the third to start, leaving Sheepshead Bay, Long Island, on 17 September. Sponsored by the Armour Meat Packing Co, Rodgers' new Wright EX was christened the *Vin Fiz* to promote the company's new grape soda. Following 4,231 miles of rail lines, accompanied by a support team in a special rail car and automobile, Rodgers complete his journey on December 10th; the epic, crash-marked flight took 84 days, with a total flying time of 82 hours and 4 minutes. Bob Fowler, who flew west to east, would not arrive in Florida until February 1912, and the other two competitors would not finish. But none would collect Hearst's prize. The magnate had already done his part by promoting the flight in the first place; he could not be faulted if no one arrived before the deadline expired.... •

ABOVE: Cal Rodgers (1879-1912) took his first lesson at Dayton's Wright Flying School on 5 June 1911. Six days later, after a half-dozen quarter-hour training flights, he bought the Wright B aircraft he'd trained on; dispensing with further instruction, he soloed that afternoon. Rodgers took to the road as an exhibition flyer in August and started his quest for the Hearst Prize in September. The fame that followed his three-month transcontinental flight faded quickly, and Rodgers returned to exhibition flying in 1912. He died in the crash of his Wright B at Long Beach, California on 3 April 1912, less than ten months after his first flight.

TOP LEFT: Rodgers and the *Vin Fiz*, in flight over Arizona. Frequent accidents meant that few original aircraft parts remained by the completion of the transcontinental flight. However, a glass bottle of Vin Fiz soda, strapped to a strut beside the aviator (see circle), survived the trip unscathed. Rodgers never again flew without this talisman, which was broken in his fatal crash of April 1912.

BOTTOM LEFT: Vin Fiz advertisements stressed the connection of Rogers' flight and their refreshing grape soda.

Rodgers' transcontinental route followed the rail line, partially to aid with navigation, partially to keep the aviator near his supply of spare parts.

With few airfields available in 1911, Rodgers landed in any available field. With the *Vin Fiz* prepared for the next leg of it's journey, curious locals gather for the event at an unidentified town in the Southwest.

This rail car advertised Vin Fiz while carrying Rodgers' replacement parts, support team, new wife, and his mother.

With his ever-present cigar, Cal Rodgers stands by his aircraft following the first successful transcontinental flight. The aviator walked away on crutches, his broken leg still mending from an earlier crash.

Fledglings and the Great War

For much of the late nineteenth century, European territorial ambitions had brought the continent to the brink of war. A complicated system of secret treaties ensured that once Austria-Hungary declared war on Serbia on 29 July 1914, all of the major powers would soon be brought into the conflict. But few could have imagined that a "local" conflict would, within a week, commit Belgium, Britain, France, Germany, Luxemburg, and Russia to war; and none believed that the war would still be raging four years later.

As the War began, the role of aviation remained undetermined. Although many Britons were certain that German dirigibles would soon cross the North Sea to bomb their factories, military facilities, and homes, most aircraft had been built to reconnoiter ground forces, supplementing the work of light cavalry. Austria-Hungary entered the war with most of its fleet of lightweight, unarmed Lohner Pfeilflieger biplanes grounded; of 79 aircraft, 40 needed new wings as war was declared. The French, long-lauded for their enlightened approach to military aviation, had less than 200 aircraft in service, most of these unarmed Farmans, Breguets, and Blériots. (Eight squadrons flew Blériot XIs, similar to the cross-Channel aircraft of 1909; the aircraft was transferred to training units in early 1915!) Most of these early observation aircraft were unarmed, though several units were equipped with newer, heavier machine-gun-armed machines, and more advanced designs were beginning to enter service. No air arm flew fighter aircraft - the need for specialized designs, equipped to pursue and destroy enemy planes, balloons, and airships, had not yet been fully recognized.

The Germans had built a fleet of eight military airships (with more to come) but had shown little interest in using them for long-range bombing attacks. Imperial Russia led the world in heavy, four-engined aircraft. Russian Il'ya Muromets bombers began long-range reconnaissance missions in October 1914, and began bombing German trenches the following February. Germany and Italy were quick to recognize the potential of such aircraft and began design of their own heavy aircraft. Britain would not field a heavy bomber until the last year of the war, and France would prove unable to produce a capable bomber. (America's eventual interest in building heavy bombers would be jump-started by license-production of British and Italian designs; none would see combat.)

Seaplane and float plane designs were also fairly advanced at the beginning of the war. Britain had purchased its first large Curtiss flying boat, and would develop the type into superlative weapons for sea patrol and anti-submarine warfare. Smaller German float planes would bomb English ports in December 1914, though they caused little damage.

Aviators would have an early impact on the ground war when reconnaissance patrols identified an advancing German army east of Paris on 2 September 1914. A French counterattack resulted in the Battle of the Marne, the Allies' first major victory. •

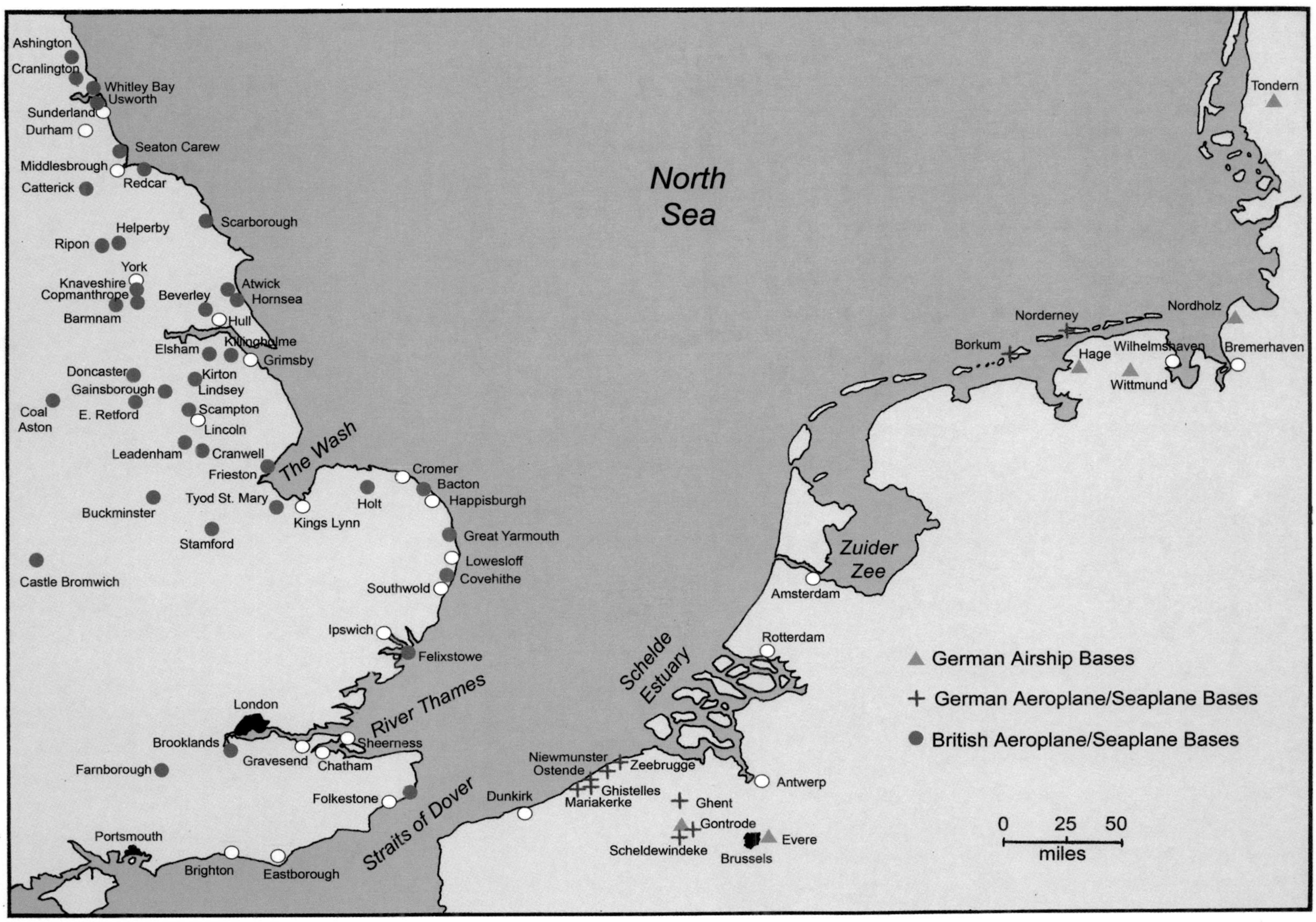

North Sea
Ashington
Cranlington
Whitley Bay
Usworth
Sunderland
Durham
Seaton Carew
Middlesbrough
Redcar
Catterick
Scarborough
Helperby
Ripon
York
Knaveshire
Copmanthrope
Beverley
Atwick
Hornsea
Barmnam
Hull
Elsham
Killingholme
Grimsby
Doncaster
Kirton
Lindsey
Gainsborough
Coal Aston
E. Retford
Scampton
Lincoln
Leadenham
Cranwell
The Wash
Frieston
Cromer
Bacton
Happisburgh
Tyod St. Mary
Holt
Buckminster
Kings Lynn
Stamford
Great Yarmouth
Lowesloff
Covehithe
Castle Bromwich
Southwold
Ipswich
Felixstowe
London
River Thames
Brooklands
Sheerness
Gravesend
Chatham
Farnborough
Folkestone
Straits of Dover
Portsmouth
Brighton
Eastborough
Dunkirk
Niewmunster
Ostende
Zeebrugge
Ghistelles
Mariakerke
Ghent
Gontrode
Scheldewindeke
Brussels
Evere
Antwerp
Schelde Estuary
Rotterdam
Amsterdam
Zuider Zee
Tondern
Norderney
Nordholz
Borkum
Hage
Wilhelmshaven
Bremerhaven
Wittmund
▲ German Airship Bases
+ German Aeroplane/Seaplane Bases
● British Aeroplane/Seaplane Bases
0 25 50
miles

British No. 70 Squadron took these new Sopwith 1-1/2 Strutters to France in September 1916. Though outclassed by German fighters within weeks, the type remained in combat in secondary areas throughout the war.

The Blériot XI served with French, British, Belgian, and Russian front-line units through the first months of the war, continuing in supporting roles through 1918. Above is an example in French service.

As with the other European nations, Czarist Russia entered the Great War armed with a large number of outmoded, single-engined, two-seat reconnaissance aircraft. The Russian forces, however, were expecting the first deliveries of their giant new Sikorsky Il'ya Muromets four-engined bombers. No nation would possess a comparable aircraft for over a year.

Most of the Austro-Hungarian military's small fleet of Lohner Pfeilflieger biplanes was grounded with structural problems as the Empire declared war - the lack of an air arm seemed little cause for concern. Red and white stripes on wings, tail, or fuselage served to identify Austria-Hungary's aircraft.

Over the Trenches

European army commanders soon learned the efficiencies of the advanced weapons they now fielded. Nearly all troops now carried high-powered, clip-loaded rifles capable of a high rate of accurate fire. Units were supported by a variety of machine guns and artillery, all with increased accuracy, rate of fire, and potency. As even the best troops proved unable to sustain an advance against such murderous fire, the armies ground to a halt. And, taught by centuries of military experience, the soldiers dug in and prepared to launch or repel the next attack.

Successful attacks required an ability to secretly concentrate forces against an opponent's weakest position before enemy reenforcements respond. In earlier wars, light cavalry could reconnoiter behind enemy lines looking for signs of enemy buildups, while infantry patrols probed enemy lines looking for weaknesses to exploit. But the trench systems that stretched the length of France left little room for cavalry sorties, and few infantry patrols could penetrate enemy lines to any depth. Against this backdrop, observation airplanes and balloons were the only assets able to gather intelligence on enemy fortifications and deployments, spot and report the accuracy of artillery barrages, and even drop the occasional bomb on enemy positions. The disruption of enemy reconnaissance and observation required a new type of aircraft, one equipped to destroy enemy airplanes and balloons.

The British fielded what can probably be considered the first fighter, the Vickers F.B. Series Gunbus. In 1913, Vickers introduced the E.F.B.1 (First Experimental Fighting Biplane), a two-seat pusher biplane with a single, flexible machine gun mounted in the nose. This developed into the E.F.B.2, E.F.B.3, F.B.4, and F.B.5 (all developed before the war began). An F.B.4 unsuccessfully attacked the Friedrichshafen floatplane that attacked London on Christmas Day 1914. The F.B.s all carried forward firing machine guns, but a general lack of power and maneuverability would prevent them from serving as effective fighter aircraft.

In France, former air racer Roland Garros found far more success with a modified Morane-Saulnier Type L. Raymond Saulnier had fitted the tractor aircraft with a single, forward-firing 8mm Hotchkiss machine gun and designed a synchronization system to help the weapon fire through the propeller arc. The unreliability of French ammunition posed a problem, with late-firing rounds occasionally reaching the front of the cowling at the same time as the wooden propeller blade. To counter the problem, Saulnier fitter deflector plates to the blades' rear faces. Flying out of Dunkerque on 1 April 1915, Garros encountered and destroyed a two-seat German reconnaissance biplane. The first fighter pilot destroyed two more aircraft (on 15 April and the morning of 18 April) before being brought down by ground fire on the afternoon of his third victory.) Garros survived, but so did his aircraft, which was examined with great interest by German authorities.

The Germans turned to Dutch aircraft designer Anthony Fokker (who had established his sole factory in Germany) for a counter to the French aerial weapon. Fokker was already producing two versions of his M.5 observation monoplane, which was copied from the earlier Morane-Saulnier Model H, and there is evidence that his firm was working on its own interrupter system before Garros had entered combat. In June, the first machine-gun equipped Fokkers (designated E.I or Eindecker - Monoplane - Type I) was at the front. The effect on the Allies, who had made little further effort to design or produce fighter aircraft, was devastating. Although not particularly fast or maneuverable, the Eindecker could destroy any aircraft that didn't flee at its approach. Called the *scourge* by the Allies, the little aircraft owned the skies until early 1916.

By that time, the French and British had introduced new fighters of their own. The Nieuport 11 was a speedy, maneuverable sesquiplane that danced through the sky, firing

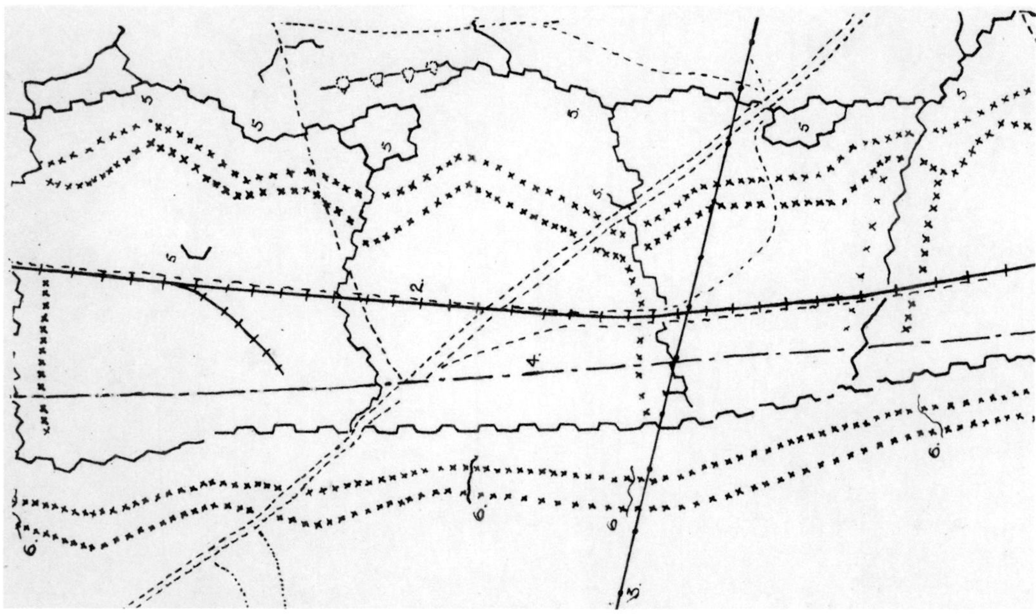

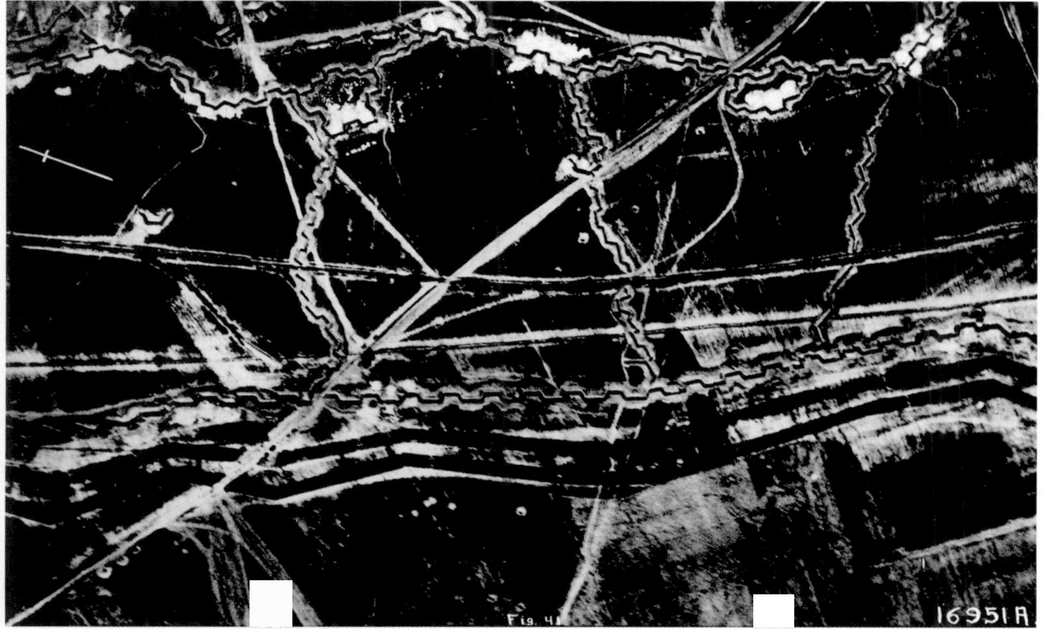

Allied intelligence experts used this aerial photo of a German trench network to create the accompanying map. Such maps were useful for planning patrols, artillery barrages, and all-out attacks.

a single machine gun above the propeller arc. Geoffrey de Havilland designed two superior pushers, the D.H.2 for Airco and the F.E.2b for the Royal Aircraft Factory, and British units were again able to hold their own against the Germans.

What followed was two-and-a-half years of accelerated development in all classes of military aircraft, with particular emphasis on fighter designs. Without fighters, few other aircraft could complete their missions. Without control of the air, ground forces were at the mercy of enemy ground forces who could find and exploit weaknesses, moving without threat of detection right up to the moment of attack. Every few months, a new fighter design would enter service and render all previous fighters obsolete (with unfortunate consequences for all pilots who had to continue to fight in older machines until their own improved designs reached the front).

In an obscene war, with tens of thousands of young men dying in the mud during each day of battle, it is little wonder that the public would consider fighter pilots knights of the air. Enjoying a hot meal, wearing clean, warm clothes and polished boots, only the pilot could range into enemy territory, killing or dying by his own skill (with little credit or blame given to the quality of his aircraft) and, hopefully, returning to a comfortable bed, a well-stocked bar, and a salute to fallen friends and enemies. •

Escorted by a Dorand A.R.2 reconnaissance plane, French heavy cavalry moves to the front in 1917.

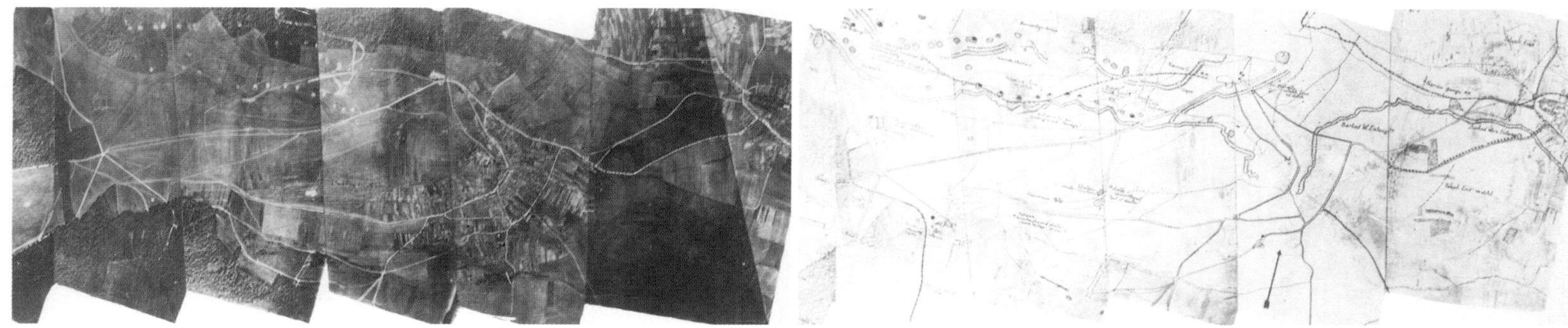

A photo mosaic of the German defenses along the Hindenberg Line in 1918, displayed with a schematic map interpreting the defenses.

A low-angle oblique image shows the effects of years of artillery on the local countryside and defenses. May 1917.

Roland Garros holds a clip of ammunition for the Hotchkiss machine gun on his Morane-Saulnier Model H. Garros would later take a similar Model L, with parasol wing, into combat. Note the triangular deflector plate mounted on the aft face of the prop blade.

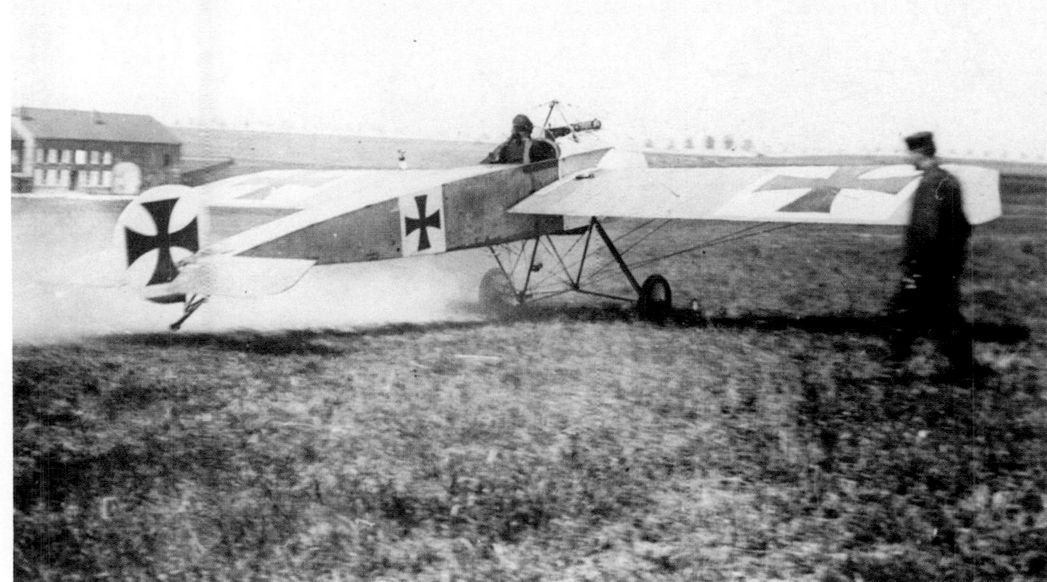

A single machine gun made the Fokker E.III Eindecker the deadliest aircraft of its day. Fewer than 475 Eindeckers were produced, and more than half of them were E.III models.

This scroll map was developed for French bombardment and observation aircraft. Somewhat heavy for its purpose, the rig was fairly effective if crews didn't fly too far north or south!

The Italian Campaign

Although World War I began on Italy's doorstep, the Italian government saw little use in joining into the conflict. The April 1915 Pact of London changed that, with British negotiators offering Italy financial and territorial incentives if the nation would join the war on the side of the Allies; Italy declared war on Austria-Hungary in May. (A declaration of war against Germany would not follow until August 1916.)

As the Austro-Hungarian troops made advances against Russia and gobbled up Serbia, Italian troops made minor gains toward Trieste between June 1915 and September 1917. A combined German and Austro-Hungarian offensive in October 1917 brought major losses for the Italians. Reeforced by the Allies, Italian troops launched a major offensive in June 1918. By late October, Austria was asking for an armistice; a week later, Hungary was ordered to disarm. On 3 November 1918, Austria, Hungary, and Italy signed a cease fire, effective at 3:00pm the next day - seven days before the armistice with Germany would take effect.

On 4 November, an Italian landing party entered the port of Trieste, party of the territory promised them in the Pact of London. They were met by members of the Yugoslav National Committee, who calmly explained that the city and region were to be part of the Kingdom of Serbs, Croats, and Slovenes. The area would remain under dispute until 1954, when it was divided between Italy and Yugoslavia. •

The Savoia-Pomilio SP.2 was an Italian development of French Farman observation aircraft. This armed example has suffered a minor landing accident.

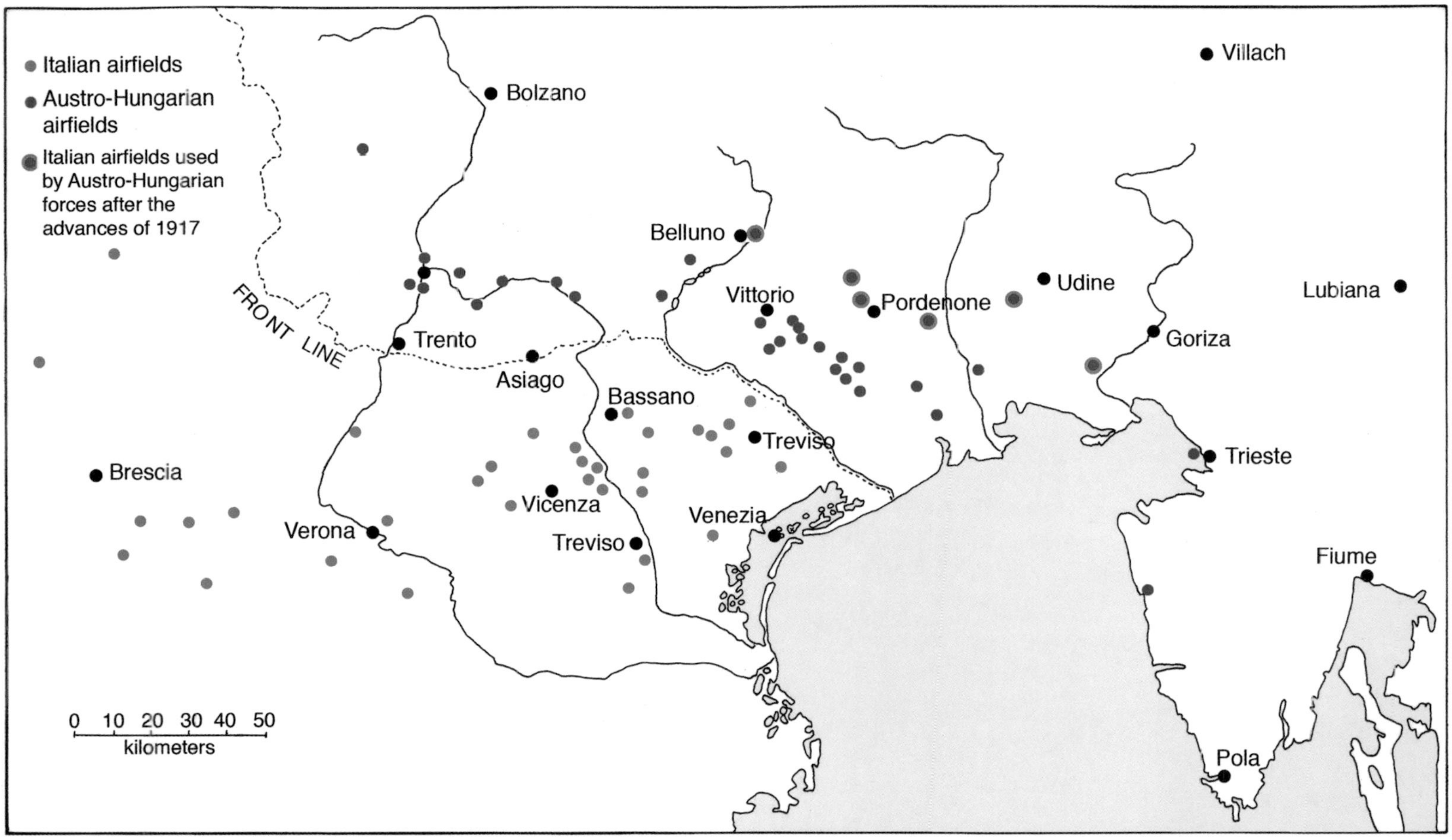

The Italian Front remained relatively stable as trench warfare set in during 1915. The Austro-Hungarian offensive of October 1917 brought British troops to Italy's aid, and by summer 1918 Italy was on the offensive once again.

The air war over the Adriatic frequently saw dogfights between opposing flying boats. Inspired by French designs, the Austrian company Lohner produced a magnificent series of flying boats; this Italian Macchi drew its inspiration from the Lohners and competing French designs.

This 1917 Austrian military map, a type issued to all Austro-Hungarian forces, was carried on air missions over the Italian lines.

Inspired by the multi-engined aircraft of Igor Sikorsky, the Italian Caproni firm turned out a number of excellent heavy bombers during the war. This contemporary giant is the Caproni Ca.5.

The Aviatik 30.07 was the largest Austro-Hungarian aircraft ever built. Although overweight, the heavy bomber still exhibited a great deal of promise at the time of its crash in July 1916. Other heavy bombers would follow.

The crew of the Caproni Ca.5 shared a single nacelle. Later Caproni variants were produced in the US under license.

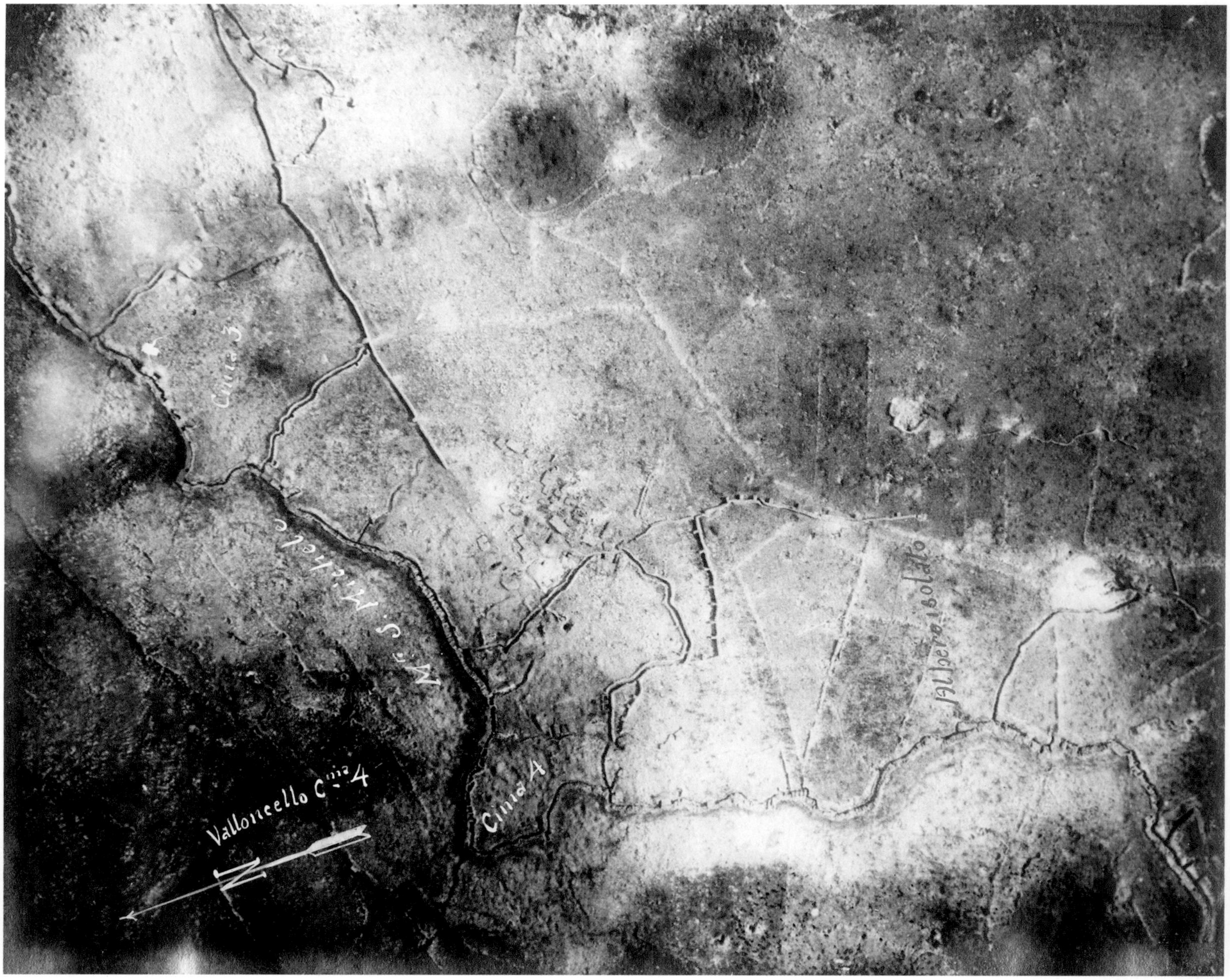

Italian reconnaissance cameras recorded this view of Austrian trenches on Mt Saint Michelle, south-west of Gorizia.

Italy's top ace was Francesco Baracca, photographed here with his French-built SPAD VII. Baracca downed 34 enemy planes before being shot down and killed on 19 June 1918.

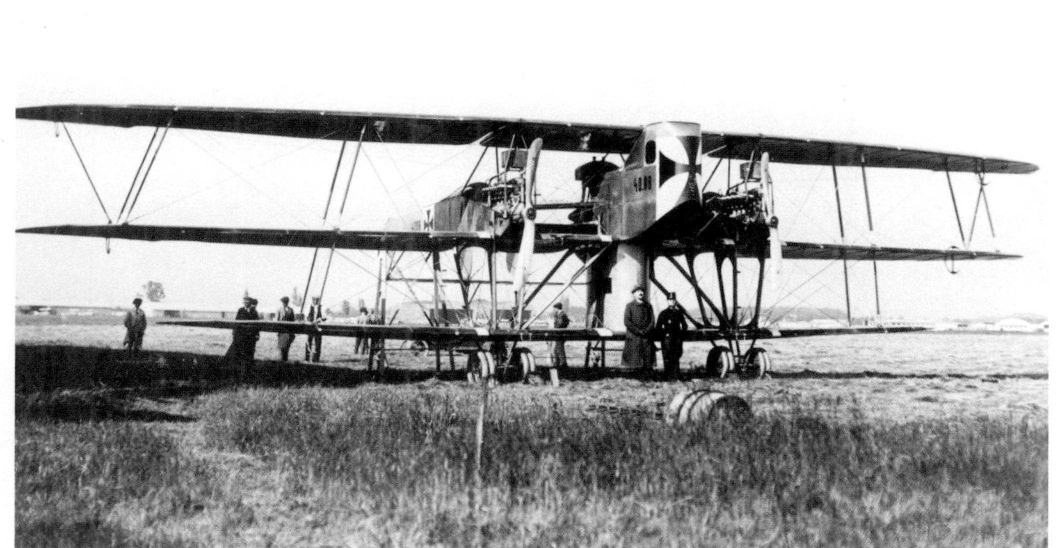
Reacting to the appearance of the first Caproni bombers in August 1915, the Lloyd company completed this LK I in June 1916. The aircraft survived several accidents during taxi tests, but apparently never flew.

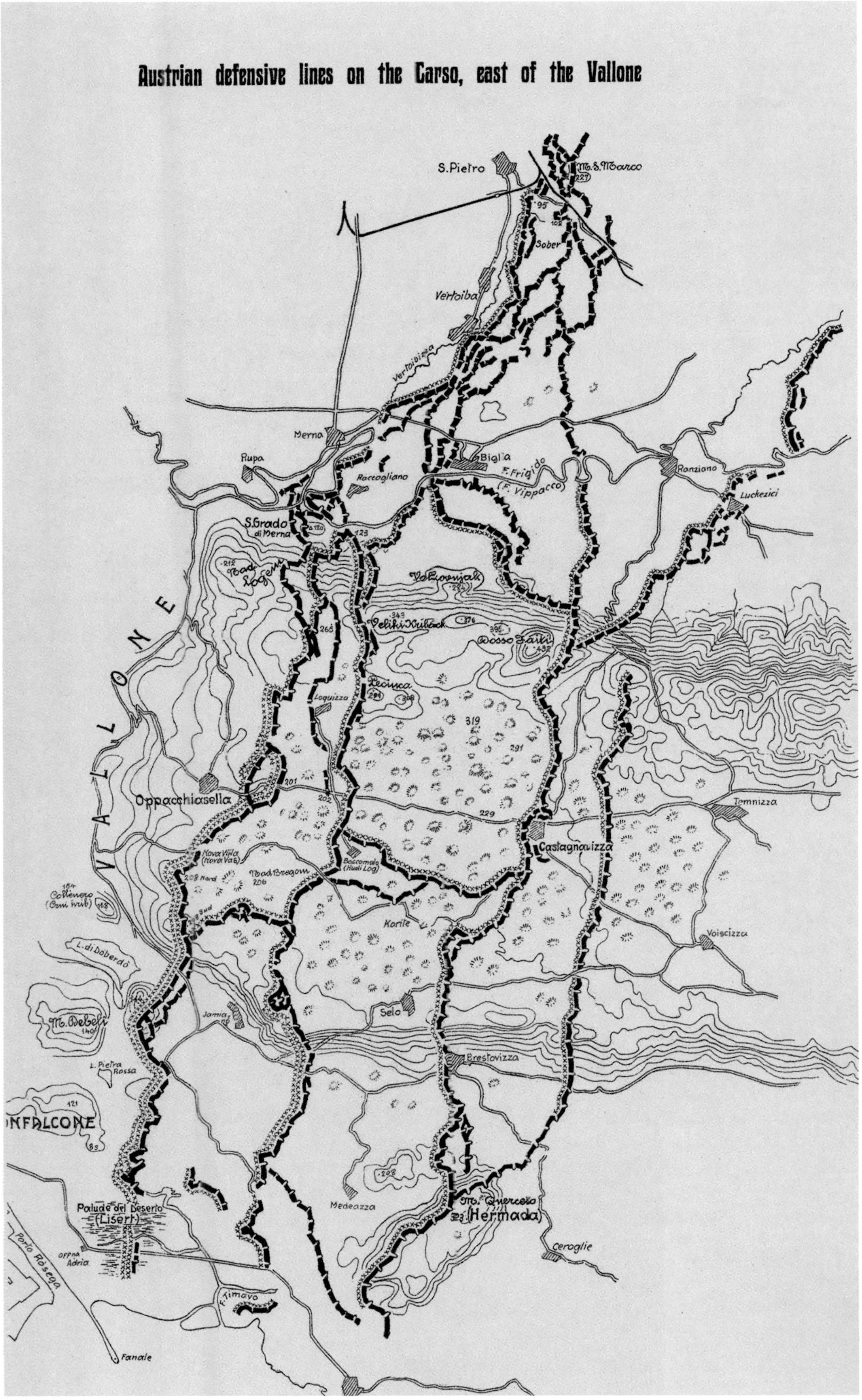

Austrian defensive lines on the Carso, east of the Vallone

The Italian military included this map of an Austrian trench system as part of its quarterly report to British allies in late 1916.

Germany exported a dozen Fokker Eindeckers to Austria-Hungary in early 1916. Designated the A.III, this fighter flew against the Italians that May.

Italy purchased and produced (under license) hundreds of French Nieuport 11s to supplement its own force during 1915 /16.

Austrian designers produced several excellent aircraft designs; this Aviatik 30.24 was not one of them. Although bearing a superficial resemblance to the successful Aviatik D.I, the underpowered 30.24 was never put into production.

Italian designers also produced a number of excellent fighters, but were unable to produce enough aircraft to meet wartime demands. As a result, Italian pilots continued to rely on French designs, such as this late-production Nieuport 17.

The Yanks are Coming

America's entry into World War I was never inevitable. The US was outraged by the slaughter in Europe and the unrestricted submarine warfare in the Atlantic. But the country was also opposed to Britain's blockade of Germany and the effect it had on the German civilian population. While most Americans preferred to stay out of the "European War," many others thought the US should support Germany, not the Allies. The final straw may have been Germany's clumsy attempts to form an alliance with Mexico. In the event the Americans should declare for the Allies, Germany proposed to support a Mexican invasion north across the Rio Grande in exchange for the restoration of territories now considered US states. British intelligence agents intercepted and decoded the telegram in January 1917 and passed its contents on to the Americans. Congress passed a declaration of war in April.

America's lack of preparedness for the war it had just declared was astounding, particularly when it came to modern aircraft. The US had purchased the world's first military aircraft in 1908; in the intervening years before the war began in Europe, the Army had purchased only 53 additional aircraft. Despite an awareness of three years of European advances, in April 1917 no US aircraft was fit for second line service on the Western Front. Europe provided the solutions, selling the Americans the latest available European aircraft while licensing US factories to produce additional modern aircraft; European designers also traveled to the US, helping to create new designs for American production. Slowly, the US got onto a war footing, though the overall contribution to the final victory had more to do with manpower than machinery.

World War I introduced America's airmen to new technologies and tactics, and convinced many of them of the potential that air power could bring to future conflicts. Thousands of young American pilots, navigators, and mechanics came home with a love of aviation. In the peace that followed the war to end all wars, many of them would join their European counterparts in a search for new avenues to develop their new skills. •

Lieutenant Harold Tittman, 94th Aero Squadron, trimmed and assembled portions of several maps to create this chart of his patrol area. The inked-in line shows the front lines, while a penciled-in arrow just north of Toul marks the aerodrome used by the 94th from July through August 1918. Again, no effort was made to preserve scale, coordinates, or compass bearings.

American squadrons found the excellent Royal Aircraft Factory S.E.5 fighter a speedy, maneuverable fighter, often using the aircraft to attack balloons or provide escorts for slower Sopwith Camels. The arrival of the German Fokker D.VII put the British-built fighter at a disadvantage, but higher morale and greater numbers often gave the Americans the advantage.

Captain Robert Rockwell, commander of the 93rd Aero Squadron, poses with his SPAD XIII.

The Italian Caproni heavy bombers were the best of their class when America entered the War. One of the US crews who learned to fly the aircraft at Foggia, Italy, was the future mayor of New York City Fiorello LaGuardia (left).

US Army Captain Albert W. Stevens learned the rudiments of aerial photography over France in World War I. He could continue to develop new photographic systems in the US after the war. Stevens is seen in the aft cockpit of a French-built Salmson 2.

US Navy aircrews flew these Curtiss HS-2L flying boats on anti-submarine patrol from the French base at Brest.

Many American units were equipped with French aircraft. This Salmson 2 observation biplane was assigned to the 1st Aero Squadron.

Captain Charles Jones, commander of the 28th Aero Squadron, poses with his SPAD XIII.

The Allies also provided training to go with their equipment. Hundreds of Americans learned to fly at British, French, and Italian schools, while others learned the essentials of combat flying from Allied instructors. Here US soldiers learn to taxi a French "grass cutter" or "penguin" (flightless bird).

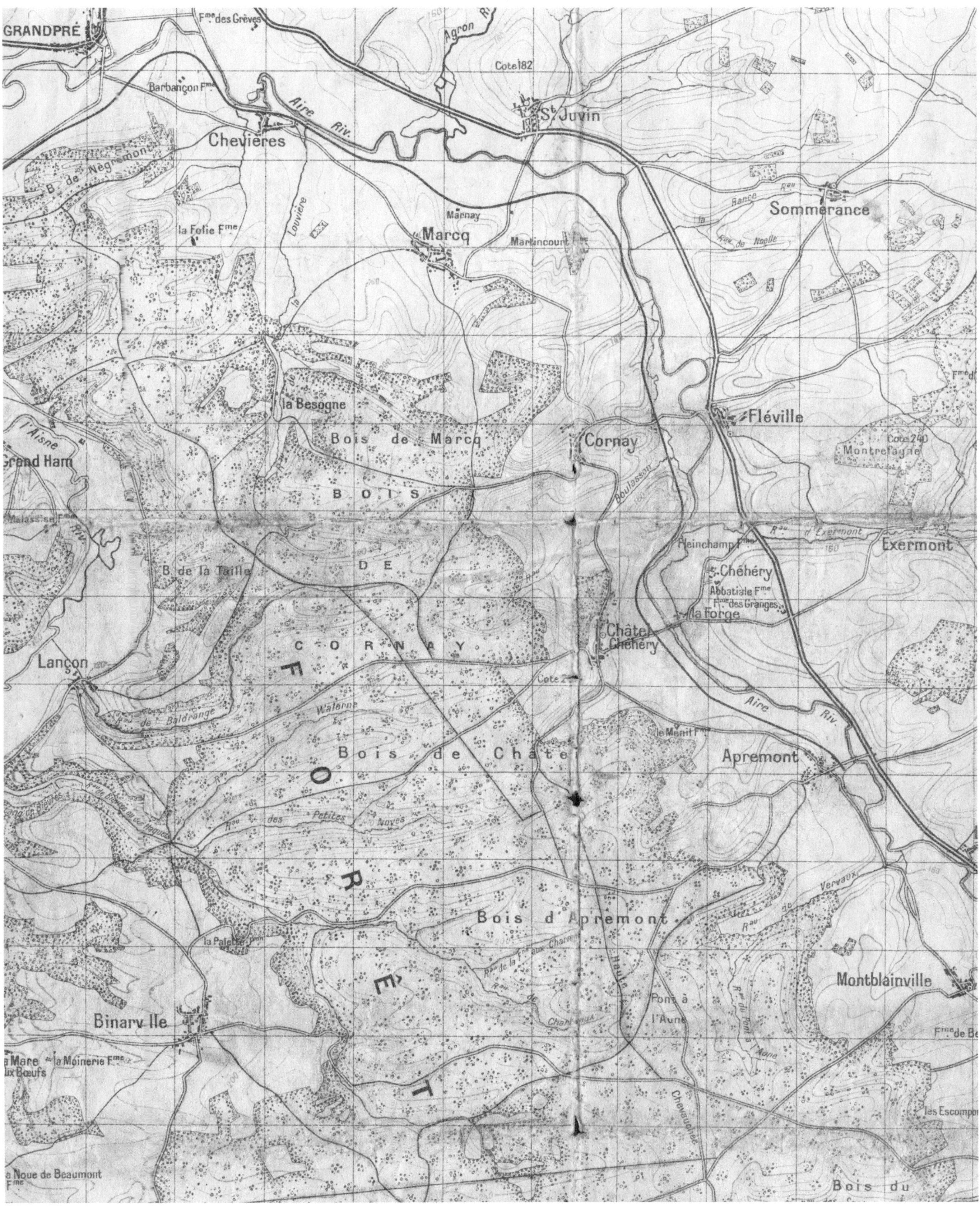

The 50th Aero Squadron's Lieutenant Maurice Graham noted that this map of the Argonne was one he had carried on infantry contact patrols. The map includes topographical information and place names, but, for ease of handling in the open cockpit of his DH-4, Graham trimmed away all coordinates, magnetic declinations, and indications of scale.

Bombers Over England

Civilian population centers have never known immunity from war. Every society has known the threat of attack, siege, occupation, or even annihilation at the hands of enemies as varied as the Golden Horde, the Vikings, the Samurai, the Normans, the Prussians, and the Yankees. But war from the skies presented a new terror - an enemy that could appear without warning to rain death and destruction with impunity. The British public had grown complacent during the nineteenth century. There were plenty of wars, of course - good wars, fought for right and noble causes, and always fought on someone else's soil. And the world's most powerful Navy ensured that any attempt to attack Britain would be turned away easily. But a century after the defeat of Napoleon had removed the last threat of invasion, Germany's giant dirigibles presented a new danger.

As Zeppelins were the first and most famous giant airships of the day, all enemy airships were generally known by the public as Zepps. The 51 Zepp raids and 52 "Gotha" raids (with German heavy bombers similarly identified as the most famous of these bombers) proved largely ineffective. From 1914 through 1918 they delivered only 280 tons of bombs, most of which missed any target of military value. They killed 1,413 people (nearly all civilians) and wounded another 3,408. Hoping to demoralize the British public and draw British fighters away from the Western Front, the raids were also unsuccessful: only eighteen British fighter squadrons would be deployed for home defense, and the British public never sued for peace. In the end, the giant airships and aircraft did convince the British to invest in long-range bombers of their own; it was the threat of retaliation that caused German war planners to suspend further attacks on Britain in August 1918.

Zepps were faster than most contemporary aircraft and could fly at higher altitudes than nearly any winged aircraft of the war. They raided at night, decreasing the risk of discovery by defending anti-aircraft gunners and fighters. Each raid could comprise a single airship or as many as sixteen (when the entire German Army and Navy airship force attempted the Great Airship Raid on the night of 2/3 September 1916). Each Zepp attacked individually; even in daylight, airships were incapable of formation flight.

Even limited fighter and aircraft defenses forced the Zepps to attack from higher altitudes, but at 15-20,000 feet, high winds hindered navigation and bomb aiming. So it was on the night of 19/20 October 1917 when eleven airships launched on the second largest

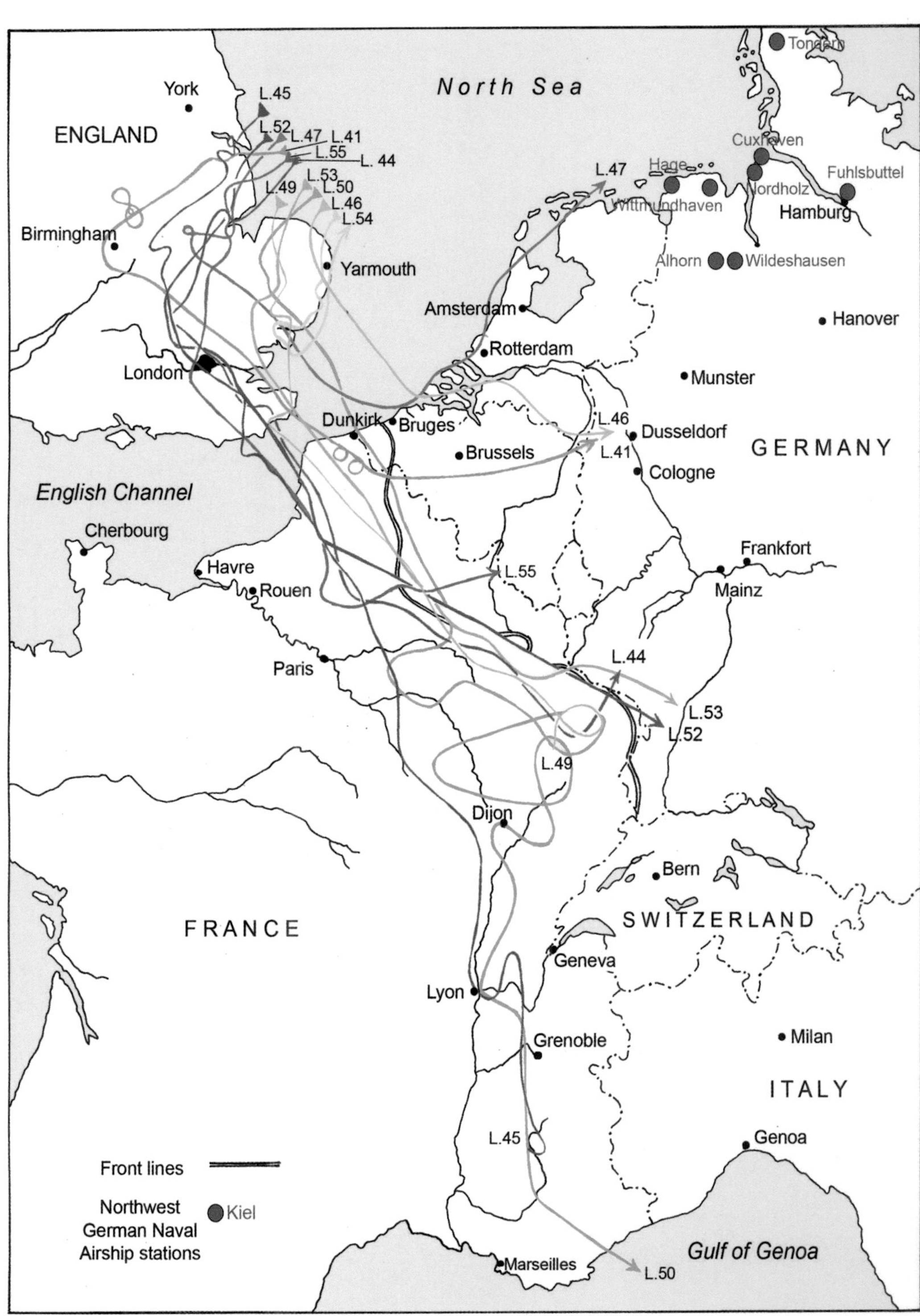

The Silent Rais: 19/20 October 1917.

the Zepps were almost inaudible on the ground; and rather than identify their positions and provide the Germans with identifiable landmarks, defensive guns and searchlights remained inactive. The attack would be remembered as the Silent Raid.

Fighting vicious cross winds, the force dropped 13.5 tons of bombs, causing minimal civilian damage, but killing 36 and injuring 55. Gale-force, high-altitude winds and ground fog hampered navigation for the returning German force, causing most of the Zepps to return over the preferred North Sea passage. On the trip home, four airships were destroyed and one captured intact.

Fates of the individual airships on the Silent Raid:

L 41 - Caused minor damage to the Austin motor works (which had not received a blackout notice) in Birmingham. Crossed to France, circled over Belgian and British armies, then returned safely to Germany.

L 44 - Bombed a number of targets, narrowly missing a major ammunition dump.

The Super Zeppelin L.33 (LZ.76) made its first flight on 30 August 1916. After bombing London just after midnight on 24 September, the airship was hit by anti-aircraft fire and began to lose height. Following an attack by a single RFC fighter, the crew force-landed in Essex, set fire to their Zepp, and surrendered to a local reserve policeman. The crew of the other airship lost that night (L.32) was less fortunate: all died when RFC incendiary rounds ignited their hydrogen cells.

Returning over France at altitude of 19,000 feet, L 44 was hit and destroyed by anti-aircraft guns at Vathimenil. All on board were lost.

L 45 - Caused some damage to civilian targets. Carried well south by winds, L 45 headed for Switzerland when the captain realized there was no longer enough fuel to reach Germany. Harried by French aircraft which failed to bring her down, L 45 attempted to land, but the captain realized too late that he was still in France. Now completely out of fuel, L 45 crash landed. Entire crew was captured after destroying the downed airship.

L 46 and L 47 - Caused little damage before returning safely home.

L 49 - Caused minor damage. On the return trip, L 49 was forced down by five French aircraft. The crew and the latest type of Zeppelin were captured by French.

L 50 - Caused no damage, became lost over fog. Noticing L 49 on the ground below, the captain thought he had returned safely to Germany. Realized error climbed to 10,000 feet, then descended again, impacting the ground. The forward car, with 16 men aboard, was torn from ship; those members of the crew were captured. The lightened airship and remaining crew were blown over Mediterranean and never seen again.

L 52 - Caused minor damage, returned home through Alsace.

L 53 - Caused no damage and returned home.

L 54 - Caused no damage, but returned home via North Sea (only one to return via the standard route).

L 55 - Caused no damage, returned home to be destroyed by a forced landing in Germany. •

German Navy Zeppelin L 43 made fourteen flights before British fighters and anti-aircraft brought it down on 14 June 1917.

German Navy Zeppelin L 48 was shot down by British fighters on 17 June 1917, less than a month after its first flight.

Zeppelin L49 participated in the Silent Raid of 19/20 October 1917. Driven off course by high winds, the giant airship was forced down and captured in France.

Formations & Maneuvers

Formation flying was unnecessary before the beginning of World War I: any situation that found more than one aircraft in the same sky was either a race or a coincidence. As the eyes of the armies, military aircraft generally flew singly, observing ground activities in their sectors, and returning home to report. When opposing armed aircraft came together, the pilots frequently flew parallel courses while their observers fired away at each other from the back seat - much like two line-of-battle ships trading broadsides. Turning and running was always an option, of course, until the advent of high-speed fighters with forward firing machine guns. Aircraft began to fly together in small formations for defense, to hunt down enemies, or even to bomb ground positions.

Unit maneuvers were nothing new to the military. Formations of ships, cavalry, and infantry trained in acting as a single force to better support each element in attack or defense. Applying those established maneuvers to aircraft was not an easy transition - after all, a horse could slow its speed to turn in formation without losing altitude!

Similar problems were faced by the new fighter pilots. Formations were useful for cohesively moving a unit to meet the enemy, but formations tended to dissolve once an attack was launched. The term dogfight described the confusion as individual aircraft tried to select a target in the wild, swirling melee. Each pilot needed an almost instinctive ability to separate friends from foes, to rapidly identify each member of his own unit, and to predict what maneuvers other aircraft were capable of executing next. (German fighter units used colorful tail and nose markings to identify each squadron, with additional markings to distinguish each member within the unit. Allied pilots, with their drab, consecutively numbered aircraft, referred to brightly painted German fighters as the "flying circus.")

By 1918, with Allied forces assembling more aircraft and units then previously imagined possible, planners devised large formations of bombers, with integral fighter escorts, to efficiently focus their attacks on enemy ground forces. The illustrations provided here depict several of the formations and maneuvers developed between 1914 and 1918. •

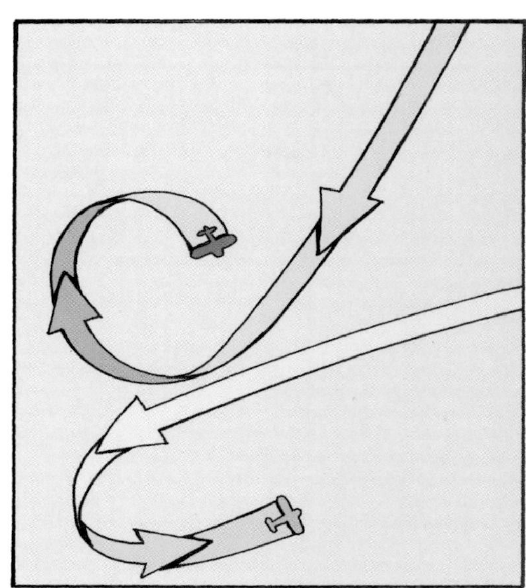

Germany's Max Immelmann perfected this climbing turn, which became widely known as the Immelmann turn, or simply the Immelmann. After a firing pass at an enemy aircraft, the attacking fighter climbed and turned into position for a second attack.

France's top ace, Rene Fonck, survived the war with 75 confirmed victories (with 52 additional unconfirmed claims). Fonck (left) is shown counting bullets with a squadron mate in front of his SPAD VII; a skilled marksman, Fonck rarely wasted a round, once claiming three German aircraft with a ten-second burst.

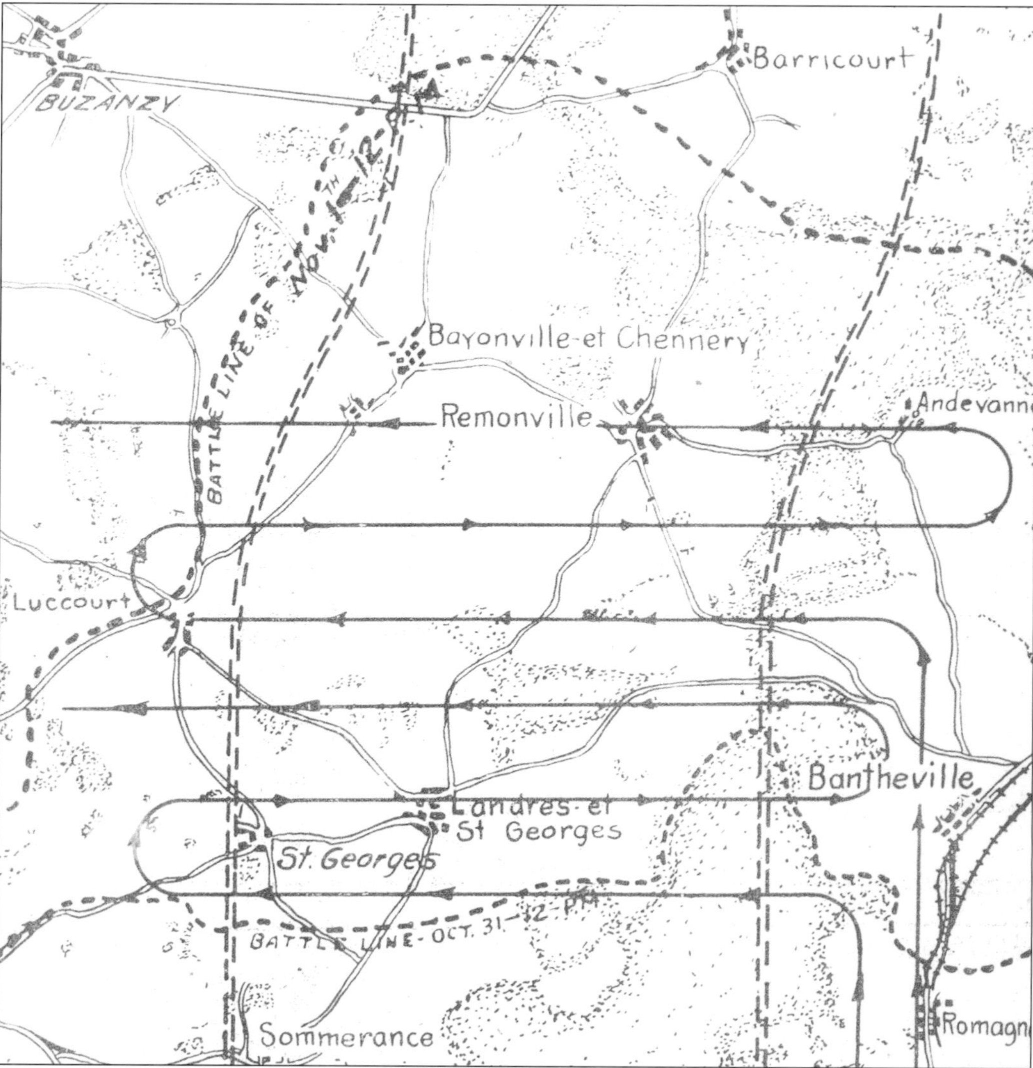

American Expeditionary Forces Lieutenant Joseph Eaton prepared this plan of a coordinated, two-plane photo reconnaissance of enemy positions in 1918. Coordination and skilled navigation ensured a thorough coverage of the area.

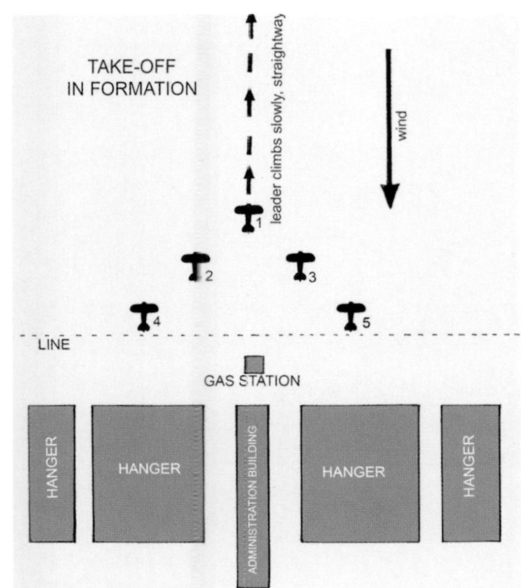

Assembly was the first challenge of formation flight. One relatively easy solution was to launch the entire unit in formation.

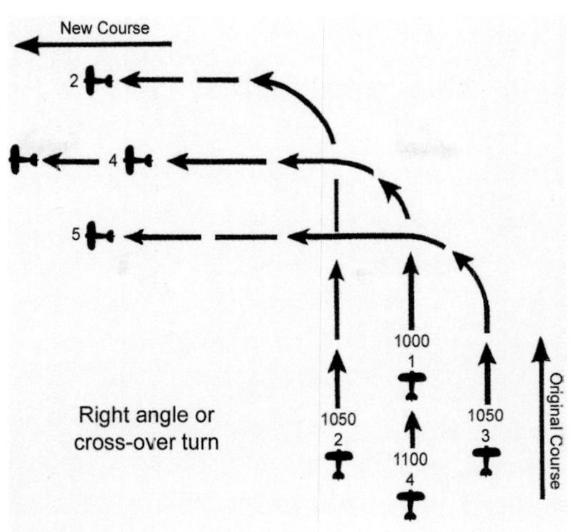

In theory, the cross-over turn allowed a formation to turn without requiring pilots to vary their speed or altitude. In practice the formation broke apart during the turn, then scrambled to reassemble as a mirror image of itself after the turn.

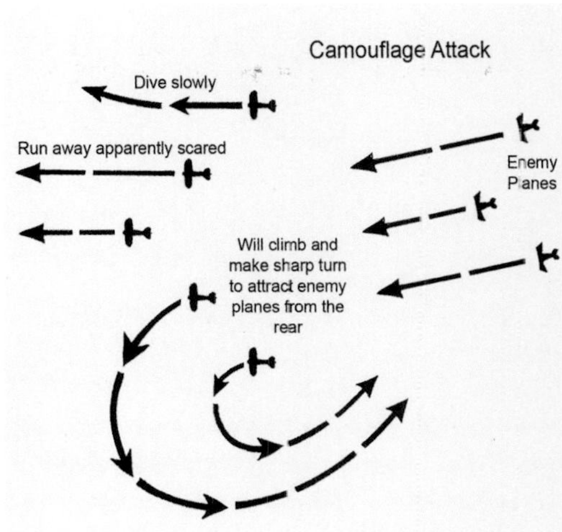

This defensive feint against enemy fighters turned three aircraft into the bait as two others maneuvered to attack.

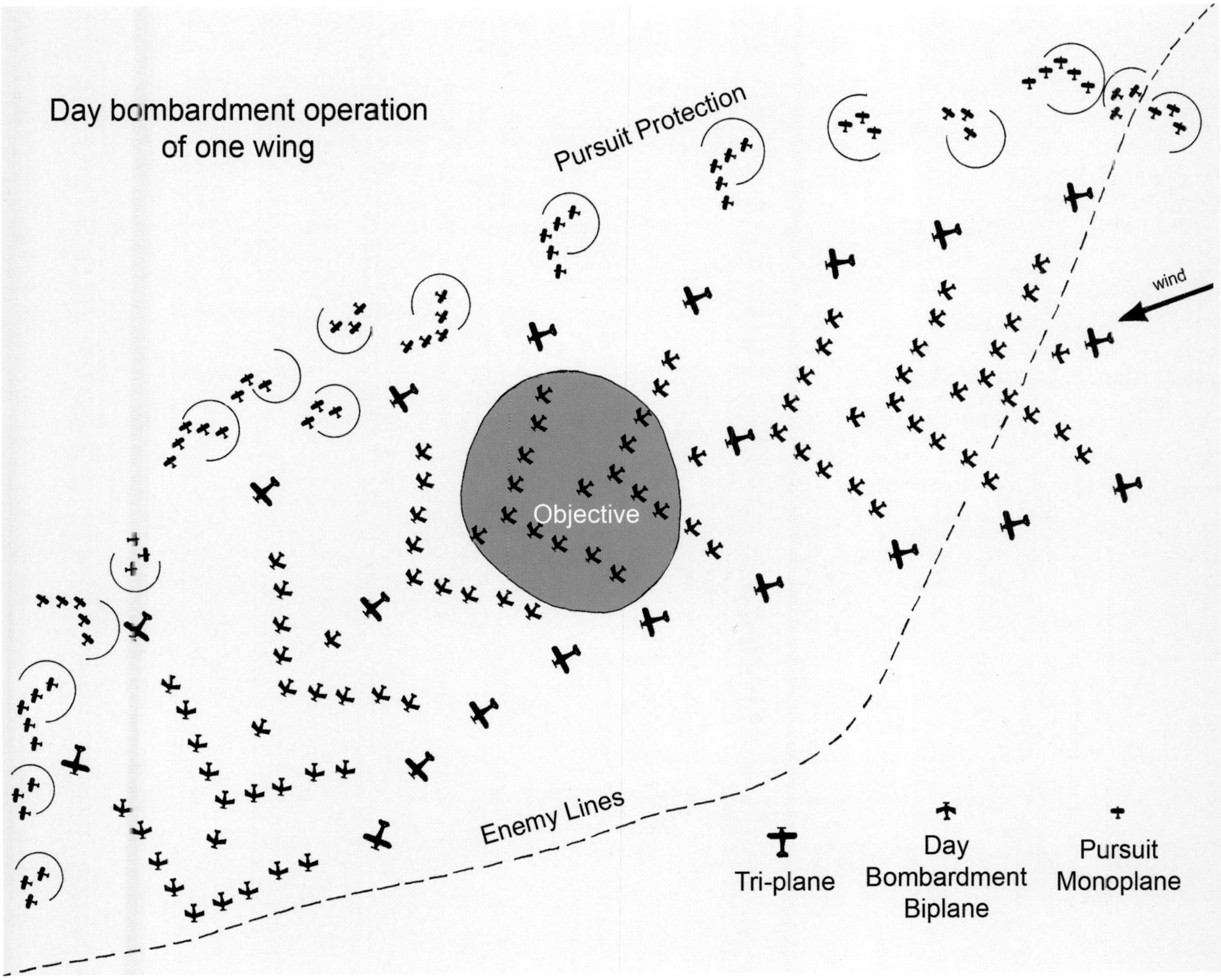

Day bombardment operation of one wing

Pursuit Protection

Objective

wind

Enemy Lines

Tri-plane

Day Bombardment Biplane

Pursuit Monoplane

In 1918 the American Expeditionary Forces devised this formation attack for three-seat and two-seat bombers, with a defensive fighter shield interfering with any enemy fighters.

Closing Positions

America's entry into the European War in April 1917 brought the Allies a boost, but not a guarantee of victory. It would take a year before the first "doughboys" would enter combat, and much could transpire in that time. Germany, of course, had been drained by severe losses on the Eastern and Western fronts, while its populace was starving under the all-too-effective Allied naval blockade - but the U-Boat offensive against Allied shipping was having a similar effect on the British people. Allied troops in France outnumbered the Germans by three to two, but the Allied offensives of 1917 failed, leaving German forces in stronger positions at the cost of thousands of casualties. In autumn 1917, the Russian Revolution ended the war on the Eastern Front, eventually freeing large numbers of German troops to redeploy West; by April 1918 the Germans outnumbered the Allies there by four to three.

In the air, the British and French were introducing fine new fighters and their first heavy bombers, but the German air arm was fielding large numbers of excellent Albatros D.V fighters and preparing to introduce the legendary Fokker Dr.I. This was followed by the Fokker D.VII - the finest fighter of the War - in early 1918.

On 21 March 1918, Germany launched its last great offensive, driving British troops back fifty miles towards Paris and threatening to swing north to take the vital Channel ports. The British and French eventually stemmed the assault, with the first 2,500 American troops entering combat in April. The stalled German offensive was the Kaiser's last chance of victory. By the summer, a half-million fresh (if untested) American troops joined the Allies in a series of offensives that drove the Germans back. •

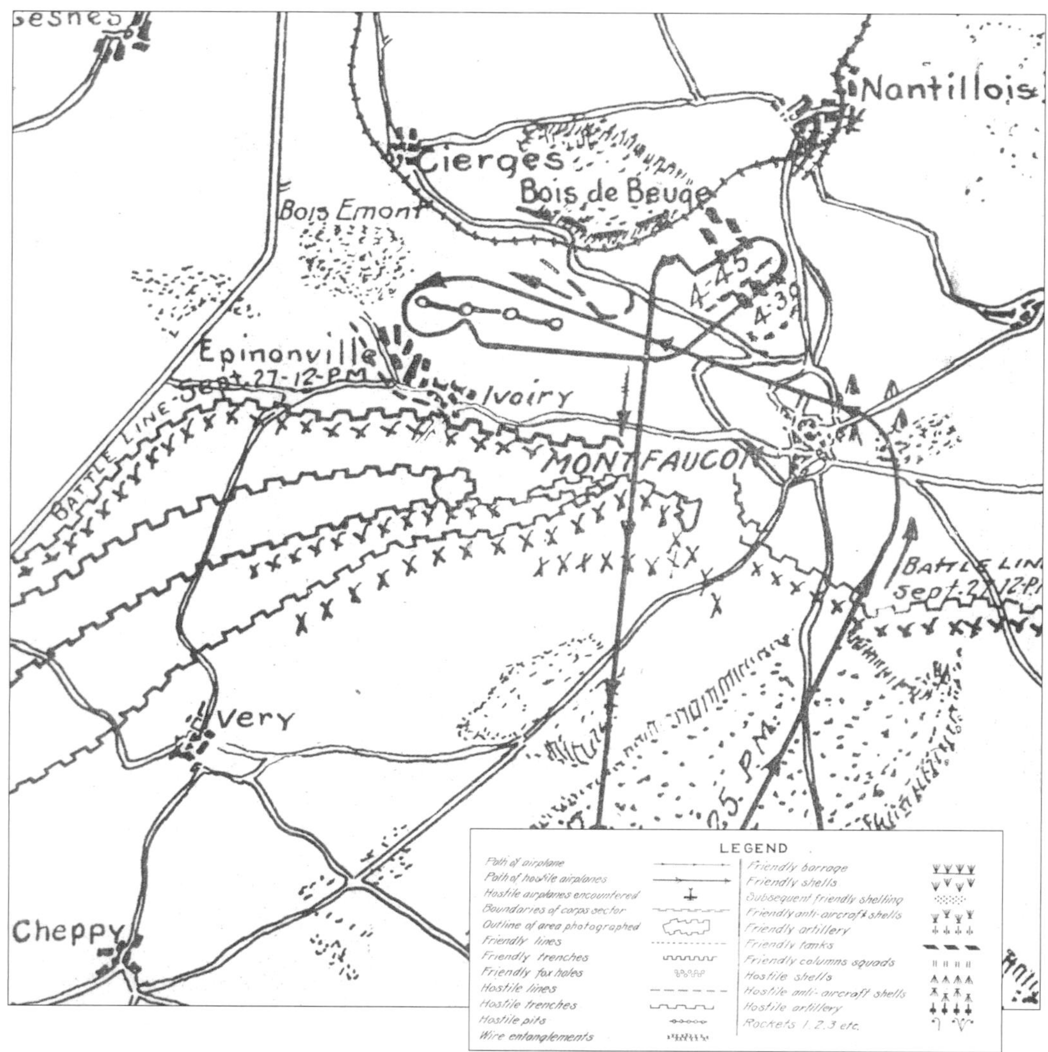

Lieutenant Joseph Eaton of the US 99th Aero Squadron prepared this map of his observations of German positions at Montfaucon, France, on 27 September 1918. The drawing shows Allied and enemy positions, with about a dozen American tanks moving in on the Bois de Beuge. German machine gun fire from those woods seriously wounded Eaton's observer, forcing an early end to the mission.

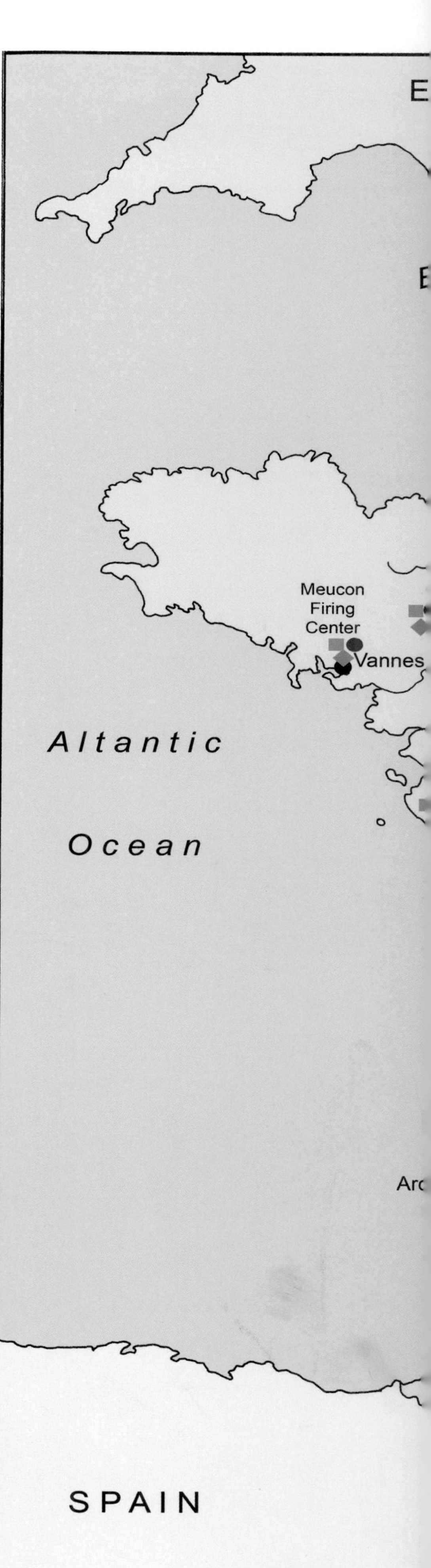

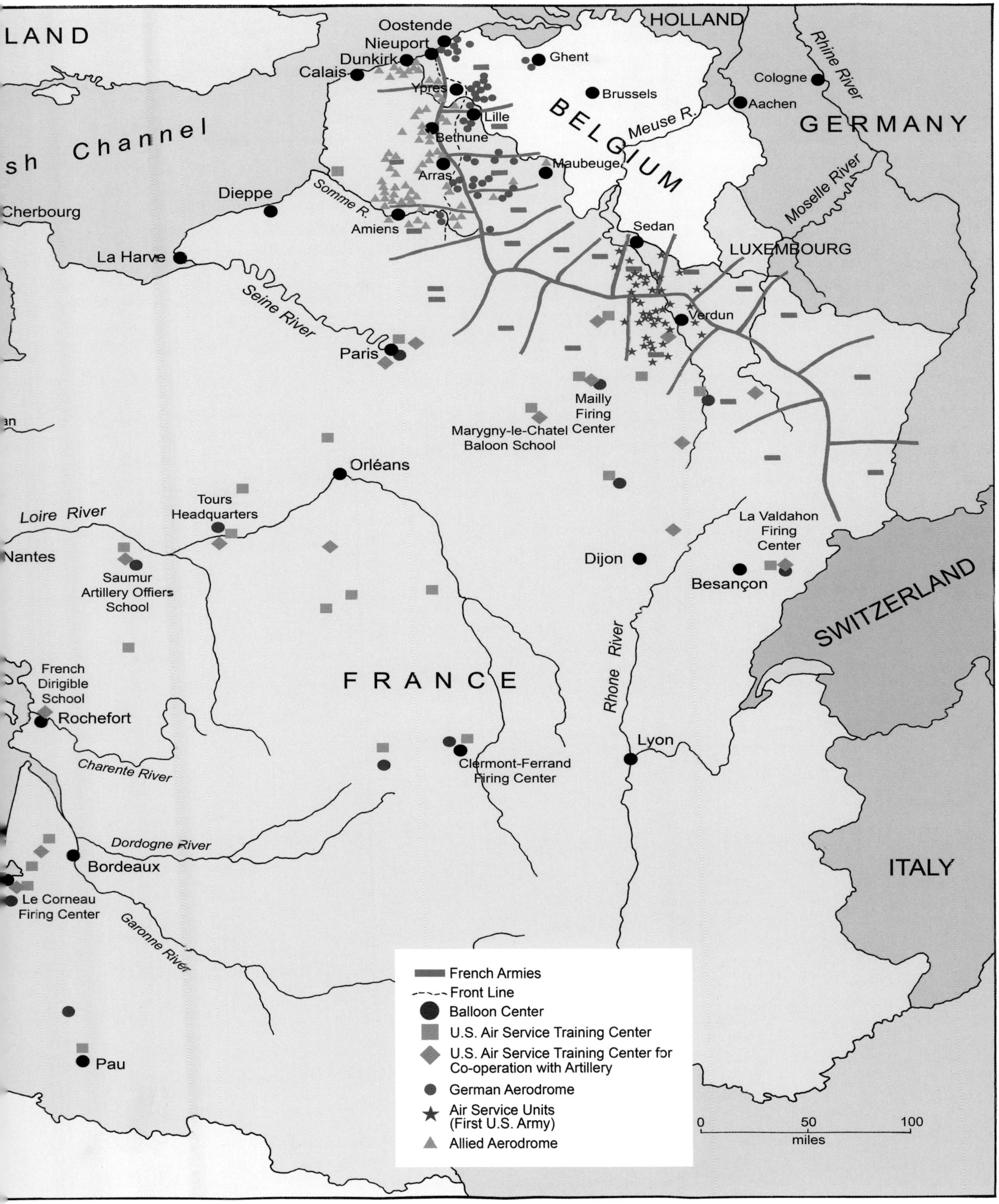

Western Front 1918.

The Armistice

By the end of 1918, the "great nations" had wearied of war. Germany, its resources depleted, its troops demoralized, and its people starving, faced defeat as the Allies increased in strength. On 6 November, a German delegation left for Rethondes, France, where an armistice was signed at 11:00 pm, 11 November (the eleventh hour of the eleventh day of the eleventh month). There was to be an immediate cessation of all hostilities followed by German withdrawal from all occupied territories and Alsace-Lorraine. Germany agreed to return all Allied citizens and prisoners of war and surrender all war materiels and weapons.

Officially, the war with Germany ended in June 1919 with the signing of the Treaty of Versailles. The Allies' peace terms were onerous; Germany was to be occupied by Allied forces, its war-making capabilities dismantled, its weapons destroyed or turned over to the Allies. Most military aircraft which had been converted to civilian purposes (as mail planes or airliners) were declared war machines and ordered destroyed. Engines built for military aircraft were likewise considered military engines and ordered destroyed; the same stipulations covered propellers, cameras, radios, and cockpit instruments. Even the manufacturing plants that created hydrogen for German airships were declared illegal and dismantled. All international sales of German military aircraft made after the armistice (which amounted to nearly 2,000 aircraft, worldwide) were also declared illegal, and the proceeds were demanded to be turned over to Allied inspectors.

German resentment over the Treaty of Versailles' punitive nature is often cited as one of the root causes of World War II, which was declared just over twenty years later. Given the nature of Hitler and the Nazi Party, there is little chance a more balanced treaty could have prevented another war. Such a treaty, however, would have eliminated one of the excuses the Germans would use to convince themselves that another war was justified.

The treaty did have one positive effect on German industry, though few would recognize it at the time. As the world slowly recovered from the economic disaster that accompanied the Great War, most aircraft and engine manufacturers found it difficult to compete in a market flooded with surplus de Havillands, Avros, Breguets, and Jennies. In the US, for example, new military aircraft would continue to use surplus Liberty engines for nearly a decade. In Germany, however, few surplus aircraft survived to be turned to civil pursuits, most "military" engines were converted into ingots, and surviving airships were destroyed or turned over to the Allies. When the nation was ready to forge ahead once more, newer designs had little competition from a war-surplus market.

The Inter-Allied Aeronautical Commission of Control (IAACC) entered Germany in May 1920, shortly before the Treaty of Versailles was signed. They met with resistance from a nation that did not consider itself defeated. German members of the inspection teams would arrange for items to be moved or hidden before the commissioner arrived (a move that has since been practiced on many occasions in many different countries). Equipment and facilities due to be turned over to the Allies were often destroyed in mysterious accidents and fires. Records were altered, protests were lodged, progress was delayed. (Some commission members found themselves arrested by local police departments, only to be released later with apologies over the "confusion.")

None-the-less, the work continued with dramatic efficiency. The map at the left has been complied from IAACC reports filed in March 1921. It shows all German military airfields examined, and the approximate numbers and types of aircraft found on each field. Few of these aircraft still existed by the time the report was filed. •

German aircraft weren't the only ones destroyed after the War; thousands of Allied aircraft (many never flown) were stripped of useful equipment and burned. The American DH-4s were easier to salvage in Europe than return to the US.

To the victors: inspections, parades, and medals. Here, American squadrons in France assemble before their French-built Salmsons shortly after the signing of the Peace Treaty.

The Zeppelin works at Staaken built this advanced R.VI bomber during the war, but converted it to civil use in 1919. "Fletcher's World," which had been painted on the nose and aft fuselage during civil operations, has been painted out with white enamel prior to the aircraft's destruction. The giant airship *Bodensee* was one of two passenger airships built by Zeppelin in 1919. Both were turned over to the Allies as war reparations.

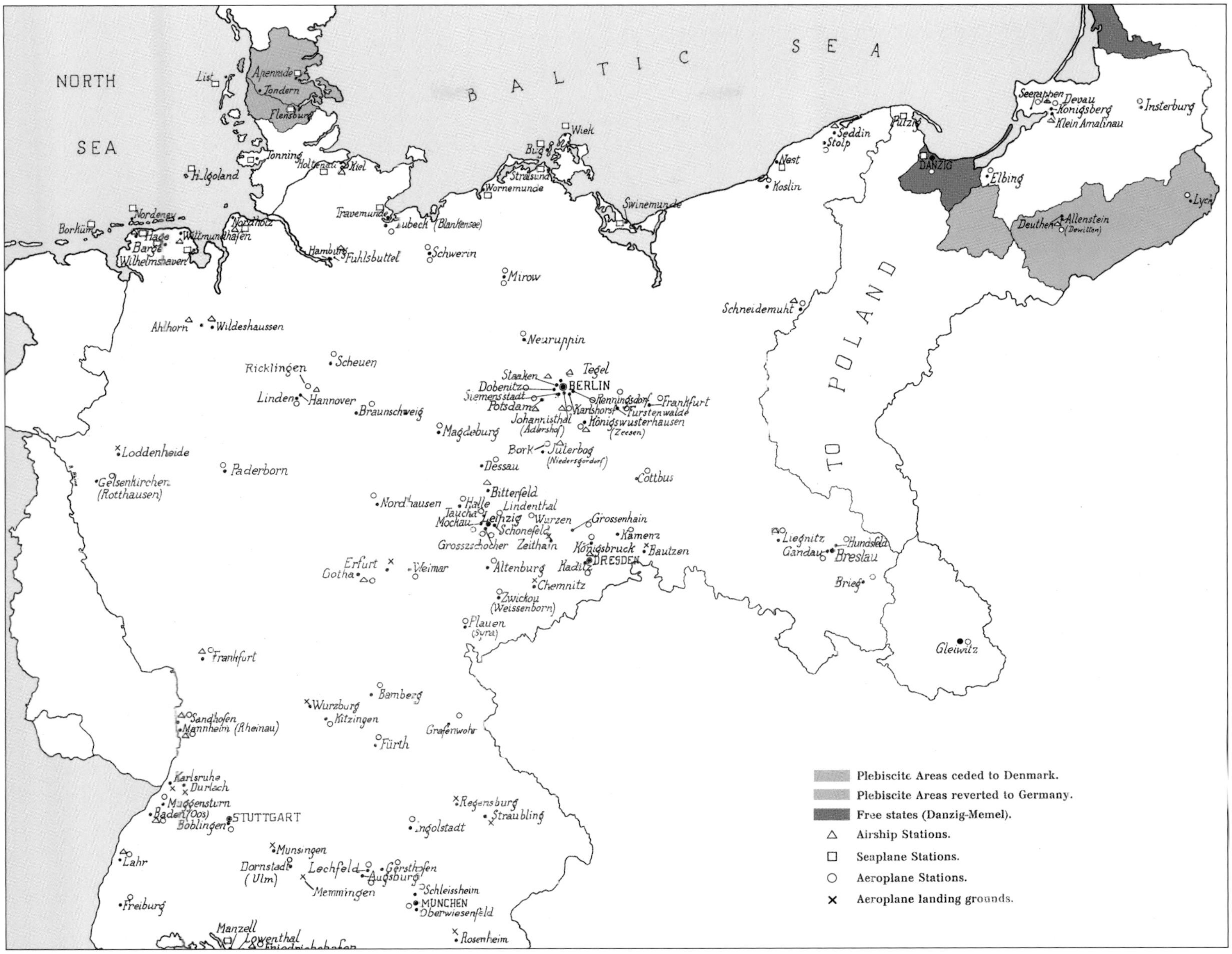

NORTH SEA
BALTIC SEA
TO POLAND

- Plebiscite Areas ceded to Denmark.
- Plebiscite Areas reverted to Germany.
- Free states (Danzig-Memel).
- △ Airship Stations.
- □ Seaplane Stations.
- ○ Aeroplane Stations.
- × Aeroplane landing grounds.

Aircraft types and approximate number found on German airfields by the Inter-Allied Aeronautical Commission of Control.

B=Bombers, R=Reconnaissance, F=Fighters, T=Trainers

	B	R	F	T		B	R	F	T		B	R	F	T
Altenburg	5	20	10	120	Gersthofen		45	15	60	Neuruppin	5	15	5	35
Baden		5			Gotha	5	195	35	185	Nordholz	5	5	5	5
Bamburg		50	10	39	Grafenwohr		5	20	5	Oberwiesenfeld		50	25	40
Barge		5	35	5	Grossenhain		135	80	50	Ricklingen		225	25	110
Boblingen	5	145	120	5	Hage				25	Rosenheim	5			
Bork		10	5	30	Halle	10	180	50	145	Sandhofen	5		5	
Braunschweig		110	105	130	Holtenau	20	10		35	Scheuen		25	20	70
Brieg		100	65	80	Hundsfeld		5	5	65	Schleissheim	5	110	50	35
Burgberg		40		20	Johannisthal	10	215	195	115	Schneidemuth		60	70	80
Cottbus	15	60	50	265	Juterbog		90	200	50	Schwerin	5	75	250	130
Danzig				50	Kaditz		5		5	Seddin				35
Debenitz	15	75	60	90	Karlshorst		5	5		Seerappen	5	85	85	35
Deveau		125	65	100	Kiel		5	5	5	Sonthofen		10	5	10
Dewitten		5	5		Kitzengen		50	40	25	Stolp		90	25	160
Elbing	5	85	5	330	Konigsbruck				75	Toucha		5	15	
Erfurt		5		5	Lechfeld		30	20	20	Travemunde			5	5
Frankfurt	5	65	15	30	Liegnitz	5	110	15	40	Weimar		10	50	
Friedrichshafen		5		10	Linden	5	95	95	190	Weissenborn				5
Furstenwalde				115	Lubeck	5	25	20		Wurzen		10	5	75
Furth	5	75	150	20	Memmingen	5		5	10					
Gandau	5	20	10	85	Mirow		10		5					

The Golden Years

The years between the two World Wars are generally considered aviation's Golden Age. A world weary of combat entered 1919 with an optimism that war had become too terrible to ever fight again. Civilization needed rebuilding - its governments, institutions, homes, and people required time and opportunity to recover. And, no longer a simple plaything for the sportsman pilot, aviation had proven itself a tool that many believed could aid in that recovery.

For four years, aviation technology had advanced in leaps and bounds. Of course, each improvement in an enemy's aircraft required a technological response, so every few months armies and navies received a new aircraft with increased range, maneuverability, ceiling, payload, speed, or durability. The end of the War didn't spell an end to those improvements, but a dramatic decrease in the numbers of new military aircraft purchased eliminated some of the urgency behind the innovations. Designers turned to the creation of postwar civilian aircraft, but again, most of these aircraft saw little production. Surplus warplanes flooded the early peacetime market, strangling many efforts to develop and market newer civilian types. A surplus Curtiss Jenny or Breguet XIV might not perform as well as the newer designs, but it certainly cost less.

Primed by interest in commercial air routes, civil air lines and private aviation slowly flourished, eventually creating new markets for the more advanced designs. Airmen, governments, and promoters provided exciting new roles for aircraft, with a host of races, endurance flights, remote explorations, and acrobatic feats. The public was encouraged to be "air minded" and schools began guiding youths to careers in aviation, even as the Great Depression, a worldwide financial catastrophe, further slowed advances in all fields.

But restrained progress is still progress. The finest fighter at the end of World War I was the Fokker D.VII biplane. With a 185hp BMW IIIA engine, the D.VII could reach 125mph with a ceiling of 18,000 feet. In 1939, the world's best fighters were the Supermarine Spitfire Mark I and the Messerschmitt Bf 109 E-1. The Spitfire's 1,030hp Rolls Royce Merlin gave a top speed of 362mph with a 31,900-foot ceiling; the Messerschmitt's 1,100hp Daimler-Benz pushed the 109 to 354mph and a ceiling of 36,000 feet.

Bombers saw similar improvements. The German Staaken R.VI had a range of 560 miles; over shorter distances, two tons of bombs could be carried. The best operational long-range bomber of 1939 was the Boeing B-17B, which carried four tons of bombs some 1,400 miles.

In 1919, a number of military airplanes were being converted for passenger service, but the best airliner of its day was the Zeppelin dirigible *Bodensee*. The giant airship, launched in 1919, carried 21 passengers over 1,060 miles. The development of the airliner during the 1920s and '30s was nothing less than remarkable. By the beginning of World War II, the passenger-carrying airship was gone from service. The best airliner in a now-thriving, worldwide industry was the Boeing 314 flying boat, which could carry up to 74 passengers over 3,500 miles.

In the two decades between the wars, aviation experienced many new records, new heros, and new tragedies. By 1939, there was no question that the aircraft would be part of the future, and that it would help carry us there.•

The Seversky P-35 was America's first modern fighter. Introduced in 1936, the aircraft featured stressed metal skin, internally braced wing and tail, enclosed cockpit, and retractable landing gear. Within three years, the aircraft would be rendered obsolete.

One of the hundreds of interwar long-distance flights involved this Tupolev ANT-25 connecting Shchyolkovo in the Soviet Union with San Jacinto, California, in July 1937. The aircraft covered 6,306 miles, via the Arctic Circle, in 62 hours, 17 minutes.

2912
A Camera Goes Up
Baker Field

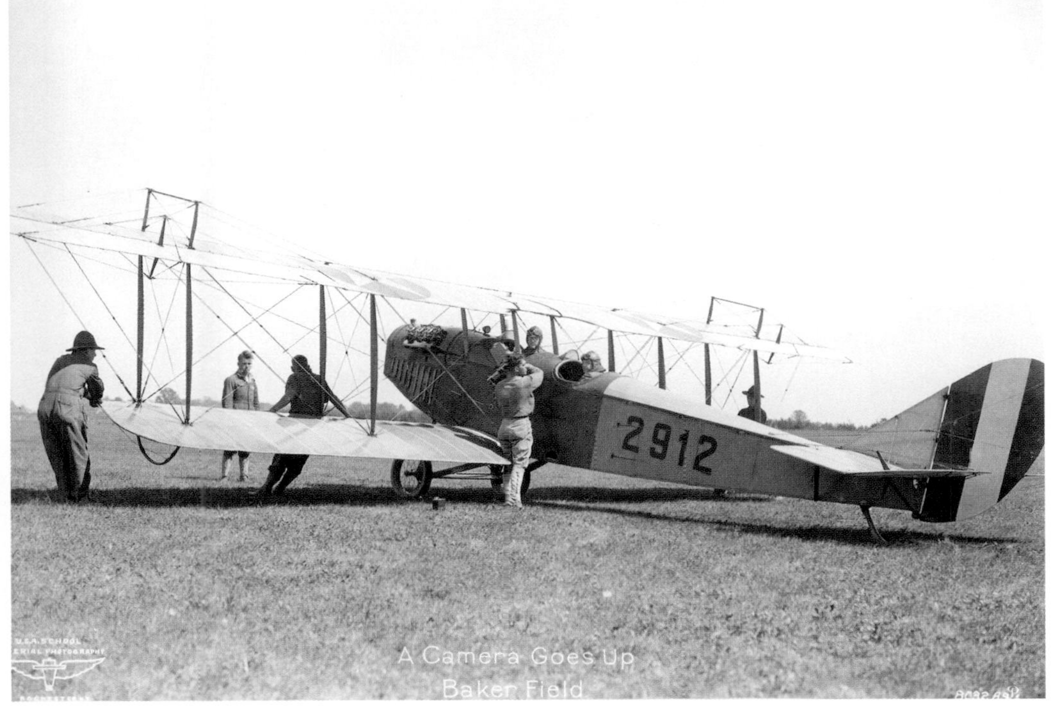

LEFT: The Curtiss JN-4D Jenny was the standard American trainer and domestic utility aircraft of World War I. With thousands produced, the Jenny remained in military service through the 1920s. Surplus aircraft flooded into the private market, where they were bought for barnstorming, aerial mapping, crop spraying, and weekend flying.

BELOW: November 1935 saw the opening of a new era of passenger travel as Pan American Airways' Martin 130 *China Clipper* landed at Manila. At a time when few aircraft had risked a trans-Pacific crossing, the success of a commercial venture demonstrated Pan American's remarkable ability to meld new aircraft technologies with improved navigational aids installed on a series of island support facilities.

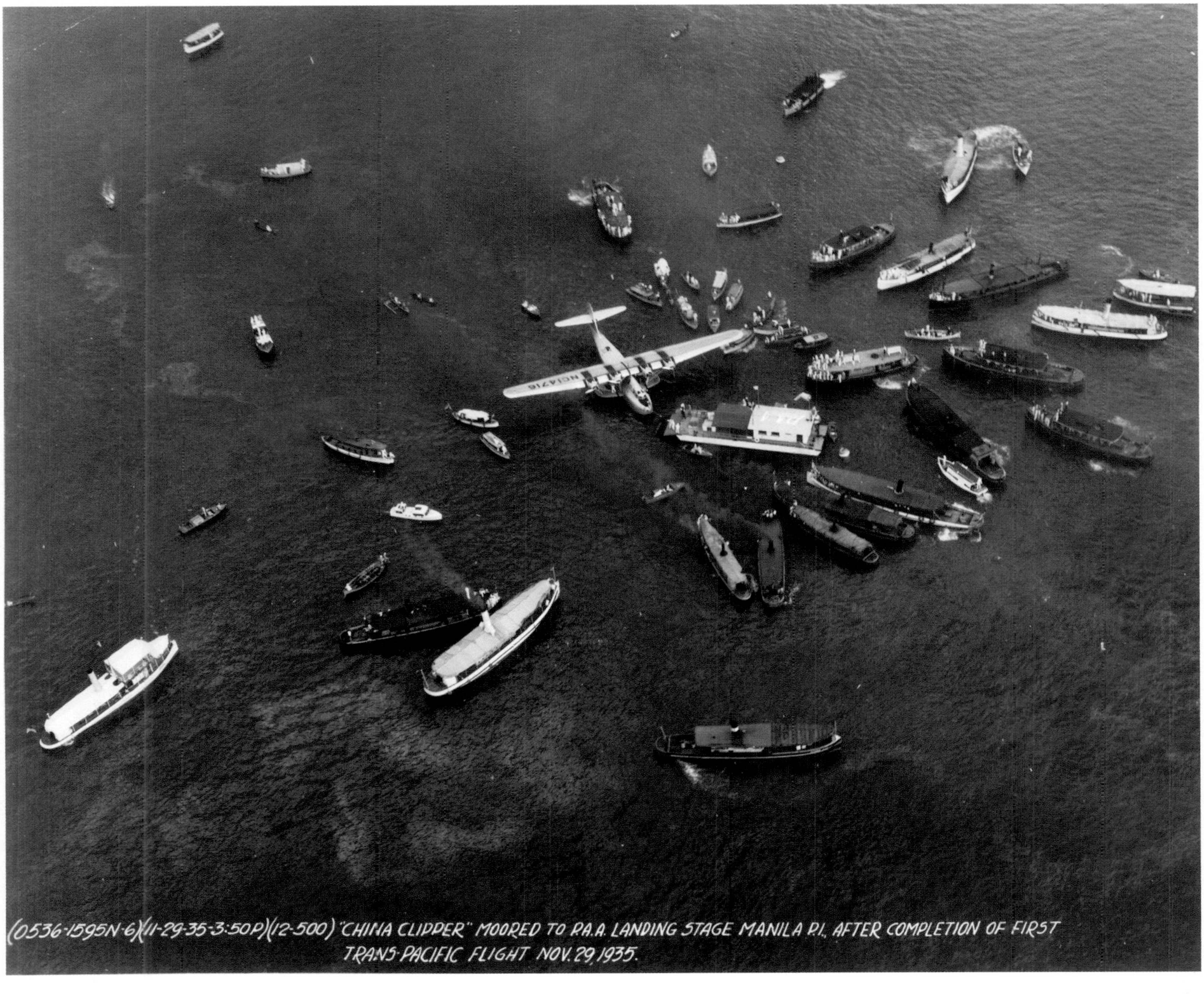
(0536-1595N-6)(11-29-35-3:50P)(12-500) "CHINA CLIPPER" MOORED TO P.A.A. LANDING STAGE MANILA P.I. AFTER COMPLETION OF FIRST TRANS-PACIFIC FLIGHT NOV. 29, 1935.

Into the Stratosphere

Hoping to increase the power of World War I engines at higher altitudes, the US National Advisory Committee for Aeronautics turned to Dr Sanford Moss, an engineer with General Electric in Lynn, Massachusetts. Moss, who had research high speed turbines before the first flight of the Wright brothers, was finally given the support to investigate an aircraft engine booster or turbo-booster, a device soon known as a turbo-supercharger.

By October 1918 Moss was ready to test the prototype, which used the engine exhaust gasses of a Liberty engine to drive a turbine wheel and compressor; the compressor, in turn, forced high-pressure air into the engine's carburetor. Moss and his team took their invention up 14,109 feet to the summit of Pike's Peak for a series of carefully calibrated tests. Their unboosted engine, which had developed 350hp at sea level, could provide only 230hp at the mountain top. With the supercharger engaged, the output increased to 356hp! Moss' success held great promise for the future, but the War's end that November forced the project's cancellation.

The LePere poses with several of the team responsible for its success. The tall officer at the right is "Shorty" Schroeder; just to his right is Dr Sanford Moss. The Moss supercharger is visible between the engine and the propellor. The photo was taken in June or July 1920, when the aircraft was testing a new Air Service aerial camouflage scheme.

A. L. "Doc" Berger of the Air Service's Powerplant Branch at McCook Field, Ohio, recognized the potential value of the Moss supercharger and, despite a slashed budget, was able to fund a second article. This GE-built unit was fitted to the Liberty engine of a LePere (LUSAC) 11 two-seat fighter in mid-1919. On 4 October, Major Rudolph W. "Shorty" Schroeder, with Lieutenant George W. Elsey as observer, took off from McCook for a test flight and attempt on the world's altitude record. Their climb was cut short when a coolant line to the supercharger's rear bearing ruptured; Schroeder switched off the supercharger and returned safely to McCook. An examination of on-board instruments determined that Schroeder and Elsey had reached 29,540 feet, a new record for an aircraft carrying two people.

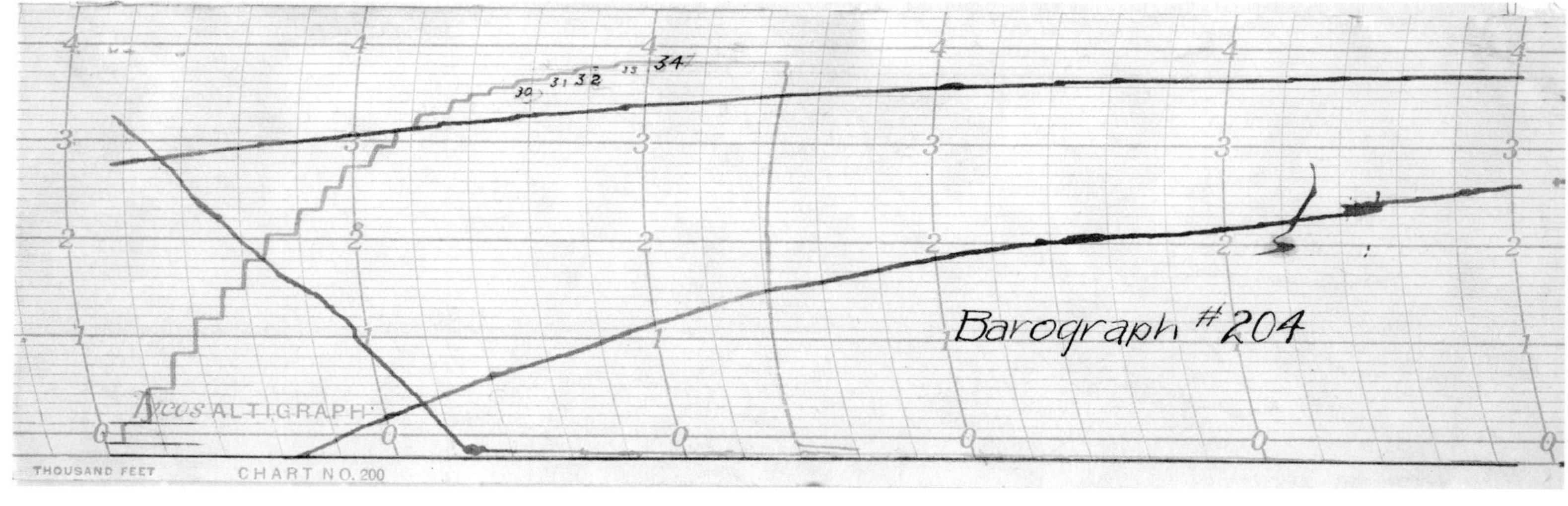

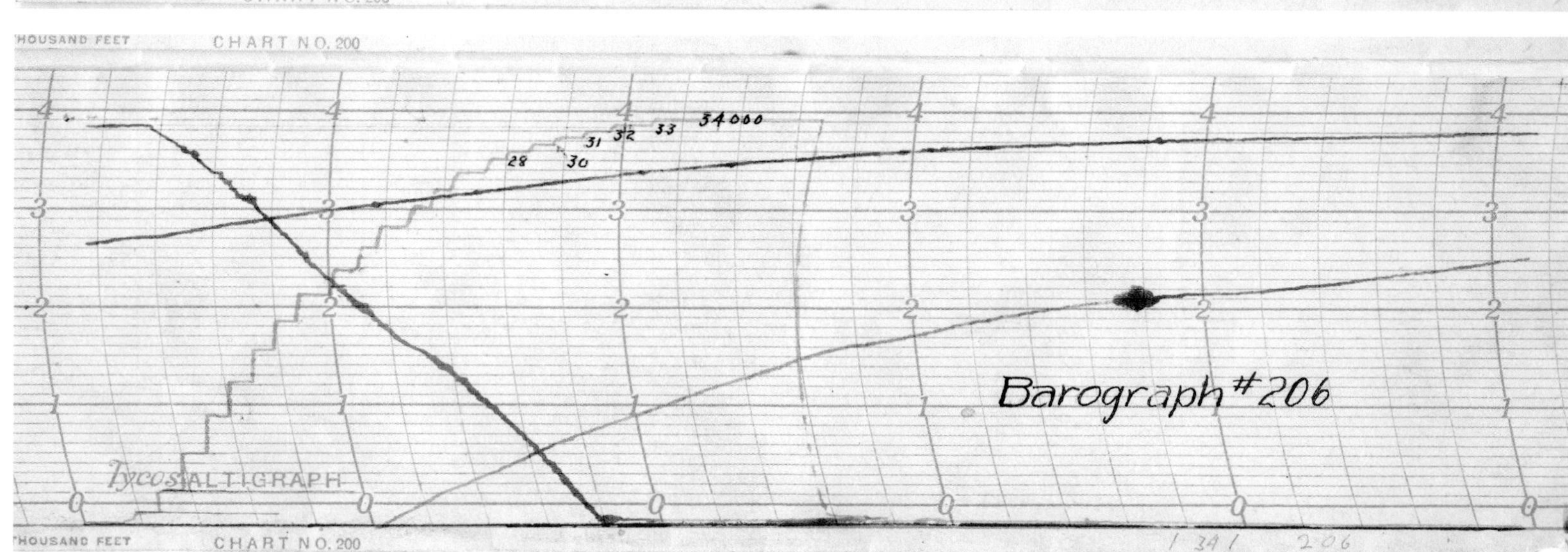

Schroeder and Elsey carried a series of instruments on their October 1919 high altitude flight, but none actually measured altitude. These barographic charts measured air pressure, which combined with data on air temperature and other parameters, could be used to calculate approximate altitude. Variations between the two charts were averaged. Using Air Service formulas, the indicated altitude averaged out at 33,335 feet. A Bureaus of Standards formula revised that figure to 31,800 feet above sea level, and an FAI formula recomputed the altitude to a world record 29,540 feet.

With the LePere 11 capable of higher altitudes, Schroeder prepared for another attempt on 27 February 1920. The barometers needed to be recalibrated - as delivered by the National Bureaus of Standards, they were capable of measuring only to 34,000 feet; McCook Field engineers tacked on another 4,000 feet. The supercharger performed flawlessly as the aircraft climbed for an hour and three-quarters. Schroeder struggled with his controls in the rough air of the Tropopause, then, a few hundred feet later, high winds began to blow the aircraft backwards at an extremely high velocity. Schroeder was in the "anti-trade winds" (known today as the "jet stream") a phenomenon that had been observed with unmanned sounding balloons, but never before experienced by a pilot. Schroeder had reached the Stratosphere.

With the cockpit temperature at -53 C, Schroeder began to experience problems with his oxygen system. He blacked out. As he fell forward onto the controls, the LePere entered a 300 mph dive. The rapidly changing air pressure crushed the main fuel tank. At about 3,000 feet, Schroeder began to regain consciousness, but his body refused to respond. His goggles were coated with ice, and his eyelids frozen shut, but he willed himself to pull out of the dive and, through eyes that would barely open, return to McCook for a "normal" landing. Lifted from the cockpit, Schroeder spent the next three weeks in a darkened room. Although he would quickly regain his sight, the pilot's heart swelled dramatically, creating a handicap that would effect him for years. Schroeder, the LePere, and the GE Moss supercharger had set a new record of 31,750 feet.

The Air Service continued its experiments with the LePere, often without the supercharger, and the aircraft was used for two further notable flights. On 27 March 1924, Major Hunter Harris, Sr, (father of a future air leader Hunter Harris Jr) took the aircraft to its absolute ceiling, which calculated out as 34,100 feet. And on 2 May 1924, lieutenants John A. Macready and Albert W. Stevens tested new cameras on a photographic mission to 33,670 feet. •

Lt Macready and official FAI observers pose with the LePere prior to a 1924 attempted record altitude flight. To the left is FAI observer Orville Wright. (The aircraft sports an Army olive drab fuselage, reapplied at the completion of the camouflage tests.)

The LePere 11 over McCook Field around the time of their 1919 record flight. Contemporary records listed the aircraft as the "LePere Supercharger" or the "P53" - the Engineering Division's individual aircraft recognition number.

Delivering the Mail

The first attempt at delivering mail by air appears to have taken place in 1785, when Jean-Pierre Blanchard and Dr John Jeffries made the first balloon crossing of the English Channel; Jeffries reportedly carried a letter to a friend in Calais, though it is doubtful the letter was delivered. As their balloon descended toward the Channel's icy waters, Blanchard and Jeffries tossed everything - including most of their clothing - over the side to lighten their craft. Blanchard had better luck in 1793, when he successfully delivered a letter from George Washington following an ascent in the United States. During the Franco-Prussian War (1870-71), the French used unmanned free balloons to float mail out of a besieged Paris. By 1911, the British were experimenting with an airmail route between Blackpool and Southport; Claude Grahame-White organized the short, ceremonial flights, eight of which were made that September. Although other experiments in France, Germany, Italy, Holland, and the US were stilled by World War I, the Germans managed to introduce regular mail and passenger Zeppelin service between Friedrichshafen and Duseldorf in June 1916.

On 15 May 1918, the US Army inaugurated the first regular American air mail service, connecting New York City, Philadelphia, and Washington, DC. Major Reuben E. Fleet organized and commanded the Air Service detachment, though he would not fly any of the mail-carrying missions. He was responsible for six new Curtiss JN-4H Jennys, facilities and supplies in the three cities, and six pilots of varied training and experience; the Post Office had selected two of the pilots based on political connections, but only one of the six, Lieutenant Howard Paul Culver, could be considered a seasoned airman.

President Woodrow Wilson and other dignitaries attended the opening ceremonies in Washington. Major Fleet gave final instructions to 2nd Lieutenant George L. Boyle, who signed for his sacks of mail, climbed into his Jenny, and took off north for Philadelphia. Boyle, who'd been flying for less than four months and had never flown more than fifteen miles from his home field, quickly became lost. Following the wrong railway, he flew south to Waldorf, Maryland, where he flipped his aircraft landing in a field. With no word of Boyle's fate (he was uninjured), Lt Culver flew on from Philadelphia to the ceremony awaiting him in New York. The mail from Washington would arrive later by rail.

On May 17th, Boyle again attempted to deliver the mail from Washington to Philadelphia. Lost again, he destroyed his aircraft in a bad landing; overriding Post Office objections, Fleet reassigned the young pilot to another unit. There would be other failures in the Army's three-month relationship with the Post Office, but no aviators would be killed. In all, 270 flights would be attempted, with 16 forced down by mechanical problems and 53 by weather. On August 12th, the Post Office took over responsibility for its own air mail deliveries.

It has often been stated that the air mail aviators used simple road maps. In fact, the Army Corps of Engineers supplied them with aviation maps, though the quality of these maps left much to be desired. Lieutenant Howard Paul Culver used the northern section of the map reproduced here during his flights on the Army's air mail route. The "aviation map" provides little navigational data - certainly no notation of ground altitudes or contours - to assist the airman, though rivers and railways are clearly marked. Latitude and longitude lines cross the page diagonally, and the magnetic declination from true north is posted at the bottom of the map west of Hampton Roads. But pilots soon learned to follow the "iron compass" - the railroad tracks connecting major cities. Culver modified his map with parallel vertical lines, one inch (representing three scale miles) apart. His drafting pen also circled the polo field (see inset), that served as the DC landing field. •

Major Reuben Fleet explains the route to Lt. George Boyle, who would carry the first air mail out of Washington, DC, on 15 May 1918.

With opening ceremonies planned before aircraft had been built, Major Fleet was able to deliver this Curtiss JN-4H to Washington only three hours before it was scheduled to carry the first sacks of mail to Philadelphia. Fleet's aviation map is folded and strapped to his right leg to prevent the slipstream from carrying it out of the cockpit.

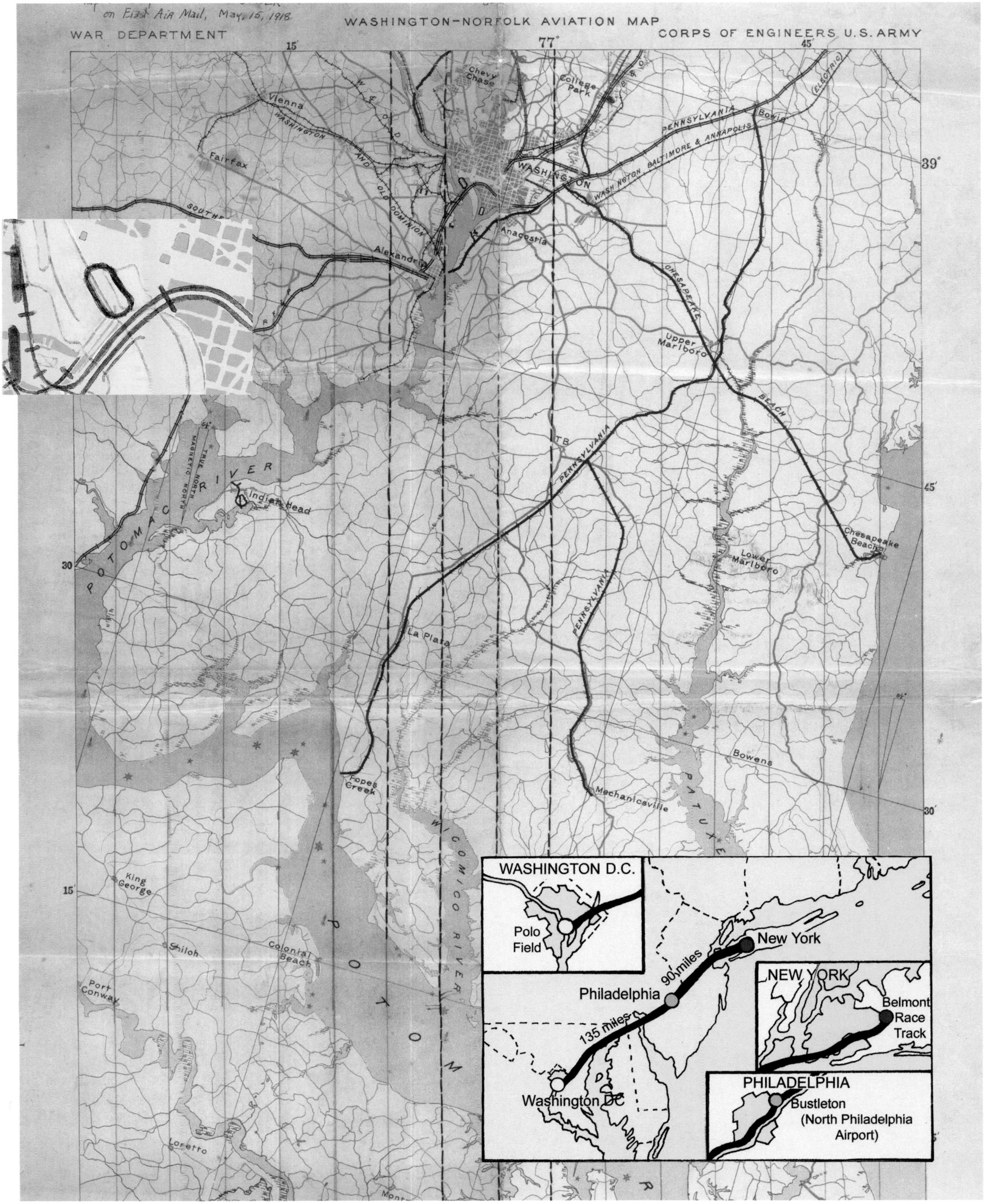

Main map caption - This War Department aviation map was carried by Lt. H. P. Culver on his early Air Service mail flights. The inset to the left shows Culver's marking around the polo field, near Washington's Tidal Basin.

Marking the Airways

Even with the best maps of the day, the aviator of 1920 had few navigation aids. Compasses, when not deflected by an engine's electrical current, might indicate magnetic north, but gave no identification of the ground below. In 1921, under the direction of General Billy Mitchell, the US Army Air Service began development of the first model airway. Connecting McCook Field (in Dayton, Ohio) with Bolling Field (in Washington, DC), the airway established a series of ground markers along the route, each providing its location and the direction of true north.

Within five years, additional information would also guide aircraft to the nearest airfield. (The lack of a circle and arrow generally meant that no nearby airfield existed.) At different times, a system could provide additional details about the type of airfield and its capabilities, though these details would prove unnecessarily complicated and be dropped.

There were, of course, many problems with the ground marking system. Most markings were designed to be read from 5,000 feet, some from higher, but the marking would be of little help to aircraft flying at 10,000 feet. Night flying could be improved by flashing beacons and illuminated markings, but these would be more expensive to maintain than paint on a roof or white stones in a field. And of course weather: rain that reduced visibility or flooded a field, snow that covered everything, or a heavy ground fog could easily obscure the markings at the very moment an aviator needed them most.

But with aviation rapidly establishing itself for sport, military use, and commercial ventures, newer improved navigational devices would become a priority for future airways. •

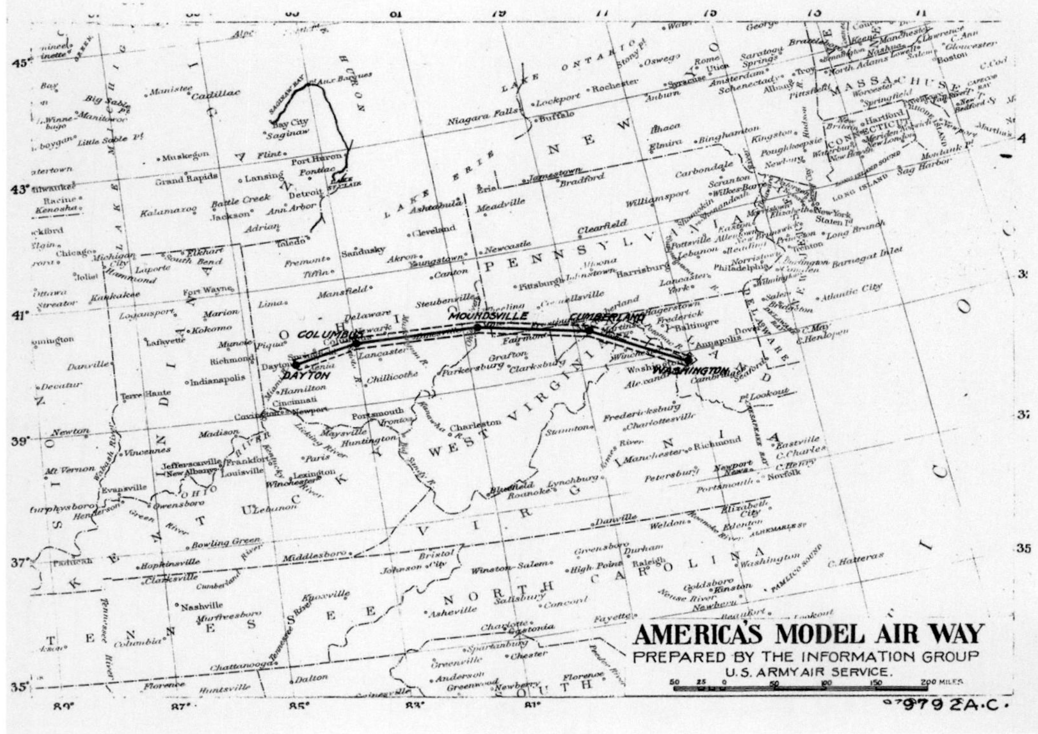

The first Model Airway was the brainchild of the Army Air Service, so it was only natural that the route connect McCook Field, the Army's experimental, developmental, and procurement center, with Bolling Field, the Air Service's headquarters.

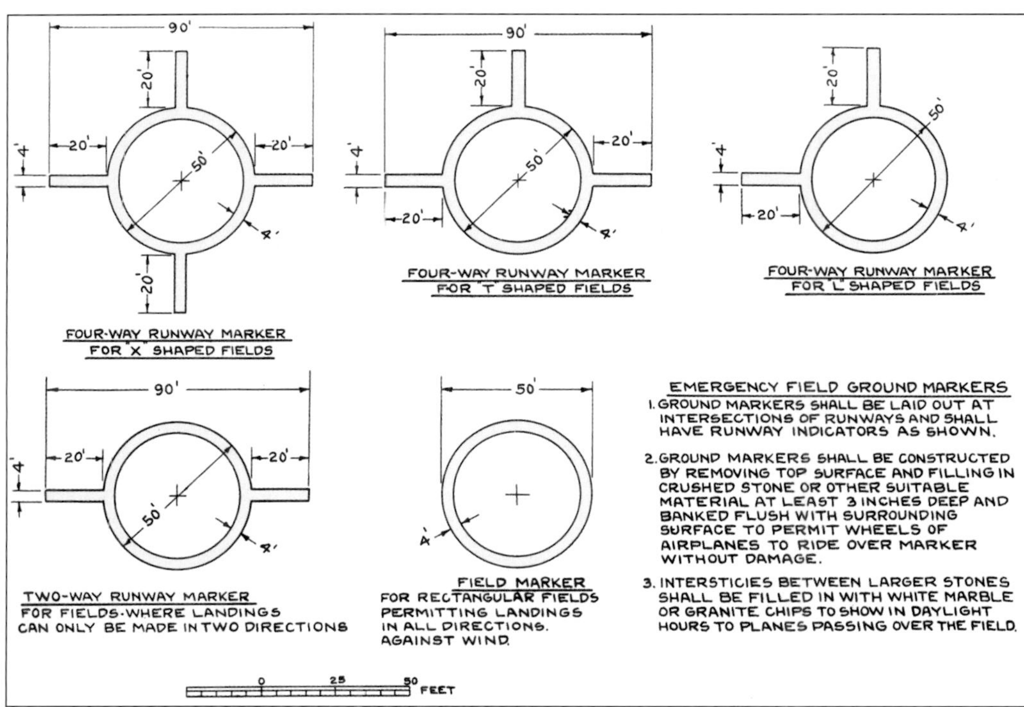

In April 1928, the Department of Commerce established approved ground markings for locating emergency landing fields. The system would be replaced in less than a year.

On 12 February 1921, General Billy Mitchell presided on the dedication of America's first Model Airway at Bolling Field, DC. As part of the ceremony, Boy Scouts arranged white stones near the airfield, marking the eastern terminus of the airway as "DC1."

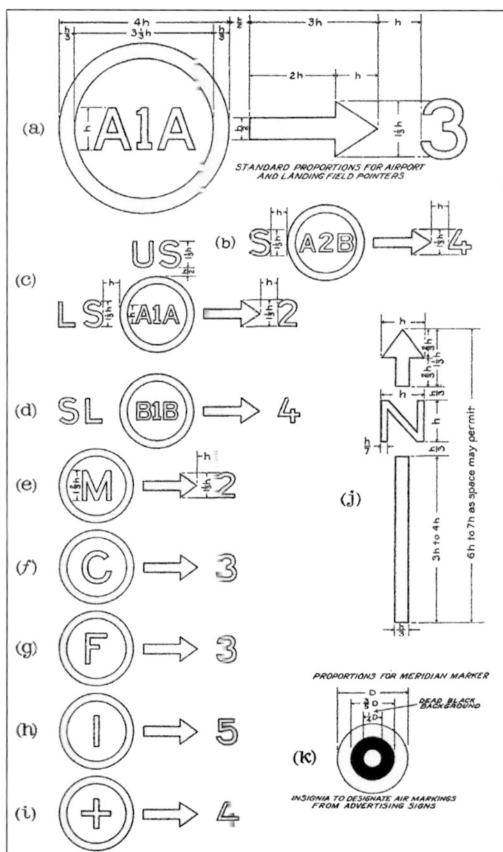

In 1935, this field marker at Champaign, Illinois, gave the direction, but not distance, to a marked auxiliary landing field.

In January 1929 the US Department of Commerce created a new national standard for air markings. Circles still gave information on airfields, but with different information on the nature of each field. This complicated system would be simplified during the 1930s. The style of north arrow was also standardized, and the paired symbols were arranged with the name of the city or town to aid with pilot orientation.

a) This arrow points to a class A1A-rated airport, three miles away.
b) This arrow points to a class A2B-rated seaplane base, four miles away.
c) This arrow points to a class A1A-rated land plane base, with facilities for seaplanes, two miles away. The "US" above this figure shows that the base is designated as a US point of entry by the Federal Government.
d) This arrow points to a B1B-rated seaplane base, with additional facilities for land planes, four miles away.
e) This arrow points to an unrated municipal airport, 2 miles away.
f) This arrow points to an unrated commercial airport.
g) This arrow points to an unrated Federal airdrome or air station.
h) This arrow points to a Department of Commerce intermediate landing field.
i) This arrow points to a marked auxiliary landing field.
j) This arrow indicates True North.
k) In areas where roofs are also used for advertising, this bull's eye is used to distinguish official air markings from all other signs.

An illuminated roof top in Los Angeles points to Grand Central Airport, nine miles away. The little-used star-and-sprocket marking signifies that approved accomodations and services are available at the indicated airport.

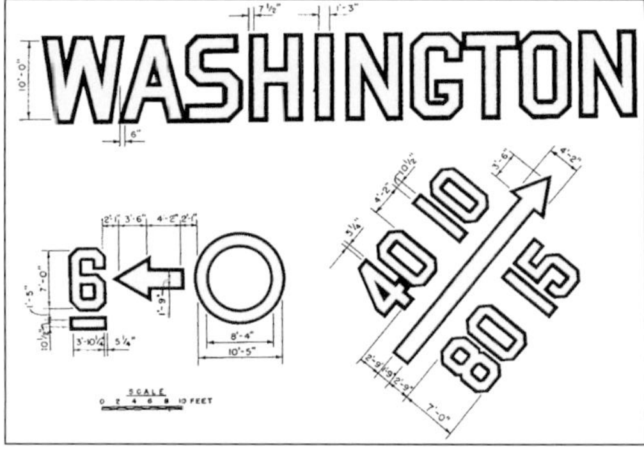

Despite the introduction of sophisticated new navigation systems during World War II, the Civil Aeronautics Administration recognized a continuing need for visible ground markers. By 1945 the information provided with the airfield circle had been simplified dramatically. The north arrow, however, now provided latitude (above) and longitude (below).

Non-Stop Coast to Coast

Just as the welded fuselage structures and advanced wing designs of Fokker fighters gave Germany some of the most effective aircraft of World War I, continuing structural advances placed Fokker's post-war transports among the most respected aircraft of the 1920s. With this in mind, the US Army asked the Dutch firm to design two larger aircraft based on the successful F.III airliner. Fokker built two of the aircraft (designated F.IV) and sold both to the Army (which designated them T-2) in June 1922. Powered by a 420-horsepower Liberty, the T-2 was the largest single-engined aircraft of its day.

One of the aircraft was converted to a flying ambulance (designated A-2) for development of air evacuation techniques. The second aircraft was developed into a long-range endurance aircraft. The cabin, normally equipped to carry 8 to 10 passengers and their baggage, was reconfigured to support additional fuel tanks and a set of auxiliary controls. Air Service engineers, calculating the fuel available at maximum takeoff weight, estimated that the aircraft was capable of a non-stop coast-to-coast flight, and Army headquarters agreed to support the effort.

Lieutenants Oakley G. Kelly and John A. Macready started their first two attempts in San Diego, hoping to take advantage of westerly winds and the higher octane fuel then available on the West Coast.

The heavy takeoff weight of the loaded aircraft meant that the Rockies would have to be threaded through its lowest passes; higher altitudes would only be attained after a significant amount of fuel had been consumed. The first flight, on 5 October 1922, turned back 50 miles east of San Diego after finding those passes blocked by fog. A second attempt, on 3 November, reached Indiana, but a cracked water jacket forced the crew to glide to an emergency landing.

The third attempt started at Roosevelt-Hazelhurst Field, New York, on 2 May 1923. Flying through the night, the crew made dawn just after crossing into New Mexico. With a greater part of the fuel load burned away, the T-2 was able to climb above 10,000 feet for an easier crossing of the Rockies. At 12:26 local time, after almost 27 hours in the air, Kelly, Macready, and their Fokker T-2 had crossed a continent and set new world's distance record. •

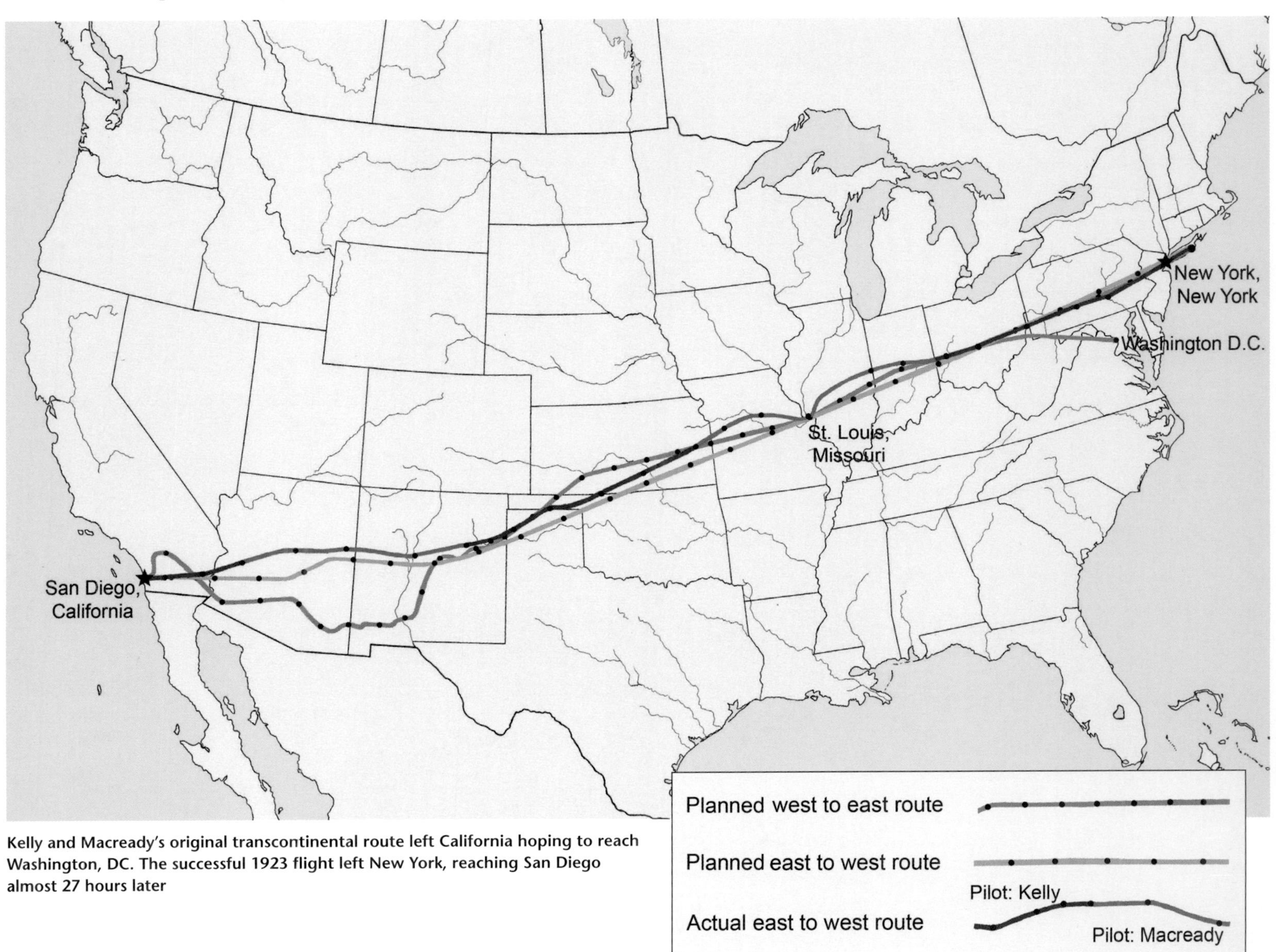

Kelly and Macready's original transcontinental route left California hoping to reach Washington, DC. The successful 1923 flight left New York, reaching San Diego almost 27 hours later

The Fokker T-2 today, displayed in the Smithsonian Institution's National Air and Space Museum.

The T-2 in flight.

Kelly (right) and Macready pose with the T-2 after completion of their historic flight.

On the West Coast prior to one of their east-bound attempts, Kelly and Macready pose with the T-2 and the fuel and oil needed for the flight.

Flying west over the American heartland, Kelly and Macready are escorted by an Army DH-4 from a local airfield.

The Emerging Airlines

Charles Lindbergh's 1927 flight from New York to Paris (see page 89) brought a fresh wave of enthusiasm for all things aeronautical. Following the Kelly Act of 1925 (which enabled private companies to compete for air mail contracts), the Air Commerce Act of 1926 (which made the US government responsible for establishing airways, navigation aids, and airway facilities), and the introduction of newer, larger, more efficient aircraft, the timing couldn't be better. Any entrepreneur with access to an airplane, half an idea how to fly it, and permission to land at two separate locations could form an airline. Those deemed capable of fulfilling their contracts could gain a contract airmail route from the Post Office, the only profitable way to stay in business. And with a profitable airmail route, passengers could be carried, increasing the profits. Not all infant airlines succeeded, and many that did merged or were bought out by larger concerns, but today's United Air Lines, Northwest Aitlines, and American Airlines all trace their roots to this period in the late 1920s.

The Airway Map shown here also traces its roots to that period. It was printed by the Department of Commerce in 1928 with the aid of the US Coast and Geodetic Survey. Oddly configured, the vertical map is designed to be read diagonally, showing the airway and lighted beacons between Greensboro, North Carolina and Richmond, Virginia. Landing fields along the route are marked, with those with lighting facilities (for night landings) coded "LF." Other than daylight visual aids, few navigational beacons appear beyond the limits of the airways. Beacons leading to Washington and Atlanta lead north and south with instructions to see other maps for those routes. None of the fields is identified with any radio contact information - few fields, and fewer aircraft, were so-equipped.

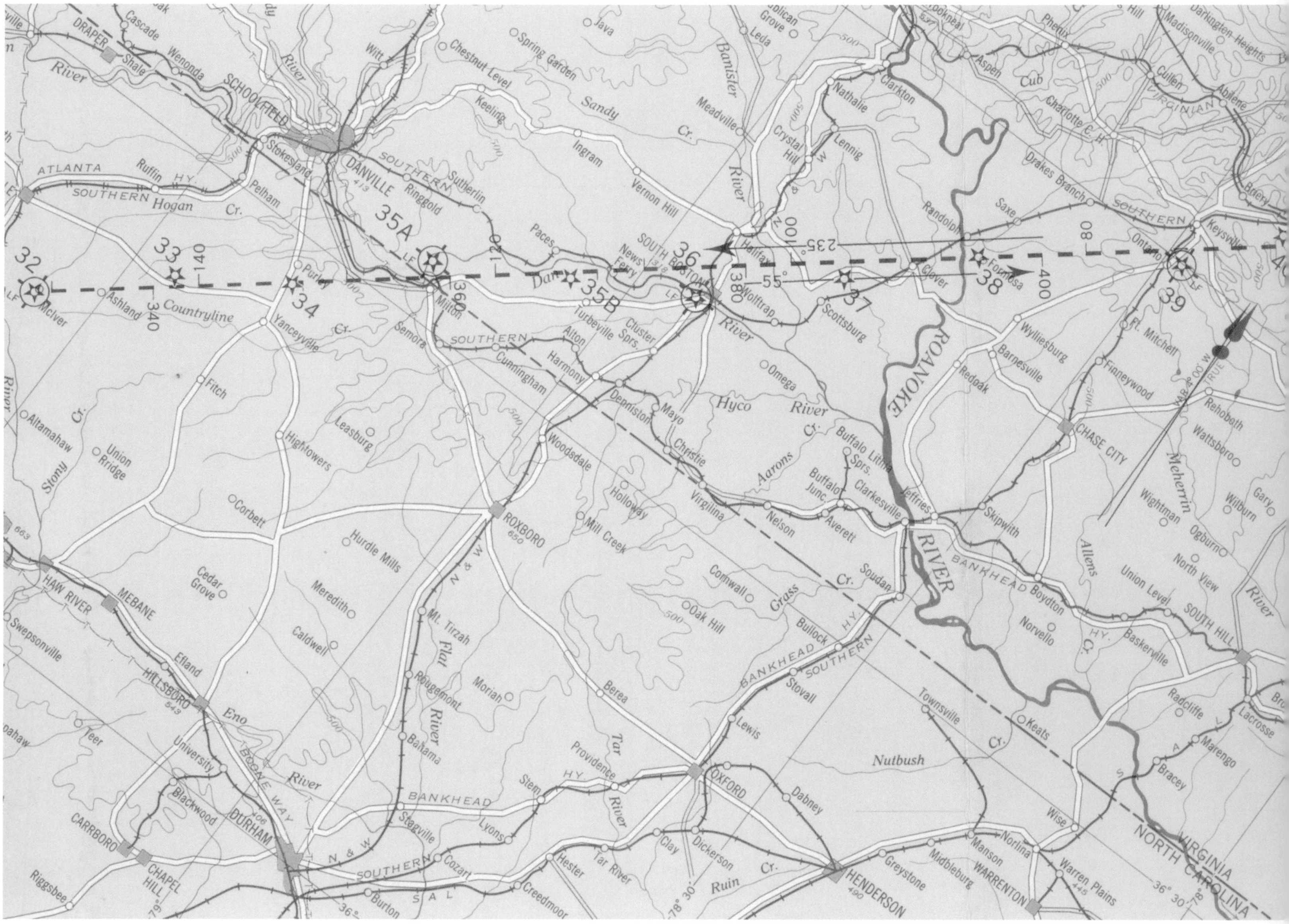

LEFT: This Ford 5-AT-B was delivered to Maddux Airlines in December 1928. TAT purchased Maddux in November 1930, then merged with Western Air Express in July 1930 to form Transcontinental and Western Air Inc; the Tri-Motor flew for three owners in twenty months.

TOP: In the 1920s, a mailplane needed speed and the capacity for a few hundred pounds of mail. This Pitcairn PA-5 Mailwing was one of eight used by Pitcairn Aviation on Contract Air Mail Route No. 19 from New York to Atlanta in 1927/28.

RIGHT: Lunch time on a Transcontinental Air Transport Ford Tri-Motor. TAT service competed with and complimented the nation's railways.

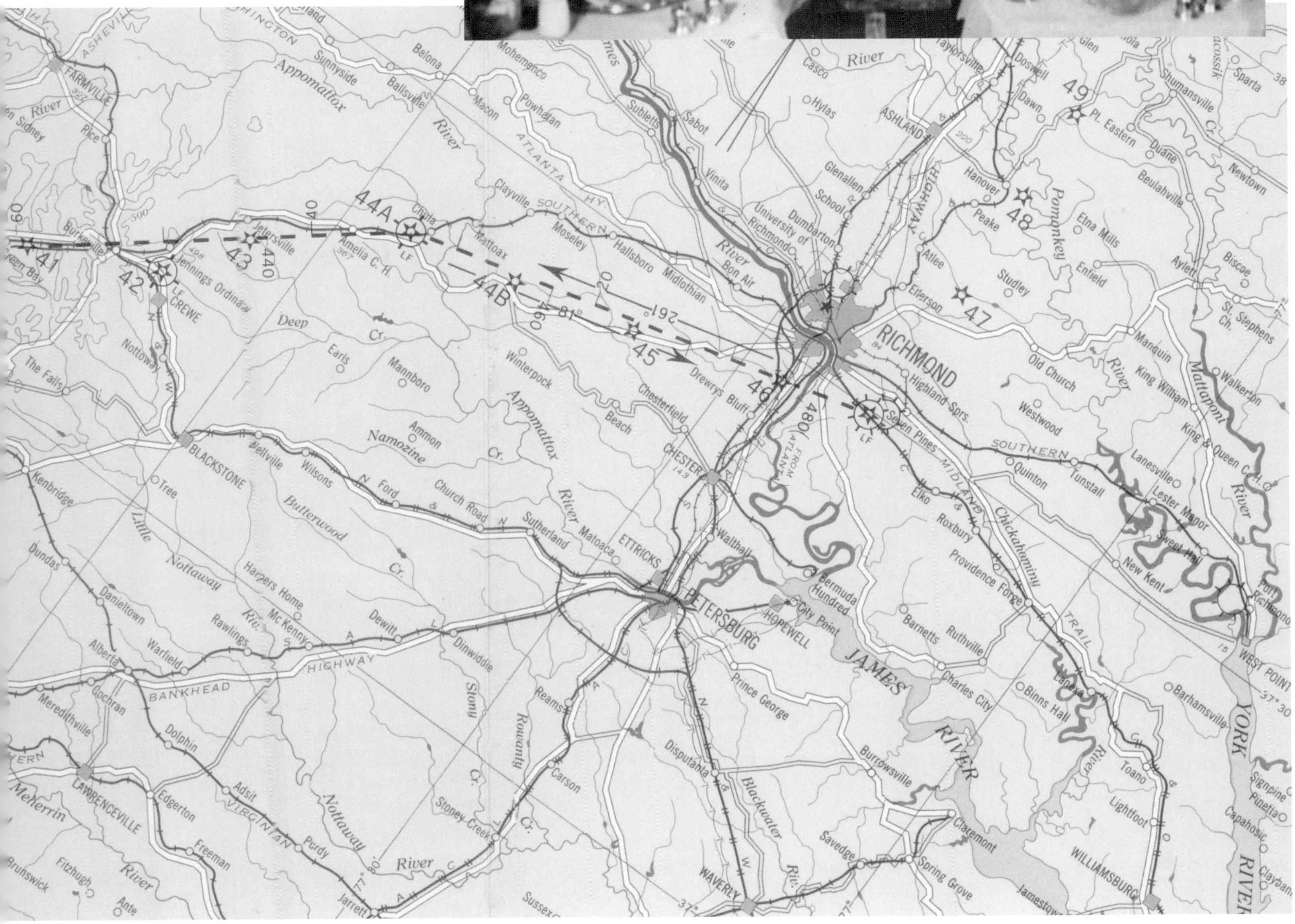

Produced by the Hydrographic Office of the US Navy, this well-used aviation chart was published in 1929 to document the airfields, markers, and radio facilities from Baltimore, Maryland, to Norfolk, Virginia. A single route connected naval facilities at Anacostia (just south of Washington) and Norfolk (home port for the US Fleet). As seen in the detail view, most of the military facilities are shown with radio station call letters - R.S.(WYC) in red to the left of Langley field, for example. Despite the increasing availability of radio equipment and trained operators, most pilots still navigated by visual identification of landmarks, many of which are depicted in grainy images printed around the map's borders. •

Two dozen Stinson Model U trimotors were purchased by American Airlines in 1932. Excessive vibrations often caused air sickness among the aircraft's ten passengers, and the aircraft was soon withdrawn from service. On this example the copilot's position has been replaced by radio equipment.

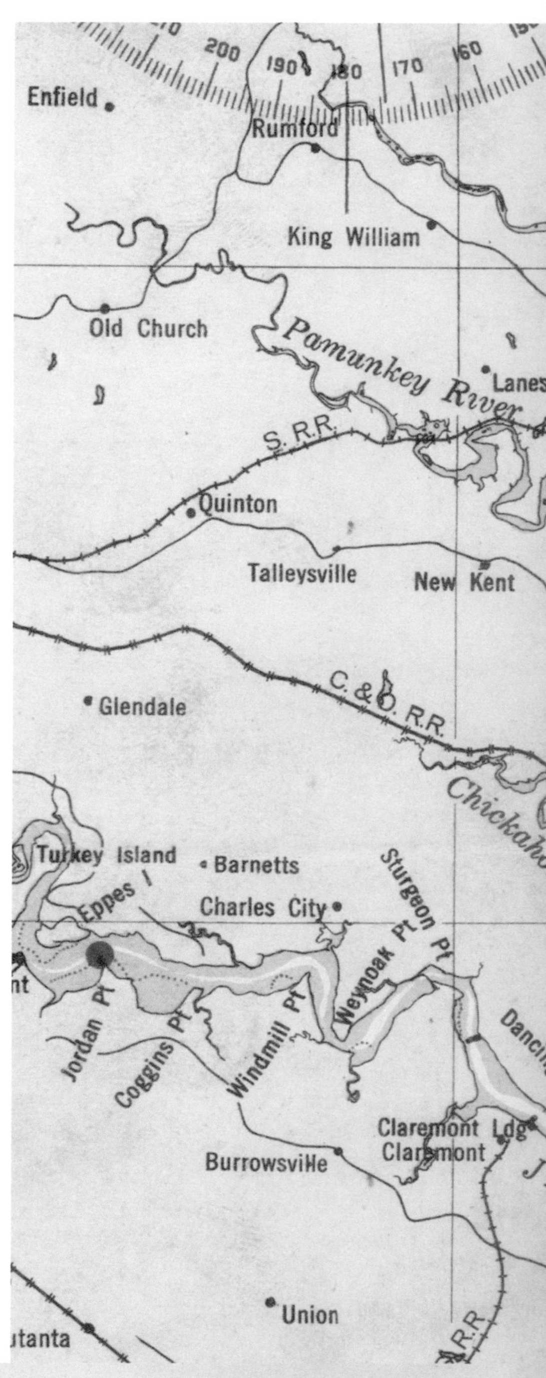

Sleek and modern, even by today's standards, the Northrop Alpha 2 was introduced on mail and (occasionally) passenger routes in 1930. This restored Alpha was the first of its kind flown by TWA in 1930. The tall mast aft of the cockpit supported the antenna wires necessary for early radio equipment.

Two giant, 32-passenger Fokker F-32s were purchased by Western Air Express in early 1930. The aircraft, which remained in service only a short time after the merger with TAT later that year, suffered continuing problems with their four engines.

SMITH POINT
RED-WHITE ROOF

GREAT WICOMICO RIVER
MARKING W10N

LANGLEY FIELD, VA.

The Transcontinental Airline

Formed on 16 May 1928, Transcontinental Air Transport (TAT) was the first major American air line to concentrate on the business of carrying passengers rather than mail. New ground terminals were built with comfort in mind, and the seating capacity on TAT's Ford Trimotors was reduced from 16 to 10, allowing room for a kitchen, serving light meals in an "aerial dining car service."

With night flying still in its infancy, passengers traveled by rail between Waynoka, Oklahoma, and Clovis, New Mexico, and between Columbus, Ohio, and New York or Washington. The trip took about 48 hours and cost between $337 and $403, depending on rail accommodations.

Informally known as the Lindbergh Line, in recognition of Charles Lindbergh's active participation in the technical side of company operations, TAT began scheduled service on 7 July 1929. Just over a year later, in financial trouble, TAT merged with Western Air Express. On 19 July 1930 the two companies reformed as Transcontinental and Western Air, Inc (TWA).

The colorful maps displayed here were part of a souvenir booklet presented to each passenger. This particular booklet was carried by passenger S. C. Burden on an east-bound trip that began 6 August 1929. •

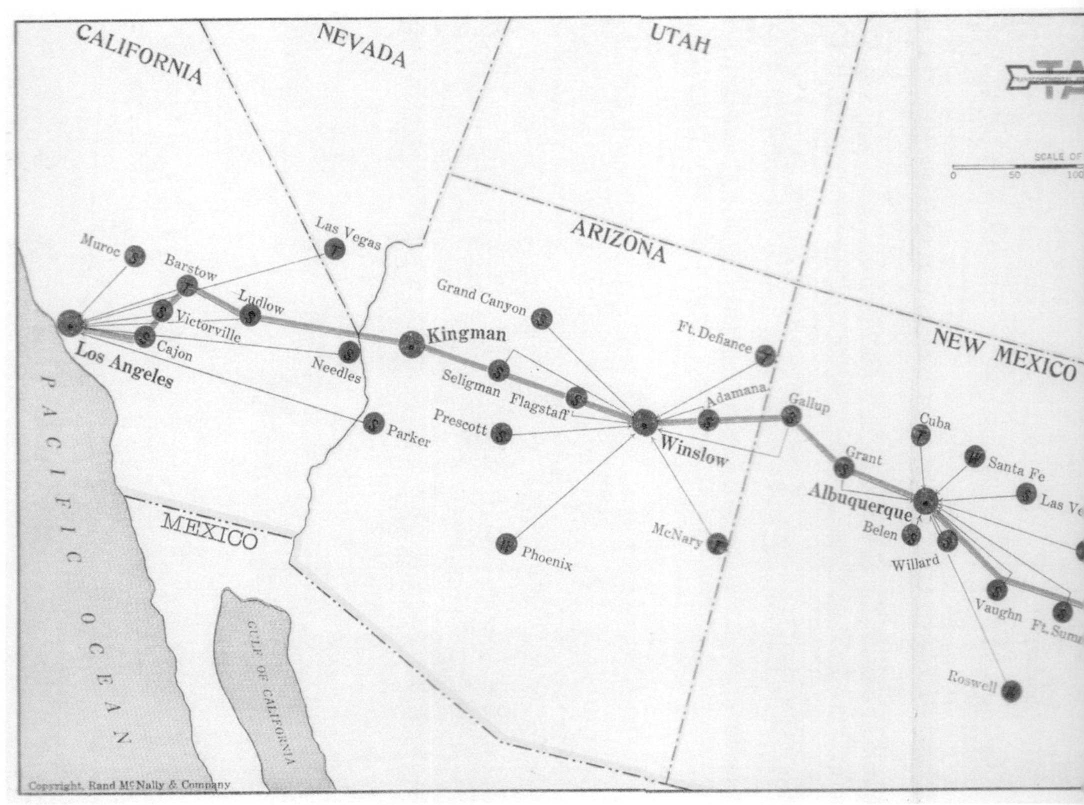

BELOW: With little time available for aerial photography, TAT staffers simply glued images of their aircraft on appropriate backgrounds.

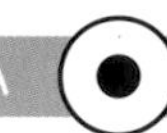

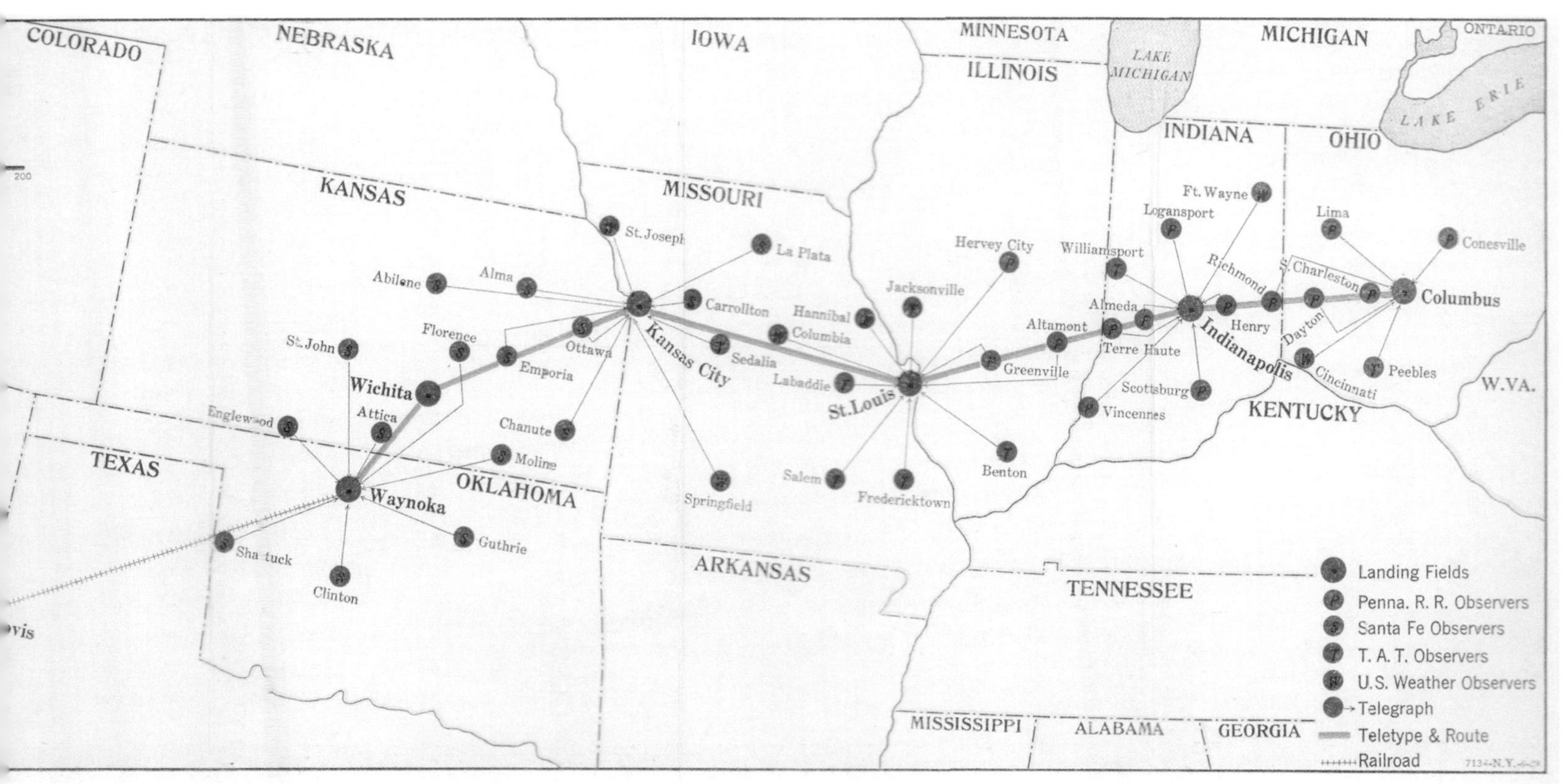

COLORADO
NEBRASKA
IOWA
MINNESOTA
MICHIGAN
ONTARIO
ILLINOIS
LAKE MICHIGAN
LAKE ERIE
INDIANA
OHIO
KANSAS
MISSOURI
Ft. Wayne
Logansport
Lima
St. Joseph
La Plata
Hervey City
Williamsport
Richmond
Conesville
Abilene
Alma
Carrollton
Jacksonville
Charleston
Columbus
Hannibal
Almeda
Columbia
Altamont
Henry
Dayton
St. John
Florence
Ottawa
Kansas City
Sedalia
Terre Haute
Indianapolis
Emporia
Greenville
Wichita
Labaddie
St. Louis
Cincinnati
Peebles
W.VA.
Scottsburg
Attica
Vincennes
KENTUCKY
Englewood
Chanute
TEXAS
Moline
Benton
Waynoka
OKLAHOMA
Salem
Springfield
Fredericktown
Sha tuck
Guthrie
Clinton
ARKANSAS
TENNESSEE
MISSISSIPPI
ALABAMA
GEORGIA
Landing Fields
Penna. R. R. Observers
Santa Fe Observers
T. A. T. Observers
U.S. Weather Observers
Telegraph
Teletype & Route
Railroad

Minneapolis
St. Paul
Milwaukee
Toronto
Chicago
Detroit
Toledo
Cleveland
Buffalo
Omaha
Des Moines
Denver
Indianapolis
Columbus
Pittsburgh
Altoona
Harrisburg
Lancaster
Philadelphia
Newark
New York
Trenton
Baltimore
Washington
Kansas City
Wichita
Cincinnati
Louisville
Richmond
Norfolk
Waynoka
Shattuck
Woodward
Albuquerque
Amarillo
Clovis
Tulsa
Oklahoma City
Nashville
Memphis
Knoxville
Atlanta

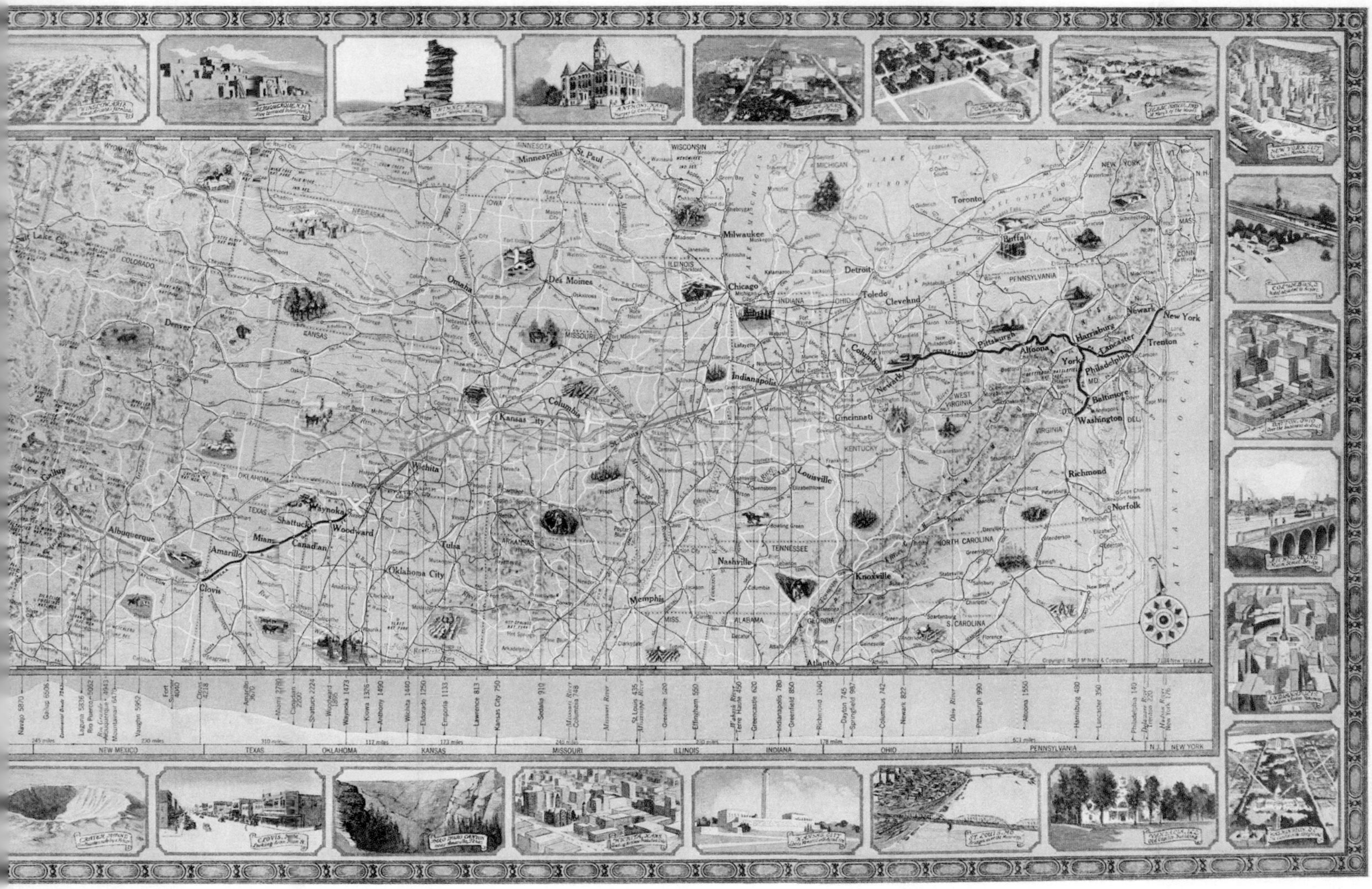

Route Maps and Sectionals

By the 1930s the US Navy's Hydrographic Office, the Army Air Corps, and the Department of Commerce were coordinating their efforts to provide aviation maps and charts. This July 1931 chart shows that progress made to that point concentrated, as one might expect, on the route maps used for military and commercial aircraft. A planned mapping of the entire US - broken down int 92 sectional maps - showed less progress. Only three sectionals had been completed, with nine more in progress.

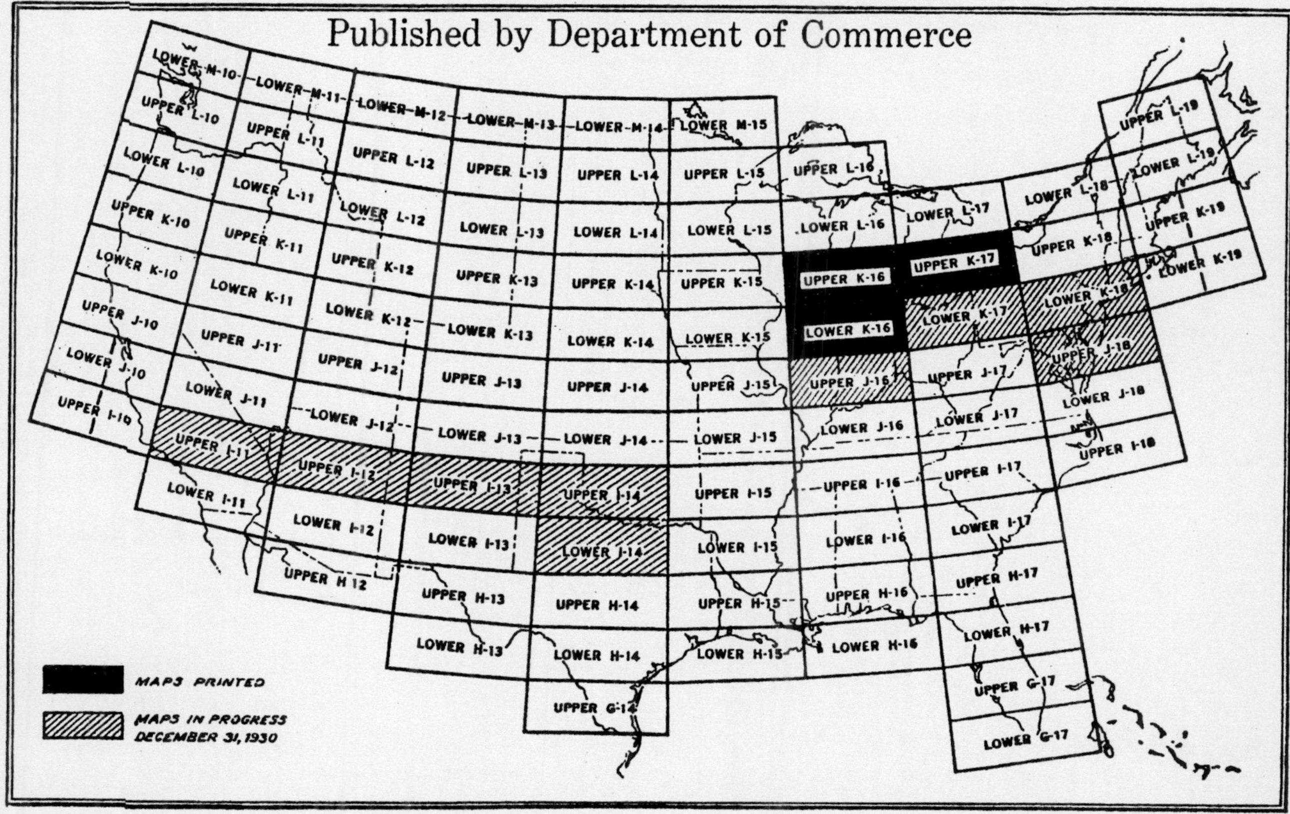

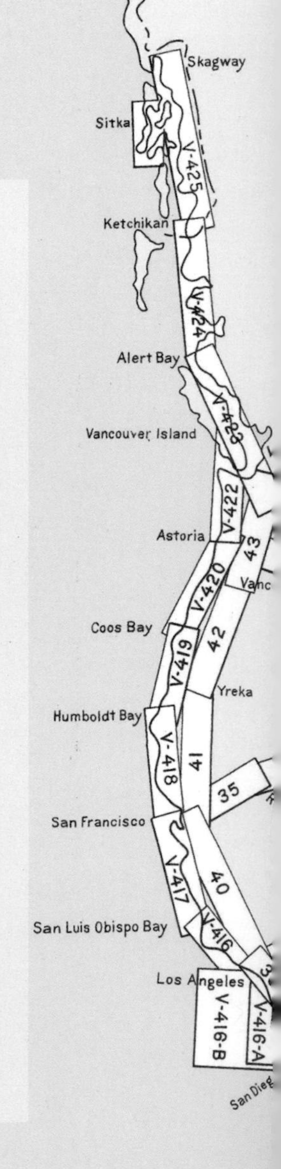

The 39th Ford 5-AT tri-motor was delivered to Southwest Air Fast Express (SAFE) in 1929, becoming the property of American Airlines when that company bought SAFE in 1930. The aircraft flew transcontinental routes through the early 1930s, "retiring" to South American carriers in 1936. American repurchased and restored the aircraft in the 1960s, donating it to the National Air and Space Museum, where it is now displayed.

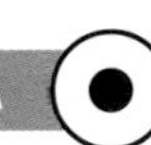

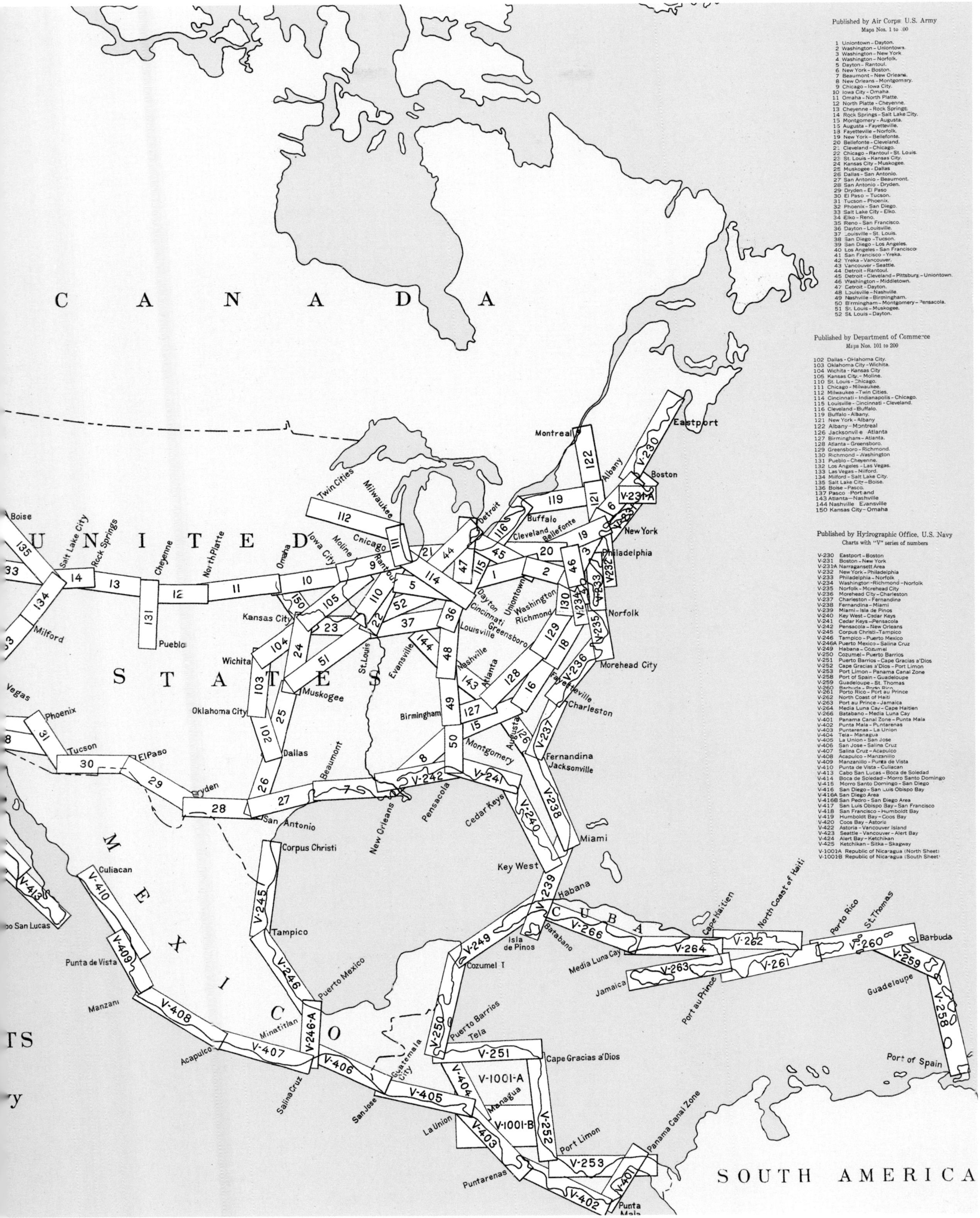
Published by Air Corps U.S. Army
Maps Nos. 1 to 100
1 Uniontown - Dayton.
2 Washington - Uniontown.
3 Washington - New York
4 Washington - Norfolk.
5 Dayton - Rantoul.
6 New York - Boston.
7 Beaumont - New Orleans.
8 New Orleans - Montgomery.
9 Chicago - Iowa City.
10 Iowa City - Omaha.
11 Omaha - North Platte.
12 North Platte - Cheyenne.
13 Cheyenne - Rock Springs.
14 Rock Springs - Salt Lake City.
15 Montgomery - Augusta.
16 Augusta - Fayetteville.
18 Fayetteville - Norfolk.
19 New York - Bellefonte.
20 Bellefonte - Cleveland.
21 Cleveland - Chicago.
22 Chicago - Rantoul - St. Louis.
23 St. Louis - Kansas City.
24 Kansas City - Muskogee.
25 Muskogee - Dallas
26 Dallas - San Antonio.
27 San Antonio - Beaumont.
28 San Antonio - Dryden.
29 Dryden - El Paso
30 El Paso - Tucson.
31 Tucson - Phoenix.
32 Phoenix - San Diego.
33 Salt Lake City - Elko.
34 Elko - Reno.
35 Reno - San Francisco.
36 Dayton - Louisville.
37 Louisville - St. Louis.
38 San Diego - Tucson.
39 San Diego - Los Angeles.
40 Los Angeles - San Francisco
41 San Francisco - Yreka.
42 Yreka - Vancouver.
43 Vancouver - Seattle.
44 Detroit - Rantoul.
45 Detroit - Cleveland - Pittsburg - Uniontown.
46 Washington - Middletown.
47 Detroit - Dayton.
48 Louisville - Nashville.
49 Nashville - Birmingham.
50 Birmingham - Montgomery - Pensacola.
51 St. Louis - Muskogee.
52 St. Louis - Dayton.
Published by Department of Commerce
Maps Nos. 101 to 200
102 Dallas - Oklahoma City.
103 Oklahoma City - Wichita.
104 Wichita - Kansas City
105 Kansas City. - Moline.
110 St. Louis - Chicago.
111 Chicago - Milwaukee.
112 Milwaukee - Twin Cities.
114 Cincinnati - Indianapolis - Chicago.
115 Louisville - Cincinnati - Cleveland.
116 Cleveland - Buffalo.
119 Buffalo - Albany.
121 New York - Albany
122 Albany - Montreal
126 Jacksonville Atlanta
127 Birmingham - Atlanta.
128 Atlanta - Greensboro.
129 Greensboro - Richmond.
130 Richmond - Washington
131 Pueblo - Cheyenne.
132 Los Angeles - Las Vegas.
133 Las Vegas - Milford.
134 Milford - Salt Lake City.
135 Salt Lake City - Boise.
136 Boise - Pasco.
137 Pasco - Portland
143 Atlanta—Nashville
144 Nashville Evansville
150 Kansas City - Omaha
Published by Hydrographic Office, U.S. Navy
Charts with "V" series of numbers
V-230 Eastport - Boston
V-231 Boston - New York
V-231-A Narragansett Area
V-232 New York - Philadelphia
V-233 Philadelphia - Norfolk
V-234 Washington - Richmond - Norfolk
V-235 Norfolk - Morehead City
V-236 Morehead City - Charleston
V-237 Charleston - Fernandina
V-238 Fernandina - Miami
V-239 Miami - Isla de Pinos
V-240 Key West - Cedar Keys
V-241 Cedar Keys - Pensacola
V-242 Pensacola - New Orleans
V-245 Corpus Christi - Tampico
V-246 Tampico - Puerto Mexico
V-246A Puerto Mexico - Salina Cruz
V-249 Habana - Cozumel
V-250 Cozumel - Puerto Barrios
V-251 Puerto Barrios - Cape Gracias a'Dios
V-252 Cape Gracias a'Dios - Port Limon
V-253 Port Limon - Panama Canal Zone
V-258 Port of Spain - Guadeloupe
V-259 Guadeloupe - St. Thomas
V-260 Barbuda - Porto Rico
V-261 Porto Rico - Port au Prince
V-262 North Coast of Haiti
V-263 Port au Prince - Jamaica
V-264 Media Luna Cay - Cape Haitien
V-266 Batabano - Media Luna Cay
V-401 Panama Canal Zone - Punta Mala
V-402 Punta Mala - Puntarenas
V-403 Puntarenas - La Union
V-404 Tela - Managua
V-405 La Union - San Jose
V-406 San Jose - Salina Cruz
V-407 Salina Cruz - Acapulco
V-408 Acapulco - Manzanillo
V-409 Manzanillo - Punta de Vista
V-410 Punta de Vista - Culiacan
V-413 Cabo San Lucas - Boca de Soledad
V-414 Boca de Soledad - Morro Santo Domingo
V-415 Morro Santo Domingo - San Diego
V-416 San Diego - San Luis Obispo Bay
V-416A San Diego Area
V-416B San Pedro - San Diego Area
V-417 San Luis Obispo Bay - San Francisco
V-418 San Francisco - Humboldt Bay
V-419 Humboldt Bay - Coos Bay
V-420 Coos Bay - Astoria
V-422 Astoria - Vancouver Island
V-423 Seattle - Vancouver - Alert Bay
V-424 Alert Bay - Ketchikan
V-425 Ketchikan - Sitka - Skagway
V-1001-A Republic of Nicaragua (North Sheet)
V-1001-B Republic of Nicaragua (South Sheet)
C A N A D A
U N I T E D
S T A T E S
M E X I C O
C U B A
SOUTH AMERICA
Montreal
Eastport
Boston
Albany
New York
Philadelphia
Buffalo
Cleveland
Bellefonte
Detroit
Twin Cities
Milwaukee
Chicago
Moline
Iowa City
Omaha
North Platte
Cheyenne
Rock Springs
Salt Lake City
Boise
Milford
Pueblo
Kansas City
Wichita
Muskogee
Oklahoma City
Dallas
Phoenix
Tucson
El Paso
Dryden
San Antonio
Beaumont
Corpus Christi
Tampico
St. Louis
Evansville
Louisville
Nashville
Atlanta
Birmingham
Montgomery
Augusta
Dayton
Cincinnati
Uniontown
Washington
Richmond
Greensboro
Norfolk
Morehead City
Fayetteville
Charleston
Fernandina
Jacksonville
Miami
Key West
Cedar Keys
Pensacola
New Orleans
Habana
Isla de Pinos
Batabano
Media Luna Cay
Cape Haitien
North Coast of Haiti
Porto Rico
St. Thomas
Barbuda
Guadeloupe
Port of Spain
Jamaica
Port au Prince
Cozumel I
Puerto Mexico
Minatitlan
Puerto Barrios
Tela
Cape Gracias a'Dios
Managua
Port Limon
Panama Canal Zone
Punta Mala
Puntarenas
La Union
San Jose
Guatemala City
Salina Cruz
Acapulco
Manzani
Punta de Vista
Culiacan
Cabo San Lucas

The 1930s saw aviation advancing dramatically in all areas. Enough new aircraft designs were entering service to fill the pages of monthly and weekly journals. Pilot training had become more formalized, with stricter government requirements introduced for each class of pilot license. Ground facilities offered improved safety features, with many fields offering two-way radio communications. Teletype systems relayed critical flight and weather information between fields. The airways themselves had more and improved visual markings, and radio beacons, with the right airborne equipment and a clear signal, could help guide aircraft through foul weather or the darkest nights.

Many of these changes were reflected in this 1934 sectional chart of southern New York. Pale, pink rays mark eight operational radio range beacons (at a time when there were just over 100 nationwide). Three of the beacons are situated with the chart's boundaries at Newark, New Jersey; Bellefonte, Pennsylvania; and Harrisburg, Pennsylvania. Four other beacons lead aircraft off the charts to Albany, New York; Boston, Massachusetts; Camden, New Jersey; and Washington, DC.

The map key (far right) shows the continuing importance of visual navigation – at the time only a few hundred US pilots had gained instrument flying ratings. Many of the symbols are still in use today, though we no longer distinguish between rail lines with single and multiple tracks and trolley lines and airship mooring masts are but a memory. Code symbols for airports and seaplane ports

This 1934 Department of Commerce sectional features the radiating pink lines of the newly installed radio beacons. The larger map shows the details of the New York City area.

were more complicated, while much of the information provided today would have had little relevance in the 1930s. (Landing speeds were still low enough that runways were rarely considered too short!)

The detail of the New York City area shows the wide variety of airfields and seaplane facilities surrounding Manhattan Island. The outer ring of each field symbol shows the type of field, with the inner symbol describing the visual beacon marking the location. In a city of skyscrapers, only the Empire State Building (completed in 1931) is marked as an obstruction, its height listed as 1002 feet (subsequently increased by nearly 475 feet). The George Washington Bridge (also completed in 1931) is shown, unlabeled, across the Hudson River; note that nearby power transmission lines are shown, though the bridge's 600-foot towers are not listed as obstructions.

As modern pilots will quickly point out, none of the airspace around the city is in any way restricted. Contemporary pilots were expected to responsibly control their aircraft, navigate the area safely, and avoid other aircraft - otherwise the skies were theirs. •

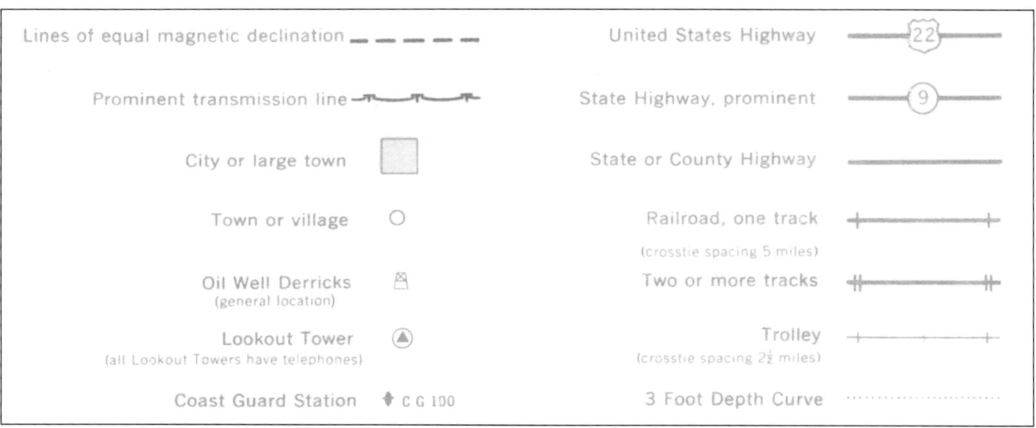

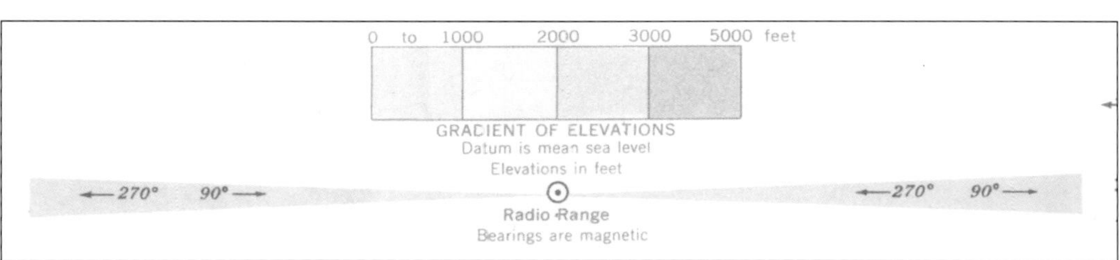

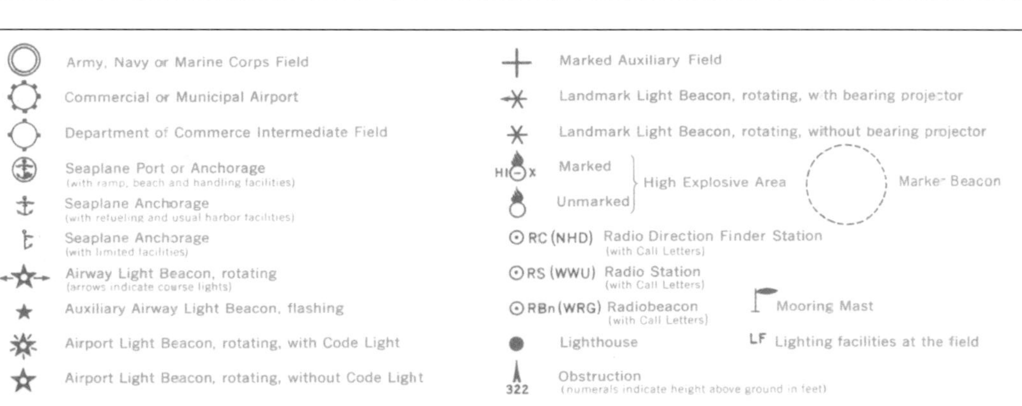

Entering service in 1933, the fabric-covered Curtiss Condor II biplanes were already surpassed by newer, all-metal designs. This American Airways Condor was the first sleeper plane in the US. It was lost in a fatal accident near Liberty, New York, in 1934.

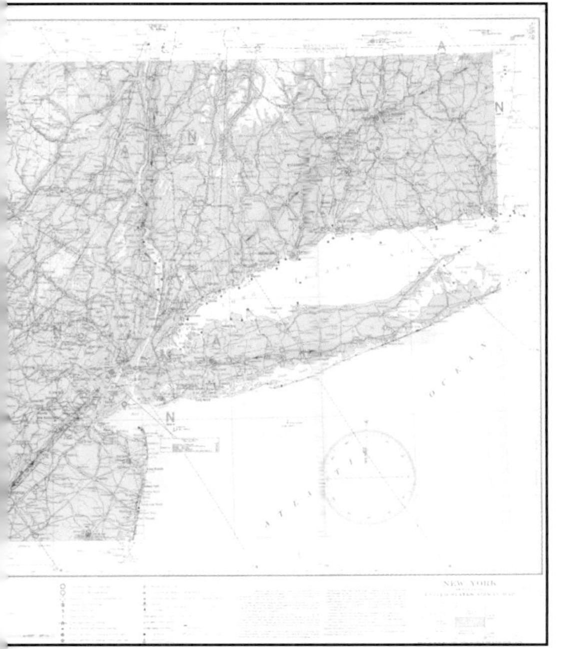

The first modern US airliner, the Boeing 247 carried its ten passengers at speeds 50-70 miles per hour faster than the Ford and Fokker trimotors it replaced. The first of seventy-five 247s began service with United Air Lines in 1933. Photographed over New York City, this 247-D was United's flight research aircraft after the DC-3 took over most passenger services. Note the large number of antenna around the 247's forward fuselage.

The Domestic Airways

By March 1938, the Bureau of Air Commerce map of American civil airways (right) covered every state in the union. Advances in radio communications and navigational aids meant that most commercial routes supported night and foul-weather operations. The approach of World War II would improve the nation's ground infrastructure dramatically, and lead to lighter and more efficient airborne radio systems. •

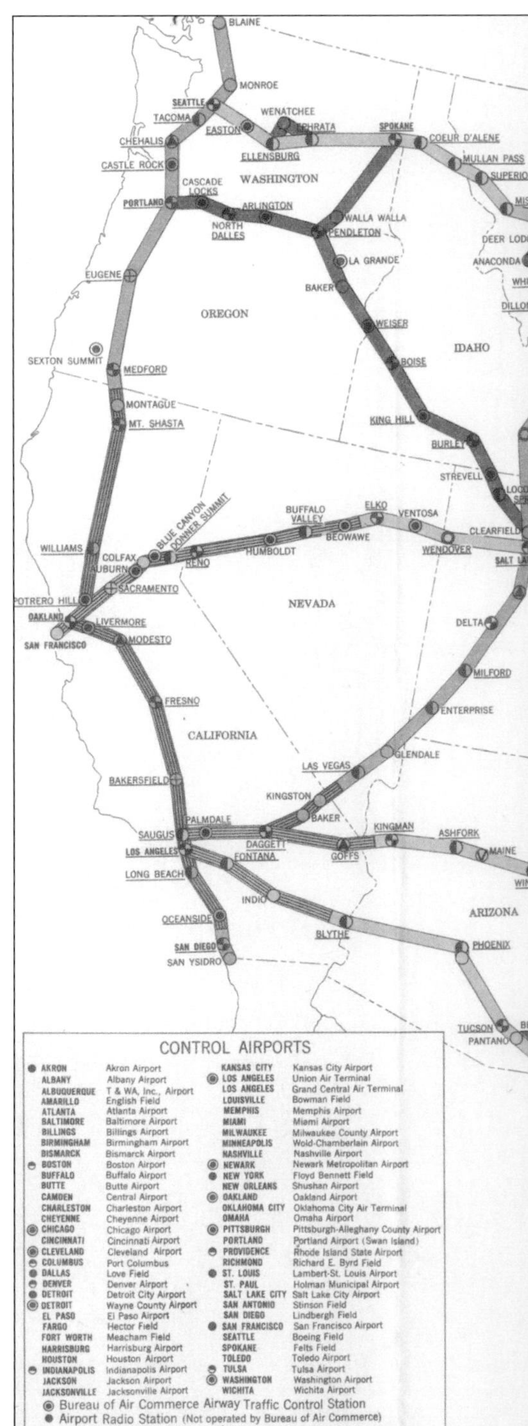

TOP LEFT: The Boeing 307 Stratoliner was the first airliner to feature a pressurized cockpit and cabin, allowing crew and passengers to fly safely and comfortably at altitudes never before possible.

MIDDLE LEFT: In the summer of 1936, American Airlines began service with two developments of the Douglas DC-2: the DST (Douglas Sleeper Transport) carried 14 berths for cross-country night flights, and the DC-3 carried 21 seats for daytime flights. The DC-3, which was the first commercial aircraft capable of turning a profit without carrying mail, would soon become the world's most widely produced airliner.

BOTTOM LEFT: Canadian Colonial Airways, an affiliate of American Airways, used its small fleet of four DC-3s from New York City to Montreal in the late 1930s through 1942.

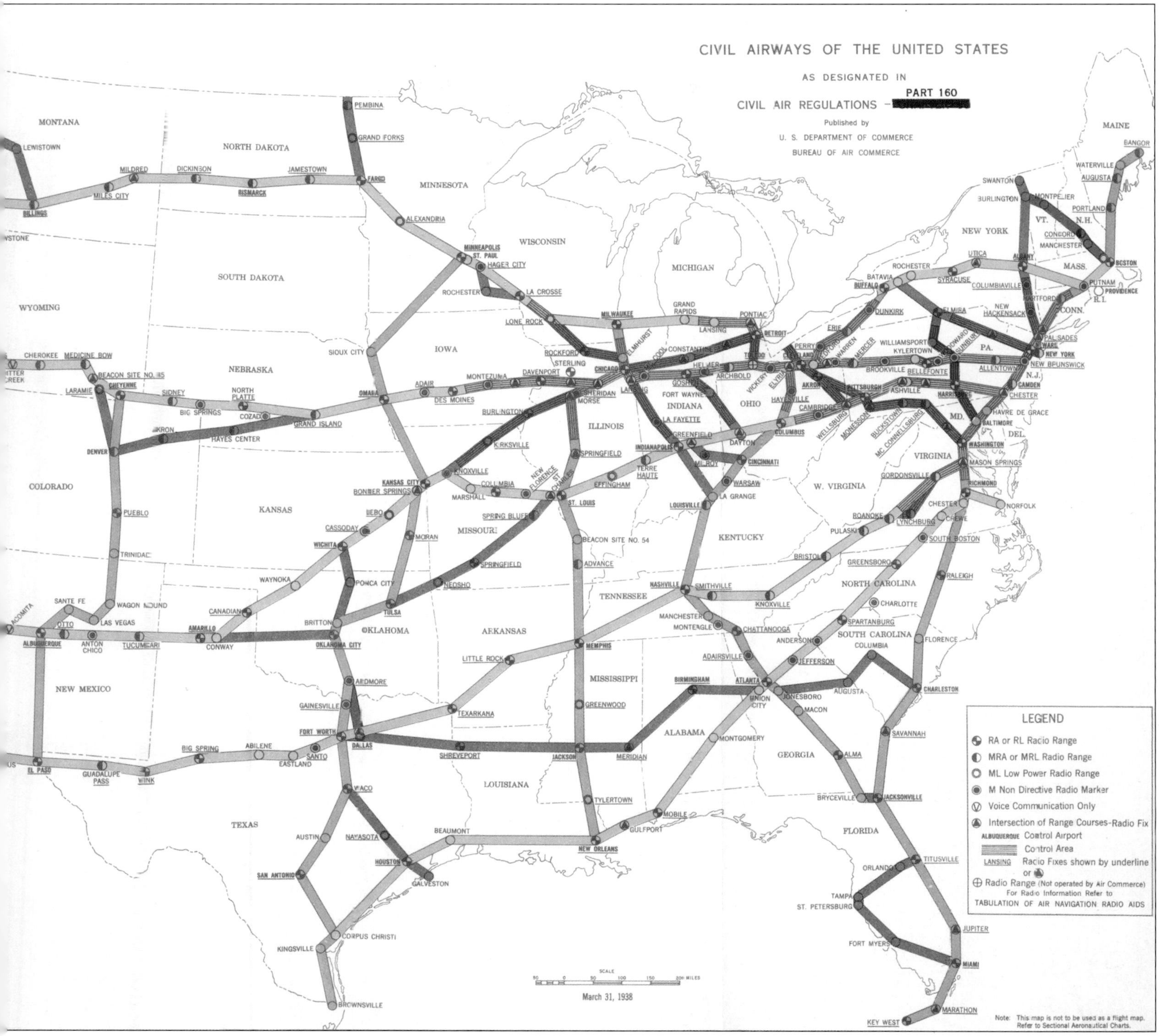

CIVIL AIRWAYS OF THE UNITED STATES

AS DESIGNATED IN

CIVIL AIR REGULATIONS – PART 160

Published by

U. S. DEPARTMENT OF COMMERCE

BUREAU OF AIR COMMERCE

LEGEND

- RA or RL Radio Range
- MRA or MRL Radio Range
- ML Low Power Radio Range
- M Non Directive Radio Marker
- Voice Communication Only
- Intersection of Range Courses-Radio Fix
- ALBUQUERQUE Control Airport
- Control Area
- LANSING Radio Fixes shown by underline or
- Radio Range (Not operated by Air Commerce)

For Radio Information Refer to TABULATION OF AIR NAVIGATION RADIO AIDS

March 31, 1938

Note: This map is not to be used as a flight map. Refer to Sectional Aeronautical Charts.

TOP: The sole Douglas DC-4 (later redesignated DC-4E) proved more complicated than its competition and failed commercially. Soon after this June 1939 visit to Wright Field, the aircraft was sold to the Japanese (who used the technology to develop a new four-engined bomber).

LEFT: Entering service in 1934, the new Douglas DC-2 rapidly established itself as the most efficient airliner of its day. Here, the mail is transferred to a Braniff DC-2 in the late 1930s.

The Early Airlines

Europe's prewar experiments with airmail service were rudely interrupted by the Great Powers' declarations of war in August 1914. Four years later, as armies mounted their last major offensives, military air arms opened aerial lines of communications between Paris, London, and other political centers. With the Armistice of November 1918, these military air routes expanded to support the peace talks and the Armistice Commission.

Civilian air transport lines formed quickly at the War's end. Most airline companies developed as adjuncts to the major manufacturing concerns - with the market for military designs rapidly evaporating, the manufacturers created the service organizations that would sustain production, even if only on a limited basis. The earliest airliners were conversions of military designs, either short-range aircraft like the British de Havilland D.H.4, or multi-engined, long-range designs like Germany's Zeppelin-Staaken heavy bombers.

With its long lead in heavy airplane and airship design, Germany was initially in a perfect position to begin the long peace with a superior line of transports. The final terms of the peace treaty, however, insisted that German war materiel be destroyed, not converted into air liners. (Ostensibly, these treaty clauses were based on fears that these rebuilt airliners could be reconverted into bombers. Many of the Allied negotiators, however, came to the table with a secondary goal of punishing Germany for is part in the conflict.) The irrepressible designers that Germany had nurtured for years would soon be developing their new aircraft at home, then manufacturing them in Italy, Sweden, and Spain.

The Russian lead in heavy aircraft development had disappeared with the Revolution; designer Igor Sikorsky fled to Paris, then to the US, where he developed the first great line of modern American flying boat transports. The Italians, with the longest Allied wartime experience in multi-engined aircraft, made only moderate advances after the war. Britain, which had the War's finest long-range flying boats and ended the war with the beginnings of a long-range land bomber force, quickly introduced civil conversions in both classes. Widely used by British and Commonwealth carriers, these fine aircraft saw little use elsewhere. The French, who had failed to develop any operational long-range aircraft during the War, produced some of the first great airliners of the immediate post-war years. But the greatest beneficiary of the postwar expansion of civil air transportation would have to have been the Dutch. The return from Germany of Dutch native Anthony Fokker gave Holland a design and manufacturing capability that would be second to none through the early 1930s. Fokker transports, including the many produced under license in Europe, Japan, and North America, would fly on every continent.

Introduced in the early 1930s, a giant (18-passenger!) Lioré et Olivier LeO 213 shares a Paris airfield with a Farman F.301.

Designed in 1918 as a bomber, the Farman F.60 Goliath became Europe's first great airliner. When *Normandie*, still in service in 1931, overran the landing field at London's Croydon Aerodrome, passengers and bystanders helped push it back from the boundary fence.

Photographed in the early 1930s, Poland's Bolesław Orliński was one of many international pilots to explore new air routes in the 1920s. In 1925 Orliński flew some 4,000 miles from Warsaw to Tokyo.

The success of civil airlines required more than a great view, a sense of adventure, and an affinity for leather jackets and helmets. Prewar experiments had shown that early aircraft could carry a passenger or mail for a short distance, but most European nations had already developed efficient railroads and postal services - the airplane might (or might not) save a few hours, but that would count for little when the postal carrier delivered only once a day. The true advantage would have to come from speed over a long distance - which required long-range aircraft and the infrastructure to support them. Prizes for distance flights - such as the trans-Atlantic and London-to-Australia purses - measured the capabilities of men and machines, but the continuing delivery of mail over these and other routes established the airlines and their support systems while teaching the lessons that led to safer and more competitive aircraft. And each mail route quickly developed into a passenger route, connecting the European nations with their colonies, friends, and business partners. •

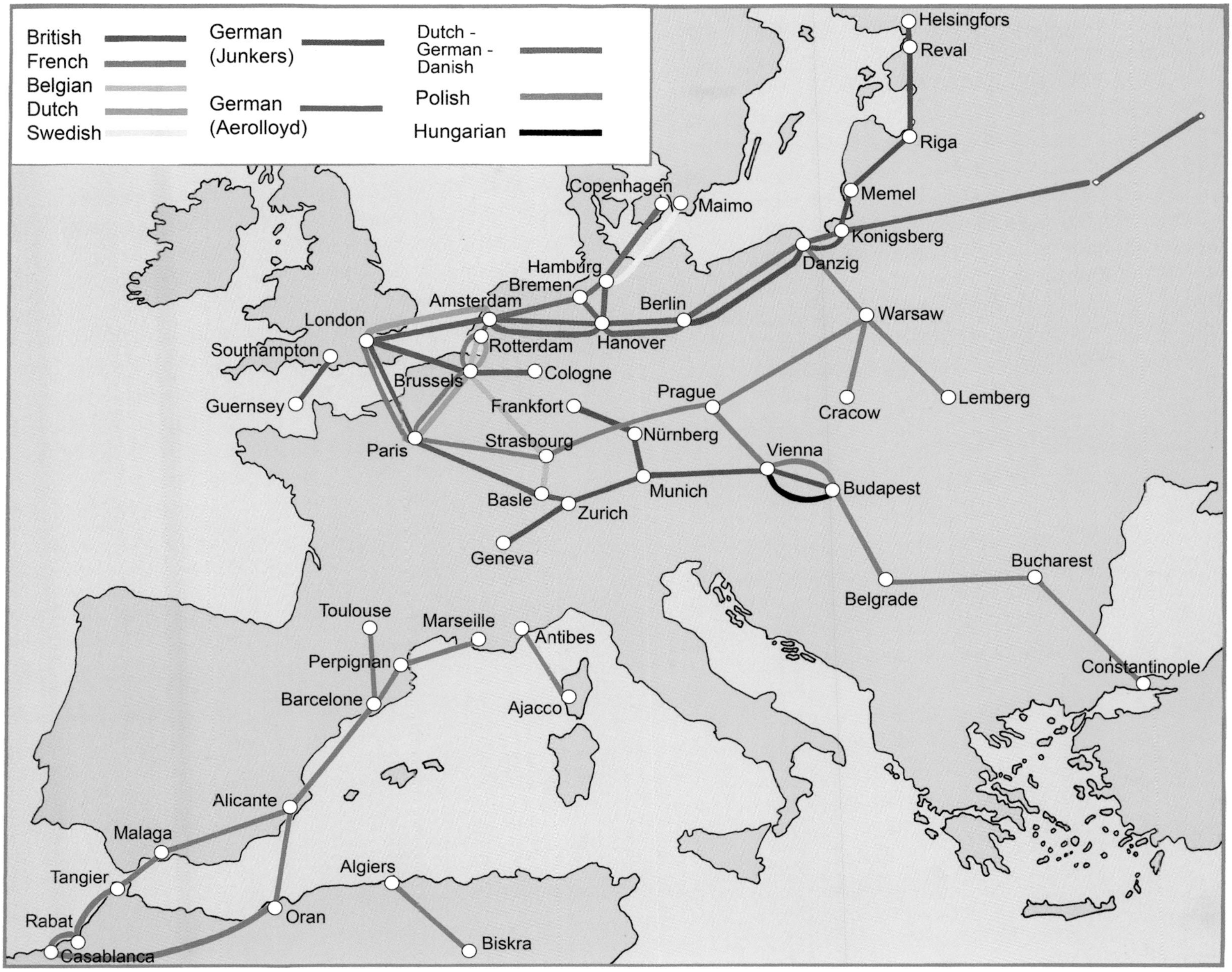

European Air Services, 1924

Introduced in 1928, the Short S.8 Calcutta was the first metal-hulled flying boat in British commercial service. With a crew of four and up to fifteen passengers, five Calcuttas began service on the Mediterranean leg or the London-India in 1929. The last aircraft were converted to trainers in 1935.

Formed in January 1919, Deutsche Luft-Reederei began the world's first sustained daily passenger service a month later. Former military aircraft such as this LVG C.VI (note the camouflage fabric) connected Berlin, Leipzig, and Weimar, before they drew the attention of Armistice inspectors.

The Zeppelin Liners

With relief that the Great War was coming to an end, Zeppelin designed and built two new civilian airships for postwar passenger service. The LZ 120 *Bodensee* and LZ 121 *Nordstern*, benefitting from four years' wartime engineering lessons, were the most advanced dirigibles of their day. Between August and December 1919, *Bodensee* carried 2,253 paying passengers and 11,000 pounds of mail, all on domestic within Germany. *Nordstern* never entered civilian service; in 1920 the Allies demanded that both airships be turned over as war reparations.

In 1928, a new dirigible was christened. The LZ 127 *Graf Zeppelin* would epitomize the finest that air travel had to offer. Comfortable passenger rooms, a dining area, and a stunning view of the earth below, the dirigible made numerous trial flights (including a twelve-and-a-half-day flight around the world) before beginning scheduled passenger service in March 1932. The *Graf Zeppelin* carried more than 13,000 passengers, covering over a million miles - including 144 ocean crossings - before retiring in 1937.

Following *Graf Zeppelin* into service in 1936, the LZ 129 *Hindenburg* benefitted from a higher top speed and increased passenger accommodation. During its first season, the *Hindenburg* carried 2,057 passengers (1,309 of them across the Atlantic) and covered more than 150,000 miles. The second season, however, began with disaster as the dirigible exploded while mooring at Lakehurst, New Jersey, on 6 May 1937. The airship was destroyed, and 35 of the 97 aboard were killed. The age of the passenger airship ended abruptly - The *Hindenburg*'s final voyage was the history's last commercial airship flight.•

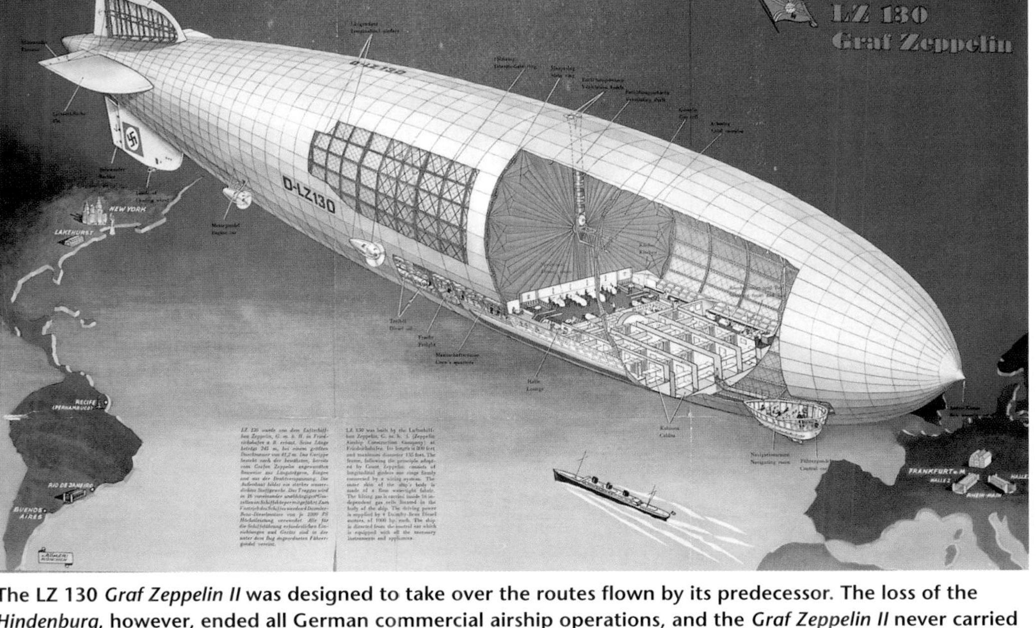

The LZ 130 *Graf Zeppelin II* was designed to take over the routes flown by its predecessor. The loss of the *Hindenburg*, however, ended all German commercial airship operations, and the *Graf Zeppelin II* never carried a paying passenger.

The death of the commercial dirigible; a rarely published view of the burning skeleton of the *Hindenburg* falling to earth at Lakehurst, New Jersey, on 6 May 1937.

Considered symbolic of Germany's technological advances in commercial aviation, the *Graf Zeppelin* and the Dornier Do X were complete opposites. The giant dirigible was easily the most successful passenger-carrying aircraft of its day, while the giant flying boat proved to be an abject failure.

A portion of the spacious dinning room aboard the *Hindenburg*.

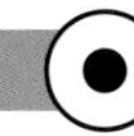

Graf Zeppelin in flight over Germany.

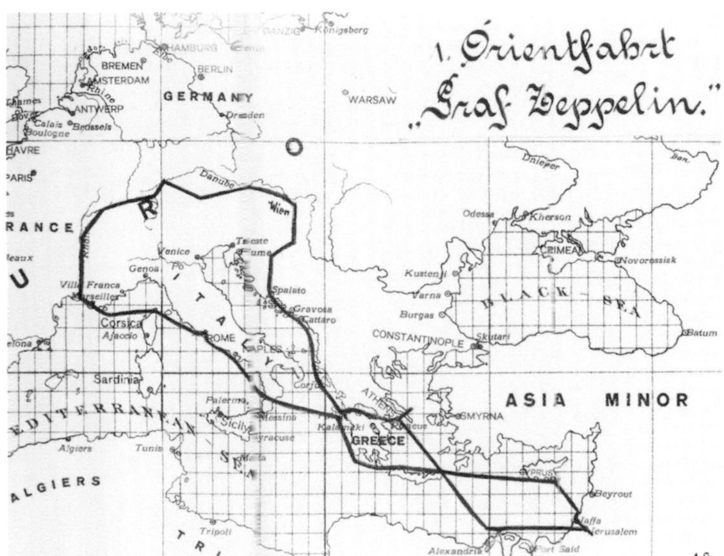

The Mediterranean routes of the *Graf Zeppelin*, March 1929.

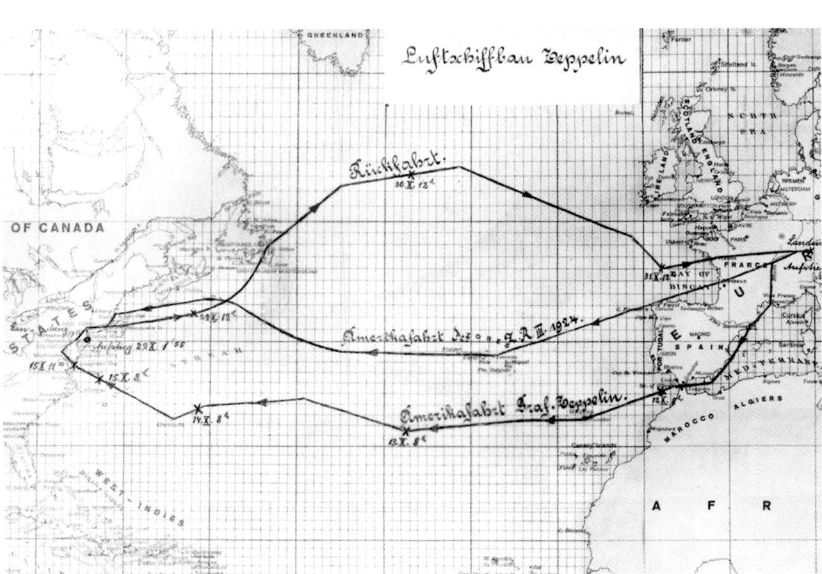

Graf Zeppelin's Atlantic routes, October 1928.

European Air Transport in the 1930s

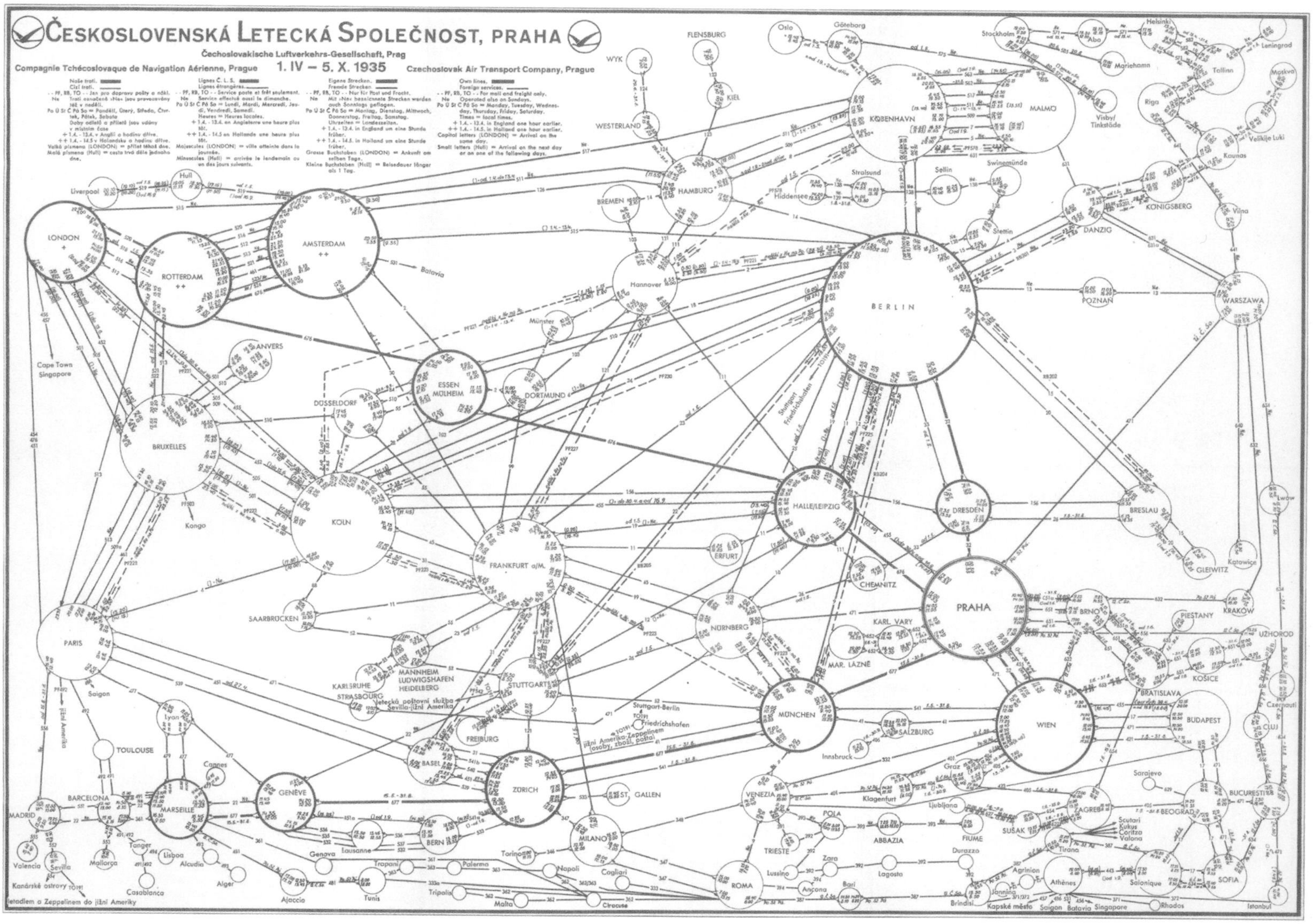
ČESKOSLOVENSKÁ LETECKÁ SPOLEČNOST, PRAHA
Čechoslovakische Luftverkehrs-Gesellschaft, Prag
Compagnie Tchécoslovaque de Navigation Aérienne, Prague
1. IV – 5. X. 1935
Czechoslovak Air Transport Company, Prague
LONDON
ROTTERDAM
AMSTERDAM
BRUXELLES
KÖLN
PARIS
FRANKFURT a/M.
HAMBURG
BERLIN
HALLE/LEIPZIG
DRESDEN
PRAHA
NÜRNBERG
MÜNCHEN
WIEN
ZÜRICH
GENÈVE
MARSEILLE
MILANO
VENEZIA
ROMA
BUDAPEST
WARSZAWA
KØBENHAVN
MALMÖ

This unusual 1935 route map shows the cities, flight numbers, and schedules of the Czech airline CLS without reference to any geographical or political boundaries.

ČESKOSLOVENSKÁ
LETECKÁ SPOLEČNOST.
COMPAGNIE
TCHECOSLOVAQUE DE NAVIGATION AÉRIENNE.
ČECHOSLOVAKISCHE-LUFTVERKEHRS-GESELLSCHAFT.

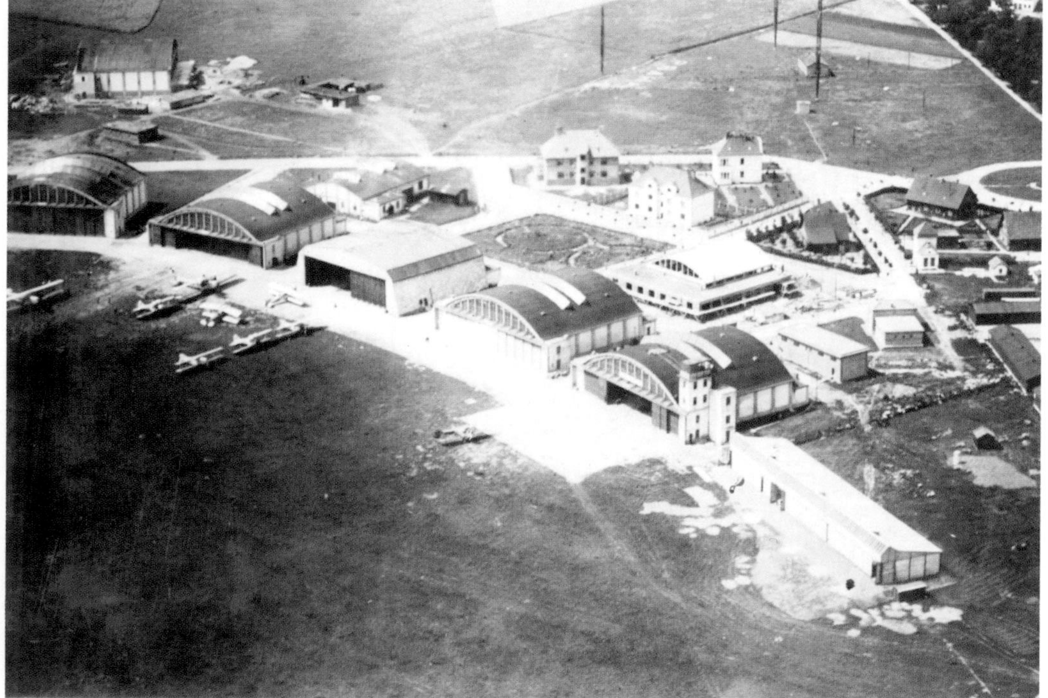

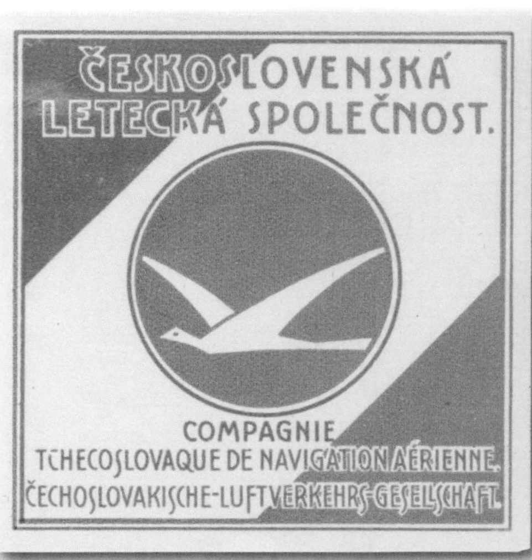

ABOVE: Baggage labels, long popular with steamship lines, were also used by most airlines through the late 1950s. (Today they are considered highly collectable!)

LEFT: The highly industrialized Czechs built modern aircraft (of domestic and licensed design) and sophisticated facilities. This aerial view shows the airport at Prague-Kbely in the early 1930s.

Air France flew its fourteen Lioré et Olivier LeO H 242s between Marseilles and North African ports from 1934 to 1940. *Ville de Tunis,* the prototype, differed little from the production standard. Each of the four-engined flying boats carried up to sixteen passengers.

On a rainy day at Milan Linate Airport, an Avio Linee Italiane Savoia Marchetti S.73 stops at the terminal to unload its passengers. Popular with Italian airlines, the S.73 was also exported throughout Europe and South America.

Macchi produced twelve of its C.94s between 1935 and 1938. The twelve-passenger aircraft were used on Ala Littoria's Adriatic routes through the 1930s, with at least three aircraft later sold to South American companies, and several others taken over by the military at the beginning of World War II.

Passengers deplane from one of Air Union's Breguet 280T *Rapid Azur* airliners in the late 1920s. Two other 280Ts are prepared for departure in front of Lyon-Bron Airport's modern terminal.

LEFT: The Scandinavian Air Express was created in late 1929, beginning operations in 1930. World War II brought the service to an end.

BELOW: This Swedish navigational map, dated 1935, covers the Amsterdam-Hamburg-Copenhagen route pioneered by the Scandinavian Air Express, a cooperative effort of Sweden's AB Aerotransport and the Netherlands' KLM. The map presents compass bearings and distances, but is notably devoid of any radio navigation or communications information.

ABOVE: With the beginning of World War II, the neutral Swedes found themselves with a mix of equipment from both sides in the conflict. All civil aircraft were heavily marked to establish their non-combatant nature, including blue and yellow national flags and large, black, block letters proclaiming the national identity. (Note the use of the German identification "Schweden" atop the Junkers Ju 52 and the English "Sweden" atop the Douglas DC-3s.)

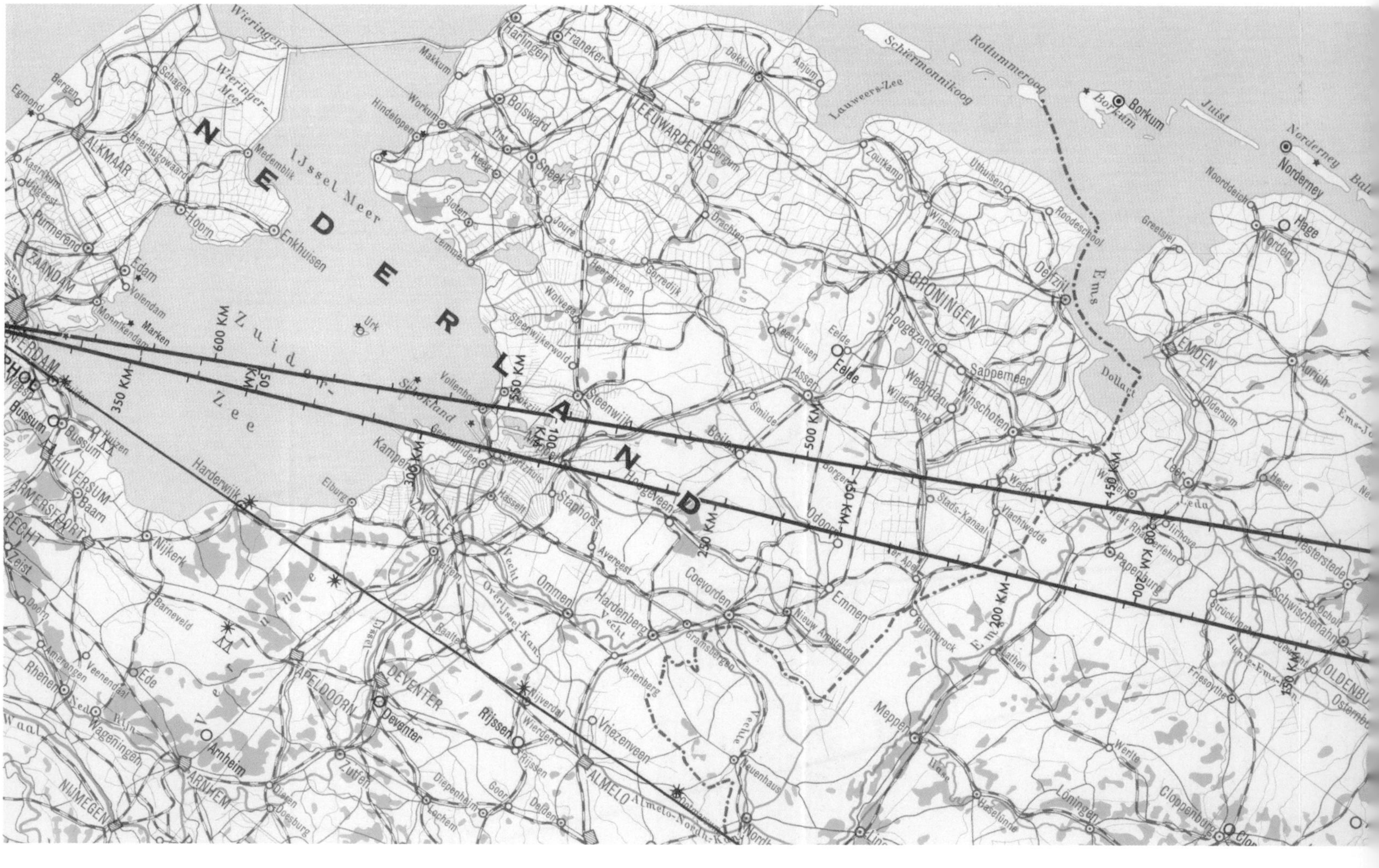

ABOVE: Spring 1937, as international travelers arrive at Le Bourget Airport, Paris. The nearer aircraft is a Dutch KLM Douglas DC-2; the other is a Belgian SABENA Savoia-Marchetti S.73 trimotor.

LEFT: Hoping to remain neutral as Europe declared war over the German and Soviet invasions of Poland, the Dutch painted the fuselages and wings of KLM's airliners in bright orange. The color scheme identified the aircraft, but did little to prevent Germany's invasion of the Netherlands in May 1940.

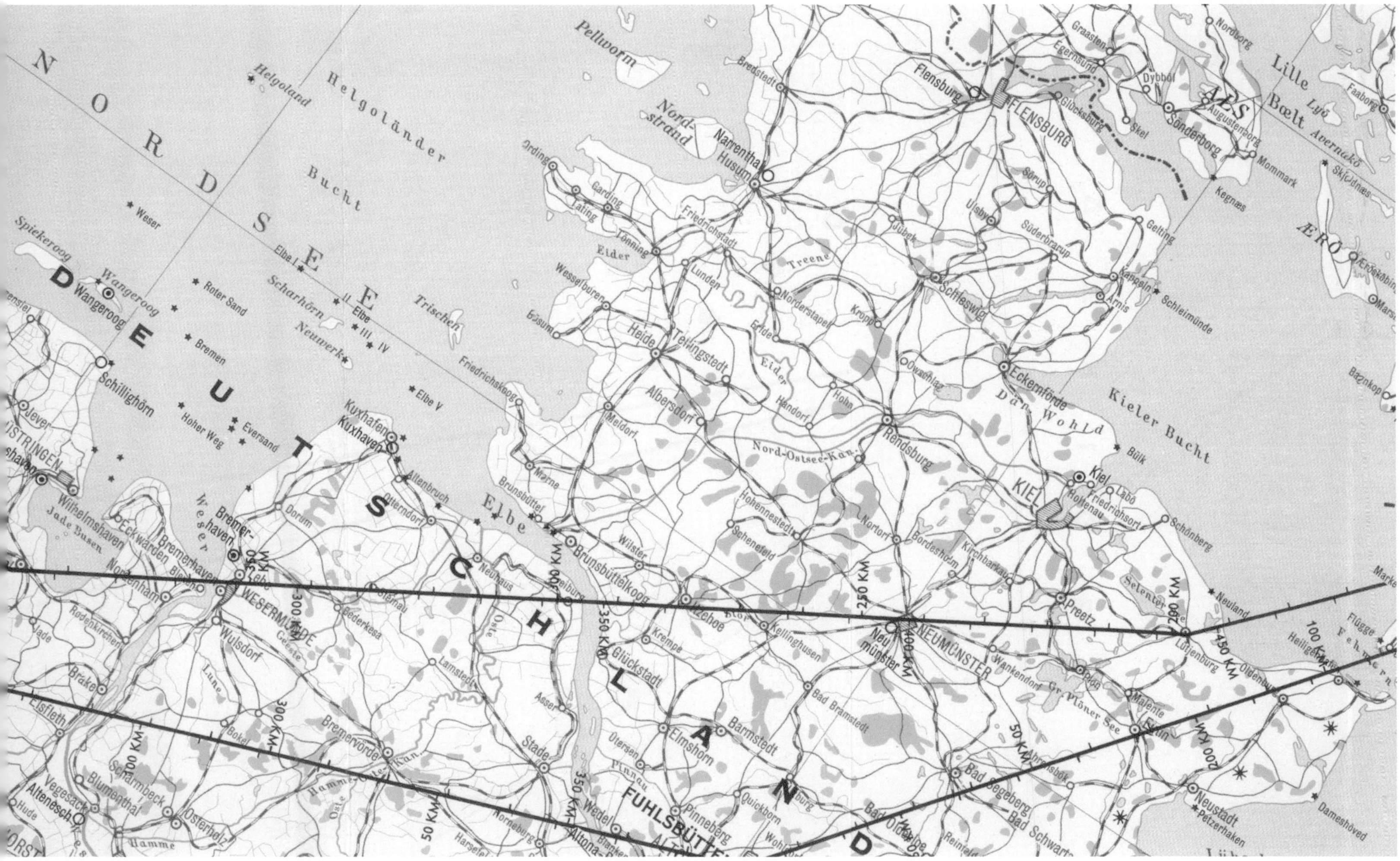

Far East Connections

This 1932 German map (below) of airline expansion into Asia and the Orient concentrates on the routes established by Germany and its partners. The routes noted in the key (map lower right) describe the following carriers:

- Deruluft (Deutsch-Russische Luftverkehrs Gesellschaft) had been jointly founded by Germany's Aero-Union and the Soviet government in 1921. The company remained in business until 1937.
- Aeroflot, the Soviet national airline was established independently in 1932, taking control of all domestic Soviet air routes not managed by Deruluft.
- Eurasia was created in 1930 by Lufthansa and the Chinese government. Equipped and supported with German equipment and materiel, Eurasia remained in service until 1939, when Germany aligned itself with Japan against the Chinese government.
- The final two route graphics describe "other companies" (including Dutch, British, and French) and routes under development. •

Designed by Filippo Zappata, the prototype Cant Z.506 floatplane seen here set several international seaplane records soon after its debut in 1936. The prototype and approximately fifteen production examples connected Italy with port cities along the Mediterranean coasts.

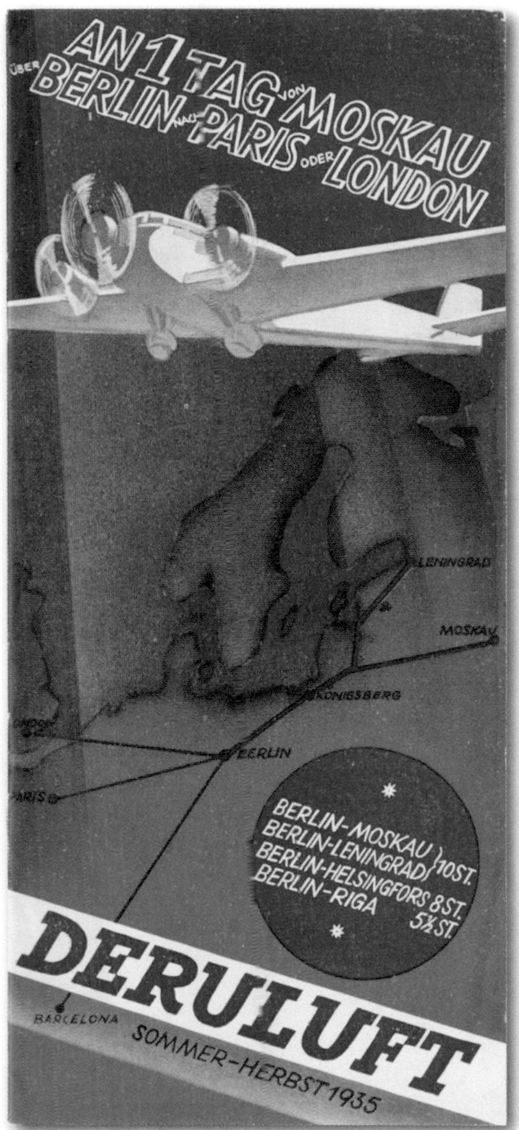

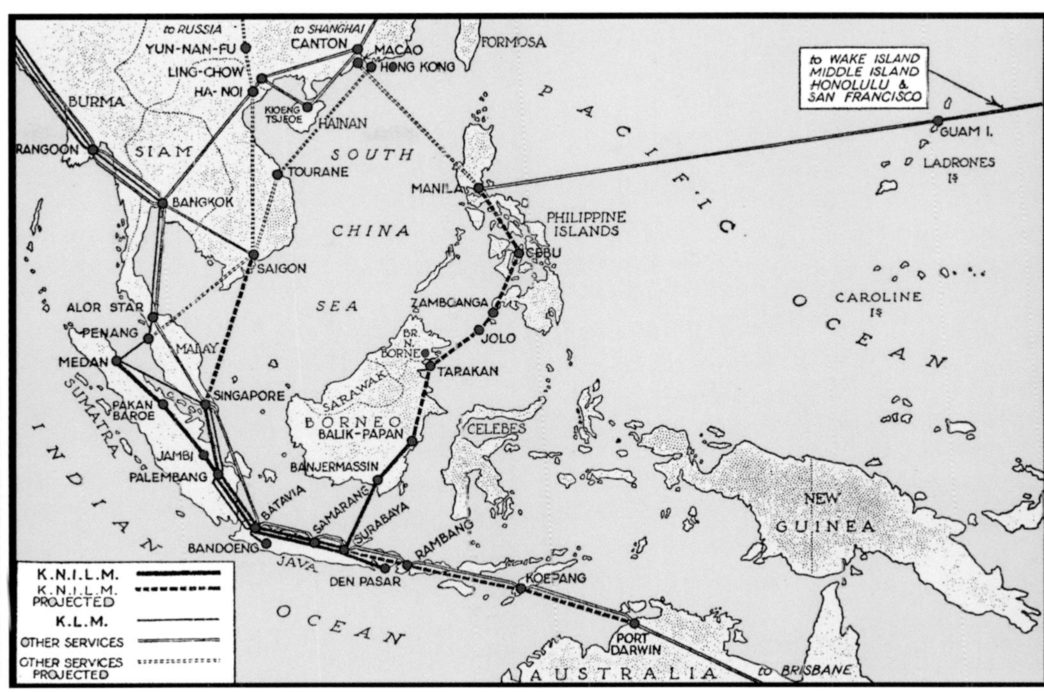

LEFT: A 1935 Deruluft timetable shows connections between London, Paris, Barcelona, Moscow, and Leningrad via Konigsberg and Berlin. As depicted in the artwork, most of Deruluft's aircraft were produced by Junkers.

ABOVE: The Dutch airlines KLM and KNILM began opening routes to the Netherlands East Indies in the 1920s; by 1936, the companies routes had successfully linked most of the region's population and resource centers.

RIGHT: The Fokker F.IX was built to KLM's specifications for travel between Amsterdam and the Dutch East Indies. Although the aircraft performed as expected, only two would be built. Both made a single flight to the Far East; one was lost and the other was reassigned to the London-Amsterdam line. The outdoor airport restaurant at Schiphol offered the public an intimate meal with some of the most advanced aircraft of the day.

As with Deruluft, Eurasia relied on Junkers for most of its aircraft. Introduced in 1932, the Ju 52/3m rapidly found its place in airlines around the world.

Britain to Australia

In March 1919, months before the first non-stop Atlantic crossing, the Australian government offered a £10,000 prize for the first flight from the UK to Australia to be completed within 30 consecutive days by an Australian flight crew. Jules Védrines, who was then planning an around the world flight, hoped at least one Frenchman could compete, but was refused. (Védrines would die in a 21 April crash while training for the world flight.) The prize would be taken by brothers Ross and Keith Smith, with W. Shiers, and J. Bennett, who covered the route between 12 November and 10 December 1919 in a Vickers F.B.27A Vimy. (None of the other five aircraft attempting the flight - including one French team - completed the flight. Four crew members died when two aircraft crashed; two other aircraft crashed without fatalities, and the French aircraft dropped out with irreparable mechanical failures.)

Others would fly between the two countries, each trying to better the time of transit. Then, in October 1934, another great England-to-Australia race began. Sir MacPherson Robertson, owner of Australia's MacRobertson Chocolate company had posted a £15,000 purse for the fastest time between London and Melbourne. The race, open to all nationalities, started with twenty entrants. Some seventy-one hours later, C. W. A. Scott and Tom Campbell Black, piloting one of three specially designed de Havilland Comet racers, landed in Melbourne to chop four and a half days from the existing record time between the two cities. The second and third place winners, however, would prove far more influential in the history of long-range aviation. The third place winners, Americans Roscoe Turner and Clyde Pangborn, flew a Boeing 247-D airliner (fitted with extra fuel tanks) to land only 23 hours later. But the second place winners, Dutch KLM pilots K. D. Parmentier and J. Moll, flew a completely unmodified Douglas DC-2 to arrive only 20 hours behind Scott and Campbell Black - this while carrying three paying passengers for all but the last, hour-long leg of the flight. The amazing performance of these two long-range, high-speed airliners heralded a new age of intercontinental travel. •

LEFT: Back home in New York, Roscoe Turner poses with his Boeing 247-D.

BOTTOM: West Australian Airways connect the coastal cities Perth and Adelaide from 1929 until the company was sold in 1936. Despite the artwork on this advertisement, the airline flew single-engined transports for most of its existence.

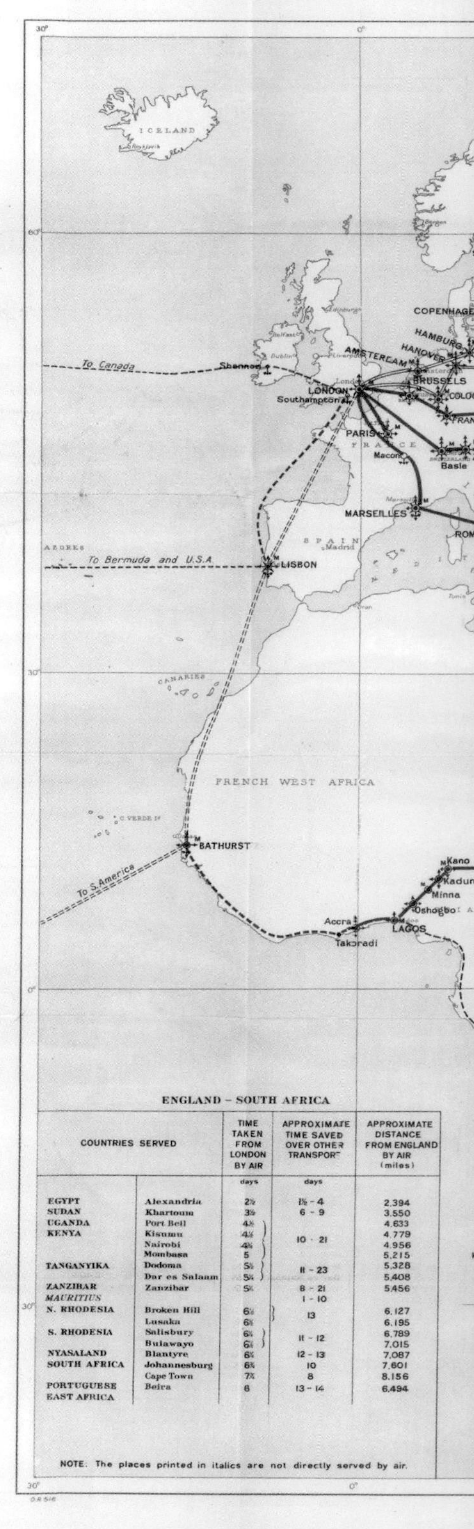

ENGLAND - SOUTH AFRICA

COUNTRIES SERVED		TIME TAKEN FROM LONDON BY AIR	APPROXIMATE TIME SAVED OVER OTHER TRANSPORT	APPROXIMATE DISTANCE FROM ENGLAND BY AIR (miles)
		days	days	
EGYPT	Alexandria	2½	1½ - 4	2.394
SUDAN	Khartoum	3½	6 - 9	3.550
UGANDA	Port Bell	4½	10 - 21	4.633
KENYA	Kisumu	4½		4.779
	Nairobi	4¾		4.956
	Mombasa	5		5.215
TANGANYIKA	Dodoma	5½	11 - 23	5.328
	Dar es Salaam	5¾		5.408
ZANZIBAR	Zanzibar	5¾	8 - 21	5.456
MAURITIUS			1 - 10	
N. RHODESIA	Broken Hill	6¼	13	6.127
	Lusaka	6½		6.195
S. RHODESIA	Salisbury	6¾	11 - 12	6.789
	Bulawayo	6¾		7.015
NYASALAND	Blantyre	6¾	12 - 13	7.087
SOUTH AFRICA	Johannesburg	6¾	10	7.601
	Cape Town	7¾	8	8.156
PORTUGUESE EAST AFRICA	Beira	6	13 - 14	6.494

NOTE: The places printed in italics are not directly served by air.

Imperial Airways ordered two landplane versions of the Kent as Short L.17 38-passenger airliners. Named *Syrinx* and *Scylla*, the pair carried passengers between London's Croydon Aerodrome and Paris, Brussels, Basle, and Zürich from 1934 to 1939.

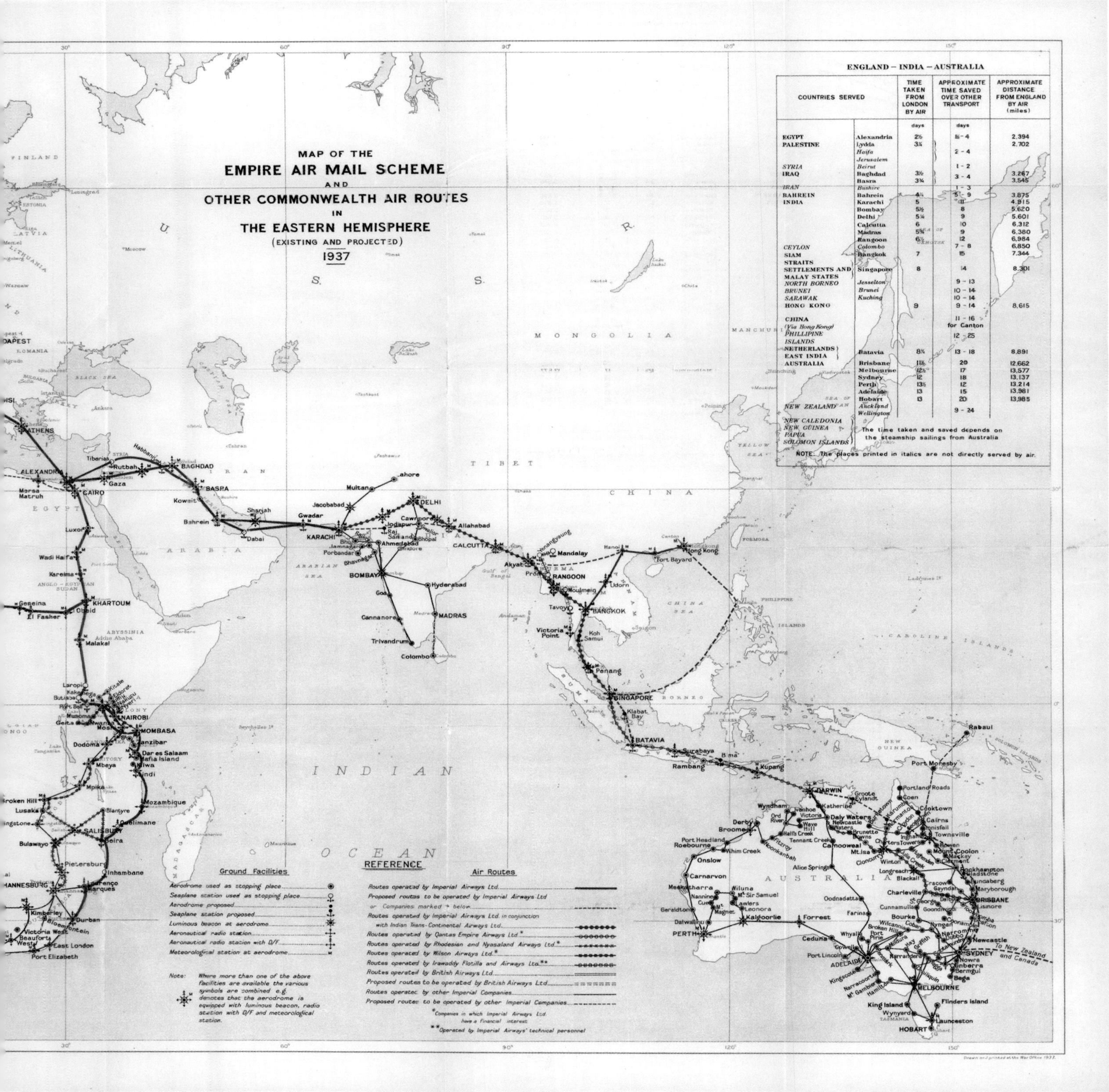

MAP OF THE
EMPIRE AIR MAIL SCHEME
AND
OTHER COMMONWEALTH AIR ROUTES
IN
THE EASTERN HEMISPHERE
(EXISTING AND PROJECTED)
1937

ENGLAND – INDIA – AUSTRALIA

COUNTRIES SERVED		TIME TAKEN FROM LONDON BY AIR	APPROXIMATE TIME SAVED OVER OTHER TRANSPORT	APPROXIMATE DISTANCE FROM ENGLAND BY AIR (miles)
		days	days	
EGYPT	Alexandria	2½	1½ - 4	2.394
PALESTINE	Lydda	3¼	2 - 4	2.702
	Haifa			
	Jerusalem			
SYRIA	*Beirut*		1 - 2	
IRAQ	Baghdad	3½	3 - 4	3.267
	Basra	3¾		3.545
IRAN	*Bushire*		1 - 3	
BAHREIN	Bahrein	4¼	5 - 9	3.875
INDIA	Karachi	5	11	4.915
	Bombay	5½	8	5.620
	Delhi	5¼	9	5.601
	Calcutta	6	10	6.312
	Madras	5¾	9	6.380
	Rangoon	6½	12	6,984
CEYLON	*Colombo*		7 - 8	6,850
SIAM	Bangkok	7	15	7.344
STRAITS SETTLEMENTS AND MALAY STATES	Singapore	8	14	8.301
NORTH BORNEO	*Jesselton*		9 - 13	
BRUNEI	*Brunei*		10 - 14	
SARAWAK	*Kuching*		10 - 14	
HONG KONG		9	9 - 14	8.615
CHINA *(Via Hong Kong)*			11 - 16 for Canton	
PHILLIPINE ISLANDS			12 - 25	
NETHERLANDS EAST INDIA	Batavia	8¼	13 - 18	8.891
AUSTRALIA	Brisbane	11½	20	12.662
	Melbourne	12½	17	13.577
	Sydney	12	18	13.137
	Perth	13½	12	13.214
	Adelaide	13	15	13.981
	Hobart	13	20	13.985
NEW ZEALAND	*Auckland*		9 - 24	
	Wellington			
NEW CALEDONIA *NEW GUINEA* *PAPUA* *SOLOMON ISLANDS*	The time taken and saved depends on the steamship sailings from Australia			

NOTE. The places printed in italics are not directly served by air.

REFERENCE

Ground Facilities

- *Aerodrome used as stopping place*
- *Seaplane station used as stopping place*
- *Aerodrome proposed*
- *Seaplane station proposed*
- *Luminous beacon at aerodrome*
- *Aeronautical radio station*
- *Aeronautical radio station with D/F*
- *Meteorological station at aerodrome*

Note: Where more than one of the above facilities are available the various symbols are combined e.g. denotes that the aerodrome is equipped with luminous beacon, radio station with D/F and meteorological station.

Air Routes

- *Routes operated by Imperial Airways Ltd.*
- *Proposed routes to be operated by Imperial Airways Ltd or Companies marked * below*
- *Routes operated by Imperial Airways Ltd. in conjunction with Indian Trans-Continental Airways Ltd.*
- *Routes operated by Qantas Empire Airways Ltd.**
- *Routes operated by Rhodesian and Nyasaland Airways Ltd.**
- *Routes operated by Wilson Airways Ltd.**
- *Routes operated by Irawaddy Flotilla and Airways Ltd.***
- *Routes operated by British Airways Ltd.*
- *Proposed routes to be operated by British Airways Ltd.*
- *Routes operated by other Imperial Companies*
- *Proposed routes to be operated by other Imperial Companies*

**Companies in which Imperial Airways Ltd. have a financial interest*

***Operated by Imperial Airways' technical personnel*

Under the Empire Air Mail Scheme, which was approved by the British governement in 1935, Imeprial Airways was to deliver mail throughout the Empire by air with no additional surcharge. This 1937 map shows those routes and other Commonwealth connections.

Into Africa

For centuries Africa has been considered a land of vast resources. By the twentieth century, most of the continent had been divided between its more-technologically developed European neighbors. Soon after the First World War, developing European airlines began charting routes to the colonial lands, starting with North Africa, then moving down the eastern coast.

Europeans also helped establish a number of local airlines that were usually put into operation as affiliates of their European counterparts. Many European-Africans had learned to fly in the War, providing a ready source of pilots, though others would move to the colonies seeking adventure and opportunity. Private aviation also grew, as ranchers and developers were joined by a new breed of bush pilots eager to provide unscheduled air service along the coast or deep into the heartland.

This 1937 map, based on a chart produced by the Shell Oil Company, shows an Africa that would be greatly changed by independence movements over the next four decades. Most of the lands seen at the left were colonies, mandates, or protectorates until the independence movements of the 1960s and '70s. (Forty years would also see dramatic realignments of some of the political boundaries.) The map shows deep disparities in the development of African air facilities. Most major development reflected the level of European investment, which was usually based on the expected return value of local resources. In 1937, these African lands were influenced by the following European powers:

- Bechuanaland - UK (Independent as Botswana in 1966)
- Belgian Congo - Belgium (Independent as Zaire in 1960)
- French Equatorial Africa - France (Independent as Chad, Gabon, Congo, and Central African Republic in 1960)
- Kenya Colony - UK (Independent in 1963)
- Northern Rhodesia - UK (Independent as Zambia in 1964)
- Nyasaland - UK (Independent as Malawi in 1964)
- Portuguese East Africa - Portugal (Independent as Mozambique in 1975)
- Portuguese West Africa - Portugal (Independent as Angola in 1975)
- South-West Africa - A mandated territory of South Africa until 1966 (Now Namibia)
- Southern Rhodesia - UK (Independent as Rhodesia in 1965)
- Tanganyika Territory - UK (Independent as Tanganyika in 1961; merged with Zanzibar as Tanzania in 1964)
- Union of South Africa - A Federal Union since 1910, with ties to the UK (Republic in 1961)

Beyond the commercial value of Africa's natural resources, the continent held an air of mystery and adventure. Among the many inter-

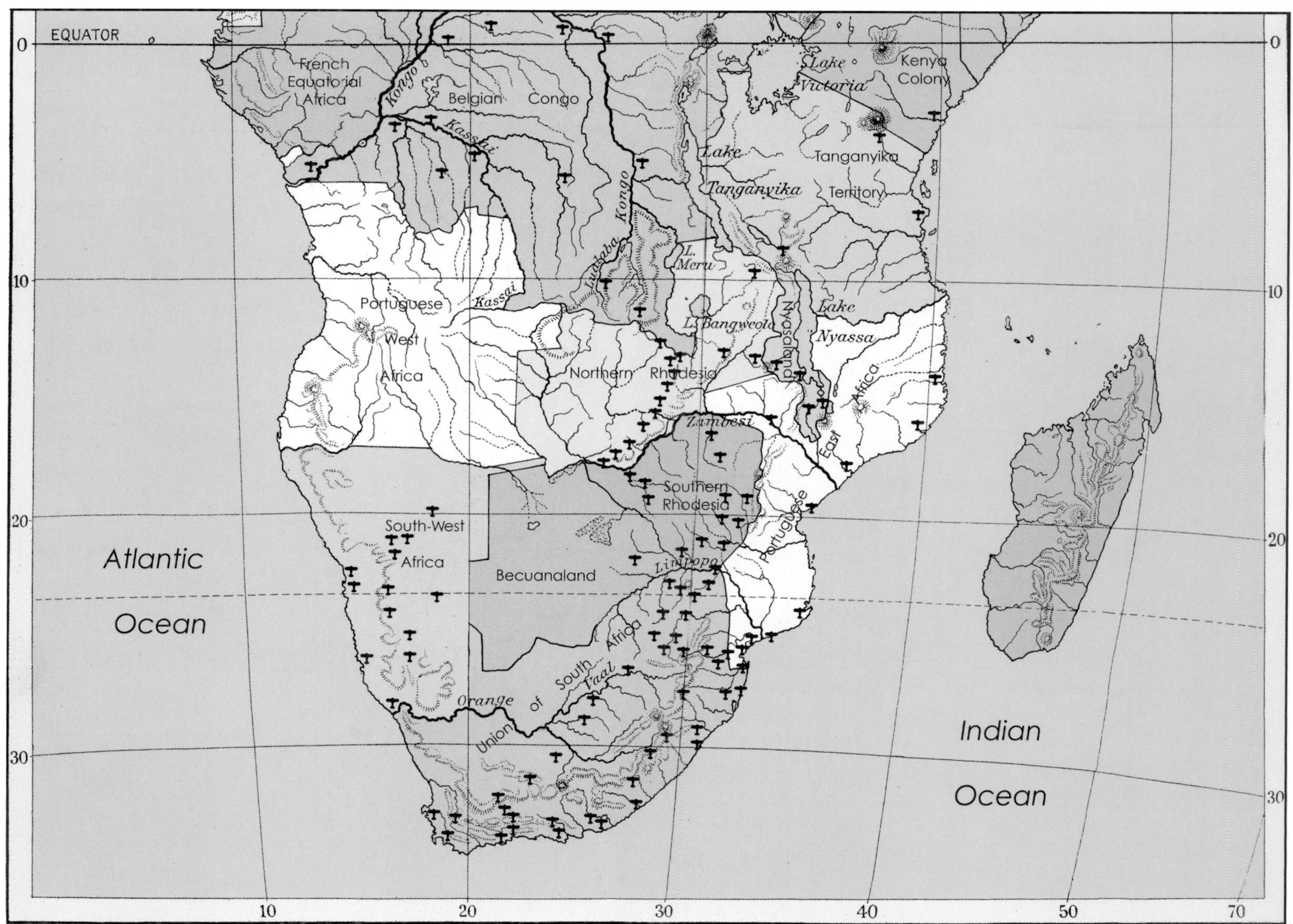

Southern African Aviation Facilities, August 1937.

Martin and Osa Johnson (right) enjoy a picnic beneath the wing of their S-38 *Osa's Ark*. Joining the couple are pilot Vern Carstens and movie sound man Robert Moreno.

The Johnsons' two Sikorsky amphibians *Spirit of Africa* (left) and *Osa's Ark*, in flight over Africa during the couple's 1933/34 expedition.

South African Airways (SAA) was formed in 1934, taking over the assets of Union Airways. With the assistance of the South African government, the company soon purchased fifteen new Junkers Ju 52 trimotors, including this example nicknamed *Lord Charles Sommerset*.

war explorers investigating the land, Martin and Osa Johnson are easily the most famous. Born in Illinois in 1884, Martin Johnson showed an early interest in photography. In 1907 he joined writer Jack London and his wife Charmian for a world cruise on the couple's yacht. London became ill in 1909, ending the tour, but bringing Johnson home with a wealth of photos, artifacts, and stories. Johnson began a lecture tour of the American Midwest that lasted into 1910.

In 1910 he met 16-year-old Osa Leighty; the two fell in love, eloping a month later. Osa Johnson had everything one could expect of a "spunky" young woman of the new century. Skilled in the domestic duties then expected of young women, she had also developed as a hunter, angler, and gardener. (In a later adventure, when the rhinoceros he was filming turned to charge Martin, it was Osa who dropped the rhino with a single shot.) Singing and dancing at school performances brought her a public confidence that would soon prove invaluable as the couple turned to the lecture circuit for the next seven years. In 1917, the couple began their first overseas adventure, a trip to film the indigenous peoples of the South Seas. A return trip followed in 1919/20 (with an added expedition along the east coast of Africa), and the couple soon released the first two documentary films of their adventures.

The Johnson's adventures in Africa would soon make them household names. Their trips in 1921-22, 1924-27, 1927-28, and 1929-31 resulted in a lucrative series of books, commercial documentaries, and lecture tours. In 1932 the couple earned their pilot's licenses and purchased a pair of Sikorsky amphibians. They named the single-engined S-39 *Spirit of Africa* and painted its hull yellow with a brown giraffe pattern; similarly, their twin-engined S-38, named *Osa's Ark*, carried black and white zebra stripes. The Johnsons took their two Sikorskys on their fifth African trip from 1933 to 1934. They became the first to fly over Mount Kilimanjaro and Mount Kenya soon produced the first aerial footage of large herds wild animals crossing the African plains.

The Johnsons made one final expedition together, flying the smaller S-39 (renamed *The Spirit of Africa and Borneo*) to Borneo in 1935-36. Home for a lecture tour, the couple were aboard a Western Air Express Boeing 247 that crashed in bad weather on 13 January 1937. Martin died of his injuries the next day. Osa would complete their lecture tour in a wheelchair while recovering from her injuries. She continued her writing, lecturing, and movie work, but her days as an explorer had come to an end. Her final trip to Africa came in 1939, when she worked as a technical consultant for the feature film *Stanley and Livingstone*. Osa Johnson died of heart failure in 1953. •

The First Atlantic Crossings

Having offered large purses for the first Channel airplane crossing and other long-distance flights, it seemed only natural that Lord Northcliff and the *Daily Mail* would offer a prize for the first airplane to cross the Atlantic Ocean between the UK or Ireland and the US or Canada. On 1 April 1913, Northcliff and his paper did just that, posting £10,000 for the feat. Several designers and pilots were preparing to accept the challenge when World War I broke out in Europe. On 14 November 1918, three days after the armistice was signed, the *Daily Mail* renewed its offer.

Despite a too-common misconception, Charles Lindbergh was not the first to cross the Atlantic. Lindbergh became the most famous to make the trip, but his flight from New York to Paris came in 1927, after eleven other successful crossings. Here are the first twelve flights to connect the new world with the old:

The US Navy's NC-4, the first aircraft to cross the Atlantic

1. Pride of place for the first Atlantic crossing goes to the US Navy and its NC-4 flying boat. The Navy-Curtiss (NC) flying boats had been designed during the War for long-range anti-submarine patrol. The NC-1, first in the series, made its initial flight in October 1918, only a month before the armistice.

By spring 1919, the Navy had four NC boats and a plan to fly three of them to Portugal via the Azores. NC-1, NC-3, and NC-4 left New York for Nova Scotia on 8 May, but NC-4 was forced down and put in to Massachusetts for repairs. Regrouped by 16 May, the three aircraft followed a course lined with 21 destroyers (one every fifty miles). NC-3 came down in heavy seas before dawn, then, over two days, taxied several hundred miles to the Azores. NC-1 came down 200 miles short of the Azores; its crew rescued by a Greek freighter, the aircraft sank in a storm. Only NC-4 flew to the Azores. A week later, on 27 May, Lt Commander Albert C. Read and his crew of five flew the NC-4 to Lisbon. The Atlantic had been crossed.

2. Less than three weeks later, on 14 June 1919, a British team completed the first direct flight between North America and the UK. Flying from Newfoundland to Ireland, John Alcock and Arthur Whitten Brown piloted a converted Vickers Vimy bomber. The flight earned the pair the *Daily Mail* prize.

3 & 4. The wreckage of German Zeppelin L.33 provided British engineers with their first useful data on heavy rigid airship construction. That technical expertise was used to build the R 33 and the R 34.

This converted British Vickers Vimy bomber made the first non-stop Atlantic crossing in June 1919.

At the invitation of the Aero Club of America, Major G. H. Scott and a crew of 30 (including one stowaway) flew the R 34 from Edinburgh to New York, landing on 6 July. The flight time of 108 hours and 12 minutes was only slightly slower that the then current steamship record. After a visit of only three days, the R 34 cast off shortly before midnight on 9 July, returning home to Norfolk just over 75 hours later. The first airship to cross the Atlantic had become the first aircraft to return across the Atlantic.

In July 1919, Britain's dirigible R.34 became the first aircraft to cross the Atlantic twice, flying from Edinburgh to New York, then returning to Norfolk.

5. The Atlantic remained quiet for two years following the two crossings by R 34. Then in 1922, Portugal's Captain Carlos Gago Coutinho announced his intentions to cross the South Atlantic and link Portugal to Brazil by air. Coutinho, a gifted navigator who had developed a number of advanced instruments for aerial navigation, also trained as a pilot for the flight. A second Portugese naval officer, Artur de Sacadura Cabral, would act as primary pilot.

The pair selected a float version of the British Fairey IIID torpedo plane, and three aircraft were purchased (two for the Portugese navy). Flying the first Fairey, nicknamed *Lusitania*, the pair left Lisbon on 30 March 1922. With fuel consumption higher than expected, they arranged to meet an escort

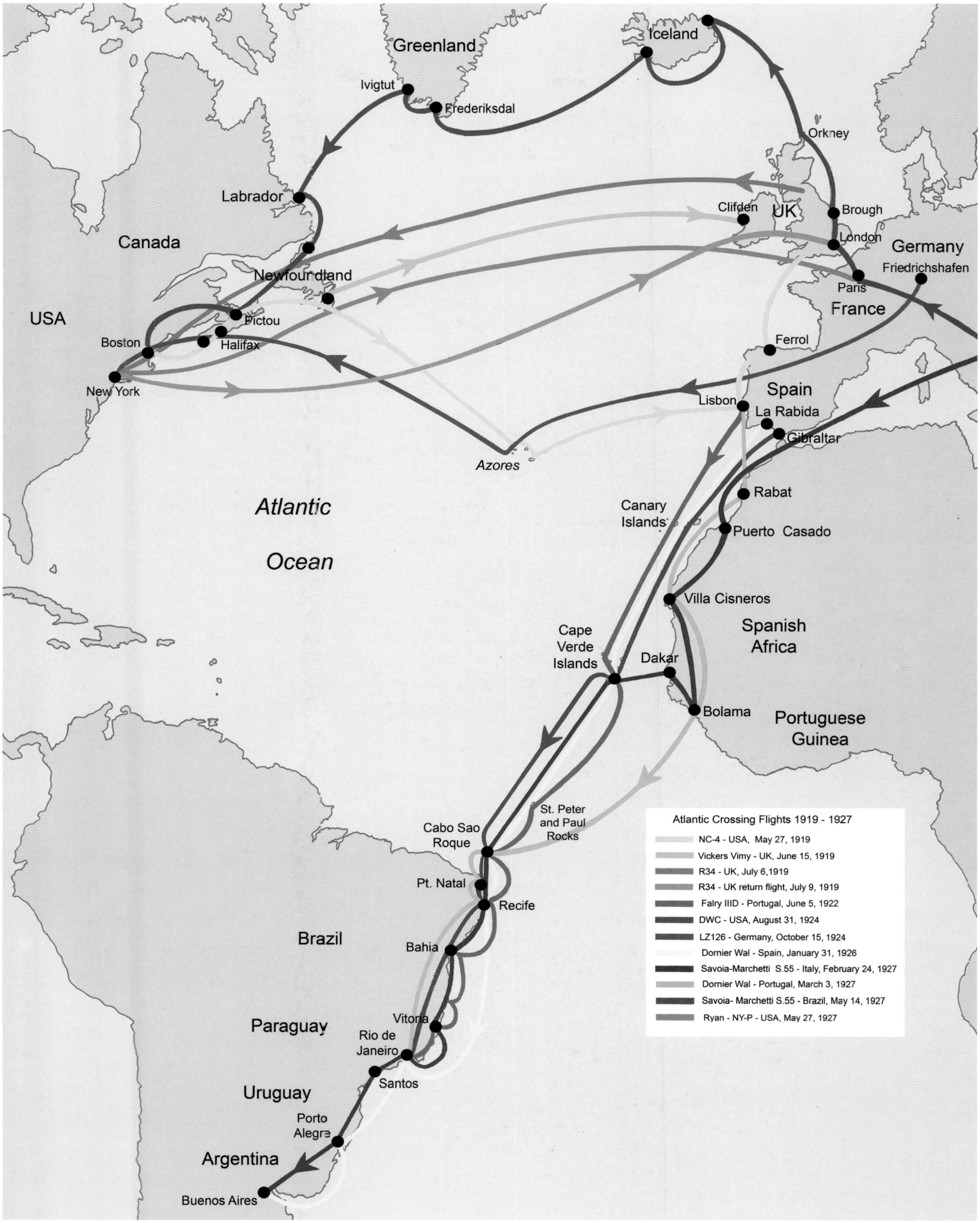

Atlantic Crossing Flights 1919 - 1927

- NC-4 - USA, May 27, 1919
- Vickers Vimy - UK, June 15, 1919
- R34 - UK, July 6,1919
- R34 - UK return flight, July 9, 1919
- Falry IIID - Portugal, June 5, 1922
- DWC - USA, August 31, 1924
- LZ126 - Germany, October 15, 1924
- Dornier Wal - Spain, January 31, 1926
- Savoia-Marchetti S.55 - Italy, February 24, 1927
- Dornier Wal - Portugal, March 3, 1927
- Savoia- Marchetti S.55 - Brazil, May 14, 1927
- Ryan - NY-P - USA, May 27, 1927

Greenland
Iceland
Ivigtut
Frederiksdal
Orkney
Labrador
Canada
Clifden
UK
Brough
London
Germany
Friedrichshafen
Paris
France
Newfoundland
Pictou
Halifax
Boston
USA
New York
Ferrol
Spain
Lisbon
La Rabida
Gibraltar
Azores
Atlantic Ocean
Rabat
Canary Islands
Puerto Casado
Villa Cisneros
Spanish Africa
Cape Verde Islands
Dakar
Bolama
Portuguese Guinea
St. Peter and Paul Rocks
Cabo Sao Roque
Pt. Natal
Recife
Brazil
Bahia
Paraguay
Vitoria
Rio de Janeiro
Santos
Uruguay
Porto Alegre
Argentina
Buenos Aires

Trans-Atlantic flights followed a number of routes across the North and South Atlantic. These are the routes followed from the first crossing in May 1919 through Charles Lindbergh's New York to Paris flight in May 1927.

vessel on 18 April at the tiny mid-ocean Rocks of St Peter and Paul; after a flight of 11 hours, Coutinho guided the aircraft directly to the 650-foot-wide rendezvous. However, rough seas damaged a pontoon, and the aircraft soon swamped and sank.

The Portugese government rewarded the intrepid flyers by sending them the second Fairey to continue the mission, which they did on 11 May. This time, however, fuel contamination forced them down at sea. The waves battered the aircraft, but a British freighter rescued the aviators before the sea claimed the second Fairey.

Support for the flight ran so high that the government sent the last Fairey, now named *Santa Cruz*. On 5 June Coutinho and Cabral took off again, reaching the Brazilian coast four and a half hours later.

6. As part of the 1924 Round the World Flight, three Douglas World Cruisers attempted an Atlantic crossing. Their story is found on pages 102–105.

7. Following World War I, the US ordered a massive new rigid airship from the German Zeppelin company. The resulting dirigible, designated LZ.126 by the Germans, was the largest airship of its day. Captain Hugo Eckner, his crew of 27, and 4 American observers departed Friedrichshafen on 12 October 1924. Three days later, following a flight of 80 hours, they landed at Lakehurst, New Jersey. With a change of markings, LZ.126 became the US Navy's ZR-3 *Los Angeles*, serving until 1932.

8. Ramon Franco, younger brother of Spain's future ruler Francisco Franco, organized his nation's first Atlantic flight. In a patriotic effort to link Spain with its former South Americana colonies, Franco secured an Italian-built Dornier Wal that he named *Plus Ultra* (Farther Still). On 22 January 1926, left the same port from which Columbus had discovered the new world. *Plus Ultra* arrived on the Brazilian coast on 31 January, becoming the first aircraft to cross the South Atlantic. The flight continued on to Rio de Janero, Montevideo, and Buenos Aires, where the Wal was presented as a gift to Argentina from the government of Spain.

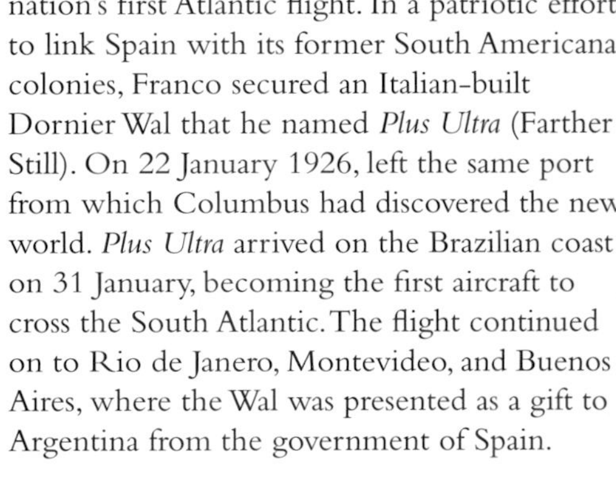

The US Navy's *Los Angeles* began life as Zeppelin's airship LZ126; her 1924 Atlantic crossing was a delivery flight.

9. On 25 October 1926, a Brazilian crew led by Commandant Joao de Barros began their Atlantic crossing in an Italian Savoia-Marchetti S.55 flying boat nicknamed *Jau*. Fuel problems, engine failures, and arguments between crew members seemed to plague the flight, which would not arrive in Brazil until 14 May 1927. Although no records were broken, the crew arrived as national heros, the first South Americans to cross the Atlantic.

10. Colonel the Marques of Pinedo would become the first aviator to cross both the North Atlantic and the South Atlantic. He named his Savoia-Marchetti S.55 *Santa Maria* after Columbus' flagship, and planned a whirlwind tour of the Americas. His flight across the South Atlantic arrived in Brazil on 24 February 1927, proceeding south as far as Buenos Aires before traveling north to the US West Coast. When an accidental refueling fire destroyed the flying boat in early April, a replacement aircraft, named *Santa Maria II*, was shipped from Italy, allowing Pinedo to resume his flight in May. He returned to Europe on 11 June.

11. Another Dornier Wal, this one named *Argos*, was chosen by Portugal's Sarament Beires for a South Atlantic crossing in early 1927. The aircraft left Lisbon on 3 March 1927, arriving in Brazil on 17 May. *Argos* made the first night crossing of the South Atlantic.

12. In 1919, American hotel owner Raymond Orteig offered a prize of $25,000 for the first non-stop airplane flight from New York

The first Atlantic crossing to South America was completed by Portugal's Carlos Gago Coutinho in this British-built Fairey IIID floatplane

Ramón Franco made Spain's first Atlantic aircraft crossing in Dornier Wal *Plus Ultra* in 1926.

to Paris. The duration of the flight would necessitate a crew of at least two. The fuel needed to cover such a distance required a large aircraft, and the limited power available from contemporary motors suggested that at least two engines would be needed to get that aircraft off the ground. Multiple engines added weight and burned more fuel, requiring an even larger aircraft, which required more power. The cyclic argument intimated that the flight couldn't be done, and for eight years technology supported that argument.

By 1926, more powerful engines and more efficient propellers brought a host of contenders for the Orteig prize. Three overloaded aircraft crashed, killing four crew members and injuring five others. A fourth flight was delayed by mechanical problems and fiery tempers. And then, French war aces Charles Nungesser and Francois Coli simply disappeared over the Atlantic.

Less than two weeks later, at 7:52 on the morning of 20 May 1927, American pilot Charles Lindbergh took off from Roosevelt Field, just outside of New York City. He flew a one-of-a-kind, single-engined, Ryan monoplane. the NY-P (New York-Paris) named *The Spirit of St. Louis*. The aircraft carried no radio or parachute, allowing capacity for additional fuel instead. The side windows were removed in hopes the cold air blowing through the cockpit would keep the pilot awake - a necessary precaution, since Lindbergh was flying solo.

Thirty-three-and-a-half hours later, Lindbergh landed in Paris. Dubbed "Lucky Lindy" and the "Lone Eagle," Lindbergh became the hero of two continents and the world's most famous aviator. His quiet, all-American, self-assured personality, melded with his skills as a pilot, mechanic, and navigator raised him to a cult status. And Lindbergh made 1927 a watershed year in public acceptance and awareness of aviation. •

Italian Francesco de Pinedo crossed the Atlantic to South America in this Savoia-Marchetti S.55 flying boat named *Santa Maria*. When the aircraft was later destroyed in a fire, de Pinedo flew home in a replacement aircraft named *Santa Maria II*.

Flown by Portuguese Sarament Bieres, Dornier Was *Argos* crossed the South Atlantic in early 1927.

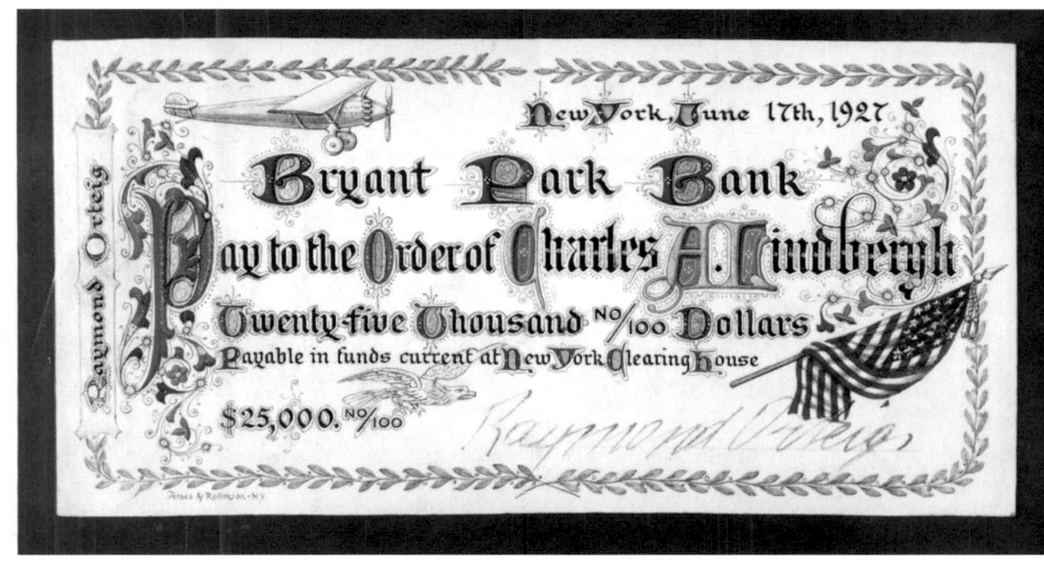

New York, June 17th, 1927

Bryant Park Bank

Pay to the Order of Charles A. Lindbergh

Twenty-five Thousand No/100 Dollars

Payable in funds current at New York Clearing House

$25,000. No/100

Raymond Orteig

Raymond Orteig

ABOVE: Charles Lindbergh, soon to be the most famous aviator of his day, poses with his Ryan monoplane *The Spirit of St. Louis* before taking off on his solo flight from New York to Paris.

LEFT: The $25,000 Orteig prize check, paid to Lindbergh a month after his famous flight.

Atlantic Crossings after Lindbergh

Charles Lindbergh ushered in a new era of trans-Atlantic flying. Several of his contemporaries continued with plans to reach Paris, while others aimed for the glory of being first to connect different Old- and New-World cities. Some would be encouraged by prize offers, others were supported by governments hoping to forge new political bonds and commercial opportunities. As fatalities mounted, governments and private sponsors often withdrew support, or (in some cases) refused takeoff permission. By the late 1930s, airlines were establishing civil trans-Atlantic airways, most of which were abandoned when war broke out in September 1939.

Here then is a brief overview of trans-Atlantic flight attempts from June 1927 through September 1939, listing the date(s), crew, aircraft, and planned route of each flight.

1927

23 May - 11 June. de Pinedo, del Prete, & Zacchetti. Savoia-Marchetti S.55 *Santa Maria II.* Newfoundland to Lisbon. See page 88.

4-6 June. Clarence D. Chamberlin & Charles A. Levine. Bellanca WB-2 Columbia. New York to Berlin. *Columbia* landed at Cottbus, some sixty miles from Berlin.

29-30 June. Richard E. Byrd, George O. Noville, Bert Acosta, & Bernt Balchen. Fokker C-2 *America.* New York to Paris. The *America* flew for 46 hours before ditching just off Ver-sur-Mer, France.

14 August. Friederich Loose, Herman Koehl, & Guenther von Huenefeld. Junkers W 33 *Bremen.* Johann Risticz, Cornelius Edzard, & Hubert R. Knickerbocker. Junkers W 33 *Europa.* Dessau to New York. *Europa* quickly became lost in impenetrable fog, developed engine trouble, and turned home to be badly damaged in a heavy landing. *Bremen* pressed on through the heavy weather, finally turning home over Ireland.

24 August. William Brock & Edward Schlee. Stinson SM-1 Detroiter *Pride of Detroit.* Newfoundland to Croydon. This was the trans-Atlantic leg of a planned world flight.

31 August. Frederick F. Minchin, Leslie Hamilton, & Princess Anne Löwenstein-Wertheim. Fokker F.VII *Saint Raphael.* Cornwall to Newfoundland. Wreckage later found at sea; no survivors.

1 September. Duke Schiller & Phil Wood. Stinson SM-1 Detroiter *Royal Windsor.* Windsor, Ontario, to Windsor, UK. Weather and mechanical problems had stalled the flight in Quebec when backers withdrew their support.

2 September. Leon Givion & Charles Corbu. Farman F.180 *l'Oiseau Bleu.* Paris to New York. This flight of Farman's latest airliner returned to base after three-and-a-half hours.

3 September. Frank T. Courtney, Downer, & Robert Little. Dornier Wal. Plymouth, UK, to Canada via the Azores and New York. Frank Courtney purchased the surviving Dornier Wal used for Amundsen's Arctic exploration (see page 114) for his first Atlantic attempt since 1919. Weather and mechanical difficulties forced him back to Spain.

6-7 September. Lloyd Bertaud, James Hill, & Philip Payne. Fokker F.VIIa *Old Glory.* Old Orchard Beach, Maine, to Rome. On the second day of the flight, Bertaud radioed an SOS; wreckage, was found in the Atlantic, but no survivors.

7 September. Terence Tully & James Medcalf. Stinson SM-1 Detroiter *Sir John Carling.* London, Ontario to London, England. Turned back in fog on 28 August. Staged out of Harbour Grace for 7 September attempt, but disappeared over the Atlantic.

16 September. James Fitzmaurice & Robert H. McIntosh. Fokker F.VII *Princess Xenia.* Dublin, Ireland, to Philadelphia. Headwinds forced the crew to return after only two hours.

12-13 October. George Haldeman & Ruth Elder. Stinson SM-1 Detroiter *American Girl.* New York to Paris. Haldeman and Elder ditched to be rescued by the tanker SS *Barendrecht.*

14 October. Friederich Loose, Paul Starke, Karl Loewe, & Lilli Dillenz. Junkers G 24. Germany to New York via Spain and the Azores. Ended in the Azores with mechanical difficulties.

14-15 October. Dieudonné Costes and Joseph Le Brix. Breguet *XIX Nungesser and Coli.* French West Africa to Brazil. This first non-stop crossing of the South Atlantic continued with a tour of Latin America and the US. The crew and aircraft shipped from San Francisco to Japan, then flew home across Asia to Paris.

4 November. Horst Merz, Wilhelm Bock, & Fritz Rhode. Heinkel Seaplane. Warnemünde to New York via Lisbon and the Azores. Crashed on take-off in the Azores.

23 December. Francis Grayson, Oskar Omdal, Brice Goldsborough, & Frank Koehler. Sikorsky S-36 *Dawn.* Harbour Grace, Newfoundland to London. The crew radioed a distress signal near Newfoundland then disappeared.

1928

13 March. Walter G. R. Hinchcliff & Elsie Mackay. Stinson SM-1 Detroiter *The Endeavour.* London to Newfoundland (?). Hinchcliff and Mackay headed over the Atlantic without announcing their intentions. They were lost at sea.

12-13 April. Baron Günther von Hoenefeld, Hermann Köhl, & James Fitzmaurice. Junkers W 33 *Bremen.* Ireland to New York. The flight ended with a hard landing on Greenly Island, Labrador.

17-18 June. Wilmer Stulz, Louis Gordon, Amelia Earhart. Fokker F.VIIb-3m *Friendship.* Newfoundland to Wales. This crossing made Earhart a celebrity, though, as a passenger, she felt her status undeserved.

28 June-2 August. Frank T. Courtney, Hugh Gilmour, Fred Pierce, & Elwood Hosmer. Dornier Wal. Lisbon to Canada via the Azores. Mechanical difficulties and severe

Crews begin repairs on the Junkers *Bremen*. The metal aircraft's Atlantic crossing ended with a hard landing in Labrador.

weather delayed the flight in the Azores until 1 August. An engine fire then forced the aircraft down in mid-Atlantic. The crew was rescued by the liner *Minnewaska,* while the aircraft was later picked up by the Italian freighter *Valprato.*

28 June. Thea Rasche, U. Koenmann, & B. Zebora. Bellanca J North Star. Cap de la Madeleine, Quebec, to Berlin. This flight was abandoned when the overloaded aircraft proved unable to take off.

3-5 July. Arturo Ferrarin & Carlo P. del Prete. Savoia-Marchetti S.64. Italy to Brazil. Ferrarin and Prete's South Atlantic flight established a new non-stop record of 4,464 miles.

22 July. Paulin Paris, Marot & Cadiou. CAMS 54 GR *La Frégate.* Brest, France, to Azores. Plagued by engine problems, this trans-Atlantic attempt ended in the Azores.

25 July. Bert R. J. "Fish" Hassell & Parker D. "Shorty" Cramer. Stinson SM-1DC Detroiter *Greater Rockford.* Rockford, Illinois, to Stockholm. Forced down shortly after takeoff.

1 August. Ramón Franco, Eduardo Gallarza, Ruiz de Alda, & Modesto Rada. Dornier Super-Wal *Numancia.* Cádiz to New York. Returned with engine troubles after 13 hours.

3-4 August. Major Ludwik Idzikowski and Major Kazimierz Kubala.
Amiot 123 *Marszalek Pilsudski.* Paris - New York. Ditched beside a freighter; crew rescued.

8 August. Maurice Drouhin, André Lanet, Gianoli, & Manuel. Couzinet 10 *Arc-en-Ciel.* Paris to New York. Sources differ as to whether this loss was a trans-Atlantic attempt or a test flight. Drouhin and Lanet died in the crash.

16-18 August. Bert R. J. "Fish" Hassell & Parker D. "Shorty" Cramer. Stinson SM-1DC Detroiter *Greater Rockford.* Rockford, Illinois, to Stockholm. Hassell and Cramer landed in Greenland, walking for two weeks before being rescued.

25 August. Louis Coudouret, Louis Mailloux, Mailly-Nesle. Bernard 191GR. Paris to NY. A heavily modified Bernard 190 airliner refused to leave the ground in Paris.

4 September. René Lefèvre & Armeno Lotti, Jr. Bernard 191GR *Oiseau Canari.* Paris to South America. Lefevre and Lotti landed in Casablanca with mechanical problems.

19 September. Cesare Sabelli, Roger Q. Williams, Pietro Bonelli & Dr. Leon Pisculli. Bellanca K Roma. Old Orchard Beach, Maine, to Rome. *Roma* returned to its point of departure after 20 minutes in the air.

11-15 October. Dr. Hugo Eckner with 38 crewmen & 19 passengers. Dirigible LZ 127 *Graf Zeppelin.* Friedrichshaven to Lakehurst, New Jersey. The first commercial Atlantic crossing; the airship completed 144 crossings in nine years. Return flight 29 October - 1 November.

12 October. Roger Q. Williams & Pietro Bonelli. Bellanca WB-2 *Columbia.* New York to Rome. Landing gear shorn off during an aborted takeoff.

17 October. H. C. MacDonald. de Havilland D.H.60G Gipsy Moth. Newfoundland to Ireland. Lost at sea.

Ground crews fuel the *Oiseau Canari* (Yellow Bird) prior to its successful 1929 trans-Atlantic flight. During the bustle of preparations, no one noticed a stowaway hiding himself inside the aircraft's tail.

1929

24-26 March. Ignacio Jiménez & Francisco Iglesias. CASA-Breguet 19 GR *Jesus del Gran Poder.* Spain to Rio de Janeiro. Crossing followed by a Latin American tour.

9 June. Albin Ahrenberg, Axel Floden, & Robert Ljungland. Junkers W 33e3e *Sverige.* Stockholm to New York via Iceland and Greenland. Swedish crew forced down south of Iceland; towed to Reykjavik, the airmen abandoned their attempt.

13-14 June. René Lefèvre, Armand Lotti, Jr., & Jean Assolant (Arthur Schreiber, stowaway). Bernard 191GR *Oiseau Canari.* Old Orchard, Maine, to Paris. Less than three weeks after their first attempt (on 29 May), this crew's second start almost ended in disaster when the aircraft's tail refused to rise due to the extra weight of a stowaway. The aircraft burned too much fuel to make Paris and landed in Spain.

13 June. Roger Q. Williams & Lewis Yancey. Bellanca Model J *Green Flash.* Old Orchard, Maine, to Rome. Crashed when the landing gear collapsed on takeoff.

21 June. Ramón Franco, Eduardo Gallarza, Ruiz de Alda, & Pedro Madariaga. Dornier Super-Wal *Numancia.* Cádiz to New York. Forced down on the Atlantic leg of a world flight, the crew was rescued by HMS *Eagle* on 29 June 1929.

3 July. Parker D. "Shorty" Cramer, Robert Gast, & Robert Wood. Sikorsky S-38 *Untin Bowler.* Chicago to Berlin. Fogged in at Labrador, Cramer watched helplessly as ice floes sank his Sikorsky.

7 July. Louis Coudouret & Louis Mailloux. Bernard 191GR. Spain to NY. Following his unsuccessful attempts in August 1928, Coudouret planned to fly from Spain. Spanish authorities refused permission, sending him home with two Spanish aviators. The aircraft crashed, killing the Frenchman and injuring the Spanish pilots.

8-9 July. Roger Q. Williams and Lewis Yancey. Bellanca J *Pathfinder.* Old Orchard, Maine, to Rome. After 31 hours in the air, the aircraft made an emergency landing in Spain, completing the flight the next day.

13 July. Ludwik Idzikowski & Kazimierz Kubala. Amiot 123 *White Bird.* Paris to New York. Engine problems over the Atlantic; crash landing on Graciosa killed Idzikowski.

13 July. Dieudonné Costes & Maurice Bellonte. Breguet XIX Super T.R. *Point d'Interrogation.* Paris to New York. Returned to Paris after a flight of 1,600 miles in bad weather.

19 August. Oscar Kaeser & Kurt Lucher. Farman 190 *Jung Schweitzerland.* Lisbon to New York via Halifax. This Swiss crew was sighted crossing the Azores, but disappeared over the Atlantic.

22 October. Urban F. Diteman. Barling B-6 *Golden Hind*. Harbour Grace, Newfoundland, to London. Diteman disappeared over the Atlantic.

15-17 December. Léon Challe & Taddeo Larre-Borges. Breguet 19 TR Bidon. Cordova to Natal, Brazil. Frenchman Challe and Uruguayan Larre-Borges followed their 41-hour crossing of the South Atlantic with a goodwill tour of South America.

1930

12-13 May. Jean Mermoz, Jean Dabry, & Leopold Gimié. Latécoère 28-3 *Comte de Vaulx*. French West Africa to Natal, Brazil. Mermoz's crossing of the South Atlantic in just over 21 hours pioneered a new airmail route for Aeropostale. The return trip was forced down at sea on 7 July, with the crew rescued by a passing ship.

18-22 May. Hugo Eckner with 40 crewmen and 22 passengers. Dirigible LZ 127 *Graf Zeppelin*. Friedrichshaven to Rio de Janeiro. *Graf Zeppelin*'s first South Atlantic crossing; the return trip crossed the North Atlantic via the United States.

24-25 June. Charles Kingsford-Smith, Evert van Dijk, Jonathan P. Saul, John W. Stannage. Fokker F.VIIb-3m Southern Cross. Portmarnock Beach, Ireland, to Harbour Grace, Newfoundland. See page 96.

6 July. C. S. Wynne-Eaton. de Havilland D.H.80A Puss Moth. Harbour Grace, Newfoundland, to London. Aircraft destroyed on takeoff; pilot escaped with minor injuries.

29 July - 1 August. R. S. Booth and crew of 40. Dirigible R.100. Cardington, UK, to Montreal. Designed for flights between the UK, India, and Australia, the R.100 was instead tested on this long-range flight between the UK and North America, returning on 13-16 August.

31 July. Wolfram Hirth & Oscar Weller. Klemm. Berlin to Chicago via Brough, UK, Greenland, and Labrador. Trans-Atlantic attempt abandoned after landing in Iceland.

2 August. Henry J. Brown & John Henry Mears. Lockheed 5B Vega *City of New York*. Harbour Grace, Newfoundland, to London. Minor injuries from takeoff crash on world flight attempt.

20-26 August. Wolfgang von Gronau, Eduard Zimmer, Franz Hack, & Fritz Albrecht. Dornier Wal *Amundsen*. Warnemunde, Germany, to New York via Iceland, Greenland, Labrador, and Nova Scotia. This was the same aircraft used by Amundsen and (later) Courtney.

1-2 September. Dieudonné Costes & Maurice Bellonte. Breguet XIX Super T.R. *Point d'Interrogation*. Paris to New York. The first non-stop flight from Paris to New York.

Jimmy Mattern waves from the cockpit of the Lockheed Vega *Century of Progress*. In July 1932, Mattern and Bennett Griffin crossed the Atlantic as part of a world flight attempt; both survived the aircraft's crash in Russia.

9-10 October. J. Errol Boyd & H. P. Connor. Bellanca WB-2 *Maple Leaf*. Harbour Grace, Newfoundland, to Berlin. The former *Colombia* was forced to land in the Scilly Isles. The crew later flew to London, Amsterdam, Berlin, and Paris.

2 November - 27 August 1931. Frederich Christiansen (later replaced by Cramer von Clausbruch), Horst Merz, Clarence H. Schildhauer (later replaced by Fritz Hammer), & crew. Dornier Do X. Friedrichshafen to New York via Lisbon, the Canaries, South America, the Caribbean, & the US East Coast. Engine fires, landing damage, weather delays, and a six-week tour of Rio de Janeiro, delayed the Do X's New York arrival for ten months. In New York, the courts delayed the return flight until 19-24 May 1932, once Dornier had paid Curtiss the money owed for the aircraft's engines.

17 December - 15 January 1931. General Italo Balbo & 55 airmen. 14 Savoia-Marchetti S.55A. Rome to Rio de Janeiro via Portuguese Guinea & Brazil. Three aircraft and five airmen were lost in crashes. The remaining aircraft were sold to Brazil, with the crews sailing home.

1931

3 January. Beryl Hart & William S. MacLaren. Bellanca CH-300 *Trade Wind*. North Beach, New York, to Paris via Bermuda and the Azores. Hart and MacLaren landed in Virginia, then disappeared over the Atlantic after taking off on the 7th.

22 June. Ruth Nichols. Lockheed 5 Special Vega *Akita*. New York to Paris. Nichols crashed on landing at St John, New Brunswick.

23-24 June. Wiley Post & Harold Gatty. Lockheed 5B Vega *Winnie Mae*. Harbour Grace, Newfoundland, to Chester, UK. Atlantic leg of an around-the-world flight.

24-25 June. Holgar Hoiriis & Otto Hillig. Bellanca J-300 *Liberty*. Harbour Grace, Newfoundland, to Copenhagen. Lost in the fog, the crew landed at Krefeld Germany, continuing to Copenhagen the next day.

15-16 July. George Endres and Sandor Wilczek. Lockheed 8A Sirius *Justice for Hungary*. Harbour Grace, Newfoundland, to Budapest, Hungary. Out of fuel, Endres and Wilczek landed just short of their goal.

27 July - 9 August. Parker D. "Shorty" Cramer & Oliver Pacquette. Bellanca Pacemaker CH-300. Detroit to Copenhagen. Cramer and Pacquette were lost over the North Sea.

28-30 July. Russell Norton Boardman & John Louis Polando. Bellanca J-300 Cape Cod. New York to Istanbul. Boardman and Polando established a distance record of 5,012 miles. (A previous attempt was canceled on 25 July.)

28-29 July. Hugh Herndon, Jr, & Clyde Pangborn. Bellanca Skyrocket CH-400 *Miss Veedol*. New York to Moylegrove, UK. The Atlantic leg of a successful around-the-world flight. (A previous attempt had turned back on 25 July.)

9-30 August. Wolfgang von Gronau, Eduard Zimmer, Franz Hack, & Fritz Albrecht. Dornier Wal *Groenlandwal*. Berlin to Chicago via Copenhagen, Iceland, Greenland, Labrador, and Montreal. Von Gronau's second trans-Atlantic flight.

19 August. Edwin L. Preston & Robert H. Collignon. Stinson floatplane. Detroit to Copenhagen. Preston and Collingnon went missing in northern Canada for two days before calling off their attempt.

12 September. Willy Rody, Christian Johanssen, & Fernando Costa Viega. Junkers W 33 Esa. Lisbon to New York. Forced down at sea, the crew floated for a week before being rescued by the steamship *Belmoira*.

26-27 November. H. J. "Bert" Hinkler. de Havilland 80A Puss Moth. Natal, Brazil, to Bathhurst, British Guinea. Hinkler's flight from Canada to London included a 22-hour crossing of the South Atlantic.

1932

13 May. Louis T. Reichers. Lockheed 8 Altair *Liberty.* New York to Paris via Harbour Grace, Newfoundland, and Dublin. Reichers was rescued after landing at sea 17 miles from Ireland.

20-21 May. Amelia Earhart. Lockheed 5B Vega. Harbour Grace, Newfoundland, to Paris. Plagued by weather and fuel problems, Earhart landed in Northern Ireland, becoming the first woman to pilot an aircraft across the Atlantic.

3 June. Stanislaus F. Hausner. Bellanca J *Santa Rosa Maria.* Newark, New Jersey to Warsaw. Forced down 550 miles from Portugal, Hausner was rescued by a British tanker after eight days. (An attempt in 28 May had turned back for bad weather.)

5-6 July. James J. Mattern & Bennett Griffin. Lockheed 5 Special Vega *Century of Progress.* Harbour Grace, Newfoundland, to Berlin. The Atlantic leg of a failed around-the-world attempt.

22-26 July. Wolfgang von Gronau, von Roth, Franz Hack, & Fritz Albrecht. Dornier Wal *Groenlandwal.* Isle of Sylt to Montreal via Iceland, Greenland, and Labrador. Von Gronau's third east-to-west crossing, the Atlantic leg of a world flight.

18-19 August. James A. Mollison. de Havilland D.H.80A Puss Moth *The Heart's Content.* Portmarnock, Ireland, to New Brunswick, Canada. The first solo east-west crossing.

23 August. Thor Solberg & Carl O. Petersen. Bellanca K *Enna Jettick.* New York to Norway. The former *Roma* was rebuilt and renamed *Enna Jettick*. The aircraft crashed in Newfoundland during a snowstorm.

23 August - 11 September. George Hutchinson, Blanche Hutchinson, Kathryn Hutchinson, Janet Lee Hutchinson, Peter H. Redpath, Joseph Ruff, Gerald Altfilisch, & Norman Alley. Sikorsky S-38 *City of Richmond*. New York to Greenland (first leg of an around-the-world flight). The Flying Family, a crew of three, and their photographer made a forced landing off Greenland, rescued two days later by a British trawler.

25 August. Clyde Allen Lee & John Bochkon. Stinson SM-1B Detroiter *Green Mountain Boy.* Barre, Vermont to Oslo, Norway, via Harbour Grace, Newfoundland. Disappeared over the Atlantic.

13 September. William Ulrich, Dr. Leon Pisciulli, & Edna Newcomber. Bellanca Skyrocket CH-400 *American Nurse.* New York to Rome. *Miss Veedol,* renamed *American Nurse* for this flight, disappeared over the Atlantic.

1933

16 January. Jean Mermoz & crew of 3. Couzinet 70 *Arc-en-Ciel.* French West Africa to Natal, Brazil. Mermoz' first crossing of the year set a speed record, he and the aircraft returned on 15 May.

3-4 June. James J. Mattern. Lockheed 5 Special Vega *Century of Progress.* New York to Norway. Mattern landed on Jomfruland Island, off Norway, in an unsuccessful around-the-world attempt.

8 June. James and Amy Mollison. de Havilland D.H.84 Dragon I *Seafarer.* Croydon, UK, to New York. *Seafarer's* landing gear collapsed while taxiing.

9-11 June. Mariano Barberán & Joaquín Collar. CASA-Breguet XIX GR Super Bidon *Cuatro Vientos.* Seville to Camaguey, Cuba. Following their Atlantic crossing, Barberán and Collar took off for Mexico City and disappeared.

1-15 July. General Italo Balbo & 99 airmen. 25 Savoia-Marchetti S.55X seaplanes. Orbetello, Italy, to Chicago via Amsterdam, Londonderry, Reykjavik, Labrador, Nova Scotia, and Montreal. One aircraft capsized in Amsterdam; the remainder completed the crossing.

15-16 July. Wiley Post. Lockheed 5B Vega *Winnie Mae.* New York to Berlin. The Atlantic leg of a solo world flight.

15-17 July. Stephen Darius & Stanley T. Girenas. Bellanca Pacemaker CH-300 *Lituanica.* New York to Kaunas, Lithuania. Darius and Girenas died when they crashed in Germany.

21 July - 26 August. Charles Lindbergh & Anne Morrow Lindbergh. Lockheed 8 Sirius Special *Tingmissartog.* Cartwright, Labrador, to Copenhagen. See page [TK].

22-24 July. James and Amy Mollison. de Havilland D.H.84 Dragon I *Seafarer.* Pendine Sands, South Wales, to New York. The aircraft suffered heavy damage landing at Bridgeport, Connecticut.

27 July. Charles Ulm, P. G. Taylor, G. U. "Scotty" Allan, & Edwards. Avro 618 Ten *Faith in Australia.* Portmarnock, Ireland, to New York. The Avro Ten was damaged when its landing gear collapsed on landing in Ireland.

5 August. John Grierson. de Havilland D.H.60A Gipsy Moth *Rouge et Noir.* Brough, UK, to Canada. This flight, planned as a test of new radio direction finding equipment, reached Reykjavik before returning to the UK.

5-7 August. Maurice Rossi & Paul Codos. Bleriot 110 *Joseph Le Brix.* New York to Rayak, Syria. A new distance record over 5,657 miles.

25 July - 13 August. General Italo Balbo & 96 airmen. 24 Savoia-Marchetti S.55X seaplanes. Chicago to Rome via New York, the Azores, and Lisbon. One aircraft capsized in the Azores, with the remainder returning safely to Italy.

8 August. Crew Joseph Adamowicz, Benjamin Adamowicz, & Bergin. Bellanca J-300 *White Eagle.* New York to Warsaw. The Adamowicz brothers purchased the Bellanca *Liberty* renaming it *White Eagle.* The aircraft was damaged in a bad landing at Harbour Grace.

2 September. Francisco de Pinedo. Bellanca

Well established as an Atlantic aviator, Francisco de Pinedo burned to death when his Bellanca *Santa Lucia* crashed during an attempted flight from New York to Rome.

Special Long Distance *Santa Lucia.* New York to Baghdad. Pinedo died in a takeoff crash.

3 October. James and Amy Mollison. de Havilland D.H.84 Dragon I *Seafarer II.* New York to Baghdad. With the engines and fuel tanks of *Seafarer* installed in a new Dragon, the Mollisons attempted three take-offs before abandoning the flight.

1934

3 January. Latécoère 300 *Croix du Sud.* French West Africa to Natal, Brazil. This was the first trans-Atlantic flight of the Laté 300.

14-15 May. George R. Pond & Cesare Sabelli. Bellanca J-300 *Leonardo da Vinci.* New York to Rome. Pond and Sabelli landed in Ireland for repairs, then continued on to Rome.

27-28 May. Maurice Rossi & Paul Codos. Bleriot 110 *Joseph Le Brix.* Paris to California. Attempting a world record flight to California, Rossi and Codos were forced to land in New York.

28 May. Jean Mermoz & crew of 3. Couzinet 71 *Arc-en-Ciel.* French West Africa to Natal, Brazil. The first crossing of the Couzinet 71, which made nine more South Atlantic runs by year's end.

28-30 June. Joseph Adamowicz, Benjamin Adamowicz, & Holgar Hoiriis. Bellanca J-300 *City of Warsaw.* New York to Warsaw. The Adamowicz brothers landed in France (where pilot Hoiriis remained) before reaching Warsaw the next day.

21 July - 27 August. John Grierson. de Havilland D.H.83 Fox Moth *Robert Bruce.* Rochester, UK, to New York. Grierson collided with a rowboat at Rekyavik. After a delay for repairs, Grierson eventually reached New York.

8-9 August. James R. Ayling and Leonard Reid. de Havilland D.H.84 Dragon I *Trail of the Caribou.* Wasaga Beach, Ontario, to Baghdad. Ayling and Reid renamed Mollison's *Seafarer II* for a record flight to Baghdad. With fuel consumption higher than expected, the pair flew to London instead.

27 August - 6 September. Richard Light & Robert Wilson. Bellanca Skyrocket CH-400 *Asulinak.* Cartwright, Labrador, to Edinburgh via Greenland, Iceland, the Faroes, and the Orkneys. Light and Wilson's trans-Atlantic crossing was part of a leisurely world tour, eventually completed in January 1935.

15 December. J. Hondong, J. Van Balkom, Van der Molen, & Stolk. Fokker F.XVIII *Snip.* Amsterdam to Curacao via Casablanca and the Cape Verde Islands. This was a delivery flight for KLM's new West Indies Division.

Douglas Corrigan greases the bearing of his Curtiss Robin before his somewhat disorienting flight from New York to California.

1935

22 June. George & Alfred De Monteverde. Bellanca J-2 Special *Magellan.* New York to Lisbon. *Abyssinia,* renamed *Marshal Pilsudski,* was again renamed for this 1935 flight, which ended with a takeoff crash.

18 July - 16 August. Thor Solberg & Paul C. Oscanyan. Loening C2C Air Yacht *Liev Eiriksson.* New York to Bergen, Norway, via Montreal, Labrador, Greenland, Iceland, and the Faroes. Weather delayed this successful flight by weeks.

21-22 September. Felix Waikus (Feliksas Vaitkus). Lockheed Vega *Lituanica II.* New York to Lithuania. Waikus' flight ended with a crash landing in Ireland.

8 December - 4 January 1936. Latécoère 521 *Lieutenant de Vaisseau Paris.* Bordeau to New York via Dakar, Natal, Martinique, and Pensacola. The first trans-Atlantic crossing of the Latécoère 521.

1936

10 January - 17 February. Antonio Menéndez Peláez. Lockheed 8 Sirius 4 de *Septiembre.* Havana to Seville via Venezuela, Brazil, & Dakar. The first Hispanic aviator to fly to Europe from the Americas.

30 March - April. Ernst Lehmann with 74 crew and passengers. Dirigible LZ 129 *Hindenburg.* Friedrichshafen to Rio de Janeiro via Recife. *Hindenberg*'s maiden Atlantic crossing.

6-9 May. Ernst Lehmann with 74 crew and passengers. Dirigible LZ 129 *Hindenburg.* Friedrichshafen to Lakehurst, New Jersey. *Hindenberg*'s first North Atlantic crossing. The airship completed sixteen North Atlantic round trips in 1936.

3 September. Henry T. "Dick" Merrill & Harry Richman. Vultee V1-A *Lady Peace.* New York to London via Harbour Grace, Newfoundland. Merrill and Richman landed in Wales, later continuing to London and Paris.

4-5 September. Beryl Markham. Percival K.1 Vega Gull *The Messenger.* Abingdon, UK, to New York. The first woman to make an east-to-west solo crossing.

11 September. Dornier Do 18 *Zephir.* The Azores to New York. The first of eight North Atlantic evaluation flights. Do 18s also made 65 South Atlantic crossings before World War II, with 18 more flights complete by Do 26s.

14 September. Henry T. "Dick" Merrill & Harry Richman. Vultee V1-A *Lady Peace*. Birkdale, UK, to New York. Ended with a forced landing in Newfoundland.

5 October. Farman 2200 *Ville de Montevidéo*. French West Africa to Natal, Brazil. Air France's first Farman 2200 crossing.

6-7 October. Kurt Bjorkvall. Bellanca Pacemaker 300-W. NY to Stockholm. Bjorkvall was forced down and rescued 100 miles from Ireland.

28-30 October. James A. Mollison. Bellanca 28-70 Flash *The Dorothy*. New York to London via Harbour Grace, Newfoundland. New trans-Atlantic record of 13 hours 17 minutes.

7 December. Jean Mermoz, Alexandre Pichodou, Henri Ezan, Edgar Cruveilher & Jean Lavidalie. Latécoère 300 *Croix du Sud*. French West Africa to Natal, Brazil. Mermoz was lost at sea on this, his 24th Atlantic crossing.

1937

3-6 May. Ernst Lehmann with 97 crew and passengers. Dirigible LZ 129 *Hindenburg*. Friedrichshafen to Lakehurst, New Jersey. *Hindenberg*'s first passenger flight of 1937 ended in disaster when the airship exploded during landing preparations.

8-9 May. Richard T. "Dick" Merrill & John Lambie. Lockheed 10 Electra. New York to London via Essex, UK. The flight connected New York and London in just under 21 hours; the return flight was made on 13-14 May.

7 June. Amelia Earhart & Fred Noonan. Lockheed 10-E Electra. Natal, Brazil, to French West Africa. This was the Atlantic leg of Earhart and Noonan's world flight attempt.

4-9 July. A. S. Wilcoxson, C. H. Bowes, T. E. Hobbs, & T. A. Vallette. Short S.23C Empire Boat *Caledonia*. Southhampton to New York via Ireland, Newfoundland and Montreal. Preparation for Imperial Airways trans-Atlantic passenger and mail service. Return trip on 12-14 July followed by two more round trip flights.

5-6 July. Harold Gray, De Lima, Masland, Chan Wright, & Walter Smith. Sikorsky S.42B *Clipper III*. Botwood, Newfoundland, to Foynes, Ireland. Test flight for Pan American's trans-Atlantic service. Return flight on 14-16 July, followed by two additional round trip surveys.

27 July - 2 August. Powell, Elder, Woods, & Lewis. Short S.23C Empire Boat *Cambria*. Southampton to New York via Foynes, Botwood, & Montreal. *Cambria*'s first Atlantic crossing, returning 6-9 August.

August. Joachim H. Blankenburg & crew of 3. Blohm und Voss Ha 139 *Noordmeer*. Germany to New York via Lisbon and the Azores.

The Short S.23C Empire Boat *Cambria* made two round-trip North Atlantic survey flights. (By convention, the name of each "C-Class" flying boat began with the letter "C.")

The first of twenty Ha 139 round-trip flights over the North Atlantic. The three floatplanes later flew regular South Atlantic mail service.

1938

4 July. Farman 2220 *Ville de Dakar*. French West Africa to Natal, Brazil. Air France's 300th South Atlantic crossing.

10 July. Howard Hughes, Harry Connor, Ed Lund, Tom Thurlow, & Richard Stoddard. Lockheed 14-N2 Super Electra Sky *Zephyr*. New York to Paris. The trans-Atlantic leg of Hughes' world flight.

17-18 July. Douglas Corrigan. Curtiss Robin J-1 Sunshine. New York to "California" (Dublin). Denied permission for a flight to Ireland, Corrigan filed a flight plan for California. Due to "compass problems," he landed in Baldonnel, Ireland, 28 hours later.

20-21 July. D. C. T. Bennett & A. J. Coster. Short S.20 *Mercury*. Foynes Harbour, Ireland, to Montreal. The upper aircraft of the Short Mayo composite flew the first commercial airplane crossing of the Atlantic carrying a half ton of mail and newspapers. Return flight 25-27 July.

10-11 August. Alfred Henke, Rudolph von Moreau, Paul Dierberg, & Walter Kober. Focke-Wulf Fw 200 Condor. Berlin to New York. A record time of just under 25 hours, returning 13-14 August in just under 20 hours.

1939

26 March - 4 April. Harold Gray, Arthur La Porte, James Walker, Adam Kalkowsky, Horace Brock, Lew Lindsey, Chan Wright, Ray Cornish, Shelby Kritzer, Addison Beideman, Bob Dutton, & William Thaler with 9 representatives of Boeing and the US government. Boeing 314 *Yankee Clipper*. Baltimore to Southampton via the Azores, Lisbon, Marseilles, Bordeaux. This was the first Atlantic crossing of the new Boeing 314, returning 11-14 April.

28-29 April. V. K. Kokkinaki & M. Kh. Gordinenko. Il'yushin TsKB.30 Moskva. Moscow to New York. With insufficient fuel, oxygen, and heat, Kokkinaki and Gordinenko were forced to land in Canada near the Gulf of St Lawrence, proceeding to New York on 15 May.

16 May. Carl Bachman. Monocoupe 90A. Gander, Newfoundland, to Stockholm. Bachman disappeared over the Atlantic.

20-21 May. Arthur La Porte & crew. Boeing 314 Yankee Clipper. New York to Marseille via the Azores & Lisbon. The first regular, scheduled, North Atlantic air mail service along the southern route.

28 May. Thomas H. Smith. Aeronca 65-C Chief *Baby Clipper*. Old Orchard, Maine, to London. Smith disappeared shortly after takeoff; the wreckage of his aircraft was discovered in August 1941, but Smith was never found.

24-28 June. Harold Gray & crew, plus 20 observers. Boeing 314 *Yankee Clipper*. Baltimore to Southampton via New York, Newfoundland, and Ireland. Opening of the northern mail route.

28-30 June. R. O. D. Sullivan, Blackmore, & crew with 22 passengers. Boeing 314 *Dixie Clipper*. New York to Southampton via the Azores, Lisbon, and Marseille. The first North Atlantic passenger service.

5-6 August. J. C. Kelly Rogers, S. G. Long, B. C. Frost, A. J. Coster, & C. E. Wilcockson. Short S.30C *Caribou*. Southampton to New York via Ireland, Labrador, and Montreal. The first S.30 to make the crossing, *Caribou* extended its range by refueling mid-air just west of Ireland. The return trip, without mid-air refueling, was made on 9-11 August. *Caribou* and sister ship *Cabot* made sixteen flights in this test program.

11 August. Alex Loeb & Richard Decker. Ryan Brougham Shalom. Cape Breton Island, Nova Scotia, to Palestine. The last trans-Atlantic flyers lost before World War II. •

Kingsford-Smith and the *Southern Cross*

In 1928, a Fokker trimotor named the *Southern Cross* became the first aircraft to cross the Pacific Ocean. Over the next few years, the aircraft and its pilot, Australian Charles Kingsford-Smith, would circle the globe, becoming the first aircraft to cross the equator in doing so. (Some would claim that Kingsford-Smith and the *Southern Cross* were first to circle the globe, since earlier world flights had only circled the Northern Hemisphere.)

The *Southern Cross* began life as two earlier Fokkers wrecked in Alaska during Hubert Wilkins' abortive 1926 Arctic survey. When accidents damaged the wing of the expedition's single-engined F.VII the *Alaskan* and the fuselage and landing gear of his trimotor F.VII-3M *Detroiter*, Wilkins returned to Washington state to repair and regroup. While the Boeing Company grafted the undamaged trimotor wing to the *Alaskan's* fuselage, Wilkins sold the aircraft to Charles Kingsford-Smith and Charles Ulm. The pair ordered the installation of more-powerful engines and additional fuel capacity, then attempted a world's unrefueled endurance record; their best flight, however, lasted just over 50 hours, a few hours short.

But 50 hours was enough for the longest leg of the pair's true goal, a trans-Pacific flight to Australia. The flight, which would be the longest yet attempted over water, would be attempted less than a year after nineteen aviators had died over the Atlantic, and seven more had died between the Hawaiian Islands and California.

Kingsford-Smith and Ulm rounded out

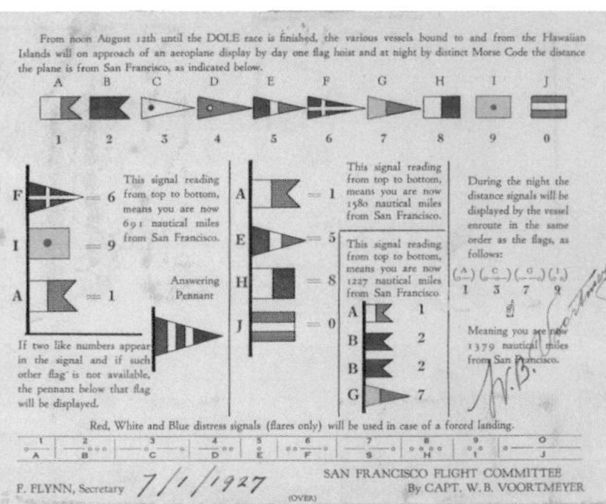

Although largely forgotten today, William B. Voortmeyer's code flag system allowed maritime navigators to relay information to passing aircraft. Contemporary radios were so heavy and unreliable that many aircraft elected to fly without them.

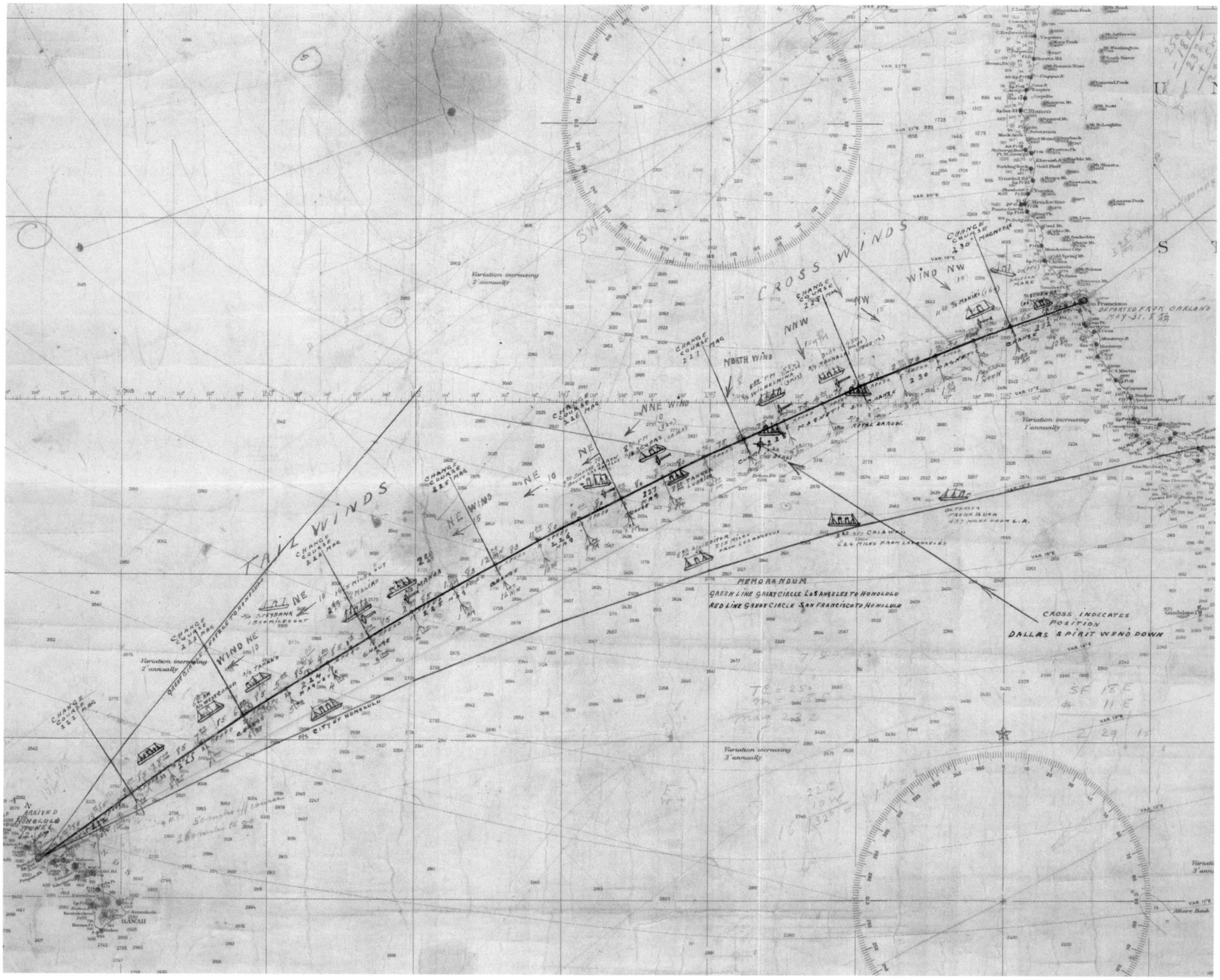

This maritime navigational map was prepared for the first leg of the *Southern Cross*' Pacific flight by William Voortmeyer, with additional inflight notations by navigator James Warner.

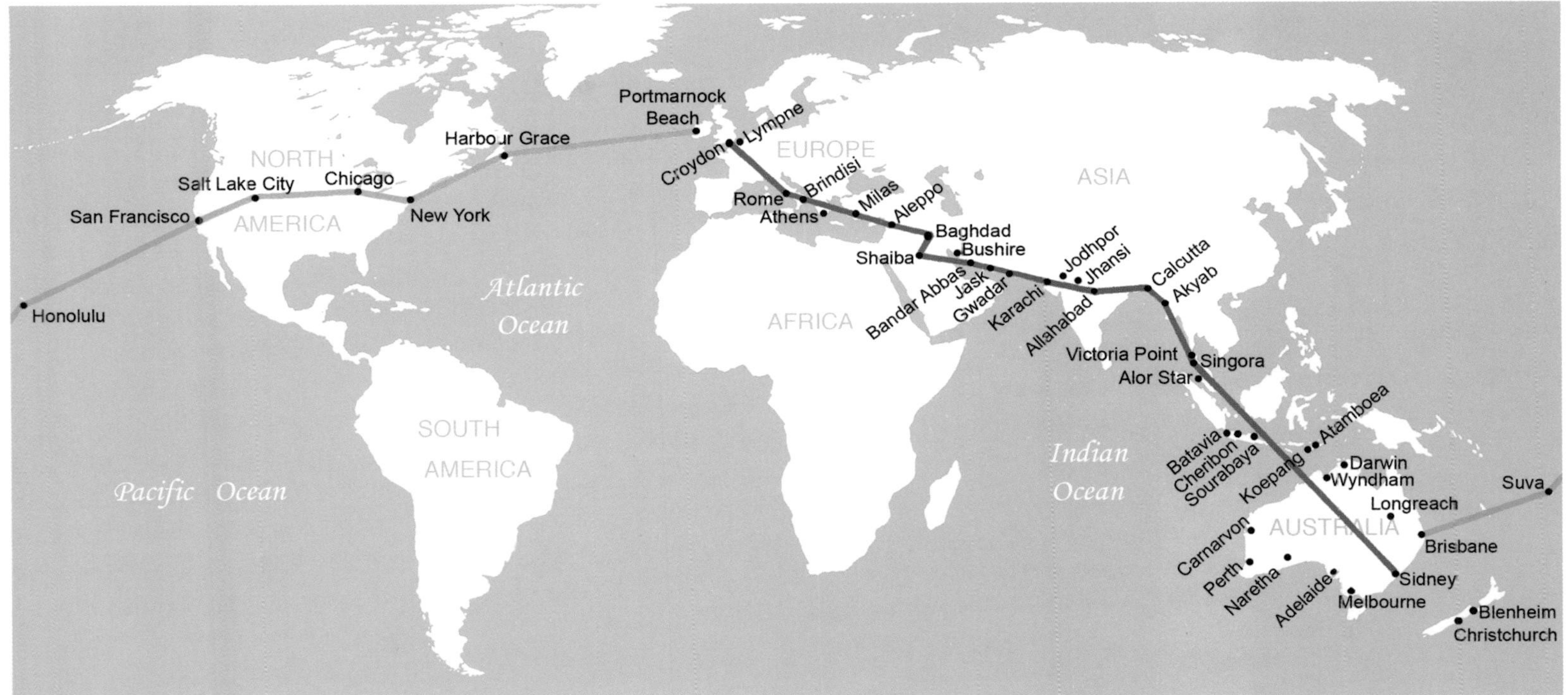

Over a period of two years, Charles Kingsford-Smith and the Southern Cross made a series of long range flights that resulted in the first circumnavigation of the globe to include equatorial crossings. The color-coded route on this map show (green) Oakland, California, to Brisbane, Australia, in May-June 1928; (blue) Sydney, Australia, to Croydon, UK, in June-July 1929; and (yellow) Portmarnock, Ireland, to San Francisco, California, in June-July 1930.

their flight crew with the addition of Harry Lyon as radio operator and James Warner as navigator. And just as critically, on the ground, they secured the support of William B. Voortmeyer. Voortmeyer, a master maritime navigator who had developed many early aerial navigation systems, had earlier assisted flyers in the 1927 Dole Race to Hawaii. For the *Southern Cross* he prepared maps along major shipping lanes. The map reproduced here shows Voortmeyer's instructions on magnetic declination and expected winds, as well as the all important positions of commercial shipping. The freighters and tankers provided hope of rescue should the Fokker be forced down, but also provided important navigational updates. Voortmeyer had enlisted the help of the ships' navigators, who used his system of signal flags and lights to advise any passing aircraft of the distance from San Francisco. Annotations above several of the ship names (SS *Makini*, 169; SS *Maunalai*, 450, etc) show Warner's inflight use of the data to verify his own computations.) One other cautionary note marked Voortmeyer's estimated position of the *Dallas Spirit*, lost with its crew attempting to return to the mainland following the Dole race.

The *Southern Cross* left Oakland at 8:52 am on 31 May 1928. By 11:30 the next morning, they were 260 miles from Honolulu and only 50 miles off course. They landed safely at 12:17. The map was sent to Voortmeyer with thanks for his help.

While Kingsford-Smith and crew rested, 1924-world-flyer Lowell Smith and a group of Army mechanics from Wheeler Field inspected and serviced the Fokker. The leg to Suva, Fiji, an incredible 3,200 miles, was started two days later and took 34-1/2 hours in the air. On 9 June, the Southern Cross completed the final leg to Brisbane, Australia. The total flying time from California was 83 hours, 38 minutes.

During the rest of 1928, Kingsford-Smith and the *Southern Cross* made numerous historic flight in the Antipodes. In June and July 1929, the Fokker set a new record flying between Sydney and the UK in 12 days and 18 hours. A long overhaul and reconditioning followed at the Dutch Fokker factory. In June 1930, Kingsford-Smith and crew flew to Newfoundland, then on to New York. Continuing to San Francisco, the *Southern Cross* landed on 4 July. Although the flight had taken just over 26 months, the *Southern Cross* and Charles Kingsford-Smith had circled the globe.

Kingsford-Smith died in November 1935 when his Lockheed Altair disappeared in the Gulf of Bengal. The *Southern Cross* did some barnstorming in Australia before retiring in 1935. Today the restored Fokker is displayed at Brisbane airport. •

Onlookers greet the *Southern Cross* and crew at Brisbane, following the first flight from the US to Australia.

Exploring with the Lindberghs

His 1927 flight from New York to Paris made Charles Lindbergh the world's most famous airman, a mantle the young aviator wore with little comfort. The parades, speeches, receptions, and banquets seemed less than a reward for one who preferred to spend his time flying. Soon after touring the US, Lindbergh began a series of exploratory flights around the Caribbean, northern South America, and Central America. Flying his Ryan monoplane the *Spirit of St Louis*, the Lone Eagle served as an American goodwill ambassador while exploring possible routes and facilities for Pan American Airways. But Lindbergh's most important discovery came at the beginning of the journey; visiting the American Ambassador in Mexico City, the airman met and fell in love with the ambassador's daughter in December 1927. Lindbergh and Anne Morrow would be married on 27 May 1929.

A year later, the newlyweds accepted the first Lockheed Sirius monoplane, which had been designed and built to Lindbergh's specifications. Charles and Anne Morrow Lindbergh then flew the aircraft from Lockheed's California factory to the East Coast, setting a new transcontinental speed record, a feat made more remarkable by the fact that Anne was seven months pregnant. The couple soon settled in with their new son while the Sirius was modified for an exploratory flight to the Far East. Between July and October 1931, the "First Couple of the Skies" examined the great circle route across Canada and Alaska to Japan and China for possible airline routes being considered by Pan American. When their Sirius was damaged before a flight from the Yangtze River, the couple and their crippled aircraft returned home by ship.

Following repairs and modifications, the Sirius was again prepared for a long flight, this time across the North Atlantic and Europe. Ostensibly planned for the development of civil air routes, the flight also offered a therapeutic escape for the couple, whose first-born had been kidnaped and murdered a year earlier. Leaving in July 1933, the Lindberghs flew up thorough Canada to Greenland, where the local children referred to their aircraft as *Tingmissartoq*, Innuit for "one who flies like a big bird;" the name seemed appropriate, and was soon painted on the Sirius' side.

The flight continued to the great cities of Europe as far east as Moscow, then south to the western coast of Africa, across the South Atlantic, north across South America, through the Caribbean, and home to New York - a trip covering 30,000 miles and visiting twenty-one countries.

The well-used first map (right) shows the Lone Eagle's 1927 route though the Caribbean and northern South America in the *Spirit of St Louis*. Lindbergh used the chart's blank spaces to record his impressions of his aircraft's performance and the fields visited.

The second map (below), a mariners' chart of the Davis Strait between Canada and Greenland, was used by the Lindberghs for their 1933 flight. Again, Charles made notes on the open areas of the folded chart. •

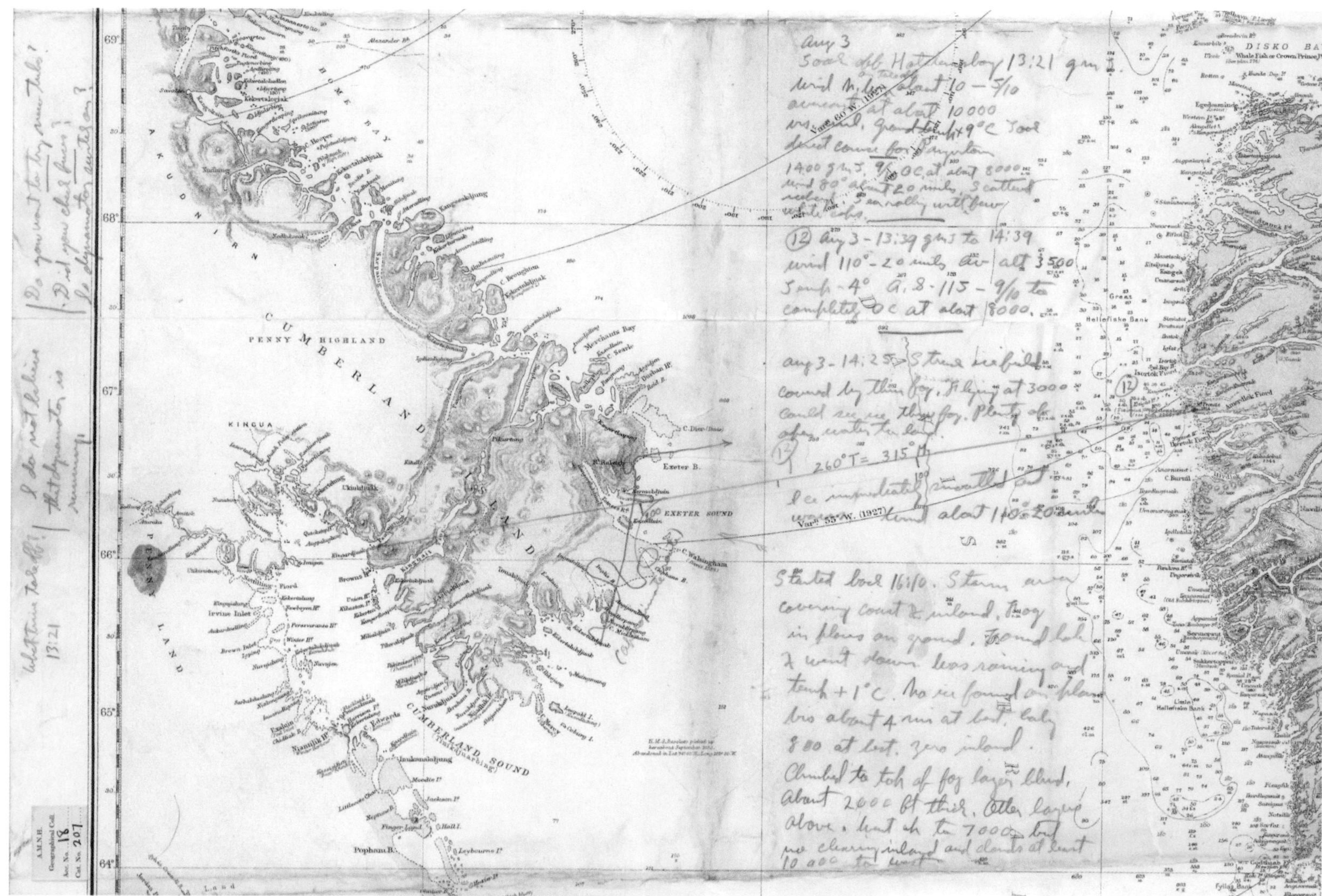

The Davis Strait proved a convenient place for Charles Lindbergh's observations on the 1933 Atlantic route exploration with wife Anne.

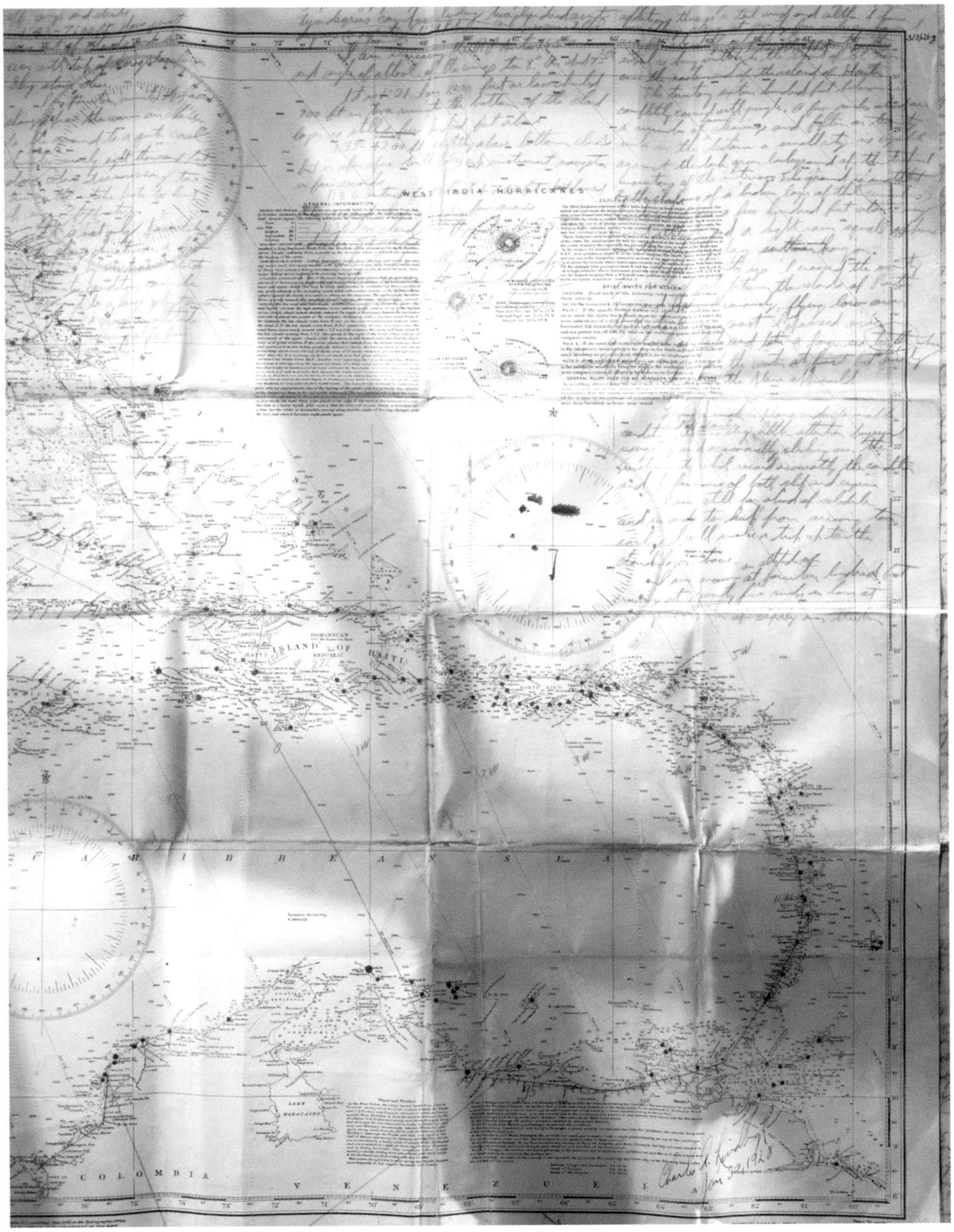

French naval personnel lower the *Tingmissartoq* into the River Seine following the 1933 visit to Paris. Charles Lindbergh stands at the wing root while two French sailors straddle the aft fuselage for added balance.

Anne Morrow Lindbergh became a full partner in the couple's explorations. She acted as copilot, navigator, and radio operator. She is seen here in the aft cockpit of the Sirius during the 1933 flights.

BELOW: Moored at Angmassalik, Greenland, the *Tingmissartoq* receives its nickname from the paintbrush of a local youth.

Pan American and the Great Flying Boats

Having completed his development of South American air routes, Juan Trippe turned his attentions to service across the Atlantic and Pacific oceans. Each project would present unique problems.

To reach the Far East, Trippe proposed to follow a great circle route through Alaska and the Aleutians. Attempts to negotiate stops in the Soviet Union came to naught; the Soviets, whose government was not yet recognized by the US, saw little advantage in supporting what some regarded as the American national air line.

Forced to fly directly across the Pacific, Pan American had no aircraft with the non-stop range, and no inter-route facilities capable of handling passengers and servicing aircraft. The solution was to build facilities on Hawaii, Midway, Wake, Guam, and the Philippines - a task often made more formidable by the lack of local resources and populations. Trippe dispatched the freighter *North Haven* west from San Francisco in March 1935. The ship included all the supplies, equipment, facilities, and personnel needed to prepare and maintain the new chain of facilities. The company stripped down one of its S-42s for a series of exploratory flights, which began a month later. April 1935 connected Alameda and Hawaii, June connected Honolulu to Midway, August established the route from Midway to Wake, and October flew on to Guam.

In the meantime, the first new Martin M-130 flying boat was being prepared for service. On 22 November 1935, the *China Clipper* made its first flight to the Philippines. (Despite the public perception that all Pan American flying boats were "China Clippers," only one airframe actually flew with that name.) The trip from San Francisco took just under sixty hours. After some political wrangling with the British government, Trippe was able to extend Pan American routes to Hong Kong and New Zealand in 1937.

By 1935, the challenges of Trans-Atlantic flight were more political than physical. Pan American's attempts to gain landing rights in the Azores and France met with years of delay. Germany pressured the Icelandic government to deny landing rights there, and other complications with the Danish government delayed approval of landing rights in Greenland.

In February 1937, the British government came to an agreement granting landing rights to Pan American in exchange for reciprocal rights for Imperial Airways. Similar agreements with France were delayed until 1939. On 20 May 1939, Boeing 314 *Yankee Clipper* began scheduled service on the southern route through the Azores. The same aircraft inaugurated service on the northern route a month later.

British and French aircraft were exploring their own routes through 1938 and 1939, but War intervened before service could be scheduled. •

Pan American's advertising maps emphasized the exotic destinations of the company's new trans-Pacific service.

Passengers board a Boeing 314. The Number 4 engine ran the flying boat's generators, providing electric power before the flight.

August 1938 saw the first of four experimental trans-Atlantic flights by Latécoère flying boats. *Lieutenant de Vaisseau Paris*, the sole Latécoère 521, made three of the flights. The start of World War II prevented the start of scheduled service.

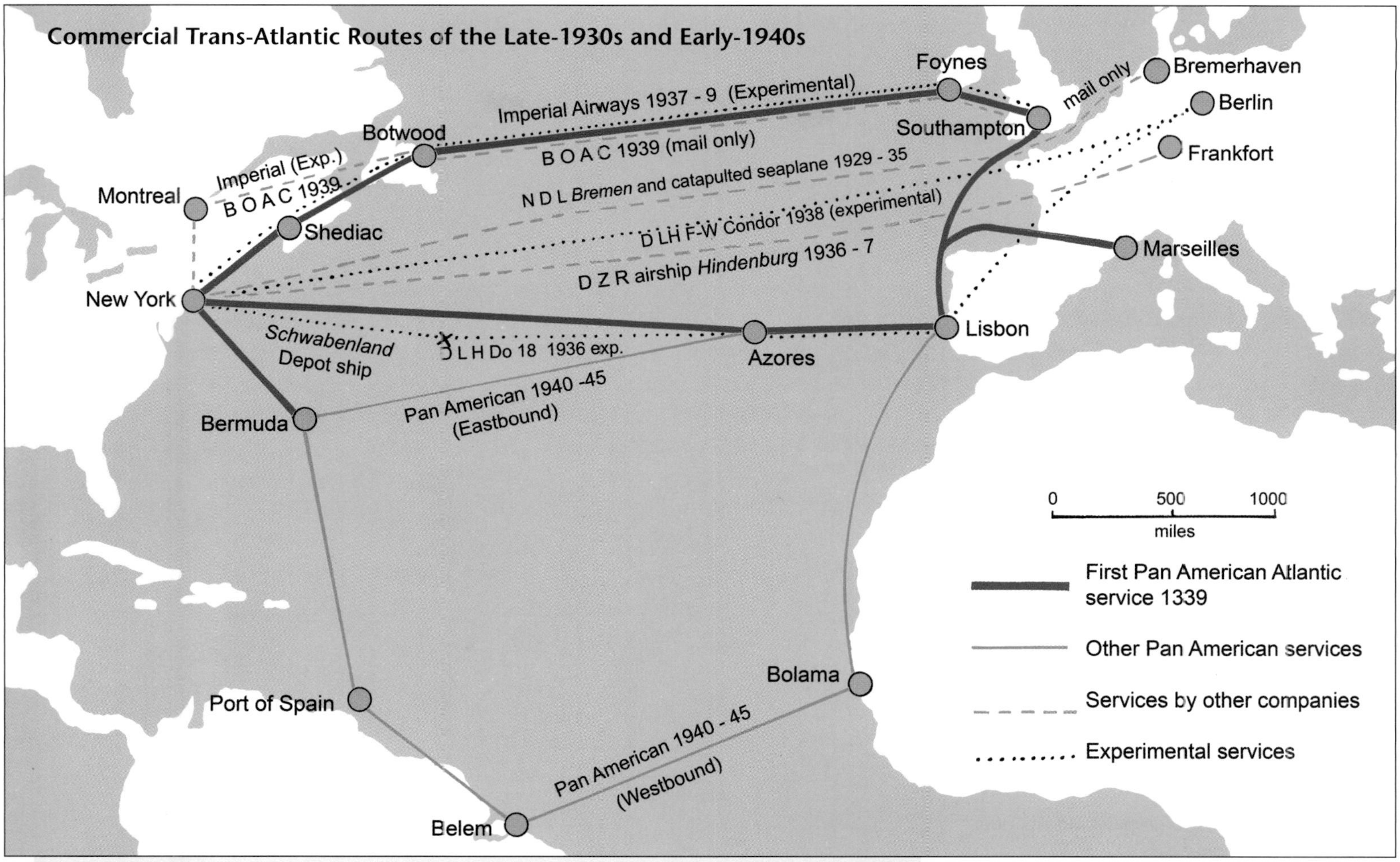

Commercial Trans-Atlantic Routes of the Late-1930s and Early-1940s

Foynes
Bremerhaven
mail only
Berlin
Imperial Airways 1937 - 9 (Experimental)
Southampton
Botwood
Frankfort
B O A C 1939 (mail only)
Imperial (Exp.)
N D L *Bremen* and catapulted seaplane 1929 - 35
Montreal
B O A C 1939
Shediac
D LH F-W Condor 1938 (experimental)
Marseilles
D Z R airship *Hindenburg* 1936 - 7
New York
Lisbon
Schwabenland Depot ship
D L H Do 18 1936 exp.
Azores
Pan American 1940 -45 (Eastbound)
Bermuda
0 500 1000 miles
First Pan American Atlantic service 1339
Other Pan American services
Services by other companies
Experimental services
Bolama
Port of Spain
Pan American 1940 - 45 (Westbound)
Belem

With the arrival of its first S-40 flying boat in 1930, Pan American began the practice of naming its aircraft Clippers. The company's fleet of giant, luxurious flying boats represented the epitome of international travel in the 1930s, a reputation built by only 25 aircraft (one of which never entered service).

TYPE	REGISTRATION	NAME
Sikorsky S-40	NC80V	*American Clipper*
Sikorsky S-40	NC81V	*Caribbean Clipper*
Sikorsky S-40	NC752V	*Southern Clipper*
Sikorsky S-42	NC822M	*Brazilian Clipper;* later *Colombia Clipper*
Sikorsky S-42	NR823M	*West Indies Clipper,* later *Pan American Clipper,* later *Hong Kong Clipper*
Sikorsky S-42	NR823M	unchristened, crashed in Trinidad, Dec 1935
Sikorsky S-42A	NC15373	*Jamaica Clipper*
Sikorsky S-42A	NC15374	*Antilles Clipper*
Sikorsky S-42A	NC15375	*Brazilian Clipper,* later *Colombian Clipper*
Sikorsky S-42A	NC15376	*Dominican Clipper*
Sikorsky S-42B	NC16734	*Pan American Clipper II,* later *Samoan Clipper*
Sikorsky S-42B	NC16735	*Bermuda Clipper,* later *Alaska Clipper,* later *Hong Kong Clipper II*
Sikorsky S-42B	NC16736	*Pan American Clipper III,* later *Bermuda Clipper*
Martin M-130	NC14714	*Hawaiian Clipper (Hawaii Clipper)*
Martin M-130	NC14715	*Philippine Clipper*
Martin M-130	NC14716	*China Clipper*
Boeing 314	NC18601	*Honolulu Clipper*
Boeing 314	NC18602	*California Clipper*
Boeing 314	NC18603	*Yankee Clipper*
Boeing 314	NC18604	*Atlantic Clipper*
Boeing 314	NC18605	*Dixie Clipper*
Boeing 314	NC18606	*American Clipper*
Boeing 314A	NC18609	*Pacific Clipper*
Boeing 314A	NC18611	*Anzac Clipper*
Boeing 314A	NC18612	*Capetown Clipper*

The prototype Boeing 314 floats near the factory a week after it's first flight in June 1938. Later named *Honolulu Clipper,* the aircraft entered service with Pan American in May 1939.

Between April and October 1935, this stripped S-42 made four Pacific survey flights for Pan American. Regular service to the Philippines began in November.

The 1924 Round the World Flight

Although no prize was offered for the first flight around the world, the prestige to be earned by such an accomplishment encouraged attempts by several nations, companies, and individuals.

The US Army Air Service was first around, partially due to the quality of its aircraft and aviators, but also due to the intricate planning, maintenance system, and supply line established

WHEELED LANDING GEAR

FLOATS/PONTOONS

CRASH OR FORCED LANDING

LEG 1: Seattle, Washington, to Prince Rupert, B.C., Canada (650 miles). Depart: April 6, 1924; Flight Time: 8 hrs, 10 min

LEG 2: Prince Rupert to Sitka, Alaska (282 miles). Depart: April 10, 1924; Flight Time: 4 hrs, 26 min

LEG 3: Sitka, Alaska, to Seward, Alaska (625 miles). Depart: April 13, 1924; Flight Time: 7 hrs, 44 min

LEG 4: Seward, Alaska, to Chignik, Alaska (425 miles) . Depart: April 15, 1924; Flight Time: 6 hrs, 38 min

LEG 5: Chignik, Alaska, to Dutch Harbor, Unalaska, Alaska (390 miles). Depart: April 19, 1924; Flight Time: 7 hrs 26 min

LEG 6: Dutch Harbor, Unalaska, Alaska, to Nazan, Atka, Aleutian Islands (365 miles). Depart: May 3, 1924; Flight Time: 4 hrs, 19 min

LEG 7: Nazan, Atka, Aleutian Islands, to Chichagof, Attu, Aleutian Islands (555 miles). Depart: May 9, 1924; Flight Time: 7 hrs 52 min

LEG 8: Chichagof, Attu, Aleutian Islands, to Komandorskiye Island, USSR (350 miles). Depart: May 15, 1924; Flight Time: 5 hrs 25 min

LEG 9: Komandorskiye Island, USSR, to Paramushiru, Kurile Islands, Japan (585 miles). Depart: May 17, 1924; Flight Time: 6 hr, 55 min

LEG 10: Paramushiru, Kurile Islands, to Hitokappu, Yetorofu, Kurile Islands (595 Miles). Depart: May 19, 1924; Flight Time: 7 hrs, 20 min

LEG 11: Hitokappu, Yetorofu, Kurile Islands, to Minato, Japan (485 miles). Depart: May 22, 1924; Flight Time: 5 hrs, 5 min

LEG 12: Minato, Japan, to Kasumigaura, Japan (350 miles). Depart: May 22, 1924; Flight Time: 4 hrs, 55 min

LEG 13: Kasumigaura, Japan, to Kushimoto, Japan (305 miles). Depart: Jun 1, 1924; Flight Time: 4 hrs, 35 min

LEG 14: Kushimoto, Japan, to Kagoshima, Japan (360 miles). Depart: June 2, 1924; Flight Time: 6 hrs, 11 min

LEG 15: Kagoshima, Japan, to Shanghai, China (550 miles). Depart: June 4, 1924; Flight Time 9 hrs, 10 min

LEG 16: Shanghai, China, to Tchinkoen Bay, China (350 miles). Depart: June 7, 1924; Flight Time: 4 hrs, 30 min

LEG 17: Tchinkoen Bay, China, to Amoy, China (250 miles). Depart: June 7, 1924; Flight Time: 2 hrs, 47 min

LEG 18: Amoy, China, to Hong Kong, China (310 miles). Depart: June 8, 1924; Flight Time 3 hrs, 24 min

LEG 19: Hong Kong, China, to Haiphong, French Indo-China (495 miles). Depart: June 10, 1924; Flight Time: 7 hrs, 26 min

LEG 20: Haiphong, French Indo-China, to Tourane, French Indo-China (410 miles). Depart: June 11, 1924; Flight Time: 5 hrs, 5 min

LEG 21: Tourane, French Indo-China to Saigon, French Indo-China (540 miles). Depart: June 16, 1924; Flight Time: 7 hrs, 38 min

LEG 22: Saigon, French Indo-China, to Kampong Saom Bay, French Indo-China (295 miles). Depart: June 18, 1924; Flight Time: 4 hrs, 28 min

LEG 23: Kampong Saom Bay, French Indo-China, to Bangkok, Siam (290 miles). Depart: June 18, 1924; Flight Time: 4 hrs, 2 min

LEG 24: Bangkok, Siam, to Tavoy, Burma (200 miles). Depart: June 20, 1924; Flight Time: 3 hrs, 55min

LEG 25: Tavoy, Burma, to Rangoon, Burma (295 miles). Depart: June 20, 1924; Flight Time: 2 hrs, 8 min

LEG 26: Rangoon, Burma, to Akyab, Burma (430 miles). Depart: June 25, 1924; Flight Time: 5 hrs, 38 min

LEG 27: Akyab, Burma, to Chittagong, Burma (180 miles). Depart: June 26, 1924; Flight Time: 2 hrs, 10 min

LEG 28: Chittagong, Burma, to Calcutta, India (265 miles). Depart: June 26, 1924; Flight Time: 3 hrs, 17 min

LEG 29: Calcutta, India, to Allahabad, India (450 miles). Depart: July 1, 1924; Flight Time: 6 hrs, 30 min

LEG 30: Allahabad, India, to Ambala, India (480 miles). Depart: July 2, 1924; Flight Time: 6 hrs, 25 min

LEG 31: Ambala, India, to Multan, India (360 miles). Depart: July 3, 1924; Flight Time: 5 hrs, 45 min

LEG 32: Multan, India, to Karachi, India (455 miles). Depart: July 4, 1924; Flight Time: 7 hrs, 8 min

LEG 33: Karachi, India, to Chahbar, Persia (410 miles). Depart: July 7, 1924; Flight Time: 4 hrs, 50 min

LEG 34: Chahbar, Persia, to Bandar Abbas, Persia (365 miles). Depart: July 7, 1924; Flight Time: 4 hrs, 5 min

LEG 35: Bandar Abbas, Persia to Bushire, Persia (390 miles). Depart: July 8, 1924; Flight Time: 4 hrs, 5 min

LEG 36: Bushire, Persia, to Bagdad, Mesopotamia (530 miles). Depart: July 8, 1924; Flight Time 6 hrs, 30 min

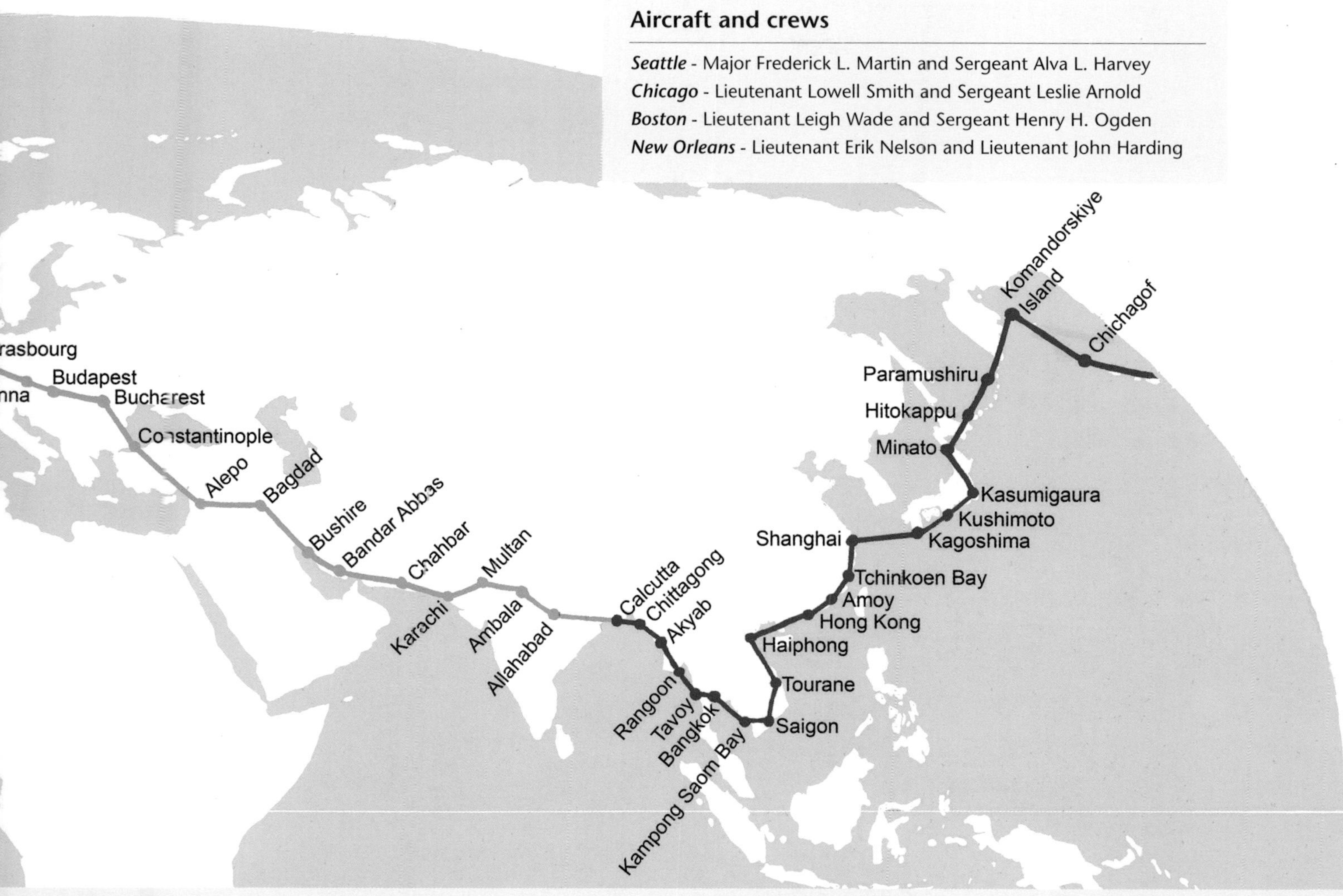

Aircraft and crews

Seattle - Major Frederick L. Martin and Sergeant Alva L. Harvey
Chicago - Lieutenant Lowell Smith and Sergeant Leslie Arnold
Boston - Lieutenant Leigh Wade and Sergeant Henry H. Ogden
New Orleans - Lieutenant Erik Nelson and Lieutenant John Harding

LEG 37: Bagdad, Mesopotamia, to Aleppo, Syria (450 miles). Depart: July 8, 1924; Flight Time: 6 hrs, 10 min

LEG 38: Aleppo, Syria, to Constantinople, Turkey (560 miles). Depart: July 10, 1924; Flight Time: 7 hrs, 38 min

LEG 39: Constantinople, Turkey, to Bucharest, Rumania (350 miles). Depart: July 12, 1924; Flight Time: 4 hrs, 40 min

LEG 40: Bucharest, Rumania, to Budapest, Hungary (465 miles). Depart: July 13, 1924; Flight Time: 6 hrs, 50 min

LEG 41: Budapest, Hungary, to Vienna, Austria (113 Miles). Depart: July 13, 1924; Flight Time: 2 hrs

LEG 42: Vienna, Austria, to Strasbourg, France (500 miles). Depart: July 14, 1924; Flight Time: 6 hrs, 30 min

LEG 43: Strasbourg, France, to Paris, France (250 miles). Depart: July 14, 1924; Flight Time: 3 hrs, 55 min

LEG 44: Paris, France, to London, England (215 miles). Depart: July 16, 1924; Flight Time: 3 hrs, 7 min

LEG 45: London, England, to Brough, England (165 miles). Depart: July 17, 1924; Flight Time: 1 hr, 55 min

LEG 46: Brough, England, to Kirkwall, Orkney Islands (450 miles). Depart: July 30, 1924; Flight Time: 5 hrs, 30 min

LEG 47: Kirkwall, Orkney Islands, to Horna Fjord, Iceland (555 miles). *Chicago* Depart: August 2, 1924; Flight Time: 6 hrs, 13 min. *New Orleans* Depart: August 3, 1924; Flight Time: 9 hrs, 3 min

LEG 48: Horna Fjord, Iceland to Reykjavik, Iceland (290 miles). Depart: August 5, 1924; Flight Time: 5 hrs, 3 min

LEG 50: Reykjavik, Iceland, to Fredricksdal, Greenland (830 miles. *Chicago* Depart: August 21, 1924; Flight Time: 10 hrs, 40 min. *New Orleans* Depart : August 21, 1924; Flight Time: 11 hrs, 17 min

LEG 51: Fredricksdal, Greenland, to Ivigtut, Greenland (165 miles). Depart: August 24, 1924; Flight Time: 2 hrs, 12 min

LEG 52: Ivigtut, Greenland, to Icy Tickle, Labrador (560 miles). Depart: August 31, 1924; Flight Time: 6 hrs, 55 min

LEG 53: Icy Tickle, Labrador, to Hawke Harbour, Newfoundland (315 miles). Depart: September 2, 1924; Flight Time: 4 hrs, 56 min

LEG 54: Hawke Harbour, Newfoundland, to Pictou Harbor, Nova Scotia (430 miles). Depart: September 3, 1924; Flight Time: 6 hrs, 34 min

LEG 55: Pictou Harbor, Nova Scotia, to Mere Point, Maine (450 miles). Depart: September 5, 1924; Flight Time: 6 hrs, 5 min

LEG 56: Mere Point, Maine, to Boston, Massachusetts (100 miles). Depart: September 6, 1924; Flight Time: 2 hrs, 8 min

LEG 57: Boston, Massachusetts, to New York, New York (220, miles). Depart: September 8, 1924; Flight Time: 3 hrs, 40 min

LEG 58: New York, New York, to Aberdeen, Maryland (160 miles). Depart: September 9, 1924; Flight Time: 3 hrs, 38 min

LEG 59: Aberdeen, Maryland, to Washington, D.C. (70 miles). Depart: September 9, 1924; Flight Time: 1 hr, 25 min

LEG 60: Washington, D.C. to Dayton, Ohio (400 miles). Depart: September 13, 1924; Flight Time: 6 hrs, 43 min

LEG 61: Dayton, Ohio, to Chicago, Illinois (245 miles). Depart: September 15, 1924; Flight Time: 2 hrs, 58 min

LEG 62: Chicago, Illinois, to Omaha, Nebraska (430 miles). Depart: September 16, 1924; Flight Time: 4 hrs 48 min

LEG 63: Omaha, Nebraska, to St. Joseph, Missouri (110 miles. Depart: September 18, 1924; Flight Time: 1 hr 48 min

LEG 64: St. Joseph, Missouri, to Muskogee, Oklahoma (270 miles). Depart: September 18, 1924; Flight Time: 3 hrs 53 mln

LEG 65: Muskogee, Oklahoma, to Dallas, Texas (245 miles. Depart: September 19, 1924; Flight Time: 3 hrs 45 min

LEG 66: Dallas, Texas, to Sweetwater, Texas (210 miles). Depart: September 20, 1924; Flight Time: 3 hrs, 6 min

LEG 67: Sweetwater, Texas, to El Paso, Texas (390 miles). Depart: September 20, 1924; Flight Time: 6 hrs 18 min

LEG 68: El Paso, Texas, to Tucson, Arizona (230 miles). Depart: September 21, 1924; Flight Time: 3 hrs, 23 min

LEG 69: Tucson, Arizona, to San Diego, California (390 miles). Depart: September 22, 1924; Flight Time: 4 hrs, 3 min

LEG 70: San Diego, California, to Los Angeles, California (115 miles). Depart: September 23, 1924; Flight Time: 1 hr 25 min

LEG 71: Los Angeles, California, to San Francisco, California (265 miles). Depart: September 25, 1924; Flight Time: 5 hrs 5 min

LEG 72: San Francisco, California, to Eugene, Oregon (420 miles). Depart: September 27, 1924; Flight Time: 5 hrs, 20 min

LEG 73: Eugene, Oregon, to Vancouver Barracks, Washington (90 miles). Depart: September 28, 1924; Flight Time: 1 hr 8 min

LEG 74: Vancouver Barracks, Washington, to Seattle, Washington (150 miles). Depart: September 28, 1924; Flight Time: 1 hr, 43 min

TOTAL MILEAGE:
28,000 miles

TOTAL FLYING TIME:
371 hrs 11 min

Beached at Dutch Harbor, the crews of the three remaining World Cruisers received word that their commander and his observer had survived the crash of *Seattle*.

for this single mission. Although World War I had made America a world power, in 1924 there were few US overseas facilities. All supplies, equipment, and support personnel needed to be available when the flyers arrived at a stop - and in most cases the system worked.

For the flight - officially called the "Round the World Flight" - the Douglas Aircraft Company designed and built five single-engined DWC (Douglas World Cruiser) biplanes. A prototype was tested at Wright Field to establish range and fuel consumption charts and maintenance requirements; the remaining four aircraft were prepared for the mission. Depending on the next destination, each aircraft could be mounted on floats or wheeled landing gear (and the appropriate replacements were also sent to the preestablished landing sites).

The four mission aircraft (named *Boston*, *Seattle*, *New Orleans*, and *Chicago*) left Seattle, Washington, for Prince Rupert, British Columbia, on 6 April 1924. The map on page 105 shows one example of the navigation aids prepared for the airmen - a large scale map of the Prince Rupert area was marked to show landmarks, landing zones, and even the local hotels. Glued to the bottom of the map were photos and post cards detailing important geographical features and structures. In the days when most navigation was visual, and most aviation maps were rudimentary or non-existent, these hand-made nav-aids would prove critical to the flight's success.

The aviators, support staffs, and local firms and individuals would assist with a number of minor difficulties even before the flight started, but the first major problem came on 15 April,

Saigon was a port city in French Indo-China when the World Cruisers visited. Later the capitol of South Vietnam, Saigon is now called Ho Chi Minh City.

When dockside facilities were unavailable, the DWCs were serviced at harbor moorings.

the fourth leg of the flight. As the four aircraft battled strong headwinds between Seward and Chignik, Alaska, *Seattle* dropped behind and eventually disappeared. The aircraft crashed into a mountain, but ten days later its crew - mission commander Major Frederick L. Martin and Sergeant Alva L. Harvey - walked out of a blizzard to reach civilization.

Poor relations with the Soviet government meant that the American flyers were not allowed to stop anywhere in Russia. However, the leg between Chicagoff in the Aleutian Islands and Paramushiru, Japan, included a peaceful layover near Komandorskiye Island. Civility was the order of the day, while local officials telegraphed Moscow for further instructions; the next morning word came that the Americans should continue on their way. Just how sly the two governments had been is unclear - both could deny having cooperated with the other; but maps prepared before the flight began included a stop at Komandorskiye Island.

The flight continued with each leg offering new adventures, celebrations, and diplomatic contacts. The three aircraft continued together whenever possible, regrouping after each separation until the 47th leg between the Orkney Islands and Iceland. With a sudden drop in oil pressure, *Boston* was forced down in heavy seas. *Chicago* circled to evaluate the situation, then dropped one message at the telegraph station on Suduroy Island, with a second later dropped to an American destroyer. After drifting for several hours, Lt Leigh Wade and Sergeant Henry H. Ogden were rescued by the cruiser *Richmond*, but *Boston* was lost.

The Army quickly named the prototype DWC *Boston II* and shipped it to Nova Scotia, where Wade and Ogden were able to rejoin their comrades for the final legs of the flight. On 28 September 1924, the three aircraft arrived back in Seattle having covered some 28,000 miles in five and a half months. •

The World Cruisers first switched to conventional landing gear in Calcutta prior to arriving here in Allahabad. The aircrew, who had borrowed British uniform shorts to better deal with the heat, landed with sunburned knees!

USS *Richmond* attempts to recover the *Boston* in mid-Atlantic. The aircraft, further damaged by a breaking crane, sank while being towed by the cruiser.

Floats attached for over-water flight, *Chicago* heads out from Seattle on the first leg.

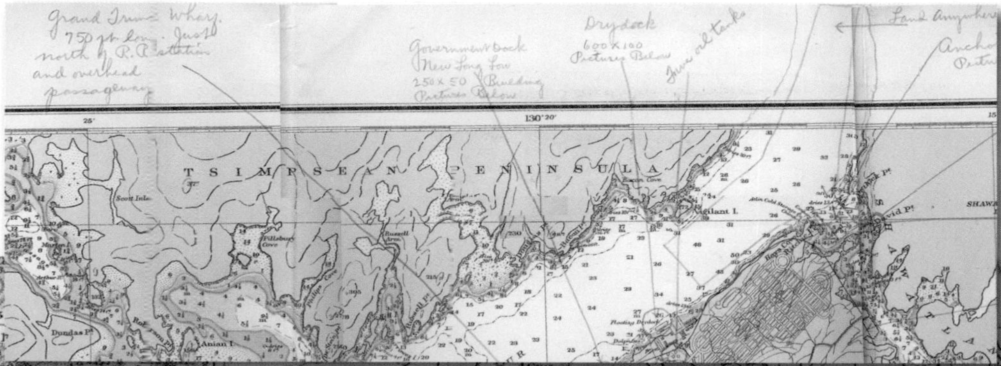

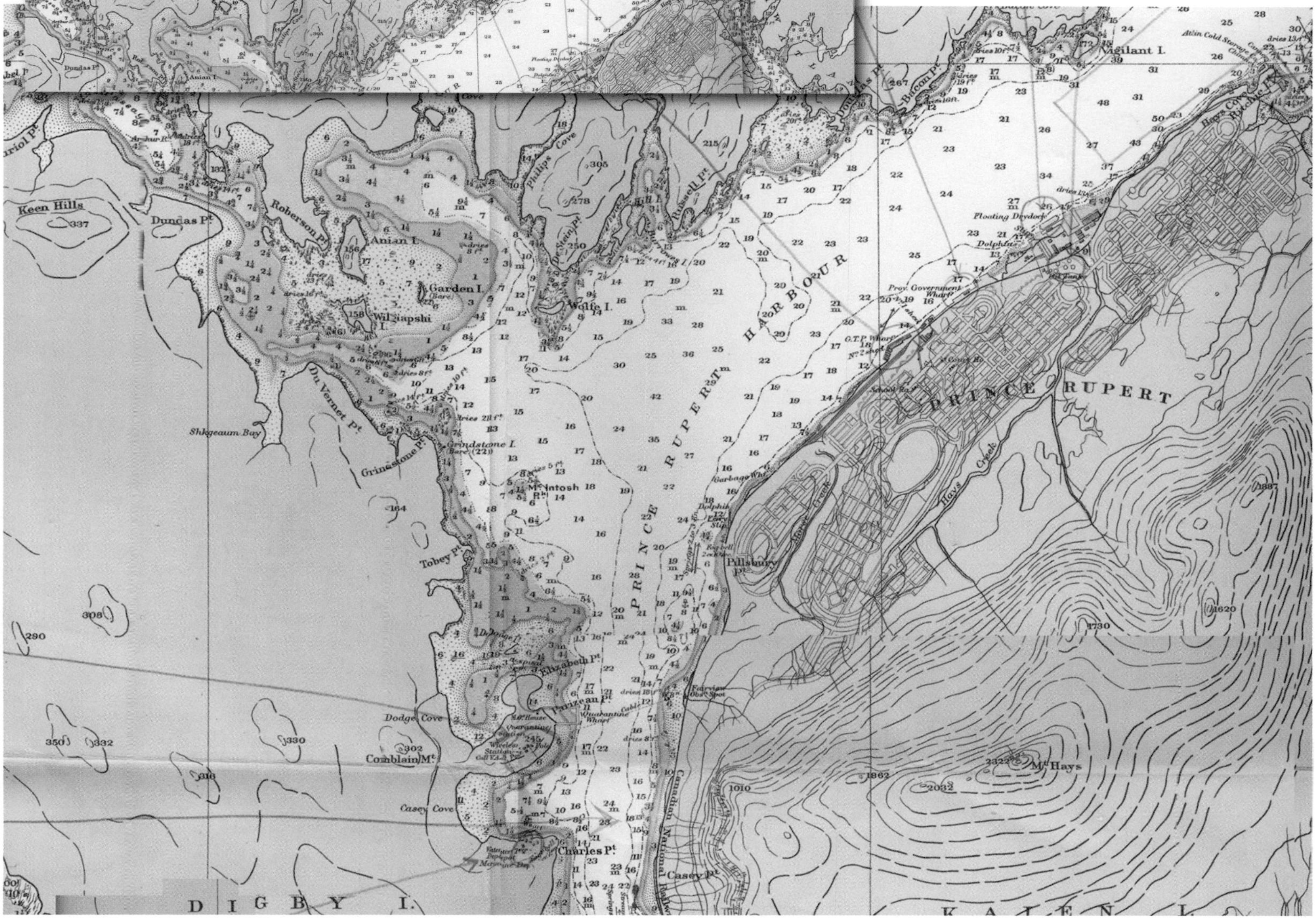

Planning the route for the Round the World Flight, US organizers visited each projected stop, determined what facilities were available or needed, and annotated the best local maps with details helpful to the aircrews.

Circumnavigation Record Flights

The US Army's 1924 Round the World Flight proved as much a success of logistical planning as aerial navigation. But as many would later note, since the World Cruisers never crossed the equator, their flight was technically a circumnavigation of the Northern Hemisphere. In fact, due to the additional hazards with flights to South America, Africa, or Australia, few Golden Age around-the-world flights would include equatorial crossings. The around the world journey of the *Southern Cross* (see page 96) was the first true circumnavigation of the globe, though the two years needed to complete the journey left room for many later aviators to improve the record.

With few prizes or commercial advantages associated with world flights, few aviators would risk the dangers. Here are some who found glory in the attempt. •

Following his third trans-Atlantic flight to America, Wolfgang von Gronau and crew continued on to circle the Northern Hemisphere in their Dornier Wal *Groenlandwal*. The flight lasted from 22 July through 9 November 1932. Here, the *Groenlandwal* approaches Manila in September 1932.

Leaving Lakehurst, New Jersey, on 8 August 1929, the *Graf Zeppelin* flew westward in the first global tour to carry passengers. The German dirigible returned to its starting point on 29 August.

BELOW: Howard Hughes' Lockheed 14 *New York World's Fair, 1939,* circled the globe in a record 91 hours, halving Wiley Post's record. The crew of five left New York on 10 July 1938, returning on the 14th.

Amelia Earhart - the first woman to cross the Atlantic and the first woman pilot to solo the Atlantic - made two attempts at becoming the first woman to circle the globe. On the first attempt, she flew her Lockheed Electra from Oakland, California, to Hawaii on 17-18 March 1937. Two days later, she damaged the aircraft attempting to take off for Howland Island. The second attempt left Miami on 2 June 1937, heading east. Earhart and navigator Fred Noonan disappeared over the Pacific, searching for tiny Howland Island, on 2 July.

Dieudonné Costes and Joseph Le Brix left Paris on 10 October 1927, flying to South America via Brazil. Swinging north to tour the USA, they and their Breguet then traveled by ship from San Francisco to Tokyo, completing - in several stages - the return flight to Paris on 14 April 1928.

The Clyde Pangborn and Hugh Herndon world flight in the Bellanca *Miss Veedol* left New York on 30 June 1931. They would end their association after landing in Seattle on 2 October. Although they did not circumnavigate, the managed to complete the first non-stop flight from Tokyo to North America.

The Pan American Goodwill Flight

The US Army's Pan American Flight was conceived in 1925 as a means of improving relations with the USA's southern neighbors. Other goals, as approved on 24 August, included evaluating and promoting potential airline routes, training pilots in long distance navigation, and evaluating the potentials of the new Loening OA-1A amphibian.

First of those OA-1As left the factory in 13 November 1926. Capt. C. E. Woolsey, the flight's engineering officer, quickly evaluated the dog ship (as prototypes were described in those days), then instituted a series of modifications in that aircraft and the five mission aircraft. Woolsey also removed all military equipment, including cameras, to avoid any suspicions that the Americans had come as spies. (Since the flyers carried no camera equipment of their own, all photos of the flight were supplied by local sources.)

Major Herbert A. Dargue, commander of the flight, had his nine pilots trained and organized by 16 December, as scheduled, only to learn that fuel supplies had not yet arrived at the initial destinations. Five days later, the fuel was in place, but weather delayed the takeoff until 21 December.

Despite the assistance of local civilians and the Brazilian military, the three remaining Loenings were unable to taxi up onto the soft sands at Victoria, Brazil.

U. S. ARMY
PAN-AMERICAN FLIGHT

Following an informal Air Corps practice, each aircraft was named for an American city. Dargue flew *New York*, followed by *San Antonio*, *San Francisco*, *Detroit*, and *St. Louis*. At France Field, in the Canal Zone, *New York* and *San Antonio* suffered hull damage in rough landings. Both aircraft would be left behind - *New York* for quick repairs, *San Antonio* for a more thorough rebuild. The remaining three aircraft proceeded with the planned mission to Colombia. In late January, they returned to France Field, where *New York* was once again ready and the dog ship had arrived to become the new *San Antonio*.

A flight of five once more, the amphibians left for Columbia, only to have the dog ship grounded for a new engine on 1 February. It would be the last time all five aircraft flew together. *New York*, *San Francisco*, *Detroit*, and *St. Louis* continued their tour down South America's west coast, crossing the Andes in southern Chile, then turning north along the Argentine coast. At Buenos Aires, *New York* and *Detroit* collided and crashed to the ground. Major Dargue and Lieutenant Whitehead parachuted to safety, but Captain Woolsley and Lieutenant Benton were killed.

The original *San Antonio* was by this time repaired and waiting in Panama; lieutenants Weddington and Whitehead were directed to find their way there by boat and rail, collect the repaired aircraft, and rejoin the flight in Venezuela. Meanwhile, the second *San Antonio* (the former dog ship) had been fitted with a replacement engine and was racing down the coast of Chile and across the Andes, rejoining the others at Montevideo, Uruguay, on 6 March.

The flyer found friendly receptions at most stops, but they encountered strong anti-American sentiment in many places. The arrival of the Marques of Pinedo in his Savoia-Marchetti on 24 February (see page 88) stole much of the Americans' thunder. One local newspaper devoted half of its sixteen pages to Pinedo, hiding word of the Pan-American flight among the remaining news stories. Pinedo, who had planned a more southerly tour, craftily turned north, arriving in Para, Brazil, within a half hour of the Americans. The planned reception for the Americans became a joint reception for all of the flyers. (Over dinner, Pineda casually informed Dargue that all his flight plans were telegraphed in from Rome.)

Original Aircraft and Crew Assignments of the 1926/27 Pan-American Flight

1. *New York* - Maj Herbert Dargue, 1Lt Ennis Whitehead
2. *San Antonio* - Capt Arthur McDaniel 1Lt. Charles Robinson
3. *San Francisco* - Capt Ira Eaker, 1Lt Muir Fairchild
4. *Detroit* - Capt Clinton Woolsey, 1Lt John Benton
5. *St. Louis* - 1Lt Bernard Thompson, 1Lt Leonard Weddington

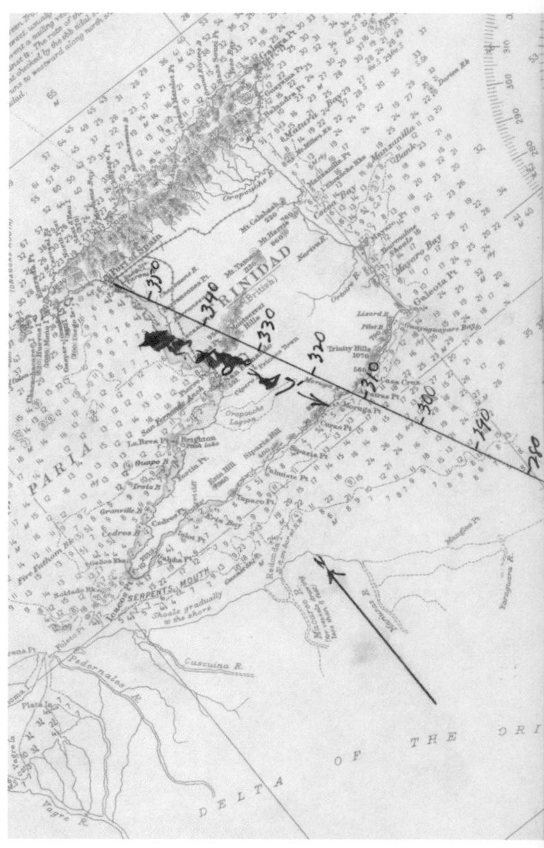

The Americans would end their journey in Washington on 2 May 1927. The ten pilots (including Woolsley and Benton) would be among the first recipients of the new Distinguished Flying Cross, and would later be awarded the Mackay Trophy for their phenomenal 133-day flight covering more than 22,000 miles. The eight surviving officers would continue to distinguish themselves in their military careers, but the Pan-American Flight's time in the public spotlight would be brief: less than three weeks after the mission returned to Washington, Charles Lindbergh would capture the world's attention with his solo flight to Paris.

Maps for the Pan-American Flight came from two sources. For general planning, the best maps available were the National Geographic Society's "Countries of the Caribbean" and "South America" - the same maps tucked into the magazine for all Society members. With no sectional aerial maps of the regions, hydrographic charts were trimmed,

glued together, and mounted on linen for in-flight use. Routes were plotted in Texas, and twelve sets of each map produced - one for each pilot, one for the advance officers at each stop, and one for the permanent file.

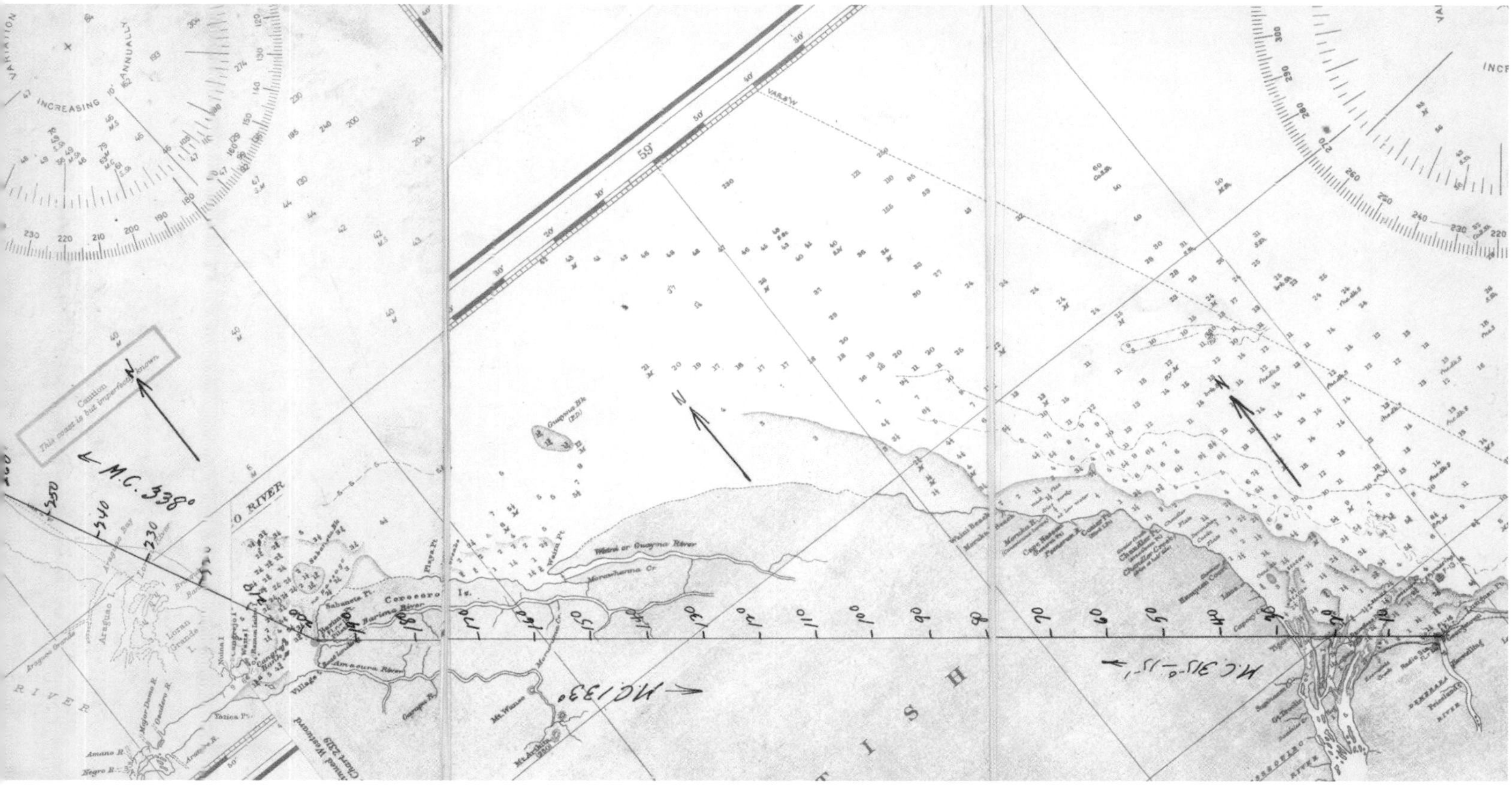

The map shown here was used by Major Dargue to navigate from Georgetown, British Guiana, to the major supply base at Port of Spain, Trinidad. Dargue made particular mention of this section of the route map, particularly the yellow-bordered warning, "Caution - This coast is but imperfectly known." The crossing of the Orinoco Delta took two hours, amazing the aviators who had already circumnavigated a continent. The maps made little note of the tidal flats at Port of Spain, where the three aircraft would find themselves stuck in the mud as they attempted to taxi to shore. Eventually freed, *San Antonio*, *San Francisco*, and *St. Louis* doubled back to Puerto Cabello, Venezuela, two days later, joining up with the original *San Antonio*, now rechristened *New York*, which Whitehead and Weddington delivered from Panama. •

ABOVE: With the damaged *New York* and *San Antonio* left at France Field, the Canal Zone, *San Francisco*, *Detroit*, and *St. Louis* proceeded on to Colombia.

LEFT: Captain Ira Eaker, second in command of the Pan-American Flight, was also responsible for press and public relations. He was photographed with *San Francisco* before the flight began.

Pan American to South America

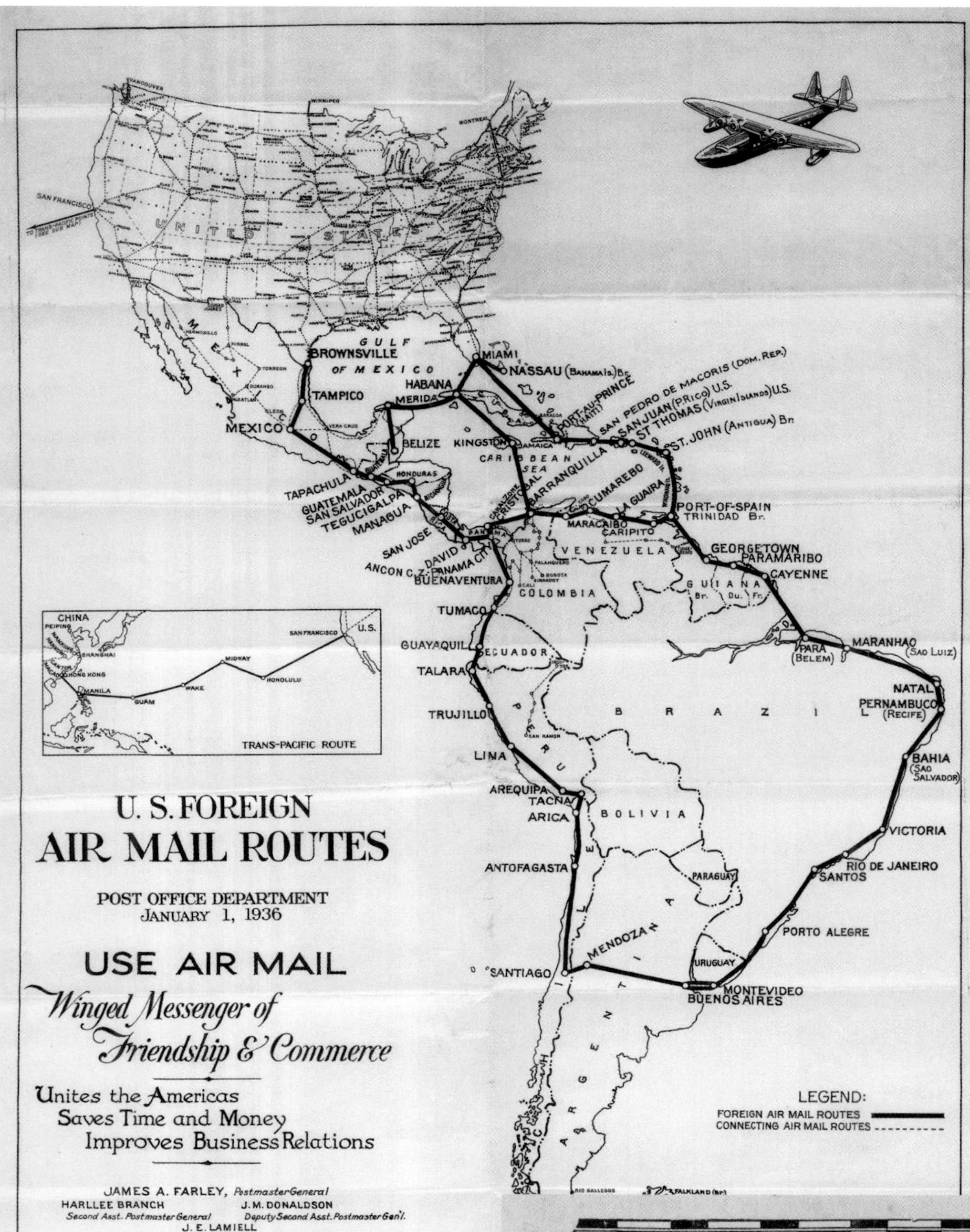

ABOVE: When the US Post Office published this map of its international air mail routes in January 1936, all of the routes were controlled by Pan American. The private company had become an international symbol of American enterprise and a representative of American interests abroad.

RIGHT: An early Pan American ticket folder shows the extend of the company's routes in early 1928.

OPPOSITE PAGE: An Army Air Corps map, produced a year later, shows the company's rapid growth.

In late 1920, Florida West Indies Airways (which would soon be renamed Aeromarine West Indies Airways) began air mail service between Key West, in the Florida Keys, and Havana, Cuba. The line flew converted war-surplus Curtiss HS-2s (which became Aeromarine 80s) and F-5Ls (rebuilt as Aeromarine 75s). The large flying boats offered plenty of room for passengers, many of whom were eager to escape Prohibition for the joys of Cuban rum. By September 1921, the airline had extended service as far north as New York and could deliver passengers to Havana in two days (or half the time required by ship and train). Aeromarine continued to grow for the next two years, but, under financial pressure, ceased operations in September 1923. With no other American airline operating in the Caribbean, the original air mail contract lapsed.

Two years later, the Colombian airline SCADTA approached the US State Department about opening service between South America and Florida. But SCADTA was backed by German money and flew German aircraft. With the memories of World War I still fresh, State rejected the Colombian request.

But Europe continued its inroads to South and Central America, and US entrepreneurs and government agencies recognized the potential loss of influence and trade. The Pan American Flight was the government's first effort to spread goodwill and evaluate potential air links. The main private venture began on 8 March 1927; on the day the Pan American flyers left Montevideo, an unrelated enterprise - Pan American Airways - was incorporated in New York City with the immediate goal of opening air routes to the Caribbean and

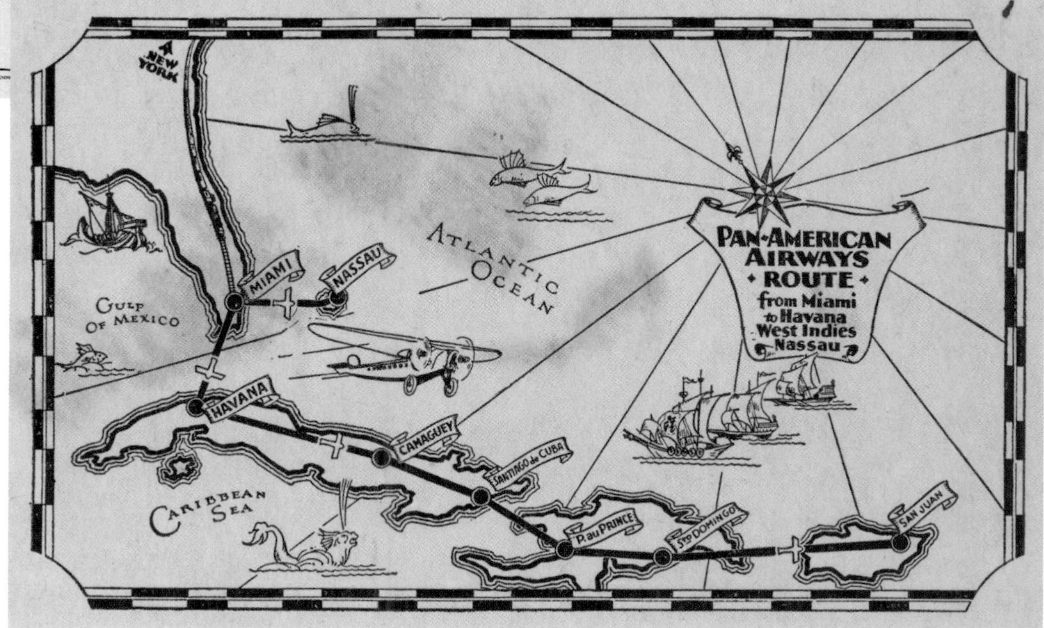

Central America. That summer two other lines formed in competition with Pan American: Aviation Corp of America and Southeastern Air Lines (which soon reincorporated as Atlantic, Gulf, and Caribbean Airways). Pan American would open service first, delivering 30,000 letters from Key West to Havana in borrowed Fairchild FC-2 on 19 October 1927. Scheduled service in Fokker F.VIIs began nine days later.

At first it would seem that Pan American had bested its competition, but the head of Aviation Corp of America was the very formidable Juan Trippe. While Pan American had negotiated with the US government for the air mail contract, Trippe had negotiated with the Cuban government for the landing rights. By 23 June 1928, Trippe was able to engineer a merger of the three groups as Aviation Corp of the Americas, with Pan American Airways Inc as the operating subsidiary. The joining of Juan Trippe with Pan American would evolve into one of air transportation's great success stories. Within seven months, Trippe would negotiate Pan American's control of routes into Mexico. Opposed by Grace Lines steamship company in his expansion down western South America, Trippe formed Pan American-Grace Airways Inc (PANAGRA) in January 1929; that July, PANAGRA opened service as far south as Santiago, Chile.

In March 1929, Pan American faced new competition in the form of the New York, Rio and Buenos Aires Line (NYRBA). On 1 September 1929, NYRBA opened an east coast route and connected Buenos Aires and Santiago from the east five weeks before PANAGRA could begin similar service from the west. But the victory was short-lived, as Trippe was able to force a buyout of NYRBA two weeks later; NYRBA investors lost about $3-million of their initial $5-million in capital. In November 1930, Trippe introduced service down the east coast to Buenos Aires. Just over three years earlier, Pan American had borrowed its first aircraft to connect Florida and Cuba; the company now connected two continents with regular, scheduled service in the finest airliners of the day. •

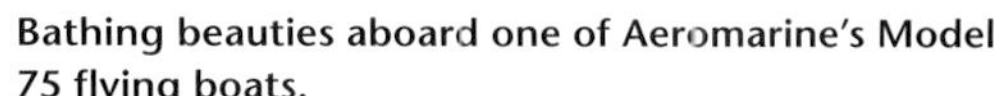
Bathing beauties aboard one of Aeromarine's Model 75 flying boats.

Pan American's Dinner Key facility in Miami, Florida, photographed in 1937. All three of the company's S-40 flying boats are present.

Cargo handlers load a Pan American S-40 bound for Latin America.

Aviation in Latin America

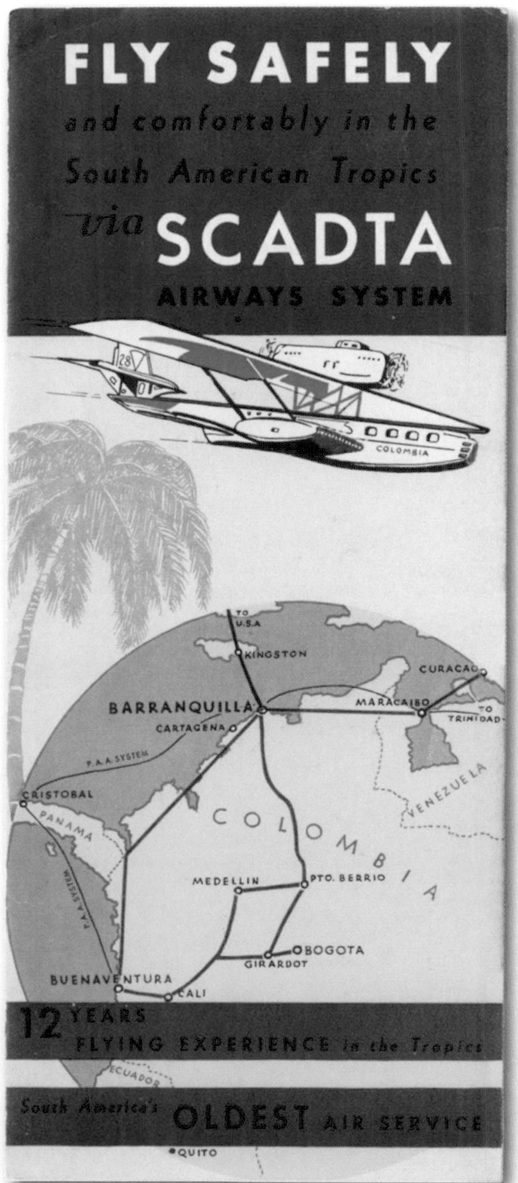

ABOVE: With the demise of the French-backed C.C.N.A. airline, Colombia's SCADTA became South America's oldest air service. Formed in 1919 with German investments, equipment, and directors, Sociedad Colombo-Alemana de Transportes Aéreos found its German ties hindered its efforts to extend service to a strongly anti-German USA in the years immediately following World War I.

BELOW: The last aircraft designed by the Granville Brothers (famous for their line of GeeBee racers) was the R-6H. Created for the London-to-Melbourne MacRobertson Race (which the aircraft did not finish), the long-range racer was eventually purchased by Francisco Sarabia, Mexico's most famous pilot of the day. In May 1939, Sarabia flew the aircraft, now named *Conquistador del Cielo,* for a ten-hour-forty-five-minute record time between Mexico City and New York. Our photo shows the aircraft at the end that flight, with Sarabia lost in the crowd of fans and reporters. The airman died two weeks later when the *Conquistador del Cielo* crashed on the flight home.

RIGHT: America's new B-17s made two goodwill flights to South America during the late 1930s. Between 16 and February 1938, six Y1B-17s flew to Buenos Aires in celebration of the inauguration of Dr. Roberto Ortiz as Argentina's new president. In November 1939, seven B-17Bs visited Rio de Janeiro in a gesture of support as Europe plunged into World War II. Here, the six Y1B-17s prepare to depart Miami at the start of the 1938 flight.

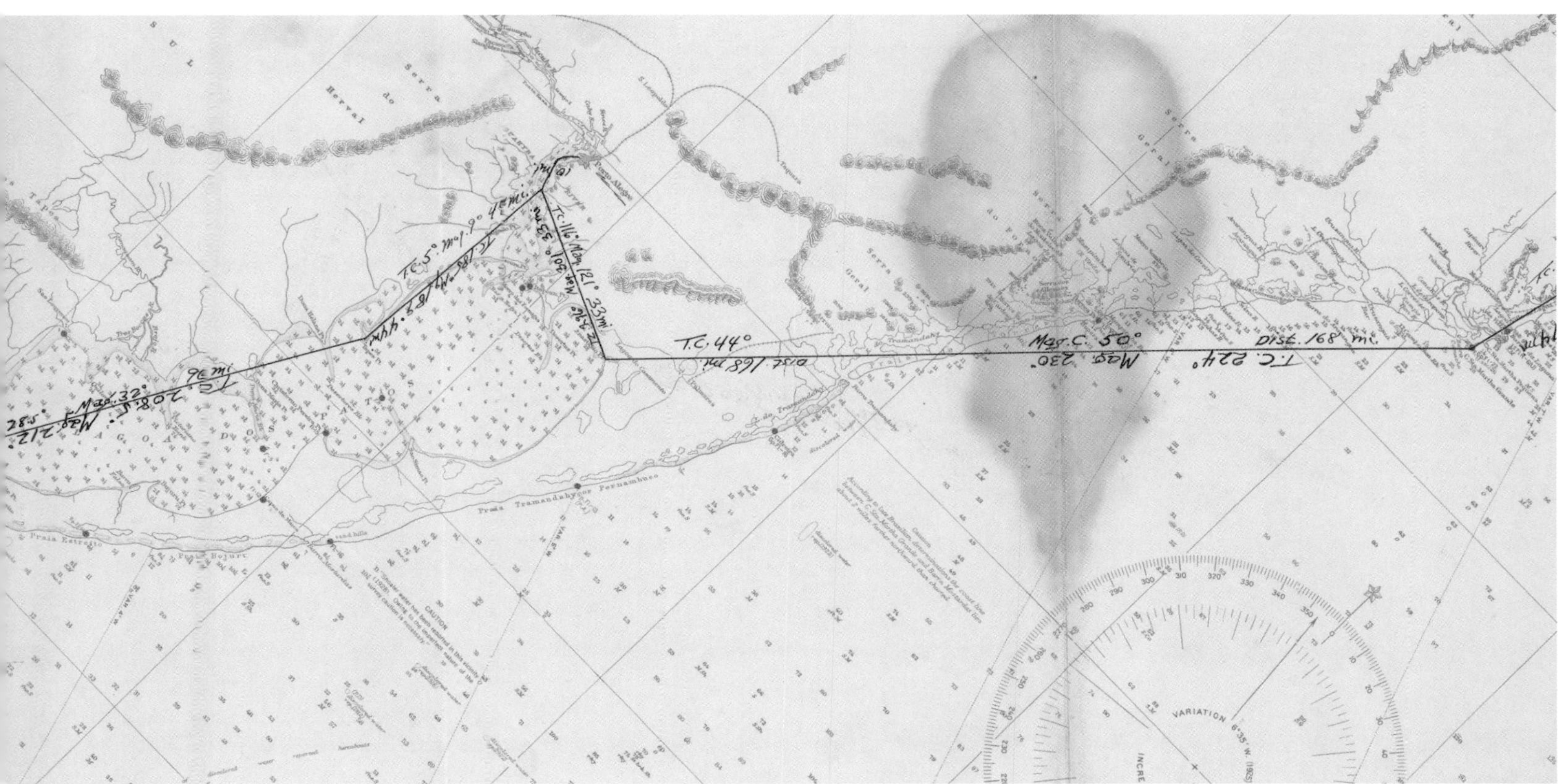

ABOVE: Humphrey Toomey, flew with the NYRBA, using this trimmed and annotated navigation chart for flights along the eastern coast of South America. Toomey inked in bearings and distances between the harbor at Florianópolis on Brazil's Santa Catharina Island, to the port city of Porto Alegre at the north end of the Lagoa dos Patos, and finally to the map's margin at Uruguay's Point San José Ignacio. (A second map provided the route on to Montevideo and Buenos Aires.)

LEFT: Continuing its reliance on German-built airliners, Syndicato Condor purchased seventeen Junkers Ju 52s. Here, *Curupira,* named for a mountain range in northern Brazil, prepares to board passengers at Rio de Janeiro's Aeroporto Santos Dumont.

LEFT: Formed in 1927, the Brazilian company Syndicato Condor incorporated the much of the equipment, facilities, and staff of the former German-owned Condor Syndikat. As this timetable shows, the fleet relied heavily on German-built aircraft, primarily smaller Junkers airliners and Dornier Wals.

BELOW: Using a half dozen Savoia Marchetti S.M.83s, Italy's Ala Littoria opened South Atlantic passenger service in 1939. The line's Linee Atlantiche subsidiary was replaced by LATI (Linee Aeree Transcontinentali Italiane) by the end of the year, but passenger and mail service was soon suspended by World War II.

Exploring the Arctic

Western explorers have been drawn to the Arctic wastes for centuries. Some have searched for wealth, some to learn what lies beneath the ice and snow, and others have hungered for adventure and the distinction of being first. The first attempt to reach the North Pole by air came in 1897, when three Swedish explorers led by Salomon August Andree attempted to fly north in the free balloon *Eagle*. The three would be forced down, dying in their attempts to return to civilization. In 1907, American aeronaut Walter Wellman attempted to pilot the *America*, a French-built airship, north from Dane Island. The dirigible was unable to fight the Arctic winds, and Wellman abandoned the attempt after a flight of three hours. Wellman's attempt with a new airship in 1909 made 70 miles, but the airship malfunctioned and was lost; the crew trekked to safety. The North Pole would be reached that year, by dog sled, in an expedition comprising Robert E. Peary, Matthew Henson, and four Inuit guides.

In 1922 and 1923, Norwegian explorers Roald Amundsen and Oskar Omdahl attempted three Arctic flights in a Curtiss Oriole and a Junkers-Larsen JL-6, only to prove that neither aircraft was satisfactory for the Arctic mission. In 1925, Amundsen and Omdahl returned to Spitzbergen with two Italian-built Dornier Wal flying boats and Lincoln Ellsworth, their new American backer. They planned an extended reconnaissance, testing the range of their aircraft, moving as close to the Pole as possible, then returning to Spitzbergen. On 21 May 1925, the two Wals, each with a crew of three, headed north. After seven hours, the first Wal, with Amundsen aboard, developed engine trouble and set down in a fissure 138 miles from the Pole. Ellsworth, in the second plane, put down three miles away, only to discover that the aircraft's hull was leaking badly. After 25 days on the ice, all six men climbed into Amundsen's repaired aircraft and took off along a path they had cleared through the ice. Hours later they put down at near Spitzbergen and beached their aircraft to be rescued by a passing whaler.

1926 found three expeditions attempting the North Pole. From Alaska, Australian George Hubert Wilkins would attempt a northern exploration with a pair of Fokker F.VIIs (one a trimotor, the other single-engined). Both aircraft would wreck, later to be combined into a new aircraft named *Southern Cross*. (See page 96.)

The other two teams formed up at Spitzbergen. American Richard E. Byrd was also equipped with a Fokker Trimotor, which he named *Josephine Ford* after the daughter of his sponsor. On 9 May 1926, Byrd and

Roald Amundsen was one of the most successful polar explorers. Using two of these Dornier Wal flying boats, Amundsen and five others landed within 138 miles of the North Pole in May 1925.

The *Alaskan* was one of two Fokker F.VIIs damaged by Wilkins and Eielson on their 1926 Arctic Expedition. Parts from the two aircraft would later be rebuilt into the *Southern Cross*.

his pilot, Floyd Bennett got away first. Their journey was expected to take 20 to 24 hours, but 15-1/2 hours later they returned. Byrd immediately claimed success, but many doubted his claim. Bennett, for the most part, left the public relations to his leader. But in private, to his friends, he told a different story. When asked about the dispute by his friend Paul Garber, aviation curator for the Smithsonian Institution, Bennett would only say, "Paul, we didn't do it."

The first flight over the Pole would be made in an Italian airship purchased by an American millionaire for an expedition headed by a Norwegian. Two days after Byrd's flight, at 10:00 am on 11 May 1926, the dirigible Norge left Spitzbergen with the same mission. On board were Amundsen, the expedition leader, Umberto Nobile, the Italian designer of the Norge and its nominal commander, Lincoln Ellsworth, the expedition backer, and a crew of seven Norwegians, five Italians, and a Swede. Just about fifteen-and-a-half hours later, the Amundsen-Ellsworth-Nobile Expedition reached the North Pole. Amundsen threw out a small Norwegian flag, Ellsworth pitched a small American flag, and Nobile (despite earlier agreements) tossed a collection of large Italian flags, banners, pennants, and emblems. Perhaps it's a truism, but from there they headed south, in this case continuing their flight across to Alaska landing at a coastal Inuit village sixty miles north of Nome . They had covered 3,290 miles in about 72 hours.

There was still much to learn about the Arctic; rumors abounded that large islands supported much of the Northern ice, and Wilkins was back in April 1927 to search for any new territories to claim. However, early in the mission Wilkins and pilot Carl Ben Eielson crashed one of their new Stinson monoplanes. They trekked out safely in thirteen days. In 1928, the pair returned with a new Lockheed Vega. This time, they successfully traversed a 2,200-mile route north of Canada and Greenland, arriving at Spitsbergen after a 24-hour flight (and four-day weather layover at Dead Man's Island). Their flight found no evidence of the land so many had expected to find. The exploratory flight led to speaking tours and National Geographic Society gold medals for both men. Wilkins would be knighted as Sir Hubert Wilkins. Eielson continued as one of the great Alaskan bush pilots, dying in on a rescue mission in November 1929. The US Air Force base at Fairbanks, Alaska, would be named in his honor.

Further honors were not fated for Italy's General Umberto Nobile, however. A national hero for his part in the Norwegian flight over the North Pole, a flight for which he claimed a lion's share of the credit, Nobile returned to the North two weeks after Wilkins and Eielson landed. Nobile's attempts to eclipse Norwegian contributions to the *Norge*'s polar flight had caused a rift with expedition leaders Amundsen and Ellsworth. With this in mind, Nobile planned a series of northern explorations with his new airship, the *Italia,* and an all-Italian crew. (Nobile did include two foreign scientists the ship's complement.)

Nobile and fifteen others soon flew to the Pole, arriving just after midnight on 24 May after a 19-hour trip. After circling for two hours to make scientific observations, the *Italia* began its return to Spitzbergen. Increasing winds plagued the trip, which was less than halfway back 25 hours later. Late on the morning of the 25th the dirigible crashed to the ice, dropping the control car, an engine, and ten of the crew. The other six crewmen drifted away on the lightened - and uncontrollable - envelope and were never seen again.

Among the ten left on the ice were one dead and three injured, including Nobile. Confusion with the Italian support team delayed any rescue attempt for weeks. Once an international rescue effort was finally launched, Roald Amundsen would insist on joining, only to be lost at sea flying from Norway to Spitzbergen on 18 June. The rescue would be completed by the Russians on 11 July; Nobile was one of the eight survivors, but his political enemies in Italy's fascist party would use the subsequent investigations to destroy his reputation. Three years later he was back in Arctic waters on a Russian ice breaker, futilely searching for the six crewmen carried away with the *Italia*'s envelope. •

In May 1926, the Italian airship Norge became the first aircraft to fly over the North Pole. *Norge* was part of a Norwegian expedition headed by Amundsen.

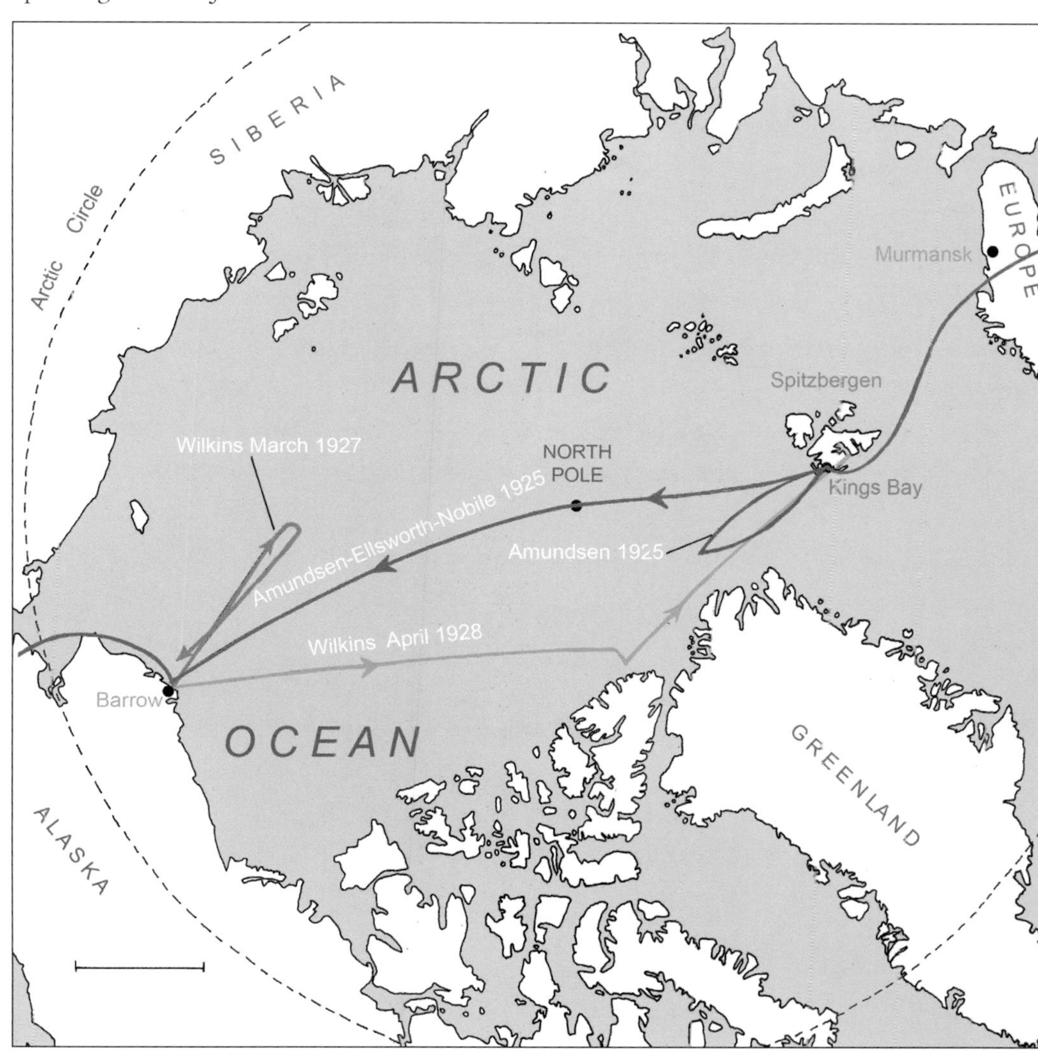

Exploring the Antarctic

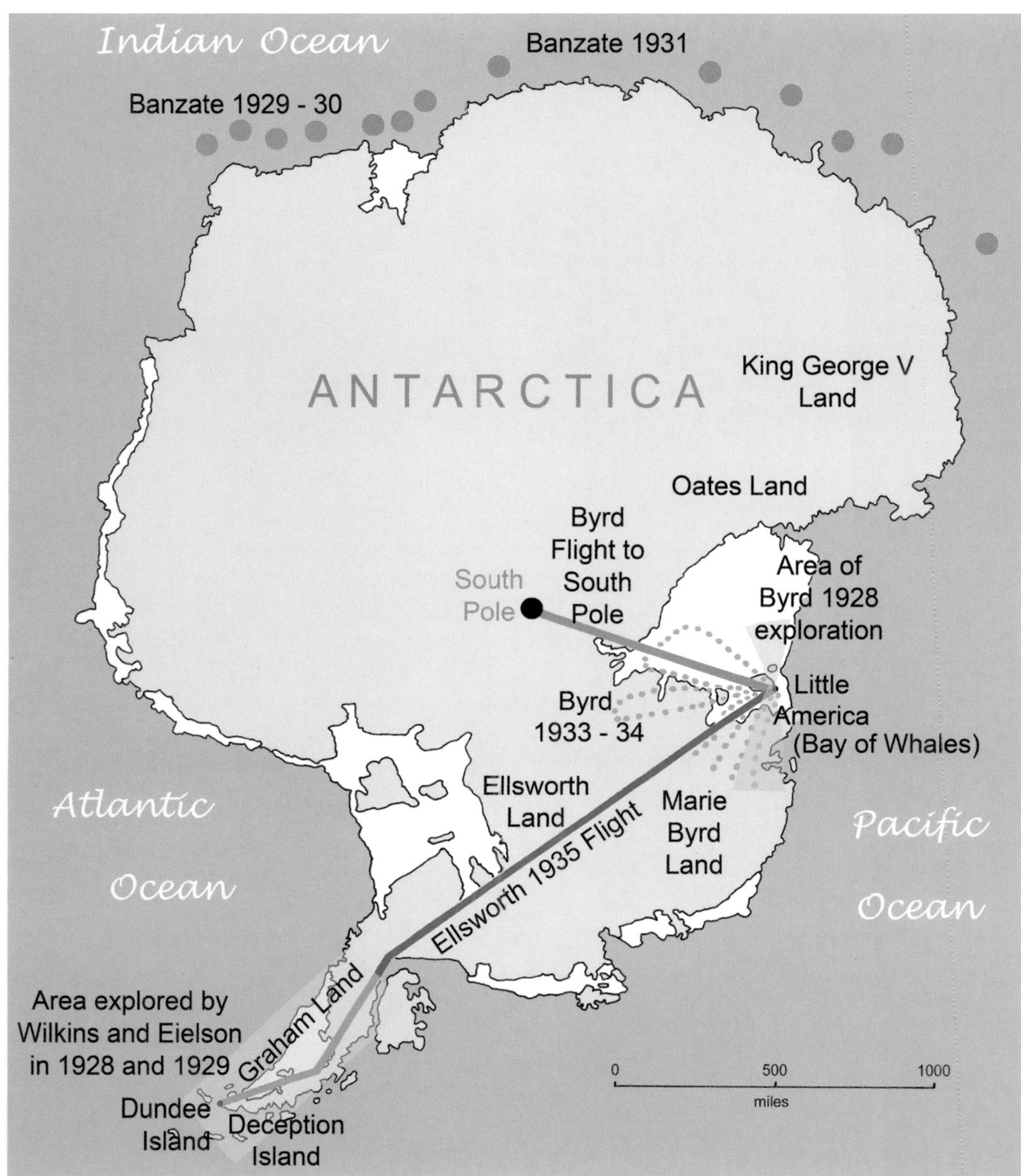

Flight has been a part of Antarctic exploration since the early 1900s. Captain Robert Falcon Scott first ascended in the tethered hydrogen balloon *Eva* at the edge of the Great Ice Barrier in February 1902. He was followed aloft by shipmate Ernest Shackleton, who took the first aerial photos of the Antarctic. In March, Eric von Drygalski took more photos from a tethered balloon as part of a German expedition. Von Drygalski rose to an altitude of almost 600 feet, twice that of his British predecessors.

The airplane first flew over the continent in November 1928, when Hubert Wilkins and Carl Ben Eielson made a short hop in the same Lockheed Vega (now named *Los Angeles*) used for their earlier Arctic flights. *Los Angeles* and a second Vega (named *San Francisco*) explored the Graham Land peninsula through early January 1929, then both planes were dismantled and stored in a whalers' shed while the explorers returned to warmer climes. Wilkins and two new pilots (Al Cheeseman and Parker D. Cramer) returned in November, loading one of the Vegas onto the exploration ship *William Scoresby* to search for a better base for aircraft operations. The trio continued to explore Graham Land from December 1929 through February 1930.

Richard Byrd began a decade of Antarctic exploration in December 1928. Arriving at Little America with three aircraft, Byrd began flight operations in January 1929 with a Fairchild FC-2 nicknamed *Stars and Stripes*. A single-engined Fokker - *The Virginian* - was destroyed by a sudden storm in March. The Ford Trimotor *Floyd Bennett* (named for the pilot of Byrd's Arctic flights) was also flown on local survey flights before all but 43 of the explorers headed north to avoid the long Antartic night that started in April 1929.

In November the reinforced expedition dug out the *Floyd Bennett* for an attempt at the first flight over the South Pole, a mission accomplished on the 28th and 29th. Byrd navigated for pilot Bernt Balchen, radio operator Harold June, and Paramount cameraman Ashley McKinley.

Today the *Polar Star* is displayed at the Smithsonian's National Air and Space Museum in Washington, DC. The forward fuselage remains wrinkled just forward of the wing's leading edge, a souvenir of the first hard landing at Camp I.

When Byrd returned to the Antarctic in late 1933, it was with an even larger expedition. Aiding the explorer for a number of survey flights were four new aircraft: Curtiss Condor *William Horlick*, Fokker *Blue Blade*, Fairchild *Miss American Airways*, and an unnamed Kellet K-4 Autogyro.

Arguments marred the British, Australian, New Zealand Antarctic Research Expedition (BANZARE) of 1929/30. For reasons never made clear, expedition leader Sir Douglas Mawson and ship's captain John King Davis disagreed over many of the goals and strategies for their project, despite their many years of friendship. None-the-less, between 29 December 1929 and 26 January 1930, the expedition, its two pilots (Stuart Campbell and Eric Douglas), and a single, well-worn de Havilland D.H.60G Gipsy Moth biplane explored vast sections of the Antarctic coast. They named the area MacRobertson Land in honor of Sir MacPherson Robertson, sponsor and owner of the Australian MacRobertson confections concern. Mawson dropped Davis when forming the second BANZARE of 1930/31 (although they remained friends). BANZARE II would again use its tiny Gipsy Moth in a series of coastal survey flights that ended in mid February.

The first BANZARE would find initially find itself in direct competition with a Norwegian expedition funded by Lars Christensen and headed by Captain Hjalmar Riiser-Larsen, veteran of Roald Amundsen's Arctic 1925 explorations with two Dornier

Wals, and 1926 voyage to the North Pole in the dirigible *Norge*. Crammed into the whaler *Norvegia*, Riiser-Larsen and crew carried two floatplanes - a World War I-era Hansa-Brandenburg and a Lockheed Vega - with which several dozen exploratory flights were accomplished. In a meeting at sea in December 1929, Mawson and Riiser-Larsen split the territory they would explore (and claim for their respective governments).

Lars Christensen headed his own Antarctic expedition in 1933, though Riiser-Larsen attended to the aerial portion of their surveys, using and Avro Avian seaplane. They worked together again in 1936/37, this time flying a Stinson floatplane. Between them, Riiser-Larsen and Christensen would eventually map more than half of the Antarctic coastline.

Like Riiser-Larsen, Lincoln Ellsworth was a veteran of Amundsen's Arctic expeditions in the Dornier Wals and in the Norge. Unlike Riiser-Larsen, Ellsworth was a millionaire who had helped fund both expeditions. Teaming with Sir Hubert Wilkins, Ellsworth turned his attention to Antarctica with plans for a flight across a portion of the continent between Graham Land and Little America. Equipped with a Northrop 2B Gamma named *Polar Star*, Ellsworth and pilot Bernt Balchen prepared for their first attempt on 12 January 1934. The aircraft was damaged as it fell through melting pack ice while the men slept, ending the season's hopes. The expedition returned later that year, but the attempted flight of 3 January 1935 caused a rift between pilot and explorer: Balchen turned back in the face of foul weather when Ellsworth insisted on continuing. Again, the expedition sailed north.

November 1935 found Ellsworth and Wilkins back in the Antarctic with a new pilot, Herbert Hollick-Kenyon. They planned a transcontinental flight with several stops on the pack ice for rest, sun fixes, and claiming new territory for the United States. They would fly to Little America and wait for Wilkins to arrive in their ship by 22 January. Weather and technical problems forced the pair to return on the first two attempts. On the third attempt on 22 November, the radio went dead and the pair disappeared.

Unbeknownst to the rest of the world, Wilkins and Kenyon were doing fairly well. They landed after 14 hours in the air, took bearings, ate, and rested for 19 hours. They took off on the 24th, but, after only a half hour in the air, landed to weather out an approaching storm. Another short hop on the 27th saw them huddled in their tent for three days of gale-force winds and snow. On 5 December they were again in the air, but ran out of fuel sixteen miles short of their goal. It took ten days to walk to Byrd's abandoned camp at Little America, which they reached on 15 December. The pair was somewhat surprised by the arrival, a month later, of an Australian rescue vessel and team. Three days later, Wilkins arrived, and after thanking the Australians for all their efforts, the expedition returned home.

These early aircraft and aviators assisted in the exploration of the last continent as they had helped north of the Arctic Circle. Nearly every subsequent expedition to Antarctica would consider aircraft essential to a successful mission. •

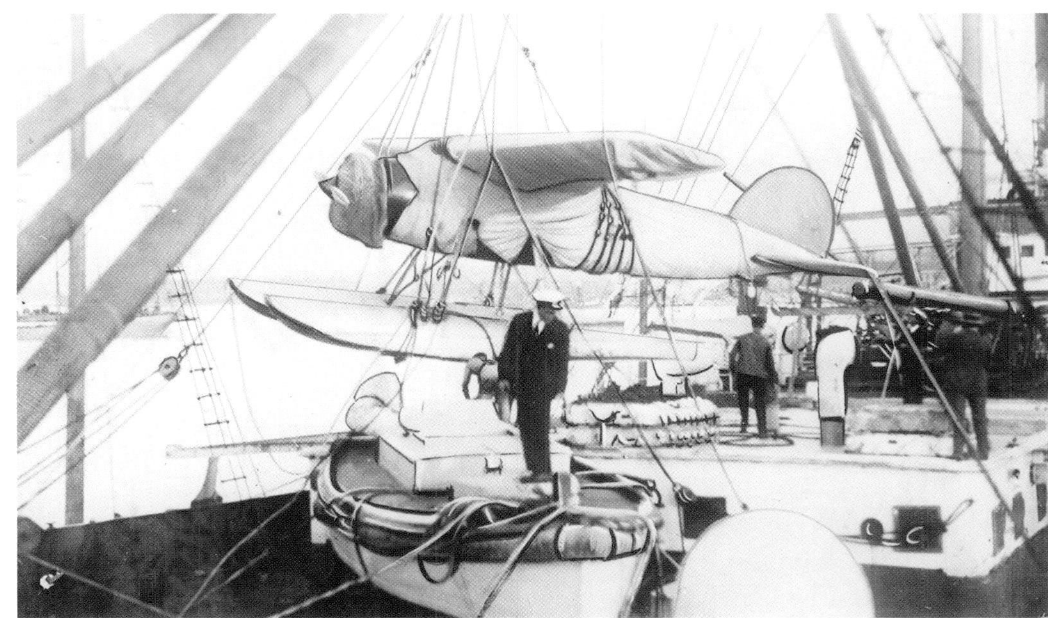

RIGHT: In late 1928, Sir Hubert Wilkins, Carl Ben Eielson, and two Lockheed Vegas boarded the whaler *Hektoria* bound for the Antarctic. Eielson and Wilkins would make the first airplane flight over the continent that November.

BELOW: Ellsworth's *Polar Star* landed four times on the polar ice cap before completing it's transcontinental flight. The roomy cargo compartment forward of the cockpit carried enough supplies and equipment to support the explorers for months, should the need have arisen.

Lightning War

In retrospect, the late-1930s' buildup of Nazi military might was clearly planned to bring Europe under the control of the Third Reich. But at the time, few recognized what the future held. Certainly, Adolf Hitler and his circle had a program in place, peacefully seizing what territories could be threatened into submission, then gradually declaring war to gobble up all the rest. But few in the world were privy to those plans, and those who warned of what was coming were easily dismissed as alarmists. The Nazi propaganda machine managed to create a curious blend of carrot and stick, convincing many with their arguments for "peaceful" annexations, while threatening the rest with the unstoppable might of the German war machine. Both arguments, of course, were spurious - Germany had no legal or moral rights to the territories it cowed the world into granting it, and the state of German arms was far below what was advertized until early 1940, when the War was well under way. Few saw the dangers - Hitler and the Nazis were easily seen as eccentrics who really knew how to put on a good show. Surely the people that entertained the world with the 1936 Olympic Games were far too civil to plunge the world into another war....

Beyond the bluff and the propaganda, the Germans participated in an ancient military ritual known as "blooding the warriors." All military planners know that raw recruits, no matter how well trained and motivated, are less prepared than soldiers who have been tested and proven in battle. And so, when the Spanish Civil War broke out in the summer of 1936, Germany allowed "volunteers" to join the Condor Legion in support of Spanish Fascists. The German forces included armor and aircraft units, which developed their combat skills while evaluating the capabilities of their tanks and aircraft. (Although Germany sent no infantry units to Spain, Italy's Fascist regime sent 35,000 ground troops. British, French, and Polish military planners sent observers to Spain, but declined the opportunity to harden their air and ground units - nations hoping for peace rarely jump at the chance to join a war.)

Despite Germany's announced intentions to reclaim some of its former territory from Poland, France and Britain still believed a peaceful solution was possible. Recognizing that the policy of appeasement had failed to block Nazi aggression, Britain and France announced that they would meet any attack on Poland with declarations of war. On paper, their combined military might would have been enough to dissuade any reasonable government from beginning another conflict.

On the early morning of 1 September 1939, German forces dressed a number of convicts in Polish uniforms, then shot them to death on the German side of the Polish border. Decrying this open invasion of German territory, Hitler soon announced that he had no choice but to respond to such treachery; German forces had swept into Poland before dawn. On 3 September, Britain and France declared war on Germany. World War II had begun.

The German forces were fully prepared and briefed on their targets. When fully mobilized

With air superiority established early in the Polish Campaign, Junkers Ju 87 dive bombers wreaked havoc on assembling regiments and retreating refugees. *Sturzkampfflugzeug* - the German word for "dive bomber" - was generally abbreviated as *Stuka,* a name most often associated with the Ju 87.

Polish forces were less than half the strength of the German army; but England and France had persuaded the Polish government to delay mobilization, fearful of the effect such a military action would have on a diplomatic solution. The Germans had trained in a new employment of combined arms they called *Blitzkrieg* - Lightning War. Armor, infantry and aviation forces moved quickly, acting together to identify and destroy opposing forces. The German propaganda machine exaggerated the Blitzkrieg's effectiveness, making little mention of Polish counteroffensives and victories while extolling the military supremacy of its own air and ground forces. On 18 September, Soviet forces attacked Poland from the east, a coordinated moved planned with Hitler in August. Poland collapsed the next day, though fighting continued through 5 October.

British and French forces had not been able to fire a single bullet in defense of their Polish ally. Worse, they now found themselves in a war to defend a country that had already been overrun. Hitler again talked peace while he rebuilt his forces and prepared for his next move into Belgium and France. Wits named the period that followed the Phoney War or the *Sitzkrieg* (sitting war) - lots of talking but not very much shooting.

By April 1940, Hitler was in position. To defend their flanks, the Germans attacked Denmark and Norway on 9 April - the Danes fell in twelve hours, with the Norwegians holding out until 10 June. In the interim, the bulk of German forces entered Belgium, the Netherlands, and France in May. France's static defenses were bypassed. French and British forces, acting independently, proved unable to respond to the coordinated German assaults; France fell in six weeks. •

ABOVE: The success of Germany's Heinkel He 111 bomber in the Spanish Civil War helped German planners convince themselves, that longer ranged, heavier bombers were unnecessary. The lack of range and payload would soon cause the Luftwaffe problems over Britain, the Mediterranean, and Russia.

BELOW: Hardly invincible, this He 111 of *Kampfgeschwader* (Bomber Wing) 51 came out in second place against French fighters at the beginning of the Battle of France.

The Battle of Britain

June 1940 was a difficult month for the forces Allied against Germany. On the 4th, the evacuation of British troops from France ended with most British guns and tanks and thousands of British soldiers abandoned and soon to be captured by the Germans. On the 17th, the French government asked for terms, with a final armistice signed on the 30th. All of continental Europe was suddenly controlled by the Germans, friendly to the Germans, or neutral (and no threat) to the Germans. Britain stood alone.

Hitler, of course, offered peace, though few Britons were fooled; it was obvious to all that the Fuhrer never negotiated in good faith. Hitler already planned to conquer the Soviet Union, but first any remaining British forces must be neutralized. Even as Hitler offered peace, he directed his staff to continue preparing for *Sealion*, the invasion of Britain.

German forces needed air supremacy to have any chance of crossing the Channel. Prior destruction of the Royal Air Force (RAF) would eliminate any British aerial threat and allow the Luftwaffe to concentrate its attacks on the Royal Navy, offsetting Britain's commanding advantage in naval forces. With an unchallenged crossing of the Channel, the superior German army would quickly sweep away any remaining ground resistance, and Britain would fall. Or so the plan went.

The first small incursions began in early July. Channel shipping and coastal ports were subjected to small raids designed to probe defenses and engage the RAF. The main attack began on 13 August. Adlertag (Eagle Day) initiated an all-out assault on RAF facilities in Southern England. With the range of its own fighters limited, the Luftwaffe expected to destroy most RAF fighters, driving the remainder to less-effective defensive positions farther north. In this war of attrition, everything favored the Luftwaffe. Fortunately, the Germans changed tactics just as the war against the RAF was beginning to show results.

In early September, a German night bomber crew became disoriented. Thinking themselves over the Channel, the crew salvoed its bombs and returned to France. In a navigational error with far-reaching consequences, the crew had dropped the first bombs on London, a city declared off limits by Hitler himself. RAF Bomber Command responded with a series of night raids on Berlin. Infuriated by these attacks on *his* capital, Hitler ordered the destruction of London. The period the British would remember as "The Blitz" focused unimaginable hardships on the peoples of London, Hull, and other major British cities, but gave the RAF the time and the air fields needed to turn the tide. Although the Luftwaffe continued to strike at Britain for several years, the last heavy day and night raids were completed on 29 October 1940. The Battle of Britain saw the destruction of 1,733 German aircraft at a cost of just over 900 British fighters. But more critically, Germany's inability to control the skies meant that there could be no invasion. For the first time in history, an entire campaign had been fought in the air, and aerial forces alone had prevented the initiation of a great naval or ground battle. •

The Heinkel He 111 was the standard German bomber during most of World War II. As day operations over England became more dangerous, much of the bomber force adopted black camouflage and switched to night operations.

Civil defense crews and ordinary citizens search the rubble for victims of the latest German attack.

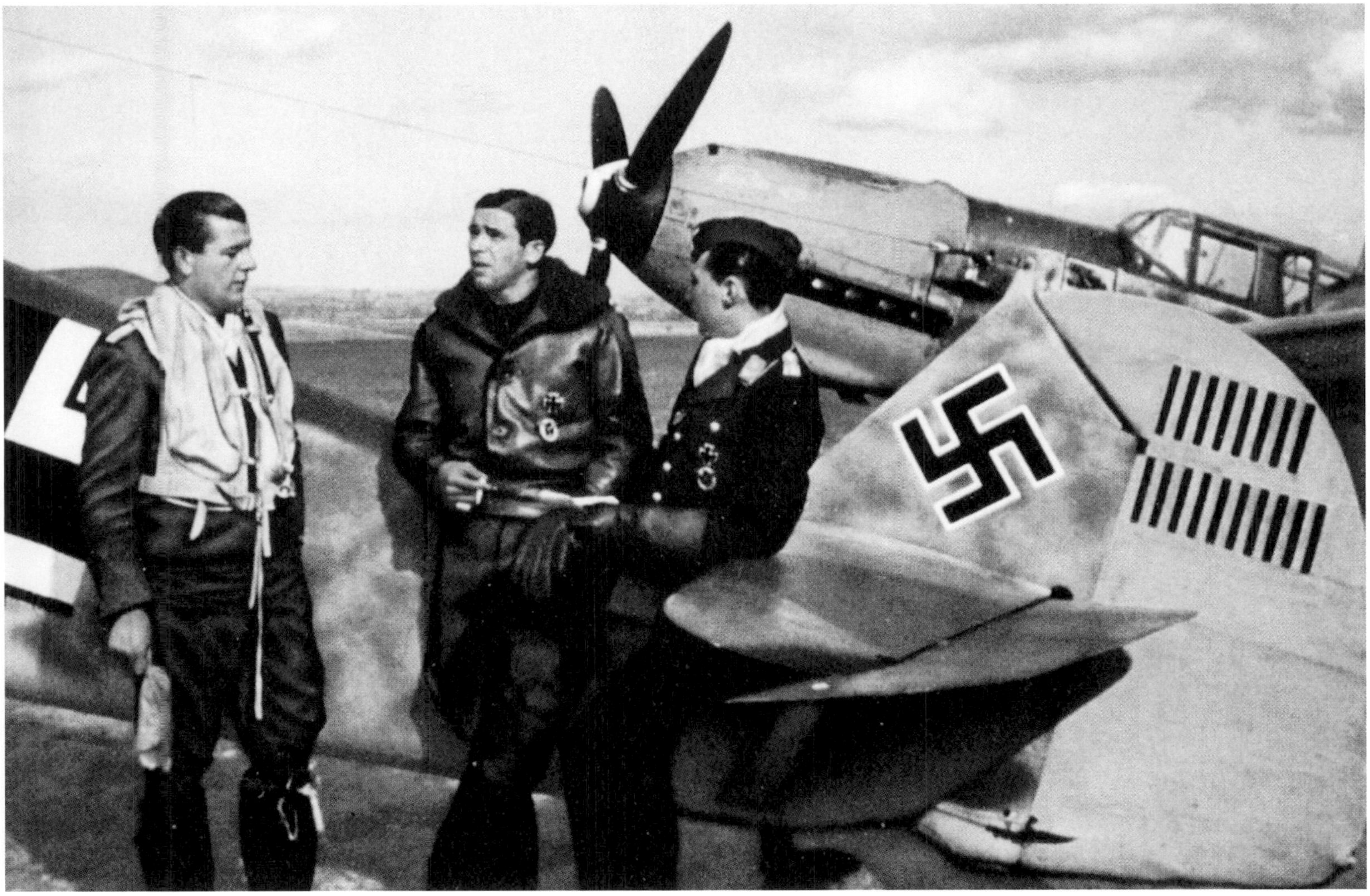

Elite fighter pilots of the German Luftwaffe pose with their Messerschmitt Bf 109E fighters during the Battle of Britain. Training and tactical experience had created in these men the best fighter force of the day, but the short range of the Bf 109 limited their time over London to only ten minutes, giving the RAF time to train, rebuild, and develop the tactics needed for victory.

THE GERMAN AIR FORCE

"Confidential"

AIRFLEET I					AIRFLEET II					AIRFLEET III					AIRFLEET IV					AIRFLEET V					AIRFLEET VI					TOTAL IN AIRFLEETS							
DIVISIONS	WINGS	GROUPS	SQUADRONS	PLANES including STAFF PLANES	DIVISIONS	WINGS	GROUPS	SQUADRONS	PLANES including STAFF PLANES	DIVISIONS	WINGS	GROUPS	SQUADRONS	PLANES including STAFF PLANES	DIVISIONS	WINGS	GROUPS	SQUADRONS	PLANES including STAFF PLANES	DIVISIONS	WINGS	GROUPS	SQUADRONS	PLANES including STAFF PLANES	DIVISIONS	WINGS	GROUPS	SQUADRONS	PLANES including STAFF PLANES	DIVISIONS	WINGS	GROUPS	SQUADRONS	PLANES	RESERVE OF COMBAT PLANES	TYPE	TOTAL NO. OF PLANES
3	9	27	81	1170	2	6	18	54	780	1	3	9	27	390	1	3	9	27	390	1	3	9	27	390	1	3	9	27	390	9	27	81	243	3510	2785	PURSUIT	6295
					1	3	9	27	390	2	6	18	54	780						1	3	9	27	390	1	3	9	27	390	5	15	45	135	1950	1490	2 ENG. FTG'S	3440
					3	9	27	81	1170	5	15	45	135	1950	4	12	36	108	1560		1	3	9	130		2	6	18	260	13	39	117	351	5070	4190	BOMBER	9260
					2	6	18	54	780	1	3	9	27	390											1	3	9	27	390	4	12	36	108	1560	970	DIVE BOMBERS	2530
3	9	27	81	1170	8	24	72	216	3120	9	27	81	243	3510	5	15	45	135	1950	2	7	21	63	910	3	11	33	99	1430	31	93	279	837	12090	9435	TOTAL COMBAT	21525
																																				NAVY	900
																																				TRANSPORT	1850
																																				OBSERVATION	1600
																																				PAT. & TORP.	780
																																				TRAINING	5545
																																				TOTAL	32200

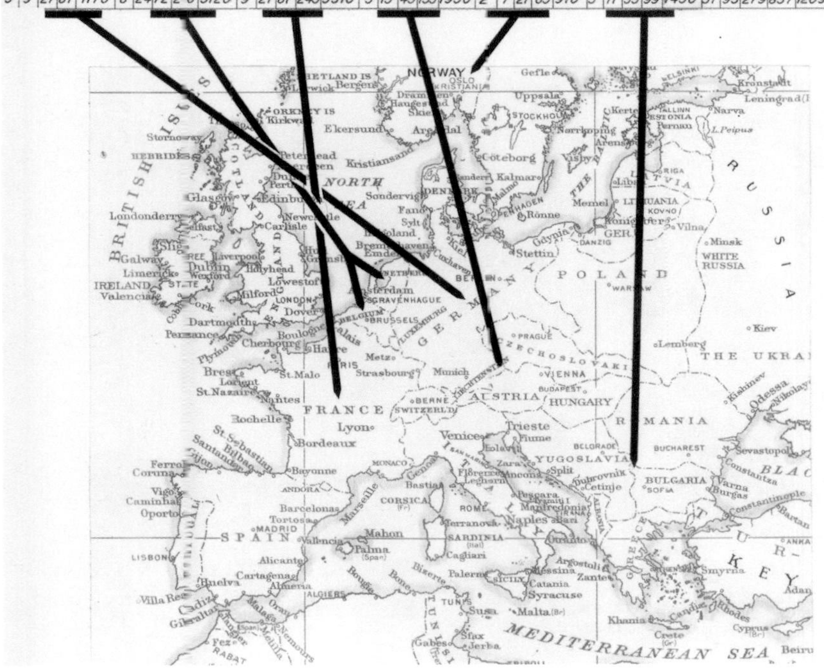

ABOVE: The standard British fighter of the Battle of Britain was the Hawker Hurricane. Carrying eight machine guns (twelve on later models), the Hurricane wreaked havoc on German bombers and held its own against the Bf 109. This Mark I of Number 87 Squadron was photographed in late August 1940.

LEFT: This April 1941 US intelligence map estimated the strengths of German *Luftflotten* (Air Fleets) in Western Europe. Great Britain was still the main target, though action in North Africa was beginning to draw the Luftwaffe into Libya. This assessment gives little indication of the coming German invasion of Russia, little more than two months away.

Reaping the Whirlwind

In the 1920s and '30s, the new proponents of air power developed the concepts of strategic bombing. Tactical bombing, the direct application of air power against enemy armies and their facilities, would continue to employ aircraft as a sort of flying artillery. In the simplest terms, theorists supporting strategic bombing believed that future wars would be won by the long-range destruction of manufacturing facilities, transportation centers, and even civilian populations. With armies thereby deprived of critical equipment, and civil populations horrified by their own defenselessness, wars would become too cruel and all-encompassing, ending more quickly, and perhaps even becoming more humane. The counter arguments generally asserted that strategic bombing wouldn't work or, even if it would work, attacks on civilian populations were immoral.

During World War II, Germany's Luftwaffe, Britain's Royal Air Force, and the US Army Air Forces each practiced versions of strategic bombing. Once Germany began the unrestricted bombing of British cities, Britons felt less inclined to temper their response. As Winston Churchill expressed the general consensus (on 30 December 1941), "Hitler and his Nazi gang have sown the wind; let them reap the whirlwind." RAF Bomber Command, which quickly recognized that its night bombing campaign stood little hope of destroying individual factory buildings, soon turned to area bombing - with a portion of a city reduced to rubble, the factory would probably also be destroyed while the nearby civilian factory workers would be "dehoused."

In Europe, American strategic bombing proponents argued for a program of precision daylight bombing. Heavily armed, four-engined bombers, equipped with the most advanced bombsight, could make every bomb count, destroying the targeted factory, but avoiding any damage to the surrounding civilian population. Fighter escorts, where available, would drive defending fighters from the sky; beyond the range of escorting fighters, the bombers' own gunners would put up enough defensive fire to protect the bomber formation.

Over occupied Europe, daylight bombing promised to minimize injury to the very people the Allies hoped to liberate. Commanders practiced formation flying, hoping to maximize the defensive capabilities of each bomb group and bring each mission's bomb load into a tight pattern centered on the target. Post-mission intelligence and reconnaissance reconstructed each mission, evaluating damage to the target, evaluating if another mission was required and if each unit was performing as expected. Despite the promises of precision daylight bombing, accuracy remained a problem, and many civilians (including those in occupied countries near German targets) paid the price.

The Luftwaffe developed new defenses against British and American bombers, whom they regarded as terror bombers. Heavier aircraft armament, increases in size, numbers, and direction of Flak (antiaircraft artillery),

The weight of most early airborne radar sets meant that they could only be carried by larger, twin-engined aircraft. Built as a bomber, this Junkers Ju 88 was converted to a night fighter by the addition of radar equipment (including the nose-mounted aerials) and forward firing armament. These modified aircraft were remarkable effective against slower, four-engined night bombers, but eventually found themselves hunted by British Mosquito night fighters.

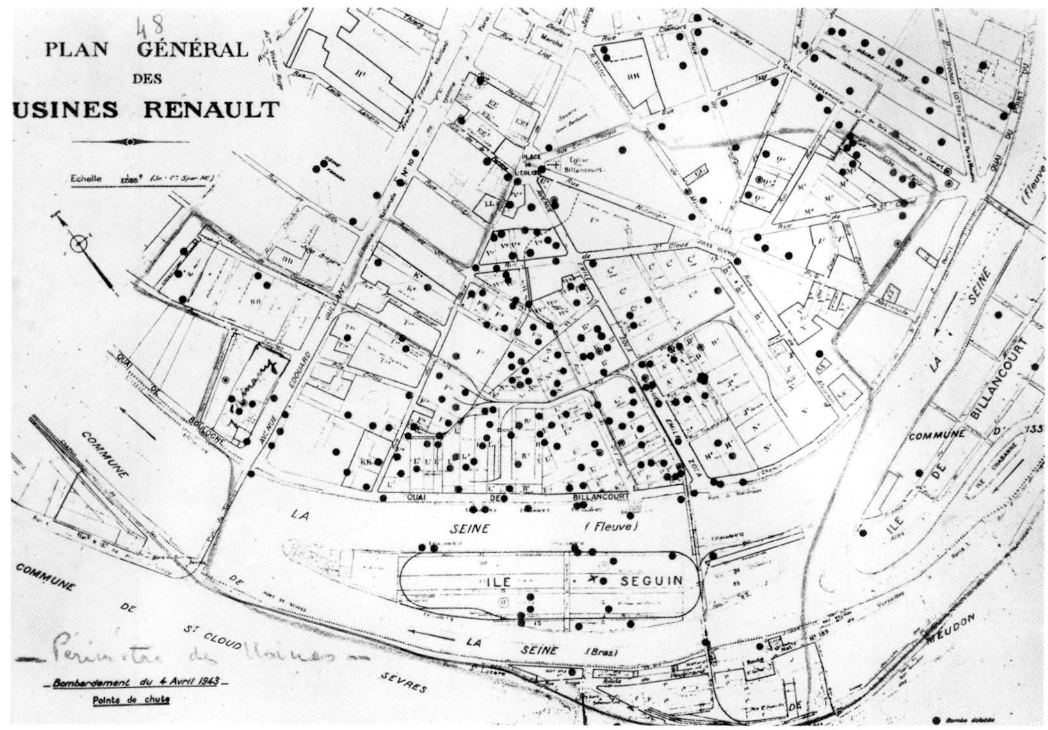

On 4 April 1943, 85 Eighth Air Force B-17s attacked the Renault factory near Paris. Four bombers were lost, with 39 crewmen missing in action, and a further six crewmen wounded. This post-mission assessment plotted where each bomb fell, noting which bombs failed to explode.

With no four-engined bombers at the beginning of the war, RAF Bomber Command relied on several twin-engined types, including the superb Vickers Wellington. Produced in greater numbers than any other British bomber, the Wellington remained the principal British strategic bomber into mid-1942.

revised aerial tactics, and improved night fighting equipment took a heavy toll on the bomber crews, particularly before very long-range escort fighters were introduced in 1944. Forced to fly at higher altitudes, bombers faced greater difficulties hitting their targets.

The arguments over the effectiveness of strategic bombing continue to this day. German aircraft production actually reached its greatest output in 1944, following several months of attacks concentrating on the German aircraft industry. Yet, in order to reach that high rate of production, German industry sacrificed in other areas. Many of the latest designs were destroyed before they could be test flown. Many newly built aircraft were destroyed before they could be delivered. And Through a remarkably fluid accounting system, used aircraft rebuilt with new engines were tallied as new aircraft; bombers rebuilt with radars counted as new nightfighters; fighters modified with a second seat became new two-seat trainers. There is little evidence to support the idea that German industry was better off for the effects of strategic bombing, and by war's end, most shortages in most equipment, supplies, and fuels limited German forces' ability to engage at will. •

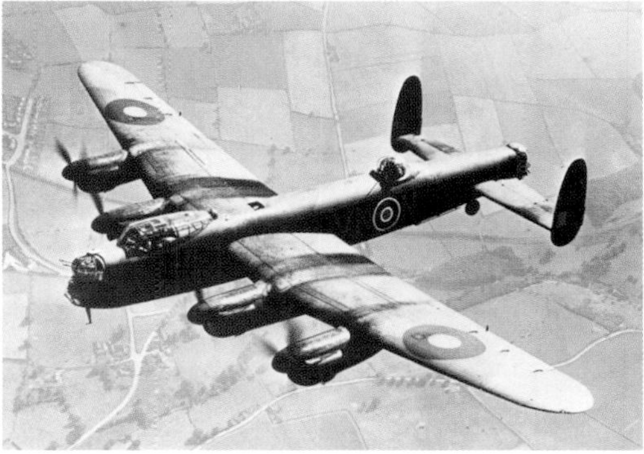

LEFT: Avro's Lancaster bomber carried a heavier bomb load than any of its American counterparts, needing fewer defensive weapons and gunners for its night missions.

BELOW: One of the war's finest defensive fighters, the Focke-Wulf Fw 190 D-9 was designed for high-altitude interception, but also performed well in low-altitude air field defensive missions.

Consolidated B-24 Liberators and (as seen here) Boeing B-17 Flying Fortresses bore the brunt of the US strategic air war against Germany. Both aircraft proved unable to survive sustained assaults by large formations of enemy fighters, but the development of long-range escort fighters increased the bombers' effectiveness, reducing crew losses to the point that many "extra" aircrews were transferred to the infantry in 1944.

Airborne Radar

Radar changed the face of World War II. Ground based systems helped plot approaching German formations during the Battle of Britain, allowing Fighter Command to adjust its defenses and inflict heavy losses on the enemy. (A similar system would detect Japanese bombers approaching Hawaii on 7 December 1941, though the signal was misinterpreted and US forces were caught unawares.) Images on airborne radar screens soon guided night fighters and anti-shipping bombers to their prey. The newer centimetric radar systems, introduced in 1943, gave bomber crews a clear image of the earth beneath them. Called H_2S by the British, and H_2X, Mickey, or BTO (Bomb Through Overcast) by the Americans, the new radars, when interpreted correctly, allowed crews to bomb targets hidden by smoke, clouds, or darkness.

In early 1944 British and American reconnaissance crews began a new series of missions to document the routes and targets soon to be attacked by the bombers. Using a camera to photograph their airborne radar screens, the recon missions gave bomber crews accurate images of what they would soon see on combat missions. Beyond the relatively distinctive coastlines, the images helped distinguish the reflections of glass roofs on factories and rail stations from surrounding wood and metal surfaces, asphalt or concrete roads, or grass-covered fields. Camouflage paint gave no protection from the radar beam, which also penetrated net and hessian camouflage covers. These rudimentary radar reconnaissance missions would eventually develop into an entire branch of radar mapping and reconnaissance, practiced today by aircraft, satellites, and space probes. •

This composite radar image of the Ligurian Sea shows the clarity with which shore lines and mountainous terrain could be viewed.

Two 93rd Bomb Group Consolidated B-24s approach a target from above the undercast. The lead aircraft mounts a Mickey radar dome beneath its fuselage, enabling the crew to attack a target it would never see.

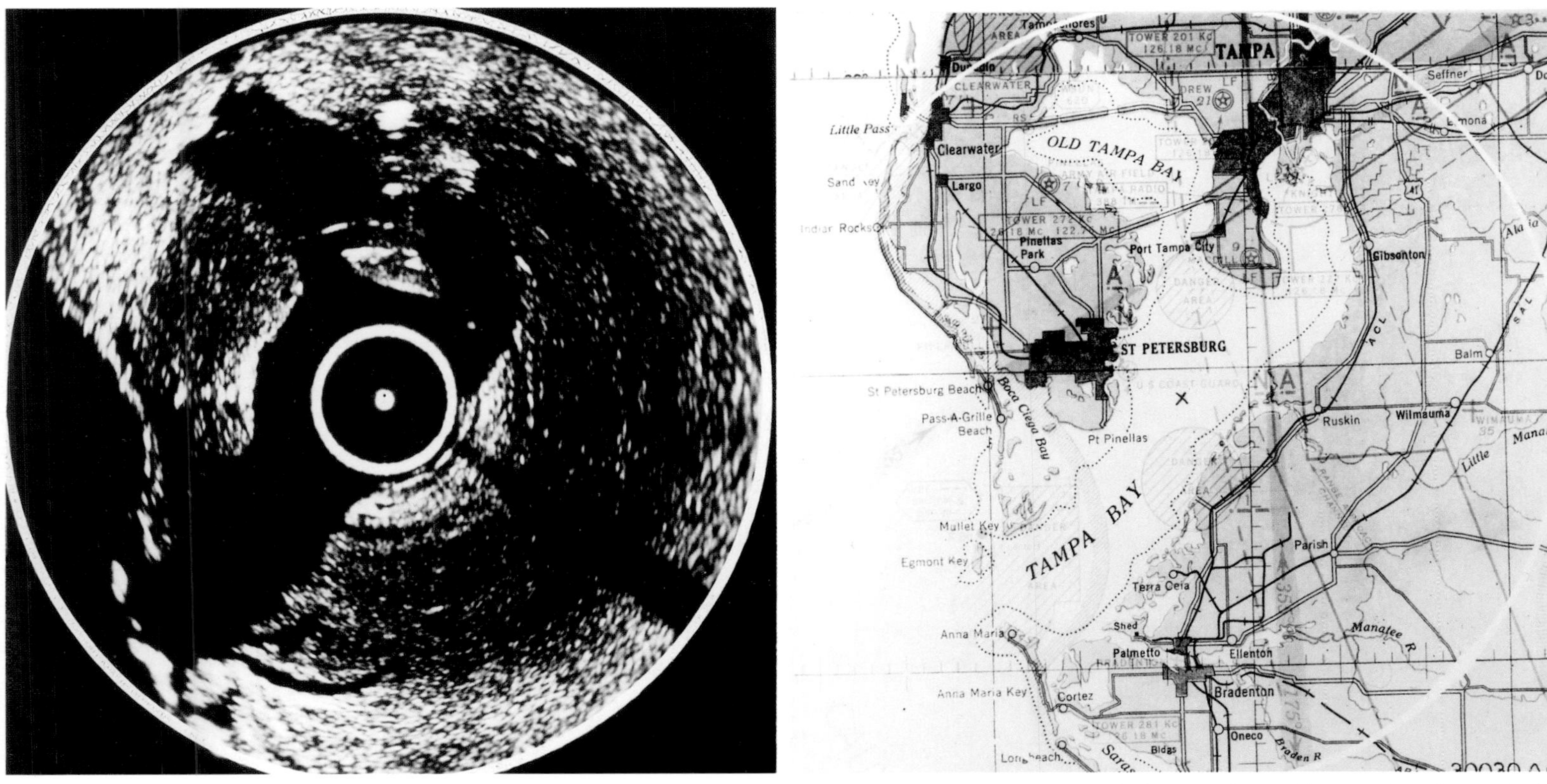

Comparing an early radar image of Tampa Bay, Florida, with an aeronautical map, even an untrained eye can distinguish the coast line, bridges, and, to the south, the Manatee River.

ABOVE: This 5th Photo Recon Group P-38 Lightning has been equipped with a Mickey radar system in the nose. The radar operator/photographer entered his cramped compartment through a small hatch under the nose.

LEFT: Naval aircraft used H2X radars to bomb land targets and locate enemy surface vessels. This Grumman Avenger tested the radar at Traverse City, Michigan, in 1945.

Hunting the U-Boat

A relatively small force of German submarines (U-Boats) terrorized the Atlantic shipping lanes through the first two years of World War II. Experience in the Great War had shown that aircraft could be useful in detecting submerged submarines. With luck, a flying boat or dirigible could drop a depth charge on a U-Boat, though most successful attacks were carried out by surface vessels guided by aircraft.

British anti-sub experience showed that a well-trained U-Boat crew could crash dive in half a minute, becoming almost undetectable in another thirty seconds. This meant that an aircraft needed to approach undetected at a high speed, closing before the submarine could escape. Radar helped - a surfaced submarine, detected at night or from behind clouds or haze, could be closed upon quickly and destroyed. German submariners were long unaware that they were being tracked on centimetric radar frequencies, and for months failed to mount any form of appropriate radar detector. More seriously, the crews never recognized that the Allies had penetrated German naval codes; every time a submarine reported its location to headquarters, anti-submarine forces could close and attack.

From bases around the North Atlantic, South Atlantic, Caribbean, and North Africa, long range bombers flew their patrols. In 1944, the US Navy added hunter-killer groups to the mix, flying high-speed fighters and bombers from smaller "jeep" carriers. •

Assigned to US Navy hunter/killer forces, Grumman TBF Avengers (and similar General Motors TBMs) attacked U-boats with depth bombs, rockets, and machine guns.

The tanker *R. P. Resor* was torpedoed off the New Jersey coast on 28 February 1942. Only three of the 50 crew members survived; the tanker was easily seen from the shore as she burned for two days.

The most effective long-range anti-submarine aircraft was the Consolidated B-24. *Tidewater Tillie* flew in Europe and North Africa with the USAAF's 480th Antisubmarine Group.

The RAF used long-range Short Sunderland flying boats as their primary anti-sub aircraft until American Catalinas and Liberators took over most patrols.

ABOVE: A depth charge explodes just aft of a U-Boat during an attack on 30 May 1943; despite the near miss, no German subs were lost that day.

LEFT: Depth charges hanging beneath their wings, US Navy Patrol Squadron 63 PBY-5A Catalinas await their next anti-submarine patrol from Natal, Brazil.

US Stations in Britain

For security purposes, the US Army Air Forces identified each station in the UK by a three-digit station number. Each installation was also named - usually for the nearest railway station - but the AAF (Army Air Field) number appeared in all official records. The code numbers were also used to identify several fields and installations outside the UK, particularly if the sites were associated with units or activities stationed in Britain. A small number of airfields established on the continent following the Normandy invasion used the number system briefly before converting to the field numbers noted on pages 132. •

KEY: Note that many of the smaller sites and all of the remote sites listed below are omitted from this map.

AAF Number, Name (Alternative name/names), Location

101 High Wycombe (Camp Lynn), Buckinghamshire
102 Alconbury, Huntingdonshire
103 Brampton Grange, Huntingdonshire
104 Hardwick, Norfolk
105 Chelveston, Northamptonshire
106 Grafton Underwood, Northamptonshire
107 Molesworth, Huntingdonshire
108 Old Catton, Norfolk
109 Podington, Bedfordshire
110 Polebrook, Northamptonshire
111 Thurleigh, Bedfordshire
112 Bovingdon, Hertfordshire Cheddington (Marsworth), Buckinghamshire
114 Hethel, Norfolk
115 Shipdham, Norfolk
116 Elveden Hall (Camp Blainey), Suffolk
117 Kimbolton, Huntingdonshire
118 Wendling, Norfolk
119 Horham, Suffolk
120 Attlebridge, Norfolk
121 Bassingbourne, Cambridgeshire
122 Steeple Morden, Cambridgeshire
123 Horsham St. Faith, Norfolk
124 Tibenham (Tivetshall), Norfolk
125 Bungay (Flixton), Suffolk
126 Rattlesden, Suffolk
127 Little Staughton, Bedfordshire
128 Deenthorpe, Northamptonshire
129 St. Eval, Cornwall
130 Glatton (Connington), Huntingdonshire
131 Nuthampstead, Hertfordshire
132 Beccles, Suffolk
133 East Wretham, Norfolk
134 Eye, Suffolk
135 Hepworth, Suffolk
136 Knettishall, Suffolk
137 Lavenham, Suffolk
138 Snetterton Heath, Norfolk
139 Thorpe Abbots, Norfolk
140 Winfarthing, Norfolk (See: 554 Fersfield)
141 Bodney, Norfolk
142 Deopham Green, Norfolk
143 North Pickenham, Norfolk
144 Old Buckenham, Norfolk
145 Rackheath, Norfolk
146 Seething, Norfolk
147 Ketteringham Hall, Norfolk
148 Beaumont, Essex
149 Birch, Essex
150 Boxted, Essex
151 Butley (Bentwaters), Suffolk
152 Debach, Suffolk
153 Framlingham (Parham), Suffolk
154 Gosfield, Essex
155 Great Ashfield, Suffolk
156 Mendelsham, Suffolk
157 Raydon, Suffolk
158 Sudbury, Derbyshire
159 Wormingford, Essex
160 Marks Hall, Essex
161 Boreham, Essex
162 Chipping Ongar (Willingdale), Essex
163 Cold Norton, Essex
164 Great Dunmow (Little Easton), Essex
165 Little Walden (Hadstock), Essex
166 Matching, Essex
167 Ridgewell, Essex
168 Rivenhall, Essex
169 Stansted (Mountfitchet), Essex
170 Wethersfield, Essex
171 Stisted Hall, Essex
172 Snettisham, Norfolk
173 Dunkeswell, Devon
174 Sudbury (Acton), Suffolk
175 Mousehole, Cornwall
176 Narborough, Norfolk
177 Ludham, Norfolk
178 Matlask, Norfolk
179 Harrington, Northamptonshire
180 Villacoublay, France (A-420)
181 Chievres, Belgium (A-84)
182 Merville, France (B-53)
183 Barisey le Cote, France
184 Charleroi, Belgium (A-87)
185 Wittem, Holland
191 Ollencourt, France
194 Martigues, France
195 Carnillon, France
196 Istres, France
231 Kirkcassock House (Nyack), County Down, Northern Ireland
232 Long Kesh, County Down, Northern Ireland
233 Belfast (Victoria Barracks), County Antrim, Northern Ireland
234 Mount Farm, Oxfordshire
235 Nutts Corner, County Antrim, Northern Ireland
236 Toome, County Londonderry, Northern Ireland
237 Greencastle, County Down, Northern Ireland
238 Cluntoe, County Tyrone, Northern Ireland
239 Maghaberry, County Down, Northern Ireland
240 Mullaghmore, County Londonderry, Northern Ireland
341 Bushey Hall (Watford), Hertfordshire
342 Atcham, Shropshire
343 Biggin Hill, Kent
344 Eglinton, County Londonderry, Northern Ireland
345 Goxhill, Lincolnshire
346 High Ercall, Shropshire
347 Ibsley, Hampshire
348 Kenley (London, Surrey)
349 Kirton-in-Lindsey, Lincolnshire
350 Lurgan, County Armagh, Northern Ireland
351 Merston, Sussex
352 West Hampnett, Sussex
353 Colerne, Wiltshire
354 Iceland
355 Coltishall, Norfolk
356 Debden, Essex
357 Duxford, Cambridgeshire
358 Earls Colne, Essex
359 Great Sampford, Essex
360 Ouston, Durham
361 Snailwell, Suffolk
362 Ford, Sussex
363 Tangmere (Chichester), Sussex
364 Gloucester, Gloucestershire
365 Halesworth (Holton), Suffolk
366 Metfield, Suffolk
367 Kingscliffe, Northamptonshire
368 Wittering, Northamptonshire
369 Martlesham Heath, Suffolk
370 Saffron Walden, Essex
371 Sawston, Cambridgeshire
372 Walcot Hall (Stamford), Northamptonshire
373 Leiston, Suffolk (Theberton)
374 Bottisham, Cambridgeshire
375 Honington, Suffolk
376 Watton, Norfolk
377 Wattisham, Suffolk
378 Fowlmere, Cambridgeshire
379 St. Germaine-en-Laye, France
380 Bath, Somerset
381 Paris (45 Sharron), France
382 Sudbury (Constitution Hill), Suffolk
383 Bolleville, France (A-25c)
384 Toussus-le-Noble, France (A-46)
385 Le Bourget, France (A-54c)
386 Paris (1 Rue de Tillsit at Champs Elysees), France
387 Northolt, Middlesex
388 Marseilles (Marignane), France (Y-14)
389 Compiegne, France
390 Bryanston Square, London
392 Boise de Boulogne (Chateau Rothschild), France
393 Verdun, France (A-82)
394 Le Francport, France
395 Rouen, France
396 Fontenay, France
397 Pierrefonds, France
398 Montdidier, France
399 Fignieres, France
400 Virton, Belgium (Y-41)
401 Haseley Court, Oxfordshire
402 Arborfield Cross, Berkshire
403 Kingston Bauize, Berkshire
404 Chibolton, Hampshire
405 Hampstead Borough (Elsworth Road and Wadham Gardens, St. Johns Wood), Middlesex (Greater London)
406 Andover, Hampshire
407 Thruxton, Hampshire
408 Beaulieu, Hampshire
409 Uxbridge, Buckinghamshire
410 Lashenden, Kent
411 High Halden, Kent
412 Headcorn, Kent
413 Staplehurst, Kent
414 Winkton, Hampshire
415 Bisterne Close, Hampshire
416 Christ Church, Hampshire
417 Ashford, Kent
418 Kingsnorth, Kent
419 Woodchurch, Kent
420 Popham, Hampshire
421 Chapel Row, Berkshire
422 Great Barrington, Gloucestershire
423 Cokethorpe, Oxfordshire
424 Sole Common, Berkshire
425 Scorton, Yorkshire
426 Stanlake Park, Berkshire
427 Langton, Dorset
428 Coleby Grange, Lincolnshire
429 Crookham Common, Berkshire
430 Drems, East Lothian
431 Dering Woods, Kent
432 Charborough Park, Hampshire
433 Bishopstrow, Wiltshire
434 Chisledon, Wiltshire
435 Erle Stoke Village, Wiltshire
436 Bois Hall, Essex
437 Norman Court, Hampshire
438 Brenzett, Kent
439 Aldergrove, County Antrim, Northern Ireland
440 Breamore, Hampshire
441 Bruern Abbey, Oxfordshire
442 Totton, Hampshire
443 St. Marys Hill, Glamorganshire, Wales
444 Stallington Grange, Staffordshire
445 Stiffkey, Norfolk
446 Taunton, Somerset
447 Weston Zoyland, Somerset
448 Start Point (Rougham), Devon
449 Middle Wallop, Hampshire
450 Zeals, Wiltshire

451 Rudloe Manor, Wiltshire
452 Stony Cross, Hampshire
453 Tarrant Rushton, Dorset
454 Warmwell, Dorset
455 Holmsley South, Hampshire
456 Eastcote, Middlesex
457 Fairford, Gloucestershire
458 Down Ampney, Gloucestershire
459 Blakehill Farm, Wiltshire
460 Winkleigh, Devon
461 Church Stanton (Culmhead, Somerset)
462 Upottery, Devon
463 Exeter, Devon
464 Merryfield, Somerset
465 Chalgrove, Oxfordshire
466 Membury, Berkshire
467 Aldermaston, Berkshire
468 Bury St. Edmunds, Suffolk 94
469 Ramsbury, Wiltshire
470 Hitcham, Suffolk (Station number used by Wattisham before April 1944; See: 377)
471 Keevil, Wiltshire
472 Ascot (Sunninghill Park), Berkshire
473 Bristol, Gloucestershire
474 Welford Park, Berkshire
475 Medmenham, Buckinghamshire
476 Aldermaston Court, Berkshire
477 North Luffenham, Rutland
478 Woolfox Lodge, Rutland
479 North Witham, Lincolnshire
480 St. Vincents (Grantham Lodge), Lincolnshire
481 Bottesford, Leicestershire
482 Balderton, Lincolnshire
483 Barkstone Heath, Lincolnshire
484 Folkingham, Lincolnshire
485 Great Saling (Andrews Field), Essex
486 Greenham Common, Berkshire
487 Charmy Down, Somerset
488 Fulbeck, Lincolnshire
489 Cottesmore, Rutland
490 Langar, Nottinghamshire
491 Bray Court, Berkshire
492 Hurn, Hampshire
493 Spanhoe (Wakerly), Northamptonshire
494 Henley-on-Thames (Phyllis Court), Oxfordshire
495 Tiverton (Knightshayes Court), Devon
496 Grane, France
497 Querqueville, Cherbourg, France (A-23C)
498 Ebrington Manor, Gloucestershire
499 Higham Heath, Suffolk
500 Prestwick, Ayrshire, Scotland
501 Stowmarket, Suffolk
502 Tostock Park, Suffolk
503 Romsey, Hampshire (Stanbridge Earls and Roke Manor)
504 Portreath, Cornwall
505 Neaton, Norfolk
506 Milton Ernest (Twinwood Farm), Bedfordshire
507 Perham Downs, Wiltshire
508 Hurst Park Site, Surrey
509 Kidderminster, Worcestershire (Also listed as Stone/Duncan Hall, Staffordshire)
510 Heston, Middlesex
511 Moulsford Manor and Bucklands, Berkshire
512 St. Mawgan (Trebelsue) Cornwall
513 Liverpool (Kirby House; BADA Silcocks Warehouse), Lancashire

US forces moved into the air base at Warton, Lancashire, in June 1942. The depot established there was officially known as Army Air Field 582.

514 Kirkby, Lancashire
515 Wapley Common, Gloucestershire
516 St. Mellons, Monmouthshire, Wales
517 Barnham (Little Heath), Suffolk
518 Stone (Beatty Hall), Staffordshire
519 Grove, Berkshire
520 Melton Mobray, Leicestershire
521 Braybrooke, Northamptonshire
522 Smethwick, Staffordshire
523 Shaftsbury (Coombe House Hotel), Dorset
524 Southport (Palace Hotel), Lancashire
525 Cranford (Meadowbank), Middlesex
526 Bures, Essex
527 Leicester, Leicestershire
528 Nether Wallop, Hampshire
529 Tetbury (Westonbirt), Gloucestershire
530 Haydock, Lancashire
531 Chrishall, Cambridgeshire
532 Ringshall, Suffolk
533 Altrincham (Dunham New Park), Cheshire
534 Cuddington, Cheshire
535 Hale, Cheshire
536 Newcastle-under-Lyme (Keele Hall), Staffordshire
537 Trowbridge, Wiltshire
538 Saltby, Lincolnshire
539 Tilshead, Wiltshire
540 Lydiard Tregoze, Wiltshire
541 Riseley, Bedfordshire
542 Crewe, Cheshire
543 Kingham, Oxfordshire
544 Ashdown Park Berkshire
545 Earsham, Norfolk
546 Potters Hill, Yorkshire
547 Abbots Ripton, Huntingdonshire
548 Eccles, Norfolk
549 Nascot Lodge, Hertfordshire
550 Williamstrip Park, Gloucestershire
551 Lymington, Hampshire
552 Huyton, Lancashire
553 Brigg, Lincolnshire
554 Fersfield, Norfolk
555 Shepherd's Grove, Suffolk
556 Alton (Aylesfield House), Hampshire
557 Pangbourne House, Oxfordshire
558 Walhampton House, Hampshire
559 Poltava, Ukraine, USSR
560 Piryatin, Ukraine, USSR
561 Mirgorod, Ukraine, USSR
562 Worcester (Spetchley Park), Worcestershire
563 Kings Somborne (Furze Down House), Worcestershire
564 Egginton, Derbyshire
565 Preston, Rutland
566 Tugby (Keythorpe Hall), Leicestershire
567 Witney (Eynsham Hall), Oxfordshire
568 Valley Anglesey, Wales
569 Bamber Bridge (Adams Hall, Lancashire)
570 Ayr, Ayrshire, Scotland
571 Poynton, Cheshire
572 Melchbourne Park, Bedfordshire
573 Stornoway, Isle of Lewis, Scotland
574 Heathrow, Middlesex
575 Hendon, Middlesex
576 London (20 North Audley Street), London
577 Maghull (Liverpool), Lancashire
578 Manchester (Bellvue Park), Lancashire
579 Padgate, Leicestershire
580 Wellingborough, Northamptonshire
581 Wortley, Yorkshire
582 Warton, Lancashire
583 Sharnbrook, Bedfordshire
584 Thrapston, Northamptonshire
585 Hull, Yorkshire
586 Camp Griffiths (Kew Gardens; Bushey Park; Teddington, London)
587 Barnham (Warren Wood St. Site), Suffolk
588 Bowes Moor, Yorkshire
589 Burton-on-Trent, Staffordshire
590 Burtonwood, Lancashire
591 Chorley (Washington Hall), Lancashire
592 Groveley Wood, Wiltshire
593 Burton Rough, Sussex
594 Stone (Jefferson Hall), Staffordshire
595 Troston, Suffolk
596 Kettering (Goghton Park), Northamptonshire
597 Langford Lodge, County Antrim, Northern Ireland
598 Litchfield, Staffordshire
599 Lords Bridge, Cambridgeshire
801 Bournemouth, Hampshire
802 Baverstock (Dinton), Wiltshire
803 Filton (Bristol), Gloucestershire
925 Remenham, Berkshire

Cross-Channel Attack

American military planners originally hoped to return to continental Europe in the spring of 1942, less than six months after the Japanese attack on Pearl Harbor. Wiser heads prevailed, however. Similarly, plans to invade France in 1943 were delayed as the Allies concentrated on the Mediterranean. In both cases, the delays were fortuitous; the weapons and trained troops available in 1942 and 43 would have assured defeat at the hands of a well supplied German army.

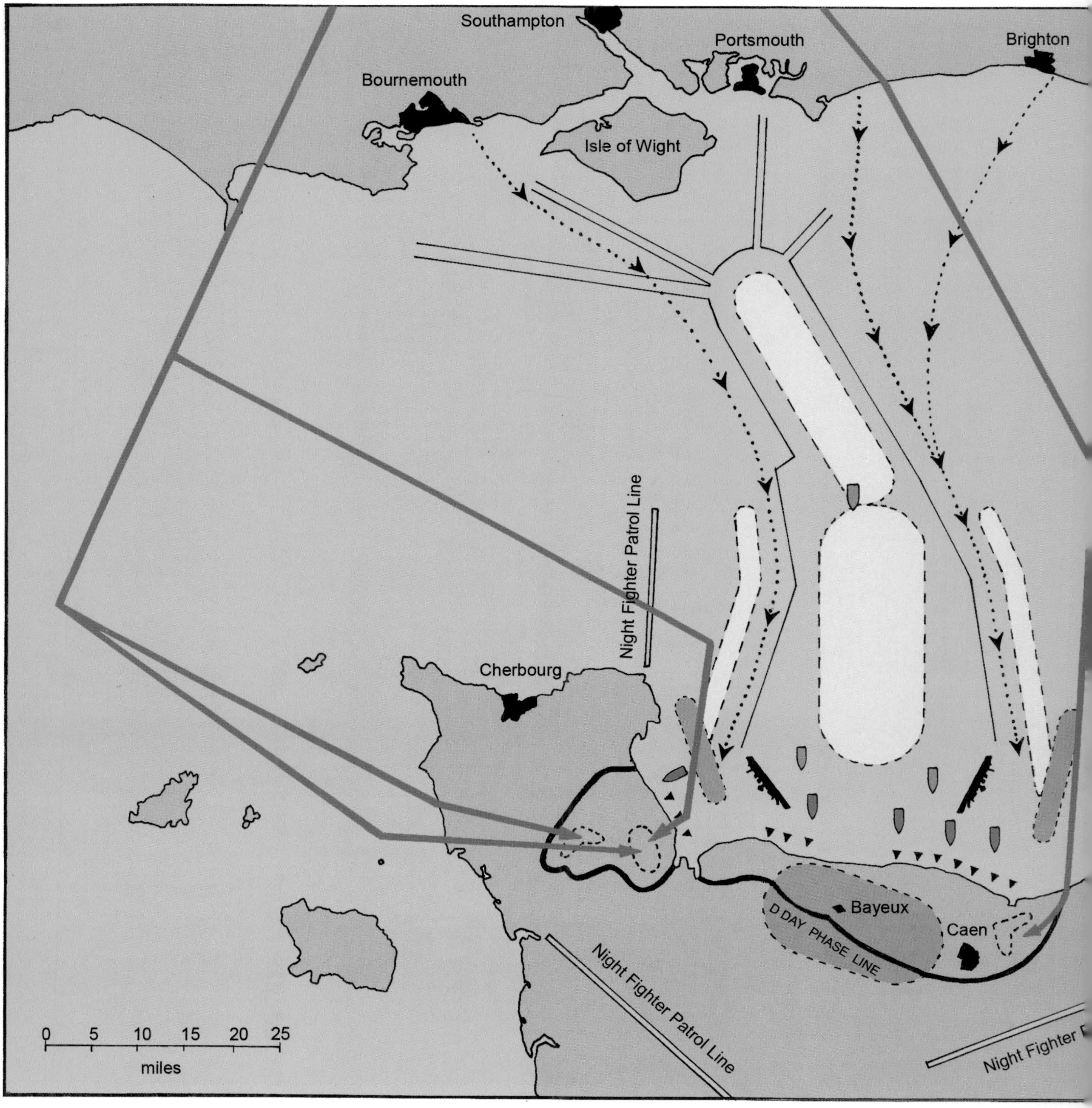

By the end of 1943 the balance had shifted. The Germans had improved their defenses along the Channel coast, and had produced more weapons of higher quality. But American and Canadian production lines and training grounds were producing weapons and troops at an amazing rate. Cadres of airmen, sailors, and soldiers had been hardened by the battles in North Africa and Sicily. New amphibious tactics and landing craft were developed, and, most critically, Allied air power was beginning to take control of the skies. General Dwight Eisenhower, Supreme Commander of the Allied Expeditionary Force, was able to assure his troops that any aircraft appearing over the beachheads would be theirs. (In fact, only two Luftwaffe fighters were able to attack the landing force.)

Overlord, the invasion of Normandy, was scheduled for 4 June 1944, though weather delayed D-Day* until the 6th. As the Allied fleet moved to the French coast, American transport aircraft dropped over 13,000 paratroopers to secure the beachhead's right flank. To the left flank, British aircraft inserted 6,000 British parachute and glider troops. Earlier experiences in Sicily had shown that nervous shipboard gunners could inflict terrible damage on their own airborne forces. To prevent a similar disaster, that night's transport aircraft, and those delivering the next two days' supplies and reinforcements, followed a route well away from the fleet.

Air units also applied special high-visibility markings - black and white wing and fuselage stripes - to lessen to possibility of friendly fire losses. Tactical bombers and fighters swept over the beaches to interdict German reinforcements before they could move to the battle area, while other fighters provided cover for the fleet and landings.

In six days the beachhead was secured to the point that the US chiefs of staff, General Eisenhower, and key members of their staffs were able to tour the landing area and observe their troops, equipments, and supplies pouring ashore. Air power's contribution was decisive; Eisenhower would observe, "If I didn't have air supremacy, I wouldn't be here." •

**In Allied practice the first day of a planned operation was designated D-Day. Days leading up to the operation were listed as D-1, etc, and days following the operation were listed as D+1, etc. Because of heavy contemporary press use of the term, "D-Day" has also become a popular name for the Normandy invasion.*

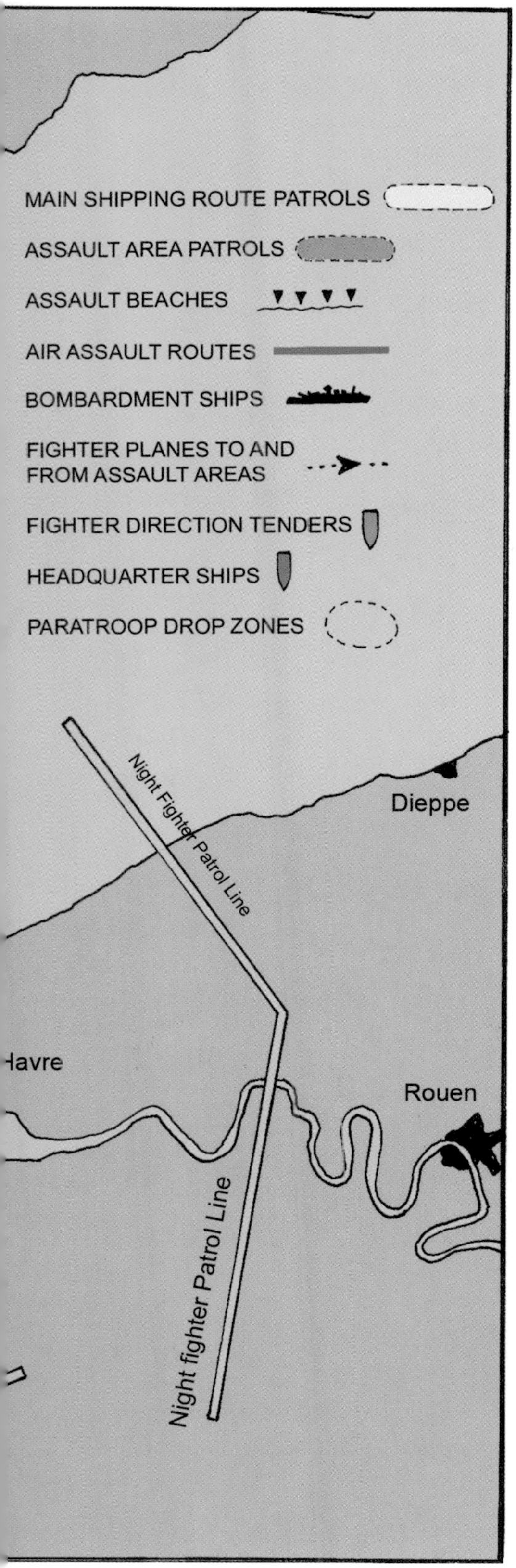

MAIN SHIPPING ROUTE PATROLS
ASSAULT AREA PATROLS
ASSAULT BEACHES
AIR ASSAULT ROUTES
BOMBARDMENT SHIPS
FIGHTER PLANES TO AND FROM ASSAULT AREAS
FIGHTER DIRECTION TENDERS
HEADQUARTER SHIPS
PARATROOP DROP ZONES
Night Fighter Patrol Line
Dieppe
Havre
Rouen
Night fighter Patrol Line

American C-47s tow their gliders to the flanks of the beachhead. Daylight glider resupply missions delivered howitzers, antitank guns, and 4,000 additional troops to reinforce paratroopers inserted the previous night.

Its bombing mission complete, an American B-26 leaves the French coast. Allied landing craft have been stranded on the beaches by the tides.

By the end of the first day, Allied engineers had prepared a rudimentary airstrip near the beachhead. This medevac C-47, with its crew and medical team, was the first aircraft to land.

Allied Continental Landing Fields

Aviation engineers were among the first specialized troops to land at Normandy on 6 June 1944. They were trained to build new airfields and rehabilitate captured airfields for use by Allied air forces, and by nightfall they had constructed the first temporary emergency landing strip. Two days later they opened a fully operational transport strip for delivery of supplies from the UK, and by month's end several American and British fighter units were operating from French fields.

For security purposes, the Allies designated each field with a letter-number code for use instead of place names in official documents, press releases, and letters home. The first fields were coded B- (for British) and A- (probably for American) with consecutive numbers assigned as commander planned the development of each site. By September, the Americans had designated fields A-1 through A-99 and adopted a Y- prefix for new fields. (The British simply began numbering fields in the one-hundred range.) After assigning code Y-99 in spring 1945, the Americans designated subsequent fields with the prefix R. By the War's end, American and British engineers had established almost 450 operational airfields. They dropped the code system in mid-September 1945, and those fields still in service became known by their geographical identities. •

CODE #	AIRFIELD & LOCATION
A-1	St Pierre du Mont, France
A-2	Criqueville, France
A-3	Cardonville, France
A-4	Deux Jumeaux, France
A-5	Chippelle, France
A-6	Beuzeville, France
A-7	Azeville, France
A-8	Picauville, France
A-9	Le Molay, France
A-10	Carentan, France
A-11	St Lambert, France
A-12	Lignerolles, France
A-13	Tour en Bessin, France
A-14	Cretteville, France
A-15	Maupertus, France
A-16	Brucheville, France
A-17	Meautis, France
A-18	St Jean de Daye, France
A-19	La Vielle, France
A-20	Lessay, France
A-21	St Laurent sur Mer, France (E-I, T-I)
A-22	Colleville, France (T-2)
A-23	Querqueville, France (T-3, AAF-497)
A-24	Biniville, France (T-4)
A-25	Bolleville, France (AAF-383)
A-26	Gorges, France
A-27	Rennes, France
A-28	Pontorson, France
A-29	St James, France
A-30	Courtils, France
A-31	Gael, France
A-32	Nantes/Chateau-Bougon, France
A-33	Vannes, France
A-34	Gorron, France
A-35	Le Mans, France
A-36	St Leonard, France
A-37	Lombron, France
A-38	Montreuil, France
A-39	Chateaudun, France
A-40	Chartres, France
A-41	Dreux, France
A-42	Villacoublay, France (AAF-180)
A-43	St Marceau, France
A-44	Peray, France
A-45	Lonray, France
A-46	Toussus Le Noble, France (AAF-384)
A-47	Orly, France
A-48	Bretigny, France
A-49	Beille, France
A-50	Orleans/Bricy, France
A-51	Morlaix, France
A-52	Etampes/Mondesir, France
A-53	Issy les Moulineaux, France
A-54	Le Bourget, France (AAF-385)
A-55	Melun, France
A-56	Le Hamil, France
A-57	Laval, France
A-58	Coulommiers, France
A-59	Cormeilles en Vexin, France
A-60	Beaumont sur Oise, France
A-61	Beauvais/Tille, France (B-42)
A-62	Reims/Champagne, France
A-63	Villeneuve/Vertus, France
A-64	St Dizier, France
A-65	Perthes, France
A-66	Orconte, France
A-67	Vitry, France
A-68	Juvincourt, France
A-69	Laon/Athies, France
A-70	Laon Couvron, France
A-71	Clastres, France
A-72	Peronne, France
A-73	Roye/Amy, France
A-74	Cambrai/Niergnies, France
A-75	Cambrai/Epinoy, France (B-72)
A-76	Athis, France
A-77	St Liviere, France
A-78	Florennes/Juzaine, Belg.
A-79	Prosnes, France
A-80	Mourmelion le Grand, France
A-81	Creil, France
A-82	Verdun, France (AAF-393)
A-83	Denain/Prouvy, France (B-74)
A-84	Chievres, Belg.
A-85	Senzeilles, Belg.
A-86	Vitrival, Belg.
A-87	Charleroi, Belg.
A-88	Maubeuge, France
A-89	Le Culot, Belg. (B-68)
A-90	Toul/Croix de Metz, France
A-91	Sedan, France
A-92	St Trond, Belg. (B-62)
A-93	Liege/Bierset, Belg.
A-94	Conflans, France
A-95	Nancy/Azelot, France

US forces moved into the wrecked German airfield at Ober Olm in March 1945, assigning the code number Y-64 for identification purposes. Here, a 354th Fighter Group P-51 Mustang is serviced near the bombed-out hangar.

When the P-38s of the 370th Fighter Group moved into the former German airfield at Florennes/Juzaine in late 1944, the facility carried the Allied code A-78.

CODE #	AIRFIELD & LOCATION
A-96	Toul/Ochey, France
A-97	Sandweiler, Luxemburg
A-98	Rosieres en Haye, France
A-99	Mars/Latour, France
Y-1	Tantonville, France
Y-2	Luneville, France
Y-3	Avril, France
Y-4	Buc, France
Y-5	Amberieu, France
Y-6	Lyon/Bron, France
Y-7	Dole/Tavaux, France
Y-8	Luxeuil, France
Y-9	Dijon/Longvic, France
Y-10	Le Culot/East, Belg.
Y-11	Cannes/Mandelieu, France
Y-12	St Raphael/Frejus, France
Y-13	Cuers/Pierrefeu, France
Y-14 (AAF-388)	Marseilles/Marignane France
Y-15	Aix/Les Milles, France
Y-16	Salon, France
Y-17 (AAF-196)	Istres/Le Tube, France
Y-18	Le Vallon, France
Y-19	La Jasse, France
Y-20	Sisteron, France
Y-21	Montelimar/Ancone, France
Y-22	Crest, France
Y-23	Valence, France
Y-24	Satolas, France
Y-25	Loyettes, France
Y-26	Lons le Saunier, France
Y-27	Besancon/Thise, France
Y-28	Verdun/Charny, France
Y-29	Asch, Belg.
Y-30	Le Havre/Octeville, France
Y-31	Bulgneville, France
Y-32	Ophoven, Belg.
Y-33	Thionville, France
Y-34	Metz, France
Y-35 (AAF-389)	Compiegne/Margny, France
Y-36	Cognac, France
Y-37	Bordeaux/Marignac, France
Y-38	Toulouse/Blagnac, France
Y-39	Haguenau, France
Y-40	Strasbourg/Entzheim, France
Y-41	Virton, Belg.
Y-42	Nancy/Essey, France
Y-43	Duren, Germ.
Y-44	Maastricht, Neth.
Y-45	Conde sur Marne, France
Y-46	Aachen, Germ.
Y-47	Namur, Belg.
Y-48	Auxerre, France
Y-49	Bourges, France
Y-50	St Avord, France
Y-51	Vogelsang, Germ.
Y-52	Nice, France
Y-53	Colmar, France
Y-54	Kelz, Germ.
Y-55	Venlo, Neth.
Y-56	Munchen-Gladbach, Germ
Y-57	Trier, Germ.
Y-58	Cologne, Germ.
Y-59	Strassfeld, Germ.
Y-60	Dunstekoven, Germ.
Y-61	Krefeld, Germ.
Y-62	Niedermendig, Germ.
Y-63	Coblenz, Germ.
Y-64	Ober Olm, Germ.
Y-65	Chantilly, Germ.
Y-66	Gollheim, Germ.
Y-67	Gelnhausen, Germ.
Y-68	Lachen/Speyerdorf, Germ.
Y-69	Mittelbronn, Germ.
Y-70	Maitzborn, Germ.
Y-71	Eudenbach, Germ.
Y-72	Braunschardt, Germ.
Y-73	Frankfurt/Rhine-Main, Germ.
Y-74	Frankfurt/Eschborn, Germ.
Y-75	Frankfurt/Rebstock, Germ.
Y-76	Darmstadt/Griesheim, Germ.
Y-77	Babenhausen, Germ.
Y-78	Biblis, Germ.
Y-79	Mannheim/Sandhofen, Germ.
Y-80	Wiesbaden, Germ.
Y-81	Ailertchen, Germ.
Y-82	Kirchellen, Germ.
Y-83	Limburg, Germ.
Y-84	Giessen, Germ.
Y-85	Ettinghausen, Germ.
Y-86	Fritzlar, Germ.
Y-87	Nidda, Germ.
Y-88	Wertheim, Germ.
Y-89	Mannheim/Stadt, Germ.
Y-90	Giebelstadt, Germ
Y-91	Hanau/Langendiebach, Germ.
Y-92	Dornberg, Germ.
Y-93	Munster, Germ.
Y-94	Handorf, Germ.
Y-95	Bracht, Germ.
Y-96	Kassel/Waldau, Germ.
Y-97	Paderborn, Germ.
Y-98	Lippstadt, Germ.
Y-99	Gutersloh, Germ.
R-1	Wenigenlupnitz, Germ.
R-2	Langansalza, Germ.
R-3	Rohrensee, Germ.
R-4	Gotha/North, Germ.
R-5	Crailsheim, Germ.
R-6	Kitzingen, Germ.
R-7	Weimar, Germ.
R-8	Eisefeld, Germ.
R-9	Erfurt/Bindersleben, Germ.
R-10	Illesheim, Germ.
R-11	Eschwege, Germ.
R-12	Kassel/Rothwesten, Germ.
R-13	Hessich/Lichtenau, Germ.
R-14	Detmold, Germ.
R-15	Oschersleben, Germ.
R-16	Hildesheim, Germ.
R-17	Gottingen, Germ.
R-18	Kolleda, Germ.
R-19	Nordhausen, Germ.
R-20	Esperstedt, Germ.
R-21	Rockau, Germ.
R-22	Rodigen, Germ.
R-23	Altenburg, Germ.
R-24	Wurzburg, Germ.
R-25	Schweinfurt, Germ.
R-26	Bayreuth, Germ.
R-27	Sachsenheim, Germ.
R-28	Furth, Germ.
R-29	Herzogenaurach, Germ.
R-30	Furth/Industriehafen, Germ.
R-31	Meresburg, Germ.
R-32	Kothen, Germ.
R-33	Gardelagen, Germ.
R-34	Stendal, Germany
R-35	Volkenrode, Germany
R-36	Wesendorf , Germany
R-37	Brunswick/Waggum, Germ.
R-38	Brunswick/Broitzem, Germ.
R-39	Helmstedt, Germ.
R-40	Bremen, Germ.
R-41	Schwabisch-Hall, Germ.
R-42	Buchschwabach, Germ.
R-43	Nuremburg, Germ.
R-44	Goppingen, Germ.
R-45	Ansbach, Germ.
R-46	Roth, Germ.
R-47	Ottingen, Germ.
R-48	Ingolstadt, Germ.
R-49	Hailfingen, Germ.
R-50	Stuttgart/Echterdingen, Germ.
R-51	Cazaux/Bordeaux, France
R-52	Leipzig/Mockau, Germ.
R-53	Zwickau, Germ.
R-54	Landesberg/East, Germ.
R-55	Salzwedel, Germ.
R-56	Nordholz, Germ.
R-57	Bremerhaven, Germ.
R-58	Friedricshafen, Germ.
R-59	Leipheim, Germ.
R-60	Neuburg, Germ.
R-61	Eutingen, Germ.
R-62	Mengen, Germ.
R-63	Wieden, Germ.
R-64	Cham, Germ.
R-65	Risstissen, Germ.
R-66	Regensburg/Prufening, Germ.
R-67	Memmingen, Germ.
R-68	Straubing, Germ.
R-69	Landau, Germ.
R-70	Kaufbeuren, Germ.
R-71	Lechfeld, Germ.
R-72	Furstenfeldbruck, Germ.
R-73	Ergolding, Germ.
R-74	Oberweisenfeld, Germ.
R-75	Schleissheim, Germ.
R-76	Pocking, Germ.
R-77	Gablingen, Germ.
R-78	Landsberg, Germ.
R-79	Schongau, Germ.
R-80	Salzburg, Germ.
R-81	Oberpfaffenhofen, Germ.
R-82	Munich/Reim, Germ.
R-83	Muhldorf, Germ.
R-84	Augsburg, Germ.
R-85	Munich/Neubiberg, Germ.
R-86	Aibling Bad, Germ.
R-87	Horsching, Austria
R-88	Innsbruck, Austria
R-89	Pilsen, Czechoslovakia
R-90	Wels, Austria
R-91	Erding, Germany
R-92	Vienna/Tulln, Austria
R-93	Hoitzkirchen/Marshall, Germ.
R-94	Nellingen, Germ.
R-95	Templehof (Berlin), Germ.
R-96	Erlangen, Germ.
R-97	Regensburg/Obertraubling, Germ.
R-98	Bad Kissingen, Germ.
BRITISH AIRFIELDS	
B-1	Asnelles sur Mer, France
B-2	Bazenville, France
B-3	St Croix sur Mer, France
B-4	Beny sur Mer, France
B-5	Camilly. France
B-6	Coulombs, France
B-7	Martragny, France
B-8	Sommervieu, France
B-9	Lantheuil, France
B-10	Plumetot, France
B-11	Longues, France
B-12	Ellon, France
B-13	(Unassigned)
B-14	Amblie, France
B-15	Ryes, France
B-16	Villoens les Buissons, France
B-17	Caen/Carpiquet, France
B-18	Cristot, France
B-19	Lingevres. France
B-20	Demouville, France
B-21	St Honorine, France
B-22	Authie, France
B-23	La Rue Huguenot, France
B-24	St Andre de l'Eure, France
B-25	Le Theil-Nolent, France
B-26	Illiers l'Eveque, France
B-27	Boisney, France
B-28	Evreux, France
B-29	Valailles, France
B-30	Creton, France
B-31	Fresnoy Folny, France
B-32	Prey, France
B-33	Campneuseville, France
B-34	Avrilly, France
B-35	Godelemesnil, France
B-36	Boussey, France
B-37	Corroy, France
B-38	La Lande, France
B-39	Ecouffler, France
B-40	Beauvais/Nivillers, France
B-41	Plouy, France
B-42	Renumbered A-61
B-43	St Omer/Ft Rouge, France
B-44	Poix, France
B-45	St Omer/Longuenesse, France
B-46	Grandvilliers, France
B-47	Construction cancelled
B-48	Amiens/Glisy, France
B-49	Construction cancelled
B-50	Vitry en Artois, France
B-51	Lille/Vendeville, France
B-52	Douai/Dechy, France
B-53 (AAF-182)	Merville, France
B-54	Achiet, France
B-55	Courtrai/Wevelghem, Belg.
B-56	Brussels/Evere, Belg.
B-57	Lille/Wambrechies, France
B-58	Brussels/Melsbroek, Belg.
B-59	Ypres/Vlamertinghe, Belg.
B-60	Grimberghen, Belg.
B-61	St Denis/Westrem, Belg.
B-62	Renumbered A-92
B-63	Bruges/St Croix, Belg.
B-64	Diest/Schaffen, Belg.
B-65	Maldegen, Belg.
B-66	Blakenberg, Belg.
B-67	Ursel, Belg.
B-68	Renumbered A-89
B-69	Moerbeke, Belg.
B-70	Antwerp/Deurne, Belg.
B-71	Coxyde, Belg.
B-72	Renumbered A-75
B-73	Moorseele, Belg.
B-74	Renumbered A-83
B-75	Nivelles, Belg.
B-76	Peer, Belg.
B-77	Gilze/Rijen, Neth.
B-78	Eindhoven, Neth.
B-79	Woensdrecht, Neth.
B-80	Volkel, Neth.
B-81	Le Madrillet, France
B-82	Grave, Neth.
B-83	Knocke/Le Zoute, Belg.
B-84	Rips, Neth.
B-85	Schijndel, Neth.
B-86	Helmond, Neth.
B-87	Rosieres en Santerre, France
B-88	Heesch, Neth.
B-89	Mill, Neth.
B-90	Petit/Brogel, Belg.
B-91	Kluis, Netherlands
B-92	Abbeville/Drucat, France
B-93	Valkenberg, Neth.
B-94	Unassigned
B-95	Teuge, Neth.
B-96	Unassigned
B-97	Amsterdam/Schipol, Netherlands
B-98 & B-99	Unassigned
B-100	Goch, Germ.
B-101	Nordhorn, Germ.
B-102	Vorst, Germ.
B-103	Plantlune, Germ.
B-104	Damm, Germ.
B-105	Drope, Germ.
B-106	Twente/Enschede, Neth.
B-107	Lingen, Germ.
B-108	Rheine, Germ.
B-109	Quakenbruck, Germ.
B-110	Achmer, Germ.
B-111	Ahlborn, Germ.
B-112	Hopsten, Germ.
B-113	Varrelbusch, Germ.
B-114	Diepholz, Germ.
B-115	Melle, Germ.
B-116	Wunstorf, Germ.
B-117	Jever, Germ.
B-118	Celle, Germ.
B-119	Wahn, Germ.
B-120	Hanover/Langenhagen, Germ.
B-121 to B-149	Unassigned
B-150	Hustedt, Germ.
B-151	Buckeburg, Germ.
B-152	Fassberg, Germ.
B-153	Bad Oeynhausen, Germ.
B-154	Reinsehlen, Germ.
B-155	Dedelstorf, Germ.
B-156	Luneburg, Germ.
B-157	Werl, Germ.
B-158	Lubeck, Germ.
B-159	Mahlen, Germ.
B-160	Copenhagen/Kastrup, Denmark
B-161	Unassigned
B-162	Stade, Germ.
B-163	Unassigned
B-164	Schleswig/Land, Germ.
B-165	Unassigned
B-166	Flensburg, Germ.
B-167	Kiel/Holtenau, Germ.
B-168	Hamburg/Fuhlsbuttel, Germ.
B-169	Unassigned
B-170	Westerland, Germ.
B-171	Unassigned
B-172	Husum, Germ.
B-173	Unassigned
B-174	Utersen, Germ.

Pearl Harbor

The Japanese attack on Pearl Harbor and other Hawaiian installations is remembered by most Americans as an act of treachery and infamy. It was also a well planned and executed tactical victory for the Japanese, though it would fail to achieve any of it's long-term strategic goals.

When America resisted Japan's imperial expansion into Asia with boycott and diplomatic resistance, Japan's military government came to regard war as inevitable. In November 1941, the Japanese fleet was ordered to sortie against the American fleet anchored at Pearl Harbor, Hawaii. Planners reasoned that destruction of the fleet would eliminate America's ability to counterstrike, forcing the US to concede defeat and grant the Japanese major concessions.

The plan called for three carrier divisions (six aircraft carriers) to launch a strike force of 183 aircraft against the base on 7 December. The aircraft were to arrive over the anchorage minutes after the Japanese ambassador in Washington delivered a declaration of war to the US State Department. At 7:55am, the attack commenced. Within thirty minutes, four of the eight battleships were sunk and three more suffered enough damage to render them unfit for further action. A second wave of 168 aircraft, which arrived just before 8:00 am, added to the destruction. Air facilities suffered similarly; by 10:00am only about a hundred Army Navy, and Marine aircraft (of nearly 400 available at sunrise) were fit for duty.

But the Japanese had blundered. Attacking the fleet in shallow water ensured that all but two battleships would be refloated, repaired, and returned to action. Also, none of the three Pacific Fleet aircraft carriers were in port during the attack, leaving all available during the critical battles of early 1942. Further, the critical tanks farms, storing millions of gallons of fuel, escaped attack; without that fuel, the fleet would have been unable to perform offensive or defensive actions of any kind.

But the most critical blunder came in Washington, where signals delays prevented the Japanese ambassador from delivering his message until after the attack was well under way. An enraged America could not forgive such a lapse, and rather than sue for peace, a nation rallied to the cry, "Remember Pearl Harbor!" •

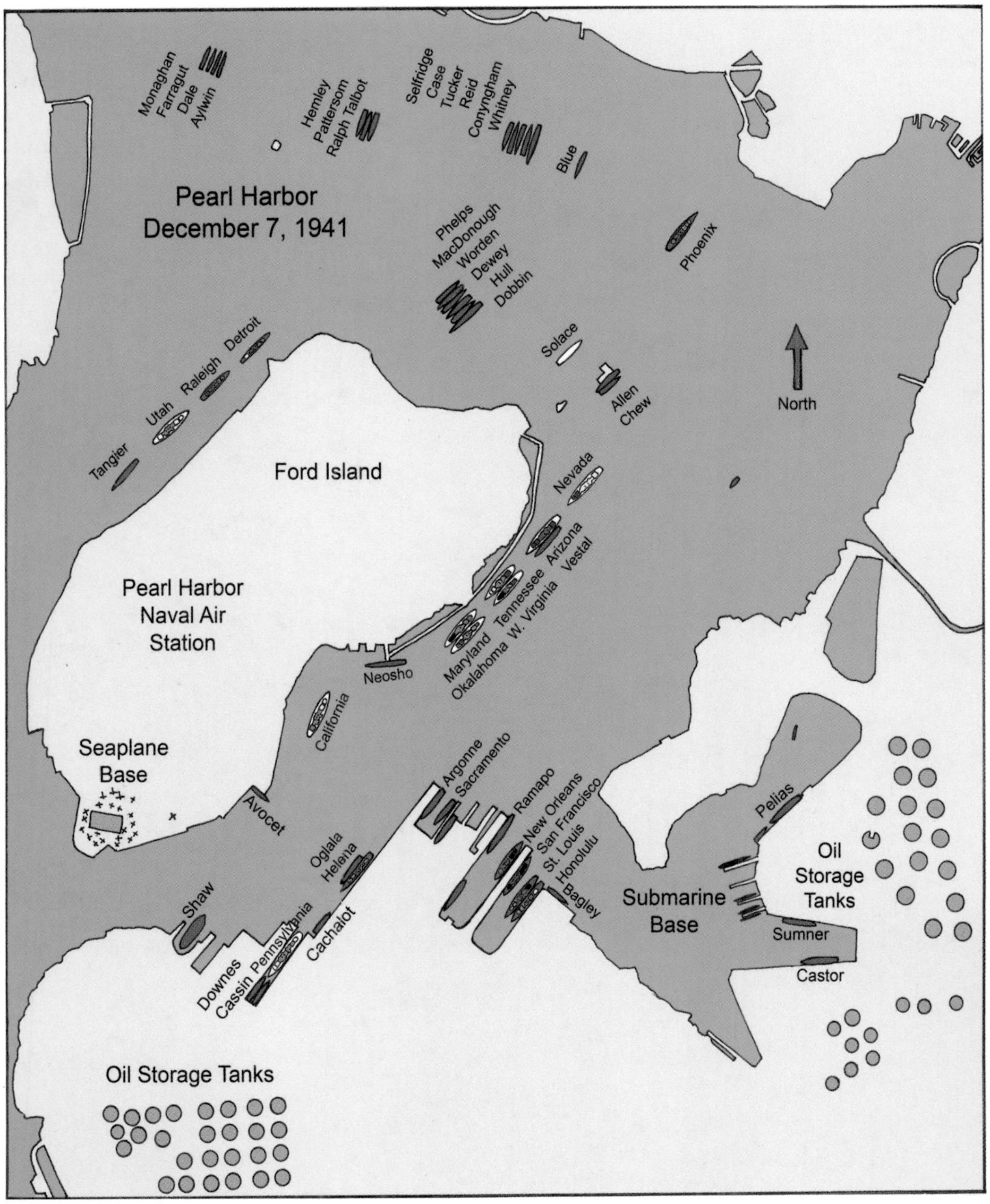

The bulk of the US Pacific Fleet was "safely" anchored in these positions when the first wave of Japanese aircraft appeared. Although the peacetime light gray color schemes had been replaced by dark camouflage blues and grays, the turrets of battleships and cruisers carried the peacetime colors that identified them to American scouting planes.

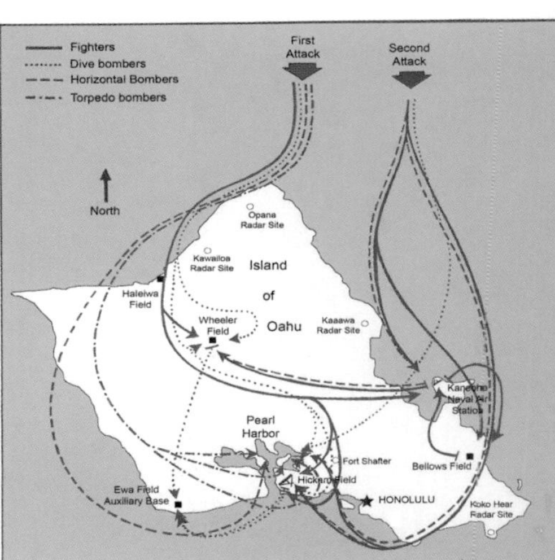

Descending from the north, the first attack wave arrived from the west and northwest. An hour later, the second wave moved in from the east and north east.

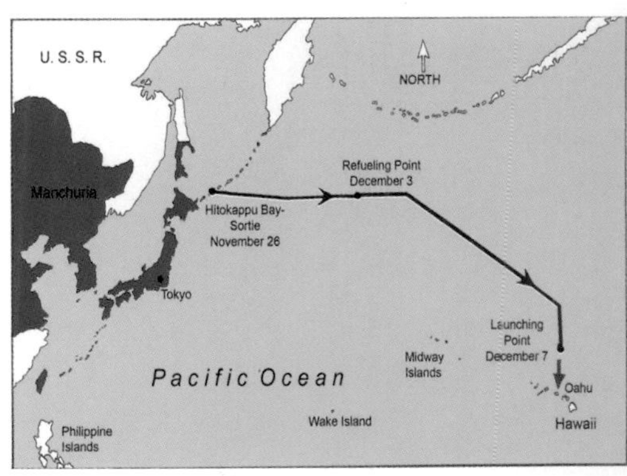

The Japanese attack force left home waters on 26 November 1941, arriving at a launch point north of the Hawaiian Islands just before dawn on 7 December (local time).

Army aircraft in Hawaii were lined up for defense against saboteurs - rather than dispersed against air attack - with predictable results. An unarmed section of B-17s, all bound for the Philippines, arrived during the attack. Most were damaged or destroyed.

Wrecked Kingfisher observation aircraft sit outside a damaged hangar on Ford Island. The least damaged aircraft of this group (2-O-3) was assigned to *Tennessee.*

Photographed three days after the attack, this US Navy image shows the damage at Battleship Row. To the right, *Arizona* hemorrhages fuel oil. Just forward, the damaged *Tennessee* is pinned in its berth by the sunken *West Virginia.* To the left, *Maryland* undergoes repairs while rescue efforts continue for the crew of the capsized *Oklahoma.*

Naval Aviation over the Pacific

The failure of the American, Dutch, British, and Commonwealth governments to appreciate Japan's military capabilities led to a stunning series of Allied defeats in the early months of 1942. The battleships of the US Pacific Fleet remained at Pearl Harbor, sunk or damaged. Great Britain's two Singapore-based battleships, the *Prince of Wales* and the *Repulse*, had been caught at sea by Japanese bombers; both were sent to the bottom in less than two hours.

However, the US Navy's aircraft carriers had escaped destruction in the Pacific war's early months. The force was not particularly large, particularly when pitted against the ten aircraft carriers available to the Japanese Navy in December 1941. The USS *Langley*, America's first carrier, had been converted to a seaplane tender. (She would be sunk in February 1942, attempting to transport a squadron of Army P-40s to Java.) The *Lexington,* sister ship *Saratoga,* and the new *Enterprise* were on duty in the Pacific at the time of Pearl Harbor. The smaller *Ranger* remained with the Atlantic Fleet, while *Yorktown* moved from the US East Coast to the Pacific at the end of 1941. The new ships *Wasp* and *Hornet* were in the Atlantic; both would be drawn to the Pacific in mid-1942 (*Hornet* in March and *Wasp* in June). Four of the carriers (*Lexington*, *Yorktown*, *Wasp*, and *Hornet*) would be lost between May and October 1942, but their replacements were already under construction. During 1943, the Pacific Fleet would gain four new *Essex* class carriers and five new light carriers; even more flattops, including dozens of smaller escort carrier, would enter the battle in 1944 and '45. •

Light and maneuverable, the Japanese Type 00 naval fighter was an unpleasant surprise for Allied planners at the beginning of the War. Although the "Zero" remained capable through 1945, heavier armor and armament would reduce the aircraft's aerobatic qualities. Japanese forces abandoned the remains of this Zero on Saipan in 1944.

The Grumman TBF - named the Avenger a few weeks before Pearl Harbor - would prove to be the US Navy's best torpedo bomber of the War. Most Avengers would be produced by General Motors under the designation TBM.

Mail call for deck crews on aboard the USS *Enterprise* in April 1942. The "Big E" was one of only two US carriers to survive the entire War.

ABOVE: The Japanese started the war with a number of Mitsubishi A5M fighters still assigned to second-line combat units. The aging monoplane's remarkable maneuverability still gave it a decided advantage over heavier British and American fighters. This 14th Air Group fighter was forced down in China in mid-1941.

RIGHT: The Japanese carrier *Akagi* dodges bombs dropped by high-altitude US Army B-17s during the Battle of Midway, 4 June 1942. Defending fighters also protected the carrier from Navy torpedo bombers, but later that day *Akagi* became one of four carriers sunk by Navy dive bombers during the battle.

Avengers warm-up their engines aboard the *Enterprise* as the elevator carries a Hellcat fighter to the flight deck. The aircraft were supporting the invasion of the Marshall Islands in December 1943-January 1944.

ABOVE: Its left engine shot away, a Japanese Kawanishi H8K flying boat attempts to escape pursuing US Navy fighters. The well-armed patrol craft would be shot down minutes later.

RIGHT: The fastest single-engined fighter of its day, the Vought F4U Corsair initially proved unsuitable for carrier operations. Operating instead with island-based Marines, the Corsair was the first US fighter to outperform Japanese fighters in combat over the Pacific.

With 34 confirmed victories, Captain David McCampbell ended the War as the US Navy's top ace - a feat made more remarkable by the fact that all of McCampbell's victories were scored within six months of combat. McCampbell's aircraft for most of this period was this Grumman F6F Hellcat nicknamed *Minsi III*.

Bombing Japan

Even without the advantages of turbojet powerplants, the Boeing B-29 Superfortress was easily the most technologically advanced aircraft of World War II. In aerodynamics, structures, and metallurgy, the B-29 used the latest engineering advances. Its crew flew in a pressurized fuselage, comfortable even at extreme altitudes. Each of four remote control gun turrets could be directed by more than one gunner. Bombing was aided by the most advanced radar systems of the day.

The first combat B-29 missions were flown from China in mid-1944, with bases in the Marianas Islands first opening in August 1944. The difficulties of moving supplies to Chinese bases forced the consolidation of all B-29 units in the Marianas in April 1945.

For all of their advances, the high-altitude B-29s missed many of their targets as bombs were redirected by variable jet stream winds, which often reached speeds of 200mph. In March 1945, the aircraft switched from precision bombing to wide-area fire bombing at lower altitudes, beginning a program of widespread destruction as incendiary bombs spread flames over small wood-frame factories and population centers.

On 6 August 1945, a single B-29 dropped the first atomic bomb on the Japanese city of Hiroshima. In a flash, the weapon reduced much of the thriving port city to rubble, destroying the headquarters of the Japanese Second Army and killing tens of thousands of civilians. Three days later, a second atomic bomb destroyed the city of Nagasaki. A military leadership that had planned to fight to the bitter end found that the end had come before a single Allied soldier landed. •

General Haywood Hansell, Commander of the XXI Bomb Command, points to the target for 24 November 1944: Tokyo.

The Marianas Islands were rebuilt as bases for hundreds of US B-29s. This section of Guam served Superfortresses of the 29th Bomb Group.

LEFT: On 7 June 1945, 409 B-29s attacked industrial and transportation targets in Osaka with high explosive and incendiary bombs. Bombing by radar through heavy undercast, the force burned out two square miles of the city, destroying over 55,000 buildings. This damage assessment chart compared new damage to the results of previous missions. Polka-dotted sections identified lightly populated areas.

Armorers carry belts of 50-caliber ammunition into a 497th Bomb Group B-29 in the Marianas.

ABOVE: A formation of Superfortresses heads home following a bombing mission to Japan.

LEFT: With 20,000 pounds of bombs, each B-29 carried an unimaginable destructive power. Here, a single mission's load of incendiary bombs waits beside the open bomb bay of a 29th BG Superfortress.

A mixed load of incendiary and fragmentation bombs descends towards Kobe, attacked on 5 June 1945.

As the second wave arrived at Kobe, smoke from the burning port city awaited them at 18,000 feet. Japanese antiaircraft guns and fighters accounted for eleven of the bombers.

Yokohama was the target on 29 May 1945; the B-29s in this photo were in the 500th BG.

On 7 April 1945, one hundred B-29s of the 73rd Bomb Wing dropped new 2,000-pound bombs on Tokyo, one of the few attempts to use such heavy ordnance against Japan.

The Japanese battleship *Hyuga* was run aground by its crew following devastating attacks by American carrier aircraft in July 1945. Destruction of naval facilities at the nearby port of Kure prevented any reclamation efforts before the War ended.

Toyama burns during the night raids of 1 August 1945.

The flash from the nuclear weapon dropped on Hiroshima bleached everything it touched; a valve handle left this shadow on the side of a storage tank.

A-11-JAPAN-HIROSHIMA-RUINS OF CENTRAL HIROSHIMA-
N3424 E13225-RESTRICTED
1802.471

The systematic destruction of Japanese industrial centers leveled most major cities, but the Hiroshima atomic bomb caused this devastation in minutes, leaving a lingering hazard from radiation.

Eyes Over the Pacific

US military doctrine of the 1930s gave little thought to combat aerial mapping. While developing mapping cameras, the Army Air Corps gave little thought to the aircraft that would carry those cameras. Officially, aerial mapping was to be carried out by any available aircraft, once air superiority had been established.

Air superiority would prove a more elusive goal than originally believed - and maps, essential to military planners, were needed even when enemy aircraft controlled the skies. The British solution had been to remove the guns from high-speed fighters and install cameras, a concept quickly accepted in the US. In March 1942, the first F-4 reconnaissance versions of the Lockheed Lightning were flown from the factory to the Southwest Pacific. In the next two months, a pair of the aircraft photographed most of New Guinea.

While F-4s and more advanced F-5s served as the primary US recon aircraft in the Pacific, specially modified B-24 Liberators (F-7s) and B-29 Superfortresses (F-13s) were employed as high-altitude, long-range reconnaissance platforms. These larger aircraft carried more cameras and flew longer ranges at higher altitudes. Assembled photos could be interpreted in theater, converted into maps as needed; images were also forwarded to Washington, where the new Aeronautical Chart Service would prepare higher-grade maps for service use. •

RIGHT: ***Limping Lizzie*****, one of the first Lockheed F-4 Lightnings produced, became one of a pair of aircraft to map New Guinea in mid-1942.**

BELOW: This provisional chart of the central Philippines was prepared by the Army Air Forces in mid-1944, several months before the American invasion. Data was collected from a variety of sources, including aerial mapping photography. Special inks allowed charts like this to be viewed at night under white, ultra-violet, red, or amber lights.

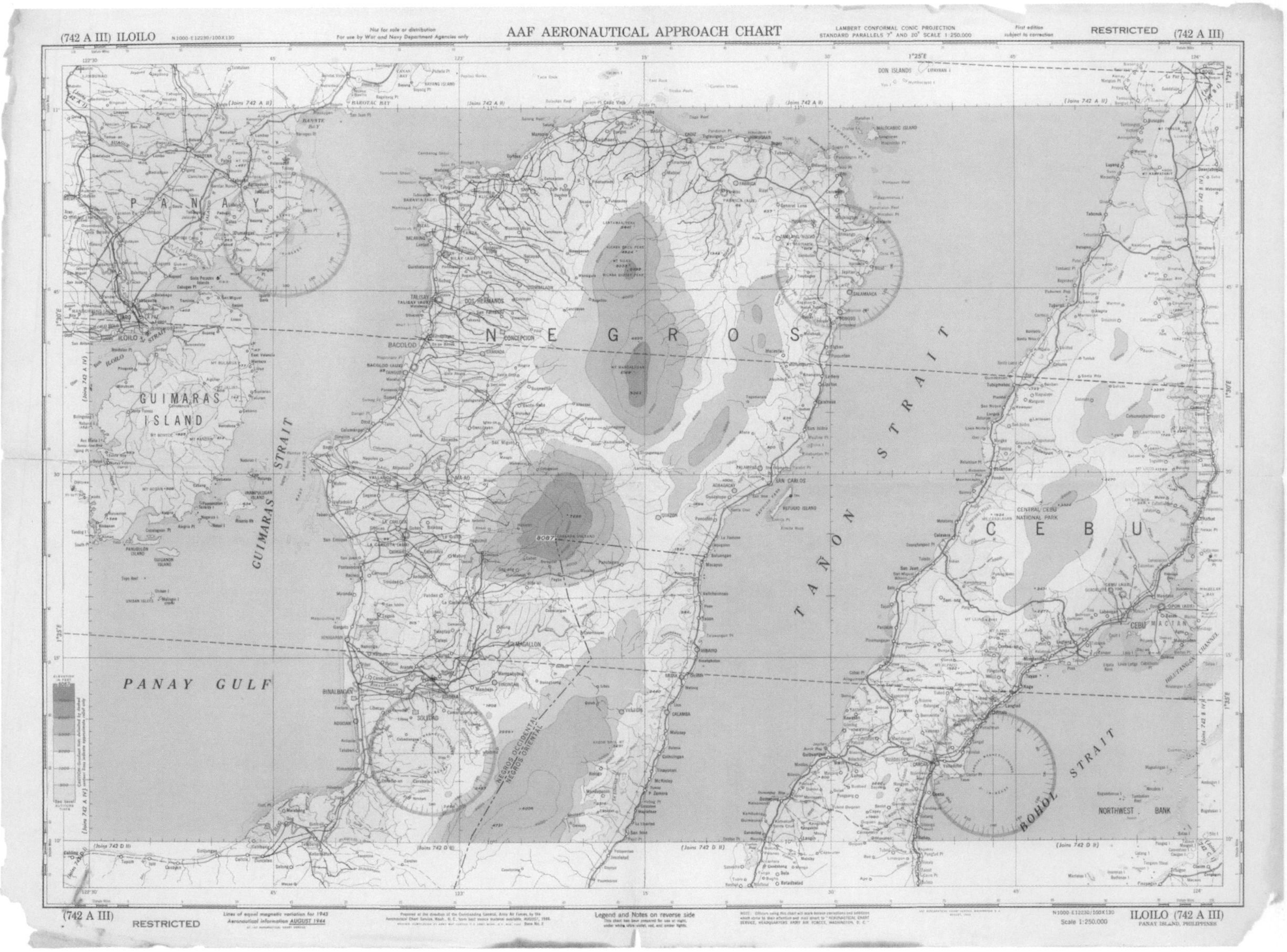

Following the first recon mission over Tokyo, US analysts prepare photo mosaics of the imagery.

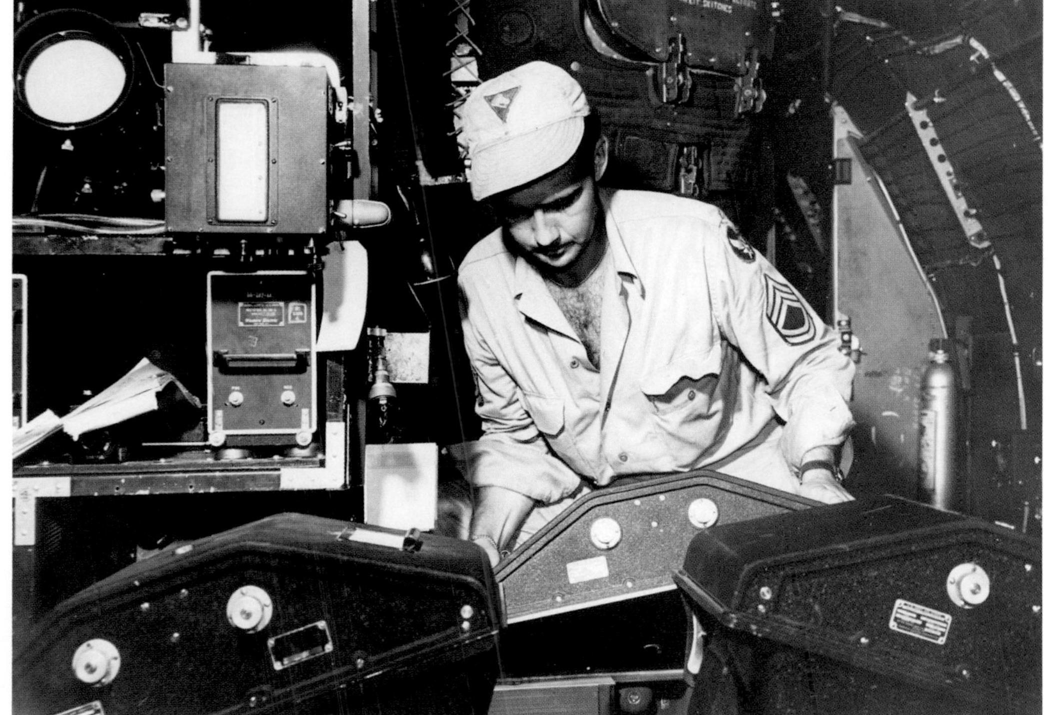

ABOVE: Technicians prepare film magazines at the nose of an F-7B Liberator.

LEFT: Cameras are prepared in the aft fuselage of *Tokyo Rose*, the Boeing F-13 that completed the first recon mission over Tokyo.

America's Air Forces

The major combat commands of the American Army Air Forces were initially created to control air assets in specific geographical areas. The number of air forces grew as American forces entered new combat theaters. Generally, geographical need continued to dictate the establishment of the newer air forces, though some were established due to political concerns. In late 1944, the first air forces were established along functional lines, with two commands sharing the same theater, but dividing forces between tactical and strategic missions.

Note that the organizational numbers of US air forces can be spelled out or presented in Roman numerals, but should never be written in Arabic numerals. ("First Air Force" or "I Air Force," but never (1st Air Force.") The letters listed in parentheses below refer to general locations on the map [at the right].

The FIRST AIR FORCE, which was established in early 1941, was originally activated as the Northeast Air District in December 1940. Charged with air defense of the US northeast (A), the First AF also trained combat units and replacements for other combat theaters.

The SECOND AIR FORCE mirrored the history of the first, though geographically responsible for the American Northwest (B). (It had been activated as the Northwest Air District in December 1940.)

The THIRD AIR FORCE - Besides antisubmarine missions, the Third trained units and crews for bomber, fighter, and recon missions in the Southeast US (C).

The FOURTH AIR FORCE - The Fourth flew air defense missions along the US West Coast in the months after Pearl Harbor (D).

The FIFTH AIR FORCE was activated as the Philippines Department Air Force in August 1941 and redesignated the Far East Air Force in October 1941, finally becoming the V Air Force in February 1942. Driven out of the Philippines (E) early in the war, the Fifth eventually rebuilt in Australia. Fighting back through New Guinea, and the Dutch East Indies, the Fifth eventually returned to the Philippines in October 1944, moving to Okinawa by the War's end.

The Panama Canal Air Force, activated in November 1940, was redesignated the Caribbean Air Force in August 1941 and the SIXTH AIR FORCE in February 1942. The Sixth controlled US air assets in Central America and the Caribbean (F).

Redesignated the SEVENTH AIR FORCE in February 1942, this organization was activated as the Hawaiian Air Force in November 1940. The Seventh, headquartered in Hawaii (G), fought throughout the Central Pacific. It's detached units in the South Pacific formed the cadre of the Thirteenth Air Force in 1943, and several of its fighter units flew escort missions to Japan, protecting the Twentieth Air Force's B-29s in 1944-45.

Activated in Georgia in January 1942, the EIGHTH AIR FORCE moved to Britain (H) in May. Engaging in the strategic bombing of Nazi targets, in October 1943 the Eighth was divided into strategic combat units (which it retained) and tactical units (which it passed to the newly reformed Ninth Air Force). In February 1944, the Eighth was redesignated the US Strategic Air Forces in Europe; at the same time, the Eighth Bomber Command was redesignated as the new Eighth Air Force. After the German surrender, the Eighth began to reform on Okinawa with B-29s in July 1945. At least two bombing missions were launched against the Japanese homeland, but both missions were recalled before reaching their targets.

The NINTH AIR FORCE was established in the US, moving to Egypt (I) to control US units fighting the German Afrika Corps in November 1942. With the Germans driven out of North Africa, the Ninth was preparing to inactivate when it was moved to England to become a tactical air force (in preparation for D-Day) in October 1943.

The TENTH AIR FORCE was activated in February 1942, moving to India (J) the next month. The Tenth initiated the India-China airlift, which was soon taken over by the Air Transport Command. The Tenth's China Air Task Force became the Fourteenth Air Force in March 1943.

The Alaskan Air Force was activated in Alaska (K) in January 1942, then redesignated the ELEVENTH AIR FORCE in February. The Eleventh helped drive Japanese forces from the Aleutian Islands after June 1942, then launched long-range bombing missions against Japan's northern islands.

The TWELFTH AIR FORCE was activated in August 1942, moving to England the same month to prepare for the invasion of Northwest Africa (L) that November. After the Allies moved into Italy, the Twelfth was reorganized as America's tactical air force in the Mediterranean.

The THIRTEENTH AIR FORCE was formed in the South Pacific (M) in January 1943, a political necessity to ensure parity with

naval forces operating in the area. (AAF units there were originally detached from the Seventh Air Force.) With the expulsion of Japanese forces from the South Pacific, the Thirteenth moved to the South-West Pacific, fighting alongside units of the Fifth Air Force. The Thirteenth ended the War based in the Philippines.

The FOURTEENTH AIR FORCE also formed for political purposes. The War Department repeatedly denied General Claire Chennault's request to have his China Air Task Force elevated to numbered air force status. After Chinese head of state Chiang Kai-shek interceded directly with President Roosevelt, the FOURTEENTH AIR FORCE was established in China (N) in March 1943.

The FIFTEENTH AIR FORCE was activated in the Mediterranean Theater in November 1943, moving to Italy (O) in December. The Fifteenth was created as America's second strategic air force, coordinating its bombing missions against Germany's industry with the Eighth Air Force in Britain.

America's final strategic air force, the TWENTIETH AIR FORCE was established in Washington, DC, in April 1944. Command remained in Washington almost to the War's end, thwarting most local command efforts to divert the Twentieth's B-29s from their missions against Japan's industrial capacity. The Twentieth's XX Bomber Command began operations from China (N) in June 1944; the XXI Bomber Command began operations from the Marianas (P) in late 1944. Both commands joined in the Marianas in mid-1945, both disbanding in July, with combat wings reporting directly to the XX Air Force, then established in theater.

The Far East Air Forces (FEAF) was created in June 1944 to coordinate logistics and operations of the Fifth and Thirteen air forces, which were both operating in New Guinea at the time. A proposal to inactivate the Thirteenth, passing its units to the Fifth, was deemed a bureaucratic nightmare; creation of FEAF solved the problems with far less confusion.

Created in early 1944, the Mediterranean Allied Air Forces coordinated the efforts of US, British, French, and Italian Republican air forces. Both the Twelfth and Fifteenth air forces coordinated logistically through the MAAF, though Fifteenth operations were directed by the US Strategic Air Forces in Europe.

The UNITED STATES STRATEGIC AIR FORCES IN EUROPE was formed in February 1944 to coordinate the strategic missions flown against Germany by the Eighth Air Force in Britain and the Fifteenth Air Force in Italy. •

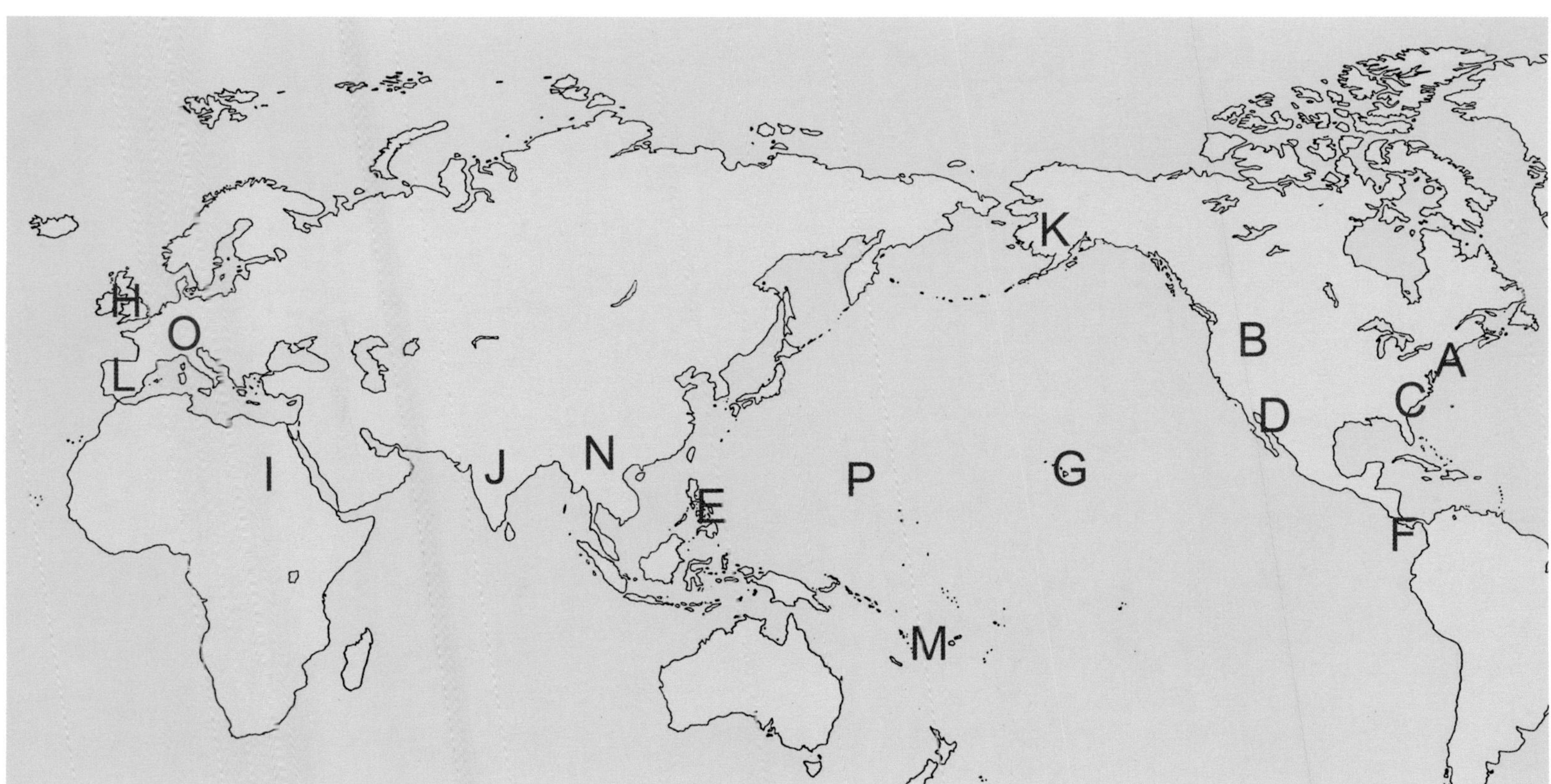

Initially unprepared for warfare on a worldwide scale, the Army Air Forces quickly reorganized and adapted to the changing situation on many fronts. The letters on this world map show the locations each air force's headquarters as referenced in the text.

Wright Field's Crash Map

In October 1917, the US Army established McCook Field in northern Dayton, Ohio, to serve as headquarters of the Air Service's Engineering Division. McCook became the center for Army research and development in aeronautical technology. To the east was the newly established Fairfield Aviation General Supply Depot, which included Wilbur Wright Field. The Army's primary aeronautical storage and distribution center, the facility was renamed Wilbur Wright Air Service Depot in 1919, Fairfield Air Intermediate Depot in 1921, and Patterson Field in 1931 (with Fairfield AID as a subsidiary organization).

In the interim, the citizens of Dayton donated land to the southwest of the depot to serve as a new Army air field. This opened as Wright Field (named for Wilbur *and* Orville) in 1927, immediately absorbing the functions and personnel of McCook Field (which closed a short time later). Although separated by function (and about three miles), Wright and Patterson fields were often united under the same commander; in January 1948 they were formally merged as Wright-Patterson Air Force Base.

Bureaucratic infighting saw Wright Field reorganized, with some of its responsibilities transferred to other locations. But the Materiel Center at Wright Field continued to function as the primary facility for evaluating aircraft and their components, flight and ground equipment, and armaments. Much of the work involved flight tests - either of the aircraft or new components - and many of those tests ended in forced or crash landings.

In order to quickly locate the sites of these emergencies, Wright Field produced a grid map for distribution to local police, fire, civil defense, and emergency units. The map divided an area 36 by 44 miles into one-square-mile grid sections, each section identified by an X and a Y coordinate. (This 1959 edition of the map has been marked - for reasons unknown - at grid coordinates X18, Y17 and coordinates X12, Y18.)

The military use of grids had been well established in the artillery and Corps of Engineers. While latitude and longitude were still useful for navigation, each coordinate identified only a point - grid coordinates identified an area. Grid coordinates could also be encoded, preventing the unauthorized and the unfriendly from listening in on critical communications. All of this fit with Wright Field's need to reach any crash site quickly; beyond the normal requirements of protecting life and property, the aircraft based around Dayton often carried classified equipment to be protected from the curious. And mobilizing local emergency resources to secure the crash site left more clues in place when investigators arrived - with the area cordoned off, untrained citizens were less likely to obscure clues that could help determine if a new system had caused the crash or if a pilot had simply flown into the ground. •

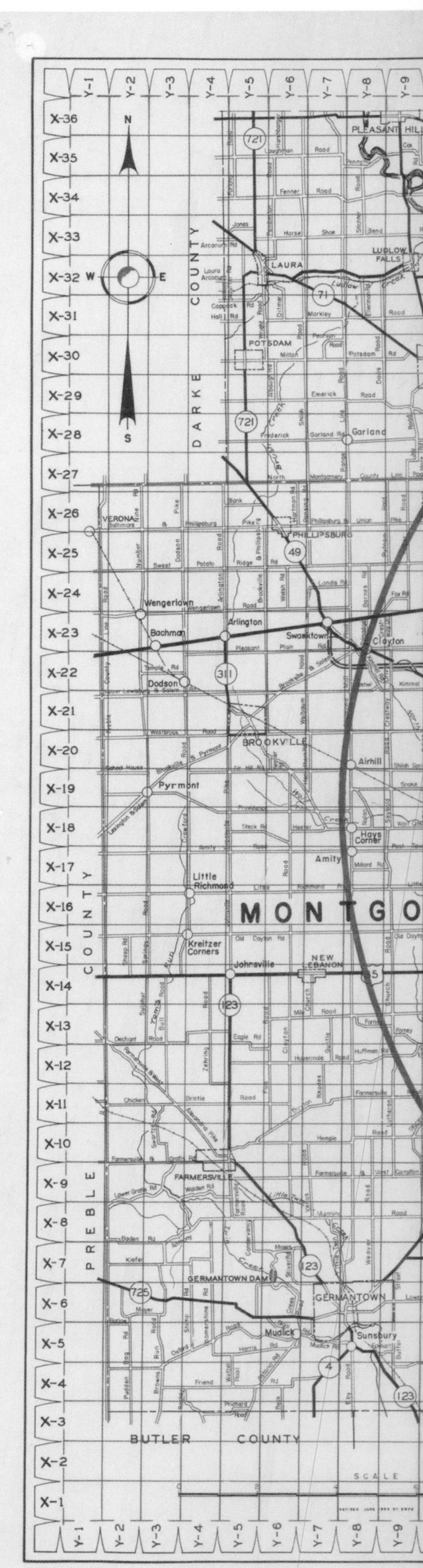

The hardstand at Wright Field shows the latest in aircraft designs in this mid-1941 photo. They are (clockwise, from the lower right corner): Republic YP-43, Bell P-39C, Curtiss P-40B, Douglas B-23, North American B-25A, Martin B-26, Boeing B-17B, and Lockheed YP-38. A B-17C is taxiing in from the field beyond.

On 8 March 1943, Lieutenant Harold Goodwin took this AT-6B up for a low-altitude speed test. When the engine began to vibrate uncontrollably, Goodwin made a wheels-up landing in a field just off Osborn Road, at X-22, Y-26.

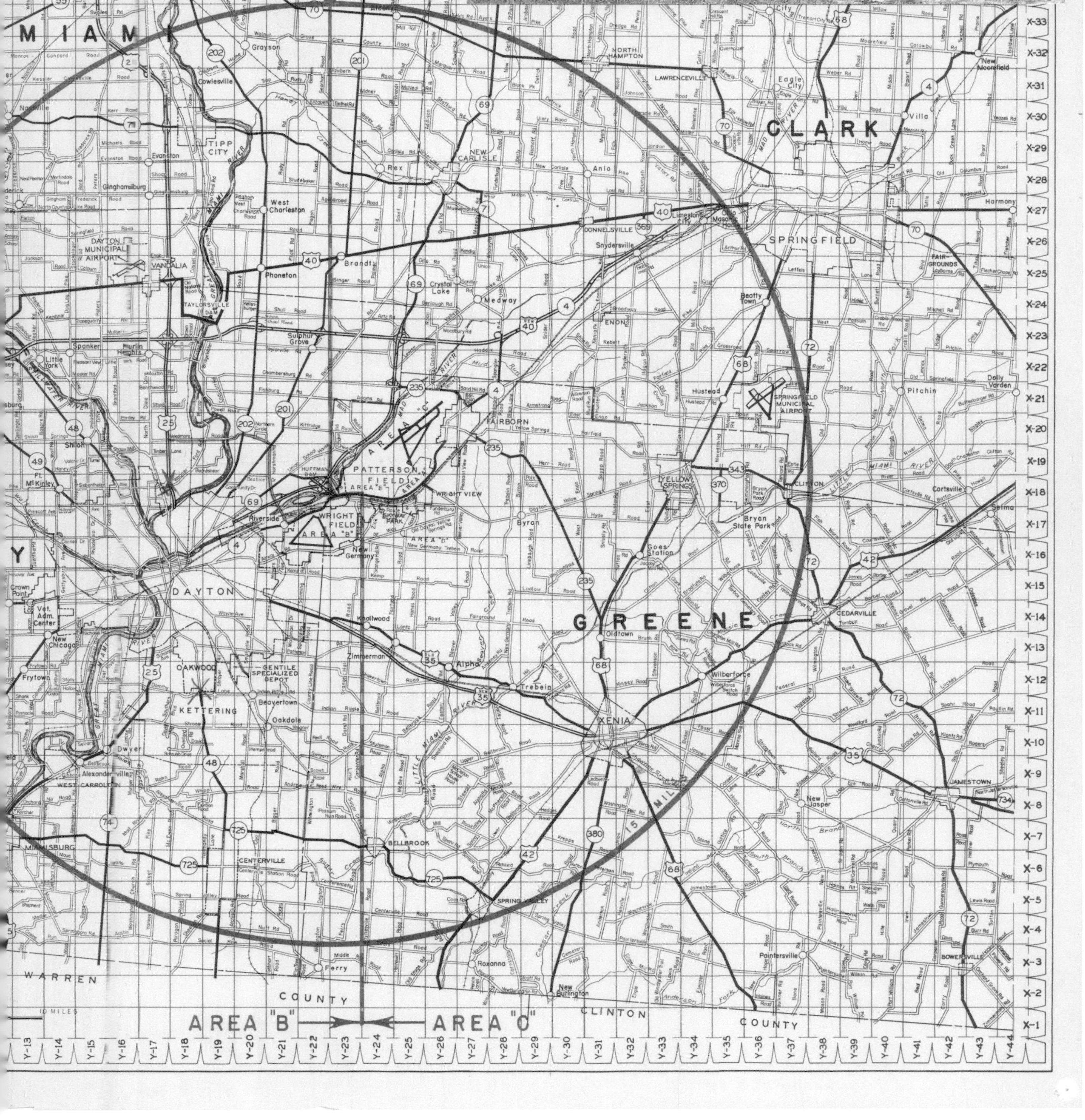

The US Image Grid

With the increase of aerial mapping photography in World War I, the Army began encoding each reconnaissance image with a common data line at the base. The data included the date and time the image was created; the focal length of the camera lens, the altitude of the aircraft when the image was created, and the coded grid coordinates of the area being photographed.

The date, time, lens length, and altitude were inscribed for more than simple record-keeping purposes: using trigonometry, a photo interpreter could approximate the length of any object or feature. Shadow lengths, which changed with date, time, and location, could be used to calculate object heights and the direction of true north.

Again, the military used a series of grid maps to identify locations. Our map shows a 1943 version of the US grid, though the same grid numbers were used as early as 1920 and continued to appear well into the 1960s. Each grid "square" (actually rectangle, as the width of each box shrunk with distance from the equator) covered one degree of latitude by one degree of longitude. These squares could be divided into sixteen further sub-squares. As the two boxes shown to the east of Florida show, one system identified these subsections with Roman numerals and compass points. From the upper left, these would be NIW, NIE, NIIW, NIIE, through SIVE. Surviving recon photos show little use of that system, the second, alphabetic system (identifying subsections as A through P) being far more common. The Army produced similar grid maps covering most of the world as the reach of US air power extended during World War II. •

Aberdeen Proving Grounds, Maryland, was and is a major test facility for Army weaponry. The legend lists this as oblique image number 4 of grid 850, subsection O, photographed by unit 2 (possibly the 2nd Air Base Squadron?). The image was created on 2 June 1932 at 10:00am with a 12-inch camera at an altitude of 900 feet.

With the war in Europe paused while forces regrouped, the Army Air Corps held a display of its latest weapons at Bolling Field, just south of the capitol. Temporary camouflage schemes adorn many of the aircraft, including in the line nearest the camera) the B-15, B-17B, B-18A, B-23, and XA-21. The legend at the foot of the image can be read as O for oblique camera angle, 1297 for a local filing number, grid square 840, subsection M, shot by the Bolling Field detachment in 19 January 1940 at 11:21am with a 12-inch lens at 800 feet. The subject - in this case, Bolling Field - was a common addition.

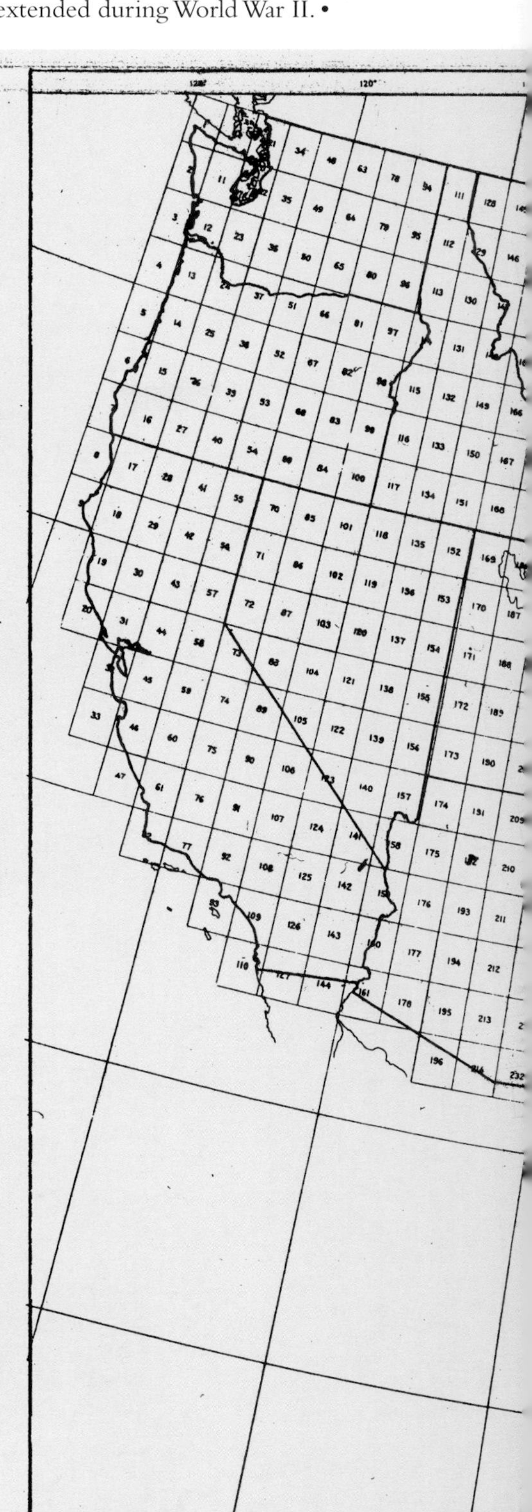

(02-304-I-4PH)(8-21-41-10:10A)(12-1400) BIGGS FIELD, EL PASO, TEXAS

(V-573-G-6AB)(9-17-41-10:30A)(12-11,000) BARKSDALE FIELD, LA. A-20371 A.C.

Decoding the information at the base of old Army images is less difficult once the system is clear. Information at the base of an image of Biggs Field, Texas, shows that this is the second photo documenting grid section 304-I taken by the 4th Photo Squadron on 21 August 1941 at 10:00am; the camera mounted a 12-inch lens and the photo was taken at an altitude of 1,400 feet. The second data strip, documenting Barksdale Field, Louisiana, was a vertical image of grid 573-G taken by the 6th Air Base Squadron on 17 September 1941 at 10:30am; the camera, mounting a 12-inch lens, was at 11,000 feet when the shutter was snapped.

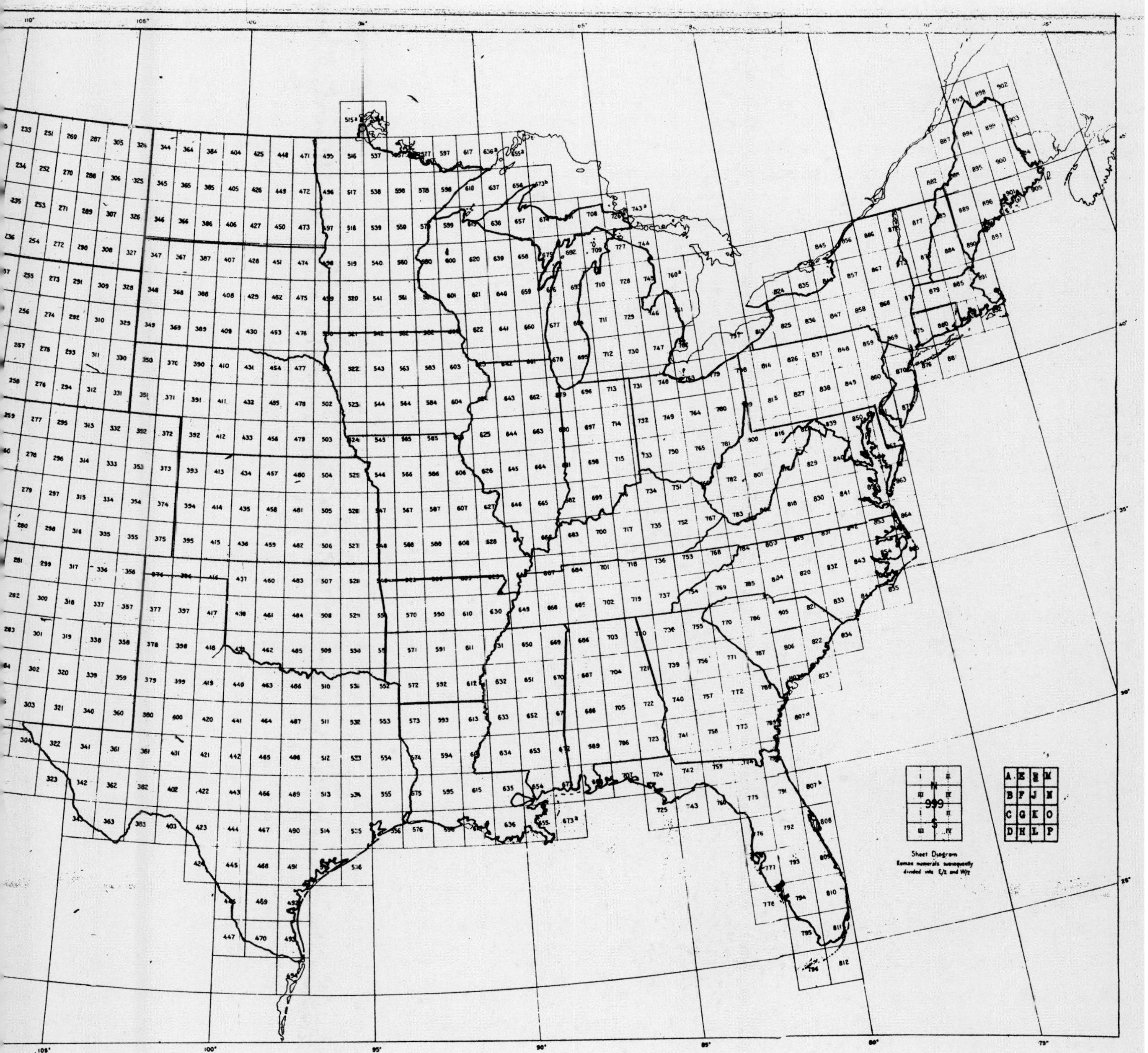

This 1943 Army map divided the continental US into numbered grid sections.

The Air Transport Command

By the end of World War II, the world's largest airline was the US Army Air Forces' Air Transport Command (ATC). The organization boasted more than 200,000 officers and men, with 3,700 aircraft on hand. In July 1945 alone, the ATC carried 275,000 passengers and 100,000 tons of cargo to military fields around the world. The ATC established or maintained hundreds of air fields, produced charts and facility maps, organized weather and air rescue services, ferried over a quarter million aircraft, trained and supported air crews, evacuated wounded personnel, and maintained its own aircraft. Allied planners knew that they could move personnel, critical components, or replacement aircraft to any combat theater in days, not weeks.

Air Transport Command was a new organization, created just over four years earlier with the establishment of the Air Corps Ferrying Command in May 1941. At the time, Lend-Lease deliveries to the UK had been placing increasing burdens on British man power. The Army Air Corps established "Ferry Command" to assume the responsibility for movement of aircraft within the US, increasing the training of American air crews in the bargain. Still holding to an unusual brand of neutrality prior to 7 December 1941, the Americans would deliver the aircraft to the Canadian border for pick up by British and Canadian pilots.

Air Corps Ferrying Command was renamed Air Forces Ferrying Command in June 1941. The attack on Pearl Harbor added to the command's responsibilities and problems and led to the creation of a new Air Forces Air Transport Command in June 1942. Charged with introducing a world-wide delivery system, Ferry Command and ATC found their best pilots (who had been on temporary assignment to gain additional flight experience) were being recalled to combat units. The Army was able to bring in several hundred trained civilian private pilots, increase their training, and rate them as service pilots - not qualified for combat, but capable of navigating and flying their assigned aircraft for ATC. The greatest single source of trained pilots would have been the civil airlines, with about 2,600 pilots employed at the beginning of the War. While many of these pilots held reserve commissions, the Army's heavy reliance on contracted airline services provided a strong argument against recalling this pool of officers. During the War's first year, airline contracts performed nearly 88 percent of ATC's transport work. This would drop to about 19 percent by the War's end, still a significant contribution to the military's effort to deliver supplies around the world. (The heavy reliance on airline support led many to quip that ATC stood for "Always Terrified Civilians." Many of those civilians would loose their lives to enemy fire, aircraft malfunctions, or rapidly changing weather conditions.)

Aircraft shortages - both complete aircraft and spare parts - would prove especially difficult during the War's first two years. Combat aircraft would have first priority on production lines, and combat organizations would have first priority on any new transports delivered. ATC was a *strategic* airlift organization, moving men and equipment between rear areas (though many of those areas were in hotly contested combat zones), while *tactical* airlift units (at the time known as troop carrier units) moved men and materiel to the front-line airfields and performed all combat airlift, including air assaults with paratroopers. Not only did troop carrier units compete for newly delivered aircraft, they could also cite situational emergencies and divert cargos and aircraft landing at their fields.

Four-engined aircraft were always the most desirable - their range and capacity allowed them to accomplish much more than their smaller, twin-engined cousins. At the end of 1942, Ferry Command controlled only twenty four-engined aircraft. Eleven were Liberator bombers jury-rigged into transports, four were Boeing 314 Clippers purchased from Pan American, and five were Boeing 307 Stratoliners purchased from TWA. The best aircraft would be the Douglas

ATC C-54s and C-47s line a Chinese airfield as local civilian crews work on the dirt hard stand.

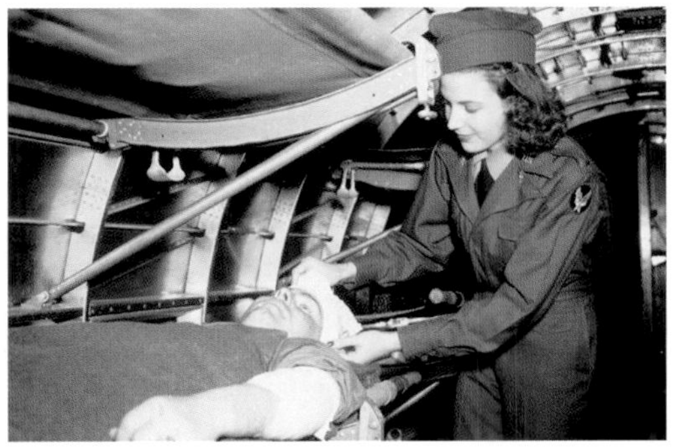

ATC's large-scale evacuation of wounded to rear areas and the US saved countless lives and helped reduce the strain on facilities near the front lines.

The Curtiss C-46 Commando showed great promise as an airlifter. The yellow markings on this C-46 identify it as an aircraft assigned to domestic air routes in the US.

C-54s (which entered large-scale production in 1942) and Lockheed C-69 Constellations (which would see little wartime production). Several hundred more four-engined Liberators were modified into C-87 or C-109 transports, but the workhorse of ATC would be the twin-engined Douglas C-47. Based on the proven Douglas DC-3 airliner, the C-47 was reliable, easy to maintain, and respected by its crews. ATC also hoped for a boost from another twin-engined transport, the Curtiss C-46 Commando. The C-46 carried nearly double the load of the C-47 at 200mph, but the early aircraft were plagued with so many flaws that ATC returned its first thirty aircraft to the factory for modifications and correction. Maintenance crews complained that the aircraft was a "plumber's nightmare," and early air crews in China regarded the aircraft a death trap. Between May 1943 and March 1945, 31 China-Burma-India Theater C-46s caught fire or exploded in flight. Many others simply disappeared over the Himalayas. By the end of the War, most problems with the C-46 had been resolved, but with the postwar fleet reduction, ATC kept only 5 of its Commandos (while retaining 402 of its less-sophisticated C-47s).

Few aircraft were based at any of ATC's air fields - base commanders were expected to provide support for transient aircrews and passengers, refuel and maintain aircraft, and onload or offload cargo as necessary. The best-known exception to this rule involved the India-China airlift, begun in June 1942 with 49 Douglas twin-engined transports. With Japanese forces controlling China's port cities, the US proposed to support its Chinese Allies by airlifting supplies over the Himalaya Mountains from eastern India and Burma, a treacherous route known to crews as the Hump. In July 1942, ATC's Hump pilots delivered its first 85 tons of materiel and passengers. By 1944 the resupply mission included support for B-29s of the Twentieth Air Force, the first aircraft to strike the Japanese homeland on a regular basis. In July 1945, ATC's greatly expanded India-China Wing (with 332 aircraft in service) delivered 71,042 tons! Of ATC's many wartime accomplishments, its success over the Himalayas provided the first glimpse of the future capabilities of military airlift.

Of the many war-time deliveries completed by the ATC, few were appreciated as much as the touring performers of the USO (United Service Organization). Here, Bob "joke-a-minute" Hope boards a C-53 following a show.

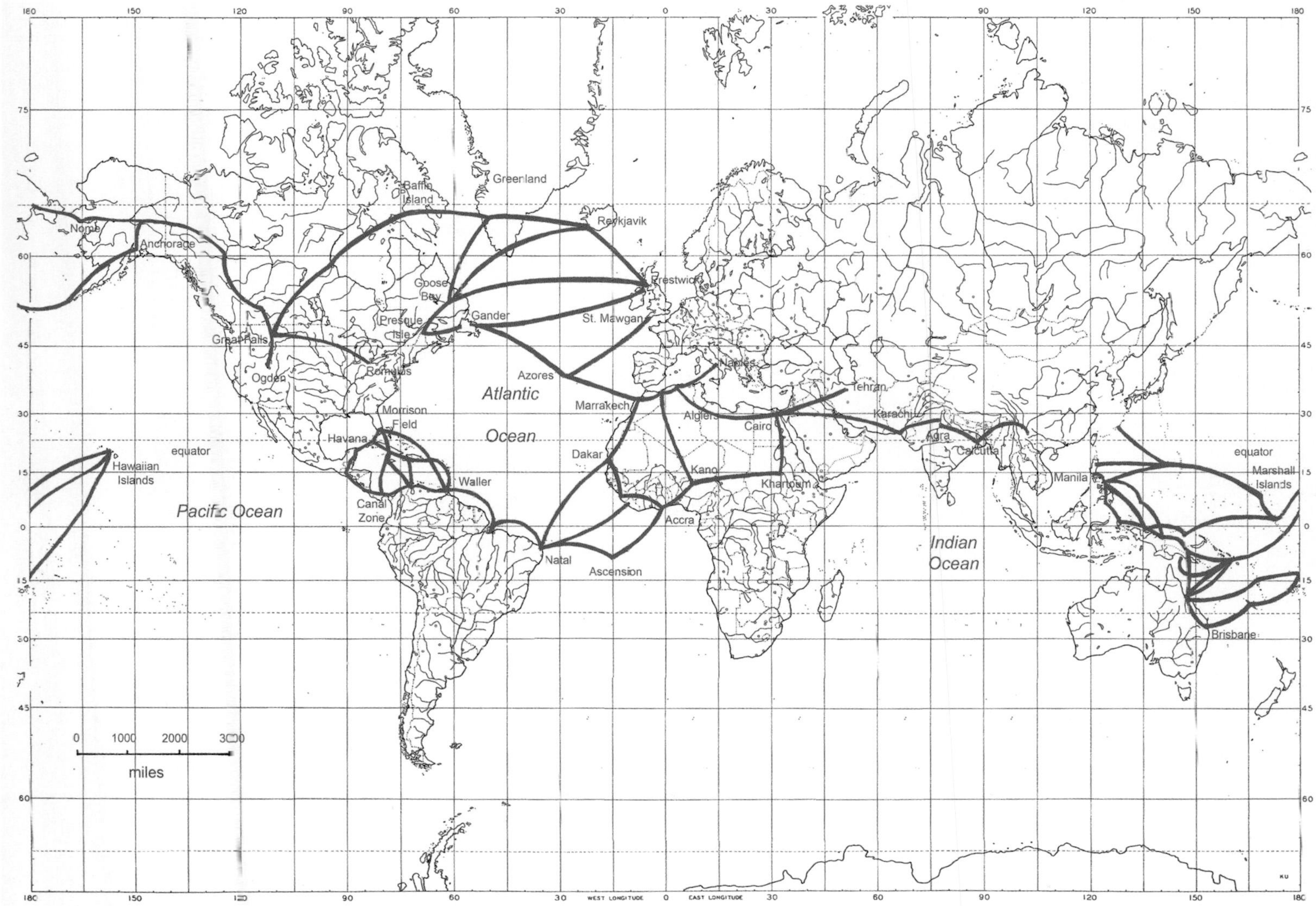

While the ATC could fly to any open field in the world, , the routes shown on this map were flown on a regularly scheduled service, similar to any civil airline.

ATC's first overseas route was established by Ferry Command in June 1941. Known as the Southeastern Air Route, the path moved aircraft from southern Florida, through the Caribbean to Brazil, and across the South Atlantic to central Africa. From there, aircraft could continue across Africa to support the Middle East or continue on to India. The opening of an ATC base on Ascension Island in late 1942 allowed long-range fighters to fly across the South Atlantic for delivery to forces building against Rommel's Afrika Korps.

In mid-1942, ATC opened the North Atlantic routes connecting Canada with Britain, developing facilities that had been opened by the British in 1940 for delivery of Lend-Lease supplies and opening new facilities on Greenland and Iceland. During BOLERO (code name for the buildup of the Eighth Air Force in Britain), US bomber and fighter groups would fly their own aircraft across "the pond," supported, refueled, and fed at ATC facilities along the way.

The map below shows the airways connecting North America with Meeks Field at Keflavik, Iceland in April 1945. Aircraft with the range could fly directly from Harmon Field, Newfoundland (1,442nm), or from Goose Bay, Labrador (1,335nm), though most aircraft made the trip in shorter hops via ATC's Greenland bases. The user of this map traveled the more southerly Greenland route, turning south at the Bluie West 3 (BW3) radio beacon, then following the Prince Christian Radio beacon across the southern tip of Greenland and on to Keflavik. All of these routes and facilities would support the return of civil trans-Atlantic passenger service in the postwar years.

A transient troop carrier C-47 under repair at a Brazilian ATC facility.

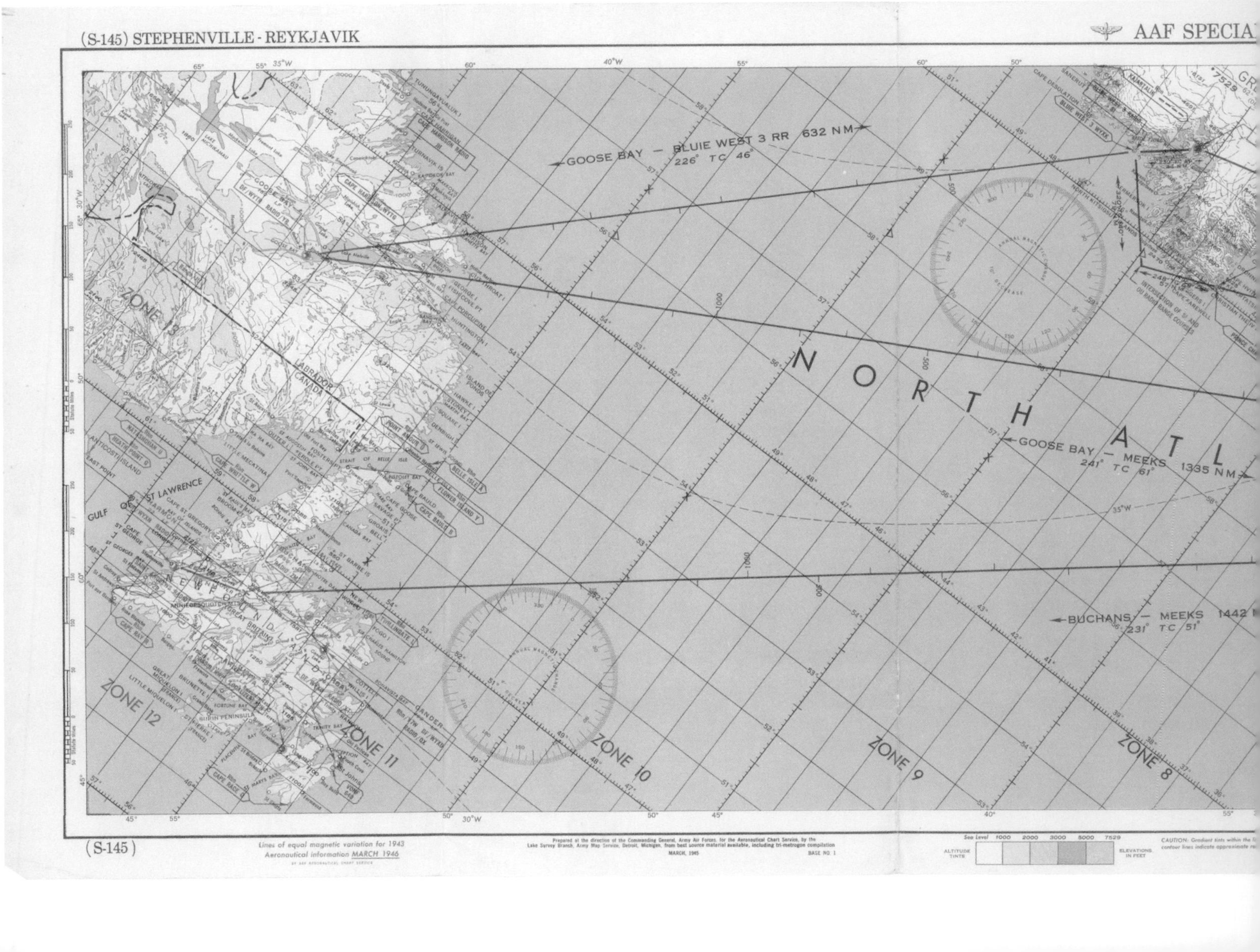

Early export Liberators were known as LB-30s; this example is one of eleven taken over by Ferry Command. The large American flags painted over the British camouflage proclaimed the aircraft's neutrality before America entered the war.

RIGHT: Work continues on improvements to Belem airfield in April 1943. The aircraft nearest the camera is a former TWA Boeing 307, now flown for the ATC on regular communications missions between Washington and Cairo. Designated C-75s by the military, each of the five 307s was named for an Indian tribe; this example was called *Zuni*.

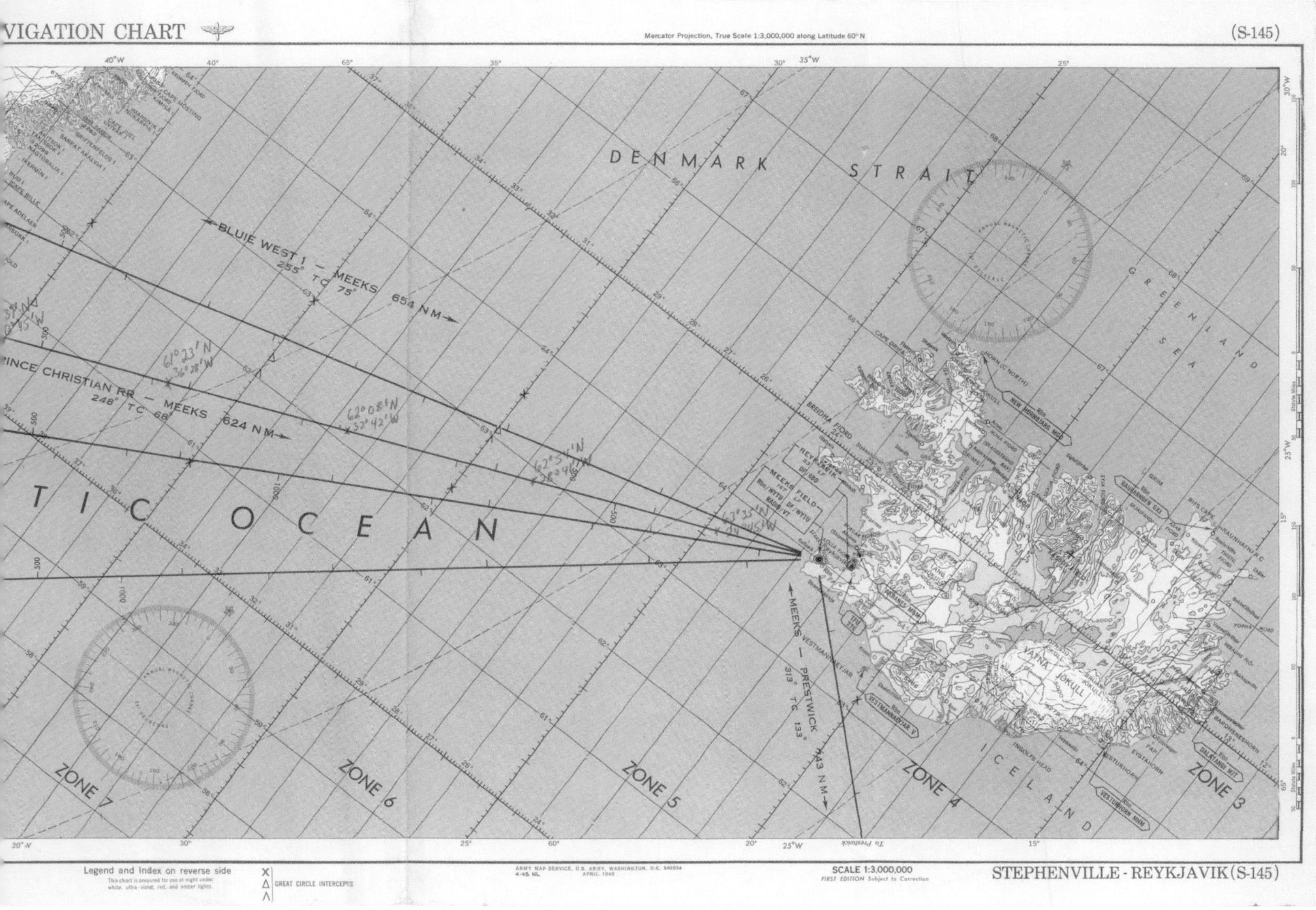

VIGATION CHART

Mercator Projection, True Scale 1:3,000,000 along Latitude 60° N

(S-145)

DENMARK STRAIT

GREENLAND SEA

BLUIE WEST 1 — MEEKS 255° TC 75° 654 NM

PRINCE CHRISTIAN RR — MEEKS 248° TC 68° 624 NM

TIC OCEAN

MEEKS — PRESTWICK 313° TC 133° 743 NM

ICELAND

ZONE 7

ZONE 6

ZONE 5

ZONE 4

ZONE 3

Legend and Index on reverse side

GREAT CIRCLE INTERCEPTS

SCALE 1:3,000,000

STEPHENVILLE - REYKJAVIK (S-145)

The South American route structure created by Pan American in the 1930s was taken over by ATC in 1942, with Pan American continuing to fly the routes under ATC contract. The arrangement came with some advantages for PanAm, which gained radio, maintenance, and base support without having to fill seats to make a profit. This map (at right) from one of ATC's 1943 Air Route Manuals includes a chart of ground altitudes for the cross-Andes flight between Santiago and Buenos Aires, a listing of course data, and a topographical map showing routes and fields. •

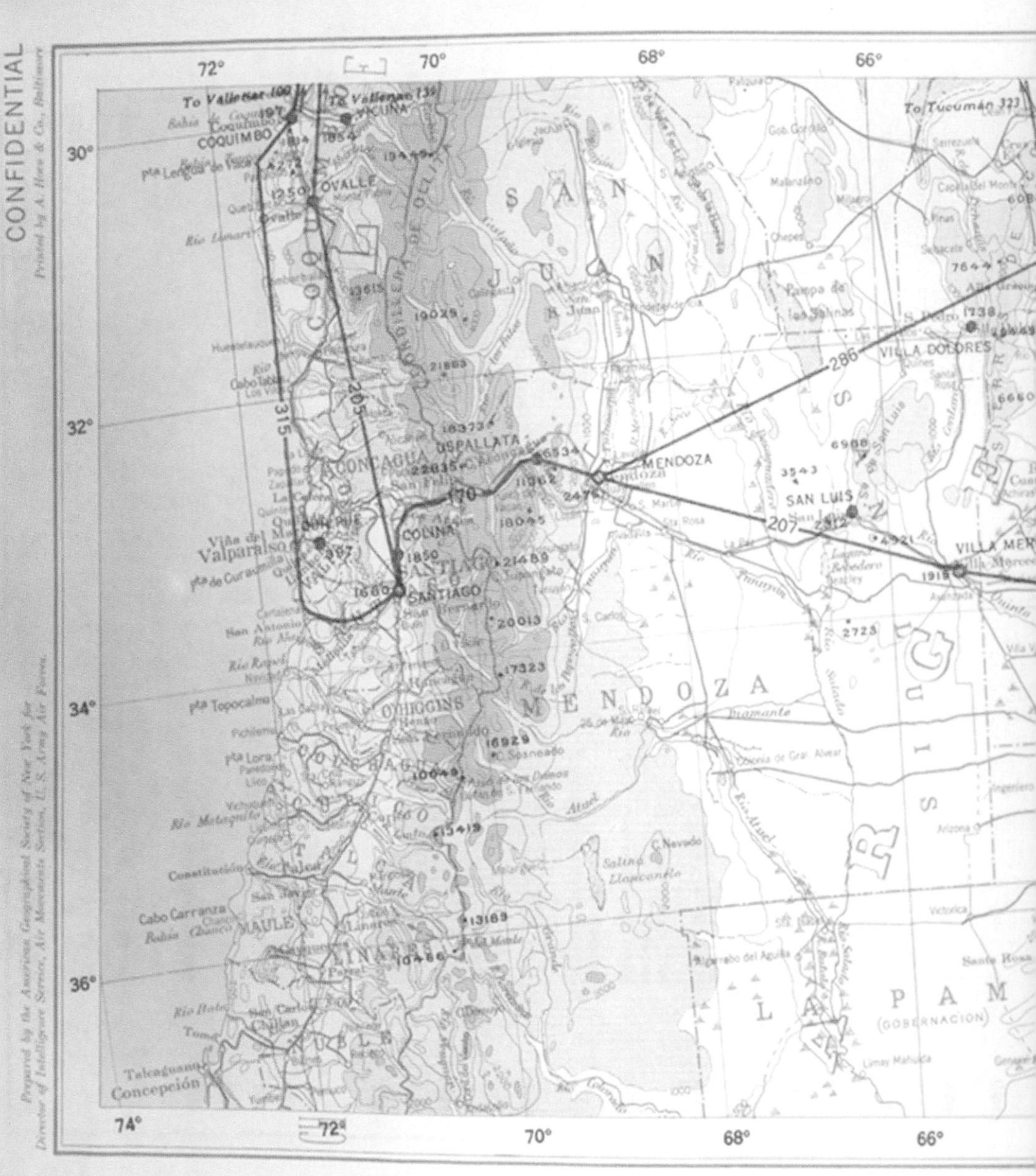

Two ATC C-46s and a C-87 at Atkinson Field, British Guiana, in early 1943. Across the field, American bombers await delivery to North Africa.

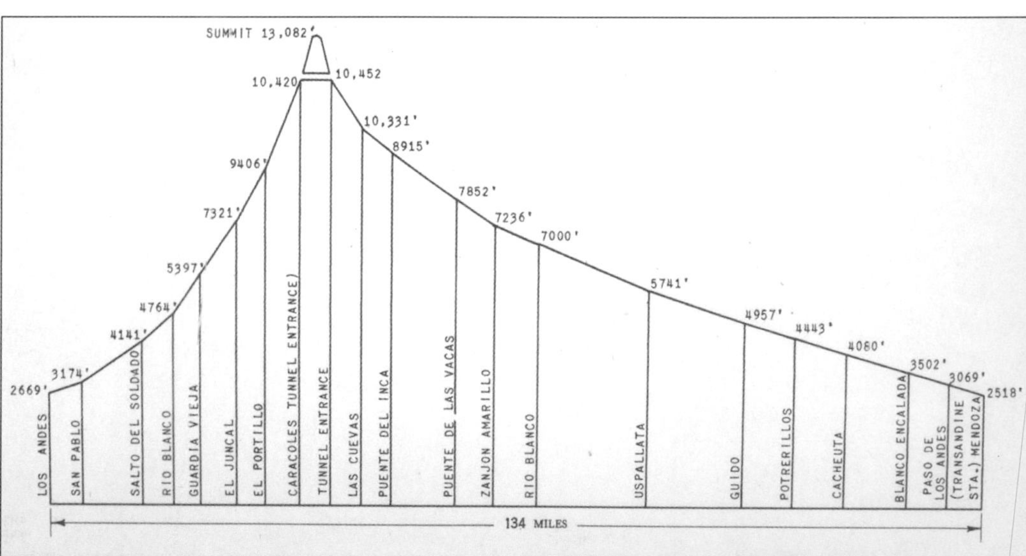

Delayed enroute, a half dozen AAF aircraft await repairs on Ascension Island before continuing on their flights to the combat zone.

LEFT: If Ascension Island's position in the South Atlantic made it an ideal location for an ATC base, the cliff at the end of the runway was not always appreciated by aircrew with bad brakes. This early-1944 image shows a variety of transient aircraft, few assigned to ATC.

ABOVE: Many route charts of the 1930s and '40s included schematic representations of ground elevations. Combined with the standard topographical charts, these altitude charts gave aircrews an immediate understanding of the terrain ahead.

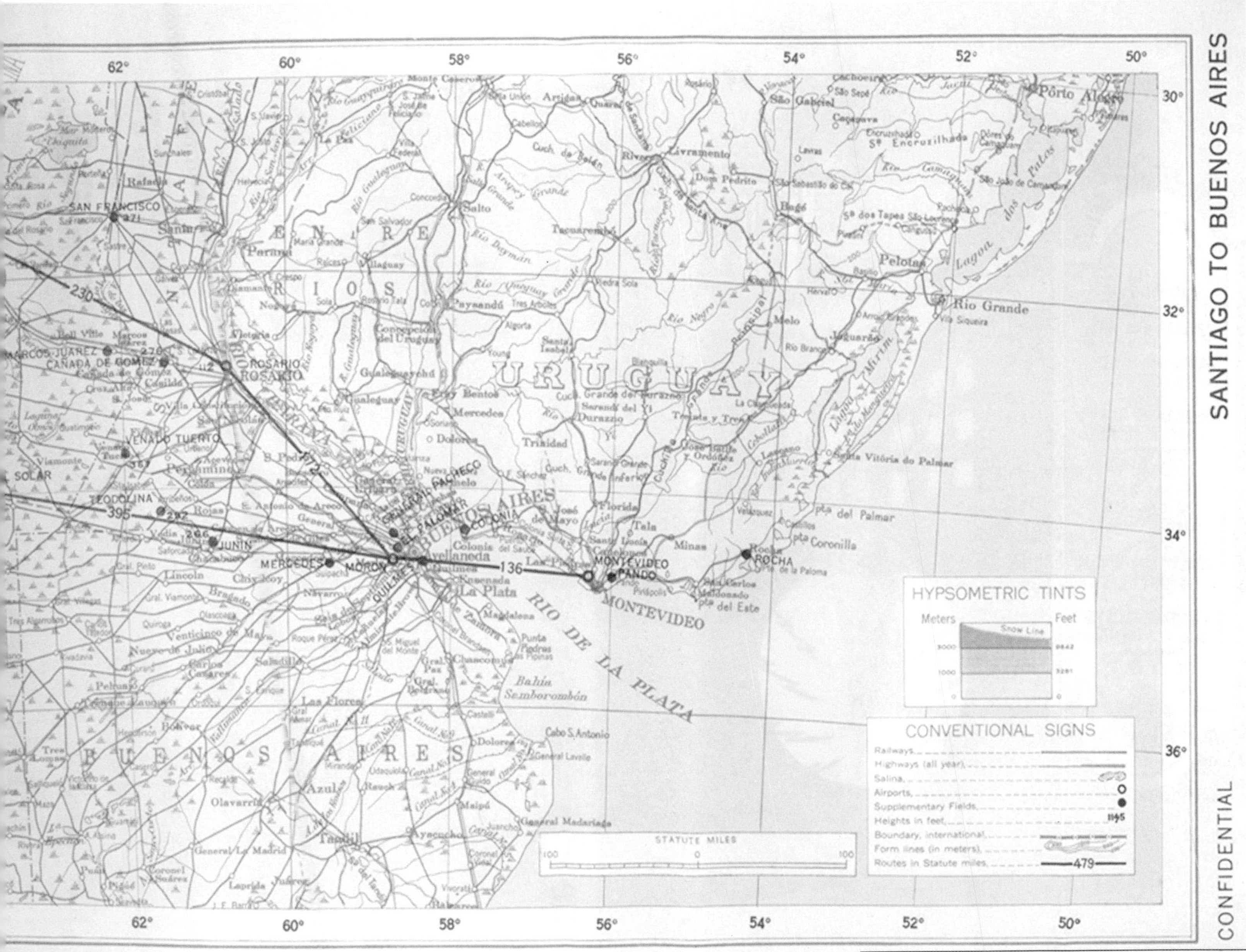

SANTIAGO TO BUENOS AIRES

HYPSOMETRIC TINTS

Meters Feet

Snow Line

CONVENTIONAL SIGNS

Railways
Highways (all year)
Salina
Airports
Supplementary Fields
Heights in feet
Boundary, international
Form lines (in meters)
Routes in Statute miles 479

STATUTE MILES

URUGUAY

BUENOS AIRES

MONTEVIDEO

RIO DE LA PLATA

CONFIDENTIAL

A strong ally in the war against Germany, Brazil supported the development of ATC air routes along the coast, provided air crews for combat in the Mediterranean theater, and supported the increased wartime demand for raw materials. This US civilian PBY-5A was used by America's Rubber Development Corporation for work along the Amazon basin.

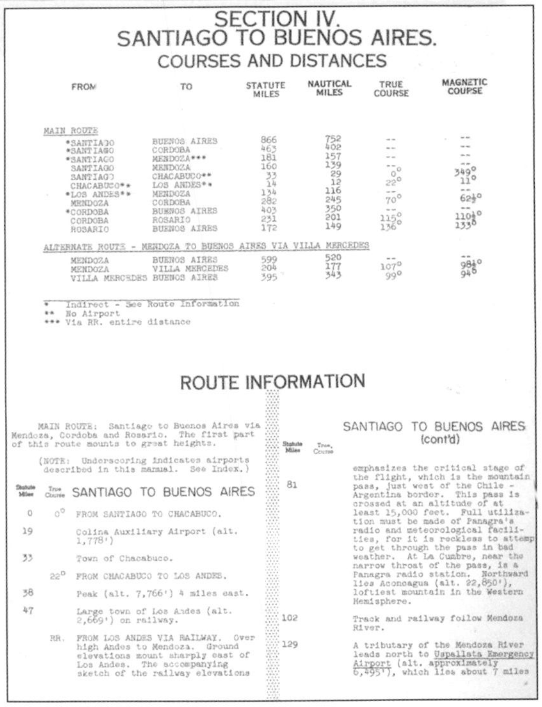

SECTION IV.
SANTIAGO TO BUENOS AIRES.
COURSES AND DISTANCES

FROM	TO	STATUTE MILES	NAUTICAL MILES	TRUE COURSE	MAGNETIC COURSE
MAIN ROUTE					
*SANTIAGO	BUENOS AIRES	866	752	--	--
*SANTIAGO	CORDOBA	463	402	--	--
*SANTIAGO	MENDOZA***	181	157	--	--
SANTIAGO	MENDOZA	160	139	--	--
SANTIAGO	CHACABUCO**	33	29	0°	349°
CHACABUCO**	LOS ANDES**	14	12	22°	11°
*LOS ANDES**	MENDOZA	134	116	--	--
MENDOZA	CORDOBA	282	245	70°	62½°
*CORDOBA	BUENOS AIRES	403	350	--	--
CORDOBA	ROSARIO	231	201	115°	110½°
ROSARIO	BUENOS AIRES	172	149	136°	133°
ALTERNATE ROUTE - MENDOZA TO BUENOS AIRES VIA VILLA MERCEDES					
MENDOZA	BUENOS AIRES	599	520	--	--
MENDOZA	VILLA MERCEDES	204	177	107°	98½°
VILLA MERCEDES	BUENOS AIRES	395	343	99°	94°

* Indirect - See Route Information
** No Airport
*** Via RR. entire distance

ROUTE INFORMATION

MAIN ROUTE: Santiago to Buenos Aires via Mendoza, Cordoba and Rosario. The first part of this route mounts to great heights.

(NOTE: Underscoring indicates airports described in this manual. See Index.)

Statute Miles	True Course	SANTIAGO TO BUENOS AIRES
0	0°	FROM SANTIAGO TO CHACABUCO.
19		Colina Auxiliary Airport (alt. 1,778')
33		Town of Chacabuco.
	22°	FROM CHACABUCO TO LOS ANDES.
38		Peak (alt. 7,766') 4 miles east.
47		Large town of Los Andes (alt. 2,669') on railway.
	RR.	FROM LOS ANDES VIA RAILWAY. Over high Andes to Mendoza. Ground elevations mount sharply east of Los Andes. The accompanying sketch of the railway elevations

Statute Miles	True Course	SANTIAGO TO BUENOS AIRES (cont'd)
81		emphasizes the critical stage of the flight, which is the mountain pass, just west of the Chile - Argentina border. This pass is crossed at an altitude of at least 15,000 feet. Full utilization must be made of Panagra's radio and meteorological facilities, for it is reckless to attemp to get through the pass in bad weather. At La Cumbre, near the narrow throat of the pass, is a Panagra radio station. Northward lies Aconcagua (alt. 22,850'), loftiest mountain in the Western Hemisphere.
102		Track and railway follow Mendoza River.
129		A tributary of the Mendoza River leads north to Uspallata Emergency Airport (alt. approximately 6,495'), which lies about 7 miles

Additional navigational data was presented in chart form; this chart supported the Santiago to Buenos Aires route map shown above.

The ATA and the WASPs

WASPs Francis Green, Peg Kirshner, Ann Waldner, and Blanche Osborne leave the flightline after a B-17 ferry flight.

Britain's drastic need for pilots at the opening of World War II led to the creation of the Air Transport Auxiliary (ATA) in August 1939. Within weeks, the first group of 30 civilian pilots had assembled to begin duties ferrying aircraft from factories to maintenance units (MUs). As the second group of 30 was raised, the Air Ministry decided to allow women pilots to join. By May 1940, the ATA was responsible for the ferrying of all aircraft between factories and MUs, with many flights crossing the Channel in support of the Battle of France. And in July 1941, ATA pilots took over all RAF ferrying operations. By September 1944, the ATA was back in France, delivering aircraft to RAF units. Over 150 ATA pilots would die during the war; the many survivors returned to civilian life following the War.

America's use of civilian ferry pilots was based, in part, on the ATA experience. The acceptance of well-qualified women pilots for ferry duties came in the summer of 1942 when Nancy Harkness Love persuaded the AAF to form The Women's Auxiliary Ferrying Squadron (WAFS) and assign 25 well qualified women, each with over 1,000 flying hours. At about the same time, Jacqueline Cochran convinced the AAF to begin a training program for new women pilots to be known as the Women's Airforce Service Pilots (WASPs). By August 1943, the two organizations, with a combined total of 303 pilots, merged as WASPs under the ATC. In August 1944, more than half of the WASPs were transferred to other commands and given flying duties more suitable for their limited training.

In all, 1,074 women would complete pilot training with the WASPs and assume operational duties. They proved themselves capable time and again, but suffered from an unfair civilian status in a military program. At the AAF's request, Congress finally considered granting commissions to WASP pilots just as the AAF began terminating many of its new pilot programs. Faced with the prospect of commissioning women while denying flight training to men, Congress terminated the WASP program on 20 December 1944. WASP pilots lost 37 of their number in fatal accidents, with seven more suffering major injuries, and 29 receiving minor injuries. In their 27 months of existence, the WAFS and the WASPs completed 12,650 ferry missions, freeing their male counterparts for other duties. It would take Congress more than thirty years to grant the survivors the benefits granted to all of their male counterparts. •

WASPs Nelle Carmody, Enid Fisher, and Lana Cusack review their map before a training flight in a PT-19A at Avenger Field, Texas.

WASP Wilda Winfield pilots a BT-13 on a photographic mission from Frederick Army Air Field, Oklahoma.

Three WASPs compare notes before a tow target mission in a Curtiss A-25 Helldiver. They women were attached to the 9th Tow Target Squadron at Camp Davis, North Carolina.

BELOW: Ann Wood, a member of the ATA, used the map below during ferry flights in Scotland. She used red ink to lay out routes between Edzell (a major aircraft maintenance and storage facility) and the training fields at Lossiemouth and Forres. She also marked in the locations of British bases at Peterhead, Kinloss, and Dalcross. The RAF modified this Ordnance Survey Map for wartime flight use by adding compass roses and several prominent facilities in red.

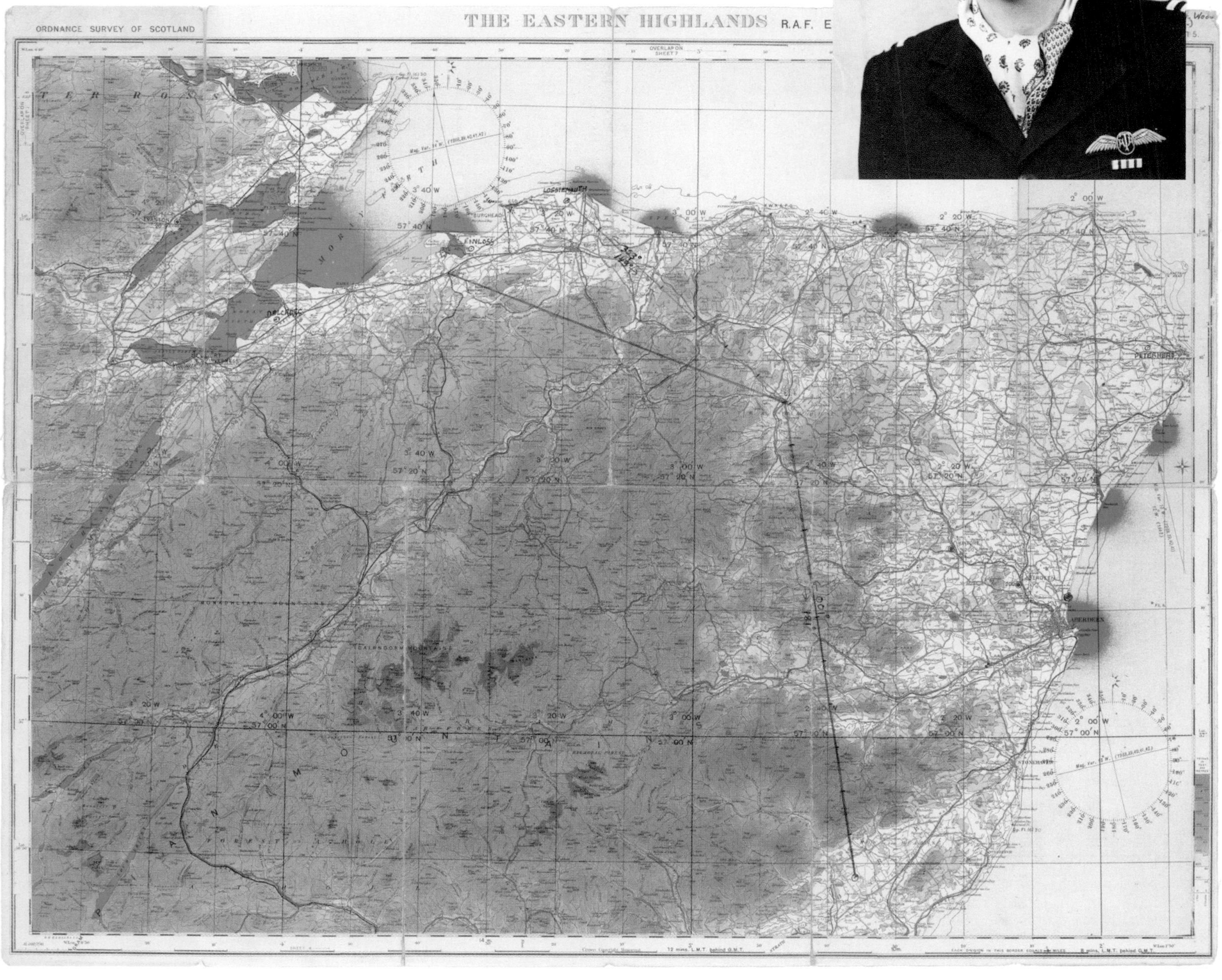

ORDNANCE SURVEY OF SCOTLAND

THE EASTERN HIGHLANDS R.A.F. E

Cold War Military Aviation

The invention of the jet engine would eventually revolutionize aviation. Although the first jet flew in the months before World War II, the technology was still only partially developed by the War's end. Several German jet fighters, reconnaissance aircraft, and bombers had flown combat missions during the War. Only one squadron of British jets became operational before the war, and American jets (developed with the aid of British technology) lagged a bit farther behind.

With the peace following Japan's surrender, all arms development and production decreased. The development of new jet engines and jet-powered aircraft continued, although not with the urgency seen during the war. Increased tensions between the West and the Soviets - what came to be known as the Cold War - were exacerbated by Russia's attempts to export revolution and assimilate its neighbors. The development of Russia's first nuclear bomb, and production of an aircraft capable of delivering that bomb sparked a new arms race, beginning decades of remarkable "peacetime" spending and expansion on both sides of the Iron Curtain.

Improved jets formed a major portion of that expansion. Jet engines gave bombers the speed to reach their targets quickly, then escape the blast of their own exploding nuclear weapons. They gave fighters the speed to intercept the bombers and outrun each other. The first experimental aircraft to exceed the speed of sound did so in 1947; within a decade, new engines, afterburners (called "reheat" in Britain, where they were invented), and improved aerodynamics were producing operational fighters capable of flying twice the speed of sound.

Fearing the destruction of its airfields in any future war, the USAF developed ZELL, the Zero-Length Launch system in the late 1950s. A massive solid-fuel rocket booster could launch a modern fighter, such as this North American F-100D Super Sabre, from the back of a truck.

All this speed required enormous quantities of jet fuel. The ability of jet aircraft to convert fuel to speed limited range enough to make most combat aircraft ineffective. The response was aerial refueling, creating a fleet of airborne tankers to "pass the gas" to fighters and bombers outside the combat zone, then refuel them again as they returned home. Experiments with aerial refueling had yielded promising results in the 1920s and '30s; by the 1950s, an operational tanker fleet was essential to most military combat missions.

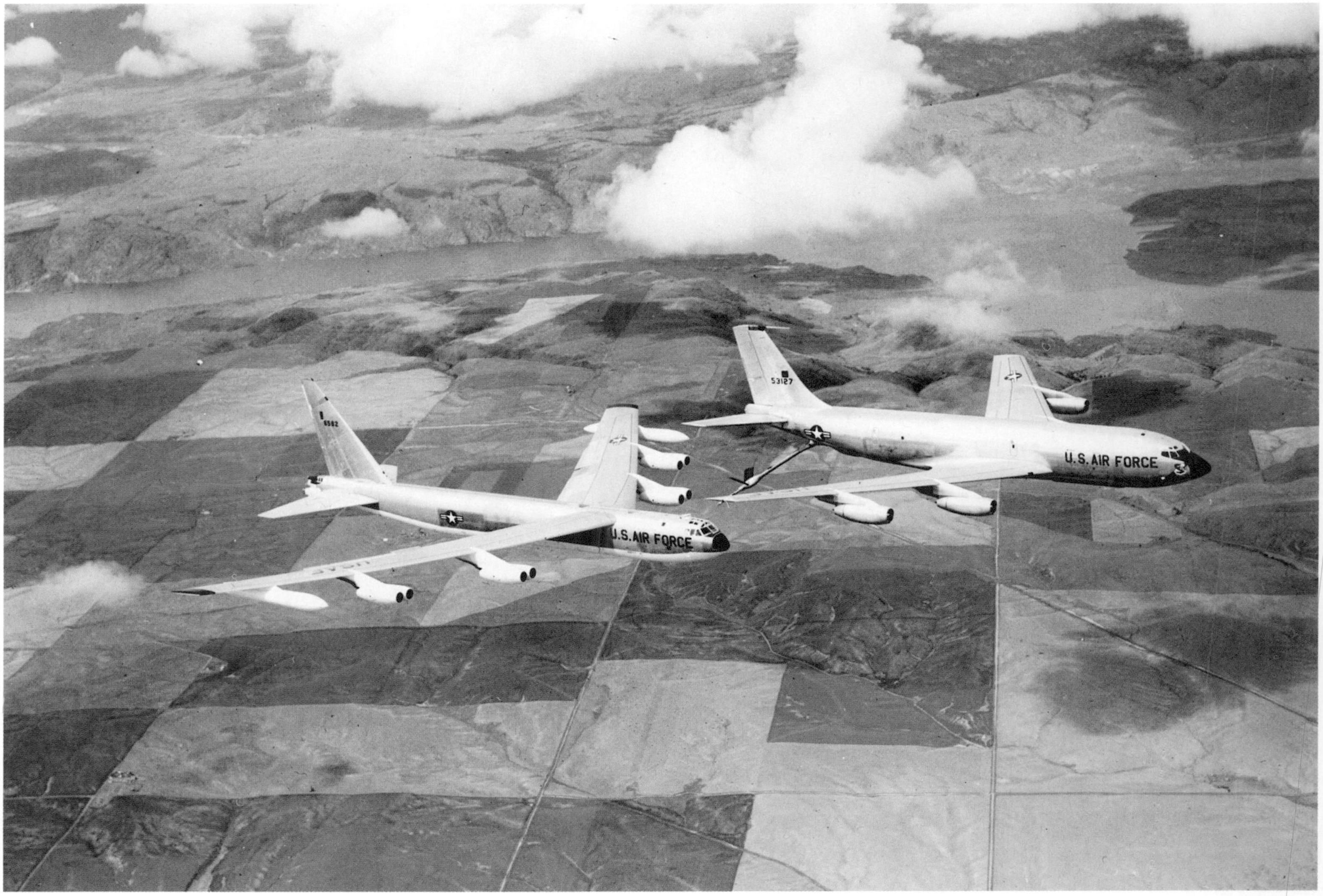

The introduction of a fleet of tanker aircraft in the 1950s helped the USAF extend the range of its fuel guzzling jets. Here a Boeing KC-135A Stratotanker prepares to refuel a Boeing B-52D Stratofortress.

New air-to-air missiles gave fighters a better chance of destroying bombers (when the thought of even one bomber getting through threatened unimaginable destruction) and other fighters - at least in theory. New airborne radar systems improved the fighters' ability to detect and attack targets. The concept of dogfighting fighters, blasting at each other with machine guns and cannon began to seem outmoded, and by the end of the 1950s, new generations of fighter aircraft relied totally on missile armament, with no guns mounted at all.

With all the planning for nuclear war, few major powers were prepared for the many smaller conventional wars they faced (or precipitated) in the 1960s. In the end, the specter of "Mutually Assured Destruction" (with appropriate abbreviation of MAD) may have done more to prevent an nuclear exchange than any fleet of interceptors. The jet aircraft of the 1950s that continued to serve into the 1960s and '70s required new defensive systems and (in some cases) the retrofitting of guns. The expectations that speed alone could provide safety met reality in the skies over the Middle East, southern Asia, Africa, and Southeast Asia. New generations of aircraft would have speed and power, though flying twice the speed of sound became less important than increasing maneuverability to dodge an enemy's missiles and guns. The first generation of gleaming, silver jets helped define the character of the late-1940s and the 1950s, a time when air power offered the potential to incinerate the whole world while offering the only hope of preventing that conflagration. •

Developed in the closing days of WWII, Britain's Hawker Sea Hawk became operational in 1953, with the last example leaving front line Royal Navy squadrons in 1960. As the aircraft started leaving British service, West Germany placed orders for 64 Sea Hawks of its own. The aircraft were fully equipped for shipboard operations, despite Germany's lack of aircraft carriers.

The McDonnell F2H Banshee was one of the US Navy's first operational jets, entering service in the late 1940s. Here, two F2H-3s prepare to launch from the deck of the USS *Oriskany* in the mid-1950s.

The Berlin Airlift

The Berlin Airlift was a concerted US, British, and French effort to supply the population of West Berlin during 15 months in 1948/49. It was history's most significant peacetime aerial supply campaign; without firing a shot, the Western allies broke a Soviet blockade designed to force the entire city to submit to Russian control.

Following World War II, Germany was partitioned into British, French, Soviet, and American control sectors. Berlin, the nominal capitol, was similarly partitioned, but it was located deep in the Soviet zone. Following a currency dispute, on 24 June 1948 the Soviets closed all Western rail and road access to Berlin, and limited air access to three narrow corridors. The Soviet plan was to force the people of Berlin to register with Soviet bureaucrats and draw their food and fuel from Soviet stocks using Soviet currency.

The Allied response was to deliver all of life's necessities to Berlin by aircraft. The city required 15,500 tons of supplies daily before the airlift began. Although that level was never reached, the Allies kept the people of Berlin alive and warm, flying up to 1,400 deliveries (and 13,000 tons) on the most successful day. On 21 May 1949 the Soviets lifted their blockade; the airlift continued four more months, ensuring that Berlin would be provisionned through the coming winter. •

TOP: PSP (Pierced Steel Planking) is loaded onto a C-47; the airport facilities in Berlin needed rebuilding and improvement - including this portable runway material - to handle the increase in air traffic.

ABOVE: West Berliners, who called the airlift Lüftbrock (air bridge), were keenly aware that each arriving aircraft carried more of the supplies and equipment needed to sustain their lives.

LEFT: A US Air Force C-54 flies over a portable instrument landing trailer during the airlfit.

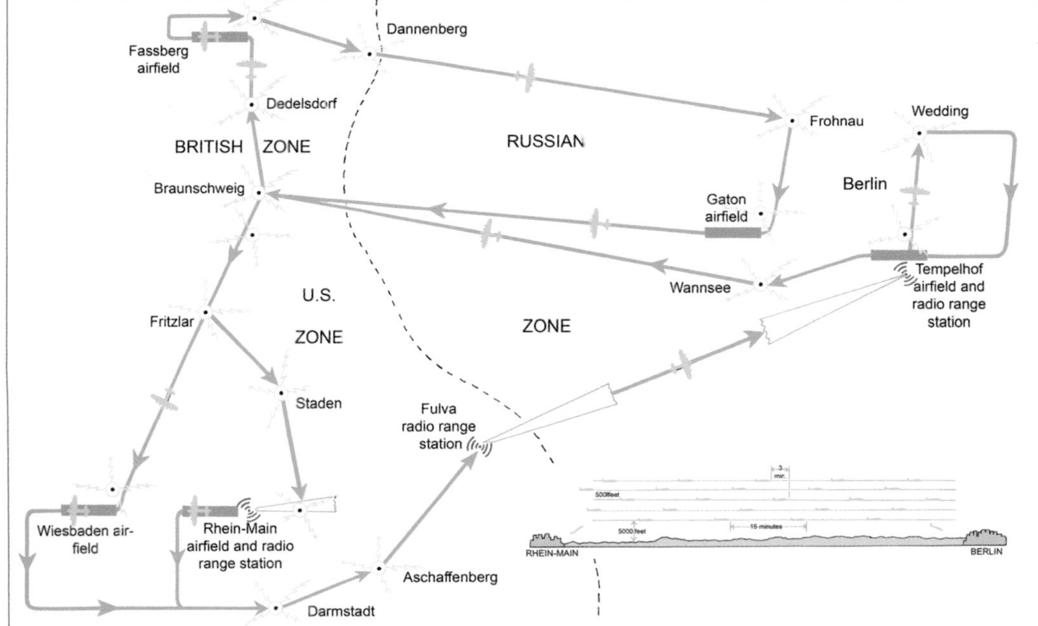

At the height of the Airlift, the new US Air Force prepared this graphic to explain the routes used to deliver supplies to Berlin. The use of radio beacons kept transports safe in their narrow corridors in even the worst weather; patrolling Russian fighters awaited any who drifted from the designated path.

TOP: The German airport at Templehof handled the lion's share of cargo deliveries. Here, cargo is transferred from C-47s to waiting trailer trucks.

ABOVE: An organization built on wartime experience ensured the airlift's success. Here, aircrews review procedures in a base operations office.

Air War over Korea

The Korean War began on 25 June 1950, when Communist troops in North Korea swept south to overrun democratic South Korea. Within days, most South Korean resistance ended. The newly formed United Nations resolved to come to South Korea's aid. For American planners, steeped in the advantages of a strategic air war, Korea would prove a nightmare: the Korean peninsula offered few strategic targets. Most military manufacturing facilities remained safe across the Chinese border or in Russia, targets that, if attacked, could easily lead to a third world war.

Korea would become the first jet war. The Communists' extremely capable Mikoyan-Gurevich MiG-15 fighter surprised Allied planners, just as the latest Japanese fighters had done a decade earlier. The North American F-86 proved a good match, but in the end it was superior training that gave the UN the advantage.

United Nations air and ground forces were able to restore most of the South, and came close to securing the North when hundreds of thousands of Chinese "volunteers" entered the ground war. The war slowly ground to a stalemate, followed by an armistice signed in July 1953. The two Korean nations have yet to sign a peace treaty, and North Korean leaders continue to speak of reunifying Korea under their control. •

Flying from the carrier USS *Kearsarge*, a McDonnell F2H Banshee dives on a Korean target.

A North Korean defector delivered this MiG-15 to American hands; the aircraft was subsequently evaluated at Wright Field.

Pilot training and the capable North American F-86 Sabre gave the United Nations air supremacy in the skies over Korea.

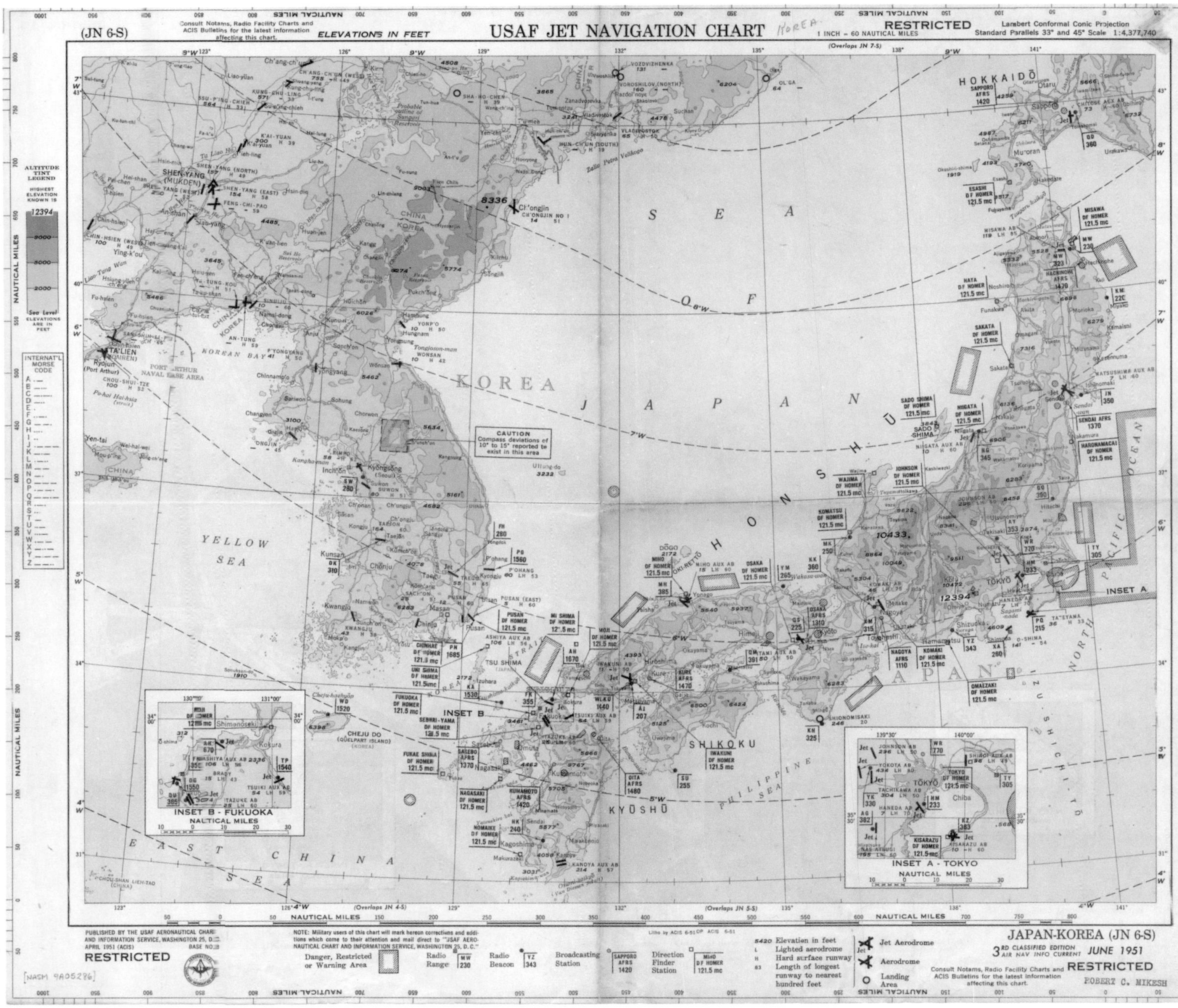

(JN 6-S) USAF JET NAVIGATION CHART RESTRICTED

ELEVATIONS IN FEET

1 INCH = 60 NAUTICAL MILES

Lambert Conformal Conic Projection Standard Parallels 33° and 45° Scale 1:4,377,740

SEA OF JAPAN

KOREA

YELLOW SEA

EAST CHINA SEA

HONSHU

SHIKOKU

KYUSHU

HOKKAIDO

NORTH PACIFIC OCEAN

INSET A - TOKYO

INSET B - FUKUOKA

CAUTION Compass deviations of 10° to 15° reported to exist in this area

JAPAN-KOREA (JN 6-S)

3RD CLASSIFIED EDITION AIR NAV INFO CURRENT JUNE 1951

RESTRICTED

ROBERT C. MIKESH

USAF Captain Robert Mikesh used this jet navigation chart when planning missions from Japan to Korea during the Korean War. Captain Mikesh flew Douglas B-26 Invaders, twin-engined medium bombers built during World War II.

Black-painted B-26 Invaders performed night interdiction missions throughout the Korean War.

The Small Wars

Although the decades following World War II have not seen the level of conflict that defined the first half of the twentieth century, the post-World War II era has rarely been at peace. The more technologically sophisticated nations managed to avoid direct confrontation, primarily due to the fear that a wrong move could leave the planet incinerated. But ideological differences meant that they would find ample reason to support each other's enemies in a number of smaller wars. The quarter century since 1945 saw the end of most colonial rule, as peoples who, hundreds of years earlier, had come under European control asserted their independence. However, independence did not always bring peace, as racial, ethnic, and religious tensions exploded, and new leaders, often tyrants, created opposition movements that were frequently courted and supplied by the Soviet Union or the West. Small wars were often launched to solve age-old disputes, usually over a valuable piece of land or ethnic dominance.

Aviation has had its role in many of these conflicts. Sometimes that role was little more than symbolic, as in the traditional bombing of the Presidential Palace (for example in South Vietnam in 1962 and in Chile in 1973)to signal the beginning of a coup d'etat. On other occasions, a few quick air battles began and ended disputes between nations. In far too many conflicts, air power has been needed to provide relief to tens of thousands of refugees, driven from their homes as the only alternative to slaughter. The existence of long-range airlifters has allowed many industrialized nations to deliver medical facilities, food, clothing, and shelter within days.

Despite all hopes and plans to the contrary, aviation has not made war too terrible to imagine. (For that matter, neither the crossbow, the machine gun, nor poison gas did much to end war forever, either.) Air power alone does not win wars, but a lack of air power can quickly lose a war. •

A pair of Fairchild-Republic A-10s covers American troops during operations in Afghanistan in 2006.

American military equipment was delivered to many Latin American nations in the form of defense aid. This Guatemalan P-51 Mustang was flown in the country's decades-long civil war.

ABOVE: Great Britain was preparing to retire its remaining Vulcan nuclear bombers when, in 1982, Argentina invaded the Falkland Islands, a self-governing British overseas territory in the South Atlantic. As a British fleet sailed to reclaim the islands, a Vulcan bomber flew from Ascension Island to destroy the Argentinian airfield at Port Stanley. The 7,860-mile round trip was, at that time, the longest operational bombing mission in history.

LEFT: Following World War II, France sought to reassert its control over French Indo-China. Opposed by a several national forces, the French were defeated by a large Vietnamese army in 1954 when French air power, limited in strength, proved unable to relieve colonial forces.

Vietnam

While most Americans agree that they don't want another Vietnam, or that we must remember the lessons of Vietnam, there is little consensus over just what Vietnam represented or what the lessons were. What is clear is that US efforts to prevent the Communist North Vietnamese from overrunning the South Vietnamese failed; just two years after all parties signed a 1973 cease fire, North Vietnamese forces invaded and overthrew the South Vietnamese government. Despite US guarantees to support their South Vietnamese allies, America proved unwilling to reenter the conflict; US support was limited to evacuation missions.

The military learned many lessons during the Vietnam War. Most of its training and equipment had been designed to counter a massive Warsaw Pact invasion of Europe or an all-out nuclear war. The guerilla war that marked most Vietnamese operations generally required more precise responses, new weapons, tactics, and training.

When the North Vietnamese and Viet Cong guerillas mounted large-scale offensives, they attempted the type of warfare for which the US was best prepared. (In military parlance, they created a "target-rich environment.") Every major Communist Offensive was turned back by combined air power and ground forces. Even the famous Tet Offensive of 1968, initiated during an agreed holiday cease fire, failed within weeks, costing the North an estimated 45,000 troops. America's first great Cold War defeat left the country's military leaders aware of a new set of rules: political support for future wars would require rapid victories that reduced casualties to friendly forces and enemy civilian populations alike. Planners began to look to new generations of aircraft, with improved bombing computers and precision-guided munitions ("smart bombs") to play a more critical part in those future victories. •

ABOVE: Heading North in 1972, a McDonnell Douglas F-4E refuels from a Boeing KC-135A. Waiting to the right is a Republic F-105G, an aircraft especially equipped to attack surface-to-air missile sites.

BELOW: This USAF chart shows the route taken by Guam-based B-52s on the 20 January 1973 Arc Light mission to South Vietnam. The last mission over South Vietnam occurred seven days later, with the final mission against Cambodia flown that August.

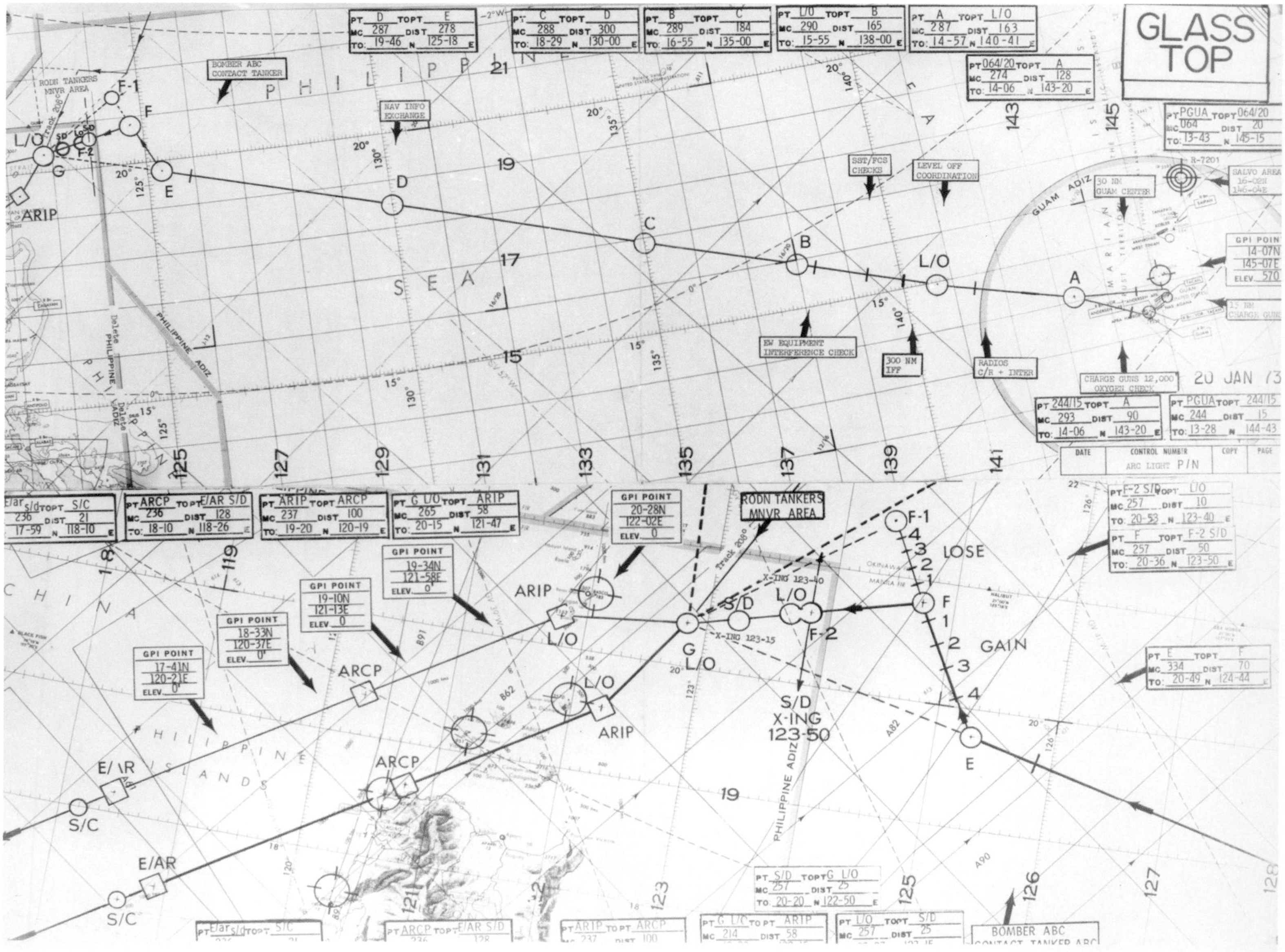

Designed at the end of World War II, the Douglas A-1 Skyraider was the perfect attack aircraft for the developing South Vietnamese air force. The rugged Skyraider could loiter over targets for hours while carrying more ordnance than a WWII B-17 bomber.

B-52 operations against Communist forces in South-East Asia came under the code name Arc Light. The first missions were flown from Guam in June 1965, with bombing raids continuing from Guam and Thailand through August 1973.

The Gulf Wars

On 2 August 1990, Saddam Hussein, ruler of Iraq, invaded the tiny neighboring kingdom of Kuwait. Despite its small size (only 6,200 square miles), Kuwait was an immensely wealthy nation. Profits from the country's vast oil deposits gave the Kuwaiti people one of the world's highest per-capita incomes and made them easy targets for the greed of their morally and financially bankrupt neighbor.

The occupation was completed in a matter of hours. The Iraqi army, the largest in the region, was equipped with some of the most sophisticated Soviet weaponry; Kuwait's armed forces were largely ceremonial in nature. The international response was overwhelming. A US-led coalition moved to the Saudi Arabian desert and the Persian Gulf to prepare to force an Iraqi withdrawal. After four-and-a-half months of failed negotiations and disregarded warnings, Coalition forces began Operation Desert Storm on the night of 16/17 January 1991.

The problem for Hussein and his military planners was doctrinal; their military buildup (including the world's sixth largest air force) had created exactly the type of enemy that NATO and allied forces had trained against. Through the use of precision-guided weapons, the Coalition quickly targeted and destroyed command centers, air defense facilities, and major depots with minimal damage to surrounding civilian population centers. Airborne control aircraft quickly identified Iraqi aircraft, which were soon targeted and destroyed by Coalition fighters.

Joint operations; A US Marine MH-53E approaches the refueling drogue of an Air Force HC-130P tanker/rescue aircraft. Fully refueled in less than a minute, the helicopter inserted Marine reconnaissance teams far behind Iraqi lines.

Developed in secret, its existence hidden from the public for over a decade, the Lockheed F-117 Nighthawk was able to strike deep inside Iraq, undetected by enemy radar systems. The first Stealth Fighters, F-117s destroyed critical command, control, and communications centers, leaving the target areas before defenses had been alerted to their presence.

For all the destructive capability of the combined allied force, every effort was made to avoid civilian and military casualties. Leaflets dropped on Iraqi positions warned troops against sleeping in their tanks on the nights that raids were scheduled; hours later, laser-guided bombs would destroy the vehicle sparing the crews to surrender later.

After six weeks of air attack, ground forces moved into Kuwait and Iraq on 24 February. Cut off from supplies, their air force and heavy weapons destroyed, more than 78,000 Iraqi soldiers would surrender in the next 100 hours. Iraq was allowed peace terms, its government left intact in exchange for an agreement to allow a supervised destruction of its chemical, biological, and nuclear weapons programs.

On 20 March 2003, US and British forces began a second attack on Iraqi forces, this time aimed at the removal of Saddam Hussein and his power structure. By the end of April, the Iraqi government had fallen.

The invasion of Iraq had again shown the ability of modern air forces to minimize civilian casualties, even when Iraqi forces positioned aircraft weapons and tanks next to schools, hospitals, and mosques. Air planners, knowing that even their smallest guided weapons were likely to cause collateral damage, fashioned new bombs out of solid concrete and attached laser guidance systems. The weapons were able to hit and destroy the military equipment without the use of explosives, avoiding further casualties.

A Lockheed-Martin F-16C refuels from a Boeing KC-10 tanker during Operation Iraqi Freedom. Considered a multi-role fighter, the F-16 carries air-to-air missiles and laser guided bombs.

Two aircraft have become critical to the new employment of air power, and neither aircraft carries a single gun, bomb, or missile. The E-3 AWACS (Airborne Warning and Control System) and E-8 J-STARS (Joint Surveillance and Target Attack System) are flying command posts, using sophisticated radars to sweep the skies (on the E-3) and the earth (on the E-8) to identify threats, then coordinate responses from friendly air and ground forces.

Even as the war continued after Saddam's fall, air power proved useful. Prior to an assault on the insurgent stronghold in Tikrit, American reconnaissance drones monitored the locations of all parked cars and trucks. Vehicles which had not moved in the weeks before the attack were identified as possible car bombs, held in reserve for the arrival of the American troops. The night before the assault, each of the vehicles was hit with a precision guided bomb; the resulting explosions confirmed that most had carried explosives. No car bombs were used against American forces during that attack. •

RIGHT: A Boeing C-17 heavy airlifter takes off beyond an Air National Guard Lockheed-Martin C-130 during an Iraqi Freedom resupply mission.

BELOW: An aging veteran, this Boeing B-52H first flew in 1962. Highly modified over the intervening four-and-a-half decades, the long-range bomber flew missions in Desert Storm and Iraqi Freedom.

A US Marine F/A-18C prepares for a strike on Iraqi radar defenses; the anti-radiation missiles beneath the wings were developed to identify, track, and destroy ground-based radar systems.

TOP: Loaded for bear, a 20th Fighter Wing F-16C launches on a Wild Weasel defense suppression mission. Besides its complement of air-to-air missiles, the aircraft carries a large, white anti-radar missile under each wing.

BOTTOM LEFT: The highly sophisticated ground attack version of the F-15 Eagle is widely known as the Beagle (Bomb-Eagle). With advanced navigation and targeting electronics, the Beagle can destroy individual targets with unprecedented accuracy.

BOTTOM RIGHT: Europe's most advanced multi-role combat aircraft is the Panavia Tornado, built in Germany, the UK, and Italy. This British Tornado is equipped for precision ground attack missions.

Modern Military Aircraft

One of the least sophisticated front-line combat aircraft in the modern arsenal, the Fairchild Republic A-10 is a dedicated ground attack aircraft. Large and slow, the "Warthog" is still capable of carrying and delivering more ordnance than any other modern fighter. This Alaskan A-10 formation is banking over Mount McKinley.

LEFT: The newest fighter in the US inventory, the F-22 Raptor is the next generation of stealth fighter. Adjustable exhaust nozzles help the engines' thrust maneuver the aircraft. The highly efficient engines make the Raptor capable of supersonic flight without the use of its afterburners.

BELOW: Tilt Rotor technology allows the V-22 Osprey to takeoff like a helicopter and fly like an airplane. The Osprey's primary roles are rescue and combat transport, but several other missions are underdevelopment.

BOTTOM: Training helps prepare the modern pilot for combat, and part of combat training involves an understanding of enemy tactics. This F-15 Eagle, painted in the garish colors of Russian export aircraft, mimics the appearance, flight characteristics, and maneuvers of potential enemies.

LEFT: The Lockheed-Martin F-35 Joint Strike Fighter combines vertical takeoff and landing capabilities with supersonic speeds, a low radar signature (stealth), and supersonic speeds. The F-35 is currently on order for the US Navy, Marines, and Air Force, and Britain's Royal Air Force and Royal Navy.

BELOW: An extremely clean, flying wing design gives the Northrop-Grumman B-2 Stealth Bomber a remarkable unrefueled range of some 6,000 miles with a 25-ton payload.

RIGHT: New technology in old airframes: the E-8 Joint Surveillance Target Attack Radar System combines the latest ground-scanning radar with rebuilt Boeing 707-320B airliners. The E-8 crew identifies ground vehicles and structures, then coordinates any necessary attacks by aircraft and ground forces.

U.S. AIR
WR

Pushing the Envelope

During the 1920s, US military designations began carrying an "X" prefix to distinguish the experimental versions of aircraft. Following tests and evaluations, aircraft could be ordered into production, without the experimental prefix. In 1947, the US Air Force introduced a new "X" designation system for aircraft designed solely to evaluate new technologies when the XS-1 (Experimental, Sonic Research Aircraft Model 1) was redesignated the X-1. The new X-planes would evaluate new aeronautical technologies for use in future projects, but even the most successful of the designs was never meant for full production. Over the following half century, X-planes have come to symbolize the most modern, futuristic technological and scientific advances, and any new test aircraft, regardless of the designation or country of origin, is generally described as an X-plane. •

BELOW: With so many new designs to test, the USAF established its Test Pilot School at Edwards AFB, California, to train the men who would fly the new aircraft. Here a pilot enters one of the school's specially marked F-80 Shooting Stars.

One of many bizarre designs of the 1950s, the Convair XFY-1 Pogo used two turboprop engines to drive contra-rotating props for a vertical takeoff. Only one of the three completed aircraft was flown before the program was canceled.

On 20 November 1953, the Douglas D-558-2 rocket plane became the first aircraft to exceed Mach 2 (twice the speed of sound). The aircraft could also carry Jet-Assist Take-Off equipment to boost take off power.

ABOVE: The XS-1 (later designated X-1) was the first aircraft to exceed the speed of sound in level flight. The pilot for that flight, Air Force Captain "Chuck" Yeager (L), is seen here with two other members of the test program.

LEFT: Dramatic technological improvements coincided with the introduction of the Century Series aircraft (which each carrying a designation over 99). Photographed together on a test flight in the later 1950s are (clockwise from the bottom) the North American F-100 Super Sabre, the Lockheed F-104 Starfighter, the McDonnell F-101 Voodoo, and the Convair F-102 Delta Dagger.

BELOW: Enhancements in the X-1 design led to the X-1E, which was continued high speed research from 1955 through 1958.

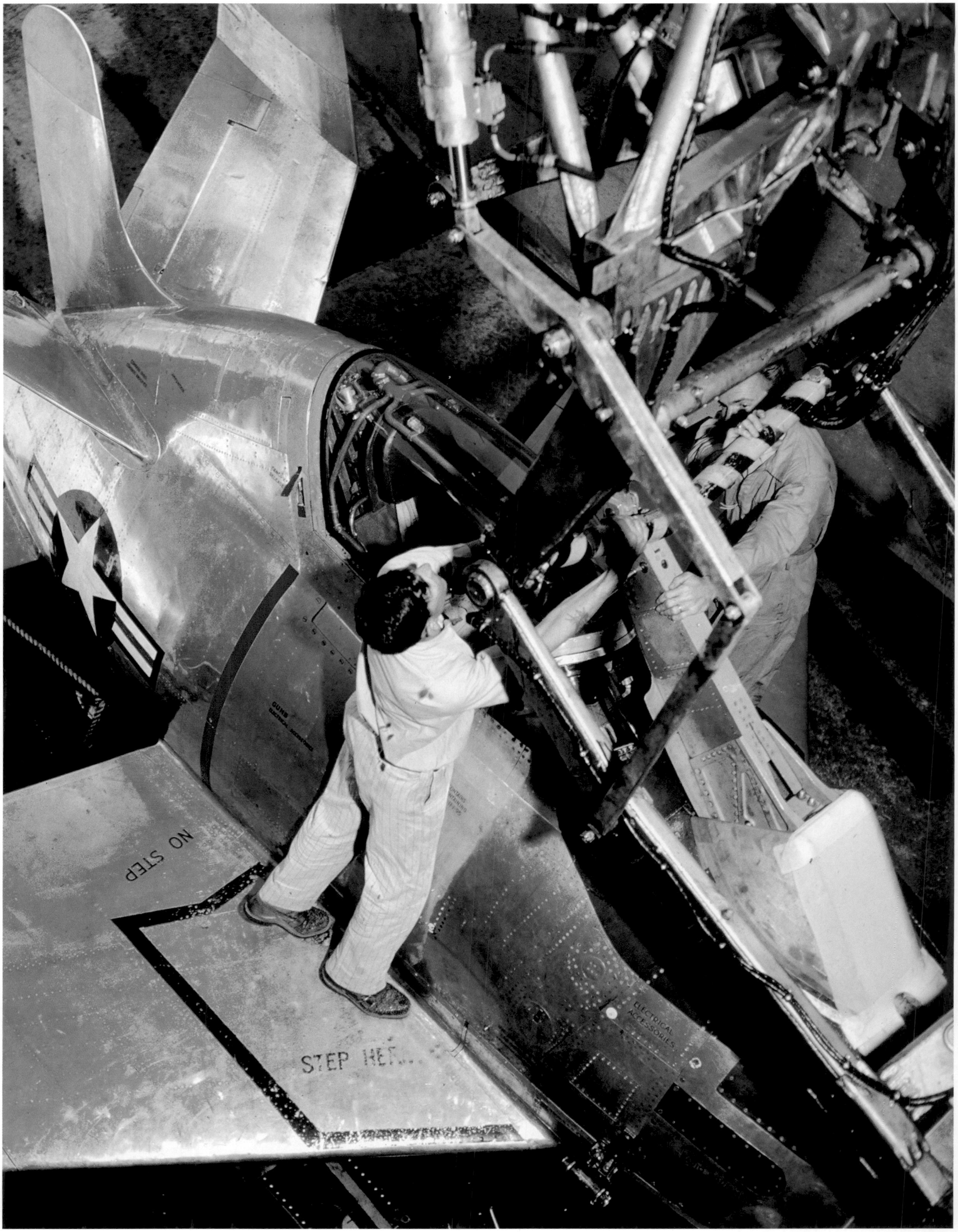
NO STEP
GUNS
ELECTRICAL ACCESSORIES

ABOVE: Britain's delta-winged Avro 707 began high speed research in the late 1940s; this model 707A continued test flights until 1967.

RIGHT: NASA's Northrop M2-F1 lifting body tested wingless flight in the mid-1960s. An unpowered glider, the M2-F1 was towed to altitude by a second aircraft.

BELOW: The XC-142 tested the fundamentals of tilt-rotor technology in the early 1960s. After a four-decade gestation, technology was finally developed enough to introduce the first operational tilt rotor aircraft early in the 21st century.

LEFT: The tiny XF-85 Goblin parasite fighter was designed to be carried inside intercontinental bombers, flying out as a defensive fighter, then returning to the bomber for the trip home. The two Goblins made only six flights, totaling 2 hours 19 minutes, before the program was canceled in mid-1949.

LEFT: The oldest F-15 still flying, NF-15B #837 was the third USAF prototype before it joined NASA to help evaluate new technologies. Mounting forward canards and a variety of test packages, the aircraft was photographed over the Tehachapi Mountains in February 2007.

BELOW: A former Pan American Boeing 747SP, SOFIA (Stratospheric Observatory for Infrared Astronomy) was modified as a high-altitude infrared observatory by NASA and the German Aerospace Center. This was SOFIA's first flight on 26 April 2007.

RIGHT TOP: The Vought F-8 Crusader, one of the finest naval fighters to come out of the 1950s, was adopted by NASA for several emerging technologies in the 1970s. In this image, the Digital Fly-by-Wire (DFBW) testbed leads the Supercritical Wing (SCW) Crusader following test flight over the Dryden test facility in 1973.

The Boeing X-36 Tailless Fighter Agility Research Aircraft was built as a drone - note the sketches of the "crew" drawn on the side of the "cockpit." Designed to test the extremes of aircraft maneuverability, the X-36 began its test program in 1997.

One of the newest X-planes, the Boeing X-48B Blended Wing Body subscale demonstrator first flew in the summer of 2007. The remotely piloted, unmanned vehicle was photographed over the desert at Edwards AFB, California, on its fifth test flight on 14 August 2007.

The Postwar Airlines

The decades following World War II have seen remarkable growth in the capabilities of civil air transport. The war itself had curtailed, but not ended, the activities of the airlines. Many lines operated under contract to military or government authorities. As peace arrived, most airlines had plans in place for growth and expansion.

The War, for all of its destruction, left the world with many more improved air fields than had been available in 1939. New navigational systems covered much of the globe, hundreds of surplus aircraft were available at a fraction of their original costs, and thousands of well-trained, ex-military flight crews needed civilian jobs. Aircraft manufacturers had also been preparing for the post-war economy. Many new designs were ready to enter production, often based, in part, on successful wartime aircraft.

Prewar air transport had been a speedier alternative to rail and steamship lines, which continued to carry the greatest numbers of passengers. The postwar success of airlines spelled the end of nearly all independent railroads and ocean liners. The airplane had arrived as a safe, economical alternative means of transportation.

By the mid-1950s, Europe had introduced the first new jet- and turboprop-powered airlines; the de Havilland Comet, the Vickers Viscount, and the Sud Caravelle shaved hours off longer journeys. American designers responded with the four-jet Boeing 707 and Douglas DC-8, which soon commanded much of the market. Plans for new fleets of supersonic airliners came to an end in the late 1960s; while a handful of Anglo-French Concorde SSTs (Supersonic Transports) served into the early 21st century, airline executives turned from the quest for speed to the practicality of economy. Oversized jumbo jets that carried hundreds, not dozens, of passengers dominated international and long-distance travel from the 1970s. New engines had to develop more power using less fuel, while creating less noise and pollution.

In the span of a generation, much of the adventure of air transport had been replaced by the business of air transport. •

RIGHT: After World War II, airlines stressed the safety and comfort of air travel. The harried businessman of the pre-war advertizing photos was noticeably absent in this post-war shot of a mom, her three daughters, and a stewardess (as female flight attendants were then known).

BELOW: America's VOR (Very-high-frequency Omnidirectional Radio range, also called Omni) was adopted as an international navigational standard in the late 1940s. This experimental Omni chart was issued in 1948 to help navigate the VOR route from New York to Chicago.

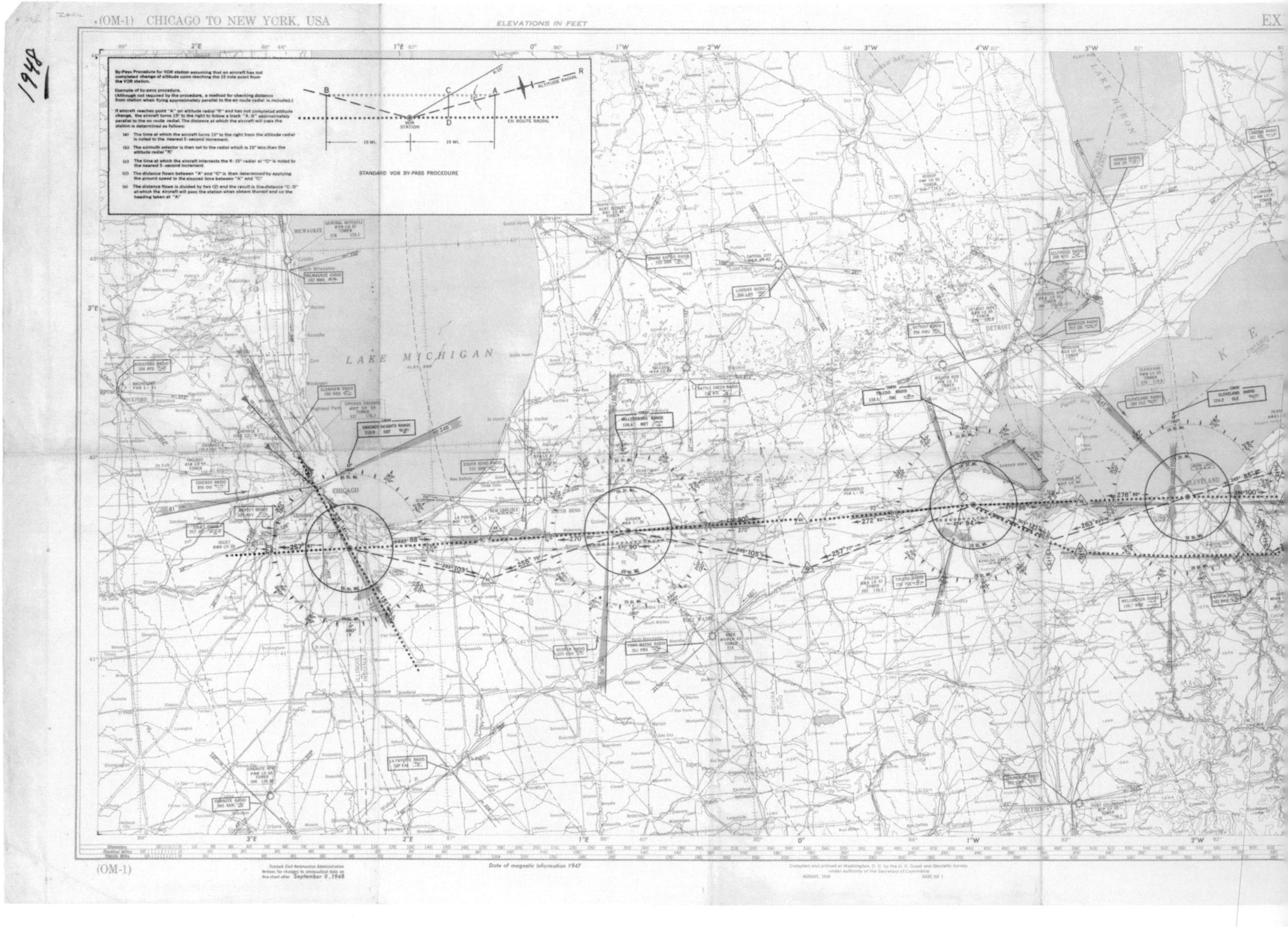

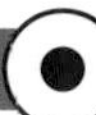

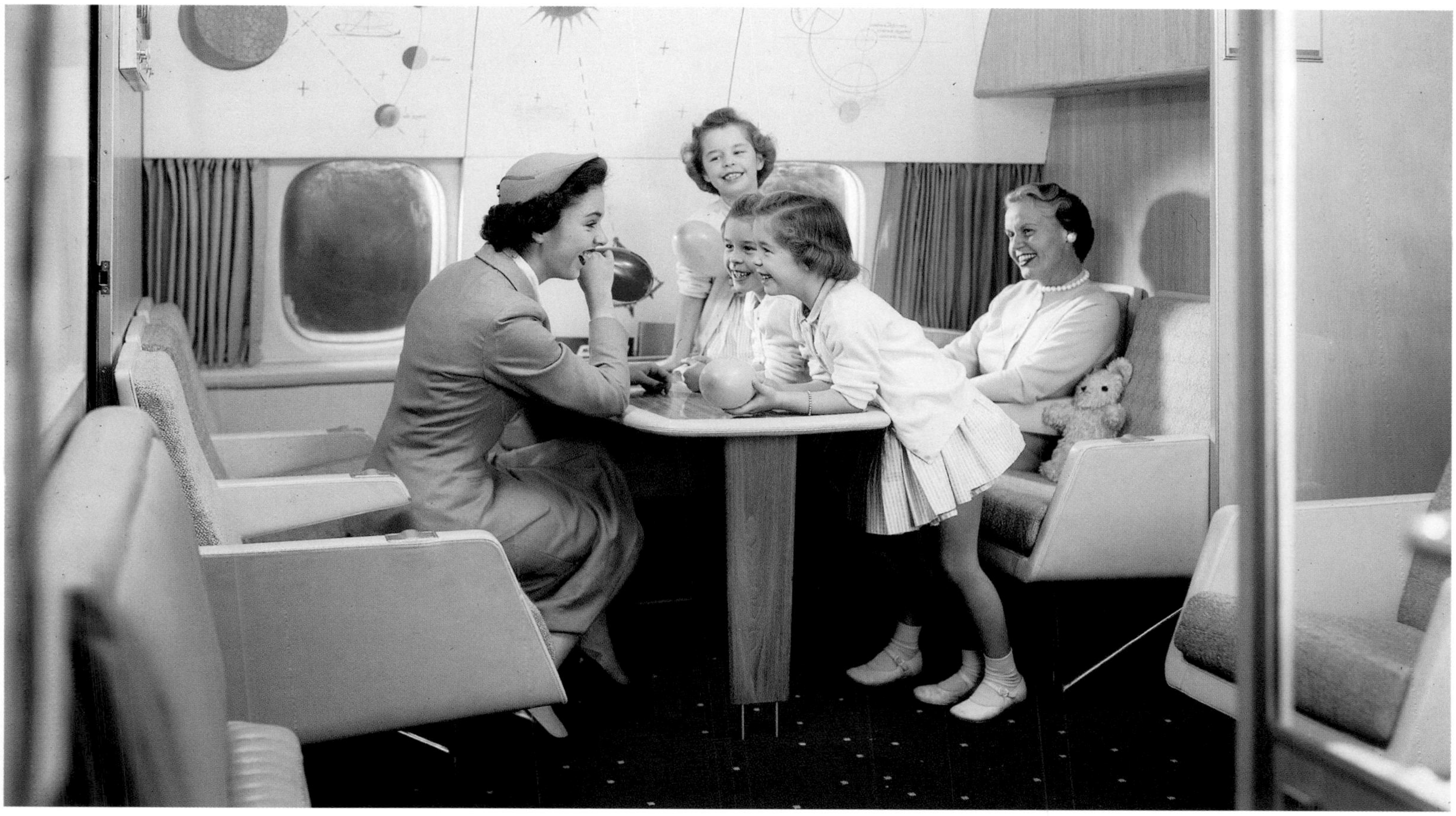

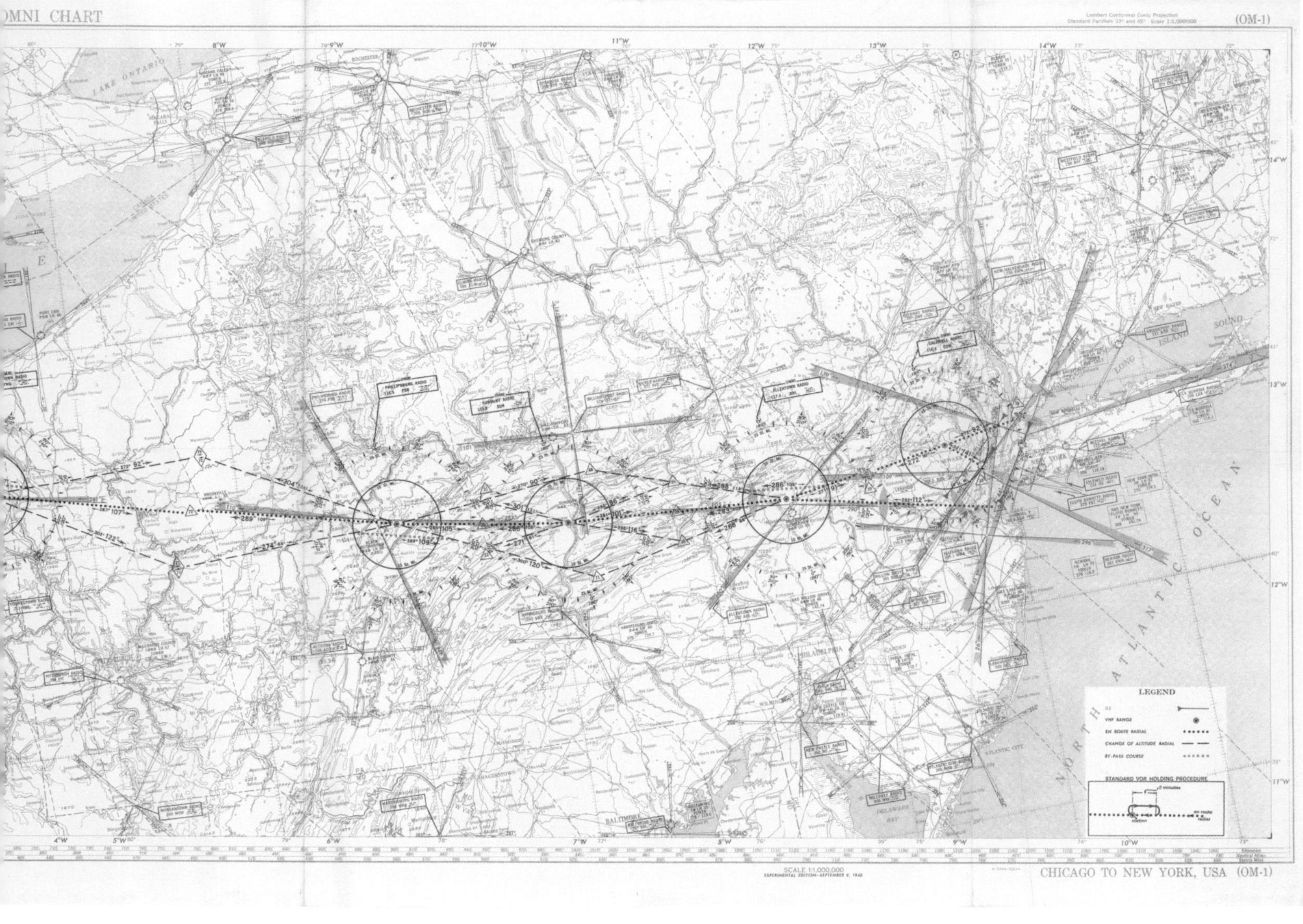
OMNI CHART
(OM-1)
LAKE ONTARIO
LONG ISLAND SOUND
NORTH ATLANTIC OCEAN
PHILADELPHIA
BALTIMORE
ATLANTIC CITY
DELAWARE BAY
LEGEND
ILS
VHF RANGE
EN ROUTE RADIAL
CHANGE OF ALTITUDE RADIAL
BY-PASS COURSE
STANDARD VOR HOLDING PROCEDURE
3 minutes
station
en route radial
SCALE 1:1,000,000
CHICAGO TO NEW YORK, USA (OM-1)

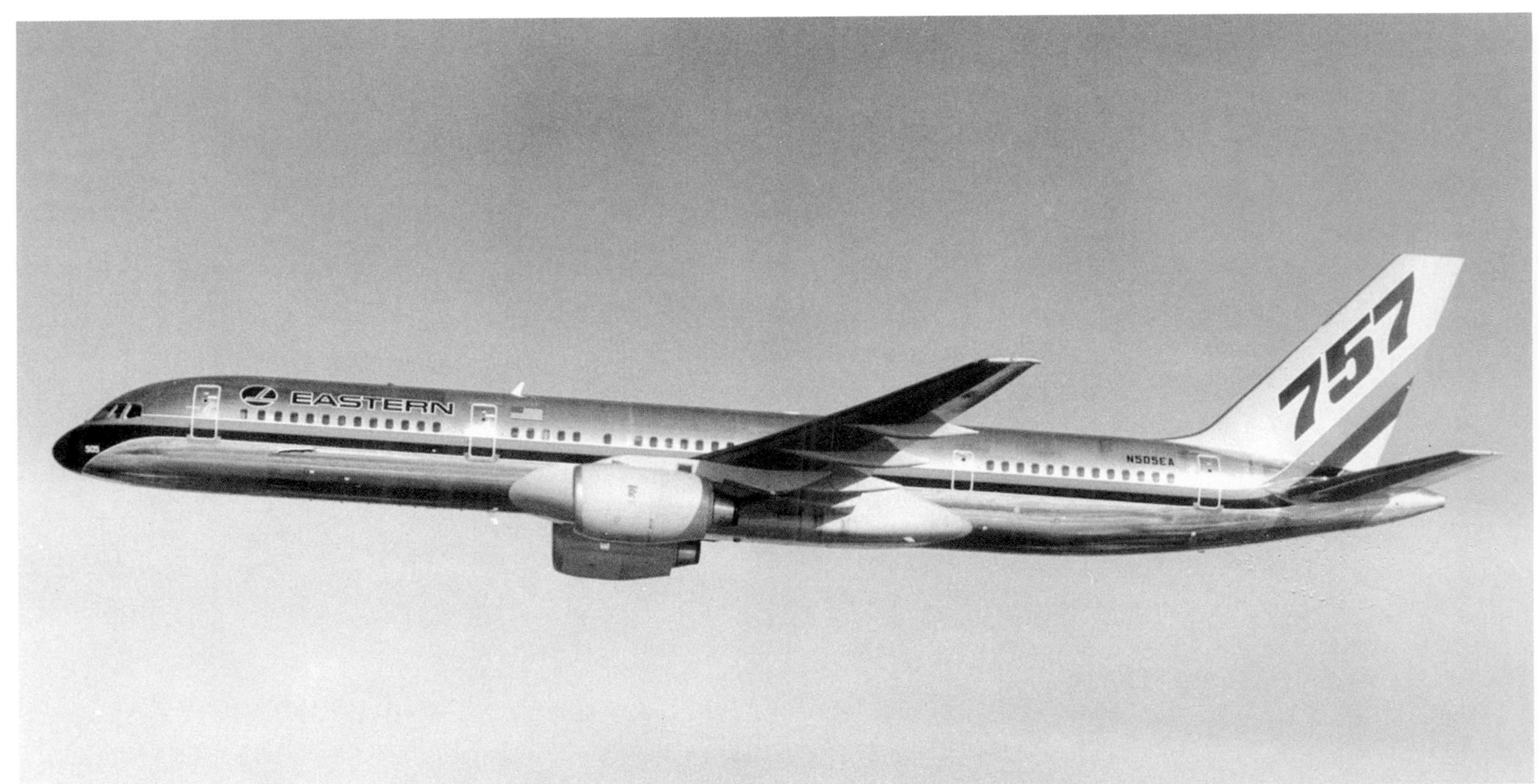

EASTERN
757
N505EA

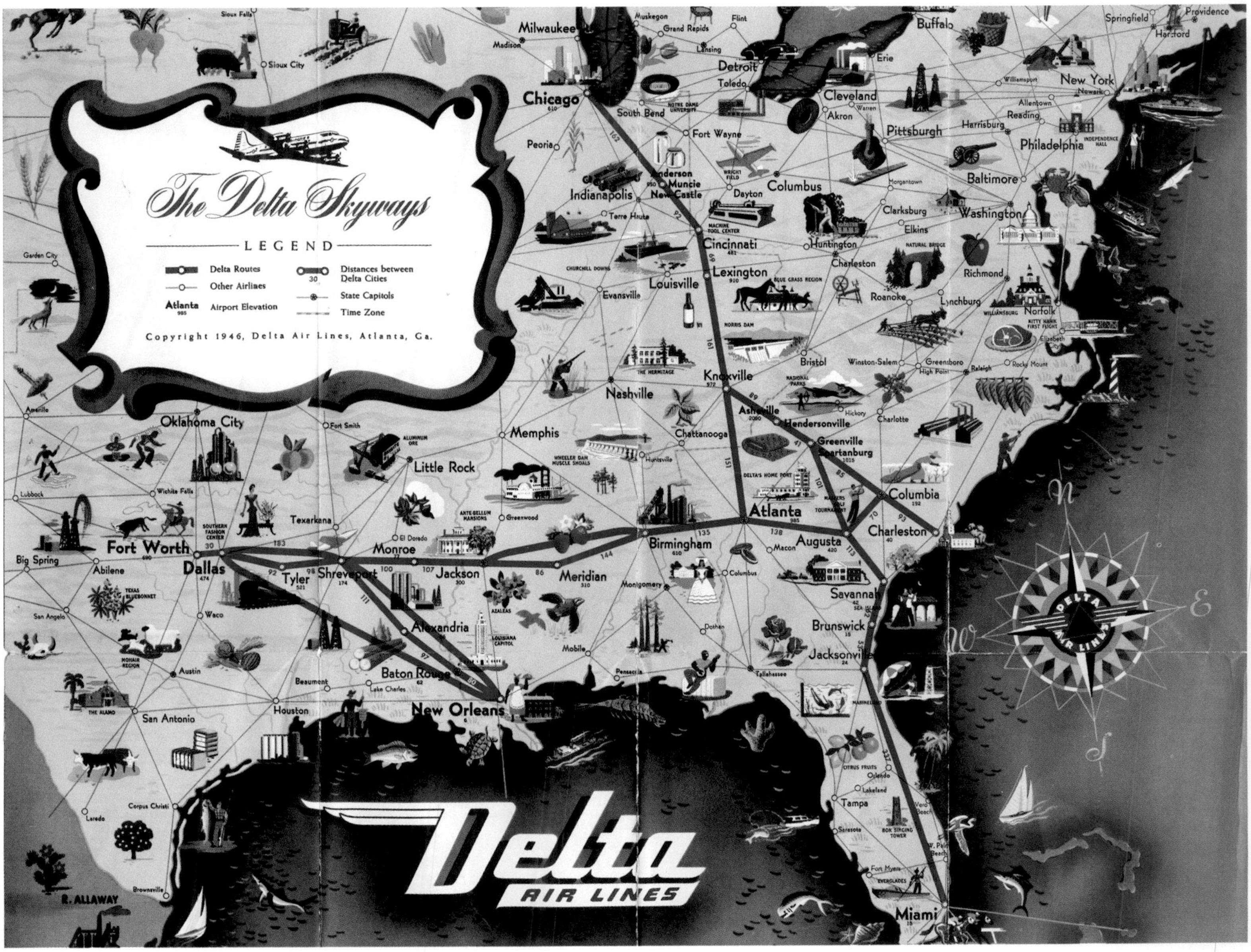
The Delta Skyways
LEGEND
Delta Routes
Other Airlines
Atlanta 985 Airport Elevation
Distances between Delta Cities
State Capitols
Time Zone
Copyright 1946, Delta Air Lines, Atlanta, Ga.
Delta
AIR LINES
R. ALLAWAY
Chicago
Milwaukee
Detroit
Cleveland
Pittsburgh
Buffalo
New York
Philadelphia
Baltimore
Washington
Richmond
Norfolk
Indianapolis
Columbus
Cincinnati
Lexington
Louisville
Knoxville
Nashville
Asheville
Hendersonville
Greenville
Spartanburg
Columbia
Charleston
Atlanta
Augusta
Savannah
Brunswick
Jacksonville
Tampa
Miami
Birmingham
Meridian
Jackson
Monroe
Shreveport
Tyler
Dallas
Fort Worth
Alexandria
Baton Rouge
New Orleans
Memphis
Little Rock
Oklahoma City
Chattanooga
Houston
San Antonio
Big Spring
Abilene

ABOVE: In 1946, the New York Yankees began traveling to some away games by air rather than by rail. This specially marked United Air Lines C-54 carried them to many of their destinations in speed and comfort.

RIGHT: Passengers pull their coats on for warmth following a cross-country flight. Although many new designs were available after the war, the venerable DC-3 continued to carry the lion's share of passengers for several years.

LEFT TOP: Introduced in the early 1980s, Boeing's 757 was the first of a new generation of airliners to employ high-bypass turbojet engines, which produce high thrust with much less pollution and noise. Eastern Airlines was among the 757's first customers.

LEFT BOTTOM: Based in the US Southeast, Delta Air Lines underwent a massive postwar expansion. This 1946 passengers' route map gives little indication what was to come; six decades later, Delta would reach 54 countries, with scheduled service to more than 900 cities.

In the years following World War II, hundreds of retired military airlifters were converted for use with civilian airlines. This former US AAF C-54 is receiving finishing touches in the US before delivery to Dutch airline KLM in 1946.

AB AEROTRANSPORTS
LINJENÄT
SOMMAREN 1947

LINES OPERATED BY
SWEDISH AIRLINES
SUMMER 1947

FLYGTID FÖR 100 KM
FLYING TIME PER 100 KM
DC-3 21½ min.
DC-4 18½ min.

This 1947 AB Aerotransports route map shows the Swedish airline's DC-3 and DC-4 connections in the new Europe. Political boundaries for Germany show the British, French, American, and Soviet occupation zones.

The first jet airliner offered by Douglas Aircraft, the DC-8 was direct competition for Boeing's 707. Introduced in 1967, the Super 63 variant featured an improved wing, new engines, and a stretched fuselage for improved performance on some shorter trans-Atlantic routes.

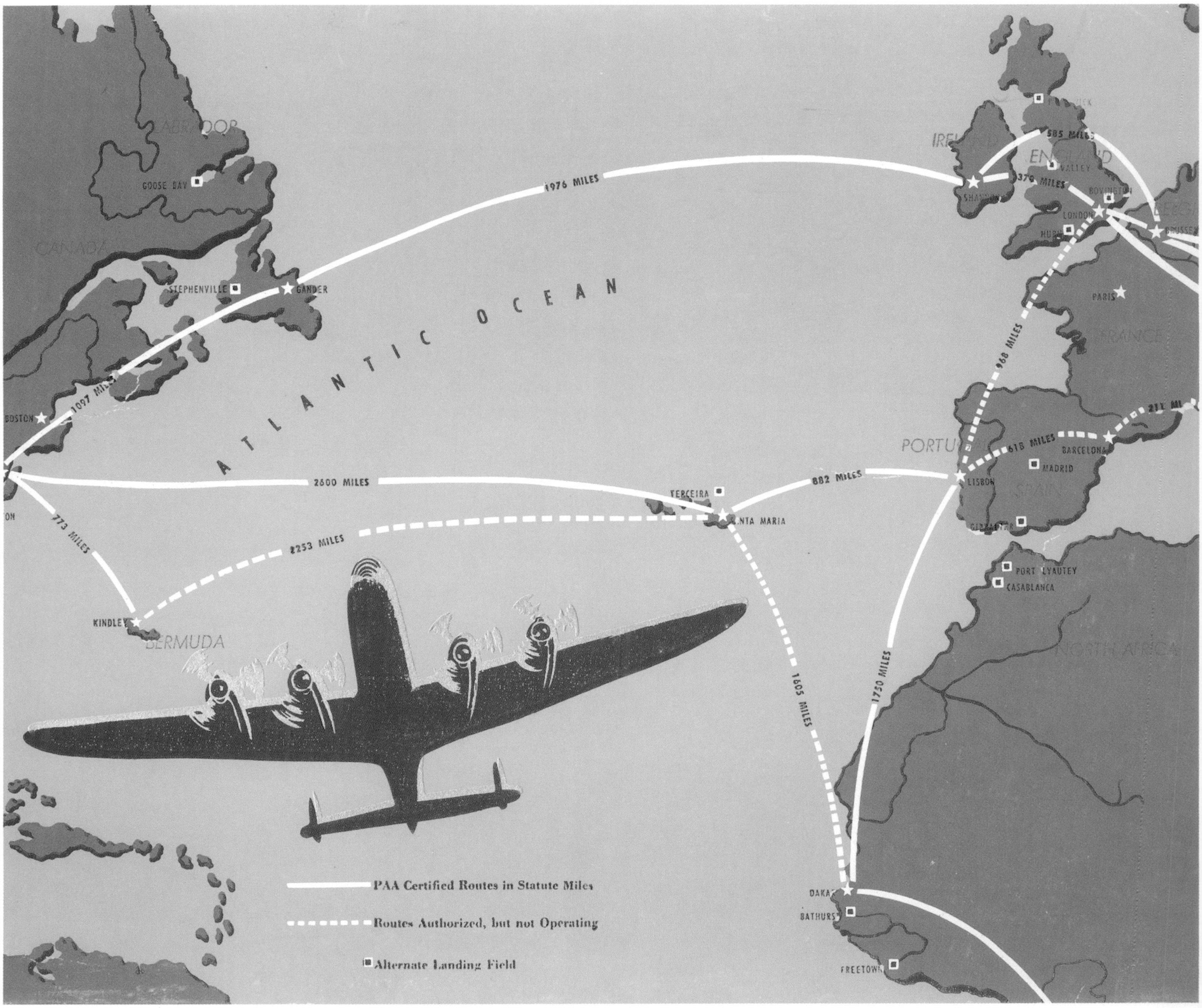

ABOVE: By the early 1950s, Pan American had resumed most of its trans-Atlantic routes, though the company's flying boats had been replaced by newer, long-range land planes.

LEFT: An Eastern Air Lines DC-3 in the company's new post-war colors.

RIGHT TOP: Introduced to commercial service in 1955, the Lockheed 1049G Super G was the most successful version of the Constellation series. Of the 101 built, 28 were delivered to TWA for use on the company's international routes.

RIGHT BOTTOM: This 1959 FAA schematic explained the latest improvements for Instrument Landing Systems.

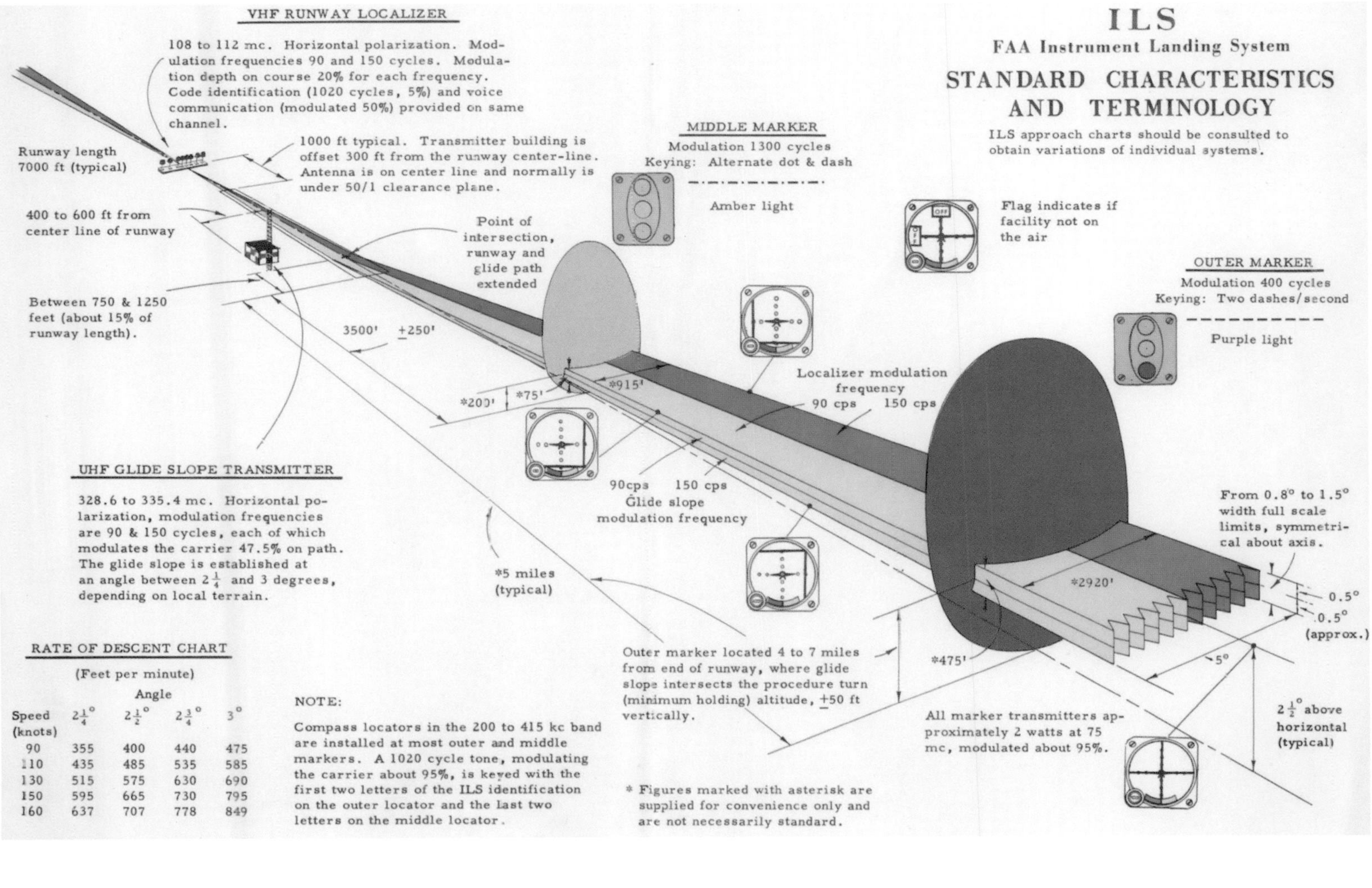

ILS

FAA Instrument Landing System

STANDARD CHARACTERISTICS AND TERMINOLOGY

ILS approach charts should be consulted to obtain variations of individual systems.

VHF RUNWAY LOCALIZER

108 to 112 mc. Horizontal polarization. Modulation frequencies 90 and 150 cycles. Modulation depth on course 20% for each frequency. Code identification (1020 cycles, 5%) and voice communication (modulated 50%) provided on same channel.

Runway length 7000 ft (typical)

1000 ft typical. Transmitter building is offset 300 ft from the runway center-line. Antenna is on center line and normally is under 50/1 clearance plane.

400 to 600 ft from center line of runway

Point of intersection, runway and glide path extended

Between 750 & 1250 feet (about 15% of runway length).

3500' ±250'

*200' *75' *915'

MIDDLE MARKER

Modulation 1300 cycles
Keying: Alternate dot & dash

Amber light

Flag indicates if facility not on the air

OUTER MARKER

Modulation 400 cycles
Keying: Two dashes/second

Purple light

Localizer modulation frequency
90 cps 150 cps

UHF GLIDE SLOPE TRANSMITTER

328.6 to 335.4 mc. Horizontal polarization, modulation frequencies are 90 & 150 cycles, each of which modulates the carrier 47.5% on path. The glide slope is established at an angle between $2\frac{1}{4}$ and 3 degrees, depending on local terrain.

90cps 150 cps
Glide slope modulation frequency

*5 miles (typical)

From 0.8° to 1.5° width full scale limits, symmetrical about axis.

*2920'

0.5°
0.5°
(approx.)

*475'

5°

$2\frac{1}{2}$° above horizontal (typical)

Outer marker located 4 to 7 miles from end of runway, where glide slope intersects the procedure turn (minimum holding) altitude, ±50 ft vertically.

All marker transmitters approximately 2 watts at 75 mc, modulated about 95%.

RATE OF DESCENT CHART

(Feet per minute)

Speed (knots)	Angle $2\frac{1}{4}$°	$2\frac{1}{2}$°	$2\frac{3}{4}$°	3°
90	355	400	440	475
110	435	485	535	585
130	515	575	630	690
150	595	665	730	795
160	637	707	778	849

NOTE:

Compass locators in the 200 to 415 kc band are installed at most outer and middle markers. A 1020 cycle tone, modulating the carrier about 95%, is keyed with the first two letters of the ILS identification on the outer locator and the last two letters on the middle locator.

* Figures marked with asterisk are supplied for convenience only and are not necessarily standard.

Freighter
G-AGVC

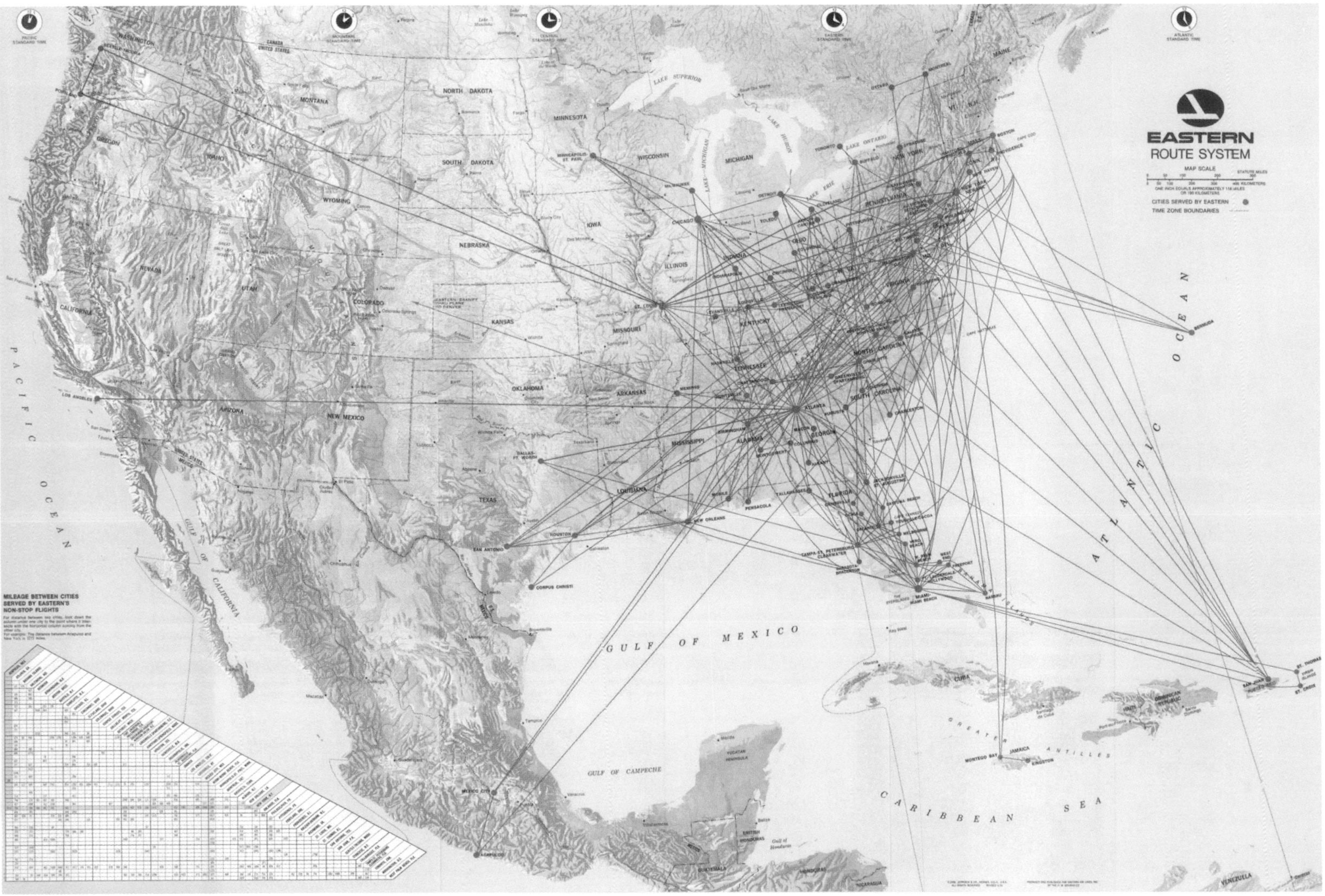

ABOVE: By the 1970s, Eastern Airlines routes covered most of the eastern US, with flights to Bermuda, Puerto Rico, Jamaica, the Bahamas, Mexico, and Canada.

RIGHT: The late 1940s commercial aviation had advanced far beyond its pre-war capabilities and was introducing new generations of prop-driven airliners. This photo includes a pair of new Lockheed Constellations (from Pan American and TWA) and, at the right, a converted C-54 from American Overseas Airlines.

LEFT: The third Bristol 170 Freighter made a demonstration tour of North and South America in 1946/48 before returning the Europe to participate in the Berlin Airlift. An outstanding cargo plane (seen here onloading four automobiles at New York's LaGuardia Airport), the Bristol Freighter saw a production run of 214 aircraft, some of which continued in service in the early 1990s.

The Growth of a Modern Airport

Today, New York's John F. Kennedy International Airport is the busiest passenger gateway to the United States, and ranks as one of the top airports for international freight. Opening to commercial traffic in 1948, "JFK" mirrors dozens of other major worldwide airports introduced since World War II

In 1942, the city of New York began the construction of a new municipal airport at Idlewild, directly across Jamaica Bay from Floyd Bennett Field. Progress on the new airport would be slowed by World War II, but on 1 July 1948 the first commercial flight left the what would soon be called New York International Airport. (The name "Idlewild" remained popular for the next fifteen years.) The terminal area was designed as a central ring surrounded by six concrete runways. (The longest two runways were each 10,000 feet in length.) By 1951, Runway 4-22 had been configured as an instrument runway with the installation of Instrument Landing System (ILS) antenna. The facilities included two hangars (increased to ten hangars in the 1950s). Early passenger, operations, and customs facilities were erected from war-surplus Quonset huts on either side of the single terminal building.

By the early 1960s, the New York Port Authority had invested more than three-hundred-million dollars in the airport. Major airlines added their own funds, creating a series of new terminals that won architectural awards and established New York International as one of the world's most beautiful air facilities. Runways were added, restored, or extended to meet the demands of new jet aircraft. Runway 4-22 (renamed 4R-22L) was extended to 11,400 feet, while the parallel 4L-22R was also lengthened by 3,000 feet.

In December 1963, New York International was renamed John F. Kennedy International Airport, honoring the memory of the US President, assassinated a month earlier.

The airport continued to grow as air traffic increased and jets became larger. By the 1970s, many of the award-winning terminal buildings were showing their age, unable to support the new jumbo jets or the growth in passenger numbers and flights. Terminals and ground traffic patterns were redesigned, runways were again lengthened. (At 14,572 feet, Runway 13R-31L is North America's second longest commercial runway.) Handling more than 42-million passengers each year (including roughly a fifth of all departing US overseas passengers), Kennedy recently ranked second in overall passenger satisfaction among all large US airports. •

TOP: This June 1948 image shows buildings nearing completion less than a month before New York International processed its first commercial flight.

BOTTOM: Luggage and food trucks service an American Airlines 767 at Kennedy International in mid 1989.

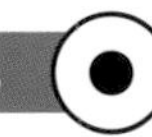

By the early 1960s, New York International nearing completion of a new series of terminal buildings, thought the wartime Quonset huts remained in service at either side of the original terminal.

Shortly after opening its new terminals and improved runways, New York International was renamed John F. Kennedy International Airport in December 1963.

Part of New York International's 1961 redesign bridged the access road to the central terminal complex with aircraft taxiways.

Late-1950s plans for improvements at New York International included new runways extending into Jamaica bay. The projected runways were never built.

Modern Flight Charts

The aeronautical charts available to today's aviators reflect a century of growth in navigational aids and aircraft capabilities. In most of the world, these capabilities also come with greater responsibilities - each pilot must be cognizant of any restrictions to his use of airspace along a route, his responsibilities for reporting in at waypoints on that route, and his need to file a flight plan for any IFR (Instrument Flight Rules) operations within controlled airspace. The charts on the next twenty pages show how some of that information is presented to the pilot. There are two other important flight planning documents that are not included in this book. NOTAMs - Notices to Airmen - are available (in the US) from Flight Service Stations. Generated by the government, each NOTAM provides the most current information about changes in status to facilities (such as runways closed for repairs, new reporting procedures, temporary NAVAID restrictions, etc.) along the flight route. The other critical chart is the weather map, warning the pilot of any possible weather hazards along the route or at the destination.

The charts presented here are generated by government agencies and commercial firms. The charts are reproduced at a 10% reduction, to fit more material on each page, and are in scale order, starting with the largest scale and ending with the smallest. The chart selected in each series includes Washington, DC, which is presented in more-or-less the same position on each page, providing the reader with a quick, visual reference when comparing charts. *All charts are reproduced for historical use only, and must not be used for navigational purposes.*

Although these charts are printed in the US, the standards and graphic icons were established by agreement within the ICAO, the International Civil Aviation Organization, eliminating the need for extensive, specialized map keys each time an aircraft crosses an national border. (Note that while most of the world navigates by the metric system, US charts measure distances in nautical miles and altitudes in feet.) The US governmental civil charts are prepared and distributed by the Federal Aviation Administration's National Aeronautical Charting Office. Our one privately produced chart comes from Jeppesen Sanderson, Inc, a Boeing company. The information in federal and commercial charts comes from the same sources - the data itself is not copyrighted - but the style of presentation varies widely within the ICAO parameters. Three of our charts are produced by the US Department of Defense's National Geospatial-Intelligence Agency (NGA).

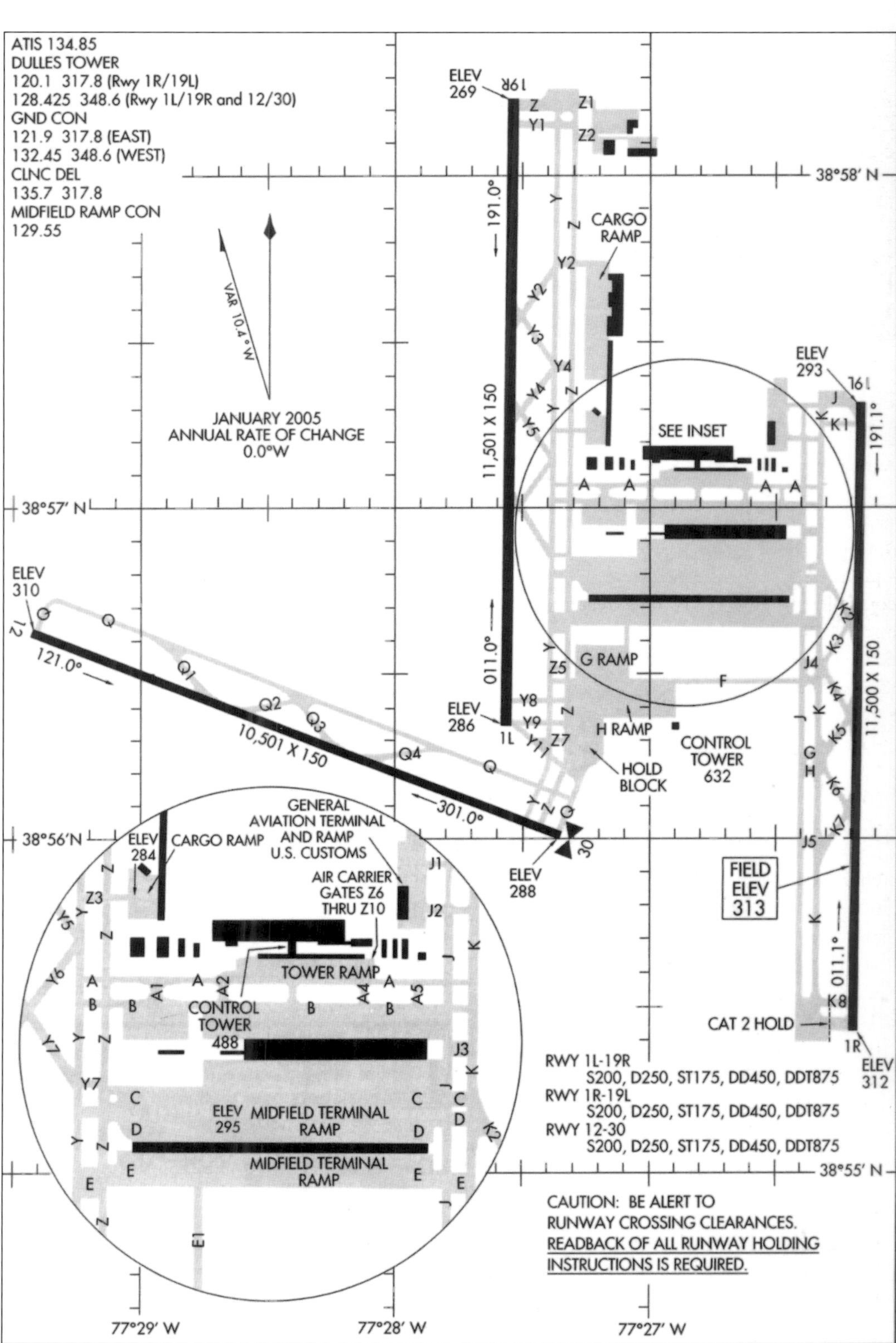

Airport Diagram - Washington Dulles International (IAD).

A few general notes on aerial charts and navigation might help keep the following charts in perspective:

Runways. Runways are identified by two digit numbers derived from the bearing on true north. A runway bearing 89.9° is rounded off to 90° and identified as Runway 9. The same surface has a bearing of 269.9° in the opposite direction and is identified as Runway 27. Using Dulles International as an example, when a field has multiple parallel runways, they can be distinguished as Runway 1R (1 Right) and Runway 1L (1 Left). A third parallel runway would be Runway 1C (1 Center). Use of the same surfaces in the opposite direction also reverses the suffix - 1R becomes 19L on a southerly heading, and 1L becomes 19R.

Airspace Classification: Airspace is classified by aids available to the pilot and capabilities

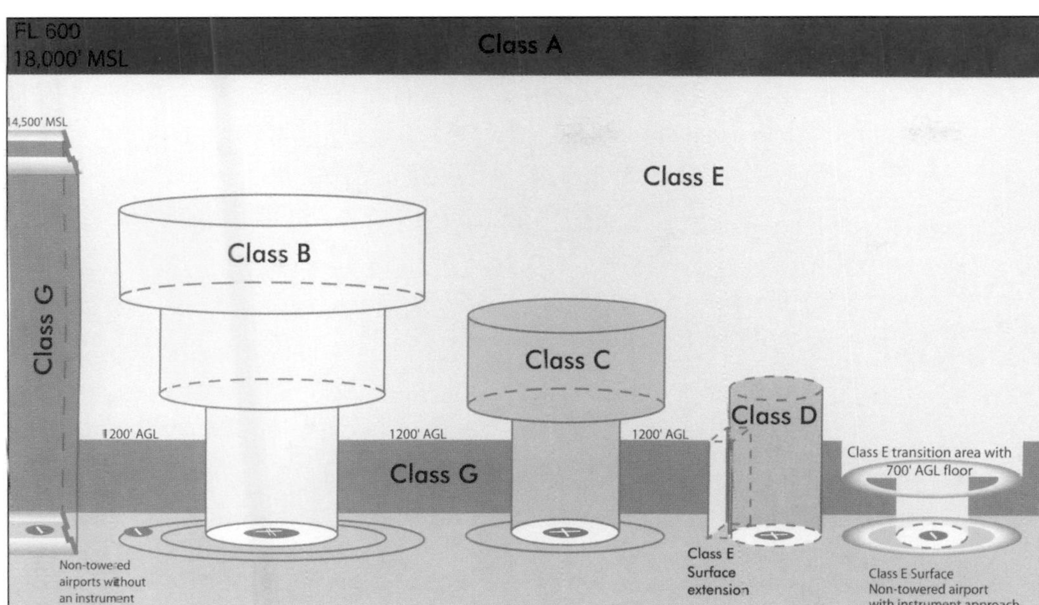

Airspace Classification, as depicted on US Visual Navigational Charts.

required of the pilot and aircraft. Classes A through E are considered controlled airspace - pilots must secure permission from ground controllers to enter. Class G is treated as uncontrolled airspace. The following simplified descriptions provide a basic explanation of those classes:

- **Class A Airspace** (formerly called PCA - Positive Control Area) ranges from 18,000 feet MSL (Mean Sea Level) to FL600. (Altitudes above 18,000 feet are listed as three-digit flight levels; Flight Level 600 represents an altitude of 60,000 feet.) All charts described as "High Altitude" cover Class A Airspace. Pilots flying at these altitudes must have Instrument Ratings where VFR flight is prohibited.
- **Class B Airspace** (formerly known as the TCA - Terminal Control Area) surrounds major airports. Extending from the surface to a designated altitude, Class B airspace is usually shown as three concentric blue rings on World Aeronautical Charts, Sectional Aeronautical Charts, and Terminal Area charts. Each chart depicts the sector's ceiling and floor altitudes in blue digits; 90/20, for example, shows that an sector is considered Class B airspace between 2,000 feet and 9,000 feet.
- **Class C Airspace** (formerly ARSA - Airport Radar Surveillance Area) generally surrounds airports where Air Traffic Controllers provide full-time radar vectoring and sequencing for all traffic. It is shown on low-altitude FAA maps as a pair of concentric magenta rings.
- **Class D Airspace** (originally called Control Zones or Airport Traffic Areas) are usually a cylinder of airspace surrounding other tower-operated airports. It is shown as a single dashed blue line.
- **Class E Airspace** is general controlled airspace, including space surrounding airports without control towers, transition areas, federal airways, and all unallocated US airspace between 14,500 feet and 18,000 feet MSL. Near the surface, Class E airspace is shown as a dashed magenta line. At higher altitudes, Class E airspace is represented by vignetted blue or magenta border lines.
- **Class G Airspace** is the remaining, uncontrolled airspace. No ATC entry permission is required and two-way radio communications are optional (unless a temporary tower is present).
- **Special Use Airspace.** Not a class of airspace, Special Use Airspace includes Prohibited, Restricted, or Warning Areas, Alert Areas, and Military Operations Areas (MOAs)

NAVAIDS are radio aids to navigation. The simplest of these can result from two-way radio communications with an air traffic controller monitoring ground-based radar. (The use of an aircraft-mounted transponder allows a ground controller to make immediate, accurate identification of any aircraft monitored by the local radar.) The controller can direct a lost pilot to a certain heading and altitude, until an airport is reached. Other on-board systems provide pilots with the means to interpret ground signals.

- **NDB (Non-Directional Radio Beacon)** - a ground beacon which transmits radio waves in all directions. Each beacon transmits a two- or three-letter identification signal in Morse Code. An onboard ADF (Automatic Direction Finder, originally known as a radio compass) provides a bearing to the beacon. Additionally, an onboard Relative Bearing Indicator (RBI) can be used to triangulate a position from two NDBs.
- **Compass Locator Beacon** - a low-power Non-Directional Beacon which is frequently used as part of an Instrument Landing System.

- **VOR (VHF - Very High Frequency - Omnidirectional Radio Range)** - a medium-range radio navigation aid similar in principle to a Non-Directional Radio Beacon, but operating at a much higher frequency.

- **DME (Distance Measuring Equipment)** uses onboard equipment to communicate with a ground beacon to determine the aircraft's range in nautical miles from that beacon. Note that the range factors in the aircraft's altitude. DME equipment can be paired with VOR or ILS equipment.
- **TACAN (Tactical Air Navigation)** was developed by the military as a UHF system combining the functions of a VOR for azimuth and DME for range; the onboard equipment is installed on military aircraft only.

- **VORTAC (VHF Omnidirectional Radio Range/TACAN)** is a ground station broadcasting VOR/DME and TACAN signals. The onboard avionics determine which signals the pilot will be reading.

- **ILS (Instrument Landing System)** a system combining onboard avionics and ground electronic beacons and light signals to guide an aircraft to a specific runway.
- **SDF (Simplified Directional Facility)** - a less-precise variation of the localizer equipment in an ILS.
- **RNAV (Area Navigation)** is a system for flying a course without the necessity of overflying ground beacons. The system establishes waypoints along a route using data from VORTACs, LORAN (Long-Range Navigation System), Inertial Navigation System (INS), Radar, or GPS (satellite locations from the Global Positioning System). Established RNAV waypoints marked along routes do not identify the locations of ground equipment. •

NAMEE

Helicopter Route Charts

The high concentrations of helicopter activity make the airspace around Washington, DC, and Baltimore, MD, one of nine American locations covered by FAA Helicopter Route Charts. (The other sections center on Boston, Chicago, Dallas-Fort Worth, Detroit, Houston, Los Angeles, New York City, and Salt Lake City.) The four-color charts depict current aeronautical information useful to helicopter pilots, including information depicting helicopter routes, and four classes of heliports with associated frequency and lighting capabilities, NAVAIDS, and obstructions. These large-scale charts also feature pictorial symbols identifying landmark buildings, roads, and easily-identified geographical features. There is no regular update schedule for Helicopter Route Charts; changes are published on an as-needed basis. The charts are printed on a heavier, synthetic paper, reflecting the expectation that each copy will remain in use longer than most other charts.

Although helicopters are capable of flying, taking-off, and landing in a variety of unique locations, during normal operations they use a series of established helicopter routes, each shown in heavy blue lines with the route number enclosed in a blue box. Required altitudes are shown in blue between two bars (for recommended altitudes), or with a bar above (for a maximum altitudes), or with a bar below (for minimum altitudes).

The air space over the US capital city is subject to a variety of restrictions for public safety and national security. Note also the bold "Warning Avoid Prohibited Area" notices around the Naval Observatory, a few miles north of the city's center. The restrictions reflect less concern that helicopters will disturb the nation's astronomers than a recognition that the grounds include the official residence of the country's vice president. •

A Bell UH-1H of the US Army's Priority Transport Division hovers over the tidal basin at Washington, DC's Jefferson Memorial.

This chart, cropped from the original and reduced to 90% its original size, is presented for informational purposes and is not to be used for navigational purposes.

Helicopter Route Chart: Baltimore-Washington (HELDC); Original Scale 1:125,000 (1″ = 1.7nm)

VFR Terminal Area Charts

Terminal Area Charts (sometimes referred to as Terminal Aeronautical Charts) help pilots identify VFR flyways and avoid major controlled traffic flows in heavily congested, high traffic areas. As such, the charts document only those areas where Class B or Class C airspace predominate. The information is similar to that found on Sectional Charts (see pages 202–203), but is presented in larger scale with much more detail. In the US these charts are published by the FAA and revised semi-annually.

Each side of the chart covers the same geography. The multi-color VFR Terminal Area Chart includes topographical contour information (though the Washington–Baltimore area has little to offer in the way of dramatic elevations). Mixed in with the topographical colors, the built-up civic areas are shown in bright yellow. Major architectural landmarks are shown with the same graphic representations used in the Helicopter Route Chart.

The flip side of the chart is a less complicated flyway planning chart showing multiple VFR routings to be used as alternatives to flight within established Class B airspace. The chart, which is not to be used for navigation, is designed solely for information and planning purposes. •

Still in use after more than seven decades, the venerable Piper J-3 Cub rarely carries the instrumentation needed for IFR flight in Class B airspace. Cub pilots often find a VFR Terminal Area Chart necessary for their flight planning.

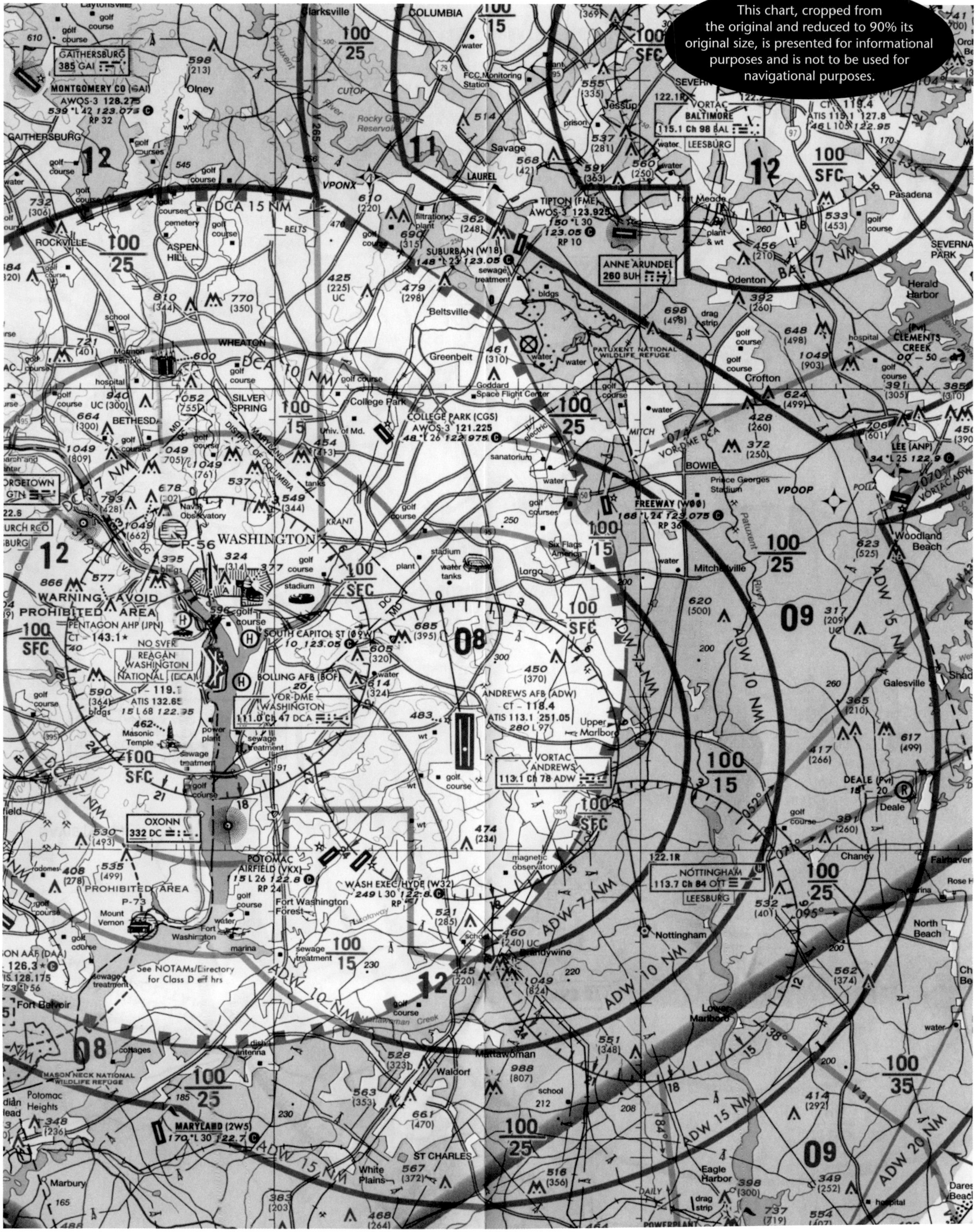

This chart, cropped from the original and reduced to 90% its original size, is presented for informational purposes and is not to be used for navigational purposes.

VFR Terminal Area Chart: Baltimore-Washington (TWAS); Original Scale 1:250,000 (1″ = 6.86nm)

Sectional Aeronautical Charts

Sectional Aeronautical Charts (usually referred to as "Sectionals") are designed for visual navigation of slow to medium speed aircraft. The maps include topographical contour data and visual checkpoints, but the pictographs identifying architectural landmarks are no longer featured. The chart's second side presents the area just south of this chart. Sectionals cover most of the worlds land areas; in the US they are released by the FAA and revised semi-annually.

The change in scale from the Terminal Area Charts is readily apparent, as is the lower level of detail - Sectionals are half the scale. The depiction of mountainous terrain introduced to the west of Washington is a feature of this chart not seen in our previous examples. This does not reflect a new style of data presentation; Virginia's Blue Ridge mountains were simply too far west to appear on the earlier charts. •

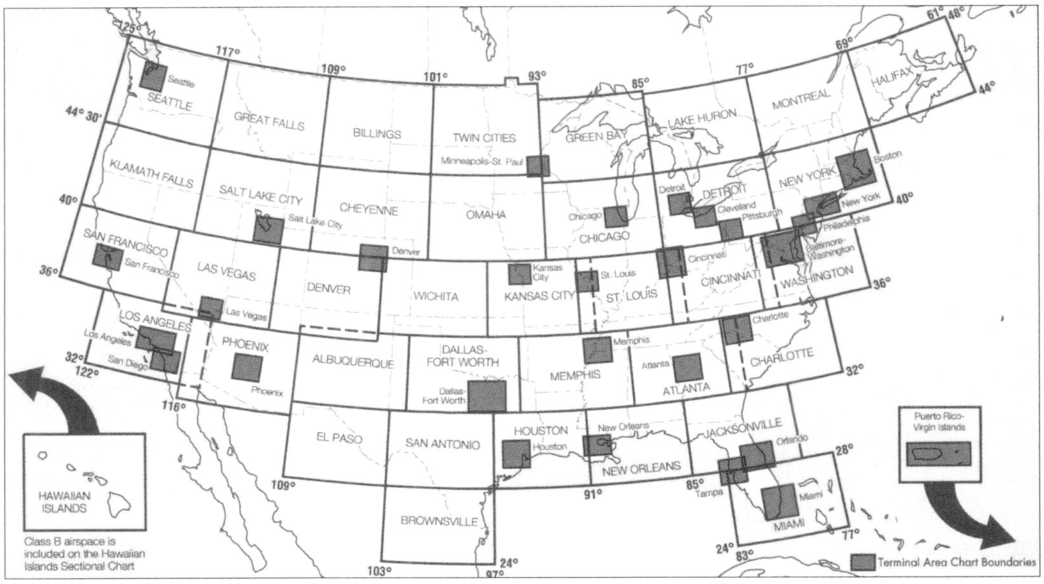

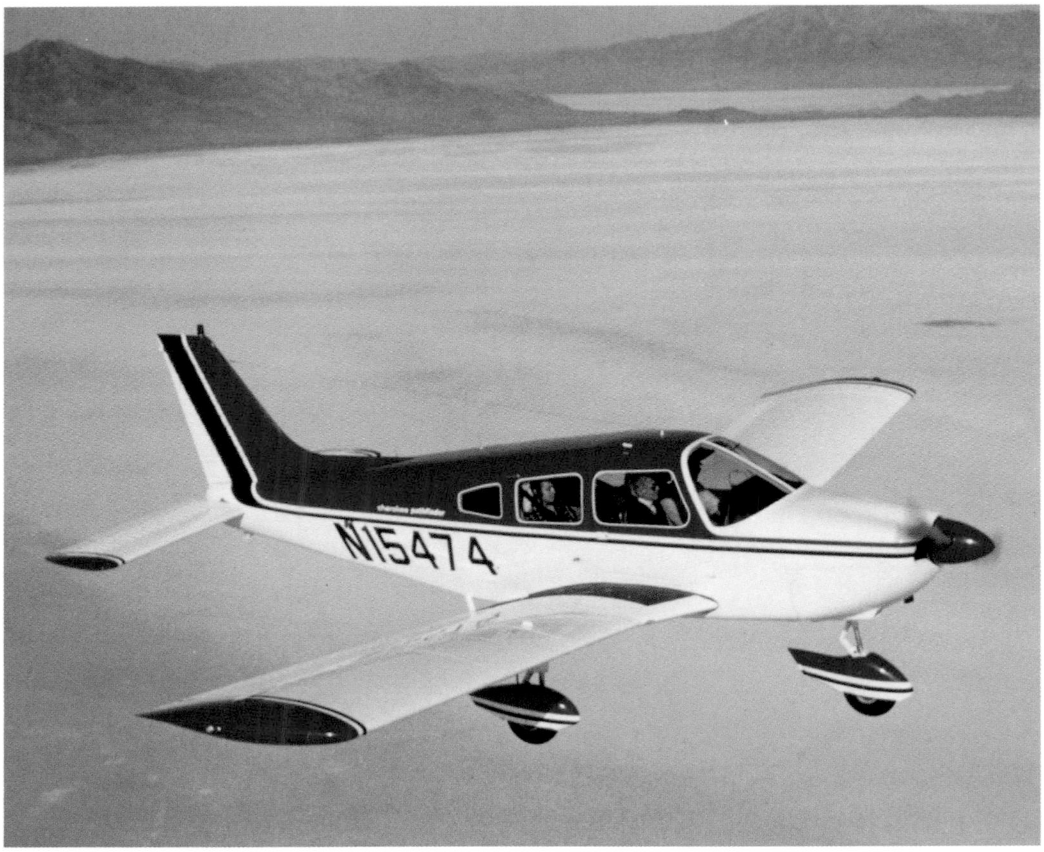

The Piper Cherokee family has been in production since 1961. The Cherokee Pathfinder version, shown here, was produced briefly in the mid-1970s.

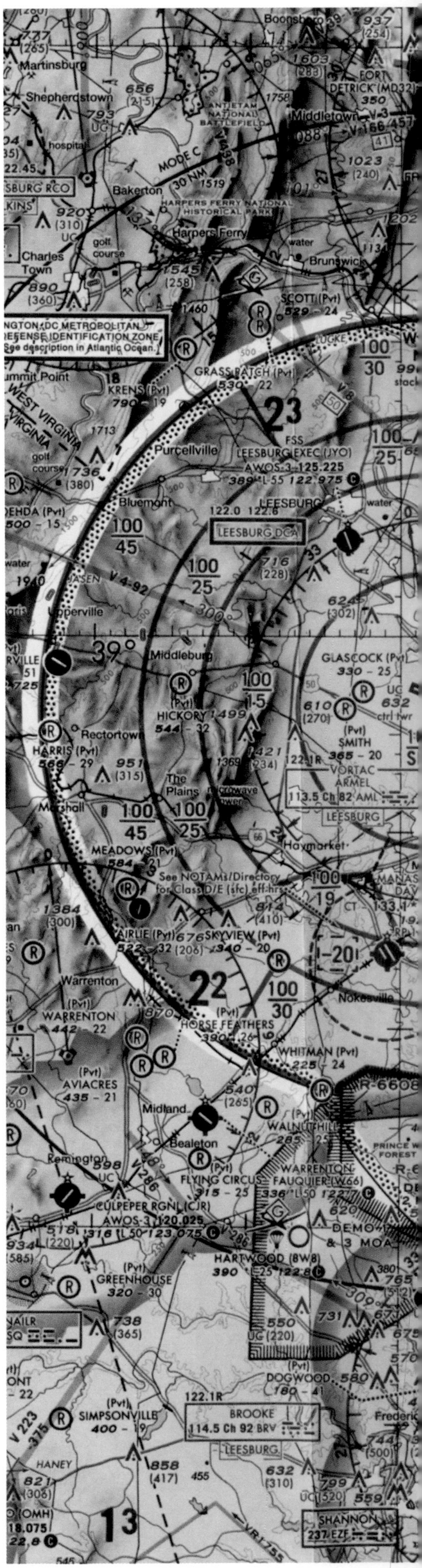

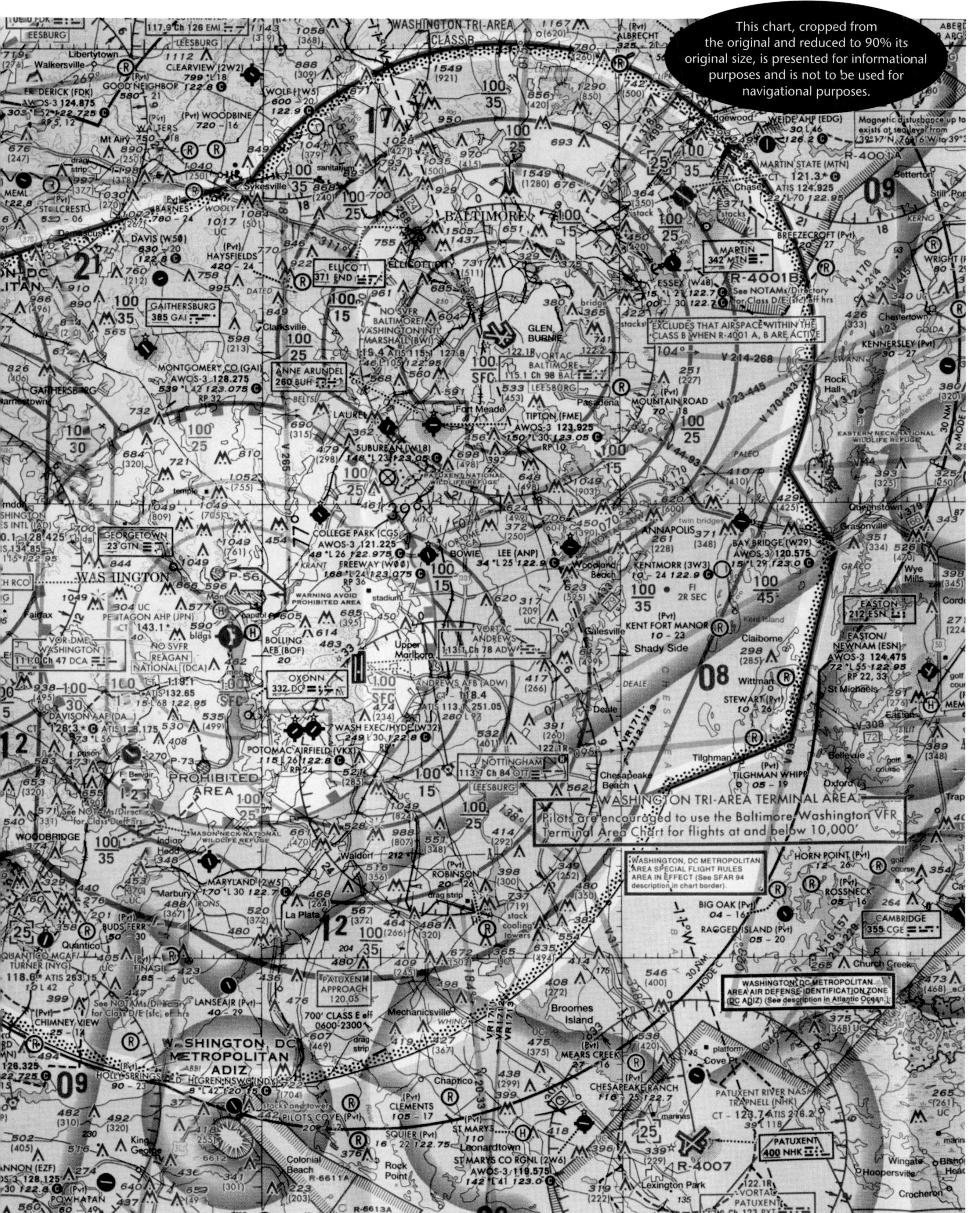

Sectional Aeronautical Chart: Washington (SWAS); Original Scale 1:500,000 (1" = 8.86nm)

Jeppesen Enroute Low Altitude

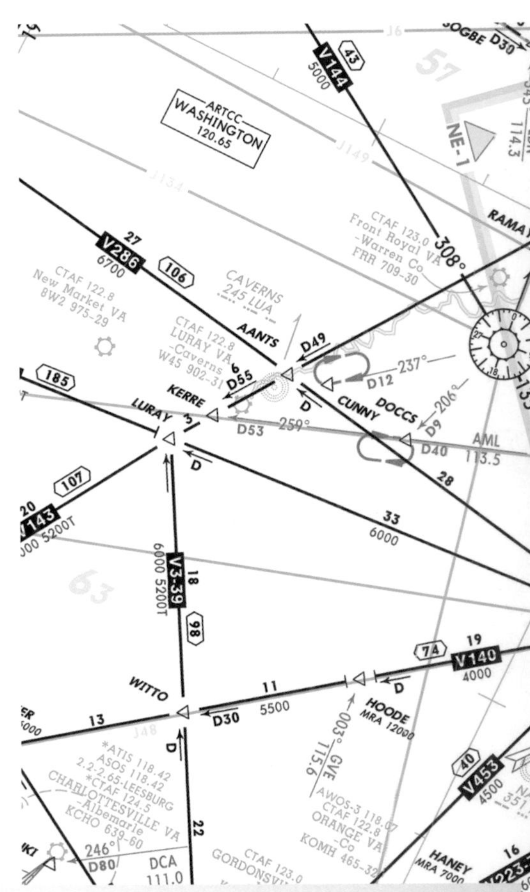

The first of our modern charts designed for instrument flight rules (IFR), this is a United States Low Altitude Northeast Coastal Enroute Chart. The chart shown here is widely known as a "Jepp," a commercially produced chart created by Jeppesen Sanderson, one of the world's most recognized producers of aviation charts and manuals. Jeppesen Sanderson charts draw their data from the same sources as government charts, but presents that data in a slightly different format. In most cases, aviators choose their chart as a matter of personal preference, and Jepps are a very popular alternative, providing direct equivalents to most of the FAA charts discussed in this book.

This chart is laid diagonally across the US East Coast, following the busy air routes of the Northeast Corridor from Boston to Atlanta, splitting into two sections at Washington, DC. Designed for instrument flight at altitudes up to 18,000 feet MSL, the chart provides little topographic information, instead using icons to depict airways and area navigation routes, limits of controlled airspace, data on radio aids to navigation, notes on airports with Instrument Approach Procedures (or 3000-foot hard surface runways), and similar safety and navigational data. Information is printed on the bias, diagonally, to be read along the east-west axis. The green lines broken with a green J-number, depict Jet Routes, while the black lines with white V-numbers depict Victor Routes - low altitude airways followed using VOR or VORTAC navigational aids. •

Photographed during the last days of Eastern Air Lines, this Eastern Metro Express British Aerospace Jetstream 31 prepares for an early morning flight. Eastern's short-range commuter aircraft plied the US Northeast Corridor through the 1980's until the company sold the operation in 1989. Eastern went out of business in January 1991.

Enroute Low Altitude Chart: United States Low Altitude Northeast Coastal Enroute Charts (Jeppesen NE1 and NE2), Original Scale 1″ = 10nm (approximately 1:729,273)

World Aeronautical Charts

World Aeronautical Charts (WACs, pronounced "Whacks") cover land areas at a standard size and scale for navigation by moderate speed aircraft and by aircraft operating at high altitudes. Considered VFR charts, they display topographical information including city tints, principal roads and railroads, distinctive landmarks, drainage patterns and relief. The aeronautical information includes visual and radio aids to navigation, airports, airways, restricted areas, obstructions and similar pertinent data. Because of their smaller scale, these charts cover larger areas than Sectionals and Terminal Area Charts, but show less detailed information. Because some information is omitted (such as Class D and Class E airspace and the limits of controlled airspace), pilots of low speed, low altitude aircraft should not rely exclusively WACs for VFR navigation.

In the US, World Aeronautical Charts are published by the FAA. They are revised and updated annually, except for a few charts covering sections of Alaska, Mexico and the Caribbean, which are revised biennially. •

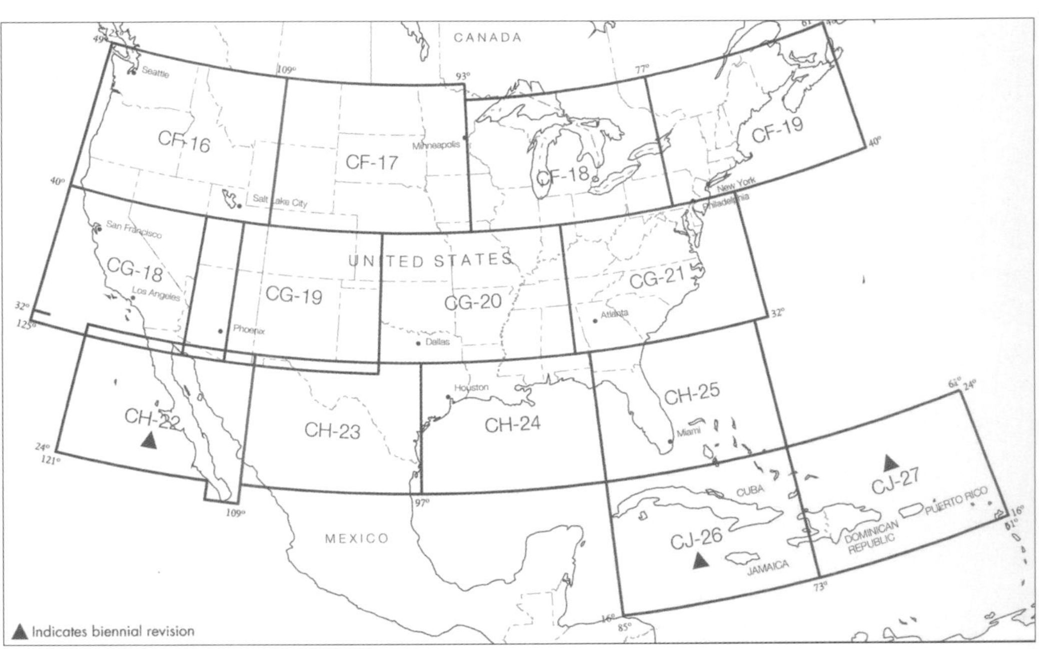

The larger scale of the World Aeronautical Chart provides less detail, but covers a the lower 48 states in only 12 charts.

Introduced in the late 1950s, the sporty Beech J35 Bonanza featured advanced instrumentation for a contemporary private aircraft.

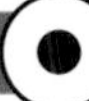

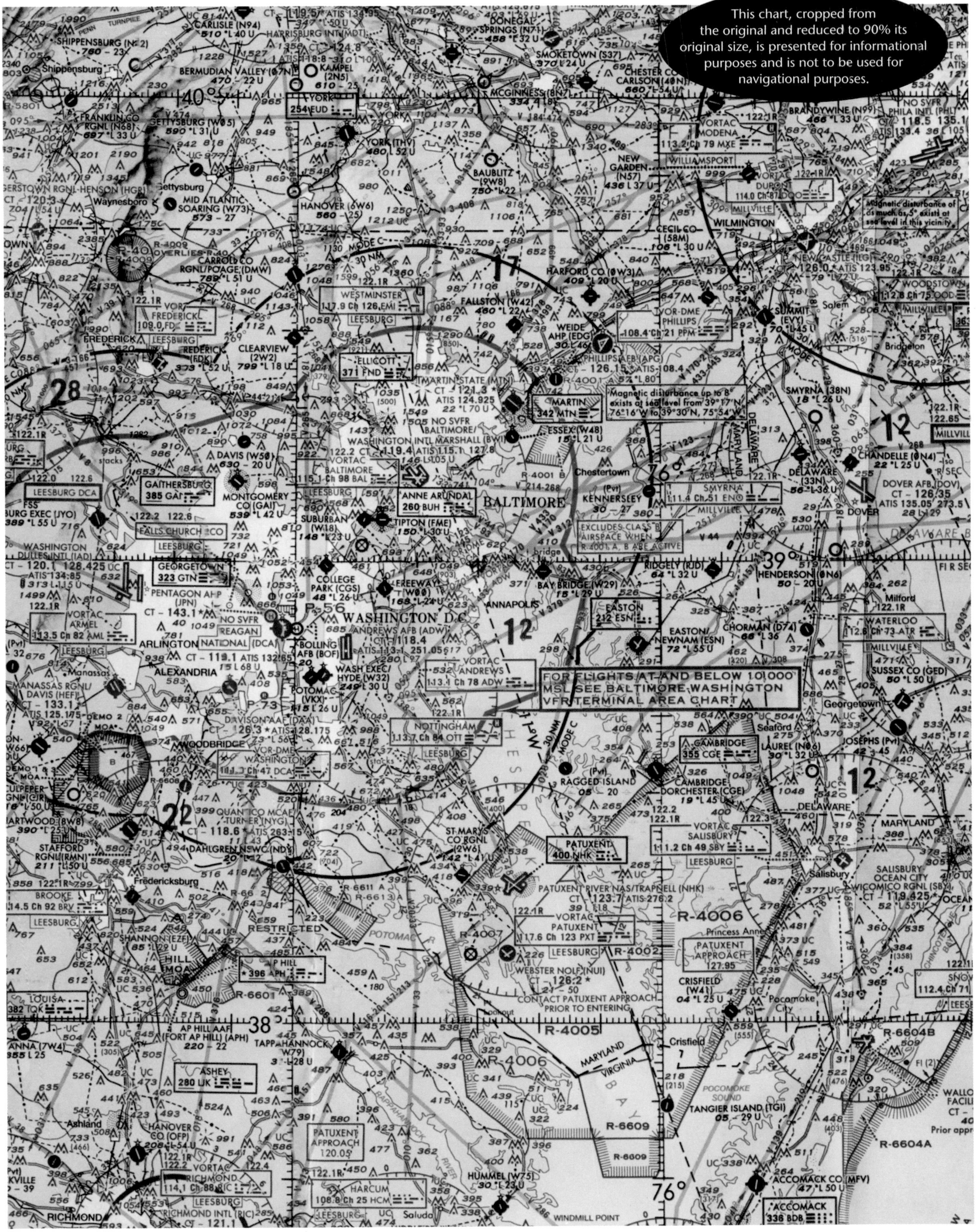
This chart, cropped from the original and reduced to 90% its original size, is presented for informational purposes and is not to be used for navigational purposes.
BALTIMORE
WASHINGTON D.C.
FOR FLIGHTS AT AND BELOW 10,000' MSL SEE BALTIMORE-WASHINGTON VFR TERMINAL AREA CHART
WILMINGTON
R-4006
R-4005
R-6609
R-6604A
R-6604B

World Aeronautical Chart: WCG21; Original Scale 1:1,000,000 (1″ = 13.7nm)

Operational Navigation Charts

Although the same scale as the WAC, Operational Navigation Charts (ONCs) are produced by the US Department of Defense to support high-speed radar navigation requirements at medium altitudes. They support visual, celestial, and radio navigation, or (if tactical charts are unavailable) low altitude visual and radar navigation. Charts in this series cover most of the world's terrain to support military combat, supply, training, or humanitarian missions as needed.

One unusual feature of the ONC involves the color coding of topographical contours. In this chart, green designates large, level expanses of terrain, regardless of their altitude above sea level. Unlike the WAC, the ONC omits established air routes, though standard navigational aids and beacons are included. Particular attention is paid to MOAs (Military Operating Areas) - established zones where military aircraft can train with little danger of colliding with private or commercial aircraft. •

ELEVATIONS IN FEET

ALL ELEVATION VALUES (AERONAUTICAL, RELIEF AND HYDROGRAPHIC) ARE BASED ON MEAN SEA LEVEL.

LEGEND

RELIEF PORTRAYAL

Elevations are in feet. HIGHEST TERRAIN elevation is *6684* feet located at *35°46′N 82°16′W*

TERRAIN CHARACTERISTIC TINTS

GREEN color indicates flat or relatively level terrain regardless of altitude above sea level.

BELOW: F-4Ds of the District of Columbia Air National Guard on a training mission over the capital in March 1989.

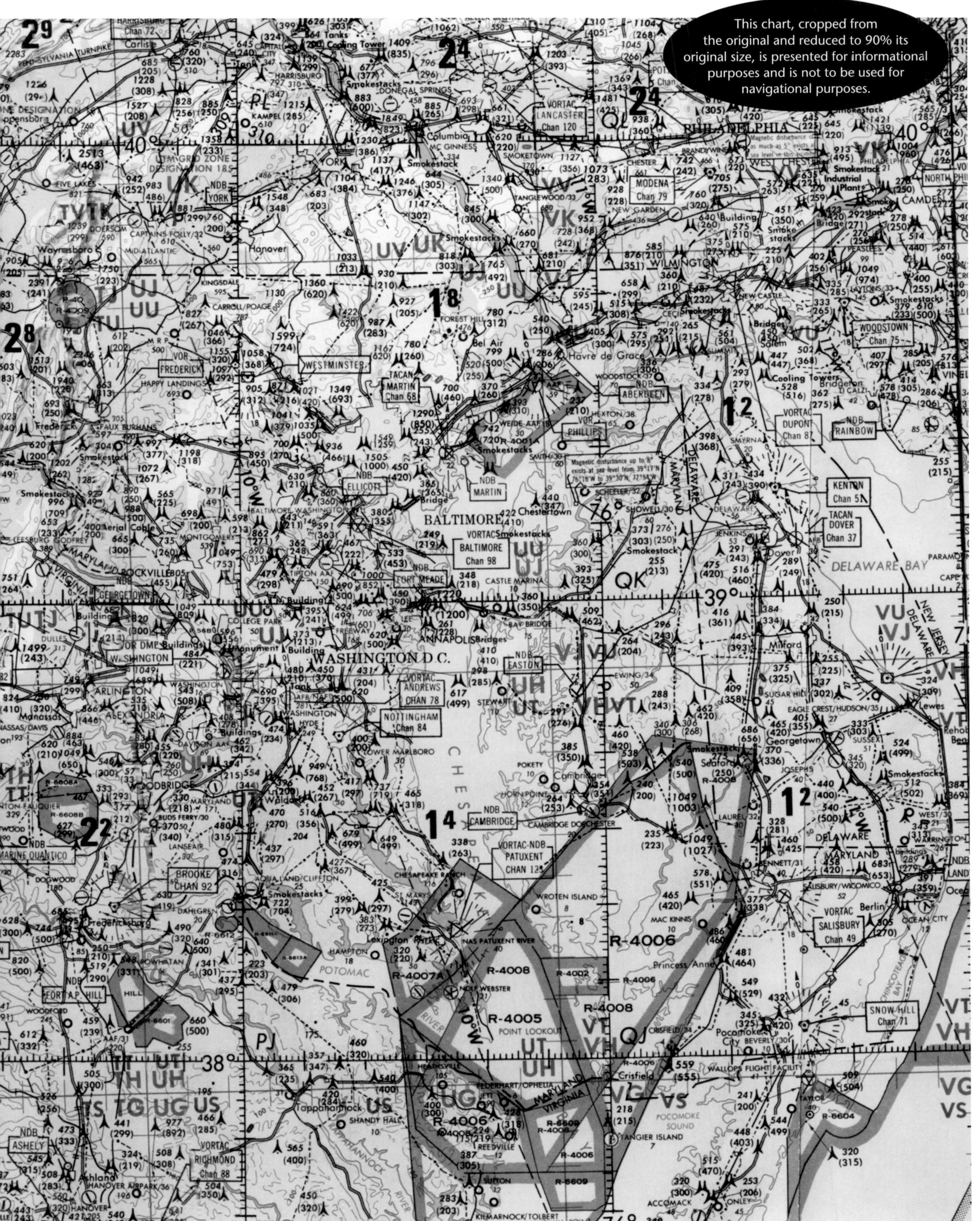

Operational Navigation Chart: ONC G-21; Original scale 1:1,000,000 (1″ = 13.7nm)

IFR Enroute High Altitude Charts

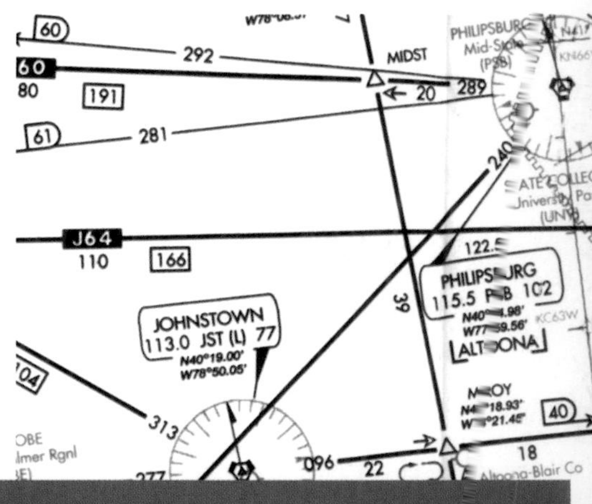

The airspace above 18,000 feet is considered Class A Airspace; all flight there is conducted under Instrument Flying Rules. IFR Enroute High Altitude Charts are designed specifically for navigation at that level. Almost all topographic information has been eliminated from the chart, as has all information on flight routes for lower altitudes. In their place is the intercity jet route structure, area navigation (RNAV) routes, VHF radio aids to navigation, notes on airports with Instrument Approach Procedures (or 5,000-foot hard surface runways), and other useful high-altitude navigation data. Published by the FAA, the charts are revised every 56 days. •

A United DC-8, photographed in Class A Airspace in the 1960s.

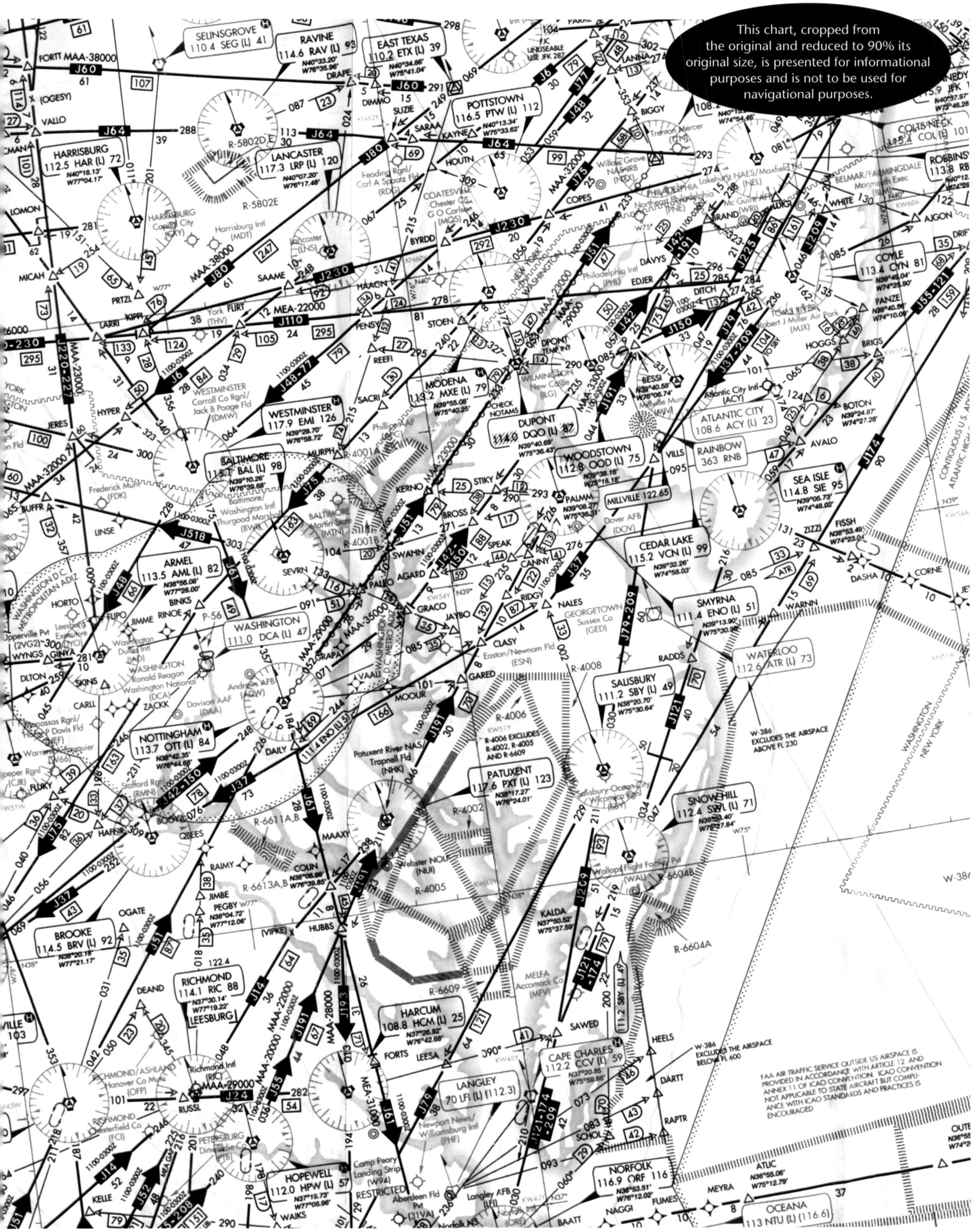

This chart, cropped from the original and reduced to 90% its original size, is presented for informational purposes and is not to be used for navigational purposes.

IFR Enroute High Altitude - US: EHUS9 - Original Scale: 1″ = 20nm (Approximately 1:1,458,547)

Jet Navigation Charts

Published by the US military, Jet Navigation Charts are designed for long-range, high-altitude, high-speed navigation. Their topographical features include large cities, roads, railroads, and drainage. Relief is shown with contour lines, spot elevations, and gradient tints (although the green sections of the chart represent level areas, regardless of their altitude above sea level). Runway patterns are included, though they are exaggerated to increase their value as visual landmarks. In all, these charts load an amazing level of detail into such a small-scale presentation.

Wearing a camouflage that led to the nickname "flying pickle," this well-worn C-5B was photographed in 1992.

Aeronautical information includes restricted areas, L/MF (Low/Medium Frequency) and VOR ranges, radio beacons, and a selection of standard broadcast stations and airports. Civil air routes and low altitude military training routes are omitted. In fact, the only standard routes included are military over-water "Echo Routes," which are shown as doubled blue lines. The dashed green lines with "GV" codes angling just west of north are isogrivs, lines of constant grid variation between true north and magnetic north. Crisscrossing the chart at approximately 45 degrees are solid green grid navigation (GN) lines. These lines are used by the military for celestial navigation; they are set on the diagonal to avoid confusion with the standard latitude and longitude grid.

Unlike the FAA's charts, which are folded for easy and continuing access in flight, Jet Navigation Charts are designed for preparation on a large surface. After appropriate routes are marked for the day's mission, excess portions of the chart are trimmed away and disposed of. •

Camouflaged perfectly against the terrain, this Air Force C-141B was photographed on a cross-country flight in 1993.

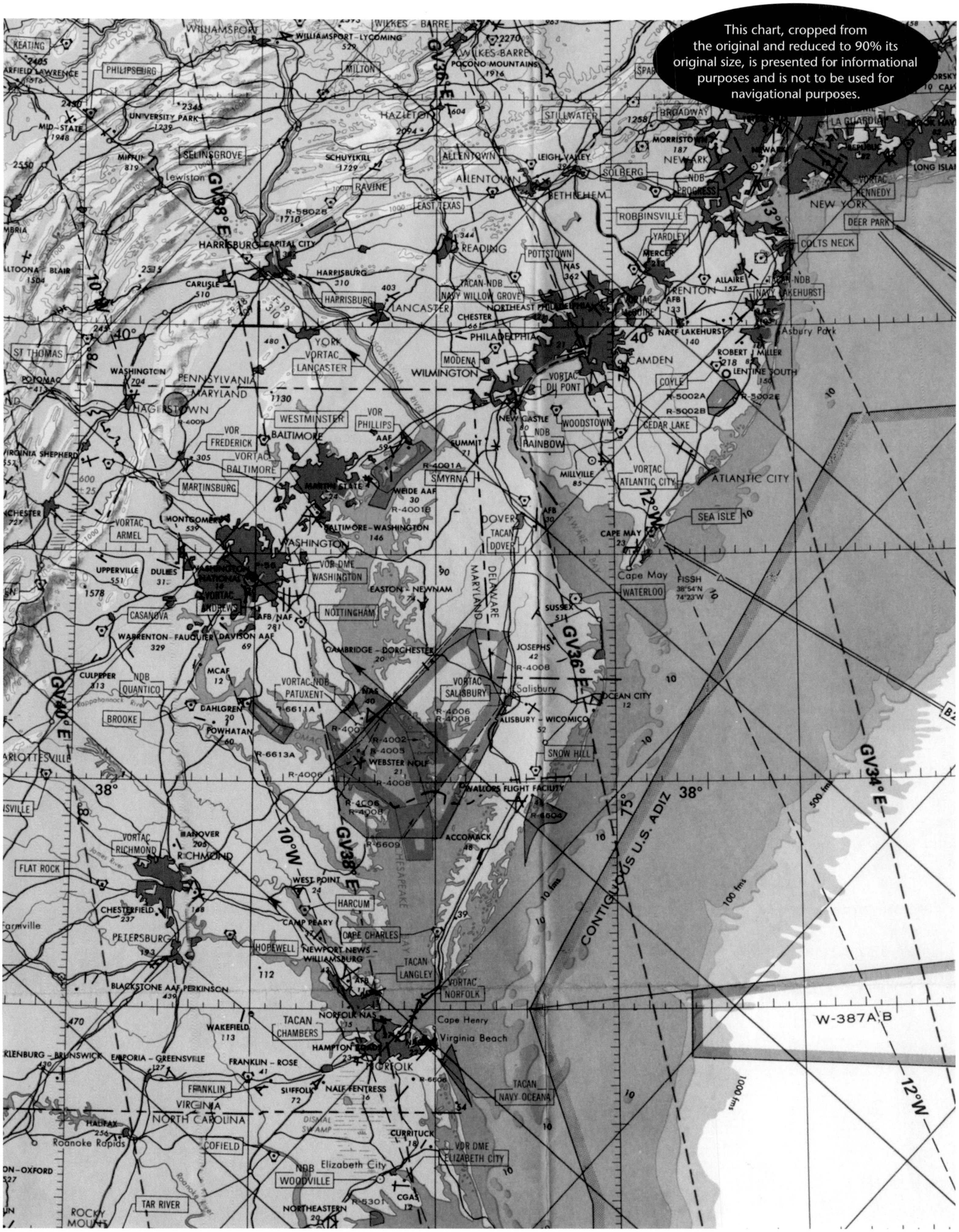

This chart, cropped from the original and reduced to 90% its original size, is presented for informational purposes and is not to be used for navigational purposes.

Jet Navigation Chart: JNC 45; Original Scale: 1:2,000,000

Jet Navigation High Altitude Charts

The US military's High Altitude Jet Navigation Charts are similar to the Jet Navigation Charts, though the much smaller scale allows one chart to cover the entire contiguous United States. At this scale, the detail of topographical features remains extraordinary. As with the larger-scaled charts, there is little information on established air routes - even the lower altitude, over-water Echo Routes are omitted. The grid navigation lines and the broken green isogrivs follow the military practice. Again, the planned route chart is to be drawn onto the chart, which is then trimmed for flight use. •

The eye in the sky, the U-2 has been flying its reconnaissance missions at extreme altitudes since the 1950s.

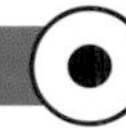

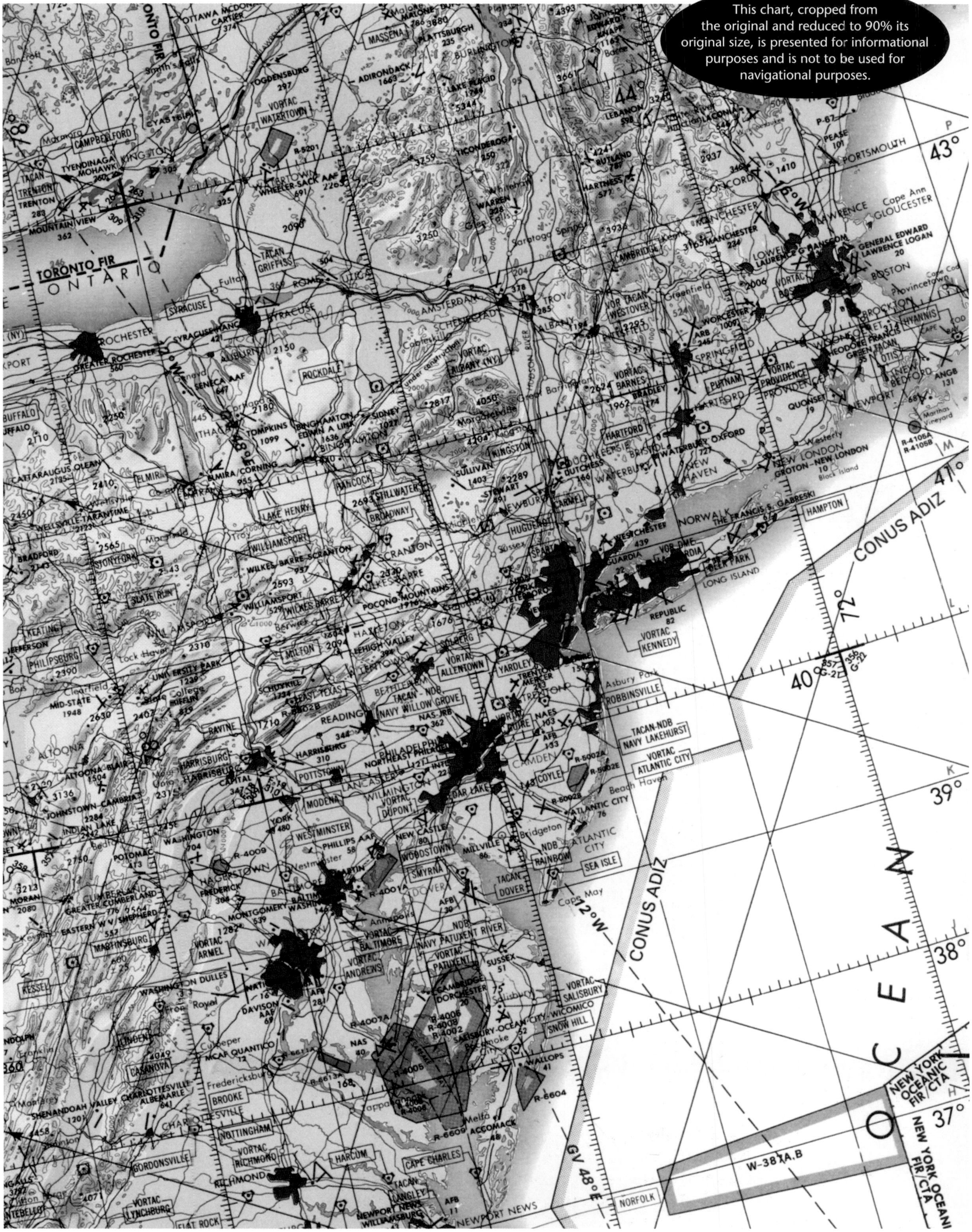
This chart, cropped from the original and reduced to 90% its original size, is presented for informational purposes and is not to be used for navigational purposes.
TORONTO FIR
ONTARIO
CONUS ADIZ
CONUS ADIZ
OCEAN
NEW YORK OCEANIC FIR/CTA
NEW YORK OCEANIC FIR/CTA
W-387A,B
43°
41°
40°
39°
38°
37°
72°

Jet Navigation Chart, High-Altitude: JNCA-5; Original Scale: 1:3,000,000

National Aircraft Markings

The signatories of The Hague Convention of 1907 agreed each military aircraft must display a conspicuously placed insignia identifying the nation it served. At that time, all military aircraft were lighter-than-air, and the military insignia took the form of a flag or streamer. Similar flags were carried by early military airplanes, though this proved impractical as aircraft improved performance quickly frayed the free-flying banners.

In the early days of World War I, painted insignia quickly replaced the flags. Germany adopted its first "Iron Cross," while France chose a three-ring cocarde similar to that worn in the hats of French revolutionaries. The British initially painted a full Union flag on wings and tails, but this complicated design (which included a white cross similar to the German insignia) was quickly replaced by a cocarde similar to the French marking. Allied nations also painted their rudders with vertical stripes, a part of the national markings that would continue into the jet age.

To the south, Austria coupled a German cross with red and white paint under wings. Their Italian foes adopted another cocarde, but also painted the underwing surfaces in red, white, and green. As America approached the War, it's military adopted a white star on a blue disc with a red center disc. But the white five-pointed star bore a distant similarity to the four pointed German cross, so American wartime forces flew with yet another variation of the cocarde.

Many books examine in detail the national military markings used over the last century. The following pages offer a simple display of some of the official insignia applied since 1914. •

Egyptian paratroops board a Lockheed C-130 in the early 1980s; the national insignia is shown on the aft fuselage, with the Egyptian flag on the vertical tail.

A Spanish CASA CN-235 transport shows reduced variations of the national markings first adopted in the 1930s. Red and yellow cocardes are positioned on the wings and aft fuselage, with a small black and white cross of St. Andrews atop the rudder.

Abu Dhabi

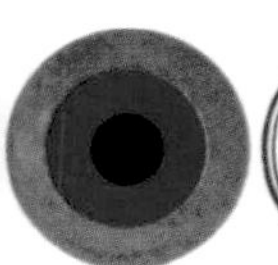

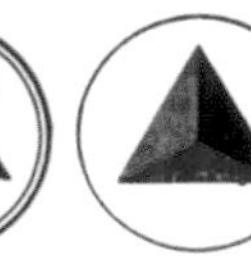

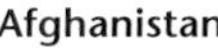

Afghanistan

Albania

Algeria

Angola

Argentina

Australia

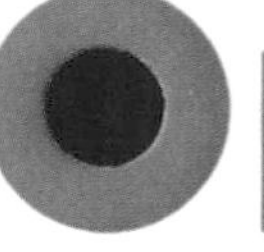

Austria

Austria-Hungary

Bahrain

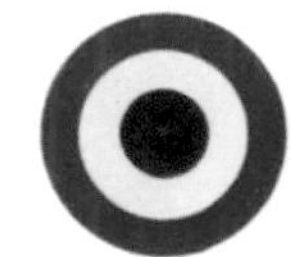

Bangladesh

Barbados

Belgium

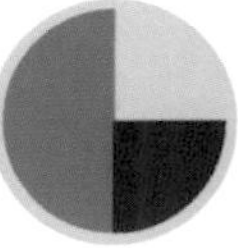

Benin

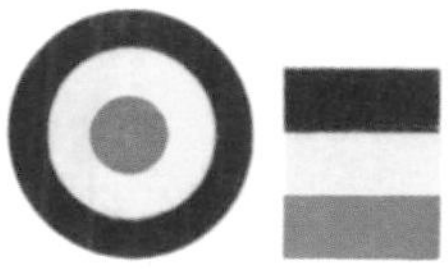

Bolivia

Botswana

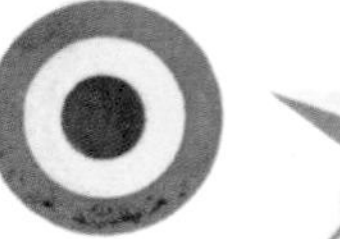

Brazil

Brunei

Bulgaria Burma Burundi

Cambodia Cameroon Canada

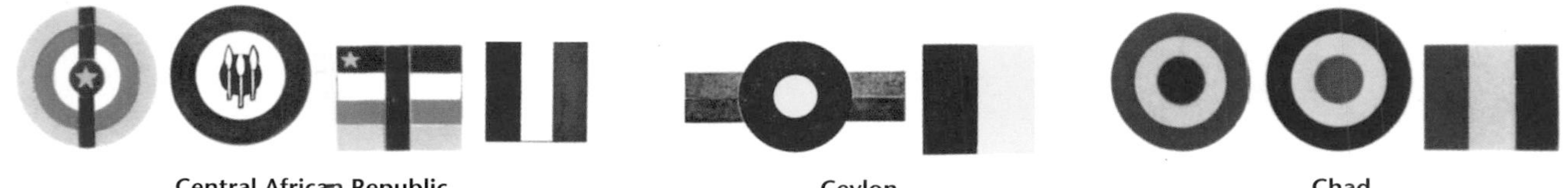
Central African Republic Ceylon Chad

Chile China, Communist China, Cochin China, Nationalist (Taiwan)

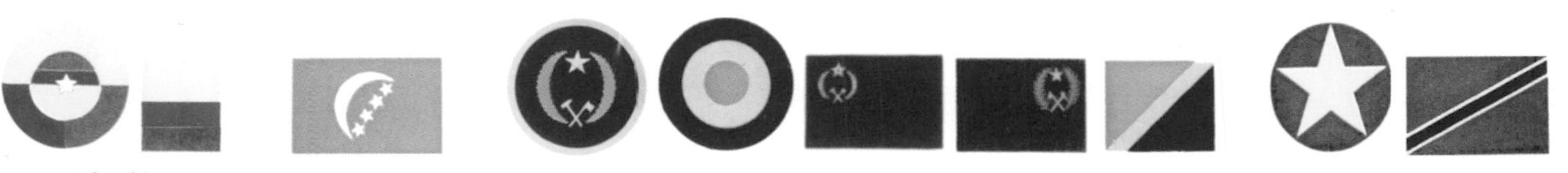
Colombia Comoro Islands Congo Congo, Leopoldville

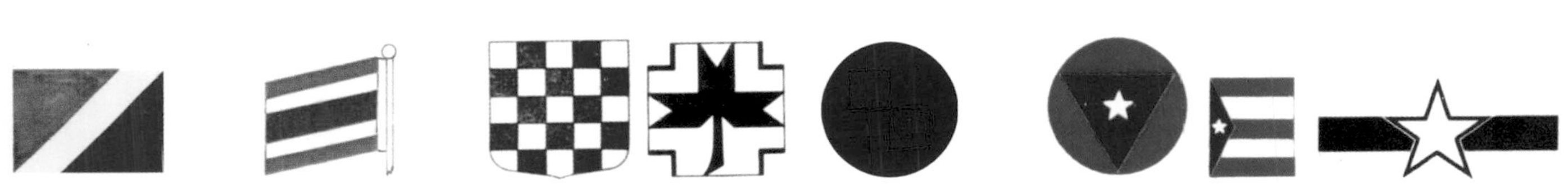
Congo, Brazzaville Costa Rica Croatia Cuba

Czechoslovakia/Czech Republic Dahomey Denmark Djibouti

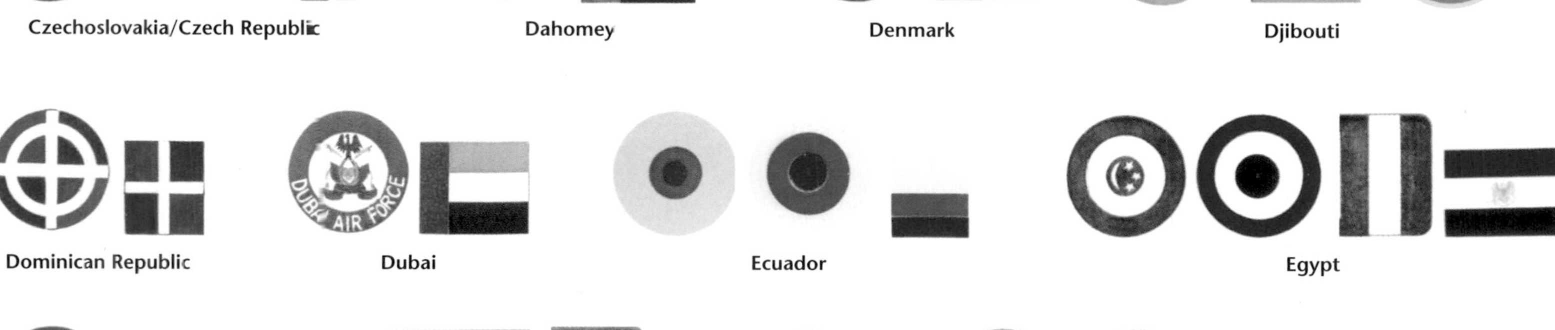

Dominican Republic Dubai Ecuador Egypt

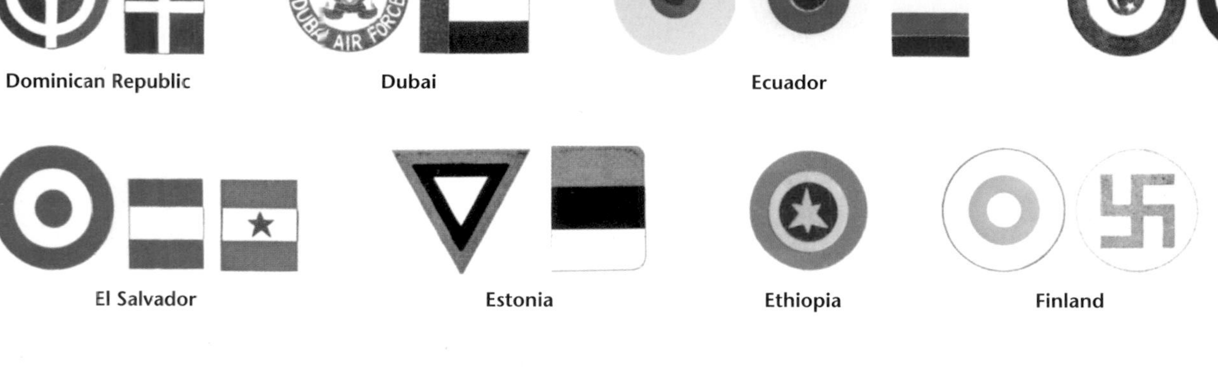
El Salvador Estonia Ethiopia Finland

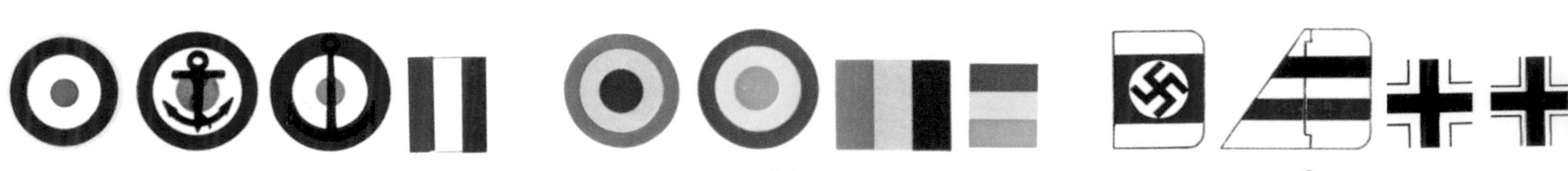

France Gabon Germany

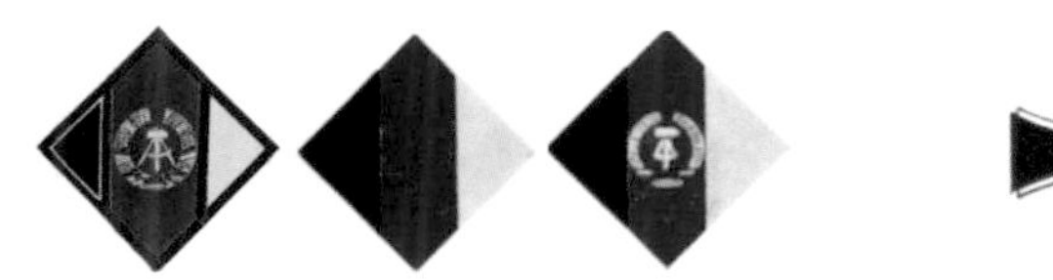

Germany, East Germany/West Germany Ghana Greece

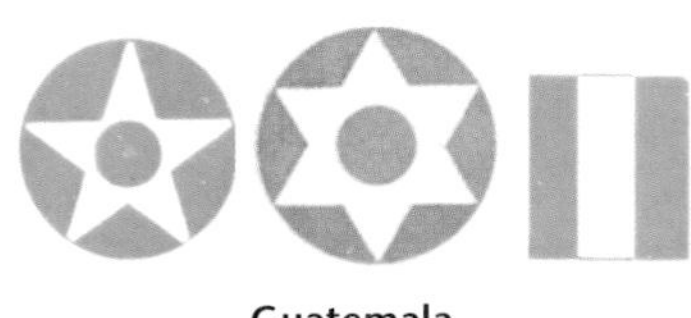

Guatemala Guinea Guinea-Bissau Guyana

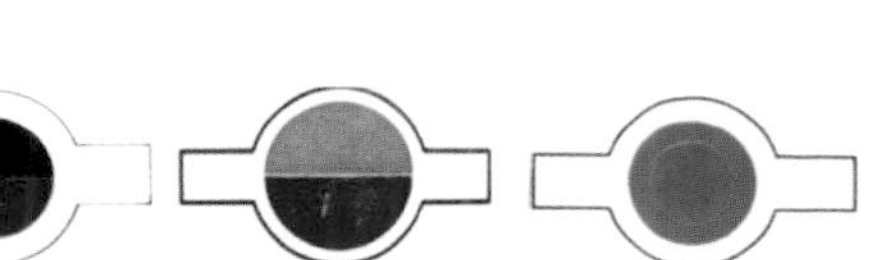

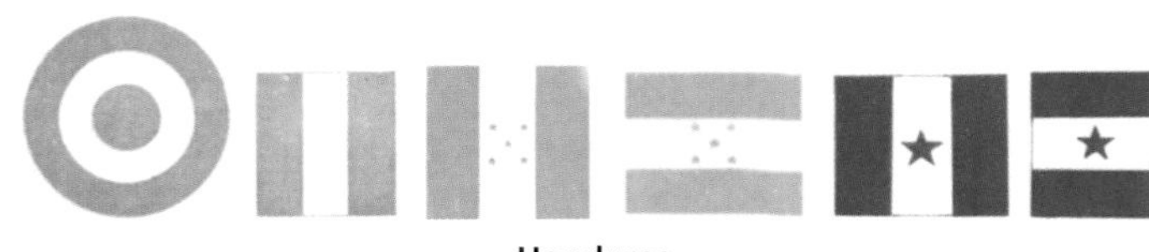

Haiti Honduras

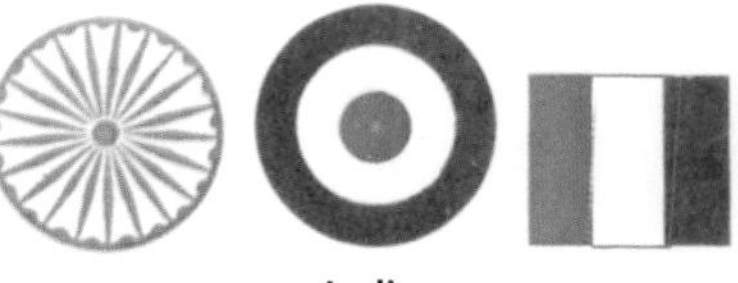

Hungary Hungarian Republic Iceland India

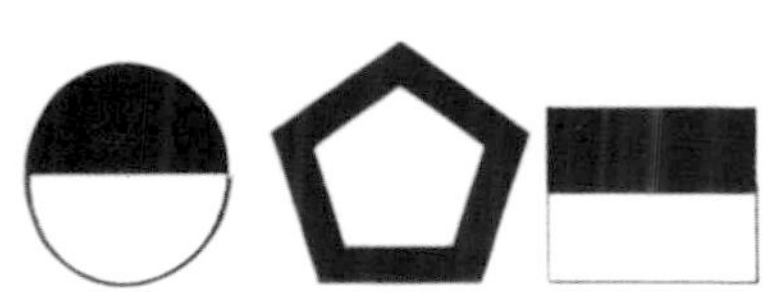

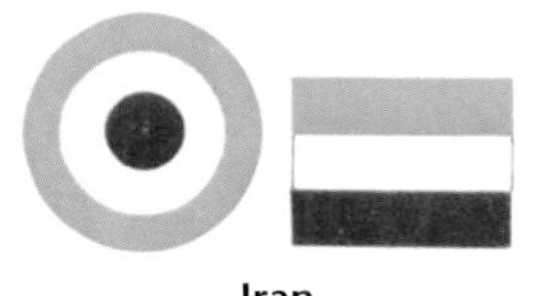

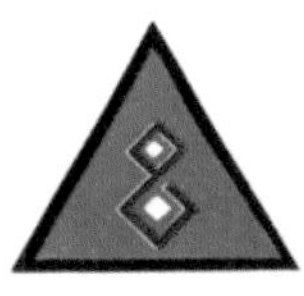

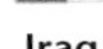

Indonesia Iran Iraq

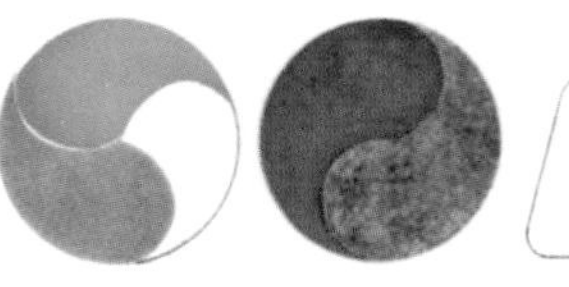

Ireland Israel

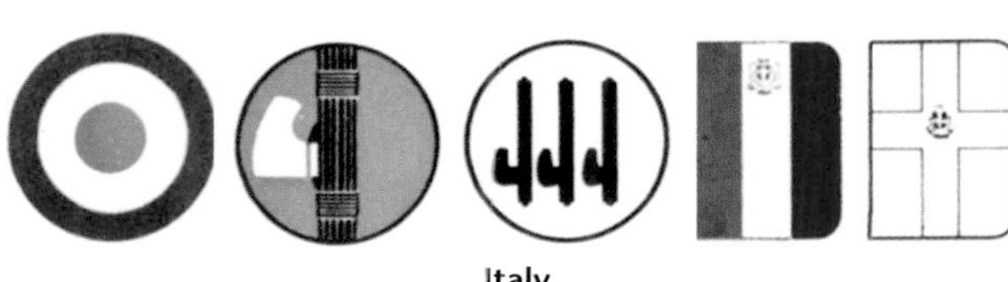

Italy

Italy, RSI

Israeli paratroops jump from the side doors of a Lockheed C-130 during a mid-1980s training exercise. The white disc with blue Star of David was adopted as the national marking soon after the formation of Israel following World War II.

Ivory Coast

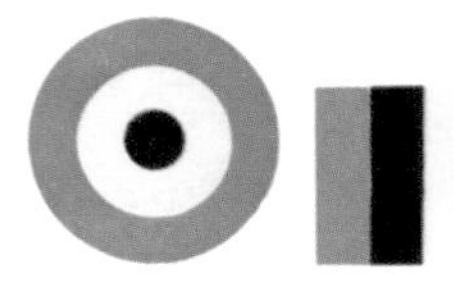
Jamaica

Japan

Jordan

Kampuchea

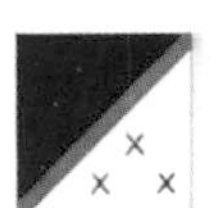
Katanga

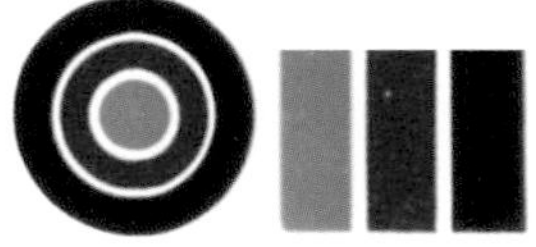
Kenya

Korea, North

Korea, South

Kuwait

Laos

Latvia

Lebanon

Lesotho

Liberia

Libya

Lithuania

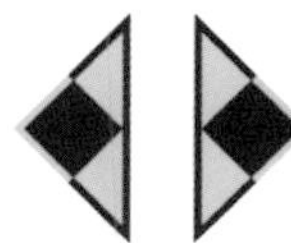
Macedonia

Madagascar

Madagascar
(Malagasy Republic)

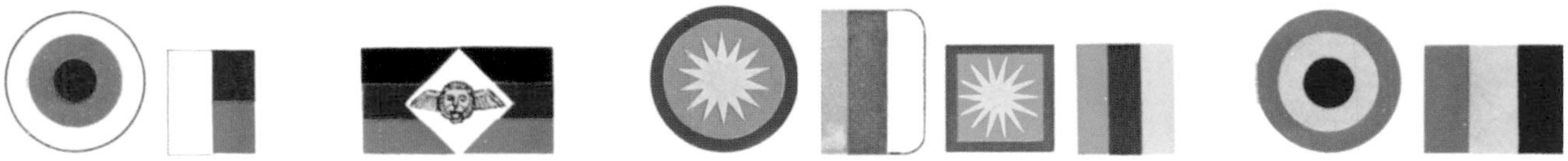

Malawi

Malaysia

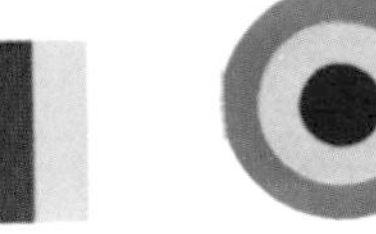
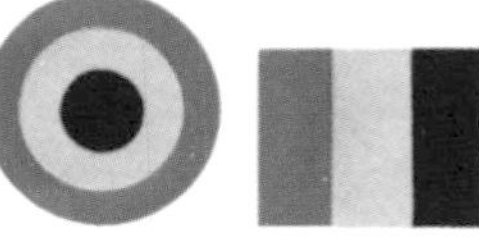
Mali

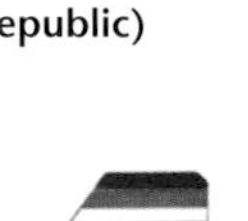
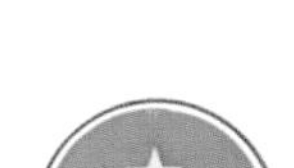
Manchuria

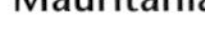

Mauritania

Mexico

Mongolia

Morocco

Mozambique

Nanking China

NATO

Nepal

Netherlands

New Zealand

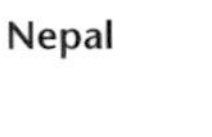

Nicaragua

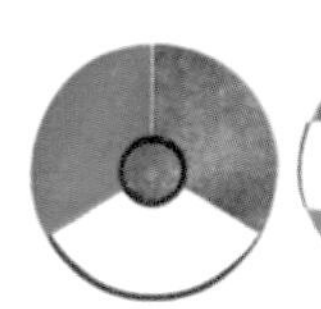

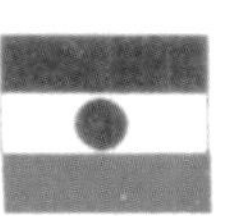
Niger

Nigeria

Norway

Oman

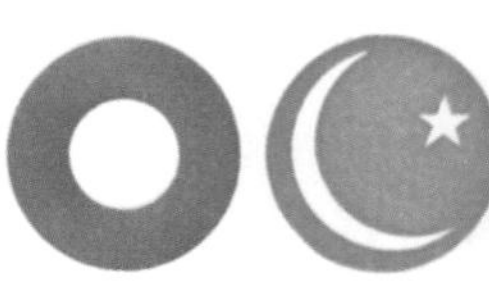

Pakistan

Panama

Papua New Guinea

Paraguay

Peru

Philippines

Poland

Portugal

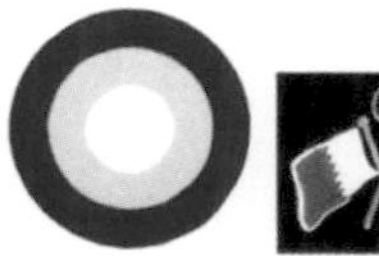
Qatar

Rhodesia

Romania

Russia

Rwanda

Saudi Arabia

Senegal

Singapore

Slovakia

Sovenia

Somalia

South Africa

Southern Rhodesia

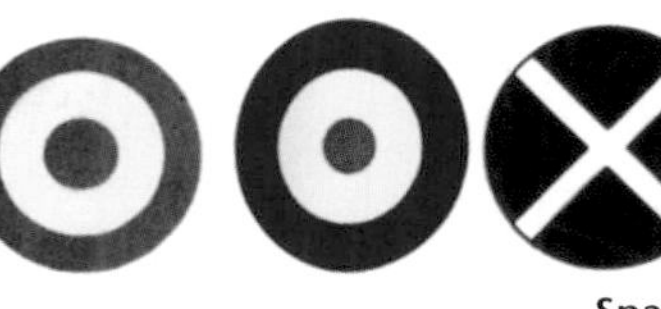

Spain

Sri Lanka

Sudan

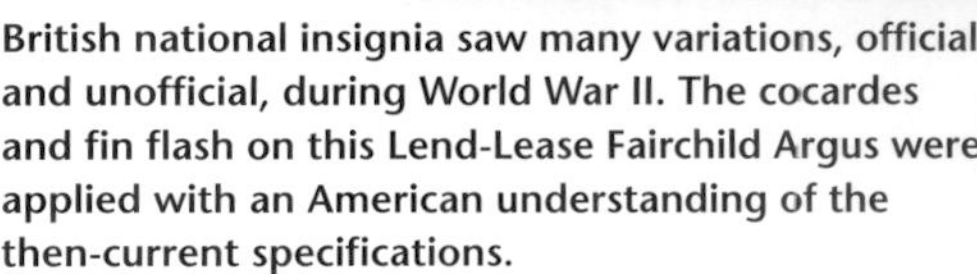
British national insignia saw many variations, official and unofficial, during World War II. The cocardes and fin flash on this Lend-Lease Fairchild Argus were applied with an American understanding of the then-current specifications.

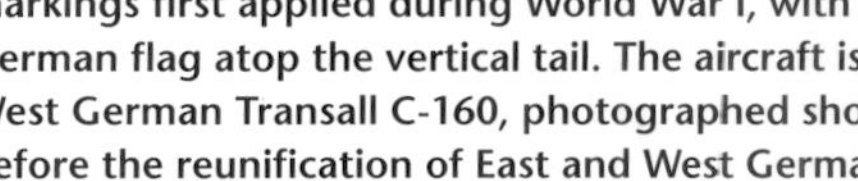
German national insignia currently resemble the markings first applied during World War I, with the German flag atop the vertical tail. The aircraft is a West German Transall C-160, photographed shortly before the reunification of East and West Germany.

Sweden

Switzerland

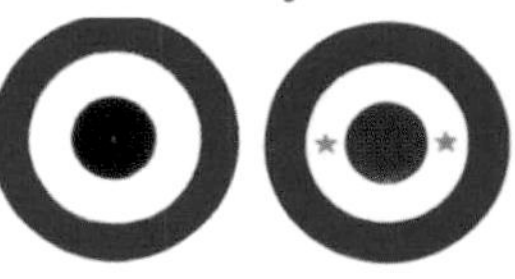

Syria

Tanzania

Thailand

Togo

Trinidad and Tobago

Tunisia

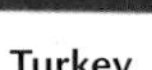

Turkey

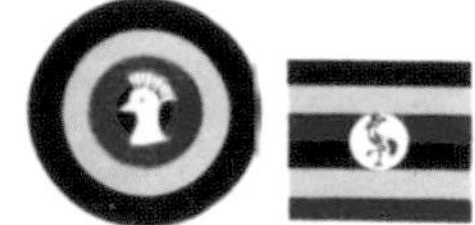

Uganda

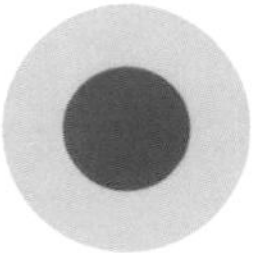

Ukraine

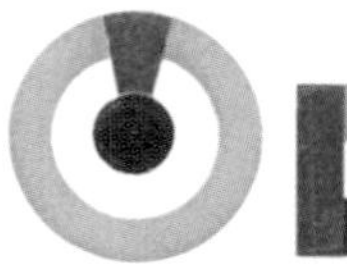

Union Air Force, UAE

United Arab Republic

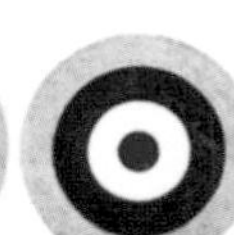

United Kingdom

United States of America

Upper Volta

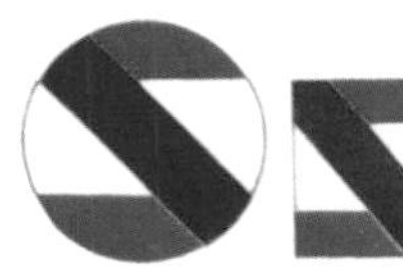

Uruguay

USSR

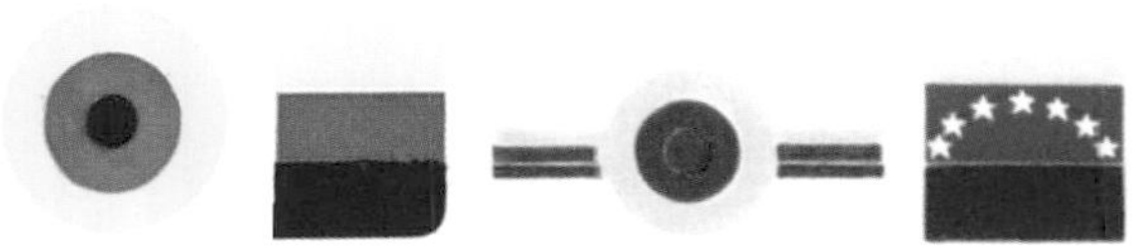

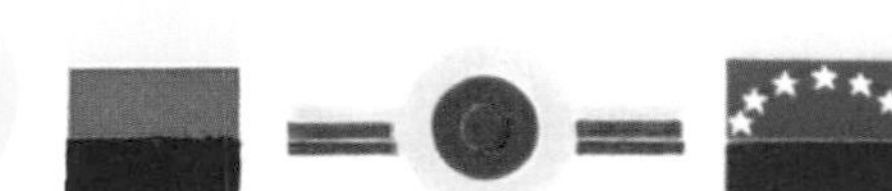

Venezuela

Vietnam/North Vietnam

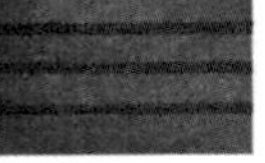

Vietnam (South)

Yemen, People's Dem. Republic of

Yemen, Arab Republic

Yugoslavia

Zaire

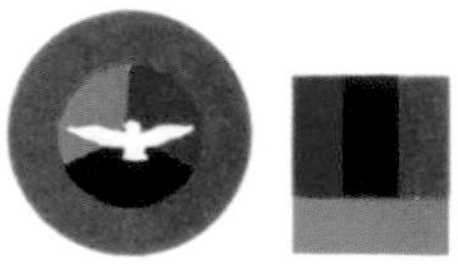

Zambia

Zimbabwe

National Civil Aircraft Codes

Delegates at the World War I Paris Peace Conference introduced the first voluntary international system of civil aircraft identification markings in 1919 . The Convention for the Regulation of Air Navigation (Commission Internationale de Navigation Aerienne or CINA) agreed that, "The nationality mark shall be represented by capital letters in Roman characters. The registration mark shall be represented by a group of four capital letters; each group shall contain at least one vowel, and for this purpose the letter Y shall be considered a vowel. The complete group of five letters shall be used as a call sign for the particular aircraft..." The nationality marks were apparently drawn from existing international wireless communications regulations, which assigned radio codes beginning with, D for Germany, F for France, G for Great Britain, I for Italy, J for Japan, N for the United States, and so on.

The US, which never ratified the 1919 accord, instituted a similar registration system in the 1920s. N was retained as the national prefix, though display of the letter was required only for those aircraft operating internationally. A second prefix letter was added: C for

National Civil Aircraft Codes, Organized by Country

Country	Code
Aden	VR-A
Afghanistan	YA-
Albania	B-A; ZA-
Algeria	7T-
Andorra	C3-
Angola (Portuguese West Africa)	CR-L; D2-
Anguilla	VP-LAA to VP-LJZ
Antigua and Barbuda	V2-; VP-L
Arabic Federation (Iraq and Jordan)	4YB-
Argentina	LQ-; LV-; R-
Armenia	EK-; RH-
Aruba	P4-
Australia	G-AU; VH-
Austria	A-; OE-
Azerbaijan	4K-
Bahamas	C6-; VP-B
Bahrain	A9C
Bangladesh	S2-; S3-
Barbados	8P-; VQ-B
Belarus	EW-
Belgium	O-B; OO-
Belize (British Honduras)	V3-; VP-H
Benin (Dahomey)	TY-
Bermuda	VR-B; VP-B (current)
Bhutan (Sikkim)	A5-
Bolivia	
Bolivia	CB-; CP-; C-V
Borneo	VR-O
Bosnia-Herzegovina	T9-
Botswana (Bechuanaland)	A2; VQ-Z
Brazil	PA; P-B; PP-; PR-; PT-
British Virgin Is lands	VP-LVA to VP-LZZ
Brunei Darussalam (British Northern Borneo)	V8; VR-U
Bulgaria	B-B; LZ-
Burkina Faso (Upper Volta)	XT-
Burundi	9U-; BR-
Cambodia (Kampuchea)	KW-; XU-
Cameroon (British Cameroons)	VR-N; TJ- (1960 - present)
Canada	CF- (C-F); CG-; CI-; G-C
Cape Verde	CR-C; D4-
Cayman Islands	VR-C; VP-C (current)
Central African Republic	TL-
Chad	TT-
Chile (Republic)	CC-
China, People's Republic	B-; X-C; XT-
Colombia	C-; HK-
Comoros	D6-
Congo (Brazzaville)	9O-; TN-
Cook Islands	E5-
Costa Rica	TI-
Croatia	9A-; RC-
Cuba	C-C; CU-
Cyprus	5B; VQ-C
Czech Republic (Czechoslovakia)	OK-
Czechoslovakia	L-B
Danzig (Gdansk)	DZ-; Y-M
Denmark	OY-; T-D
Djibouti (French Somalia)	J2-
Dominica	J7-
Dominican Republic	HI-
Ecuador	E-E; HC-
Egypt	SU-
El Salvador	YS-
Equatorial Guinea (Rio Muni)	3C-
Eritrea	E3-; ER-
Estonia	E-A; ES-
Ethiopia	ET-
Falkland Islands	VP-F
Fiji	DQ-; VQ-F
Finland	K-S; OH-
France	F-
Free France	FC-
French Overseas Departments/Territories	F-O
Gabon	TR-
Gambia	C5; VP-X
Georgia (Grusinia)	4L-
Germany	D-
Germany (Democratic Republic of Germany)	DDR-; DM-
Ghana (Gold Coast)	9G-; VP-A
Gibraltar	VR-G
Greece	S-G; SX-
Grenada	J3-; VQ-G
Guadeloupe	F-OG
Guatemala	L-G (LG-); TG-
Guinea	3X-
Guinea-Bissau (Portuguese Guinea)	CR-G; J5-
Guyana (British Guiana)	8R; VP-G
Haiti (Republic)	H-H (HH-)
Honduras	HR-; X-H (XH-)
Hong Kong	B-H; B-K; B-L (1997-present)
Hungary	HA-; H-M
Iceland	TF-
India	G-I; VT-
Indonesia (Irian Jaya, West Irian)	PK-
Iran (Persia)	EP-; RV-
Iraq	YI-
Ireland	EI-; EJ-
Israel (British Palestine)	4X; VQ-P
Italy	I-
Ivory Coast	TU-; VP-A
Jamaica	6Y; VP-J
Japan	J-; JA
Johore	VR-J
Jordan	JY-; TJ-
Katanga	KA-
Kazakstan (1991 - present)	UN-
Kenya	5Y-; VP-K
Kiribati (Gilbert Islands)	T3; VP-P
Korea (Democratic People's Republic, North)	P-
Korea (Republic of Korea, South Korea)	HL
Kuwait	9K-; K-
Kyrgyz Republic (Kyrgyzstan, Kirghizia)	EX-
Laos	F-L; RDPL-; XW-
Latvia	B-L (1930s); YL-
Lebanon	LR-; OD-
Lesotho (Basutoland)	7P-; VQ-Z
Liberia	EL; LI-; L-L
Libya	5A
Lichtenstein	HB-
Lithuania	LY-; RY-; R-Z
Luxembourg	L-U; LX-; UL-
Macau	CR-M
Macedonia	Z3-
Madagascar (Malagasy)	5R-

commercial aircraft, G (used from 1929 to 1937) for gliders, P (used only during 1927) for privately owned aircraft, R for restricted aircraft, S for state (that is, government-operated) aircraft, and X for experimental aircraft. The four-letter registration was replaced with a numeric system and later with a numeric system allowing letter suffixes.

Following World War II, control of international civil registration codes passed to the International Civil Aviation Organization (ICAO), an agency of the United Nations. (It was at this time that the US required the N prefix to be displayed on all American-registered aircraft.)

Other national registration markings found many variations over the years. France, Portugal, and the United Kingdom commonly assigned blocks of code letters to their colonies. The codes used by the United Kingdom, for example, have been assigned sequentially beginning with G-AAAA in 1919. (The range of G-AAAA through G-ZZZZ, which comprises some 331,776 registration codes, is still in use today.) Within that system, codes G-AUAA through G-AUZZ were reserved for Australia, G-CAAA through G-CZZZ for Canada, G-IAAA through C-IZZZ for India, G-NZAA through G-NZZZ for New Zealand, and G-UAAA through G-UZZZ for South Africa. Each of these former members of the commonwealth has long since received its own national codes.

As wars, independence movements, and political reorganizations have changed the world map, the civil aircraft codes have also changed. The following lists present national registration prefixes, whether established by international agreement or used simply as a national practice, since the CINA of 1919. •

National Civil Aircraft Codes, Organized by Country

Country	Code
Malawi (Nyasaland)	7Q-; VP-N
Malaysia (Malaya)	9M; VR-R
Maldives	8Q-
Mali	TZ-
Malta	9H-; VP-M
Marshall Islands	MI-; V7-
Martinique	F-OM
Mauritania	5T-
Mauritius	3B-; VQ-M
Mexico	M-S; X-A; X-B; XC-
Micronesia	V6-
Moldova	RM-; ER- (1991 - present)
Monaco	3A-; CZ-
Monaco (Monte Carlo)	MC-
Mongolia	BNMAU-; HMAY-; MONGOL-; MPR-; MT-
Montserrat	VP-LMA to VP-LUZ
Morocco	CN-
Mozambique (Portuguese East Africa)	C9; CR-A; CR-B
Myanmar (Burma)	XY-; XZ-
Namibia	V5-
Nauru	C2-
Nepal	9N-
Netherlands	H-N; PH-
Netherlands Antilles (Curacao)	PJ-
Netherlands East Indies	JZ-
New Zealand	G-NZ; ZK-; ZL-; ZM-
Newfoundland	VO-
Nicaragua	A-N (AN-); YN
Niger	5U-
Nigeria	5N; VR-N
Norway	LN-; N-
Oman	A4O
Pakistan (Belutshistan)	AP-
Panama	HP-; R-; RX-; S-P
Papua New Guinea (Niugini)	P2-
Paraguay	ZP-
Peru	OA-; OB-; O-P
Philippines	PI-C-; RP-C
Poland	SP-
Portugal	C-P; CS-
Portuguese India (Goa)	CR-I
Portuguese Overseas Provinces	CR-
Qatar	A7
Rumania	C-R; CV; YR-
Russia	IS-; RA; RF-
Rwanda	9XR-
Saarland	EZ-; SL-; TS-
Saint Helena	VQ-H
Saint Kitts and Nevis	V4-; VP-LKA to VP-LLZ
Saint Lucia	J6; VQ-L; VR-L
Saint Vincent and the Grenadines	J8-; VP-V
Samoa	5W-
San Marino	T7-
Sao Tome and Principe	CR-S; S9-
Saudi Arabia (Hejaz, Nedjd)	A-H; HZ-; UH-
Senegal	6V-; 6W-
Serbia	X-S
Seychelles	S7-; VQ-S
Sierra Leone	9L; VR-L
Singapore	9V-; VR-S
Slovakia	OM-; S5-; SL- (1990s)
Solomon Islands	H4-; VP-P
Somalia (Somaliland)	6O-; 6OS; VP-S
South Africa	G-U; ZS-; ZT-; ZU-
Soviet Union (Russia)	CCCP-; R; RR; URSS; USSR (Cyrillic CCCP)
Spain	EC-; M-
Sri Lanka (Ceylon)	4R-; CY-; VP-C
Sudan	FT-; SN-; ST-
Surinam (Netherlands Guyana)	PZ-
Swaziland	3D-; VQ-Z
Sweden	S-A; SE-
Switzerland	CH-; HB-
Syria	SR-; YK-
Taiwan (Republic of China, Formosa)	B-
Tajikistan	EY-; YT-
Tanganyika	VR-T
Tanzania (United Republic of Tanganyika and Zanzibar)	5H-
Thailand (was Siam)	H-S (HS-)
Timor (East Timor)	CR-T
Togo	5V-
Tonga	A3-
Trinidad and Tobago	9Y-; VP-T
Tunisia (1956 - present)	TS-
Turkey	TC-
Turkmenistan (1991 - present)	EZ-
Turks and Caicos Islands	VQ-T
Tuvalu	T2-
Uganda	5X-; VP-U
Ukraine	UR-
United Arab Emirates (UAE)	A6
United Kingdom (Great Britain)	G-
United Nations (UN)	4U
United States of America (USA)	N-
United States of America, Commercial	NC-
United States of America, Glider	NG-
United States of America, Limited	NL-
United States of America, Private	NP-
United States of America, Restricted	NR-
United States of America, State	NS-
United States of America, Experimental	NX-
Uruguay	C-U; CX-
Uzbekistan	UK-
Vanuatu (New Hebrides)	VP-P; YJ-
Vatican City	HV-
Venezuela	YV-
Vietnam (also North Vietnam)	VN-
Vietnam (Pre-1959)	3W-; F-VN
Vietnam, South	XV-
Wei-Hai-Wei	VP-W
Yemen	YE-
Yemen (also People's Democratic Republic/ South Yemen)	7O-
Yemen (North Yemen)	4W-
Yugoslavia	UN-; YU-
Zaire (Belgian Congo)	9Q-; 9T-; OO-C
Zambia (North Rhodesia)	9J-; VP-R
Zansibar	VP-Z
Zimbabwe (Southern Rhodesia)	VP-W; VP-Y; Z-

National Civil Aircraft Codes, In Code Order

Code	Country
3A-	Monaco
3B-	Mauritius
3C-	Equatorial Guinea (Rio Muni)
3D-	Swaziland
3W-	Vietnam (Pre-1959)
3X-	Guinea
4K-	Azerbaijan
4L-	Georgia (Grusinia)
4R-	Sri Lanka (Ceylon)
4U	United Nations (UN)
4W-	Yemen (North Yemen)
4X-	Israel (British Palestine)
4YB-	Arabic Federation (Iraq and Jordan)
5A	Libya
5B	Cyprus
5H-	Tanzania (United Republic of Tanganyika and Zanzibar)
5N-	Nigeria
5R-	Madagascar (Malagasy)
5T-	Mauritania
5U-	Niger
5V-	Togo
5W-	Samoa
5X-	Uganda
5Y-	Kenya
6O-	Somalia (Somaliland)
6OS	Somalia (Somaliland)
6V-	Senegal
6W-	Senegal
6Y-	Jamaica
7O-	Yemen (also People's Democratic Republic/ South Yemen)
7P-	Lesotho (Basutoland)
7Q-	Malawi (Nyasaland)
7T-	Algeria
8P-	Barbados
8Q-	Maldives
8R-	Guyana (British Guiana)
9A-	Croatia
9G-	Ghana (Gold Coast)
9H-	Malta
9J-	Zambia (North Rhodesia)
9K-	Kuwait
9L-	Sierra Leone
9M-	Malaysia (Malaya)
9N-	Nepal
9O-	Congo (Brazzaville)
9Q-	Zaire (Belgian Congo)
9T-	Zaire (Belgian Congo)
9U-	Burundi
9V-	Singapore
9XR-	Rwanda
9Y-	Trinidad and Tobago
A-	Austria
A2	Botswana (Bechuanaland)
A3-	Tonga
A4O	Oman
A5-	Bhutan (Sikkim)
A6	United Arab Emirates (UAE)
A7	Qatar
A9C	Bahrain
A-H	Saudi Arabia (Hejaz, Nedjd)
A-N (AN-)	Nicaragua
AP-	Pakistan (Belutshistan)
B-	China, People's Republic
B-	Taiwan (Republic of China, Formosa)
B-A	Albania
B-B	Bulgaria
B-H	Hong Kong
B-K	Hong Kong
B-L	Hong Kong (1997-present)
B-L	Latvia (1930s)
BNMAU-	Mongolia
BR-	Burundi
C-	Colombia
C2-	Nauru
C3-	Andorra
C5-	Gambia
C6-	Bahamas
C9-	Mozambique (Portuguese East Africa)
CB-	Bolivia
C-C	Cuba
CC-	Chile (Republic)
CCCP-	Soviet Union (Russia)
CF- (C-F)	Canada
CG-	Canada
CH-	Switzerland
CI-	Canada
CN-	Morocco
C-P	Portugal
CP-	Bolivia
C-R	Rumania
CR-A	Mozambique (Portuguese East Africa)
CR-	Portuguese Overseas Provinces
CR-B	Mozambique (Portuguese East Africa)
CR-C	Cape Verde
CR-G	Guinea-Bissau (Portuguese Guinea)
CR-I	Portuguese India (Goa)
CR-L	Angola (Portuguese West Africa)
CR-M	Macau
CR-S	Sao Tome and Principe
CR-T	Timor (East Timor)
CS-	Portugal
C-U	Uruguay
CU-	Cuba
C-V	Bolivia
CV-	Rumania
CX-	Uruguay
CY-	Sri Lanka (Ceylon)
CZ-	Monaco
D-	Germany
D2-	Angola (Portuguese West Africa)
D4-	Cape Verde
D6-	Comoros
DDR-	Germany (Democratic Republic of Germany, GDR)
DM-	Germany (Democratic Republic of Germany, GDR)
DQ-	Fiji
DZ-	Danzig (Gdansk)
E3-	Eritrea
E5-	Cook Islands
E-A	Estonia
EC-	Spain
E-E	Ecuador
EI-	Ireland
EJ-	Ireland
EK-	Armenia
EL-	Liberia
EP-	Iran (Persia)
ER-	Eritrea
ER-	Moldova (1991 - present)
ES-	Estonia
ET-	Ethiopia
EW-	Belarus
EX-	Kyrgyz Republic (Kyrgyzstan, Kirghizia)
EY-	Tajikistan
EZ-	Saarland
EZ-	Turkmenistan (1991 - present)
F-	France
FC-	Free France
F-L	Laos
F-O	French Overseas Departments/Territories
F-OG	Guadeloupe
F-OM	Martinique
FT-	Sudan
F-VN	Vietnam (Pre-1959)
G-	United Kingdom (Great Britain)
G-AU	Australia
G-C	Canada
G-I	India
G-NZ	New Zealand
G-U	South Africa
H4-	Solomon Islands
HA-	Hungary
HB-	Lichtenstein
HB-	Switzerland
HC-	Ecuador
H-H (HH-)	Haiti (Republic)
HI-	Dominican Republic
HK-	Colombia
HL	Korea (Republic of Korea, South Korea)
H-M	Hungary
HMAY-	Mongolia
H-N	Netherlands
HP-	Panama
HR-	Honduras
H-S (HS-)	Thailand (was Siam)
HV-	Vatican City
HZ-	Saudi Arabia (Hejaz, Nedjd)
I-	Italy
IS-	Russia
J-	Japan
J2-	Djibouti (French Somalia)
J3-	Grenada
J5-	Guinea-Bissau (Portuguese Guinea)
J6-	Saint Lucia
J7-	Dominica
J8-	Saint Vincent and the Grenadines
JA	Japan
JY-	Jordan
JZ-	Netherlands East Indies
K-	Kuwait
KA-	Katanga
K-S	Finland
KW-	Cambodia (Kampuchea)
L-B	Czechoslovakia
L-G (LG-)	Guatemala
LI-	Liberia
L-L	Liberia
LN-	Norway
LQ-	Argentina
LR-	Lebanon
L-U	Luxembourg
LV-	Argentina
LX-	Luxembourg
LY-	Lithuania
LZ-	Bulgaria
M-	Spain
MC-	Monaco (Monte Carlo)
MI-	Marshall Islands
MONGOL-	Mongolia
MPR-	Mongolia
M-S	Mexico
MT-	Mongolia
N-	Norway
N-	United States of America (USA)
NC-	United States of America, Commercial

National Civil Aircraft Codes, In Code Order

Code	Country
NG-	United States of America, Glider
NL-	United States of America, Limited
NP-	United States of America, Private
NR-	United States of America, Restricted
NS-	United States of America, State
NX-	United States of America, Experimental
OA-	Peru
OB-	Peru
O-B	Belgium
OD-	Lebanon
OE-	Austria
OH-	Finland
OK-	Czech Republic (Czechoslovakia)
OM-	Slovakia
OO-	Belgium
OO-C	Zaire (Belgian Congo)
O-P	Peru
OY-	Denmark
P-	Korea (Democratic People's Republic, North Korea)
P2-	Papua New Guinea (Niugini)
P4-	Aruba
PA	Brazil
P-B	Brazil
PH-	Netherlands
PI-C-	Philippines
PJ-	Netherlands Antilles (Curacao)
PK-	Indonesia (Irian Jaya, West Irian)
PP-	Brazil
PR-	Brazil
PT-	Brazil
PZ-	Surinam (Netherlands Guyana)
R	Soviet Union (USSR)
R-	Argentina
R-	Panama
RA-	Russia
RC-	Croatia
RDPL-	Laos
RF-	Russia
RH-	Armenia
RM-	Moldova
RP-C	Philippines
RR	Soviet Union (USSR)
RV-	Iran (Persia)
RX-	Panama
RY-	Lithuania
R-Z	Lithuania
S2-	Bangladesh
S3-	Bangladesh
S5-	Slovenia
S7-	Seychelles
S9-	Sao Tome and Principe
S-A	Sweden
SE-	Sweden
S-G	Greece
SL-	Saarland
SL-	Slovenia (1990s)
SN-	Sudan
S-P	Panama
SP-	Poland
SR-	Syria
ST-	Sudan
SU-	Egypt
SX-	Greece
T2-	Tuvalu
T3-	Kiribati (Gilbert Islands)
T7-	San Marino
T9-	Bosnia-Herzegovina
TC-	Turkey
T-D	Denmark
TF-	Iceland
TG-	Guatemala
TI-	Costa Rica
TJ-	Cameroon (British Cameroons) (1960 - present)
TJ-	Jordan
TL-	Central African Republic
TN-	Congo (Brazzaville)
TR-	Gabon
TS-	Saarland
TS-	Tunisia (1956 - present)
TT-	Chad
TU-	Ivory Coast
TY-	Benin (Dahomey)
TZ-	Mali
UH-	Saudi Arabia (Hejaz, Nedjd)
UK-	Uzbekistan
UL-	Luxembourg
UN-	Kazakstan (1991 - present)
UN-	Yugoslavia
UR-	Ukraine
URSS	Soviet Union (USSR)
USSR	Soviet Union (USSR)(Cyrillic CCCP)
V2-	Antigua and Barbuda
V3-	Belize (British Honduras)
V4-	Saint Kitts and Nevis
V5-	Namibia
V6-	Micronesia
V7-	Marshall Islands
V8-	Brunei Darussalam (British Northern Borneo)
VH-	Australia
VN-	Vietnam (also North Vietnam)
VO-	Newfoundland
VP-A	Ghana (Gold Coast)
VP-A	Ivory Coast
VP-B	Bahamas
VP-B	Bermuda (current)
VP-C	Cayman Islands (current)
VP-C	Sri Lanka (Ceylon)
VP-F	Falkland Islands
VP-G	Guyana (British Guiana)
VP-H	Belize (British Honduras)
VP-J	Jamaica
VP-K	Kenya
VP-L	Antigua and Barbuda
VP-LAA to VP-LJZ	Anguilla
VP-LKA to VP-LLZ	Saint Kitts and Nevis
VP-LMA to VP-LUZ	Montserrat
VP-LVA to VP-LZZ	British Virgin Islands
VP-M	Malta
VP-N	Malawi (Nyasaland)
VP-P	Kiribati (Gilbert Islands)
VP-P	Solomon Islands
VP-P	Vanuatu (New Hebrides)
VP-R	Zambia (North Rhodesia)
VP-S	Somalia (Somaliland)
VP-T	Trinidad and Tobago
VP-U	Uganda
VP-V	Saint Vincent and the Grenadines
VP-W	Wei-Hai-Wei
VP-W	Zimbabwe (Southern Rhodesia)
VP-X	Gambia
VP-Y	Zimbabwe (Southern Rhodesia)
VP-Z	Zansibar
VQ-B	Barbados
VQ-C	Cyprus
VQ-F	Fiji
VQ-G	Grenada
VQ-H	Saint Helena
VQ-L	Saint Lucia
VQ-M	Mauritius
VQ-P	Israel (British Palestine)
VQ-S	Seychelles
VQ-T	Turks and Caicos Islands
VQ-Z	Botswana (Bechuanaland)
VQ-Z	Lesotho (Basutoland)
VQ-Z	Swaziland
VR-A	Aden
VR-B	Bermuda
VR-C	Cayman Islands
VR-G	Gibraltar
VR-J	Johore
VR-L	Saint Lucia
VR-L	Sierra Leone
VR-N	Cameroon (British Cameroons)
VR-N	Nigeria
VR-O	Borneo
VR-R	Malaysia (Malaya)
VR-S	Singapore
VR-T	Tanganyika
VR-U	Brunei Darussalam (British Northern Borneo)
VT-	India
X-A	Mexico
X-B	Mexico
X-C	China, People's Republic
XC-	Mexico
X-H (XH-)	Honduras
X-S	Serbia
XT-	Burkina Faso (Upper Volta) (1960 - present)
XT-	China, People's Republic
XU-	Cambodia (Kampuchea)
XV-	Vietnam, South
XW-	Laos
XY-	Myanmar (Burma)
XZ-	Myanmar (Burma)
Y-M	Danzig (Gdansk)
YA-	Afghanistan
YE-	Yemen
YI-	Iraq
YJ-	Vanuatu (New Hebrides)
YK-	Syria
YL-	Latvia
YN	Nicaragua
YR-	Rumania
YS-	El Salvador
YT-	Tajikistan
YU-	Yugoslavia
YV-	Venezuela
Z-	Zimbabwe (Southern Rhodesia)
Z3-	Macedonia
ZA-	Albania
ZK-	New Zealand
ZL-	New Zealand
ZM-	New Zealand
ZP-	Paraguay
ZS-	South Africa
ZT-	South Africa
ZU-	South Africa

Bibliography

Allen, Peter. *The 91 Before Lindbergh.* Egan, MN: Flying Books, 1984.

Anderson, Barry J. *Army Air Forces Stations; A Guide to the Stations Where US Army Air Forces Personnel Served in the United Kingdom During World War II.* Maxwell AFB, AL: USAF Historical Research Center, 1985.

Andersson, Lennart. *Soviet Aircraft and Aviation; 1917-1941.* London: Putnam, 1994.

Banks, Arthur. *The Military Atlas of the First World War.* Barnsley, UK: Pen and Sword Books, Ltd, 1997.

Banning, Gene. *Airlines of Pan American since 1927.* McLean, VA: Paladwr Press, 2001.

Barnes, C. H. *Bristol Aircraft since 1910.* London: Putnam, 1964

————, and Derek James. *Shorts Aircraft since 1900.* London: Putnam, 1989

Berg, A. Scott. *Lindbergh.* New York: G. P. Putnam's Sons, 1998.

Bluth, John A. *Stinson Aircraft Company.* Charleston, SC, Chicago, Portsmouth, NH, San Francisco: Arcadia Publishing, 2002.

Bowers, Peter M. *Boeing Aircraft Since 1916.* Annapolis: Naval Institute Press, 1989.

————. *Curtiss Aircraft; 1907-1947.* London: Putnam, 1979.

Brooks, Peter W. *Zeppelin: Rigid Airships; 1893-1940.* London: Putnam, 1992.

Bruce, J. M. *The Aeroplanes of the Royal Flying Corps (Military Wing).* London: Putnam, 1982.

————. *British Aeroplanes; 1914-18.* New York: Funk & Wagnalls, 1957.

Burke, David. *Moments of Terror; The Story of Antarctic Aviation.* Kensington, NSW, Australia: New South Wales University Press, 1994.

Cole, Christopher, and E. F. Cheesman. *The Air Defense of Britain; 1914-1918.* London: Putnam, 1984.

Combs, Harry, and Martin Caiden. *Kill Devil Hill; Discovering the Secret of the Wright Brothers.* Boston: Houghton Mifflin Company, 1979.

Courtney, Frank T. *The Eighth Sea.* Garden City, New York: Doubleday & company, Inc, 1972.

Craven, Wesley Frank, and James Lea Cate, eds. *The Army Air Forces In World War II.* 7 vols. Chicago: The University of Chicago Press, 1958.

de la Croix, Robert. *They Flew the Atlantic.* New York: W. W. Norton & Company, Inc, 1959.

Crouch, Tom. *The Bishop's Boys; A Life of Wilbur and Orville Wright.* New York and London: W. W. Norton and Co, 1989.

Culver, Edith Dodd. *The Day the Air-Mail Began.* Kansas City, KS: Cub Flyers Enterprises Inc, N.d.

Davies, R. E. G. *Airlines of Asia since 1920.* McLean, VA: Paladwr Press, 1997.

————. *Airlines of Latin America since 1919.* Washington: Smithsonian Institution Press, 1984.

————. *Airlines of the United States since 1914.* Washington, DC: Smithsonian Institution Press, 1972.

————. *A History of the World's Airlines.* London, New York, and Toronto: Oxford University Press, 1967.

Davilla, James J., and Arthur M. Soltan. *French Aircraft of the First World War.* Mountain View, CA: Flying Machines Press, 1997.

Dierikx, Marc. *Fokker; A Transatlantic Biography.* Washington and London: Smithsonian Institution Press, 1997.

Durkota, Alan, Thomas Darcey, and Victor Kulikov. *The Imperial Russian Air Service; Famous Pilots and Aircraft of World War One.* Mountain View, CA: Flying Machines Press, 1995.

Eaton, Joseph E. *Methods in Observation Practiced with Fifth Corps First American Army on the Fronts; St. Mihiel Sector, September 12 to 16, 1918; Argonne-Meuse Sector, September 12 to November 11, 1918.* Washington: US Air Service, 1920.

Ellison, Norman. *Flying Matilda; Early Days in Australian Aviation.* Sydney: Angus and Robertson, 1957.

FAA, National Aeronautical Charting Office. *Aeronautical Chart User's Guide* (7th Ed). Washington: FAA, 2006.

————. Worldwide Aeronautical Charts and Products (8th Ed). Washington: National Geospatial Intelligence Agency, 2006.

Francillon, René J. *Lockheed Aircraft since 1913.* London: Putnam, 1982.

Franks, Norman L. R., Frank W. Bailey, and Russell Guest. *Above the Lines; The Aces and Fighter Units of the German Air Service, Naval Air Service and Flanders Marines Corps, 1914-1918.* London: Grub Street, 1993.

Gentilli, Roberto, Antonio Iozzi, and Paolo Varriale. Italian Aces of World War I and Their Aircraft. Altglen, PA: Schiffer Military History, 2003.

Gilbert, Martin. *The Routledge Atlas of the First World War,* 2nd Ed. London and New York: Routledge, 1994.

Glines, Carroll V. *Polar Aviation.* New York: Franklin Watts, Inc., 1964.

————. *Round-The-World Flights.* New York: Van Nostrand Reinhold, 1982.

Gray, Peter, and Owen Thetford. *German Aircraft of the First World War.* London: Putnam, 1962

Grosz, Peter M., George Haddow, and Peter Schiemer. *Austro-Hungarian Army Aircraft of World War One.* Mountain View, CA: Flying Machines Press, 1993.

Gwynn-Jones, Terry. *The Air Racers; Aviation's Golden Era 1909-1936.* London: Pelham Books, 1984.

————. *Aviation's Magnificent Gamblers.* Sydney, Auckland, London, New York: Lansdowne Press, 1981.

————. *Farther and Faster: Aviation's Adventuring Years, 1909-1939.* Washington and London: Smithsonian Institution Press, 1991.

Hallion, Richard P. *The Rise of the Fighter Aircraft, 1914-1918.* Baltimore: The Nautical & Aviation Publishing Co of America, Inc, 1984.

Harrison, Gordon A. *Cross-Channel Attack.* Washington: Office of the Chief of Military History, 1951.

Inter-Allied Aeronautical Commission of Control. *Execution of the Air Clauses of the Peace Treaty of Versailles; Part 1; Execution Report*, (Vol II) Germany: Inter-Allied Aeronautical Commission of Control, 1921.

Jakab, Peter L. *Visions of a Flying Machine; The Wright Brothers and the Process of Invention.* Washington and London: Smithsonian Institution Press, 1990.

Jackson, A. J. *Avro Aircraft since 1908*. London: Putnam, 1990

————. *Blackburn Aircraft since 1909.* London: Putnam, 1989.

————. *British Civil Aircraft; 1919-1972*. 3 vols. London: Putnam, 1974.

————. *De Havilland Aircraft since 1909.* London: Putnam, 1962.

Jarrett, Philip, ed. *Modern Air Transport; Worldwide Air Transport from 1945 to the Present*. London: Putnam Aeronautical Books, 2000.

————. *Pioneer Aircraft; Early Aviation before 1914*. London: Putnam Aeronautical Books, 2002.

Johnson, David C. *U.S. Army Air Forces Continental Airfields (ETO); D-Day to V-E Day.* Maxwell AFB, AL: USAF Historical Research Center, 1988.

Leary, William M. *Aerial Pioneers; The U.S. Air Mail Service, 1918-1927.* Washington, DC: Smithsonian Institution Press, 1985.

Long, Eric F., Mark A. Avino, Tom Alison, and Dana Bell. *At the Controls: The Smithsonian National Air and Space Museum Book of Cockpits.* Erin, Ontario: Boston Mills Press, 2001.

Luff, David. *Mollison; The Flying Scotsman.* Washington: Smithsonian Institution Press, 1993.

Maurer, Maurer. *Aviation in the U.S. Army; 1919-1939.* Washington: The Office of Air Force History, 1987.

————, ed. *The US Air Service in World War I*. 4 vols. Washington: The Office of Air Force History, 1979.

McDonough, Kenneth. *Atlantic Wings*. Hemel Hempstead, UK: Model Aeronautical Press, Ltd, 1966.

McMillan, Peter. *The Greatest Flight.* Atlanta: Turner Publishing, Inc., 1995.

Monk, F.V., and H. T. Winter. *Air Mail.* London: The Percy Press, 1936.

Montague, Richard. *Oceans, Poles, and Airmen; The First Flights over Wide Waters and Desolate Ice.* New York: Random House, 1971.

Morris, Joseph. *The German Air Raids on Great Britain; 1914-1918*. London: H. Pordes, 1969.

Morrow, John H., Jr. *The Great War in the Air; Military Aviation from 1909 to 1921.* Washington and London: Smithsonian Institution Press, 1993.

Mueller, Robert. *Air Force Bases, Vol. I; Active Air Force Bases Within the United States of America on 17 September 1982.* Washington: The Office of Air Force History, 1989.

O'Connor, Mike. *Airfields and Airmen; Arras.* Barnsley, UK: Pen & Sword Books, Ltd, 2004

————. *Airfields and Airmen; Cambrai.* Barnsley, UK: Pen & Sword Books, Ltd, 2003

————. *Airfields and Airmen; Somme.* Barnsley, UK: Pen & Sword Books, Ltd, 2002

————. *Airfields and Airmen; Ypres.* Barnsley, UK: Pen & Sword Books, Ltd, 2001

————. *Airfields and Airmen of the Channel Coast.* Barnsley, UK: Pen & Sword Books, Ltd, 2005

Olson, Lynne, and Stanley Cloud. *A Question of Honor; The Ko ciuszko Squadron: Forgotten Heros of World War II.* New York: Alfred A. Knopf, 2003

Penrose, Harald. *British Aviation; The Pioneer Years, 1903-1914.* London: Putnam, 1967.

————. *British Aviation; The Great War and Armistice.* London: Putnam, 1969

————. *British Aviation; The Adventuring Years.* London: Putnam, 1973

Polmar, Norman, and Dana Bell. *One Hundred Years of World Military Aircraft.* Annapolis, MD: Naval Institute Press, 2004.

Robertson, Bruce. *Aircraft Markings of the World; 1912-1967.* Letchworth, Hertfordshire, UK: Harleyford Publications Ltd, 1967.

Rogers, Les. *British Aviation Squadron Markings of World War I.* Atglen, PA: Schiffer Military History, 2001.

Roseberry, C. R. *The Challenging Skies, The Colorful Story of Aviation's Most Exciting Years - 1919-1939.* Garden City, New York: Doubleday & Company, Inc 1966.

von Schiller, Hans. *Zeppelin; Wegbereiter des Weltluftverkehrs.* Bad Godesberg: Kirschbaum Verlag, 1967.

Sims. Phillip E. *Adventurous Empires: The Story of the Short Empire Flying-boats.* Shrewsbury, UK: Airlife Publishing Ltd, 2000.

Spick, Mike. *The Complete Fighter Ace; All the World's Fighter Aces, 1914-2000.* London: Greenhill Books, 1999.

Stein, E. P. *Flight of the Vin Fiz.* New York: Arbor House, 1985.

Stroud, John. *European Transport Aircraft since 1910.* London: Putnam, 1966.

Tunner, William H. *Over the Hump.* Washington, DC: Office of Air Force History, 1985.

Underwood, John W. *The Stinsons; The exciting chronicle of a flying family and the 'planes that enhanced their fame.* Glendale, California: Heritage Press, 1969.

Vaeth, J. Gordon. *Graf Zeppelin; The Adventures of an Aerial Globetrotter.* London: Frederick Muller Ltd, 1959.

Villard, Henry Serrano. *Contact! The Story of the Early Birds.* New York: Thomas Y. Crowell Co, 1968.

Wallace, Graham. *Claude Grahame-White; A Biography.* London: Putnam, 1960.

Whitehouse, Arch. *The Early Birds.* Garden City, New York: Doubleday & Co, Inc, 1965.

Williams, Roger Q. *To the Moon and Halfway Back.* Oakland, CA: Roger Q. Williams, 1949.

Wood, Derek, with Derek Dempster. *The Narrow Margin; The Battle of Britain and the Rise of Air Power, 1930-1940.* (3rd edition) Washington, DC: Smithsonian Institution Press, 1990.

Index

AB Aerotransport, 78, 189
Acosta, Bert, 90
Adamowicz, Benjamin and Joseph, 93, 94
Ader, Clément, 9, 10
Ader *Eole*, 9
Ader *Eole III*, 9, 10
Aero-Union, 80
Aeroflot, 80
Aeromarine 75, 110, 111
Aeromarine 80, 110
Aeromarine West Indies Airways, 110
Aeronca 65-C Chief *Baby Clipper*, 95
Aéropostale, 95
Ahrenberg, Albin, 91
Air France , 77, 95
Air Union, 77
Ala Littoria, 77, 113
Albatros biplane (Farman copy), 23
Albatros D.V, 46
Albrecht, Fritz, 92, 93
Alcock, John, 86
Allan, G. U. "Scotty", 93
Alley, Norman, 93
Altfilisch, Gerald, 93
American Airlines (Airways), 60, 62, 69, 70, 194
American Overseas Airlines, 193
Amiot 123 *Marsza lek Pi lsudski*, 91
Amiot 123 *White Bird*, 91
Amundsen, Roald, 90, 92, 114, 115 ,116
Andree, Salomon August, 114
Antoinette monoplane , 20
Archdeacon, Ernest, 14
Archimedes , 2
Arnold, Leslie, 103
Assolant, Jean, 91
Atlantic, Gulf, and Caribbean Airways, 111
Aviatik 30.07, 35
Aviatik 30.24, 37
Aviation Corp of the Americas, 111
Aviation Corp of America, 111
Avio Linee Italiane, 77
Avro 618 Ten Faith in Australia, 93
Avro 707, 181
Avro Lancaster, 123
Avro Vulcan, 167
Ayling, James R., 94
Bachman, Carl, 95
Balbo, Italo, 92, 93
Balchen, Bernt, 90, 116, 117
Baldwin, Thomas Scott, 5, 7
balloon *Eagle*, 114
balloon *Eva*, 116
Baracca, Francesco, 36
Barberán, Mariano, 93
Barling B-6 *Golden Hind*, 91-92
Beech J35 Bonanza, 206
Beideman, Addison, 95
Beires, Sarament, 88
Bell, Hugh, 4
Bell UH-1 Huey , 198
Bell P-39 Airacobra, 148
Bell V-22 Osprey, 175
Bell X-1 (XS-1), 178, 179
Bellanca, Giuseppe, 90
Bellanca 28-70 Flash *The Dorothy*, 95
Bellanca 28-70 Flash *Irish Swoop*, 95
Bellanca J *Green Flash*, 91
Bellanca J *North Star*, 91
Bellanca J *Pathfinder*, 91
Bellanca J *Santa Rosa Maria*, 93
Bellanca J-2 Special *Abyssinia*, 93, 94
Bellanca J-2 Special *Magellan*, 94
Bellanca J-2 Special *Francesco de Pinedo*, 94
Bellanca J-2 Special *Marshal Pilsudski*, 94
Bellanca J-300 *Liberty*, 92, 93, 94
Bellanca J-300 *Cape Cod*, 92
Bellanca J-300 *White Eagle*, 93
Bellanca J-300 *City of Warsaw*, 94
Bellanca J-300 *Leonardo da Vinci*, 94
Bellanca K *Enna Jettick*, 93
Bellanca K *Roma*, 91, 93
Bellanca Pacemaker 300-W, 95
Bellanca Pacemaker CH-300, 92
Bellanca Pacemaker CH-300 *Lituanica*, 93
Bellanca Pacemaker CH-300 *Trade Wind*, 92
Bellanca Skyrocket CH-400 *American Nurse*, 93
Bellanca Skyrocket CH-400 *Asulinak*, 94
Bellanca Skyrocket CH-400 *Miss Veedol*, 92, 107
Bellanca Special Long Distance *Santa Lucia*, 94
Bellanca WB-2 *Columbia*, 90, 91, 92
Bellanca WB-2 *Maple Leaf*, 92
Bellonte, Maurice, 91, 92
Bennett, D. C. T., 95
Bennett, Floyd, 90, 115
Bennett, J., 82
Benton, John, 108
Benz, Karl, 4
Berger, A. L. "Doc", 52
Bernard 191GR *Oiseau Canari*, 91
Bertaud, Lloyd, 90
Bjorkvall, Kurt, 95
Blanchard, Jean-Pierre, 54
Blankenburg, Joachim H., 95
Blériot, Louis, 14, 18, 20
Blériot monoplane, 21
Blériot XI, 18, 20, 26, 27
Blériot 110 *Joseph Le Brix*, 93, 94
Blohm und Voss Ha 139 Noordmeer, 95
Boardman, Russell Norton, 92
Bochkon, John, 93
Bock, Wilhelm, 90
Boeing Company, 96
Boeing 247 , 69, 82, 85
Boeing 307 Stratoliner, 70
Boeing 314, 50, 153
Boeing 314 *Dixie Clipper*, 95
Boeing 314 *Honolulu Clipper*, 101
Boeing 314 *Yankee Clipper*, 95, 100, 101
Boeing 707, 177, 184, 189
Boeing 747, 182
Boeing 757, 186
Boeing 767, 194
Boeing B-15, 150
Boeing B-17 Flying Fortress, 50, 112, 122, 123, 137, 148, 150
Boeing B-29 Superfortress, 140, 141, 142, 143, 144
Boeing B-52 Stratofortress , 160, 168, 169, 172
Boeing (McDonnell-Douglas) C-17 Globemaster III, 172
Boeing C-75 (307) Stratoliner, 153, 155
Boeing KC-135 Stratotanker, 160, 168
Boeing E-3 AWACS, 172
Boeing E-8 J-STARS, 172, 176
Boeing F-13 (B-29) Superfortress, 144, 145
Boeing X-36, 183
Boeing X-48, 183
Bonelli, Pietro, 91
Booth, R. S., 92
Bowes, C. H., 95
Boyd, J. Errol, 92
Boyle, George L., 54
Braniff Airways, 71
Breguet 19 TR Bidon, 92
Breguet XIV, 50
Breguet XIX *Nungesser and Coli*, 90
Breguet XIX Super T.R. *Point d'Interrogation*, 91, 92
Breguet 280T Rapid Azur, 77
Brinkley, W. C., 13
British Aerospace Jetstream 31 , 204
British, Australian, New Zealand Antarctic Research Expedition (BANZARE), 116
Brock, Horace, 95
Brock, William, 90
Brossy, Frederic, 93
Brown, Henry J., 92
Burden, S. C., 64
Byrd, Richard E., 90, 114, 115, 116
C.C.N.A., 112
Campbell Black, Tom, 82
Campbell, Stuart, 116
CAMS 54 GR La Frégate, 91
Canadian Colonial Airways, 70
Cant Z.506, 80
Caproni bomber, 39
Caproni Ca.5, 35
Carling, John, 90
Carstens, Vern, 85
CASA CN-235, 216
CASA-Breguet 19 GR *Jesus del Gran Poder*, 91
CASA-Breguet XIX GR Super Bidon *Cuatro Vientos*, 93
Cavallo, Tiberius, 2
Cavendish, Henry, 2
Cayley, George, 4, 8
eskoslovenská Letecká Spole nost (CLS), 76
Challe, Léon, 92
Chamberlin, Clarence D., 90
Chanute, Octave, 9, 10, 11, 12
Charles, J. A. C., 3
Cheeseman, Al, 116
Chennault, Claire , 146
Chiang Kai-shek, 146
Christensen, Lars, 116
Christiansen, Frederich, 92
Churchill, Winston, 122
Cochran, Jacqueline, 158
Codos, Paul, 93, 94
Cody, Samuel, 21
Cody *Flying Parish Church*, 21
Coli, Francois, 89
Collar, Joaquín, 93
Collignon, Robert H., 93
Columbia Aircraft Corp, 90
Concorde SST, 184
Condor Syndikat, 113
Conneau, Roger (aka Andre Beaumont), 21
Connor, H. P., 92
Connor, Harry, 95
Consolidated B-24 Liberator , 152
Consolidated B-24 Liberator *Tidewater Tillie* , 127
Consolidated C-87 Liberator, 153, 156
Consolidated C-109 Liberator, 153
Consolidated F-7 (B-24) Liberator, 144, 145
Consolidated LB-30 Liberator, 155
Consolidated PBY-5A Catalina, 127, 157
Convair F-102 Delta Dagger, 179
Convair XFY-1 Pogo, 178
Corbu, Charles, 90
Cornish, Ray, 95
Corrigan, Douglas, 95
Costa Viega, Fernando, 93
Coster, A. J., 95
Costes, Dieudonné, 90, 91, 92, 107
Coudouret, Louis, 91
Courtney, Frank T., 90
Couzinet 10 Arc-en-Ciel, 91
Couzinet 70 Arc-en-Ciel, 93
Couzinet 71 Arc-en-Ciel, 93, 94
Cramer, Parker D. "Shorty", 91, 92, 116
Cruveilher, Edgar, 95
Culver, Howard Paul, 54, 55
Curtiss, Glenn Hammond, 5, 7
Curtiss A-25 Helldiver, 159
Curtiss C-46 Commando, 152, 156
Curtiss Condor II *William Horlick*, 116
Curtiss Condor II, 69
Curtiss F-5L, 110
Curtiss HS-2L, 40, 110
Curtiss JN-4 Jenny, 46, 50, 51, 54
Curtiss Oriole, 114
Curtiss P-40 Warhawk, 135, 136, 148
Curtiss Robin J-1 *Sunshine*, 95
Cusack, Lana, 158
d'Arlandes (Marquis), 2, 3
Dabry, Jean, 92
Daily Mail (London), 19, 20, 21, 86
Daniels, John, 13
Dargue, Herbert A., 108, 109
Darius, Stephen, 93
Davis, John King, 116
de Alda, Ruiz, 91
de Barros, Joao, 88
de Havilland (Airco) D.H.2 , 29
de Havilland D.H.4 (DH-4), 41, 46, 72
de Havilland D.H.60A Gipsy Moth *Rouge et Noir*, 93
de Havilland D.H.60G Gipsy Moth, 91, 116
de Havilland D.H.80A Puss Moth, 92 ,93
de Havilland D.H.80A Puss Moth *The Heart's Content*, 93
de Havilland D.H.83 Fox Moth *Robert Bruce*, 94
de Havilland D.H.84 Dragon I *Seafarer*, 93
de Havilland D.H.84 Dragon I *Trail of the Caribou*, 94
de Havilland D.H.84 Dragon I *Seafarer II*, 94
de Havilland D.H.88 Comet, 82, 184
de Havilland D.H.98 Mosquito, 122
de Lana, Francesco, 2
de Pinedo, Francesco, 88, 90, 94, 108
de Sacadura Cabral, Artur, 86, 88
De Monteverde, Alfred and George, 94
Decker, Richard, 95
del Prete, Carlo, 90, 91
Delagrange, Léon, 14
Delta Air Lines, 186
Deperdussin racer, 21
Deruluft (Deutsch-Russuche Luftverkehrs Gesellschaft), 80, 81
Deutsche Luft-Reederei , 73
Dierberg, Paul, 95
Dillenz, Lilli, 90
dirigibles
America, 6, 114
California Arrow, 5
L 33 (LZ.76) , 43, 86
L 41, 42
L 43 , 43
L 44 , 43
L 45 , 43
L 46 , 43
L 47 , 43
L 48 , 43
L 49, 43
L 50, 43
L 52, 43
L 53 , 43
L 54, 43
L 55, 43
La France, 4
Le Jaune, 4
LZ 1, 4
LZ 2, 4
LZ 3, 4
LZ 120 *Bodensee*, 46, 50, 74
LZ 121 *Nordstern*, 74
LZ 126 , 88
LZ 127 *Graf Zeppelin* , 74, 75, 91, 92, 106
LZ 129 *Hindenburg*, 74, 94, 95
LZ 130 *Graf Zeppelin II*, 74
Norge, 115, 116
R 33 , 86
R 34, 86
R 100, 92
S.L.1, 6
Signal Corps No.1, 7
ZR-3 *Los Angeles*, 88
Diteman, Urban F., 91-92
Dorand A.R.2 , 28
Dornier Do X , 74, 92, 93
Dornier Do 18 Zephir, 95
Dornier Wal, 90, 91. 113, 114, 116
Dornier Wal *Amundsen*, 92
Dornier Wal *Argos*, 88, 89
Dornier Wal *Groenlandwal*, 92, 93, 106
Dornier Wal *Plus Ultra*, 88
Dornier Super-Wal *Numancia*, 91
Dough, W. S., 13
Douglas A-1 Skyraider, 169
Douglas A-26 (B-26) Invader, 165, 167
Douglas B-18 Bolo, 150
Douglas B-23 Dragon, 148, 150
Douglas C-47 Skytrain, 131, 152, 153, 154, 162, 167
Douglas C-53 Skytrooper, 153
Douglas C-54 Skymaster, 152, 153, 162, 163, 188
Douglas D-558-2 Skyrocket, 178
Douglas DC-2, 70, 71, , 82
Douglas DC-3, viii, 70, 78, 153, 187, 189, 190
Douglas DC-4, 187, 189
Douglas DC-4E (DC-4), 71
Douglas DC-6, 193
Douglas DC-8, 184, 189, 210
Douglas DST, 70
Douglas DWC (Douglas World Cruiser), 88, 104, 105
Douglas DWC *Boston*, 103, 104
Douglas DWC *Boston II*, 104
Douglas DWC *Chicago*, 103, 104, 105
Douglas DWC *New Orleans*, 103, 104
Douglas DWC *Seattle*, 103, 104
Douglas, Eric, 116
Drouhin, Maurice, 91
du Temple, Felix, 8
Dupuy de Lôme, Henri, 4
Dutton, Bob, 95
Eaker, Ira, 108, 109
Earhart, Amelia, 90, 93, 95, 107
Eastern Airlines (Air Lines), viii, 186, 187, 190, 193, 204
Eastern Metro Express, 204
Eaton, Joseph, 44, 46
Eckner, Hugo, 88, 91, 92
Edzard, Cornelius, 90
Eielson, Carl Ben, 115, 116
Eisenhower, Dwight D., 131
Elder, Ruth, 90
Ellsworth, Lincoln, 114, 115, 117
Elsey, George W., 52
Endres, George, 92
Esnault-Pelterie, Robert, 14
Etheridge, A. D., 13
Eurasia, 80, 81
Ezan, Henri, 95
Fairchild Argus, 220
Fairchild FC-2 , 111
Fairchild FC-2 *Stars and Stripes*, 116
Fairchild *Miss American Airways*, 116
Fairchild PT-19A, 158
Fairchild-Republic A-10A Thunderbolt II, 166, 174
Fairey IIID *Lusitania*, 86, 88
Fairey IIID *Santa Cruz*, 88
Farman F.60 Goliath *Normandie*, 72
Farman F.180 *l'Oiseau Bleu*, 90
Farman F.301, 72
Farman 190 *Jung Schweitzerland*, 91
Farman 2200 *Ville de Montevidéo*, 95
Farman 2220 *Ville de Dakar*, 95
Ferrarin, Arturo, 91
Fiedler (Paul) 1911 monoplane, 23
Fisher, Enid, 158
Fitzmaurice, James, 90
Fleet, Reuben E., 54
Floden, Axel, 91
Florida West Indies Airways, 110
Focke-Wulf Fw 190 D-9 , 123
Focke-Wulf Fw 200 Condor *Brandenberg*, 95
Fokker, Anthony, 28, 72
Fokker A-2 (F.IV), 58
Fokker A.III Eindecker, 37
Fokker *Blue Blade*, 116
Fokker C-2 *America*, 90
Fokker D.VII, 38, 46, 50
Fokker Dr.I, 46
Fokker E.I , 28
Fokker E.III, 31
Fokker F.III , 58
Fokker F.VII, 111, 114
Fokker F.VII *The Alaskan*, 96, 114
Fokker F.VII *Duif* , 94
Fokker F.VII *Josephine Ford* , 114
Fokker F.VII *Princess Xenia*, 90
Fokker F.VII *Saint Raphael*, 90
Fokker F.VII *Spider* , 90
Fokker F.VII-3m *Detroiter*, 96
Fokker F.VIIa *Old Glory*, 90
Fokker F.VIIb-3m *Friendship*, 90
Fokker F.VIIb-3m *Southern Cross*, 92, 93, 96, 97, 106, 114
Fokker F.IX , 81
Fokker F.XVIII *Oenoe* (*Oriol*), 94
Fokker F.XVIII *Snip*, 94
Fokker F-32, 62
Fokker M.5 , 28
Fokker T-2 (F.IV), 58, 59
Fokker *The Virginian* , 116
Fonck, Rene, 44
Ford trimotor, 60, 61, 64
Ford trimotor *Floyd Bennett*, 116
Fournier, Henri, 18
Fowler, Bob, 24
Franco, Francisco, 88
Franco, Ramón, 88, 91
Franklin, Benjamin, 3
Frey, Andrea, 21
Friedrichshafen floatplane, 28

Frost, B. C., 95
Gago Coutinho, Carlos, 86, 88
Gallarza, Eduardo, 91
Garber, Paul E., 115
Garros, Roland, x, 20, 21, 28, 31
Gast, Robert, 91
Gatty, Harold, 92
General Electric, 52
George VI (King of England), 95
Giffard, Henri, 4
Gilmour, Hugh, 90, 91
Gimié, Leopold, 92
Girenas, Stanley T., 93
Givion, Leon, 90
Gloster Meteor, 20
Goldsborough, Brice, 90
Goodwin, Harold, 149
Gordinenko, M. Kh., 95
Gordon, Louis, 90
Gotha bomber, 42
Grace Lines, 111
Grade 1911 monoplane, 23
Grade, Hans, 23
Graham, Maurice, 41
Grahame-White, Claude, 20, 54
Granville R-6H *Conquistador del Cielo*, 112
Gray, Harold, 95
Grayson, Francis, 90
Grierson, John, 93, 94
Griffin, Bennett, 93
Grumman F4F Wildcat, 137
Grumman F6F Hellcat Minsi III, 139
Grumman TBF Avenger, 125, 126, 136, 138
Guest, Amy, 90
Guest, Frederick, 90
Gusmão, Laurenço de, 2
Hack, Franz, 92, 93
Haenlein, Paul, 4
Haldeman, George, 90
Hamilton, Charles K., 18
Hamilton, Leslie, 90
Hammer, Fritz, 92, 93
Hansa-Brandenburg, 116
Hansell, Haywood, 140
Harding, John, 103
Harry Houdini (nee Eric Weisz, later Ehrich Weiss), 16
Hart, Beryl, 92
Harvey, Alva L., 103, 104
Hassell, Bert R. J. "Fish", 91
Hausner, Stanislaus F., 93, 94
Hawker Hurricane, 121
Hawker Sea Hawk, 161
Hearst, William Randolph, 24
Heinkel He 111, 119, 120
Heinkel Seaplane, 90
Henke, Alfred, 95
Henson, Matthew, 114
Henson, William Samuel, 8
Herndon, Hugh, Jr, 92, 107
Herring, Augustus, 10, 11, 12
Hill, James, 90
Hillig, Otto, 92, 94
Hinchcliff, Walter G. R., 90
Hinkler, H. J. "Bert", 93
Hirth, Wolfram, 92
Hitler, Adolf, 46, 118, 120
Hobbs, T. E., 95
Hoiriis, Holgar, 92, 94
Hollick-Kenyon, Herbert, 117
Hondong, J., 94
Hope Bob, 153
Hosmer, Elwood, 90, 91
Hughes, Howard, 95, 106
Humphrey Toomey, 113
Hunter Harris, Jr, 53
Hunter Harris, Sr, 53
Hussein, Saddam, 170
Hutchinson, Blanche, 93
Hutchinson, George, 93
Hutchinson, Janet Lee, 93
Hutchinson, Kathryn, 93
Idzikowski, Ludwik, 91
Iglesias, Francisco, 91
Il'yushin TsKB.30 Moskva, 95
Immelmann, Max, 44
Imperial Airways, 82, 83, 90, 100
Inchcape (Lord), 90
Jeffries, John, 54
Jiménez, Ignacio, 91
João V (King of Portugal), 2
Johanssen, Christian, 93
Johnson, Martin, 85
Johnson, Osa Leighty, 85
Jones, Charles, 40
Joseph Le Brix, 107
Julian, Hubert Fauntleroy, 93, 94
June, Harold, 116
Junkers aircraft, 113
Junkers G 24, 90
Junkers Ju 52, 78, 81
Junkers Ju 52 *Curupira*, 113
Junkers Ju 52 *Lord Charles Sommerset*, 85
Junkers Ju 87 Stuka, 118
Junkers Ju 88, 122
Junkers-Larsen JL-6, 114
Junkers W 33 *Europa*, 90
Junkers W 33 *Bremen*, 90
Junkers W 33 *Esa*, 93
Junkers W 33e3e *Sverige*, 91
Kaeser, Oscar, 91
Kalkowsky, Adam, 95
Kawanishi H8K, 138
Kellet K-4 Autogyro, 116
Kelly, Oakley G., 58, 59
Kelly Rogers, J. C., 95
Kennedy, John F., 194
Kingsford-Smith, Charles, 92, 93, 96, 97
Klemm floatplane, 92
KLM, 78, 79, 81, 82, 94, 188
Knickerbocker, Hubert R., 90
KNILM, 81
Kober, Walter, 95
Koehl, Herman, 90
Koehler, Frank, 90
Koenmann, U., 91
Köhl, Hermann, 90
Kokkinaki, V. K., 95
Krebs, A. C., 4
Kritzer, Shelby, 95
Kubala, Kazimierz, 91
La Porte, Arthur, 95
LaGuardia, Fiorello, 39
Lambie, John, 95
Lanet, André, 91
Langley, Samuel Pierpont, 9
Langley *Aerodrome A*, 9, 11
Larre-Borges, Taddeo, 92
Latécoère 28-3 *Comte de Vaulx*, 92
Latécoère 300 *Croix du Sud*, 94, 95
Latécoère 301 *Ville de Rio de Janeiro*, 94
Latécoère 301 *Ville de Buenos Aires*, 94
Latécoère 301 *Ville de Santiago de Chile*, 94
Latécoère 521 *Lieutenant de Vaisseau Paris*, 94, 100
Latham, Hubert, 20
LATI (Linee Aeree Transcontinentali Italiane), 113
Lavidalie, Jean, 95
Le Brix, Joseph, 90
Lebaudy, Paul and Pierre, 4
Lee, Clyde Allen, 93
Lees, Walter, 93
Lefebvre, Eugène, 18
Lefèvre, René, 91
Lehmann, Ernst, 94, 95
Leonardo Da Vinci, 8
LePere (LUSAC) 11, 52, 53
Levine, Charles A., 90
Light, Richard, 94
Lilienthal, Otto, 9
Lindbergh, Anne Morrow, 93, 98, 99
Lindbergh, Charles, 60, 64, 86, 89, 90, 93, 98, 99, 108
Lindbergh Line, 64
Lindsey, Lew, 95
Linee Atlantiche, 113
Lioré et Olivier LeO 213, 72
Lioré et Olivier LeO H 242, 77
Little, Robert, 90
Ljungland, Robert, 91
Lloyd LK I, 36
Lockheed 5 Special Vega *Akita*, 92
Lockheed 5 Special Vega *Century of Progress*, 93
Lockheed 5B Vega *City of New York*, 92
Lockheed 5B Vega *Winnie Mae*, 92, 93
Lockheed 8 Altair *Liberty*, 93
Lockheed 8 Altair, 97
Lockheed 8 Sirius Special *Tingmissartog*, 93, 98, 99
Lockheed 8 Sirius *4 de Septiembre*, 94
Lockheed 8A Sirius *Justice for Hungary*, 92
Lockheed 10 Electra, 95, 107
Lockheed 14-N2 Super Electra *Sky Zephyr*, 95
Lockheed 14 *New York World's Fair, 1939*, 106
Lockheed 49 Constellation, 191, 193
Lockheed C-5 Galaxy, 212
Lockheed C-69 Constellation, 153
Lockheed C-130 Hercules, 170, 172, 216, 218
Lockheed C-141 Starlifter, 212
Lockheed F-4 Lightning, 144
Lockheed F-5 Lightning, 144
Lockheed (Lockheed-Martin) F-16 Fighting Falcon, 171, 173
Lockheed F-80 Shooting Star, 178
Lockheed-Martin F-22 Raptor, 175
Lockheed-Martin F-35, 176
Lockheed F-104 Starfighter, 179
Lockheed F-117 Nighthawk, 170
Lockheed P-38 Lightning, 125, 132, 148
Lockheed U-2, 214
Lockheed Vega, 93, 115, 117
Lockheed Vega *Lituanica II*, 94
Lockheed Vega *Los Angeles*, 116
Lockheed Vega *San Francisco*, 116
Loeb, Alex, 95
Loening C2C Air Yacht *Liev Eiriksson*, 94
Loening OA-1A *Detroit*, 108, 109
Loening OA-1A *New York*, 108, 109
Loening OA-1A *St. Louis*, 108, 109
Loening OA-1A *San Antonio*, 108, 109
Loening OA-1A *San Francisco*, 108, 109
Loewe, Karl, 90
Lohner C Pfeilflieger, 26, 27
Lohner flying boat, 33
London, Charmian, 84
London, Jack, 84
Long, S. G., 95
Loose, Friederich, 90
Lotti, Armeno, Jr., 91
Love, Nancy Harkness, 158
Lowe, Thaddeus, 3
Lowell Smith, 97
Löwenstein-Wertheim, Anne, 90
Luca-Girardville, Paul N., 15
Lucher, Kurt, 91
Ludlow, Israel, 18
Lufthansa, 80
Lunardi, Vincent, 4
Lund, Ed, 95
LVG C.VI, 73
Lyon, Harry, 97
Macchi C.94, 77
Macchi flying boat, 33
McBride, James D. (aka J. C. "Bud" Mars), 17
McCampbell, David, 139
MacDonald, H. C., 91
McDonnell XF-85 Goblin, 180
McDonnell F-101 Voodoo, 179
McDonnell F2H Banshee, 161, 164
McDonnell-Douglas F-4 Phanton II, 168, 208
McDonnell-Douglas (Boeing) F-15 Eagle, 173, 175, 182
McDonnell-Douglas (Boeing) F/A-18, 172
McIntosh, Robert H., 90
Mackay, Elsie, 90
McKinley, Ashley, 116
MacLaren, William S., 92
Macready, John A., 53, 58, 59
Madariaga, Pedro, 91
Maddux Airlines, 60
Mailloux, Louis, 91
Markham, Beryl, 95
Mars, J. C. "Bud" (nee James D. McBride), 17
Martin 130 *China Clipper*, 51, 100
Martin B-26, 131, 148
Martin, Frederick L., 103, 104
Mary, Duchess of Bedford, 90
Mattern, James J., 93
Mawson, Douglas, 116
Maxim, Hiram, 9
Mears, John Henry, 92
Medcalf, James, 90
Menéndez Peláez, Antonio, 94
Mermoz, Jean, 92, 93, 94, 95
Merrill, Richard T. "Dick", 94, 95
Merz, Horst, 90, 92, 93
Messerschmitt Bf 109, 50, 121
Mikesh, Robert, 165
Mikoyan-Gurevich MiG-15, 164
Minchin, Frederick F., 90
Mitchell, William "Billy", 56
Mitsubishi A5M, 137
Mitsubishi A6M "Zero", 136
Moll, J., 82
Mollison, Amy Johnson, 93, 94
Mollison, James A. "Jimmy", 93, 94, 95
Monocoupe 90A, 95
Montgolfier, Etienne and Joseph, 2, 3
Moore, Johnny, 13
Moore-Brabazon, J. T. C., 20
Morane Borel monoplane, 20
Morane-Saulnier H, 28, 31
Morane-Saulnier L, 28
Moreno, Robert, 85
Morrell, John A., 7
Moss, Sanford, 52
Mussolini, Benito, 93
Navy-Curtiss NC-1, 86
Navy-Curtiss NC-3, 86
Navy-Curtiss NC-4, 86
Nelle Carmody, 158
Nelson, Erik, 103
New York, Rio and Buenos Aires Line (NYRBA), 111, 113
Newcomber, Edna, 93
Nichols, Ruth, 92
Nieuport 11, 28, 37
Nobile, Umberto, 115
Noonan, Fred, 95, 107
North American AT-6 Texan, 149
North American B-25A, 148
North American F-86 Sabre, 164
North American F-100 Super Sabre, 160, 179
North American P-51 Mustang, 132, 166
Northcliff, Lord, 86
Northrop 2B Gamma *Polar Star*, 116, 117
Northrop Alpha 2, 62
Northrop M2-F2, 181
Northrop-Grumman B-2 Spirit, 176
Noville, George O., 90
Nungesser, Charles, 89
Ogden, Henry H., 103, 104
Olieslangers, Jean, 18
Omdahl, Oskar, 90, 114
Orli ski, Boles aw, 72
Orteig Prize, 89, 90
Orteig, Raymond, 89
Ortiz, Roberto, 112
Oscanyan, Paul C., 94
Pacquette, Oliver, 92
Pan American Airways, 98, 110, 111, 190, 193
Pan American-Grace Airways Inc (PANAGRA), 111
Panavia Tornado, 173
Pangborn, Clyde, 82, 92, 107
Paris, Paulin, 91
Parmentier, K. D., 82
Paulhan, Louis, 20, 24
Payne, Philip, 90
Peary, Robert E., 114
Pénaud, Alphonse, 8
Percival K.1 Vega Gull *The Messenger*, 95
Petersen, Carl O., 93
Pichodou, Alexandre, 95
Pierce, Fred, 90, 91
Pilâtre de Rozier, Jean-François, 2, 3
Pilcher, Percy, 9, 11
Pilcher *Hawk*, 9, 11
Piper Cherokee Pathfinder, 202
Piper J-3 Cub, 200
Pisciulli, Leon, 91, 93
Pitcairn Aviation, 61
Pitcairn PA-5 Mailwing, 61
Polando, John Louis, 92
Pond, George R., 94
Post, Wiley, 92, 93, 106
Preston, Edwin L., 93
Prier, Pierre, 20
Rada, Modesto, 91
Rasche, Thea, 91
Read, Albert C., 86
Redpath, Peter H., 93
Reichers, Louis T., 93
Reid, Leonard, 94
Renard, Charles, 4
Republic F-105 Thunderchief, 168
Republic P-43, 148
Rhode, Fritz, 90
Richman, Harry, 94, 95
Riiser-Larsen, Hjalmar, 116
Risticz, Johann, 90
Robertson, MacPherson, 82, 116
Rockwell, Robert, 39
Rodgers, Calbraith Perry "Cal", 24, 25
Rody, Willy, 93
Roosevelt, Franklin D., 146
Rossi, Maurice, 93, 94
Royal Aircraft Factory F.E.2b, 29
Royal Aircraft Factory S.E.5, 38
Ruff, Joseph, 93
Rumpler Taube, 23
Russian Revolution, 46
Ryan Brougham *Shalom*, 95
Ryan NY-P *The Spirit of St. Louis*, 89, 98
Sabelli, Cesare, 91, 94
SABENA, 79
Salmet, Henri, 19
Salmson 2, 39, 40
Santos-Dumont, Alberto, 4, 14, 17
Sarabia, Francisco, 112
Saul, Jonathan P., 92
Saulnier, Raymond, 28
Savoia-Marchetti S.55, 92, 93, 108
Savoia-Marchetti S.55 *Jau*, 88
Savoia-Marchetti S.55 *Santa Maria*, 88, 89
Savoia-Marchetti S.55 *Santa Maria II*, 88, 90
Savoia-Marchetti S.64, 91
Savoia-Marchetti S.73, 77, 79
Savoia-Marchetti S.M.83, 113
Savoia-Pomilio SP.2, 32
SCADTA (Sociedad Colombo-Alemana de Transportes Aéreos) 110, 112
Scandinavian Air Express, 78
Schildhauer, Clarence H. "Dutch", 92
Schiller, Duke, 90
Schlee, Edward, 90
Schreiber, Arthur, 91
Schroeder, Rudolph W. "Shorty", 52
Scott, C. W. A., 82
Scott, G. H., 86
Scott, Robert Falcon, 116
Seversky P-35, 50
Shackleton, Ernest, 116
Shiers, W., 82
ships:
Akagi, 137
Arizona, 135
Barendrecht, 90
Belmoira, 93
California, 90
Conte Rossa, 92
Eagle, 91
Enterprise, 136, 137, 138
Essex, 136
Hektoria, 117
Hornet, 136
Hyuga, 142
Kearsarge, 164
Langley, 136
Lexington, 136
Makini, 97
Maryland, 135
Maunalai, 97
Minnewaska, 91
North Haven, 100
Norvegia, 116
Oklahoma, 135
Oriskany, 161
Prince of Wales, 136
R. P. Resor, 126
Ranger, 136
Repulse, 136
Richmond, 104, 105
Saratoga, 136
Tennessee, 135
Trent, 6
Valprato, 91
Wasp, 136
West Virginia, 135
William Scoresby, 115
Yorktown, 136
Short Kent, 83
Short L.17 *Scylla*, 83
Short L.17 *Syrinx*, 83
Short Mayo composite, 95
Short S.8 Calcutta, 73
Short S.20 *Mercury*, 95
Short S.23C Empire Boat *Caledonia*, 95
Short S.23C Empire Boat *Cambria*, 95
Short S.30C *Cabot*, 95
Short S.30C *Caribou*, 95
Short Sunderland, 127
Sikorski *Il'ya Muromets*, 26, 27
Sikorsky (Sikorski), Igor, 35, 72
Sikorsky MH-53E 170
Sikorsky S-36 *Dawn*, 90
Sikorsky S-38 *City of Richmond*, 93
Sikorsky S-38 *Osa's Ark*, 85
Sikorsky S-38 *Untin Bowler*, 91
Sikorsky S-39 *Spirit of Africa*, 85
Sikorsky S-39 *The Spirit of Africa and Borneo*, 85
Sikorsky S-40, 111

Sikorsky S-42, 100, 101
Sikorsky S-42B *Clipper III*, 95
Smith, Keith, 82
Smith, Lowell, 103
Smith, Ross, 82
Smith, Thomas H., 95
Smith, Walter, 95
Solberg, Thor, 93, 94
Sopwith 1-1/2-Strutter, 27
Sopwith Camel, 38
South African Airways (SAA), 85
Southeastern Air Lines, 111
SPAD VII, 36, 44
SPAD XIII, 40
Staaken bombers, 72
Staaken R.VI, 46, 50
Stannage, John W., 92
Starke, Paul, 90
Stearman XA-21, 150
Steiner, John, 3
Stevens, Albert W., 39, 53
Stinson floatplane, 93, 117
Stinson monoplane, 115
Stinson SM-1 Detroiter *American Girl*, 90
Stinson SM-1 Detroiter *The Endeavour*, 90
Stinson SM-1 Detroiter *Pride of Detroit*, 90
Stinson SM-1 Detroiter *Royal Windsor*, 90
Stinson SM-1 Detroiter *Sir John Carling*, 90
Stinson SM-1B Detroiter *Green Mountain Boy*, 93
Stinson SM-1DC Detroiter *Greater Rockford*, 91
Stinson U, 62
Stoddard, Richard, 95
Stringfellow, John, 8
Stulz, Wilmer, 90
Sud Caravelle, 184
Sullivan, R. O. D., 95
Supermarine Spitfire, 50
Syndicato Condor, 113
Taylor, P. G., 93
Thaler, William, 95
Thurlow, Tom, 95
Tittman, Harold, 38
Trans World Airlines (TWA), 60, 62, 193
Transall C-160, 220
Transcontinental Air Transport (TAT) , 60, 61, 62, 64
Transcontinental and Western Air, Inc (TWA), 60, 64
Trippe, Juan, 100, 111
Tully, Terence, 90
Tupolev ANT-25 , 50
Turner, Roscoe, 82
Ulm, Charles, 93, 96, 97
Ulrich, William, 93
Union Airways, 85
units:
1st Aero Squadron (US), 40
First Air Force (US), 146
2nd Air Base Squadron (US), 150
Second Air Force (US), 146
Third Air Force (US), 146
Fourth Air Force (US), 146
4th Photo Sq (US), 151
Fifth Air Force (US), 146
5th Photo Recon Group (US), 125
6th Air Base Sq (US), 151
Sixth Air Force (US) , 146
Seventh Air Force (US), 146
Eighth Air Force (US), 146
Ninth Air Force (US), 146
9th Tow Target Squadron (US), 159
Tenth Air Force (US) , 146
Eleventh Air Force (US), 146
Twelfth Air Force (US) , 146
Thirteenth Air Force (US), 146
14th Air Group (Japan), 137
Fourteenth Air Force (US), 146
Fifteenth Air Force (US) , 146, 147
Twentieth Air Force (US), 147
XX Bomber Command (US), 147
20th Fighter Wing (US), 173
XXI Bomber Command (US), 140, 147
28th Aero Squadron (US), 40
29th BG (US), 141
50th Aero Squadron (US), 41
Patrol Sq 63 (US), 127
No.70 Squadron (UK), 27
73rd BW (US), 142
No.87 Squadron (RAF), 121
93rd Aero Squadron (US), 39
94th Aero Squadron (US), 38
99th Aero Squadron (US), 46
354th FG (US), 132
480th Antisubmarine Group (US), 127
497th BG (US), 141
Air Corps Ferrying Command (US), 152
Air Transport Auxiliary (ATA), 158, 159
Air Transport Command (ATC)(US), 146, 152, 158, 159
Alaskan Air Force (US), 146
Caribbean Air Force (US), 146
Condor Legion (Germany), 118
Engineering Division (US), 148
Far East Air Force (US), 146
Far East Air Forces (FEAF)(US) , 147
Hawaiian Air Force (US), 146
Mediterranean Allied Air Forces , 147
Northeast Air District (US), 146
Northwest Air District (US), 146
Panama Canal Air Force (US), 146
Philippines Department Air Force (US), 146
Southeast Air District (US), 146
US Strategic Air Forces in Europe, 146, 147
Women's Airforce Service Pilots (WASPs)(US), 158, 159
Women's Auxiliary Ferrying Squadron (WAFS)(US), 158, 159
United Air Lines (Airlines), 60, 69, 187, 210
Valentine, James , 21
Vallette, T. A., 95
Van Balkom, J., 94
van Dijk, Evert, 92
Vaniman, Melvin , 6
Védrines, Jules, 20, 21 82
Vickers E.F.B.1 Gunbus, 28
Vickers E.F.B.2 Gunbus, 28
Vickers E.F.B.3 Gunbus, 28
Vickers E.F.B.4 Gunbus, 28
Vickers F.B.5 Gunbus, 28
Vickers F.B.27A Vimy, 82, 86
Vickers Viscount, 184
Vickers Wellington, 122
Vidart, Rene, 21
von Clausbruch, Cramer, 92, 93
von Drygalski, Eric, 116
von Gronau, Wolfgang, 92, 93, 106
von Hoenefeld, Günther, 90
von Moreau, Rudolph, 95
Voortmeyer, William B., 97
Vought XC-142, 181
Vought F-8 Crusader, 183
Vought F4U Corsair, 138
Vought OS2U Kingfisher, 135
Vultee BT-13, 158
Vultee V1-A Lady Peace, 94, 95
Wade, Leigh, 103, 104
Waikus, Felix (Feliksas Vaitkus), 94
Walker, James, 95
Warner, James, 97
Washington, George, 54
Weddington, Leonard, 108, 109
Weiss, Ehrich (Eric Weisz, aka Harry Houdini), 16
Weller, Oscar, 92
Wellman, Walter, 6, 114
West Australian Airways, 82
Western Air Express, 60, 62, 64, 85
Whitehead, Ennis, 108, 109
Whitten Brown, Arthur, 86
Wilcockson, C. E., 95
Wilcoxson, A. S., 95
Wilczek, Sandor, 92
Wilkins, George Hubert, 96, 114, 115, 116, 117
Williams, Roger Q., 91
Wilson, Robert, 94
Wilson, Woodrow, 54
Winfield, Wilda, 158
Wölfert, Hermann, 4
Wood, Ann, 158, 159
Wood, Phil, 90
Wood, Robert, 91
Woolsey, C. E., 108
Woolsley, Clinton, 108
Wright, Orville , 1, 9, 12, 13, 14, 24, 52, 53
Wright, Wilbur , 1, 9, 12, 13, 14, 15, 24, 52
Wright 1900 glider, 12
Wright 1901 glider, 12
Wright 1902 glider, 12, 13
Wright 1903 Flyer, 13
Wright, Chan, 95
Wright EX *Fin Fiz* , 24, 25
Wright Model A , 1, 14, 15
Wynne-Eaton, C. S., 92
Yancey, Lewis , 91
Yeager, Charles "Chuck", 179
Zacchetti, Vitale, 90
Zappata, Filippo, 80
Zebora, B., 91
Zeppelin, Ferdinand Adolf August Heinrich von, 4
Zimmer, Eduard, 92

Photo Credits

vi 2nd from top; Carl H. Claudy, Sr. via NASM
vi 2nd from bottom; USAF
vi (all others); NASM
vii upper; USAF
vii 2nd from bottom; USN
vii (all others); NASM
viii; NASM
x-5 (all); NASM
6 lower left & lower right; USAF
6 (all others); NASM
7 lower; Carl H. Claudy, Sr., via NASM
7 upper; USAF
8-10 (all); NASM
11 lower; USAF
11 (all others); NASM
12-13 (all); USAF
14-17 (all); NASM
18 lower; NASM
18 (all others); USAF
19; Library of Congress via NASM
20 right; USAF
20 (all others); NASM
21 (all); NASM
23 lower; Shell Company via NASM
23-25 (all); NASM
27 lower & upper center; NASM
27 (all others); USAF
28 (all); USAF
29; NASM
30 (all); USAF
31 (all); NASM
32; NASM
33; RCAF Photo establishment Collection, NASM
34; NASM
35 upper right; NASM
35 (all others); USAF
36-37 (all); NASM
38 lower; USAF
38 (all others); NASM
39 upper right; NASM
39 (all others); USAF
40 upper left; USN
40 (all others); USAF
41; NASM
42 upper right; USAF
43 lower right; NASM
43 (all others); USAF
44 left; NASM
48 (all); USAF
50 lower; SOVfoto
50 upper; Hans Groenhoff Collection, NASM
51 lower; NASM
51 upper; USAF
52-53 (all); USAF
54 lower; NASM
54 upper; USAF
55; NASM
56 (all); USAF
57 lower; NASM
57 upper; USAF
59 upper left; NASM
59 (all others); USAF
60 lower; NASM
60 upper; TWA
61 upper left; Walter Wright Collection
61 upper right; C. R. Smith Museum
62 lower; Walter Wright Collection
62 center; TWA
62 upper; American Airlines
63-64 (all); NASM
68; NASM
69 left; American Airlines
69 right; Walter Wright Collection
70 upper; TWA
70 (all others); Rudy Arnold Collection, NASM
71 lower right; USAF
71 left; Walter Wright Collection
71 upper; NASM
72 lower left; Walter Wright Collection
72 upper left; NASM
72 upper right; USAF
73 left; Bombardier
73 right; NASM
74 upper left; Zeppelin Museum
74 (all others); NASM
75 upper; NASM
75 (all others); Zeppelin Museum
76 (all); NASM
77 upper left; Air France via NASM
77 (all others); NASM
78 lower; NASM
78 upper left; KLM
78 upper right; Visual Studies Workshop
79 (all); NASM
80; NASM
81 lower; Lufthansa via NASM
81 center right; KLM
81 upper left; NASM
82 lower; NASM
82 upper; Rudy Arnold Collection, NASM
83 lower; NASM
83 upper; Shell Company via NASM
85 (all); NASM
86 upper; USN
86 (all others); NASM
88 lower left; Museu de Marinha
88 (all others); NASM
89-90 (all); NASM
91; AP
92-95; Rudy Arnold Collection, NASM
96 lower; NASM
96 upper; Carol Nickisher
97-99 (all); NASM
100 lower; Rudy Arnold Collection, NASM
100 (all others); NASM
101 (all); USAF
104 (all); USAF
105 lower right; NASM
105 (all others); USAF
106 lower; Rudy Arnold Collection, NASM
106 upper left; USAF
106 upper right; NASM
107 lower; Museum of Flight
107 upper left; Rudy Arnold Collection, NASM
107 upper right; USAF
108 (all); USAF
109 lower right; USAF
109 upper; NASM
110-111 (all); NASM
112 lower; USAF
112 center right; Rudy Arnold Collection, NASM
112 left; NASM
113-114 (all); NASM
115; New York Times
116-118; NASM
119 lower; USAF
119 upper; NASM
120 (all); NASM
121 lower left; USAF
121 lower right; Walter Wright Collection
121 upper; DaimlerChrysler
122 upper; Walter Wright Collection
122 (all others); USAF
123 center; NASM
123 (all others); USAF
124 (all); USAF
125 lower; USN
125 (all others); USAF
126 lower; USAF
126 upper; USN
127-129 (all); USAF
131-132 (all); USAF
135 center; USAF
135 (all others); USN
136 lower; Hans Groenhoff Collection, NASM
136 upper; USAF
137 upper; USN
137 (all others); USAF
138 lower left; USAF
138 (all others); USN
139; USN
140-143 (all); USAF
144 lower; NASM
144 upper; USAF
145 (all); USAF
148 lower; Rudy Arnold Collection, NASM
149 lower; NASM
149 upper right; USAF
150 (all); USAF
152 lower; National Museum of the USAF
152 center left; NASM
152 center right; USAF
153 upper; USAF
154 lower; NASM
154 upper; USAF
155-158 (all); USAF
159 lower left; USAF
159 upper left; USAF
160 (all); USAF
161 lower; Ralph Stell
161 upper; Walter Wright Collection
162 (all); USAF
163 (all); USAF
164 upper left; Robert Dreesen
164 (all others); USAF
165-166 (all); USAF
167 lower; USAF
167 upper; Walter Wright Collection
168 lower; NASM
168 upper; USAF
169-171 (all); USAF
172 lower; USN
172 (all others); USAF
173-176 (all); USAF
177 upper; USAF
178 upper right; USN
178 (all others); USAF
179 upper; USAF
179 (all others); NASA
180; USAF
181 upper right; NASA
181 (all others); USAF
182-183 (all); NASA
184; NASM
185 upper; Rudy Arnold Collection, NASM
186 lower; Delta
186 upper; NASM
187 lower; NASM
187 upper; Rudy Arnold Collection, NASM
188; Rudy Arnold Collection, NASM
189 lower; NASM
189 upper; SAS
190 (all); NASM;
191 lower; NASM;
191 upper; TWA;
192; Rudy Arnold Collection, NASM
193 lower; Rudy Arnold Collection, NASM
193 upper; NASM
194 lower; author
194 upper; NASM
195 (all); NASM
198; author
200; Rudy Arnold Collection, NASM;
202; Walter Wright Collection;
204; author
206; Walter Wright
208; author
210; Rudy Arnold Collection, NASM
212 (all); Walter Wright
214; Walter Wright
216 lower; USAF
216 upper; author
218; USAF
220 lower; author
220 upper; Hans Groenhoff Collection, NASM